SYSTEM CENTER CONFIGURATION MANAGER 2007 R3 COMPLETE

BRAD PRICE AND DANIEL EDDY

Course Technology PTR
A part of Cengage Learning

COURSE TECHNOLOGY
CENGAGE Learning™

Australia • Brazil • Japan • Korea • Mexico • Singapore • Spain • United Kingdom • United States

COURSE TECHNOLOGY
CENGAGE Learning

System Center Configuration Manager 2007 R3 Complete
Brad Price and Daniel Eddy

Publisher and General Manager, Course Technology PTR: Stacy L. Hiquet

Associate Director of Marketing: Sarah Panella

Manager of Editorial Services: Heather Talbot

Marketing Manager: Mark Hughes

Acquisitions Editor: Heather Hurley

Project Editor: Jenny Davidson

Technical Reviewer: Leonard Volling

Interior Layout Tech: MPS Limited, a Macmillan Company

Cover Designer: Mike Tanamachi

Indexer: Sharon Shock

Proofreader: Sara Gullion

005.36
M626p

For product information and technology assistance, contact us at **Cengage Learning Customer & Sales Support, 1-800-354-9706**

For permission to use material from this text or product, submit all requests online at **www.cengage.com/permissions** Further permissions questions can be emailed to **permissionrequest@cengage.com.**

All trademarks are the property of their respective owners.

All images © Cengage Learning unless otherwise noted.

Library of Congress Control Number: 2011923926

ISBN-13: 978-1-4354-5650-1

ISBN-10: 1-4354-5650-5

Course Technology, a part of Cengage Learning
20 Channel Center Street
Boston, MA 02210
USA

Cengage Learning is a leading provider of customized learning solutions with office locations around the globe, including Singapore, the United Kingdom, Australia, Mexico, Brazil, and Japan. Locate your local office at: **international.cengage.com/region**

Cengage Learning products are represented in Canada by Nelson Education, Ltd.

For your lifelong learning solutions, visit **courseptr.com**

Visit our corporate website at **cengage.com**

Printed in the United States of America
1 2 3 4 5 6 7 13 12 11

For DeAnn, Jami, and Becca
Brad

I dedicate this book to my Dad, David Eddy
Daniel

ACKNOWLEDGMENTS

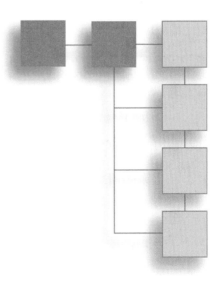

Brad Price

The work that I did on this book wouldn't be possible if not for the support of my family. DeAnn—I owe everything to you. You have been so very patient and understanding when it comes to my long work days and weeks away from home. One of these days I am going to repay you for all that you have done for me. To my beautiful daughters Jami and Becca—I think you know how very proud I am to be your Dad. Watching you grow up has been a joyous experience. You have become intelligent, kindhearted, and honest adults with bright futures ahead of you. To Dad and Mom—Thanks for your support through everything. It should come as no surprise that I think the world of you. To the rest of my family—I am glad I can call each and every one of you a friend. Danny—It is a privilege to work with someone as intelligent, dedicated, conscientious, and caring as you. This book would not be nearly as good without your work. You have a great future ahead of you. I am honored to call you my friend.

I also need to thank my Cengage family. Matt and Apurva—Thank you for your expertise in areas that I am weak in. You have helped make this book stand out. Heather and Jenny—Thank you for being patient when things became a little bit crazy. You were great to work with. Leonard—Your technical expertise was greatly appreciated. I hope I didn't drive you crazy as you were editing.

Daniel Eddy

I should start by saying thank you to Max Burgstahler for giving me the opportunity to grow and learn in the IT field. I wouldn't be where I am today without his trust and guidance. I should also thank Jim Andrews for his friendship over the past 10 years. His kindness, willingness to listen, and wisdom has been invaluable to me.

Another person I need to thank is Brad Price. Brad gave me the opportunity to co-author this book and has been a helpful teacher along the way. His knowledge of Configuration Manager 2007 never ceases to amaze me.

Thank you to Matt Webb for being an awesome friend, contributing author, and cousin. Matt is responsible for Chapters 10 and 20 and is my go-to guy for any and all development/database questions. Matt is a great guy and I always look forward to our technical discussions during our "geek nights."

Thank you to Courtney Wiedenkeller for sticking by my side as I wrote this book. This was a long and tedious process; not only for me, but for her as well. Somehow, she was able to keep me motivated and reminded me to be confident in myself even when stress levels were running high. I couldn't have done this without her. Thank you for everything, CW.

I can't say thank you enough to my family—specifically Marcie Wigginton, Jeff Wigginton, and Tim Eddy for always being there for me. You guys mean the world to me, and I love you all very much.

Finally, thank you to Cengage for allowing me to write this book and for giving me some great editors to work with. Heather Hurley, our acquisitions editor, and Jenny Davidson, our project editor, have been essential in getting this book published. Heather and Jenny were always patient and understanding while making sure we didn't fall too much behind schedule. Leonard Volling was our technical editor and went through hundreds of pages of mind numbing details to make sure that we got everything just right. His suggestions made a world of difference. I simply could not have asked for a better group of people to work with.

ABOUT THE AUTHORS

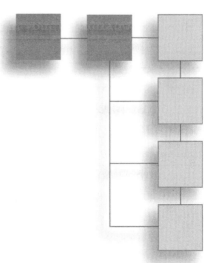

Brad Price has been in the IT field for 18 years, working as a consultant and Microsoft Certified Trainer for 12 of those. He has taught System Center Configuration Manager 2007 and System Management Server courses throughout the United States and Europe. Brad is a published author, writing books for Sybex Press and Wiley Publications. Brad has also designed and deployed rollouts of Microsoft System Center Configuration Manager 2007 for clients in the small to mid-sized markets as well as Fortune 500 companies with more than 25,000 users in four countries.

Daniel D. Eddy has worked in the IT industry for the past ten years. He is experienced in many desktop management products and specializes in Configuration Manager 2007. For the past three years, he's been responsible for all aspects of the Configuration Manager infrastructure at a large school district in the Midwest. During that time, he helped automate many complex processes and streamlined application deployment using Microsoft's Application Virtualization (App-V) technology. In his spare time, Daniel contributes to the Configuration Manager community through technical blogs and training videos.

Contents

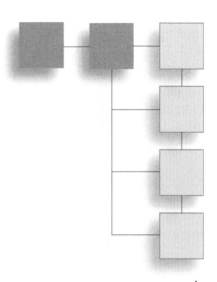

INTRODUCTION

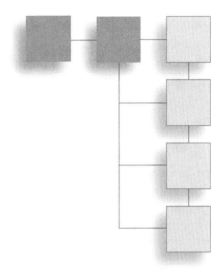

Thank you for picking up *System Center Configuration Manager 2007 R3 Complete.* Whether you are evaluating before implementation, or working with Configuration Manager on a day-to-day basis, this book is meant to give you a well-rounded look at what Configuration Manager can help you do.

If this is your first look at Configuration Manager, you may be surprised at the number of technologies included in this product. The Configuration Manager product team has done an exceptional job of tying several management technologies together to form a cohesive system management solution. If, on the other hand, you are familiar with previous versions, either Systems Management Server (SMS) or Configuration Manager, and want to brush up on the new technologies, you will find that the product team has done a commendable job of including some of the most requested features.

WHO SHOULD BE READING THIS BOOK

Well, we believe that everyone should be reading this book. Okay, maybe not everyone, but anyone who is involved with Configuration Manager, or has systems that they need to manage more efficiently. System Center Configuration Manager 2007 R3 is covered from design and planning options, to implementation, to configuration and management. For those who are in the process of evaluating Configuration Manager and the impact it may have on your environment, this book details the requirements and implementation details you are looking for. Administrators who are new to Configuration Manager will find detailed management and configuration options within these pages. And for those who already have Systems Management Server or an earlier release version of Configuration Manager, you will find discussion of the new features and how to use them efficiently.

CHAPTERS

The 21 chapters that make up this book reflect the components within Configuration Manager and how to implement and manage those components. Each chapter gets right to the information without a lot of extraneous details. We feel that if you want a lesson on ITIL or MOF, you can easily find books that are dedicated to those subjects. We wanted you to be able to pick up the book and start digesting the pertinent information quickly and easily. Within the chapters you will find:

Chapter 1—This is an introduction to Configuration Manager and the technologies that make it the powerful tool that it is. The new technologies from Configuration Manager 2007 R3 are also spotlighted within the chapter.

Chapter 2—Proper design and planning are critical to a functional Configuration Manager site and hierarchy. This chapter is a primer on the myriad options available when creating a site, and the decision criteria that should be taken into account when designing and planning the site hierarchy.

Chapter 3—As with designing and planning the site, care should be taken to ensure the site database is efficient and functional. This chapter digs into the tasks and options available to keep the database groomed and stable. There are several options to consider when scheduling tasks and status message details, and this chapter is used to make sure you have the information you need when configuring these tools.

Chapter 4—After taking all of the design and planning options under advisement, you are ready to create your first site. This chapter presents the prerequisites and the installation options for a primary site.

Chapter 5—Most organizations require more than one site to support their organization. This chapter is handy to have when you need to create child sites within the hierarchy.

Chapter 6—This chapter is a one-stop shopping center for installing Site System roles. Instead of digging through multiple chapters trying to find the installation options for each of the roles, they are presented here.

Chapter 7—Servers and workstations cannot be managed without the Configuration Manager client. This small piece of software needs to be installed on each system that will be managed. This chapter details the installation options available to a Configuration Manager administrator.

Chapter 8—Managing systems is what Configuration Manager is all about. This chapter details how clients can be managed while they are connected to the Internet instead of the organization's intranet, how administrators can use remote control tools to manage systems, and how the systems can be managed even when they are shut down.

Chapter 9—Once the managed systems have the Configuration Manager client installed, information about those systems can be obtained. This chapter presents how the managed system's hardware and software inventory is collected, as well as the details on which software is actually used.

Chapter 10—One of the most widely used, though often misunderstood, technologies within Configuration Manager is queries. Queries are used to present data from the database, either for reporting purposes or to create collections of managed objects. This chapter details how queries are created and managed.

Chapter 11—When most people think of Configuration Manager, they think of software deployment. Within this chapter you will find a detailed presentation of how software distribution is configured and used.

Chapter 12—Vulnerabilities exist within all software. Keeping systems up-to-date with the latest patches that plug those vulnerabilities is critical to all organizations. Configuration Manager includes a very robust software patching solution. This chapter includes an in-depth look at how to manage software updates.

Chapter 13—Maintaining and upgrading operating systems is very labor intensive. Configuration Manager includes technologies that can make operating system deployment easier and more cost effective for an organization. This chapter introduces and explains how to manage operating system deployments efficiently.

Chapter 14—Most organizations have systems that have specific configuration requirements. This chapter is devoted to Desired Configuration Management

(DCM) and how it can be used to validate that a system is still compliant or has become non-compliant.

Chapter 15—As more and more systems are used both within the organization's networks and from outside the corporate network, the more critical it becomes that administrators know which systems are configured correctly. This chapter discusses how Windows Server 2008's Network Access Protection and Configuration Manager tie together to validate systems when they come online, and then remediate those that are not compliant.

Chapter 16—Windows Mobile devices can be managed in much the same way as servers, workstations, and laptops. This chapter presents the configuration and management options available for mobile devices.

Chapter 17—As with any technology, disaster recovery is critical. This chapter introduces the backup and recovery options that are available for Configuration Manager, and the responsibilities that you have when protecting the Configuration Manager hierarchy.

Chapter 18—Built into Configuration Manager are several tools that you can use to manage the site and the managed resources. This chapter shows you how to use the tools that are built into the administrator's console.

Chapter 19—The Configuration Management team has made tools available as a download from Microsoft. This chapter shows you how you can use these tools, known collectively as the Toolkit.

Chapter 20—There is a lot of power built into the administrator's console and the Toolkit tools, but they may not completely meet the needs of all administrators. This chapter discusses one of the most underutilized tools within the administrator's arsenal—the Software Development Kit.

Chapter 21—The final chapter is used to discuss troubleshooting issues. With such a large collection of technologies built into Configuration Manager, there are plenty of parts that can break. Proper troubleshooting is critical. This chapter can be used as a reference to help you troubleshoot and understand the issues that administrators encounter.

SECTION I

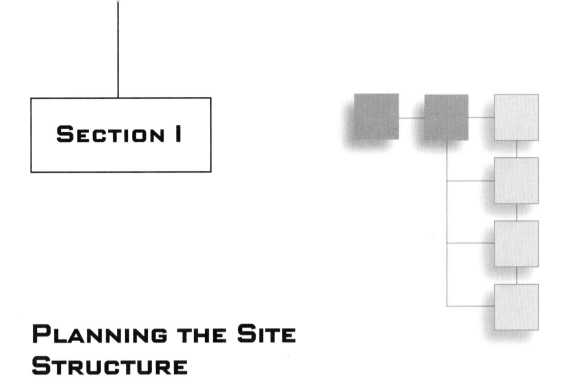

PLANNING THE SITE STRUCTURE

Throughout the next three chapters, we will be discussing the benefits of System Center Configuration Manager 2007 and the planning that is needed to prepare your site for a successful installation. This section provides you with valuable background information that will help you understand the concepts that are introduced in future chapters. Whether you are new to or familiar with Configuration Manager, these next three chapters are a good place to start!

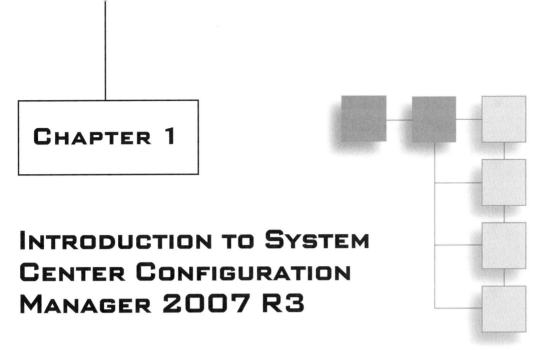

CHAPTER 1

INTRODUCTION TO SYSTEM CENTER CONFIGURATION MANAGER 2007 R3

System Center Configuration Manager 2007 (formally Systems Management Server or SMS) is designed to help IT administrators manage dynamic and complex environments by giving them an abundance of features to employ. Some of these features include software distribution, inventory, and operating system deployment. Configuration Manager is built around the rock-solid SMS architecture and uses other proven systems like Windows Deployment Services, Windows Server Updates Services, and Microsoft SQL Server, which has helped make it one of the top change and configuration management solutions in the IT industry today.

Configuration Manager 2007 uses an administration console built on top of the Microsoft Management Console (MMC) to help administrators manage all of its features from one location. It's broken down into five sections based on the management task at hand.

The five sections (nodes) that are available in the Configuration Manager 2007 console are as follows:

- Site Management
- Computer Management
- System Status
- Security Rights
- Tools

3

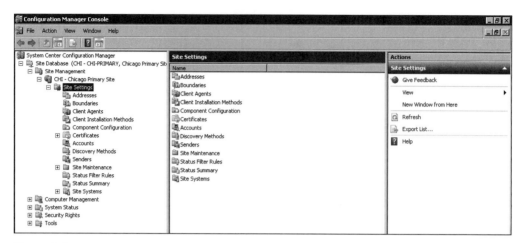

Figure 1.1
Site Management Node

- **Site Management**—This node (Figure 1.1) contains options pertaining to the overall site such as configuring site systems and roles.

- **Computer Management**—This node (Figure 1.2) contains options regarding client settings and features. This is where you will likely spend most of your time.

- **System Status**—This node (Figure 1.3) contains options for monitoring the health of the site. The options within this node give you a quick

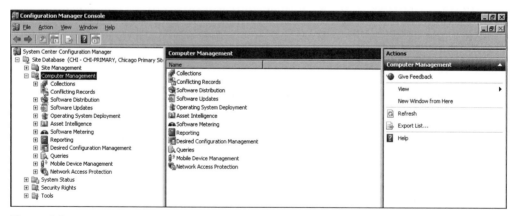

Figure 1.2
Computer Management Node

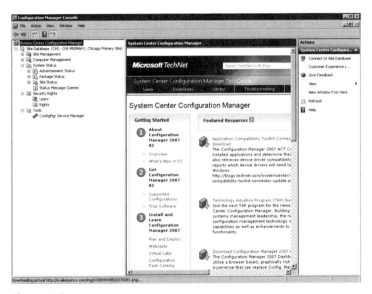

Figure 1.3
System Status, Security Rights, Tools

overview of the site status and let you quickly review logs in case there is something working incorrectly.

- **Security Rights**—This node (Figure 1.3) lets you configure the security based on users or groups that you define within Active Directory. The rights within this node are extensive and can be configured granularly or broadly depending on the scenario.

- **Tools**—This node (Figure 1.3) lets you control Configuration Manager 2007 components throughout the entire hierarchy. Components can be services or threads that are running on a Configuration Manager site system. These components are managed in a similar way to that of a Windows service in that they can be stopped, started, paused, or queried against.

INITIAL RELEASE

Configuration Manager 2007 was officially released to manufacturing in August of 2007. When it was initially released, it added many new features that were not in its predecessor, SMS 2003. These features were both evolutionary and revolutionary and were a direct result from its customers' wants and needs.

Note

Note that support for Configuration Manager 2007 (with no service pack applied) ended on July 14, 2009 and support for Configuration Manager 2007 SP1 ended on January 11, 2011.

Operating System Support

Table 1.1 lists the supported operating systems included in the initial release of Configuration Manager 2007:

Configuration Manager 2007 RTM Features

The following features were included in the initial release of Configuration Manager 2007:

Inventory

When enabled, Configuration Manager 2007 will collect software and hardware inventory from clients and store this information in the database. Inventory settings are controlled by two separate client agents—one for hardware and one for software. These settings control whether the agent is enabled, schedules for inventory scans, and what type of information to collect. Because these settings are controlled through separate client agents, you have the ability to control each agent individually, allowing you to decide what is best for your environment. Once the inventory data has been collected for client machines, this data can be used throughout Configuration Manager in a variety of ways like building reports, creating collections, running queries, or by using Resource Explorer to look at detailed information about a specific computer. To learn more about inventory, see Chapter 9, "Managing Assets."

Queries

Queries put your inventory data to work. They are used to find information quickly and easily. A good example of using a query is to identify all computers that have Office 2003 Professional installed so that you can later upgrade them to Office 2007 Professional. You start off by creating the query using a wizard that lets you define specific criteria through the use of drop-down lists. The

Table 1.1 Initial Operating System Support

Operating System	Version	Service Pack	Architecture[1]
Windows 2000	Professional, Advanced Server, Datacenter[2]	SP4	x86
Windows XP	Professional	SP2 or SP3	x86 or x64
Windows XP Tablet PC	N/A	SP2	x86
Windows XP Embedded	N/A	SP2	x86
Windows Embedded Standard 2009[3]	N/A	N/A	x86
Windows Embedded Point of Sales	N/A	N/A	x86
Windows Embedded POS Ready 2009	N/A	N/A	x86
Windows Fundamentals for Legacy PCs	N/A	N/A	x86
Windows Vista	Business, Enterprise, Ultimate	No SP, SP1	x86 or x64
Windows Server 2003	Web	SP1 or SP2	x86
Windows Server 2003	Standard	SP1 or SP2	x86 or x64
Windows Server 2003	Enterprise, Datacenter, Storage Server	SP1 or SP2	x86, x64, or IA64
Windows Server 2003 R2	Standard Edition	N/A	x86 or x64
Windows Server 2003 R2	Enterprise, Datacenter	N/A	x86 or x64 or IA64
Windows Server 2008[4]	Standard, Enterprise, Datacenter	SP1	x86, x64
Windows Server 2008 (Itanium)	N/A	SP1	IA64

[1] Configuration Manager 2007 only supports 64-bit operating systems by running 32-bit code.
[2] Configuration Manager 2007 supports Datacenter versions but are not certified.
[3] Configuration Manager 2007 does not support Operating System Deployment to Windows Embedded versions other than Windows Embedded Standard 2009.
[4] Configuration Manager 2007 does not support client installation on Windows Server 2008 Core.

options you select in the drop-down lists are eventually converted into WMI Query Language (WQL), which is the underlying technology behind queries. If you are proficient using WQL, you can create your own custom queries without using the wizard. We'll dive deeper into that in Chapter 10, "Creating and Managing Queries and Reports." Continuing with our example, our query looks to see if "Microsoft Office 2003 Professional" is in the Add/Remove Programs list. If so, all computers matching these criteria are then listed in your query. Once you determine that your query is correct and is gathering the right information, you can then start performing actions on these computers through the use of collections. To learn more about queries, see Chapter 10.

Collections

Collections are designed to group clients together based on criteria that you define. Collections are created much like queries but cannot return data such as serial numbers and memory amounts. Collections are designed only to display client results. Although queries can display clients in their results, they do not allow you to perform actions on them such as software distribution, software updates, or operating system deployment. Collections can be created from scratch or can be created using a previously defined query such as the one to find computers with a specific version of Microsoft Office as described in the previous example. Collections are useful to group computers for organizational purposes as well. Many administrators use collections as "containers" to group computers based on department or location. To learn more about collections, see Chapter 11, "Managing Software Distribution."

Distribution Points

Distribution points (DPs) are used to store content such as software installation files, scripts, operating system images, and drivers. DPs are typically spread throughout the organization so that slow links (such as wireless bridges or WAN links) are not overloaded when data is distributed to clients. Before Configuration Manager 2007, setting up a DP required you to install a Configuration Manager site system onto a server class operating system. Server licenses and server class hardware can be expensive and hard to justify when needed at a branch location with only a few client machines. To solve this problem, Configuration Manager 2007 introduced branch distribution points (BDPs).

BDPs can be installed to any supported Configuration Manager client system and require no extra hardware or software. BDPs use standard client systems to house content and deliver it locally to clients as they request it. This keeps costs low and allows you to administer multiple systems using one management console. To learn more about distribution points, see Chapter 11.

Maintenance Windows

Maintenance windows are a new feature in Configuration Manager 2007 and specify when changes can occur on client machines. Maintenance windows affect software distribution, software updates, and operating system deployment and are configured on a per collection basis (Figure 1.4). They are designed to keep downtimes to a minimum by not allowing potentially

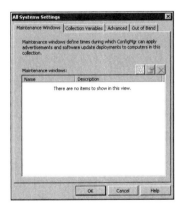

Figure 1.4
Maintenance Window Settings Are Defined Per Collection

dangerous operations from occurring during production hours. Maintenance windows are cumulative in nature because they can be defined on multiple collections. Since one client can be a member of multiple collections, the client will adhere to all of the rules set by each of the maintenance windows in each collection. Maintenance windows can be ignored, however, if necessary. If you need to push an immediate security update or an urgent piece of software, the advertisement can be configured to ignore the rules in a maintenance window and will occur at the time that is set in the advertisement schedule. To learn more about maintenance windows, see Chapter 11.

Software Distribution

One of the major features of Configuration Manager 2007 is the ability to distribute software to machines throughout an organization. Software distribution, like operating system deployment and software updates, makes use of many Configuration Manager features to efficiently and effectively deploy software to targeted machines. When you create a new software package, you are able to spread out the installation bits to distribution points that have been strategically located throughout the organization, advertise the software to collections containing specific client machines (using inventory data), and then deploy the software during non production hours via schedules that have been defined within a maintenance window. To learn more about software distribution, see Chapter 11.

Operating System Deployment (OSD)

The operating system deployment feature has been majorly upgraded and revamped compared to what was available in SMS 2003. Because many organizations typically have a multitude of hardware, software, and unique situations that require many customized actions to be performed, Configuration Manager 2007 introduced the concept of a task sequence (Figure 1.5). Task

Figure 1.5
The Task Sequence Editor

sequences give you the ability to perform customized actions when deploying operating systems (or software) by providing you with a set of tools to organize and order the sequence of events. This is very powerful and can solve many problems that occur with traditional distribution methods. Configuration Manager 2007 also solves the driver nightmare by allowing you to import the necessary drivers and deploying them to the correct hardware. Task sequences and driver catalogs can all be modified without having to update the reference image. To learn more about operating system deployment, see Chapter 13, "Managing Operating System Deployment."

Wake on LAN

Wake on LAN is built into Configuration Manager 2007 and allows you to wake up any powered off or sleeping computer as long as it is able and configured to do so. If enabled in the advertisement, Configuration Manager 2007 sends WOL packets to the targeted machines and allows them to wake up in time for the advertised program to run. This allows you to keep energy costs to a minimum by keeping your machines powered down until a change needs to occur. Wake on LAN settings are defined on a per advertisement basis (Figure 1.6). To learn more about advertisements and Wake on LAN, see Chapters 11–13.

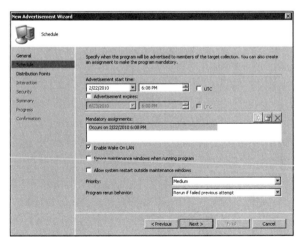

Figure 1.6
Wake on LAN Settings in an Advertisement

Reporting

Configuration Manager 2007 comes pre-loaded with over 200 pre-canned reports to help you monitor the activities in your organization. You can, for example, run a report on an advertisement to see if it ran successfully on a client or group of clients. If the report shows a failure for a specific client, you can drill down until you find the exact cause of the problem. The reporting capabilities help immensely with troubleshooting and can save a lot of time. If you find that you need to build a custom report, you can do so using Structured Query Language (SQL). To learn more about reporting, see Chapter 10.

Software Updates

The software updates mechanism is built on top of Windows Server Update Services (WSUS) but gives you more deployment and monitoring capabilities than are available with WSUS alone. Software updates are easy to deploy using update lists and deployment templates, which allow you to distribute multiple updates to a variety of computers. Once the updates have been applied, the reporting functionality within Configuration Manager 2007 allows you to verify that each update was installed successfully. To learn more about software updates, see Chapter 12, "Managing Software Updates."

Desired Configuration Management

Desired configuration management (DCM) is new to Configuration Manager 2007 and allows you to easily identify systems that suffer from configuration changes (drift). Configuration drift occurs when a setting on the local system does not meet the requirement as specified by an administrator. For example, an administrator may require that Windows 7 Service Pack 1 is installed on all clients in order for them to be compliant with company security regulations. With DCM, you can monitor (by using built-in reports) which systems are out of compliance and optionally remediate them by placing them in collections designed specifically to fix these problems. DCM works by an administrator creating (or downloading from Microsoft) configuration baselines that specify the desired configuration of client systems. DCM then evaluates machines and reports back on any machine that does not meet the configuration as defined in the baseline. To learn more about desired configuration management, see Chapter 14, "Managing Desired Configuration Management."

Software Metering

The software metering functionality in Configuration Manager 2007 allows you to gather data about how often software is used and on which computers it is installed. Like the inventory client agent, software metering also uses a client agent to collect information from the client machine. The client agent can be configured with multiple settings, such as which software to inventory and how often usage data is sent to the site server. Software metering can be very useful when trying to audit software licenses and conform to compliance. To learn more about software metering, see Chapter 9, "Managing Assets."

Mobile Device Management

Configuration Manager 2007 allows you to perform many tasks such as inventory and software distribution on devices running supported versions of the Windows Mobile or Windows CE operating systems. To learn more about mobile device management, see Chapter 16, "Managing Mobile Devices."

Network Access Protection

Network access protection (NAP) is used to disallow non-compliant systems from accessing the corporate network. A system will be deemed non-compliant if it does not meet a rule or rules defined in a NAP policy such as outdated antivirus signatures or missing security updates. This feature uses new technology built into Windows Vista, Server 2008, Windows 7, and Server 2008 R2 and is only available when used on these platforms. To learn more about network access protection, see Chapter 15, "Managing Network Access Protection."

Remote Control

Configuration Manager 2007 includes a remote control feature that allows you to remote view or remote control a client machine. By using the secure and standardized Microsoft RDP protocol, remote control operations are safe, fast, and efficient. Configuration Manager differs from normal remote desktop functions, however, by giving you the ability to remotely view and operate a user's computer while she is actively using it. This means that the remote computer's screen is not locked when you log into the computer to fix a problem. This feature existed in SMS 2003 but has been updated to support

Windows Vista and beyond. Unlike SMS 2003, however, administrators cannot remote control a user's computer unless they are logged into the computer. If the computer is at the Ctrl+Alt+Delete screen, they must use the standard remote desktop feature to remote control the computer. To learn more about the different remote tools included in Configuration Manager 2007, see Chapter 7, "Deploying Clients."

Internet Based Client Management

Laptops have become an issue for many network administrators because they are next to impossible to manage while off of the corporate network. Users who are constantly on the road are not able to get critical updates such as software updates or anti-virus signatures and are potentially at risk for viruses and other malware infections. This is where Internet based client management comes into play. This is a new feature to Configuration Manager 2007 and allows you to manage computers that are not connected to the corporate network. It's able to do this securely by using certificates to pass data through the Internet—allowing users to receive updates anywhere in the world. Note that this does require your site to be in native mode.

Native Mode

Native mode is a new installation type for Configuration Manager 2007. It allows site systems and clients to securely exchange information using security certificates. This is the recommended site mode for organizations that require secure data transmissions in their environment. The features and installation requirements for native mode are discussed in Chapter 4, "Installing a Primary Site."

Configuration Manager SDK

Configuration Manager 2007 provides a software development kit to administrators who want to extend the capabilities of the product by writing their own code based on the documentation included in the kit. This code could be a simple VB script or even a sophisticated program written in C#. To learn more about the Configuration Manager SDK, see Chapter 20, "Overview of the System Center Configuration Manager SDK."

CONFIGURATION MANAGER 2007 SERVICE PACK 1

Configuration Manager 2007 SP1 was released in May of 2008 and added new features and enhancements to the product.

New Features and Enhancements

The following new features and enhancements are included in the Configuration Manager 2007 SP1 release:

Out of Band Management

Out of Band Management is a new feature to SP1 and allows you to remotely manage offline computers with chipsets that support Intel Active Management Technology (AMT). Using Out of Band Management and AMT, you can diagnose a problem even if the client's operating system fails to boot by connecting to the computer's management controller. Depending on the controller, you have the ability to reboot the system, change BIOS settings, or even PXE the computer and push an image to it from the network.

The following hardware prerequisites are needed to use Out of Band Management:

- Intel AMT version 3.2 (minimum revision of 3.2.1)
- Intel AMT version 4.0 and 4.1
- Intel AMT version 5.0

To learn more about Out of Band Management, see Chapter 8.

Asset Intelligence 1.5

Although Asset Intelligence 1.1 was included in the initial release of Configuration Manager 2007, it was limited in functionality and usability. Asset Intelligence was upgraded from 1.1 to 1.5 with Configuration Manager 2007 SP1 and was made a first-class citizen by giving it a dedicated node within the Configuration Manager console (Figure 1.7). Asset Intelligence lets you identify, inventory, and manage your hardware and software assets through the Asset Intelligence catalog. Starting with SP1, you can now edit this catalog to include your own custom information or can even synchronize it with System Center online to give you the most up-to-date information available. Once this information has been gathered, you can use the built-in reports to find any

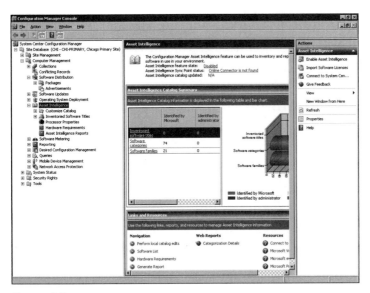

Figure 1.7
Asset Intelligence 1.5 Node

data that you need. Three types of reports are included with Asset Intelligence 1.5: Hardware, License Management, and Software. To learn more about Asset Intelligence, see Chapter 9.

CONFIGURATION MANAGER 2007 R2

Configuration Manager 2007 R2 was released in September of 2008 and added notable features such as support for Microsoft Application Virtualization. Other existing features were enhanced with this release including many areas within operating system deployment.

New Features and Enhancements

The following features and enhancements were included in the R2 release of Configuration Manager 2007.

Microsoft Application Virtualization Support

Microsoft Application Virtualization (App-V) allows you to package and deploy applications in a new and innovative way. App-V allows you to deploy software to remote machines without modifying other software that might be installed by creating a bubble around the virtualized software. This means that the application running within the virtual environment (the bubble) has isolated copies of the settings and files it needs to run the application—never modifying data outside of the bubble. The only exception is user data which is allowed to pass in and out of the bubble as needed (such as saving a document to the local hard drive). Using App-V, administrators can save time on packaging (referred to as sequencing), testing, and deploying software to client machines. Although App-V includes its own management and deployment server, it requires additional infrastructure and is completely separate from Configuration Manager 2007. With the release of R2, App-V applications can now be deployed and managed within the Configuration Manager console. To learn more about App-V and its integration with Configuration Manager, see Chapter 11, "Managing Software Distribution."

SQL Reporting Services

The SQL Reporting Services feature that is included with the R2 is designed to replace the legacy reporting services feature within Configuration Manager 2007. SQL Reporting Services provides many features compared to the legacy reporting system, such as higher performance, subscription-based reporting, and easier report creation. To learn more about enabling SQL Reporting Services within Configuration Manager, see Chapter 6.

Client Status Reporting

Client Status Reporting is designed to give you up to date information regarding the status of clients within your Configuration Manager 2007 site. When Client Status Reporting is installed, you can generate advanced reports about your clients, such as clients that are not requesting a policy, clients with nonfunctioning client components, or clients with out-of-date inventory/discovery information. Note that Client Status Reporting is designed to show information about your clients. Client Status Reporting cannot fix problems once they have been identified.

Unknown Computer Support (OSD)

With the addition of unknown computer support in Configuration Manager 2007 R2, you can now deploy an operating system to a computer without the

Configuration Manager client. Prior to R2, unknown computers had to be provisioned for OSD by inputting MAC addresses manually to the Configuration Manager database. This made OSD extremely difficult for bare metal systems. When unknown computer support is enabled in the PXE service point role, unknown computers are categorized as unprovisioned and are then eligible to receive task sequences that are advertised to the unknown computers collection (Figure 1.8). To learn more about unknown computer support, see Chapter 6 and Chapter 13.

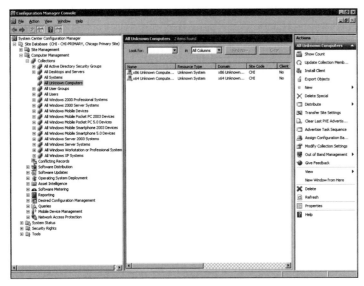

Figure 1.8
Unknown Computers Collection

Multicast Deployment (OSD)

With Configuration Manager 2007 R2, you can deploy operating system images and packages in the WinPE environment by using the multicast protocol. Multicast reduces network bandwidth by sending one stream of data to multiple clients instead of sending multiple streams of data to multiple clients. To learn more about multicast deployment, see Chapter 13.

Specify Credentials on Run Command Line Task Sequence (OSD)

This feature allows you to specify an account to use if you want to run a command as something other than System. This is typically used when accessing network shares that the computer account does not have access to.

CONFIGURATION MANAGER 2007 SP2

Configuration Manager 2007 SP2 was released in October of 2009 and added operating system support along with new features and enhancements.

Operating System Support

Support for the following operating systems was added with the SP2 release of Configuration Manager 2007.

- Windows Vista SP2
- Windows Server 2008 SP2
- Windows 7
- Windows Server 2008 R2

Adding support for these operating systems means that they can be managed by the client agent (with supported configurations). Also, these servers can now be configured to host all of the available site roles.

New Features and Enhancements

The following features and enhancements were included in the SP2 release for Configuration Manager 2007.

Branch Cache Support

Branch Cache is a new feature that was introduced with Windows 7 and Windows Server 2008 R2. It is designed to reduce network bandwidth by caching data on peer computers so that data access stays local whenever possible. Configuration Manager 2007 SP2 takes advantage of these new features and allows computers to use locally cached data instead of asking for it from distribution points. To learn more about Branch Cache support in Configuration Manager 2007, see Chapter 11.

ExtADSch.exe Logging Changes

ExtADSch.exe is a tool used to extend the Active Directory schema for Configuration Manager 2007. Before SP2, this tool only generated a log file that documented the install status. With SP2, command console feedback is provided in addition to the log file. To learn more about ExtADSch.exe and extending the Active Directory schema, see Chapter 4.

Asset Intelligence Changes

SP2 removes the System Center Online certificate requirement when installing the Asset Intelligence synchronization point site system role.

Operating System Deployment Changes

SP2 includes the Windows Automated Installation Kit (WAIK) 2.0, which updates the User State Migration Tool (USMT) to 4.0 and Windows PE to 3.0. These updated features enable the following:

- Bitlocker support
- Hard-links for user state migration
- New operating system deployment logs

SP2 also allows you to multi-select and delete drivers from the driver catalog in the Configuration Manager console. Although this seems like a minor issue, it can be very frustrating when trying to delete hundreds of drivers without the ability to multi-select and delete.

Client Policy Evaluation Improvements

- Faster policy evaluations by removing a two-minute policy execution wait.
- Software distribution at user login is nearly instantaneous by removing a ten-minute policy request wait. This is ideal for situations where applications need to be instantly available such as App-V applications.

64-bit Architecture Support

- Windows XP x64 and Windows Server 2003 x64 are now supported for remote control operations.

- The Operations Manager 2007 management pack now supports 64-bit operating systems.

- The Operations Manager 2007 client agent now supports 64-bit operating systems.

- App-V version 4.6 is now supported with SP2. App-V 4.6 supports 64-bit operating systems.

Out of Band Management Changes

Out of Band Management was significantly updated in SP2. Some of the more notable changes are briefly documented below.

802.1x Support   Adds the ability to use Out of Band Management on an 802.1x authenticated network.

Wireless Support   Adds the ability to use Out of Band Management over a wireless connection.

Audit Logging   Adds the ability to enable or disable audit logging on supported AMT controllers. These logs can be viewed through the Out of Band Management console.

Data Storage   Adds the ability to write to the 3rd Party Data Store (3PDS) through the Out of Band Management console on supported AMT controllers.

Power Management   Adds the ability to select different power control options per collection for provisioned resources.

CONFIGURATION MANAGER 2007 R3

R3 was a significant release for Configuration Manager 2007. The new features that were added focused around improved functionality, scalability, and power management. Listed below are the new features and enhancements that come with R3.

New Features and Enhancements

The following features and enhancements are included in the Configuration Manager 2007 R3 release.

Power Management

As energy costs rise and concerns about the environment grow, companies across the globe are being forced to think about energy conservation whenever possible. Configuration Manager 2007 R3 was designed to help meet these needs. R3 contains major enhancements around power management like giving you the ability to report on power consumption and showing you peak and non peak hours. Based on these reports, you can then build custom power policies that meet the needs of your environment. Power management settings are built in at the collection level to give you maximum control over how your computers and servers are affected. Some of these settings include when the computer sleeps, when the display turns off, and even when to wake up from sleep.

Operating System Deployment Enhancements

A new feature included with R3 is something called pre-staged media. This allows you to create a custom WIM image that contains both the boot image and the operating system. This image is then applied (typically by an OEM manufacturer) so that the image is located on the hard drive before the computer ships to the customer. When the customer boots the computer for the first time, it boots to the network and finishes the task sequence without ever having to go to the network for the image.

Scalability and Performance Improvements

One of Configuration Manager 2007 R3's biggest focuses was around scalability and performance. Enhancements were made in regards to collection evaluation and discovery methods, which increased the number of supported clients.

Fast Collection Evaluation   Fast collection evaluation allows Configuration Manager to find a newly discovered machine in as little as five minutes compared to the default evaluation period of 24 hours. This is done by comparing new machines with previously discovered machines and only processing the deltas (changes). Because these changes are typically small, this process is quick and easy, requiring minimal server resources. To learn more about fast collection evaluation, see Chapter 11.

Delta Active Directory Discovery   Delta Active Directory Discovery uses the same premise as fact collection evaluation. It scans for changes in Active Directory, only processing information about new resources such as users or computers. Because these evaluations do not require much processing power, they can be done more frequently. When Delta Discovery is enabled, it will look for changes every five minutes compared to the default of 24 hours. To learn more about Delta Active Directory Discovery, see Chapter 11.

Console Enhancements

The console has been updated in Configuration Manager 2007 R3 to help with common resource and collection membership tasks. For example, by right-clicking on a computer, you can now add it to a new collection or to an existing collection. You can also do this in reverse order by right-clicking on a collection and adding a resource to it. Although these features are now built into the Configuration Manager console, you still have the option to extend the console by using third-party applications or even writing your own. To learn more about extending the Configuration Manager console, see Chapter 20.

Forefront Endpoint Protection Integration

Although Forefront Endpoint Protection (FEP) 2010 was not included with R3, it was released around the same timeframe. FEP 2010 is Microsoft's newest anti-malware client (the successor to Forefront Client Security) and is managed using Configuration Manager 2007's infrastructure. FEP 2010 uses the built-in software distribution and desired configuration management components to deploy software updates and policy settings as well as monitor client health. FEP automatically creates collections in which computers are dynamically added and removed based on items such as health or policy distribution status. FEP 2010 adds a node to the Configuration Manager console under the Computer Management node called Forefront Endpoint Protection. For more information about FEP 2010 and its integration with Configuration Manager 2007, follow this link: http://www.microsoft.com/forefront/endpoint-protection/en/us/default.aspx.

THE FINAL WORD

The next chapter deals with the planning options that need to be taken into consideration when designing a site hierarchy. We'll discuss things like single and multi-site deployments and what needs to be in place for these types of scenarios.

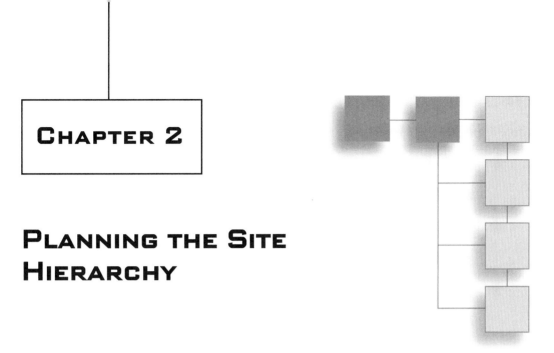

CHAPTER 2

PLANNING THE SITE HIERARCHY

When you take a look at a System Center Configuration Manager site, all you are really seeing is an administrative construct that is based on a set of IP address ranges. When you create a site, you are setting the options that control how systems within the address ranges will be managed. In much the same way as your local city government creates laws and tax structures for the city, a site has rules and configuration options for the systems within the site. Within the city limits you get the benefit of sewer and water services, plus other amenities depending on the municipality. If you live outside the city limits, you are not controlled by all of the laws, but you also don't have access to all of the amenities of living in town.

The Configuration Manager planning and deployment process can be broken down into three phases. Microsoft has identified these phases as preplanning, planning, and deployment. The remainder of this book is devoted to the deployment phase. In this chapter we are going to discuss the decision criteria that you need to take into consideration during the preplanning and planning phases. We will also take a look at the reasoning behind those decisions and some of the site planning options that are available. There are many choices you can make when planning out the site design. Thorough research and careful decision making are vital to a successful design.

PREPLANNING CRITERIA

Before you start planning how you are going to deploy System Center Configuration Manager, you need to start gathering information about your current environment. This information includes network diagrams, Active Directory configuration, network services, administrative design, and system types supported. All of this information will be used to create an efficient and manageable design. Without this information, you could introduce Configuration Manager into your current network and create more problems than solutions.

Some of the supporting documentation that you will be gathering may seem at first like it is a lot of superfluous information. However, as you start configuring the Configuration Manager components, you will find that there are good reasons for collecting the information. This is not just an exercise in futility or a way for us to make you do some extra work.

Network Topology

Your network topology will probably be the number one criteria that you use when building your site hierarchy. As we mentioned at the opening of this chapter, a site is nothing more than the IP addresses that define which systems will be managed. The information that you gather about the network will be used to determine which IP addresses will be configured for each site. You should also document the LAN and WAN connectivity to each location, the size of the network, the total bandwidth, the available bandwidth, network protocols, and traffic patterns.

Most of the information that you gather from this research will be used to determine if you can include a location within a site. Sites typically include systems that can access the site systems from a reliable connection. If you have systems that reside in a location that is connected to the corporate network through a slow or unreliable connection, or there are several systems and they are consuming the connection, you should consider creating multiple sites to control the traffic.

Active Directory Structure

Active Directory is a very important complimentary technology to Configuration Manager. While you don't have to have Active Directory to get

Configuration Manager to work, there are several benefits to integrating Configuration Manager and Active Directory. When gathering information about Active Directory, you should document the following items:

- **Forests and Domains**—used to determine the authentication realms that the managed systems belong to. Configuration Manager can manage systems in domains from trusted and untrusted domains. When a managed system is in a domain from an untrusted forest, additional components need to be configured. The managed systems in the untrusted forest will not be able to use Active Directory to locate site systems. A Server Locator Point will need to be configured so that the managed clients from the untrusted domain can communicate with the management point from the site.

- **Sites**—used to manage boundaries of sites within the Configuration Manager hierarchy. Active Directory sites can be used instead of IP addresses when defining the boundaries for a site. Of course a site is nothing more than a construct within Active Directory that is used to define one or more subnets. Identifying the Active Directory sites and the IP subnets that they manage allows you to determine if you can use a site as a boundary or if you will have to use IP addresses or subnets instead.

Server Environment

Full understanding of the servers that you have in your organization will help you determine which systems can be used to support Configuration Manager. As you document the servers, take note of services that they provide. File servers, DNS, DHCP, WINS, web servers, domain controllers, and terminal servers all lend functionality to Configuration Manager. For instance, file servers can easily become distribution points. DNS servers provide name resolution for the systems, but can also provide service location lookup. Web servers can host reporting points.

Virtualization has played an important role in many organizations. Reducing the number of physical servers, which in turn reduces the power consumption and cooling requirements, has saved organizations millions of dollars. Virtualization does present some interesting obstacles. Once the decision is made to virtualize the site systems, you need to make sure the host system has enough resources to allocate to the site system. If the site system gets "choked" off due to lack of resources, you could be facing severe problems managing your systems.

Configuration Manager is very data driven. There is a lot of data that is collected and stored within the database. As you will come to find out, there are several logs that record information as processes run. Where you store this information is also critical to how well the site server and site systems behave. The site server stores log files in the Configuration Manager installation directory by default. The site database server collects information about all of the managed systems as well as site information. With this in mind, you need to make sure that the storage subsystems that you use for either of these systems can handle the stress they are going to be under.

Client Environment

Document the clients installed at each location. This information should include the number of clients at each site and specific information about the clients. This information should include the operating systems, resources, applications, connection types, and mobility of each client. The collected information will help you determine which systems are laptops that may be moving to different locations from time to time, the operating systems and whether you can support them, and the applications that are already installed on the systems. Documenting the resources on each of the systems allows you to determine which systems can support being a branch distribution point if necessary.

Client mobility should be noted as you document client configurations. The mobility information that you need to collect will include the connection types that the client uses. If the client connects to the network using a VPN or SSL-VPN connection, note the connection information, including the VPN type, the subnet information used by the connection. If the client does not connect to the corporate network but does connect to the Internet, include that information also so you know how many clients may need to be managed via Internet based client management.

Organizations that have more than 100,000 systems will need to divide their system management into multiple sites. A management point can support 25,000 clients. If the management point is actually multiple systems running the management point role within a network load balanced cluster, up to 100,000 clients can be supported. Up to four systems can be included within a management point NLB cluster.

Finally, document the group policies, logon scripts, startup scripts, and shutdown scripts that are applied to each machine. This information will be used when determining the components that are affected by GPOs and scripts. You may want to remove or leverage these components when managing systems.

Organizational Structure

Although we typically think of Configuration Manager managing the systems within our organization, we need to take into consideration the organizational structure also. With this information in hand, you will be able to determine the departments within the organization, where applications need to be delivered, who has the authority to approve the applications, the persons who may need access to the console, and who you will need to give access to reports.

Geographic Profile

We now live in a global economy with offices located around the world. Take time to document the locations that you will need to support. This information should include languages that you will need to support, geopolitical limitations, and the time zones for each location. This information will help you determine whether you need to include the International Client Pack in your Configuration Manager installation as well as the settings that will need to be applied as you are deploying software, updates, and operating systems.

Security

Security documentation should include Active Directory security settings, including password restrictions, lockout restrictions, security groups, and members of the Domain Admins group. Using this information you can determine who has administrative control over the systems within the organization. You will also be able to plan a password change policy if you are going to use a domain account for services instead of the system accounts on site systems.

The level of security that is needed by the organization may also play a role in which site mode is selected. When a company needs to guarantee that the data sent between systems is encrypted, and that systems are authenticated to one another before they send data, then native mode needs to be used. If none of these requirements are necessary, and the organization doesn't need to support Internet based client management, then mixed mode will suffice.

Information Technology Organization

The information that you collect should also include details of the IT staff and their roles. This information will come in handy when you are determining who you will need to interface with when configuring systems and supporting services. Make sure that you not only include the members of the Windows Server team, but also note the owners of network services such as DNS and DHCP if those services are provided by UNIX or Linux systems. Network infrastructure teams should also be included for when you need to work with routers and switches.

Current and Previous Installations

If you have had, or currently support, another configuration management tool, document the information surrounding it. This information should include the product type and the configuration settings that were applied. If the other management solution included a client agent that needed to be added to the managed systems, make sure you determine how to uninstall the client so that it does not consume additional resources.

IDENTIFYING OBJECTIVES

You probably have an idea of why you want to install Configuration Manager. Some companies want inventory and metering information. Other companies want to utilize the software distribution and software updates functionality. Others want to use every component available. No matter what your needs, you should document the features that you want to enable, and the settings that you need to configure. This will help you determine what you need to configure, not only on the site server or site systems, but on other supporting services as well.

Let's assume that you want to install Configuration Manager for collecting hardware and software inventory and applying software updates to servers. Once that decision is made, you will know that you need to install WSUS on a server and enable the software inventory client agent, hardware inventory client agent, software updates client agent, and computer client agent. On top of those settings, you will also need to determine which systems will be the distribution points used to store the deployment packages.

If you take a look at the client agents, they represent most of the functionality present within a Configuration Manager site. Each agent has its own set of requirements and add configuration complexity to the site. Additional SQL Server resources are consumed as you enable each agent. The more data that you enable for inventory collection, the larger the database will grow. Software metering will also increase the size of the database as you enable more metering rules and add more clients into the site. Software updates will add additional configuration item information for every update that is synchronized. Every client will also report compliance information for all of the software updates synchronized within the site. Not every organization needs all of the functionality that Configuration Manager has to offer. Making a list of the functionality that you need will help ascertain how you are going to configure the site.

CONFIGURING A TEST LAB

The best way to learn any product is to work with it. With the advent of server virtualization, it has become very easy to create a lab environment. Testing new configuration settings and then reverting the systems back to a previous configuration setting allows you to test several options without having to worry about rebuilding systems. Leveraging virtualization for a lab environment can quickly get you on the path to understanding how Configuration Manager works.

Configuration Manager has a special setup option that can get a site configured and running very quickly. After installing the operating system on a virtual machine and loading all of the required prerequisites, you can start the Configuration Manager installation. The Installation Wizard includes an option for Simple Setup. For the most part, it is not recommended that you use this option. However, it is perfect for building your first lab Configuration Manager system.

The Simple Setup option installs everything. Well, nearly everything. Network access protection settings are not configured. Some of the components, such as operating system deployment, software distribution packages, and desired configuration management are not configured. It is up to you to configure these components after the site is created.

What the Simple Setup does is installs all of the components onto a single server and builds a mixed mode site. The site database, site server, management point, and distribution point roles are configured and started. All of the client agents are enabled with the exception of the network access protection client agent. Automatic Client Push Installation is enabled. With all that the Simple Setup does, you get a functional site very quickly, but at a cost. You do not get to choose how the components are configured at install time. They can always be changed later, but default settings are applied when the setup runs.

For a lab, the Simple Setup option is a great way to start working with Configuration Manager. If you are unfamiliar with the Configuration Manager console, you can start navigating and familiarizing yourself with all of the settings and features. Take the time to review all of the options and the settings that are available. When you install your production systems, you will have a better understanding of where components are configured and know how to navigate the components that are used for troubleshooting.

After you have familiarized yourself with the test site, you can start planning your site deployment. All of the planning decisions that you make need to be documented so that you can build a full test environment that will mimic the production environment. Having all of the planning decisions documented will assist you in fine-tuning the deployment settings when you find something that doesn't work quite the way you intended in your test lab.

Once you have the test lab built, make sure you have all of the installation and configuration criteria saved so that you can use those settings when installing the production site. Also, make sure you create a backup of the test lab so that you can go back to it when you want to try changing configuration settings. Having a test lab to work out changes before you introduce them into your production site will help you determine if the changes will adversely affect other components.

Site Planning Options

It can probably be said that no two Configuration Manager installations are created equal. Every organization is unique and every Configuration Manager installation is configured uniquely for each organization. Granted, there will be similarities, but you cannot take a cookie cutter approach to designing a site hierarchy. There are far too many variables that need to be taken into account. Evaluating those variables and making sound decisions for your site hierarchy are what this chapter is all about.

When evaluating, the primary decision criteria that will determine if you create a single or multiple site hierarchy are:

- Network bandwidth
- Administrative controls
- Site-level options
- Geo-political constraints

Network Bandwidth

Network bandwidth, and making sure that there is enough of it for the applications and services that need to use it, is extremely important. As most administrators have found, if an application does not have enough bandwidth to perform the tasks required, it will fail to return results to the user. When it comes to Configuration Manager, there are many components that require sufficient bandwidth to perform correctly. Components such as software distribution, operating system deployment, and software updates need to have enough bandwidth to deliver packages to clients as well as copy the necessary files to the appropriate site system roles.

When determining bandwidth requirements, make sure you not only look at the total bandwidth between locations, make sure you take into consideration available bandwidth. You don't want to adversely affect other applications, and you want to make sure that Configuration Manager has enough bandwidth to perform efficiently. There is nothing worse than trying to get the latest software package delivered to your user's workstations in a remote office, and the connection is so slow that it literally takes days to deliver the package.

Site server to site systems and site system to site system traffic patterns need to be evaluated, as well as the traffic patterns between clients and site systems. The storage of site data within the database is performed by the site server, but certain site systems, such as the management point and fallback status point, query the site database server. The site server is responsible for distributing software packages, operating system deployment packages, and software updates to the distribution points. Clients download software distribution packages, operating system deployment packages, and software updates from distribution points. They also download policies from, and upload status messages, state messages, inventory information, and software metering logs to management points.

All of this network traffic needs to be taken into account when you are planning your site hierarchy. If you have multiple locations where you support systems, the bandwidth and traffic patterns will be the primary decision point on whether you should create multiple sites or support all systems in one site. The other options that we are going to review next are also critical decision points, but nothing will cause more headaches than trying to manage systems across a slow or over-consumed link.

Administrative Controls

Let's take a moment and evaluate the administrative structure for your organization. Do all of the administrators have the same level of control over objects? Or do they have their own responsibilities? If each member of your administrative team shares the same responsibilities, there is a possibility that you will be able to use the default permissions and keep all of your resources within a single site. Of course the other options that are mentioned in this section will need to be evaluated before you can definitively say that a single site will meet your needs.

When determining the administrative options, you should always keep in mind that a simple design is always preferable to more complex options. As you increase the complexity of your design, you also increase the troubleshooting complexity. When you create a simple design however, you limit your ability to have more granular security and segmented administration.

Review the organization chart for your organization to determine who will need access to review information within the site. This will help you determine who will need to run reports, view status messages, and use queries. Also review the administrative needs of the organization. This information will help you determine who will need access to configure and manage components within the site. If you have administrative teams that need to have autonomous control over the site settings for a site, you may need to build another site for them to use. However, if they only need to manage computer configuration settings, you may be able to use security settings to limit what they can manage.

Site-Level Options

The settings configured within the Site Settings node affect all of the managed systems within the site. When you set the software inventory client agent to scan and collect information on all of the .exe and .vbs files, every managed system will perform the same type of scan. Accounts configured for client deployment and network access are used by every managed system.

If a certain number of the managed system population has to have different settings than the rest of the systems in the site, you will need to create another site to support them. This should not be taken lightly however. Evaluate the cost of administrative overhead when managing multiple sites to the management needs of specific systems. If there are different settings that need to be applied to client agents, evaluate whether you can include all of the settings within one site or if there are enough differences that it only makes sense to create a new site.

Geo-Political Constraints

Finally, review the geographic and political requirements when working with locations in other countries. You may have to abide by the laws of the country where the managed systems are located. This could include security regulations that control the encryption of data to the languages installed at the site. Most countries work well with regulations from other countries, but you should verify what the local regulations are before deploying sites. Many times it is easier to create a new site for the foreign location than to try to integrate all of the settings into an existing site.

PLANNING SITE DEPLOYMENT

The simplest site hierarchy is not really a hierarchy at all—it is the single site. This is the easiest configuration to implement, and it makes sense for many organizations to use. All of your systems are contained within the single site and the configuration and management of all of the systems is handled through a single set of configuration options. A single site implementation should be your initial goal when planning the site hierarchy. However, as you have been reading, you don't always have the luxury of having everything in one site. Other requirements may force you into creating another site and adding it to the hierarchy.

Begin your planning with a single site structure and then look at all of the information that you have collected in the preplanning phase. Review the planning criteria that we have discussed in the previous section. Then apply all of that knowledge to the following site planning questions.

Are the Locations Well-Connected?

If you have locations that are not well-connected, or the connections between sites are already saturated, and you don't want to minimize the traffic across the connection, you will need to create multiple sites. You will need a site for each of the locations that have communication limitations.

An exception to this planning option is a remote site that has very few clients. Even though the site may not be well connected, it will probably be too small for a dedicated site. With small locations, determine which site has the best connection to the location and add the small location as a boundary. Some of the technologies included within Configuration Manager 2007 allow you to minimize the traffic, even when the systems are within the same site, but not well connected. You can create a branch distribution point on a workstation. The branch distribution point will act as a distribution point for the systems within the remote location, allowing them to be considered on a well-connected connection to the distribution point when running software distribution, operating system deployment, and software update packages.

Do Administrators Need to Control Their Own Resources?

Administrative autonomy may be a requirement for some of the systems within your organization. There may be different organizational units, different departments, and even different management teams handling different system types. When administrative control over systems is divided up between administrative teams, you may have to create separate sites to control the administrative needs.

Take, for example, an organization that has two distinct administrative teams. One team is responsible for all of the workstations and another team manages all of the servers. While it is possible to create administrative structures within the console to manage each type of system separately, to have autonomy over the systems, it may be necessary to create a site to manage servers and another to manage workstations. Doing so will divide up the responsibilities and create a barrier so that one team doesn't accidentally affect the wrong type of system.

Although some level of autonomy can be obtained, as long as the sites are within the same hierarchy, there is always the possibility of another account having the ability to affect the sites within the hierarchy. The central site has the ability to affect how any child site beneath it functions. Administrators at the central site can create objects and manage settings that will "flow" down to the child sites. Also, any parent site can affect the child sites beneath them. To maintain the highest level of administrative autonomy, make sure the administrators at the parent site are conscientious about what they are manipulating. Complete autonomy can only be obtained by having sole control of the site. In very high security situations, that may mean creating a site that is not part of a hierarchy.

Do Resources Need to Be Managed Differently?

There are several site settings options that affect every system within the site. These settings become the default settings for all of the managed workstations and servers within the site. Settings that control the client agents, such as the hardware inventory and software inventory client agents have settings that control what is inventoried on a managed system. These settings will be used by every system, and every system will inventory the same type of information.

If there are any systems that need special settings that collect different inventory information, those systems will need to belong to a different site that has settings specifically configured for their needs. This holds true for most of the client agents. The remote tools client agent contains a setting that is used to manage the accounts that can start the remote tools on systems. If any systems have security restrictions and need to limit the users who can use the remote tools, they will need a different site.

DOCUMENTING THE DETAILS OF EACH SITE

After deciding how many sites need to be created, you will need to determine whether each site will be a primary or secondary site, what each site's site code will be, a name that you will use to identify the site, and site boundaries. Determining the three characters that you will use for each site can be difficult. Some organizations base the site codes on locations, others by department, and yet others will create a numbering scheme while using the site name as the primary visual identifier. Because the site code cannot be changed, make sure that you review your decision before creating the site.

The site boundaries must be unique to the site. No two sites should have overlapping boundaries. When an IP address exists in two sites, the Configuration Manager client becomes "confused." If you are using automatic client assignment, the client will not be able to determine which site it should be assigned to. If the client is able to move from one site to another, also known as roaming, the client will think that it is within its assigned site, even though it is actually located within a different site.

Site boundaries can either be IPv4 subnets, IPv6 prefixes, IPv4 address ranges, or Active Directory sites. If you have the luxury of your Active Directory site structure matching your Configuration Manager site structure, you can manage all of your sites by using the Active Directory Sites and Services snap-in. In a single site, this will probably be the case. Once you start creating a hierarchy, maintaining both site structures to match might not be feasible.

Primary Site Considerations

Primary sites require more functionality and resources than secondary sites, but also provide more features and flexibility. Primary sites require a SQL database to support the site. Determine if you have the resources available to install a SQL Server instance to support the site. If the resources are not available, you will have to create a secondary site.

If the resources are available, you need to determine if you need to have the additional administrative support at the site, or if you will administer the site from the parent. Secondary sites do not have their own administrative functionality. All of the configuration changes are managed at that parent primary site.

Licensing is also a consideration. Primary sites require a full Configuration Manager 2007 license. Secondary sites do not require additional Configuration Manager licensing. A SQL Server license is also required, although a version of Configuration Manager 2007 with a SQL Server license can be purchased. This version of SQL Server can only be used to support the Configuration Manager database however.

The final question you should ask yourself when considering a primary or secondary site; do you need to retain functionality of the site if the parent site fails, or do you have a need to change the parent site in the future? A secondary site needs to be uninstalled and reinstalled if you plan on moving its functionality to another parent site. Without the primary parent site, the secondary site doesn't truly exist. Primary sites can exist autonomously from other sites. If the parent site fails, the primary child will continue to function.

Moving primary sites to have another parent is also an option. You can restructure your hierarchy by changing the parent site that the primary child reports to. Making a structural change to the site hierarchy will affect how the sites will function. Parent sites control many of the settings for the primary child site. When you change the parent site, the primary child site will start "reconfiguring." This reconfiguration will include changes to collections, packages, security settings, and other properties.

You should plan for the change before moving the site to another parent within the hierarchy. The change will affect who is able to manage the site. All of the objects that are replicated to the primary child will no longer be available. The accounts responsible for managing the original parent will no longer have the ability to create objects that are replicated to the primary child site. At the same time, accounts within the new parent site will now be able to create objects that will be replicated to the primary child site. Review the administrative design of the site hierarchy and verify that the changes will not adversely affect the management of the new site structure.

In a single site hierarchy, the central site is the only primary site for the organization. Any configuration that includes more than a single site calls for one or more primary sites to be created.

Central Site Considerations

The central site is the top-most site within the site hierarchy. Many of the configuration items that are managed at the central site will be replicated and passed down to the lower sites in the hierarchy. Most of the data that is collected at the lower sites within the hierarchy is sent up to the central site. The central site database will contain information from all of the sites in the hierarchy. Because there is so much data that is stored within the central site's site database, many organizations use the central site as a reporting site, leaving the management of resources to the lower sites in the hierarchy.

If you have decided to create two or more primary child sites because you need to have administrative autonomy over resources, consider creating a central site that will be the parent site to the primary sites. The central site should be managed by a group that does not need to control resources, but does have a stake in reporting information about the resources within the organization. You want to make sure that you can trust the administrators of the central site. Being able to affect settings at the lower sites in the hierarchy can cause problems with how systems are managed. The fewer administrators you have at the central site, the easier it is to manage accountability.

There are some settings that need to be configured at the central site however. For instance, if you are planning on using the software update functionality built into Configuration Manager, the active software update point at the central site will be the software update point that will be responsible for retrieving the update catalog from Microsoft Updates. Once the central site's software update point has synchronized the updates, the other sites within the hierarchy are notified that they need to synchronize with their upstream servers. With this in mind, you will need to allow the administrators who are responsible for managing software updates to have access to the software updates configuration settings at the central site.

Secondary Site Considerations

Unlike primary sites, secondary sites do not require an additional Configuration Manager license and they do not require a SQL database. Secondary sites are created to primarily manage traffic between two locations. The same types of senders exist for a primary parent/secondary child relationship as a primary parent/primary child relationship. The difference between creating a primary child site and a secondary child site is the primary parent site needs to already exist when creating a secondary site. With primary sites, each primary site is installed and can be configured independently of the others. Only when you want to create a hierarchy do you need to identify which site will be the parent. With secondary sites, you need to identify which site will be the parent site when installing the secondary site.

All of the clients that are within the boundaries of the secondary site are actually assigned to the parent primary site. Although secondary sites use components from the parent site, such as the management point and site database server, you do not have to rely on the clients communicating with those remote systems. If you determine that the client systems are sending too much data across the WAN link that connect the two locations, you can create "replicas" of the management point and site database at the secondary site.

When moving the functionality of the management point to the secondary site, you will need to install the management point role on a system. This new management point is not truly a management point for the secondary site; it is actually a replica of the management point from the parent primary site. The term used for this new management point is proxy management point. All of the client systems within the secondary site will communicate with the proxy management point for the same type of data as they would any other management point. Policy information is retrieved from the proxy management point and inventory data, status, and state messages are sent to the proxy management point.

As for the site database, a SQL replica of the site database can be stored locally at the secondary site so that site systems within the secondary site can have local access to the data stored in the database. When determining whether to create a replica database, determine if the amount of data sent across the WAN link is greater when the site systems are accessing the database or when the SQL replication is occurring. Whenever you are working with replication of data, take note that the data at the secondary site may not be as up-to-date as the data stored within the site database at the primary site.

Note

Although it is possible to locate a SQL Server replica within the secondary site, it is not a common practice. Usually budget constraints and limited network availability restrict this practice.

Determining Parent/Child Relationships

Once the basic site decisions have been made, the site hierarchy needs to be designed. This is where you need to determine which site is going to be a parent and which will be a child site. The central site will also need to be chosen. Information that was gathered to determine whether or not to create an additional site and the types of sites that will be created, will be used here.

When creating a secondary site, it is rather easy to determine how the parent/child relationship will be configured. Secondary sites are created to manage network traffic between locations that should otherwise all exist within a primary site. Determining which primary site should be the parent and which should be the child in a primary parent/primary child relationship could be a little more difficult. Ultimately, it comes down to which administrators need to exert control over each site and where reporting of information is required.

As mentioned earlier in this chapter, when you create a hierarchy, the parent sites have the ability to control settings and objects within the child sites. Data that is collected at the child sites is passed up the hierarchy and stored within the site databases at each parent site. Carefully plan which site will become the child of another site if for no other reason than to make sure that the databases do not populate incorrectly.

Planning Site Connections

There are really only three types of connections used for communication between sites. These "connections" are called senders. Senders come in three flavors, standard, remote access (RAS), and courier. By far the most common type of sender is the standard sender. With a standard sender, all data communications between sites is performed using an "always on" connection. There is no need for any type of demand dial when sending the data between sites; it is assumed that the two systems can communicate with each other at any time.

RAS senders are used when there is some type of demand dial required for the two systems to communicate with one another. Typically, this involves some type of remote access server that controls an ISDN, X.25, modem, or VPN connection.

A courier sender is a special type of sender that is used when there is no communication between systems, or there is such a limited, unreliable connection that you would not want to send data using that connection. Instead, the data that needs to be sent from one system to another is stored on some type of removable media and delivered to the remote system by way of a courier, such as UPS, FedEx, or USPS. Once delivered, the administrator at the remote system unpackages the data on the appropriate system.

No matter which of the senders that you use, you have options to control how the data is transferred. Each sender needs addresses so that the sender knows where and when to deliver data. There are both timing settings and bandwidth control settings that can be configured on each address. When determining how you want to deliver data, make sure you take into account the high traffic periods of the WAN link so that you can throttle the data accordingly.

Physical Considerations

Every site needs to have a site server. The remaining site system roles are dependent upon the type of site and the functionality required at the site. Careful planning of the roles is required when designing the site. Some of the site system roles can reside on the same system as other site system roles, but there are some that you may not want to share system resources, and others that cannot be installed on a system where other site system roles already exist.

Site Server

The site server is the primary component within the site. Site servers are responsible for controlling most of the functionality within the site and between site systems. For instance, when a package is created or updated, the site server is responsible for sending the package to the chosen distribution points within the site and is responsible for sending the packages to remote sites according to the schedule set on the address defined for the remote site. Site servers are also responsible for aggregating the data that is collected from each of the managed systems and the other site systems within the site. Several summarizers evaluate and store data within the site database. Collected inventory is processed by the site server. Collection membership is evaluated and updated based upon the schedule assigned to the collection.

With all of this activity, the site server needs to have adequate resources to process the required data. In large environments, or organizations that do not have systems with high-end resources, it is advisable to reduce the number of site system roles assigned to the site server system. By default, the distribution point and management point roles are installed on the site server when installed to the site. Moving these roles to other systems will allow the site server to perform better.

Virtualizing the site server is a viable option in many cases. As long as the host system has enough resources to support the site server, which includes bandwidth, processor, drive allocation, and memory allocation. The primary bottlenecks that you will encounter with the site server are network bandwidth and drive performance.

SQL Server

Nearly all of the site's information is stored within the site database. Careful planning of the data that is collected within the site will help maintain the site database at an acceptable level. Baseline the database with only a few clients installed to determine how much data is stored within the site database. As you install the client on other systems, monitor the database growth. Most systems will consume approximately the same amount of space within the database. Once you have a baseline for the amount of data, you can estimate how large the database will be when all of the systems are managed.

For best performance, the site database should reside on a dedicated SQL Server. If the SQL Server instance used to host the site database has dedicated spindles for storing the database and log files, the SQL Server can be used to host other databases. We recommend co-locating the SQL Server with the site server only in those cases where you may have a smaller site.

Virtualizing the SQL Server is supported, but testing to determine if the SQL Server will perform as needed is critical. SQL Servers are very disk and memory intensive, so verify that you have enough resources to efficiently process the data from the site. For most implementations, if the site is only going to support up to 5,000 clients, it is a safe bet that the SQL Server can be co-located on the same system as the site server. As you increase the client support, it is best to divide up the roles onto separate systems. As with everything though, make sure you are monitoring performance and place the roles accordingly.

Management Point

The management point role is another vital role within the site. All of the clients use the management point to retrieve their policy and to send collected information. The management point requires a lot of network bandwidth to support the managed systems within the site. The management point is often installed on the site server, but it does not have to remain there. Management points are good candidates for virtualization. The primary bottleneck for a management point is network bandwidth. With all of the clients within the site sending status messages, state messages, and inventory data to the management point, you can see where it can get pretty busy.

Management points do have an upper limit to the number of clients they can support. Microsoft supports a total of 25,000 clients per management point. If your site has more than 25,000 clients, the management point role can be installed on up to four systems, but for all management points to respond to clients, you will need to create an NLB cluster. When doing so, make sure that the management points, if virtualized, are located on different virtual hosts. This will allow you to distribute the network load.

Fallback Status Point

The fallback status point is a perfect candidate for virtualization. When you deploy the fallback status point, you should not install it on a system that hosts any other Configuration Manager roll within the site. When site is in native mode, all of the site systems need to have a certificate in place to allow them to communicate securely. The fallback status point is the exception to the rule. When a client system has a problem communicating with the management point, it will send the information to the fallback status point instead. In the case where the client cannot communicate due to a problem with the certificate, the data needs to be sent unencrypted. If the fallback status point was installed on a system that hosts another site system role, then the unencrypted communication would be rejected.

Distribution Point

Distribution points are glorified file servers. As a matter of fact, if you have file servers that have enough available drive space, you can install the distribution point role on the file server. The bottlenecks that will occur on a distribution point are storage and network bandwidth. Distribution points need to have enough bandwidth to efficiently distribute packages, updates, and operating system images, as well as receive packages that are sent from site servers.

Drive storage is the critical component for distribution points however. When you are planning the amount of drive space for a distribution point, assume you will need close to triple the size of the packages you are planning to install. The additional space required for packages is used to store compressed packages when the package is sent to another site, and for signed versions that are used when remote differential compression is used with a package.

Reporting Point

Depending upon how many users want to run reports, you could co-locate your reporting point with another site system role. Reporting is a resource intensive task however, and if there are several users accessing reports, you may want to install the reporting point role on a dedicated site system. When configuring the reporting point for the central site, make sure you have adequate resources to support the role. All of the data collected within the hierarchy will be stored in the central site's database. This could potentially be a lot of data for the SQL Server to process against.

Software Update Point

Before you can install the software update point site system role, you will need to install Windows Server Update Services. If you already have a WSUS system, you can integrate it into your Configuration Manager site. When you do so, the WSUS functionality will change. Clients will still contact the WSUS system in order to receive the update catalog that they need when scanning for required and installed updates. The results of those scans are sent to the management point as state messages. Updates that are approved and packaged for delivery to the clients are stored on distribution points and not the WSUS server.

Software updates points have a network bandwidth bottleneck. As clients request the update metadata from the catalog, the software update point in a large site can become quite busy. Two mechanisms have been implemented that allow the software update point to perform efficiently. The first is a random offset for the client systems. When the software update client agent is scheduled to run at a specific time, a random amount of time, up to two hours, is added to the start time. This guarantees that not all of the clients will request information from the software update point at the same time.

The other is network load balancing. When a site has more than 25,000 clients, the software update point can be configured as part of an NLB cluster. Up to four systems can be configured within the software update point NLB cluster. As clients request the update information, they will be connected to the site system with the lightest performance load.

PXE Service Point

The PXE service point uses the PXE components from Windows Deployment Services. The PXE service point integrates and adds additional functionality to the PXE services within WDS, allowing Configuration Manager to perform zero-touch operating system deployments. The PXE service point also provides a PXE distribution point to the site. The PXE distribution point is used to store boot images used during operating system distribution. Make sure you have enough free disk space on your system running WDS to support all of the boot images you will use.

Site Settings Planning Options

Once you have decided on what site systems are going to be installed within the site and how the site hierarchy is going to be created, you should turn your attention to the finer details of how the site settings will be configured. These settings include discovery methods, client installation properties, hardware and software inventory, and maintenance tasks. Some of these settings require interaction with other services within your organization, such as Active Directory. Proper functionality requires that you configure them correctly and maintain the settings according to policies within your organization. Starting at the top of the settings tree, the following settings should be taken into consideration:

- **Client Agents**—For each of the components that you decided to run within your site, you will need to configure the associated client agent. There are several to configure, and you should only configure those that you want to support within the site. Most of the client agents have schedules for when they run. Evaluate how often you need to run each of the client agents. Some will need to be set a little more aggressive than others. The advertised programs client agent typically needs to run more often than the hardware inventory and software inventory client agents. Make sure the schedule you set makes sense for the component. Running an inventory once an hour is too often. You are only going to inundate the site server with needless information. Running the advertised program client agent once an hour is a valid option. Any new program that is advertised will be detected by the client in a relatively efficient manner. The client agents that can be configured are:
  - Hardware inventory client agent
  - Software inventory client agent
  - Advertised programs client agent
  - Computer client agent
  - Desired Configuration Management client agent
  - Mobile device client agent
  - Power management client agent
  - Remote tools client agent
  - Network access protection client agent
  - Software metering client agent
  - Software updates client agent

  Each of the client agents are discussed in the chapters that detail the components they are used with.

- **Client Installation Methods**—The two installation methods found here can be configured so that the client will be installed on new systems. When evaluating the settings that you want to apply, the following questions should be asked:

- Do you want to automatically install the client on any discovered system?
- If you are going to automatically install the client, do you want to install it on workstations, servers, domain controllers, and site systems?
- What account or accounts will be used to install the client?
- What installation switches will be applied when the client is installed?
- Will the client be installed automatically from the software update point?

Once you have answered these questions, the configuration options can be applied accordingly. See Chapter 7 for more information on configuring client installation properties.

- **Discovery Methods**—Once you have determined the resource types that you plan to manage, you will need to enable discovery methods to "find" the resources. All of the discovery methods have a schedule for when they run. Determine how often you need to look for new resources and make sure the settings are not too aggressive. Once you have determined how often you will discover resources, configure the search location. The Active Directory discoveries can be configured to search only specific locations within Active Directory. The Network discovery can be used to locate systems on the intranet, either by locating them via subnets, SNMP, or DHCP. The discovery methods that can be configured are:
  - **Active Directory System Group Discovery**—Used to discover the groups and organizational units that systems are a member of. The Active Directory locations and the schedule can be configured for this discovery.
  - **Active Directory System Discovery**—Used to discover the workstations and servers within the domains. The Active Directory locations, additional object attributes, and the schedule can be configured for this discovery.
  - **Active Directory Security Group Discovery**—Used to discover the security groups that user resources are members of. The Active Directory locations and the schedule can be configured for this discovery.
  - **Active Directory User Discovery**—Used to discover the user accounts within the domains. The Active Directory locations,

additional object attributes, and the schedule can be configured for this discovery.

- **Heartbeat Discovery**—The client sends a discovery information on a scheduled basis. The schedule can be configured for this discovery.
- **Network Discovery**—Used to discover objects within the network that may not be members of the organization's domains. The schedule for running this discovery can be configured, as well as the following discovery options:
  - Detail level of client information
  - Slow network discovery
  - Subnets to search
  - Domains to include in the search
  - SNMP community strings
  - SNMP devices to query
  - DHCP servers to query
  - Length of time to allow the discovery to run

For more information on Discovery Methods, see Chapter 7.

- **Site Maintenance**—There are several built-in tasks that are used to maintain the site database. These tasks need to be configured so that they run efficiently, yet not too often. Each of the tasks has a schedule as to when it will run, and the deletion tasks are configured with the length of time an object is allowed to age within the database before it is deleted. The schedule that you set for these tasks should allow them to run when other site functions are dormant. The tasks and their respective settings can be found in Chapter 3.

- **Status Filter Rules**—Status filter rules are used to control the status messages that are stored within the database. Not every status message needs to be stored within the database. And some status messages need to be stored quicker than others. You want to make sure that any critical messages are stored immediately, while other less important messages are queued up for processing. For more information on status message filters and how to manage them, see Chapter 3.

The Final Word

Proper planning is vital to a healthy site. Anyone can simply install the components and start using Configuration Manager 2007. Installing it correctly and having the components working efficiently is not always so easy. Taking into consideration the types of systems that you need, the site system roles that will be needed, the location of the site systems, and the configuration settings that define how everything works, takes a lot of planning. Once implemented however, the site should only need occasional tweaking.

In the next chapter, we are going to discuss how to maintain the site database. There are several options that can be used to manage database growth and performance. As with the planning of the site, the maintenance planning is critical to efficient site performance.

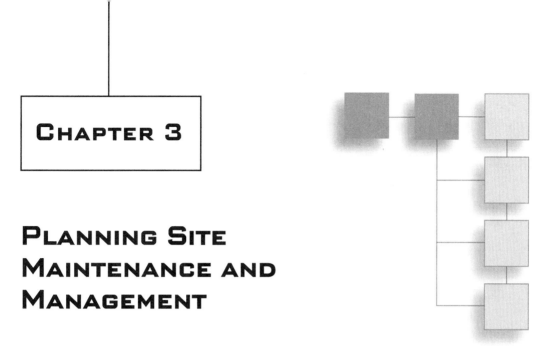

CHAPTER 3

PLANNING SITE MAINTENANCE AND MANAGEMENT

In the previous chapters, we have discussed the feature set of System Center Configuration Manager 2007 R3 and how to plan your site hierarchy. This chapter is going to remain in the planning phase, but will focus on configuring settings that will be used for troubleshooting and maintaining the database.

WORKING WITH SITE STATUS

Status messages are an extremely important part of your site. They can let you know when a component is not performing as it should, inform you of important processes that are running, and display the details of warnings and errors that appeared within the site. As you administer your site on a day-to-day basis, you will find that you will be reviewing status messages on a regular basis. It is with the status messages that you will typically start your initial trouble-shooting when a problem occurs.

Every component within Configuration Manager generates status messages. Status messages are stored within the database so that you can use them for troubleshooting purposes. Hundreds of status messages are generated within the site on a daily basis. For the most part, these messages are very useful. You will find that you can determine what is happening with all aspects of the site just by perusing the status messages that are available. Many of the status messages that are generated by the Configuration Manager components are informational messages. Most informational messages are innocuous and will only take up

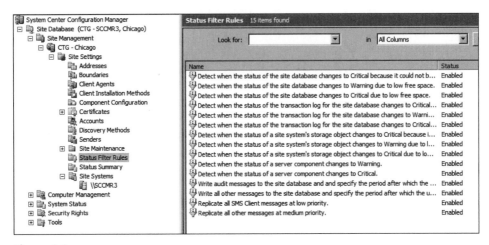

Figure 3.1
Status Filter Rules Node

additional space within the database. To make sure that only the valid status messages are stored in the database, status filter rules are used to control the messages that are stored in the database and how long the status messages remain in the database. Status filter rules are also used to detect when site components are reporting that they are having problems.

Status filter rules are found within the site settings of the site. Figure 3.1 shows the Status Filter Rules node and the default filters that are included with the default installation of Configuration Manager. You can create additional filters if you find a need to store additional status messages in the database. The processing priority can also be controlled from this screen. The order of processing precedence is top-down in this list. The first status filter is evaluated, and then the next, until the end of the list is reached. If the criterion of the status message matches one of the rules, that action is taken, and typically, the remainder of the status filter rules continues evaluating the rule. You do have the option to stop processing of any lower priority rules if you do not want to perform any other actions on a status message.

Figure 3.2 shows the settings that are available on the General tab of a status message filter. It is here that you can configure the criterion that is evaluated when a status message is received at the site server. The criteria can include any of the following settings:

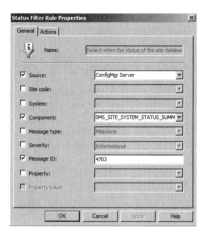

Figure 3.2
Status Filter Rule General Properties Tab

- **Source**—Where the status message was generated. Available options are as follows:
  - ConfigMgr Client
  - ConfigMgr Provider
  - ConfigMgr Server

- **Site Code**—Site where the status message originated. Only sites within the hierarchy are available from the drop-down.

- **System**—The site server or site system where the status message originated. Only site systems or the site servers within the hierarchy appear in the drop-down.

- **Component**—The component that generated the status message. Only components that are installed within the site are available from the drop-down.

- **Message Type**—Specifies the type of status message. Available options in the drop-down are as follows:
  - **Audit**—References to objects being added, modified, or deleted.
  - **Detail**—Process information that is generated during component activity.
  - **Milestone**—The start or ending of a process or component activity.

- **Severity**—Specifies the severity level of the status message. Available severity levels included in the drop-down are as follows:

- **Informational**—Event record of a component performing an activity.
- **Warning**—Notice that a component had a problem while processing, but is not typically a fatal problem within the site.
- **Error**—Notification that a component had a problem while processing and the administrative staff should take notice and troubleshoot the issue.

- **Message ID**—The message identifier of the status message.

- **Property**—The property of the status message that will be evaluated. Available options from the drop-down include:
  - Advertisement ID
  - Collection ID
  - Package ID
  - Policy Assignment ID
  - Policy ID
  - Software Metering Rule ID
  - Unique CIA ID

- **Property Value**—The value that is associated with the Property that is selected in the Property drop-down. The drop-down will display the available items from the site hierarchy.

The status message filter in Figure 3.3 is the Detect When the Status of the Site Database Changes to Warning Due to Low Free Space filter. There are three

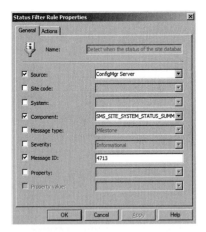

Figure 3.3
General Tab of the Detect When the Status of the Site Database Changes to Warning Due to Low Free Space Filter

options selected for evaluation—Source, Component, and Message ID. Any status message that is evaluated by the site server that originates from the SMS_SITE_SYSTEM_STATUS_SUMMARIZER component on the site server (ConfigMgr server) that has a message ID of 4713 will be processed by this status message filter.

Status messages that match the criteria are then processed based upon the settings found on the Actions tab. It is here that you can control the messages that are delivered to the site database or processed using another method. As with the options available on the General tab, all of the available actions on the Actions tab can be selected at the same time. Typically, that is not the case. You will probably want to either put the status message in the database or have it reflected within a log file. The available options are as follows:

- **Write to the ConfigMgr database**—Used to store the status message in the database.

- **Allow the user to delete messages after how many days**—Controls the grooming of status messages stored in the database. The value specified here is used to control when the status message will be expired. The Delete Aged Status Messages task uses this value when evaluating the status messages that it will remove from the database.

- **Report to the event log**—When selected, the status message is forwarded to the Application log.

- **Replicate to the parent site**—Used to control which messages are forwarded to the parent site.

- **Replication priority**—Used to control the priority level that is used when replicating the status message to the parent site.

- **Run a program**—Used to trigger the start of a program after a status message is detected.

- **Program**—Specifies the program that will be run once a matching status message is detected.

- **Do not forward to status summarizers**—When selected, the status message will not be evaluated by status summarizers and will not affect site or component status.

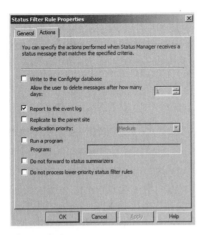

Figure 3.4
Actions Tab of the Detect When the Status of the Site Database Changes to Warning Due to Low
Free Space Filter

- **Do not process lower-priority status filter rules**—When selected, any matching status message will not be evaluated by status message filters that have a lower priority.

Looking at Figure 3.4, the Actions tab of the status filter rule Detect When the Status of the Site Database Changes to Warning Due to Low Free Space is shown. Because the status message matched the criteria on the General tab, this status message will be forwarded to the Application event log. That is not the end of the processing line for this status message however. Because the Do Not Process Lower-Priority Status Filter Rules option has not been selected, any status message that meets the criteria will continue to be processed by other status message filters.

Many organizations never make any changes to the default status filter rules. Chances are, you will not need to do anything within your sites. But there are some good reasons to modify and create status filter rules. You may find that you want to send a specific status message to a parent site for reporting purposes. Or you may want to filter out messages so that you don't have excess data in the database. One common reason for creating new status filter rules is to make monitoring of your site easier. You can create a status filter rule that sends a status message to the Application event log, which is then read by System Center Operations Manager 2007. Operations Manager can then alert or perform an action when the status message is detected.

Evaluating what data you want to keep within the database is critical to maintaining an efficient database. If you don't need to report on informational status messages, you may want to groom them more frequently than warning or error messages. You can create a new status filter rule that is used to store informational messages in the database, but has an expiration time shorter than that of the warning or error messages. To do so, let's assume that you want to groom informational messages after 14 days. You would follow these steps to create the status message filter:

1. Expand Site Database > Site Management > Site > Site Settings > Status Filter Rules.

2. Right-click Status Filter Rules and select New Status Filter Rule.

3. In the Name field, enter Informational Message Expiration and Replication.

4. Select the checkbox next to Severity.

5. Verify Informational is listed in the drop-down.

6. Click Next.

7. Select the checkbox next to Write to the ConfigMgr Database.

8. In the Allow the User to Delete Messages after How Many Days field, enter 14.

9. Select the checkbox next to Replicate to the Parent Site.

10. In the Replication Priority drop-down, verify Low is selected.

11. Select the checkbox next to Do Not Process Lower-Priority Status Filter Rules.

12. Click Next twice and click Close.

13. In the Status Filter Rules details pane, right-click the Informational Message Expiration and Replication filter rule and select Increment Priority.

14. Continue right-clicking and selecting Increment Priority until the rule is listed above the Write All Other Messages to the Site Database and Specify the Period after Which the User Can Delete the Messages rule.

CREATING STATUS MESSAGE QUERIES

Status message queries are very similar to data queries. The primary difference is that status message queries only return status messages. As you can see in Figure 3.5, there are several status message queries included within the default installation of Configuration Manager. These can be used to quickly reference status messages that have been stored in the database. Do take note that the status messages that are returned from queries are only those that have been processed by a status message summarizer. If the status message has not been summarized and placed in the database yet, you will not see it reflected in the results of the query.

The primary benefit of having status message queries is being able to extract the information you need from the database very quickly. The same information can typically be found within the status message viewer for a component, but with a

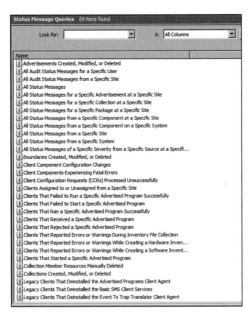

Figure 3.5
Status Message Queries

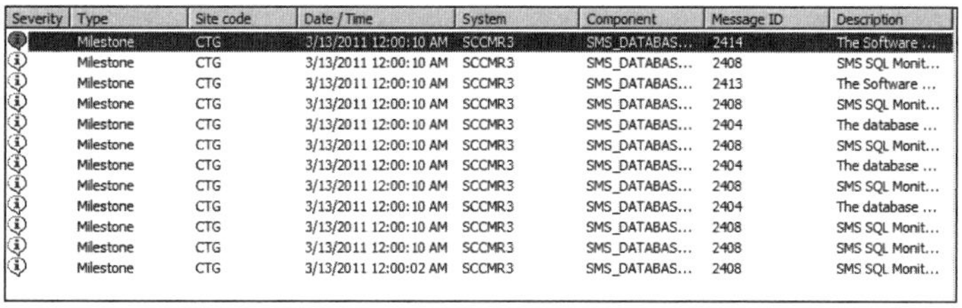

Severity	Type	Site code	Date / Time	System	Component	Message ID	Description
	Milestone	CTG	3/13/2011 12:00:10 AM	SCCMR3	SMS_DATABAS...	2414	The Software ...
	Milestone	CTG	3/13/2011 12:00:10 AM	SCCMR3	SMS_DATABAS...	2408	SMS SQL Monit...
	Milestone	CTG	3/13/2011 12:00:10 AM	SCCMR3	SMS_DATABAS...	2413	The Software ...
	Milestone	CTG	3/13/2011 12:00:10 AM	SCCMR3	SMS_DATABAS...	2408	SMS SQL Monit...
	Milestone	CTG	3/13/2011 12:00:10 AM	SCCMR3	SMS_DATABAS...	2404	The database ...
	Milestone	CTG	3/13/2011 12:00:10 AM	SCCMR3	SMS_DATABAS...	2408	SMS SQL Monit...
	Milestone	CTG	3/13/2011 12:00:10 AM	SCCMR3	SMS_DATABAS...	2404	The database ...
	Milestone	CTG	3/13/2011 12:00:10 AM	SCCMR3	SMS_DATABAS...	2408	SMS SQL Monit...
	Milestone	CTG	3/13/2011 12:00:10 AM	SCCMR3	SMS_DATABAS...	2404	The database ...
	Milestone	CTG	3/13/2011 12:00:10 AM	SCCMR3	SMS_DATABAS...	2408	SMS SQL Monit...
	Milestone	CTG	3/13/2011 12:00:10 AM	SCCMR3	SMS_DATABAS...	2408	SMS SQL Monit...
	Milestone	CTG	3/13/2011 12:00:02 AM	SCCMR3	SMS_DATABAS...	2408	SMS SQL Monit...

Figure 3.6
Status Message Viewer

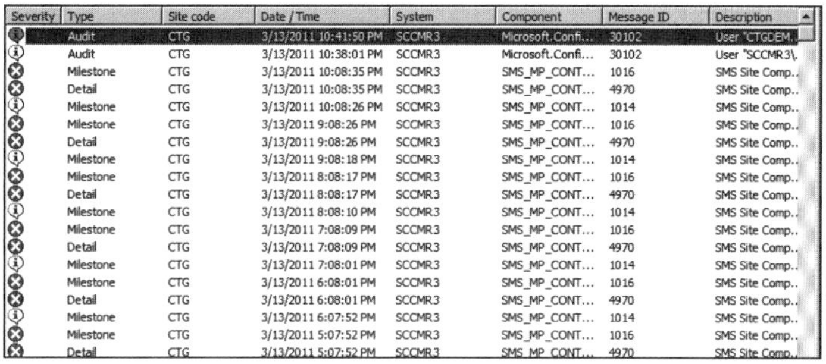

Severity	Type	Site code	Date / Time	System	Component	Message ID	Description
	Audit	CTG	3/13/2011 10:41:50 PM	SCCMR3	Microsoft.Confi...	30102	User "CTGDEM...
	Audit	CTG	3/13/2011 10:38:01 PM	SCCMR3	Microsoft.Confi...	30102	User "SCCMR3\...
	Milestone	CTG	3/13/2011 10:08:35 PM	SCCMR3	SMS_MP_CONT...	1016	SMS Site Comp...
	Detail	CTG	3/13/2011 10:08:35 PM	SCCMR3	SMS_MP_CONT...	4970	SMS Site Comp...
	Milestone	CTG	3/13/2011 10:08:26 PM	SCCMR3	SMS_MP_CONT...	1014	SMS Site Comp...
	Milestone	CTG	3/13/2011 9:08:26 PM	SCCMR3	SMS_MP_CONT...	1016	SMS Site Comp...
	Detail	CTG	3/13/2011 9:08:26 PM	SCCMR3	SMS_MP_CONT...	4970	SMS Site Comp...
	Milestone	CTG	3/13/2011 9:08:18 PM	SCCMR3	SMS_MP_CONT...	1014	SMS Site Comp...
	Milestone	CTG	3/13/2011 8:08:17 PM	SCCMR3	SMS_MP_CONT...	1016	SMS Site Comp...
	Detail	CTG	3/13/2011 8:08:17 PM	SCCMR3	SMS_MP_CONT...	4970	SMS Site Comp...
	Milestone	CTG	3/13/2011 8:08:10 PM	SCCMR3	SMS_MP_CONT...	1014	SMS Site Comp...
	Milestone	CTG	3/13/2011 7:08:09 PM	SCCMR3	SMS_MP_CONT...	1016	SMS Site Comp...
	Detail	CTG	3/13/2011 7:08:09 PM	SCCMR3	SMS_MP_CONT...	4970	SMS Site Comp...
	Milestone	CTG	3/13/2011 7:08:01 PM	SCCMR3	SMS_MP_CONT...	1014	SMS Site Comp...
	Milestone	CTG	3/13/2011 6:08:01 PM	SCCMR3	SMS_MP_CONT...	1016	SMS Site Comp...
	Detail	CTG	3/13/2011 6:08:01 PM	SCCMR3	SMS_MP_CONT...	4970	SMS Site Comp...
	Milestone	CTG	3/13/2011 6:07:52 PM	SCCMR3	SMS_MP_CONT...	1014	SMS Site Comp...
	Milestone	CTG	3/13/2011 5:07:52 PM	SCCMR3	SMS_MP_CONT...	1016	SMS Site Comp...
	Detail	CTG	3/13/2011 5:07:52 PM	SCCMR3	SMS_MP_CONT...	4970	SMS Site Comp...

Figure 3.7
Status Message Query Results

status message query, you can isolate the information you are looking for. For instance, if you are looking for status message 4405, you can look through the despooler status messages, or you can run a status message query that displays only those status messages.

If you look at Figures 3.6 and 3.7, you will see the information that is returned from both methods. In Figure 3.6, the status message viewer displays not only the status messages that you are looking for, but you will also find every other status message that is associated with that component. In Figure 3.7, the results of a status message query are shown. Notice that you can refine the results to show only the status messages that you want to view.

When creating a status message query, you will need to open the Configuration Manager console and navigate to Site Database > System Status > Status Message Queries, as seen in Figure 3.8. When you select this node, you will see several

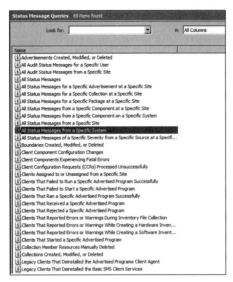

Figure 3.8
Status Message Queries

status message queries appear within the details pane. To run a status message query, right-click the query and select Show Messages. Some of the status messages queries will execute and display the results immediately, while others will prompt you to provide values to query.

Figure 3.9 shows the Criteria tab properties of a status message query. The query shown, All Status Messages from a Specific Component at a Specific Site, is a prompted query. All three of the search criteria are configured as prompted values. Looking at Figure 3.10, you can see the actual WQL query statement that is created when you build the query. If you are so inclined, you can enter and edit WQL queries instead of using the query builder. Just make sure you have your syntax correct when you do so.

To create a new status message query, right-click the Status Message Queries node and select New Status Message Query. Doing so will start the New Status Message Query Wizard. On the General page of the wizard, enter a descriptive name for the query. This name can be whatever you would like to call the query. It can even be named the same as an existing query. This is due to the fact that Configuration Manager is really only concerned about the Query ID of the query

Figure 3.9
Status Message Criteria Tab

Figure 3.10
All Status Messages From A Specific Component At A Specific Site WQL Query

and not the name that you supply. Do yourself a favor though, and keep the names unique.

You can also include additional information about the query by entering it into the Comment section. The more detailed you are about the information that is supplied, the easier it will be for other administrators to know what the query is going to do when it runs.

Figure 3.11
Status Filter Message Import Query Statement Dialog

There are two buttons that you can use when creating the query—Import Query Statement and Edit Query Statement. If you select Edit Query Statement first, you will be given the opportunity to create a query from scratch. If you know that you do not have any existing queries that you want to base your new query on, you should select this button and start building. If on the other hand you know that there is an existing query that would make a good starting point for your new query, you should select the Import Query Statement button. When importing an existing query, you are essentially reusing the settings that have been defined, saving yourself time. When you select the Import Query Statement button, you are presented with a dialog that looks like Figure 3.11. Scroll down and select the query that you want to use, and then click OK.

Once you select the Edit Query Statement button, you are presented with the configuration options for the query. On the General tab you will find three lines within the Results pane. Notice that you are not able to make any changes to these three lines. This is because all status message queries return the same information—the status message, the status message strings (text details), and status message properties.

On the criteria tab, you are able to enter the settings that have to match for a result to be returned. If you use the query builder options that are available in Figure 3.12, you can quickly build the query. However, as you saw in Figure 3.10, you can also enter the query as a raw WQL statement by clicking the Show Query Language button. After entering the criteria for the query, you can always click the Show Query Design button to check your work. As long as the information

Figure 3.12
Status Message Query Builder

that you entered for the query is syntactically correct and the criteria is supported by the query builder, the view will change to show the design view.

On the criteria tab, if you click the New button (the star shape), you are presented with the options that are available for creating a query. The criterion properties are broken down into the following options:

- **Criterion Type**—Used to define how the criteria is evaluated. The selections available are as follows:
  - **Null Value**—Used to validate if the defined attribute has a null value.
  - **Simple Value**—Used to validate if the defined attribute matched a constant value.
  - **Prompted Value**—Used to prompt the user running the query for a value that will be used to evaluate the attribute within the database.
  - **Attribute Reference**—Used to compare the selected attribute with the value contained in another attribute within the database.
  - **SubSelected Value**—Used to compare the selected attribute with the results of another query.
  - **List of Values**—Used to compare the selected attribute with a list of values. Depending on the operator used, the object is returned if the query matches any of the listed values.

- **Where**—The attribute that is used within the query. Clicking the Select button allows you to select the attribute that will be used when comparing data in the database.

- **Operator**—The operator used to control the results returned from the database.

The remaining options available within the query builder are dependent upon the Criterion Type selected. When you select a criterion type, the query builder screen changes to reflect the options that are available for that criterion:

- **Null Value** (Figure 3.13) only displays the Operator field—After selecting the attribute that will be used in the query, the Operator field displays a drop-down with two options—Is Not NULL, Is NULL.

- **Simple Value** (Figure 3.14) displays two fields when selected—Operator and Value. The available Operators are: Is Equal To, Is Greater Than, Is Greater Than Or Equal To, Is Less Than, Is Less Than Or Equal To, Is Like, Is Not Equal To, and Is Not Like. There are also uppercase and lowercase specific versions of all of these operators. The Value field can be populated by typing in the value or clicking the Select button and selecting the appropriate value that is already stored within the database. The value that you enter can also be wildcarded by using the % symbol.

Figure 3.13
Query Null Value Options

Figure 3.14
Simple Value Options

Figure 3.15
Prompted Value Options

- **Prompted Values** (Figure 3.15) presents two fields, although only the Operator field can be modified. The operators that are available are: Is Equal To, Is Greater Than, Is Greater Than Or Equal To, Is Less Than, Is Less Than Or Equal To, Is Like, Is Not Equal To, and Is Not Like. There are also uppercase and lowercase specific versions of all of these operators. Users will be presented with a dialog that allows them to select items from the database.

Figure 3.16
Attribute Reference Value Options

■ **Attribute Reference** (Figure 3.16) displays two fields—Operator and Reference. The available operators are: Is Equal To, Is Greater Than, Is Greater Than Or Equal To, Is Less Than, Is Less Than Or Equal To, Is Like, Is Not Equal To, and Is Not Like. There are also uppercase and lowercase specific versions of all of these operators. The Reference field can be used to identify the attribute that will be used for the query comparison.

■ **SubSelected Values** (Figure 3.17) presents two fields—Operator and Subselect. The available operators are Is In, Is Not In. The SubSelect field is used to enter the initial query. You can click the Browse button to select an existing query that you want to use as the SubSelected query. After selecting the SubSelected query, the query appears within the SubSelect text field.

■ **List of Values** (Figure 3.18) presents three fields—Operator, Value to Add, and Value to Match. The available operators are Is In, Is Not In. The Value To Add field is used to type in the values that will be compared to the selected attribute. You can click the Values button to retrieve existing values from the database. The Add button is used to add the entries from the Value To Add text field to the Values To Match text field. The Remove button is used to remove the selected value from the list.

Figure 3.17
SubSelected Value Options

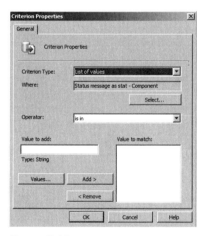

Figure 3.18
List of Values Options

After selecting the criteria that will be used with the query, you can test the query by right-clicking it and selecting Show Messages. If you have not created any prompted criteria, the query will run and display the results within a Status Message Viewer window as seen in Figure 3.19.

One word of caution when creating status message queries—they can return large amounts of data from the database, so make sure you have a means of

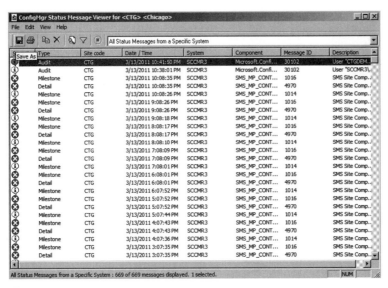

Figure 3.19
Status Message Results

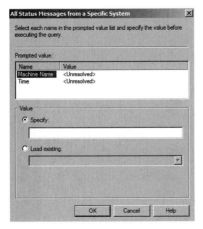

Figure 3.20
Status Criterion Properties

filtering. One of the best ways, and most recommended option, to reduce the amount of data that is returned from a status message query is to prompt for a timeframe. This is a very easy criterion to add to the query. Figure 3.20 shows the criterion properties that are used for the prompt. Every status message has a

Figure 3.21
Status Message Prompt

time associated with it. When the status message query is executed, the user will receive a prompt that appears like the one seen in Figure 3.21. The user will have the option to choose how far back in the status message history he wants to go. The options that are presented include:

- 1 Hour Ago
- 6 Hours Ago
- 12 Hours Ago
- 1 Day Ago
- 2 Days Ago
- 1 Week Ago
- 2 Weeks Ago
- 1 Month Ago
- 3 Months Ago
- 6 Months Ago
- 1 Year Ago

When creating a status message query, you have the ability to import in an existing status message query. This aids in the creation of queries that are similar, and you just want to modify a couple of settings. On the properties of the status message query, simply click the Import Query Statement button and select the query from the resulting list. Once imported, clicking the Edit Query Statement button will allow you to make modifications to the imported settings.

One final note before leaving status message queries. You may notice that there are several of the existing status message queries that display a time when you

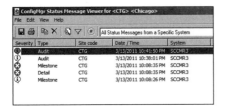

Figure 3.22
Time Displayed in Results Pane

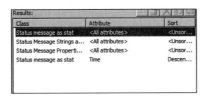

Figure 3.23
Adding stat.time to Query

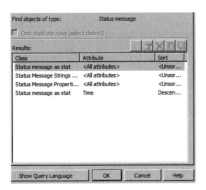

Figure 3.24
Attributes Displayed from Status Message Query

run the query. However, when you create your own status message query, you do not have the ability to add in that attribute in the Results pane, as seen in Figure 3.22. Earlier we mentioned that the attributes that are available in the Results pane cannot be changed. This is not completely true, because you do have the ability to edit the query language directly. If you click the Show Query Language button, you can add in the attribute stat.time as seen in Figure 3.23. However, as you can see in Figure 3.24, the status message viewer only displays a subset of the attributes that are available from status messages. Adding in any additional information into the results pane is a moot point.

CONFIGURING SITE MAINTENANCE TASKS

Most of the site maintenance tasks are used to control the amount of data that is stored in the database. If you take a look at the tasks shown in Figure 3.25, you can see that most of them are either summarizers or deletion tasks. Summarizers are used to condense status message information into bite-sized chunks that can be efficiently stored within the database. Without summarizers, there would be a lot of redundant information stored within the database. The sheer number of status messages that are generated would cause the database growth to get out of hand very quickly.

Summarization and Deletion Tasks

Summarizing status messages and other types of data, such as software metering data, hardware inventory, and software inventory does consume system resources. You don't want to continually summarize the data that is coming in from the various components. Instead you want to make sure that you are summarizing the data when critical processing is not being performed.

Deletion tasks are used to groom data from the database. These tasks run at the time that you configure, and remove data from the database that has aged past a

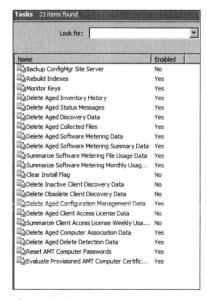

Figure 3.25
Site Maintenance Tasks

specified number of days. For many organizations, the default settings work very well. The data is stored in the database and is available for reporting purposes, but is groomed out after the data has grown stale. Some organizations may find that they need to keep the data for a longer period of time, or they want to reduce the amount of data in the database and reduce the number of days that they keep the data.

When trying to ascertain how long to keep the data that has been collected within your site, keep in mind how large your database is growing. While it may seem like a good thing to have a historical view of your site that spans back to the installation, backing up and restoring that data may take more time, and consume more resources than you are willing to commit. Backups not only consume space on drive or tape media, typically you are sending the saved data across the network. Having terabytes of data within a backup will start costing your department. However, the worst part of having a massive database is restoring the data. Many systems need to be rebuilt quickly, and if the database is overly large, it will take time to get it back to a functional state. Weigh the need for having extensive reporting capabilities with the cost of backing up and restoring the data.

The deletion tasks typically have a time period that is used to control how long the data can remain in the database. As you can see in Figure 3.26, each deletion

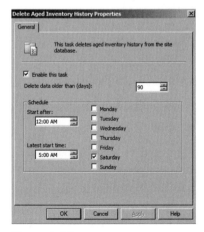

Figure 3.26
Deletion Tasks Schedule

task has a schedule for when it will run. The day or days of the week that you want to run the task appear on the right side of the window. On the left, a run time can be defined. The run time is configured with a time that the task can start, and also with the latest time that the task can start. These two times are then used to control the execution. A thread to start the task is placed within the processing queue at the start time. If that thread is acted upon at or before the latest start time, the thread is allowed to be processed. If the thread processing time is after the latest start time, a warning is issued and the thread is cancelled. The deletion tasks that are included within Configuration Manager are as follows:

- **Delete Aged Status Messages**—This maintenance task will delete status messages from the database after they have expired. The expiration age is configured using status message filters. Each status message type can have a unique expiry.

- **Delete Aged Collected Files**—Used to remove files that have been stored within the database. Enabled by default. Deletes collected files older than 90 days. Runs between midnight and 5:00 AM on Saturday.

- **Delete Aged Software Metering Data**—Used to remove metering data from the database. The data that is removed is associated with the raw information that is collected from the client systems within the site. Enabled by default. Deletes software usage data older than 5 days. Runs daily between midnight and 5:00 AM. (Can be configured between 2 and 255 days.)

- **Delete Aged Software Metering Summary Data**—Used to remove the summarized software metering data from the database. This data is typically retained longer than the raw data and is used for reporting purposes. Enabled by default. Deletes software metering summary data older than 270 days. Runs between midnight and 5:00 AM on Sunday.

- **Delete Inactive Client Discovery Data**—Used to delete the discovery data from systems that have not reported a heartbeat within the configured number of days. The number of days configured should exceed the number of days associated with the Heartbeat Discovery method. Disabled by default. Deletes inactive client discovery data older than 90 days. Runs between midnight and 5:00 AM every Saturday.

- **Delete Obsolete Client Discovery Data**—Used to remove the discovery information from systems that have been marked as obsolete. Disabled by default. Deletes obsolete client discovery data older than 7 days. Runs between midnight and 5:00 AM on Saturday.

- **Delete Aged Configuration Management Data**—Used to remove the configuration item definition of expired desired Configuration Management settings. Enabled by default. Deletes configuration data older than 90 days. Runs between midnight and 5:00 AM on Saturday.

- **Delete Aged Client Access License Data**—Used to delete client access license information that has exceeded the number of days configured for the task. Not enabled by default. When enabled, configured to delete data older than 180 days. Runs Saturday between midnight and 5:00 AM.

- **Delete Aged Computer Association Data**—Used to remove computer association data used with operating system deployment. Enabled by default. Deletes computer association data older than 30 days. Runs between midnight and 5:00 AM on Saturdays.

- **Delete Aged Delete Detection Data**—Not used within any current version of Configuration Manager.

- **Delete Aged Discovery Data**—Used to remove discovery data from the database that has aged longer than the number of days specified. This task removes discovery data that is stored from any of the discovery methods. Enabled by default. Deletes data older than 90 days. Runs every Saturday between midnight at 5:00 AM.

- **Delete Aged Inventory History**—Used to delete hardware inventory history information for any inventory data that has exceeded the number of days specified. Enabled by default. Deletes hardware inventory history data older than 90 days. Runs between midnight and 5:00 AM on Saturday.

- **Summarize Software Metering File Usage Data**—Used to aggregate data from multiple log files into general file usage data that is stored in the database. Runs daily between midnight and 5:00 AM.

- **Summarize Software Metering Monthly Usage Data**—Used to aggregate software metering data that is older than a month into monthly reporting data. Runs daily between midnight and 5:00 AM.

- **Summarize Client Access License Weekly Usage Data**—Used to aggregate the raw client access license usage into weekly data points. Disabled by default. Runs between midnight and 5:00 AM on Saturday.

Some of the tasks in this list rely on other processes to work correctly. The Delete Aged Status Messages task does not have an option to set the number of days that a status message can age. Instead, you have to set the number of days on each individual status message type within the Status Message Filter section. The Software Metering tasks rely on software metering components being enabled at the site. The same goes for the Delete Aged Client Access License Data task—asset intelligence components need to be enabled for this task to work.

Once you have determined the components that you want to enable within your site, you should review the maintenance tasks and determine which ones you want to enable or disable. If you are not performing any operating system deployment operations within your site, you can disable the Delete Aged Computer Association Data task. Once disabled, the site server will not have to process any task threads based around the task. This will only make your site server a tiny bit more efficient, but efficiencies add up over time.

Other Tasks

Up to this point we have discussed the deletion and summarization tasks that are used to keep the database optimized, but there are other tasks that are used to maintain the site. Most of these have been added over the lifetime of SMS/ SCCM so that administrators do not have to create their own SQL commands to perform these actions.

Clear Install Flag

The first of the tasks that we will discuss is the Clear Install Flag task. This is a simple task that will clear the install flag entry within the database and allow the client to be reinstalled. When you configure this task, you want to make sure that you are not causing the client to be needlessly reinstalled. The task keys off of the heartbeat discovery. By default, the heartbeat discovery is scheduled to run once a week. The default setting for the Clear Install Flag task is 21 days. In this case, 21 days would need to elapse without a heartbeat being detected from a client before the Install flag is reset. If automatic client installation is configured, after the Install flag is cleared, the client will be reinstalled during the next discovery cycle when the client system can be contacted. This task is not enabled by default. When enabled, it will run every Sunday between midnight and 5:00 AM.

Rebuild Indexes

The Rebuild Indexes task is used to keep the table indexes within the database optimized. When configured, this task will run and verify that the indexes are properly configured. Due to the ever-changing data that is collected within the Configuration Manager database, this task reviews the data within the database and creates indexes accordingly. Whenever a database column is more than 50 percent unique, this task will index the column. If the column falls beneath the 50 percent unique threshold, the Rebuild Indexes task will drop the column from the index. Rebuilding the indexes in this manner guarantees that the searches within the database are optimal. This task is enabled by default and runs every Sunday between midnight and 5:00 AM.

Monitor Keys

The Monitor Keys task does exactly what its name implies—monitors the unique keys within the database. This task runs every Sunday between midnight and 5:00 AM and will warn when any of the keys are corrupted.

Backup ConfigMgr Site Server

This task is used to back up not only the site server configuration data, it also backs up the database in a primary site. This is the only task that is available within a secondary site, although the secondary site task only backs up configuration data due to the absence of a database. Of course it is the lack of a database that is the reason for the lack of any other tasks. All of the tasks, with the exception of the Backup ConfigMgr site server, modify or optimize the database. The Backup ConfigMgr site server task is covered in greater detail within Chapter 18.

STATUS SUMMARIZERS

Besides the summarization tasks that are used to summarize data that comes in from client systems, there are three other summarizers that are used to validate the data within the site. We use these summarizers to give us a quick view into how the site is performing. They keep track of the components within the site and can give us a quick "heads-up" view of what is happening with the components. There are three summarizers that are responsible for monitoring the site components—component status summarizer, site system status summarizer, and advertisement status summarizer.

Component Status Summarizer

The component status summarizer is used to review the number of status messages within the site, determine how many of each criticality there are, and change the status of the components accordingly. There are three primary options that you need to set within the component status summarizer for it to work properly. The first is enabling the component status summarizer. By default, the component status summarizer is enabled. You can disable it if you do not want to have the automatic changing of the component's status.

The second option is to configure the threshold period. The threshold period is the timeframe that is used when determining the status of a component. By default, the threshold period is set to Since 12:00:00 AM, as seen in Figure 3.27. Using this default option, status messages that arrive at the site server after midnight are used when determining the status. This default setting allows you to quickly see how your site is performing during the current day. As the day goes on, and more status messages arrive, the component's status could change from OK to Warning to Critical.

The actual settings for when the site status gets escalated are found on the Thresholds tab, seen in Figure 3.28. The three types of status messages can be found in the Message Type drop-down. When you select a message type from the drop-down, the threshold levels for that message type appears in the Thresholds pane. The first column of the Thresholds pane lists the components that are installed within the site. The second column lists the number of messages of the selected type that will signal the summarizer to change the status of the component to a Warning level. The third column lists the number

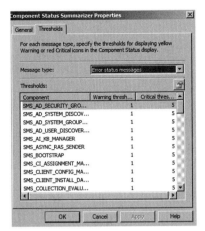

Figure 3.27
Threshold Period

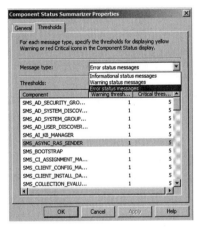

Figure 3.28
Threshold Escalation Properties

of messages of the selected type that will signal the summarizer to change the status of the component to a Critical level.

When the informational message type is selected, the default warning threshold is set to 2000 while the critical threshold is set to 5000. This means that as soon as 2000 informational messages are stored in the database within the threshold period that was selected on the General tab, the component will show in a

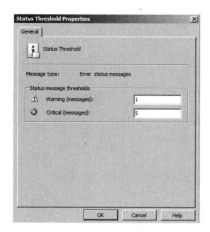

Figure 3.29
Status Thresholds Properties

warning state. 5000 Informational messages have to be stored within the database for the component to appear in a critical state. Selecting the other two options from the drop-down reveal that 10 Warning messages will turn the component to a warning level; 50 Warning messages will turn a component to Critical; 1 Error message will turn the component to a warning state; and 5 Error messages will turn the component Critical.

If you determine that you want to change these thresholds, you can select the message type and then double-click the components you want to change. The status thresholds properties, seen in Figure 3.29 are used to configure the threshold levels that you want to change. Changing the threshold levels only affect the site that you are currently focused on. If you want to change the threshold in other sites you will have to do so at each one. If you want to change the settings on every site within your hierarchy so that they use the same settings, you can use the Transfer Site Settings Wizard to force the changes.

To use the Transfer Site Settings Wizard to change the thresholds on multiple sites, configure the threshold settings on one site and then:

1. Navigate to Site Database > Site Management > *SiteName.*

2. Right-click *SiteName* and select Transfer Site Settings.

3. When the wizard starts, click Next.

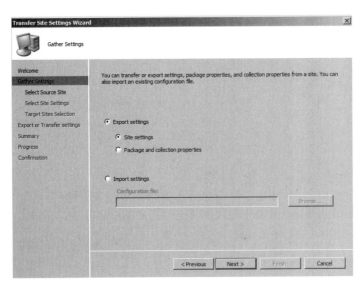

Figure 3.30
Gather Settings Page Properties

4. On the Gather Settings page, verify Export Settings and Site Settings are selected (Figure 3.30), and click Next.

5. On the Select Source Site page, verify the site where you modified the threshold levels is selected and click Next.

6. On the Select Site Settings page, expand Status Summary > Component Status Summarizer.

7. Select the checkbox next to Component Threshold (Figure 3.31) and click Next.

8. In the Target Sites Selection page, select the destination sites that you want to configure with the new threshold settings (Figure 3.32) and click Next.

9. On the Export or Transfer Settings page, select the checkbox next to Transfer Settings Now and click Next twice.

Site System Status Summarizer

Whereas the component status summarizer is used to notify when too many informational, warning, or error status messages are appearing for a

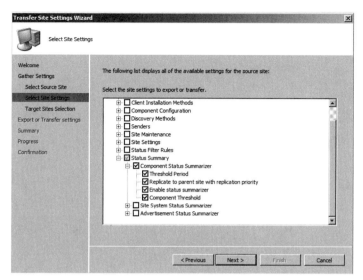

Figure 3.31
Component Threshold Settings

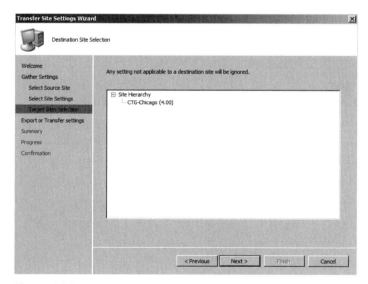

Figure 3.32
Target Sites Selection Page

component, the site system status summarizer is used to monitor the free space on any of the storage components on the site systems within the site. This summarizer can be set on a schedule so that it will evaluate the storage objects at predefined times.

Figure 3.33
Status Summarizer General Tab

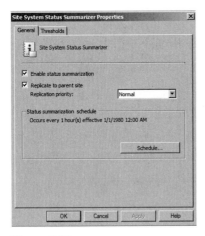

Figure 3.34
Schedule Properties

The General tab, seen in Figure 3.33, is used to enable status summarization, control the replication priority to parent sites, and set the schedule. Clicking the Schedule button presents the schedule properties as seen in Figure 3.34. This is the standard scheduling dialog that is available in nearly every component that you can configure a schedule. The default summarization time is once an hour, on the hour.

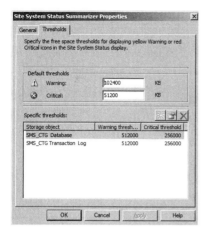

Figure 3.35
Default Thresholds Settings

The Thresholds tab is used to control the warning and critical storage levels. Within the Default Thresholds section, seen in Figure 3.35, you can set the levels that will be used by any storage object that is not configured within the Specific Thresholds section. To determine the storage components that would fall under the default settings, click the New (star shape) button. Each of the storage objects that do not have a specific threshold set appear within the Storage Object drop-down. You can set threshold levels for any of these components by selecting them in the drop-down and then configuring a warning and critical level in KB.

Advertisement Status Summarizer

There is not much that you can configure within the settings of the advertisement status summarizer. Shown in Figure 3.36, you can see that there are only two options to configure, enabling the summarizer and configuring the replication settings to the parent site. This summarizer is responsible for making sure details about the advertisements are up-to-date when you view the advertisement status. After the summarizer runs, you can see the results of the data that it found within the database by opening the Advertisement Status node. It is here that you can quickly determine how the clients have performed

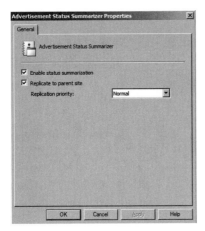

Figure 3.36
Storage Object Settings

when an advertisement is targeted at them. For more information about advertisements and advertisement status details, see Chapter 11.

THE FINAL WORD

Keeping the database at an optimal size makes it easier to maintain and back up the data stored within the database. There are several tools available to use when maintaining the site database. Status message filters and site maintenance tasks can be configured to control how data is stored within the site database, as well as how much of the data is stored in the site database. Careful management of the settings will allow you to maintain the size of the database while retaining enough data for reporting purposes. In the next chapter, we will be discussing the options available when deploying components within the site.

SECTION II

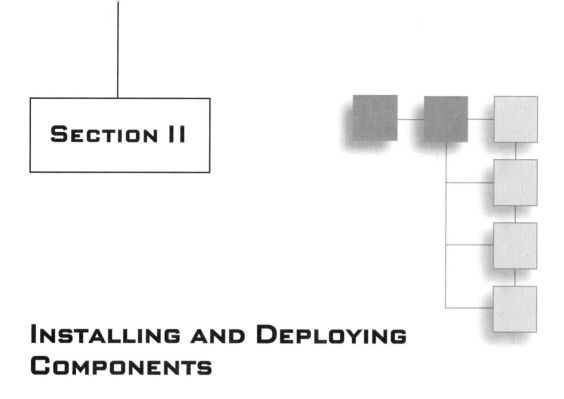

INSTALLING AND DEPLOYING COMPONENTS

This section is dedicated to the installation and setup of Configuration Manager 2007. We'll go through the steps needed to install Configuration Manager's core features and then move onto optional components and how to set them up for your environment. Whereas Section I contained many aspects regarding planning and design, this section contains the "meat and potatoes" of the book and is focused on getting the components installed and configuring them to work properly.

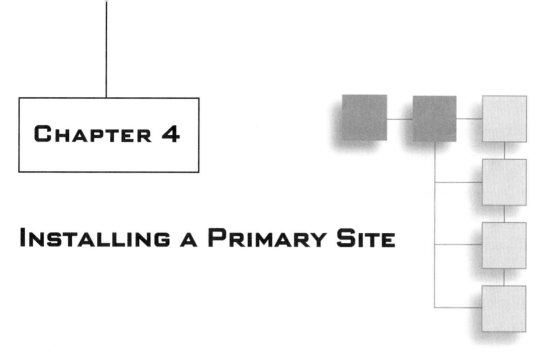

CHAPTER 4

INSTALLING A PRIMARY SITE

Configuration Manger 2007 relies on a site hierarchy for data collection, administration, and scalability. This hierarchy begins with a primary site, which must be installed during the initial setup of Configuration Manager 2007. Depending on your environment, you might have more than one site, which might include a secondary site or a central site.

In this chapter, we'll discuss the different server components that make up a primary site, the prerequisites needed to install a primary site, and the steps that must be followed to complete the installation.

QUICK INTRO TO SITE RELATIONSHIPS

Before we install a primary site, it's good to understand exactly what a site is. The term "site" in Configuration Manager can be somewhat confusing because it is often used in multiple contexts. It might help to think of the term "site" in two different ways: "types of sites" and "organizational sites". "Types of sites" refer to an operational aspect within Configuration Manager, whereas "organizational sites" refer to a hierarchical design. To make it even more confusing, a "type of site" might also be classified as an "organizational site," depending on how the Configuration Manager hierarchy is designed. To learn more about Configuration Manager hierarchies, see Chapter 5, "Creating a Site Hierarchy."

There are three types of sites:

- Primary sites
- Secondary sites
- Central sites

In the next chapter, we'll discuss the differences between primary, secondary, and central sites to ensure that you have a clear understanding of these terms.

PRIMARY SITE INSTALLATION OPTIONS AND PREREQUISITES

Before you install a primary site, you need to have a good understanding of the options that are available and what is required by these options. Below, we'll cover what options are available when installing a primary site and what prerequisites you'll need to have in place to support these options. Later in this chapter, we'll go over the installation steps so you can see these options in action.

Hardware Prerequisites

Configuration Manager 2007 is designed for high availability and scalability as long as the recommended hardware guidelines are followed correctly. These guidelines are listed in the table below:

Table 4.1 Central-Primary Site Server Recommendations

Hardware	Specifications
Memory (RAM)	16GB
Processor	Eight Cores
Disk Array	RAID 0: (2)15k Drives per Logical Volume or RAID 10: (4)15k Drives per Logical Volume
Disk Space	At least 5GB Free. 15GB Free Recommended if using Operating System Deployment

Note

Although it's not listed as a requirement, I'd also recommend that a gigabit network adapter be used on a central or primary site server.

Software Prerequisites

Configuration Manager 2007 has a multitude of options and features that are available. Understanding these options and features and what they require, however, can be quite confusing. The following software guidelines must be followed to successfully install Configuration Manager 2007.

Configuration Manager Console Component

The Configuration Manager console is the tool that administrators use to set up and configure Configuration Manager 2007 and its components. For more information about the Configuration Manager console, see Chapter 1.

When you install a primary site server, the Configuration Manager console is installed by default. If the prerequisite check for the Configuration Manager console fails, you will not be able to complete the installation of the primary site. The following items must be installed prior to installing the Configuration Manager console:

- Microsoft Management Console (MMC) 3.0
- .NET Framework 2.0

Note

The prerequisites are the same for any system that needs the Configuration Manager console installed. If you wish to install just the console on your workstation, these prerequisites must be installed there as well.

SMS Provider

The SMS provider acts as an intermediary between the site database and management tools such as the Configuration Manager console. The SMS provider implements a WMI layer (a WMI provider) allowing access to the database. The SMS provider also helps manage security by giving appropriate access to data based on the logged in user's permissions. The SMS provider can be installed to the Configuration Manager site server or another computer in the domain. The computer or server you choose for your SMS provider is not eligible if:

- It is already hosting an SMS provider for another site
- It is on a different domain than the site server or the site's database server
- It is hosting an SQL Server cluster

Note

The SMS provider should be installed to a system with high availability. If the SMS provider goes down, administrators will not be able to access the site database.

SQL Database Server

As stated earlier, primary sites (and central sites) must be attached to a SQL Server database to store their site information. The SQL Server database can be installed locally to the site server, on a remote server, or on a virtual SQL Server cluster. If your site hierarchy contains more than one primary site, there will be multiple SQL Server databases; one corresponding to each primary site. The following prerequisite apply:

- Must be at least SQL Server 2005 SP2.
- Must be a full edition of SQL Server—Express editions are not supported.
- SQL Server 2008 is fully supported starting with Configuration Manager 2007 SP1. Prior to SP1, hotfix 955229 should be applied if using SQL Server 2008 as the site database server.

Caution

Be sure to follow the hardware and software guidelines about setting up a SQL Server. This is a critical component to Configuration Manager 2007 and can drastically affect the performance of not only the console but the systems depending on the SQL Server as well.

PKI Infrastructure Requirements

Configuration Manager 2007 comes with three new features that require you to have a functioning PKI infrastructure in place before these features can be used. These new features are as follows:

- **Native mode**—Native mode is a new installation type for Configuration Manager that can be specified during setup. Native mode allows your clients and site systems to transmit data securely through the use of server signing certificates, web server certificates, and client certificates. Setting up a PKI infrastructure is out of the scope of this book but depending on your organization's security requirements, this might be a factor to think about before starting the installation.

- **Internet Based Client Management**—If your site is set up using Native mode, you have the option to use Internet Based Client Management. This feature allows you to manage certain aspects of your clients when they are not connected to the corporate network like laptops or home office computers. Although Internet Based Client Management can be very useful to administrators, it is limited in its functionality compared to when a client is on the network. For more information, see Chapter 8, "Managing Clients."

- **Out of band management**—Out of band management lets you control certain aspects of computers with AMT management chipsets like changing power states and console/IDE redirection. Out of band management requires that a PKI infrastructure be set up in your environment since it functions by using a provisioning certificate, a web server certificate, and in some cases client certificates (802.1 x authentication). For more information about out of band management, see Chapter 8.

Note

For a step-by-step guide of how to install the required certificates for native mode, follow this link: http://technet.microsoft.com/en-us/library/cc872789.aspx

IIS Requirements

IIS is used to transmit data between site systems and clients. The data that is transmitted includes policy information, state messages, and packages. Note that not all site systems require that IIS be installed. IIS is only required when the following site system roles are installed:

- BITS-enabled distribution point
- Management point

- Reporting point
- Software update point
- Server locator point

Another requirement of Configuration Manager is that WebDAV be installed and configured properly. WebDAV is required for management points and BITS-enabled distribution points. The correct version of WebDAV is included in Windows Server 2008 R2 but not with prior versions of Windows Server. If you are not running Windows Server 2008 R2, make sure you download, install, and configure WebDAV properly. We will cover this step later in this chapter.

The site system roles listed above are discussed in detail in Chapter 6, "Configuring Site System Roles."

Server 2008 Requirements

Microsoft Windows Server 2008 or 2008 R2 is required when using the network access protection feature. Network access protection checks client systems to make sure they are in good health before they are considered compliant. If they are deemed non-compliant, actions can be taken to remediate these machines. Network access protection is covered in detail in Chapter 15, "Managing Network Access Protection."

Microsoft Windows Server 2008 or 2008 R2 is also required when deploying operating systems using the multicast feature (which was added in the R2 release). Multicast uses Windows deployment services, which is only available in Server 2008 or higher. Operating system deployment is covered in Chapter 13, "Managing Operating System Deployment."

WSUS SDK

If your primary site will be set up to host the software update point, you must have the WSUS SDK installed even if the primary site does not host the actual WSUS server role. The WSUS SDK is installed when the WSUS administration console is installed, which makes the appropriate APIs available to allow communication with the WSUS server responsible for managing the updates. The primary site server can host the WSUS role or it can be located on another server in the organization. Software updates are covered in Chapter 12, "Managing Software Updates."

CONFIGURING PREREQUISITES

This section covers the installation steps needed to prepare a Microsoft Windows 2008 R2 Server to host a primary site and the site roles that can be installed. Note that these steps may differ slightly if your operating system is something other than Microsoft Windows 2008 R2 Server.

Extending the Active Directory Schema for Configuration Manager 2007

If you want to get the full benefit from Configuration Manager 2007, it needs to be able to publish site information to Active Directory. By publishing site information to Active Directory, clients can retrieve this information, securely and automatically, without any extra setup. By extending the schema, these settings are automatically configured:

- **Client installation settings**—Client deployment options like the fallback status point and server locator point are retrieved automatically during client setup when the schema is extended.

- **Native mode settings**—Information like site mode and CRL checking are retrieved by clients automatically when the schema is extended.

- **Roaming settings**—Clients that are in roaming mode can request content from different management points when the schema is extended.

- **Port configuration settings**—During setup, communication ports are defined for the site so that clients can send data back and forth to different site systems. If the ports are changed after setup, this information is distributed to the clients if the schema is extended.

- **Secure key exchange**—Configuration Manager sites are able to exchange public keys when the schema is extended.

- **Network access protection**—Clients can use the network access protection feature when the schema is extended.

- **Site failures**—If clients are connected to a management point on a central site and the central site fails, they can be configured to communicate with a new central site without any extra configuration.

▪ **Management point settings**—When the schema is extended, clients can trust any management point that you configure within your site hierarchy. If not, trusted root keys must be deployed to your clients beforehand when in mixed mode.

To extend the schema, you can use one of two methods: The ExtADSch.exe command line utility that is included with the Configuration Manager 2007 media or by using the LDIFDE.exe command line utility with a custom LDF import file.

Note

Make sure you are logged in as a user who has schema admin permissions in Active Directory before extending the schema. If not, the schema extension may fail.

Caution

Make sure that you back up the Active Directory system state of your schema master prior to extending the schema. Then, take the schema master offline and start the schema extension. If the schema extension fails, you can revert the changes using the backup you took without having to worry about a damaged copy of the schema being replicated to all of your domain controllers in the forest.

Extend the Active Directory Schema Using the ExtADSch.exe Utility

The easiest method to extend the Active Directory is to use the ExtADSch.exe utility since it requires no extra setup or configuration. To extend the Active Directory schema using the ExtADSch.exe utility:

1. Log in to the schema master using an account that has schema admin rights.

2. Navigate to the root of the Configuration Manager 2007 media, hold down Shift on the keyboard, and right-click into an empty space in the folder. Choose Open command window here from the menu.

3. Navigate to the I386 folder by typing cd \smssetup\bin\i386 and press Enter.

4. Type extadsch.exe and press Enter. The results of the schema extension are displayed.

5. The ExtADSch.exe utility writes a log file called extadsch.txt to the root of the system volume. The results of the schema extension are written to this file for troubleshooting purposes.

Extend the Active Directory Schema Using the ExtADSch.exe Utility

The Microsoft recommended method of extending the Active Directory schema is by using the LDIFDE command line utility with a custom LDF import file. A generic version of the LDF import file is located in the I386 folder on the Configuration Manager 2007 media. This file is called CONFIGMGR_AD_ SCHEMA.LDF. To edit and import this file (to extend the Active Directory schema), do the following:

1. Log in to the schema master using an account that has schema admin rights.

2. Navigate to the \SMSSETUP\BIN\I386 directory on the Configuration Manager 2007 installation media and open the CONFIGMGR_AD_ SCHEMA.LDF file with Notepad.

3. When the file is opened in Notepad, go to Edit > Replace. In the Find What field, type DC=x. In the Replace with field, type the fully qualified domain name of your domain. In our example we'll use DC=LearnIT Stuff,DC=local and click Replace All.

4. Save this file to an accessible location like the root of the C: drive.

5. Open a command prompt and type LDIFDE.exe –i –f <location of LDF file> -v –j <location of the LDIFDE log file> and press Enter. In our example, we'll type LDIFDE.exe –i –f c:\CONFIGMGR_AD_SCHEMA. LDF –v –j c:\LDIFDELOG and press Enter.

6. The results of the schema extension are displayed. If need be, you can review this information in the log file that was created in the previous step.

Note

The –i switch is for import, the –f switch points to the location of the custom LDF file, the –v switch turns on verbose logging, and the –j switch outputs the log file to the location you choose.

Configuring the System Management Container

Now that the Active Directory schema has been extended for Configuration Manager 2007, site servers can publish information for client systems. Before any site server can publish information to Active Directory, it has to be given the correct permissions to do so.

The system management container is where Configuration Manager 2007 site information is published and resides under the system container in Active Directory. The system management container can be created automatically when site information is first published or manually by using the ADSI Edit utility. If you choose to have Configuration Manager 2007 create the system management container automatically, you must give your site server full control permissions to the system container prior to installation. If your site server becomes compromised, however, it is conceivable that your Active Directory infrastructure could become compromised from the excess rights given to the system container. Because of this risk, Microsoft recommends that you manually assign the appropriate rights by using the ADSI Edit utility. In this chapter, we will manually create the system management container.

Caution

Your Active Directory database could be permanently damaged or destroyed if you use the ADSI Edit utility improperly. Make sure you know how to use this utility before making any changes. Also, you might want to take a backup of your Active Directory database prior to editing any information with the ADSI Edit utility.

Note

If you choose to have Configuration Manager automatically create the system management container, use the principals below to modify the permissions of the system container instead of the system management container.

To create and set up the system management container, do the following:

1. Log in to a workstation or server with the remote server administration tools installed.

2. Go to Start > Administrative Tools > ADSI Edit.

3. When the ADSI Edit window opens, expand the Default Naming Context node, expand the node that identifies your domain, and then highlight the system container.

4. Right-click the system container and choose New > Object (Figure 4.1).

5. Select container from the Select a class list and click Next (Figure 4.2).

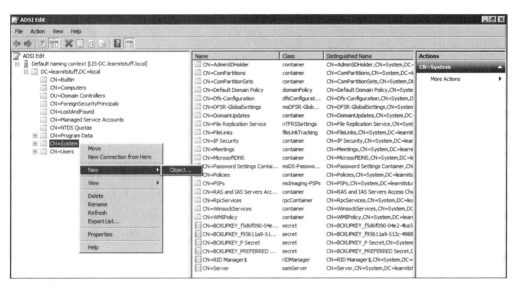

Figure 4.1
Create New Object

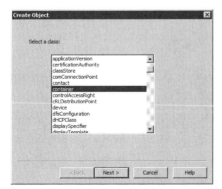

Figure 4.2
Create Container

Figure 4.3
Create Object Window

6. Type System Management into the Value field and click Next
   (Figure 4.3).

7. When prompted, click Finish to complete the creation of the system
   management container.

8. Now that the system management container has been created, we need
   to give rights to your site server so that it can publish information to
   this container. To do this, right-click on the system management
   container and click Properties.

9. Click the Security tab, click Add, and type the name of the server that
   will host your site to the list and click Check Names to verify that the
   server name is correct. In our example, CHI-PRIMARY is the site server
   that will host our primary site. Click OK to continue. Note that
   computers must be selected in the object types list for this to work
   properly (Figure 4.4).

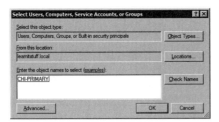

Figure 4.4
Security

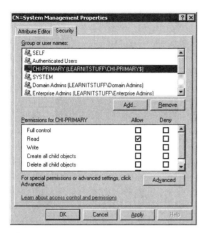

Figure 4.5
System Management Properties Window

10. Your site server is now listed in the Group or User Names field (Figure 4.5).

11. Now that your server is added in the Security window, we have to give it the appropriate rights. To do this, highlight the server object and click the Advanced button. Under the Name column, find your server and highlight it again and click the Edit button.

12. The Permission Entry window for your server object is displayed. On the Apply to drop-down list, select This Object and All Descendent Objects. Under the Allow column, click the checkbox for Full control. Click OK when you are finished (Figure 4.6).

13. Once these steps are complete, your server can now publish information to Active Directory.

Note

Each site server that will host a primary, secondary, or central site will need these same permissions set on the system management container. Depending on the number of site servers you will have in your environment, you may want to create a group and apply the permissions to the group instead of on each server object.

Installing Internet Information Services (IIS)

1. Open the server manager by going to Start, right-clicking on Computer, and left-clicking on Manage (Figure 4.7).

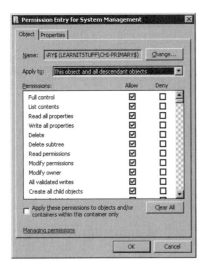

Figure 4.6
Permission Entry Window

Figure 4.7
Start > Computer > Right Click > Manage

2. Once the server manager opens, left-click on the Roles node (Figure 4.8).

3. The Roles Summary window is displayed. Click on Add Roles.

4. The Before You Begin window is displayed. Click Next to continue (Figure 4.9).

5. The Server Roles window is displayed. Click the checkbox next to Web Server (IIS) and click Next (Figure 4.10).

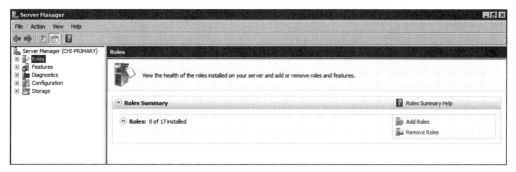

Figure 4.8
The Server Manager

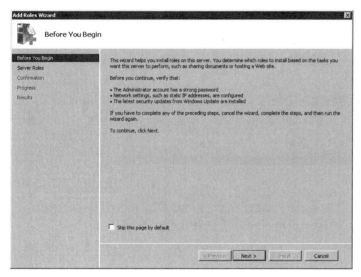

Figure 4.9
Before You Begin Window

6. The Web Server (IIS) introduction window is displayed. Click Next to continue (Figure 4.11).

7. When the IIS Role Services window is displayed, check WebDAV Publishing, ASP.NET, ASP, Windows Authentication, IIS 6 Metabase Compatibility, IIS 6 WMI Compatibility, and then click Next (Figure 4.12).

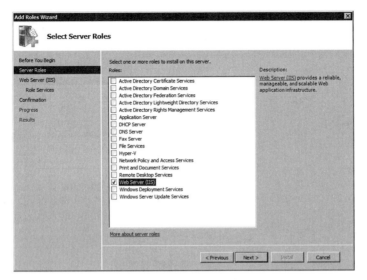

Figure 4.10
Add Server Roles Window

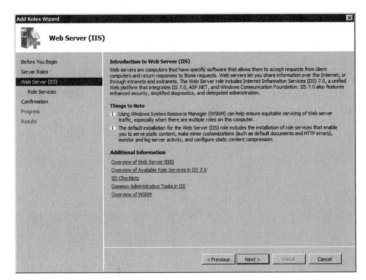

Figure 4.11
IIS Introduction Window

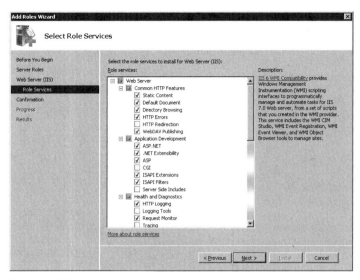

Figure 4.12
IIS Select Role Services Window

Note

You may be prompted to Add Required Role Services when adding certain components of IIS because they are dependent on other IIS components. If prompted, click Add Required Roles Services.

8. When the IIS Confirmation window is displayed, click Install.

9. When the IIS Results window is displayed, click Close.

Installing Remote Differential Compression (RDC)

1. Open the server manager by going to Start, right-clicking on Computer, and left-clicking on Manage.

2. Once the server manager opens, left-click on the Features node (Figure 4.13).

3. Click the Add Features link.

4. When the Features window opens, scroll down to Remote Differential Compression and click in the checkbox until a check appears in the box and then left-click Next (Figure 4.14).

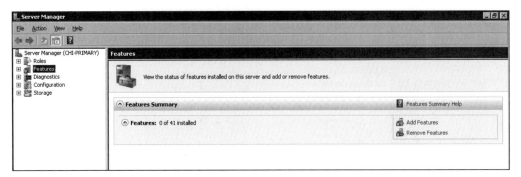

Figure 4.13
Server Manager Features Page

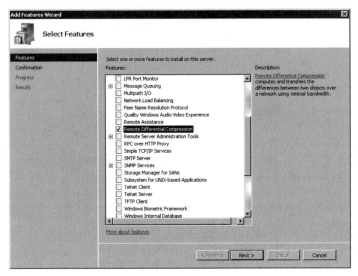

Figure 4.14
Remote Differential Compression Checked

5. Wait for the Confirmation window to be displayed and click Install (Figure 4.15).

6. Wait for the Results window to be displayed and click Close (Figure 4.16).

Installing Background Intelligent Transfer Service (BITS)

1. Open the server manager by going to Start, right-clicking on Computer, and left-clicking on Manage.

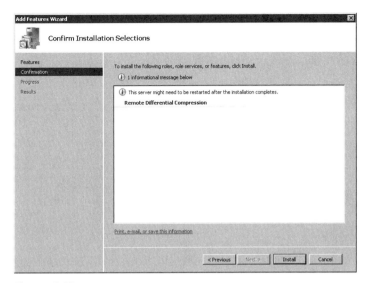

Figure 4.15
Confirmation Window

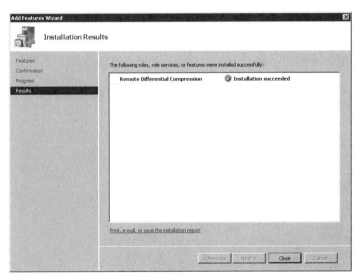

Figure 4.16
Results Window

2. Once the server manager opens, left-click on the Features node.

3. Click the Add Features link.

4. When the Features window opens, scroll down to Background Intelligent Transfer Service (BITS) and click in the checkbox until you are prompted

Figure 4.17
Add Required Role Services

with the Add Required Role Services dialog box since BITS requires IIS to be installed. Click the Add Required Role Services button to continue (Figure 4.17).

5. Once you are returned to the Features window, click Next.

6. Because BITS requires that IIS be installed, you are taken to the IIS Role Services introduction window. Click Next to continue (Figure 4.18).

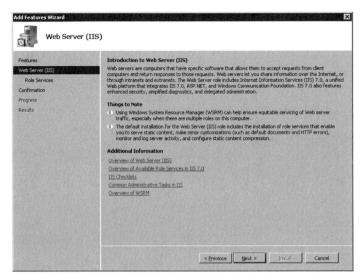

Figure 4.18
IIS Role Services Introduction Window

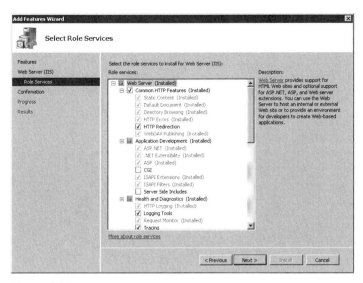

Figure 4.19
IIS Role Services Selection Window

7. Wait for the IIS Role Services window to open. The IIS features that are required for BITS are automatically checked. Click Next to continue (Figure 4.19).

8. When the Confirmation window is displayed, review the features that will be installed. Click Install to begin the installation (Figure 4.20).

9. When the installation completes, the results window will be displayed. Click Close to complete the BITS setup (Figure 4.21).

Configuring WebDAV

WebDAV stands for Web-based Distributed Authoring and Viewing and is an extension of the HTTP protocol. WebDAV is required for management points and BITS-enabled distribution points. WebDAV comes by default in Windows Server 2008 R2 and can be added during IIS installation.

Once WebDAV is installed, it must be enabled and configured to work for Configuration Manger 2007. The following steps must be followed to configure WebDAV for Configuration Manager 2007:

1. Open the IIS Manager by going to Start > Administrative Tools > Internet Information Services (IIS) Manager (Figure 4.22).

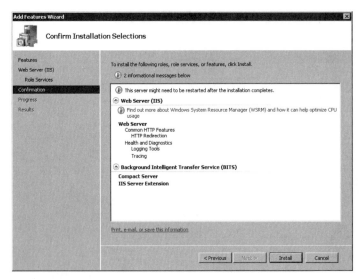

Figure 4.20
IIS Role Services Confirmation Window

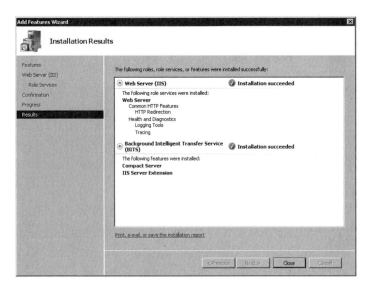

Figure 4.21
IIS Role Services Results Window

2. Expand the Server node (this should be the name of your server), expand the Sites node, click on Default Web Site, and then click on WebDAV Authoring Rules (Figure 4.23).

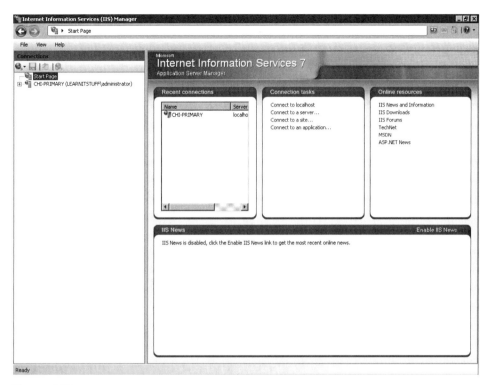

Figure 4.22
Internet Information Services (IIS) Manager Window

3. Double-click WebDAV Authoring Rules or click the Open Feature link from the Actions pane.

4. Click the Add Authoring Rule link from the Alerts pane. Make sure the All Content, All Users, and Read options are selected and click OK (Figure 4.24).

5. Click the WebDAV Settings link from the Alerts pane.

6. Under the Property Behavior section, set Allow Anonymous Property Queries to True.

7. Under the Property Behavior section, set Allow Custom Properties to False.

8. Under the Property Behavior section, set Allow Property Queries with Infinite Depth to True.

9. Under WebDAV behavior, set Allow Hidden Files to be Listed to True (only needed for BITS-enabled distribution points).

Figure 4.23
Default Web Site Home and WebDAV

10. Review your settings and click Apply in the Actions pane (Figure 4.25).

11. Click WebDAV Authoring Rules in the Actions pane.

12. Click Enable WebDAV in the Actions pane.

13. Click WebDAV Authoring Rules in the Actions pane.

14. Close the Internet Information Services (IIS) Manager.

Request Filtering Options

Before IIS7, a tool was made available by Microsoft called UrlScan, which raised the level of security on IIS web servers. IIS7 (and higher) incorporates the core functionality of UrlScan into a new feature called request filtering.

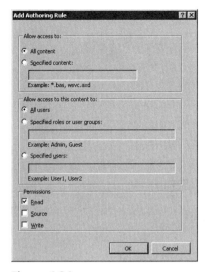

Figure 4.24
Add Authoring Rule Window

Request filtering may cause an issue for packages located on BITS-enabled distribution points, however. If a package contains folders or file extensions disallowed by the request filtering tool, your package may not get distributed to your clients.

To edit the default settings put in place by request filtering, you must modify the applicationHost.config file located in %windir%\System32\inetsrv\config.

Caution

Before you make changes to the applicationHost.config file, make a backup just to be safe.

To modify the request filtering settings within this file:

1. Open Notepad as an administrator by going to Start > All Programs > Accessories. Right-click on Notepad and click on Run as Administrator. If a User Account Control dialog box is displayed, click Yes.

2. Click File > Open and browse to %windir%\System32\inetsrv\config\ applicationHost.config and click Open.

3. When the applicationHost.config file is open, find the requestFiltering XML element (Figure 4.26).

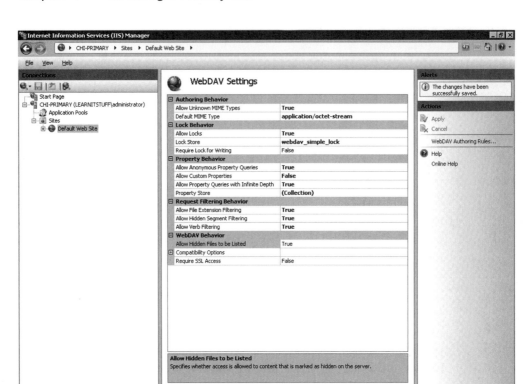

Figure 4.25
WebDAV Settings Window

4. If your package contains a file with an extension of .vb for example, change the text from allowed=false to allowed=true (Figure 4.27).

5. Make any other modifications as necessary. Once you are finished, go File > Save.

6. In order for the new settings in the applicationHost.config file to take effect, IIS must be restarted.

Note

Note that you can use the appcmd command line utility to change the parameters in the applicationHost.config instead of directly editing it with a text editor. For more information about appcmd, see http://learn.iis.net/page.aspx/114/getting-started-with-appcmdexe/.

```
applicationHost.config - Notepad
File Edit Format View Help
        <clear />
        <add path="C:\Windows\system32\bitssrv.dll" allowed="true" groupId="BITSEXTS
        <add path="%windir%\system32\inetsrv\asp.dll" allowed="true" groupId="ASP" d
        <add path="%windir%\system32\inetsrv\webdav.dll" allowed="true" groupId="WEBI
        <add path="%windir%\Microsoft.NET\Framework64\v2.0.50727\aspnet_isapi.dll" a
        <add path="%windir%\Microsoft.NET\Framework\v2.0.50727\aspnet_isapi.dll" all
    </isapiCgiRestriction>

    <requestFiltering>
        <fileExtensions allowUnlisted="true" applyToWebDAV="true">
            <add fileExtension=".asax" allowed="false" />
            <add fileExtension=".ascx" allowed="false" />
            <add fileExtension=".master" allowed="false" />
            <add fileExtension=".skin" allowed="false" />
            <add fileExtension=".browser" allowed="false" />
            <add fileExtension=".sitemap" allowed="false" />
            <add fileExtension=".config" allowed="false" />
            <add fileExtension=".cs" allowed="false" />
            <add fileExtension=".csproj" allowed="false" />
            <add fileExtension=".vb" allowed="false" />
            <add fileExtension=".vbproj" allowed="false" />
            <add fileExtension=".webinfo" allowed="false" />
            <add fileExtension=".licx" allowed="false" />
            <add fileExtension=".resx" allowed="false" />
            <add fileExtension=".resources" allowed="false" />
            <add fileExtension=".mdb" allowed="false" />
            <add fileExtension=".vjsproj" allowed="false" />
            <add fileExtension=".java" allowed="false" />
            <add fileExtension=".jsl" allowed="false" />
            <add fileExtension=".ldb" allowed="false" />
            <add fileExtension=".dsdgm" allowed="false" />
            <add fileExtension=".ssdgm" allowed="false" />
            <add fileExtension=".lsad" allowed="false" />
            <add fileExtension=".ssmap" allowed="false" />
            <add fileExtension=".cd" allowed="false" />
```

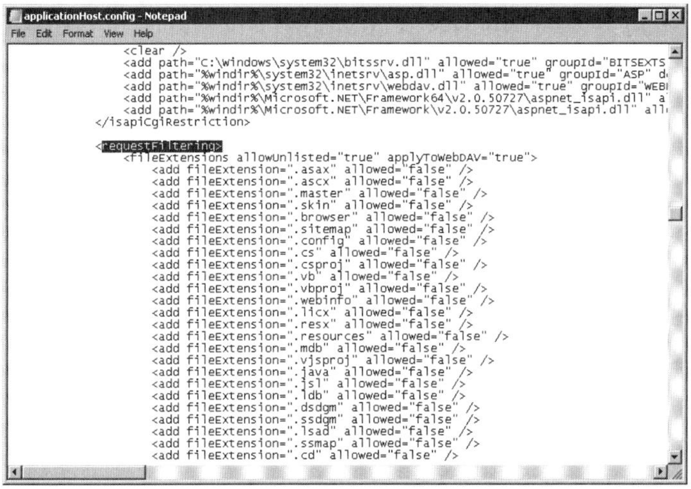

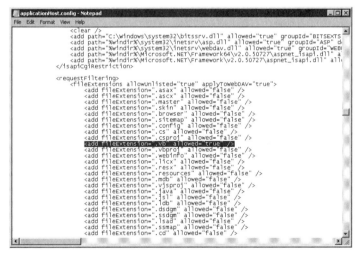

Figure 4.26
applicationHost.config—requestFiltering element

```
applicationHost.config - Notepad
File Edit Format View Help
        <clear />
        <add path="C:\Windows\system32\bitssrv.dll" allowed="true" groupId="BITSEXTS
        <add path="%windir%\system32\inetsrv\asp.dll" allowed="true" groupId="ASP" d
        <add path="%windir%\system32\inetsrv\webdav.dll" allowed="true" groupId="WEBI
        <add path="%windir%\Microsoft.NET\Framework64\v2.0.50727\aspnet_isapi.dll" a
        <add path="%windir%\Microsoft.NET\Framework\v2.0.50727\aspnet_isapi.dll" all
    </isapiCgiRestriction>

    <requestFiltering>
        <fileExtensions allowUnlisted="true" applyToWebDAV="true">
            <add fileExtension=".asax" allowed="false" />
            <add fileExtension=".ascx" allowed="false" />
            <add fileExtension=".master" allowed="false" />
            <add fileExtension=".skin" allowed="false" />
            <add fileExtension=".browser" allowed="false" />
            <add fileExtension=".sitemap" allowed="false" />
            <add fileExtension=".config" allowed="false" />
            <add fileExtension=".cs" allowed="false" />
            <add fileExtension=".csproj" allowed="false" />
            <add fileExtension=".vb" allowed="true" />
            <add fileExtension=".vbproj" allowed="false" />
            <add fileExtension=".webinfo" allowed="false" />
            <add fileExtension=".licx" allowed="false" />
            <add fileExtension=".resx" allowed="false" />
            <add fileExtension=".resources" allowed="false" />
            <add fileExtension=".mdb" allowed="false" />
            <add fileExtension=".vjsproj" allowed="false" />
            <add fileExtension=".java" allowed="false" />
            <add fileExtension=".jsl" allowed="false" />
            <add fileExtension=".ldb" allowed="false" />
            <add fileExtension=".dsdgm" allowed="false" />
            <add fileExtension=".ssdgm" allowed="false" />
            <add fileExtension=".lsad" allowed="false" />
            <add fileExtension=".ssmap" allowed="false" />
            <add fileExtension=".cd" allowed="false" />
```

Figure 4.27
applicationHost.config—modified

Installing a Primary Site

Once all of the software and hardware prerequisites are in place, you are ready to install your primary site. The prerequisites that we covered above play an integral part in the success or failure of your site installation. Make sure these prerequisites are configured before you begin!

In this example, we will be installing Microsoft System Center Configuration Manager 2007 SP2 on a Windows Server 2008 R2 Standard machine. Because this is not the only supported configuration, you might see different results in your environment.

When you install a primary site, you have three installation options:

- Simple installation
- Custom installation
- Unattended installation

We will cover each type of these installations in the remainder of this chapter.

Simple Settings Installation

The simple settings installation type for Configuration Manager 2007 appears to have been made for evaluation purposes only or for administrators who are not interested in all of the pesky details of the installation. It basically installs everything and turns everything on so you don't have to do any extra setup once the install is finished. The problem with this idea is that if you don't want to think about the details, you probably shouldn't be installing Configuration Manager 2007 in the first place. Even Microsoft recommends that you don't use this option in a production environment since you have little say as to what occurs during the install.

Consider the following details prior to installing a primary site using the simple settings installation mode:

- **Requires a local install of SQL Server**—If you wish to have the site database reside on a remote system, you cannot use the basic settings install method.

- **Management point is installed by default**—If you don't want your primary site to host a management point, you will have to uninstall it after the basic settings install has finished.

- **All client agents are enabled by default**—If you only want specific client agents to be enabled, you will have to disable these after the basic settings install has finished.

■ **Client push is enabled**—If you don't want clients to automatically install the Configuration Manager 2007 client, you must disable this feature after the basic settings install has finished.

Since the custom settings install method goes through all of the options in the simple settings setup, we will cover the actual install steps in that section.

Custom Settings Installation

The custom settings installation method is the recommended method to install Configuration Manager 2007. This option will take you through every detail of the setup process and lets you make decisions regarding how your site will function.

Caution

> Before you begin your installation, please make sure that you've planned your site carefully by using the guidelines in the previous chapters.

To start the installation, obtain the Configuration Manager 2007 SP2 installation media (whether it be on physical media or the network), browse to the root folder, and follow the steps below:

1. Double-click on SPLASH.HTA.

2. After double-clicking on SPLASH.HTA, the installer program starts and displays the initial setup window as seen in Figure 4.28. Click Configuration Manager 2007 SP2 under the Install section to begin the install.

3. Wait for the Configuration Manager 2007 SP2 Install Wizard window to be displayed and review the information. If you followed the steps prior to and including this chapter, you should be in good shape. Click Next to start the wizard (Figure 4.29).

4. When the Available Setup Options window is displayed, choose the Install a Configuration Manager site server option. Note that you can choose to only install the Configuration Manager console from this setup wizard as well. This is useful for installing the admin console to your workstation. Click Next to continue (Figure 4.30).

Figure 4.28
Configuration Manager 2007 SP2 Setup Window

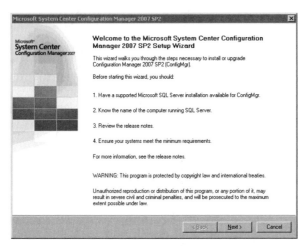

Figure 4.29
Configuration Manager 2007 SP2 Install Wizard

5. If you agree to the license terms, click Next on the Microsoft Software License Terms window to continue (Figure 4.31).

6. At this point, the Installation Settings window is displayed. This is where you can choose to install Configuration Manager with simple or custom settings. Remember that if you choose to install with simple settings, you

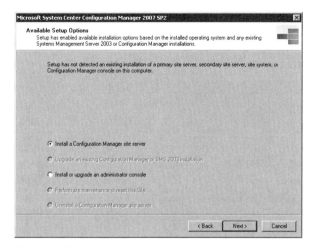

Figure 4.30
Available Setup Options Window

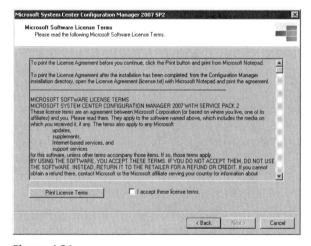

Figure 4.31
Microsoft Software License Terms Window

will not have the ability to configure important aspects of your site. For this example, we'll install Configuration Manager 2007 using the custom settings option. Click Next to continue (Figure 4.32).

7. When the Site Type window is displayed, you can choose between a primary site or a secondary site. Remember that the first Configuration

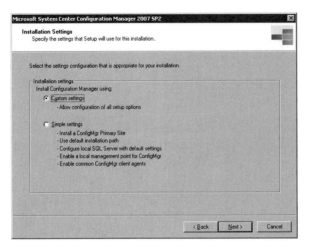

Figure 4.32
Installation Settings Window

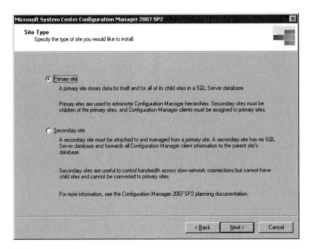

Figure 4.33
Site Type Window

Manager 2007 in your environment must be a primary site. This is the option we will choose in this example. We will install a secondary site in the next chapter. Click Next to continue (Figure 4.33).

8. The Customer Experience Improvement Program window is displayed. If you wish to send data to Microsoft about your installation experience,

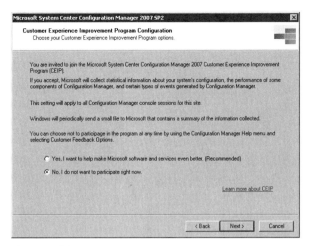

Figure 4.34
Customer Experience Improvement Program Window

choose Yes. If you do not wish to participate, choose No. In this example, we'll choose No. Once your option is set, click Next to continue (Figure 4.34).

9. If you are prompted to enter your 25-character product key, enter this here. Once your product key has been entered, click Next.

10. When you are prompted to choose your destination folder, either keep the defaults or enter another location. We'll keep the defaults in this example. Click Next to continue (Figure 4.35).

11. At this point, the Site Settings window is displayed. This is where you enter your three-digit site code. The site code must be unique and is used to identify each site as well as the primary site that clients are attached to. For more information on client assignment, see Chapter 7. Some organizations base the site code on location, department, or company name. In our example, we'll use CHI for Chicago. The site name is used to further identify the site since a three-character code is very limited in detail. The site name is not used by Configuration Manager or its clients but is only for administrators to help identify the site. Click Next to continue (Figure 4.36).

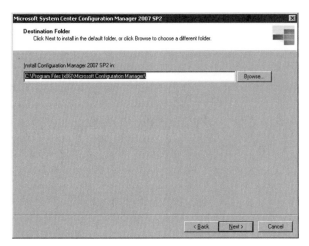

Figure 4.35
Destination Folder Window

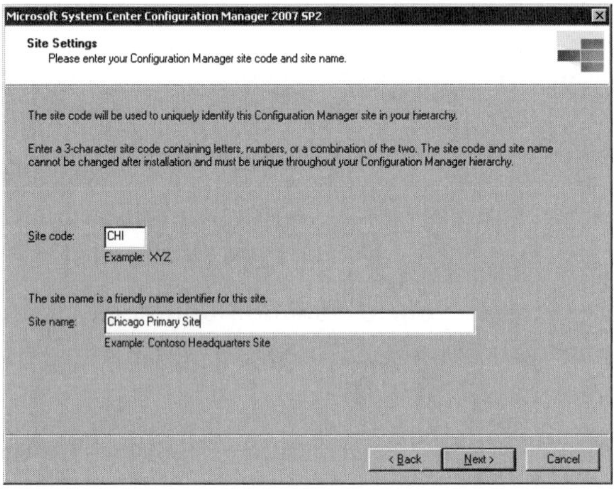

Figure 4.36
Site Settings Window

12. The next window that is displayed is the Site mode window. You can choose between native mode or mixed mode. As we talked about earlier, native mode uses PKI certificates to transmit data securely throughout the site. Mixed mode does not use certificates so the data is unencrypted. Because mixed mode does not require certificates, no PKI infrastructure needs to be in place for this option. Also, if you still have SMS 2003

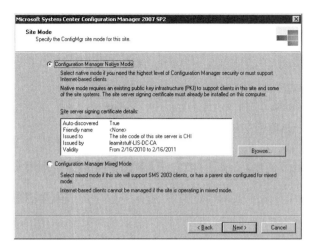

Figure 4.37
Site Mode Window

clients in your organization, you will need to use mixed mode. In our example, we'll use native mode so that we can discuss these options later in the book. In practice, however, most organizations choose to first set up their site in mixed mode and then transition to native mode. Click Next to continue (Figure 4.37).

13. The Client Agent Selection window is displayed, which lets you select which client agents are enabled from the get go. By default, network access protection is not enabled since there are other prerequisites that have to be in place prior to using this feature. Note that this step is not available in the simple settings installation. All of these client agents are enabled during setup without giving you any options. We'll leave the defaults checked in this example. Click Next to continue (Figure 4.38).

14. The next window to be displayed is the Database Server window. Since we are installing a primary site, it must be attached to a Microsoft SQL database to store its site information. This step allows you to specify the database server name, the database instance name, and the name of the database itself. In our example, we'll specify that our database server is a remote server (LIS-DB) and leave the rest of the options at their defaults. Click Next to continue (Figure 4.39).

Figure 4.38
Client Agent Selection Window

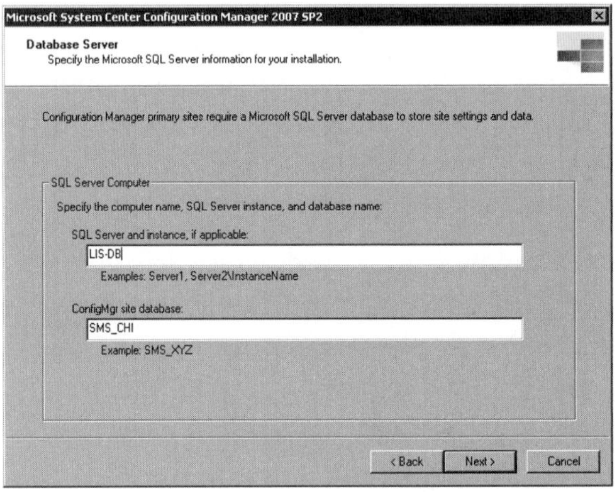

Figure 4.39
Database Server Window

15. The SMS Provider window is the next to be displayed. If you recall, we talked about the SMS provider earlier in this chapter. Its function is to be the middle man between you and the site database. This window is where you can specify where the SMS provider will be installed. We'll install it to our primary site server in this example. Click Next to continue (Figure 4.40).

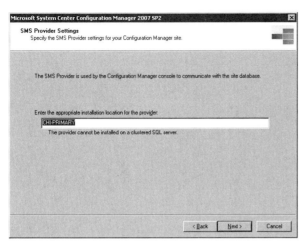

Figure 4.40
SMS Provider Settings Window

16. The Management Point window, which is displayed next, gives you the option to install a management point during the initial Configuration Manager 2007 setup. Management points are required in most situations and are the mechanism used to communicate with the clients in a site. We'll talk more about management points in Chapter 6. We'll choose the defaults and install a management point to our primary site server. Click Next to continue (Figure 4.41).

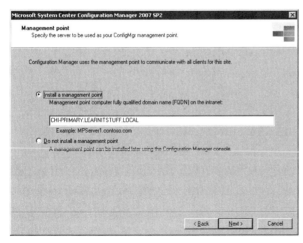

Figure 4.41
Management Point Window

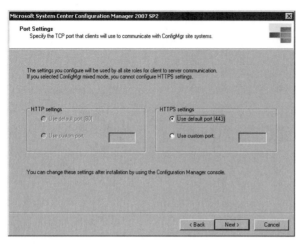

Figure 4.42
Port Settings Window

17. The next window to be displayed allows you to configure the port settings used in your site. If you are installing Configuration Manager 2007 to a system that is already using port 80 (HTTP) or port 443 (HTTPS), then you can choose a custom port that your clients and site systems will use to communicate over. Since we chose to install Configuration Manager in native mode, we can only use HTTPS settings. We'll leave the defaults in this example. Click Next to continue (Figure 4.42).

18. The next window allows you to configure options regarding updated prerequisite components. These prerequisites are for your client systems and are used to update them so that they are ready for the Configuration Manager client. Configuration Manager downloads these components on demand to a path you specify so that setup can continue. After the files have been downloaded, you can skip the download step and point directly to the directory containing these pre-downloaded updates. This is good for systems that are not connected to the Internet. Since this is our first Configuration Manager 2007 site server, we have to download the updates from the Internet, which is what is checked by default. Click Next to continue (Figure 4.43).

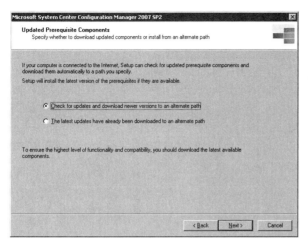

Figure 4.43
Update Prerequisites Components Window

Note

If you want to download the client prerequisites without having to go through the default Configuration Manager 2007 setup, you can use the command line setup.exe /download <path> to accomplish this.

19. Because we chose to check for updates and download the client prerequisites on demand, we now have to specify where to download the prerequisites in the Updated Prerequisites Component Path window. We'll choose C:\Downloads in our example. Click Next to continue (Figure 4.44).

Note

The directory that you specify in this step must be created prior to clicking Next. If the directory does not exist, you will not be able to continue.

20. When you have been notified that all of the prerequisites downloaded successfully, click OK.

21. The Settings Summary window is now displayed. This gives you an overview as to what will be installed and where it will be installed. Carefully review this information to make sure that you have not made a mistake. Click Next to start the Prerequisite Checker (Figure 4.45).

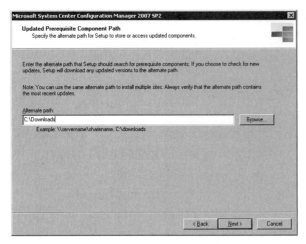

Figure 4.44
Update Prerequisites Components Path Window

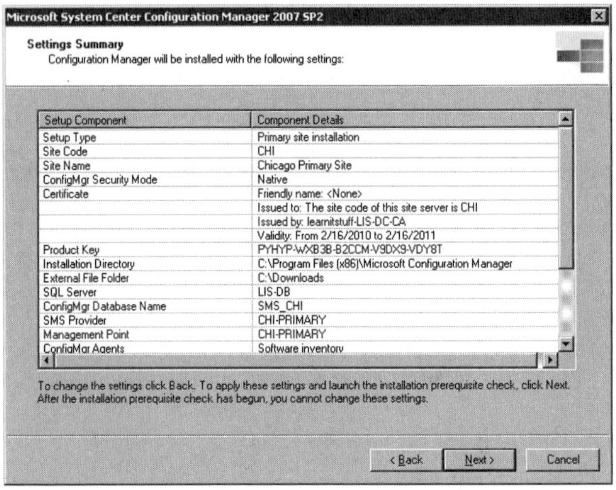

Figure 4.45
Update Prerequisites Components Window

22. The installation prerequisite checker starts automatically. This goes through and checks to make sure that the required components and permissions are in place prior to starting the installation. This gives you a chance to go back and fix any issues that are found so that your installation can be successful. In our example, no issues were found. Click Begin Install to start the installation (Figure 4.46).

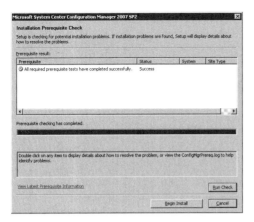

Figure 4.46
Installation Prerequisite Check Window

Note

To see exactly what the prerequisite checker looks for, visit http://technet.microsoft.com/en-us/library/bb680951.aspx.

23. When the installation begins, you are presented with the Setup Action Status Monitoring window. This window shows you the progress of the installation as well as the status of each step. If there is a failure, you are notified about it here. Once the installation completes, click Next to continue (Figure 4.47).

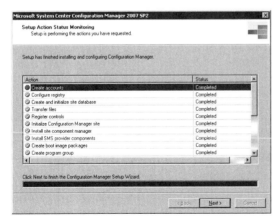

Figure 4.47
Setup Action Status Monitoring Window

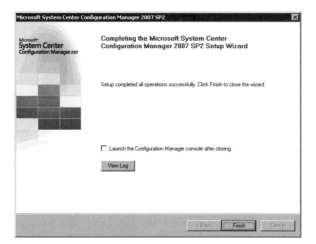

Figure 4.48
Wizard Completion

24. The last window to be displayed shows the results of the installation. If an error was detected, you can view the results of the log file by clicking the View Log button. This window also allows you to start the Configuration Manager console once the wizard is closed. Click Finish to close the wizard (Figure 4.48).

Note

We'll talk more about the log files that setup creates later in this chapter.

Unattended Installation

Configuration Manager 2007 gives you the ability to do an unattended install using a custom INI file (the unattended file). This allows you to install Configuration Manager 2007 consistently on multiple servers without having to manually step through the installation. Unattended installation is only available for new installations of Configuration Manager 2007. Upgrades from SMS 2003 are not supported using unattended installation. An unattended setup is started by using the setup /script <path to unattended file.ini> command. Other command line switches are available with Configuration Manager 2007's setup program besides /script. These switches are listed here:

- **/TRACING:OFF**—Turns off logging during setup.

- **/NODISKCHECK**—Turns off disk space checking during setup.

- **/UPGRADE**—Upgrades a site in unattended mode.

- **/DEINSTALL**— Uninstalls a site.

- **/DONTSTARTSITECOMP**—Installs a site without starting the component manager service.

- **/NOUSERINPUT**—Disables user input.

- **/NODEFAULTCOLL**—Only creates the All Systems collection during setup.

- **/RESETSITE**—Performs a site reset.

- **/SCRIPT**—Performs an unattended installation using a custom INI file.

- **/HIDDEN**—The Setup Wizard interface is not displayed. Used with the /SCRIPT switch.

- **/TESTDBUPGRADE**—Performs a test on the site database.

- **/ICPUNATTENDED**—International client pack unattended setup.

The following switches are used for the prerequisite checker:

- **/PREREQ**—When used by itself, this switch checks systems with existing installations.

- **/PREREQ /PRI**—Checks primary site prerequisites.

- **/PREREQ /SQL <SQL Server Name>\<SQL Instance Name>**—Checks the SQL server prerequisites on the server and instance specified.

- **/PREREQ /SDK**—Checks the connectivity between the SQL Server and SMS provider.

- **/PREREQ /MP <FQDN of MP>**—Checks for prerequisites on the management point specified.

- **/PREREQ /SEC**—Checks the prerequisites of the secondary site server that this command is run on.

- **/PREREQ /UI**—Checks the prerequisites for the Configuration Manager console on the computer that this command is run on.

The unattended INI file that Configuration Manager 2007 uses cannot be generated during setup and must be created from scratch using the settings provided below. It is broken down into sections, keys, and values like other INI files for organization and consistency. Each section and its keys and values are described next.

[Identification] Section

The [Identification] section is where you can specify which type of site is installed. This is done through the required action key. The possible values are as follows:

- **Action=InstallPrimarySite**—Installs a primary site.
- **Action=InstallSecondarySite**—Installs a secondary site.
- **Action=InstallAdminUI**—Installs the Configuration Manager console.

[Options] Section

The [Options] section lets you specify the details of how Configuration Manager 2007 is installed. This is done through multiple keys—some required and some optional. The keys and their values are listed here:

- **ProductID=xxxxx-xxxxx-xxxxx-xxxxx-xxxxx**—This required key specifies the product key that is used when installing a primary site or the Configuration Manager console.
- **PrerequisiteComp=x**—This required key specifies whether the client prerequisite files have been downloaded or not when installing a primary or secondary site. 0 for no, 1 for yes.
- **PrerequisitePath=<filepath>**—This required key specifies the path to the client prerequisite files when installing a primary or secondary site.
- **SiteCode=xxx**—This required key specifies the three-digit site code that will be used when installing a primary or secondary site.
- **SiteName=x**—This required key specifies the site name (description name) when installing a primary or secondary site.

- **ParentSiteCode=xxx**—This required key is used to identify the parent's site code when installing a secondary site or the Configuration Manager console.

- **ParentSiteServer=x**—This required key specifies the parent's site server name when installing a secondary site.

- **AddressType=<type>**—This required key is used to specify the default address type when installing a secondary site server. The values for this key can be MS_ASYNC_RAS, MS_ISDN_RAS, MS_LAN, MS_SNA_RAS, or MS_X25_RAS.

- **LanUser=x**—This optional key is used to specify the standard sender account that is used at a secondary site.

- **LanUserPassword=x**—This optional key is used to specify the password for the LanUser account at a secondary site.

- **RasUser=x**—This optional key is used to specify the account name for the RAS sender account at a secondary site.

- **RasUserDomain=x**—This optional key specifies the domain where the RasUserAccount was created. This is used by a secondary site.

- **RasUserPassword=x**—This optional key specifies the password for the RasUser. This is used by a secondary site.

- **RasPhoneBook=x**—This optional key specifies the phone book name for the RAS Sender to use. This is used by a secondary site.

- **SMSInstallDir=x**—This required key specifies the directory where Configuration Manager 2007 will be installed when installing a primary or secondary site. This is also used when installing the Configuration Manager console.

- **ManagementPoint=X**—This optional key specifies the name of the computer that will host the default management point for the site. This is used by a primary site.

Note

The server name must be in uppercase for this to work properly.

- **DistributionPoint=x**—This optional key specifies whether or not to install the distribution point role during the setup of a primary or secondary site. 0 for no, 1 for yes.

- **SDKServer=x**—This required key specifies the name of the computer that will host the SMS provider for the site. This is used by a primary site.

Note

The server name must be in uppercase for this to work properly.

- **ClientAgents=x**—This optional key specifies which client agents are enabled during the setup of a primary site. By default, setup will enable all of the client agents except for network access protection (just like in the GUI setup) if this key is not specified in the unattended.inf file. If you wish to only enable certain client agents, you can do so using the options below. Note that if you want to enable multiple options, separate them with a comma. For example: ClientAgents=SINV,HINV,DCM

  - **SINV**—Software inventory client agent
  - **HINV**—Hardware inventory client agent
  - **ADPROG**—Advertised programs client agent
  - **NAP**—Network access protection client agent
  - **SUM**—Software update management client agent
  - **SWM**—Software update metering client agent
  - **DCM**—Desired configuration management client agent
  - **RT**—Remote tools client agent

- **SiteSecurityMode=x**—This optional key specifies whether to use mixed mode or native mode when installing a primary site. Use mixed for mixed mode and native for native mode.

- **Port=x**—This optional key specifies which custom port to use when installing a primary site. If not specified, port 80 will be used when in mixed mode and port 443 will be used when in native mode.

- **SiteServerSignCert=x**—This key is only required when installing a primary site in native mode. The value needs to equal the signing certificate thumbprint (with no spaces).

[SQLConfigOptions] Section

The [SQLConfigOptions] section specifies options regarding the SQL database. These options are described below:

- **SQLServerName=X**—This required key specifies the name of the server or clustered instance name that is running SQL server when installing a primary site.

Note

The server name must be in uppercase for this to work properly.

- **CreateSQLDevice=x**—This required key specifies if the database should be created when installing a primary site. 0 for No, 1 for Yes.
- **DatabaseName=x**—This required key specifies the name of the database when installing a primary site.

Below is an example of an unattend.ini file that will install a primary site just as we did in the Custom Installation section:

```
[Identification]

Action=InstallPrimarySite

[Options]

ProductID=xxxxx-xxxxx-xxxxx-xxxxx-xxxxx
PrerequisiteComp=0
PrerequisitePath=C:\Downloads
SiteCode=CHI
SiteName=Chicago Primary Site
SMSInstallDir=C:\Program Files (x86)\Microsoft Configuration Manager
ManagementPoint=CHI-PRIMARY
SDKServer=CHI-PRIMARY
SiteSecurityMode=Native
SiteServerSignCert=a909502dd82ae41433e6f83886b00d4277a32a7b

[SQLConfigOptions]

SQLServerName=LIS-DB
```

```
CreateSQLDevice=1
DatabaseName=SMS_CHI
```

Verifying the Installation

Once Configuration Manager 2007 has been installed, you should verify that the installation was successful by looking at the installation log files that are created during install time. These log files can be very long and difficult to read so Microsoft has made a tool available in the Configuration Manager 2007 Toolkit called Trace32.exe. This tool interprets log files and outputs them in a readable fashion. If there are any warning or error events contained in the log file, these events are highlighted in yellow and red respectively. The Configuration Manger 2007 Toolkit can be downloaded from http://www.microsoft.com/downloads/en/details.aspx?FamilyID=5A47B972-95D2-46B1-AB14-5D0CBCE54EB8

Use Trace32.exe to review the log files that get written to the root of the system drive during the installation process. These log files are as follows:

- **ConfigMgrSetup.log**—This is the log file that Configuration Manager 2007 setup writes to when going through the install process. Most every aspect of the install phase is written to this file.

- **ComponentSetup.log**—Once the initial setup is complete, Configuration Manager components start to get installed by the component manager. The component manager outputs its setup information to this log file.

- **ConfigMgrPrereq**—This is the log file that gets created when the prerequisite checker runs before installing Configuration Manager 2007 to your site server. The results of the prerequisite checker are written to this file.

Tip

Trace32.exe, as shown in Figure 4.49, allows you to view log files and the events that are written to them as they happen (unlike Notepad). As long as you know the name and location of the log file, you can watch events occur in real time such as the Configuration Manager 2007 setup process. Simply open ConfigMgrSetup.log as soon as it is created by the Configuration Manager 2007 setup process to watch the setup results.

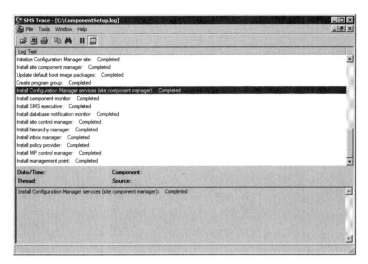

Figure 4.49
Trace32.exe

Configuration Manger 2007 includes a multitude of log files that can be used for troubleshooting purposes. These log files are covered in Chapter 21, "Troubleshooting Common Issues."

INSTALLING CONFIGURATION MANAGER 2007 R3

Once you have verified that your site is up and running correctly, you can install the R3 update to your site server. Because R3 contains all of the updates included in the R2 release, we can skip the installation of R2 and move on to R3.

Note

Hotfix KB977384 must be applied to your site server prior to installing R3. During the installation, you are prompted to create a software package to update the Configuration Manager client software on your client machines so that they are compatible with the new R3 power management features. Once this update is applied to your client machines, the client version number will be 4.00.6487.2157. If KB977384 is not applied to your site server, you will receive an error message and the installation will fail. For more information about KB977384 and how to obtain the hotfix, visit this URL: http://support.microsoft.com/kb/977384.

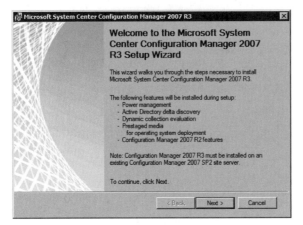

Figure 4.50
Configuration Manager 2007 R3 Install Wizard

To start the installation, obtain the Configuration Manager 2007 R3 installation media (whether it be on physical media or the network), browse to the root folder, and follow the steps below:

1. Double-click on SPLASH.HTA.

2. After double-clicking on SPLASH.HTA, the installer program starts and displays the initial setup window. Click Configuration Manager 2007 R3 under the Install section to begin the install.

3. Wait for the Configuration Manager 2007 R3 Install Wizard window to be displayed and review the information. Click Next to start the wizard (Figure 4.50).

4. If you agree to the license terms, click Next on the Microsoft Software License Terms window to continue.

5. The registration information window is displayed. Enter the correct registration information and click Next to continue.

6. A warning message is displayed. If you have any sites higher in the hierarchy that have not been upgraded to R3, abort the installation and upgrade those sites first. When finished, continue the R3 installation at this site. Because we have no sites higher in the hierarchy, we can ignore

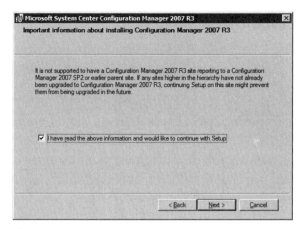

Figure 4.51
R3 Upgrade Warning

this message by checking the checkbox and clicking Next to continue (Figure 4.51).

7. The installation window is displayed. Click Next to start the installation.

8. The Setup Complete window is displayed. If any errors were experienced during installation, these messages would be displayed on this screen. Click Finish to close the wizard.

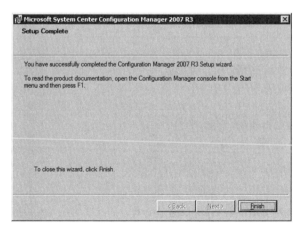

Figure 4.52
Setup Complete

Post Installation Tasks

Once Configuration Manager 2007 SP2 and R3 have been installed, you may want to do some post setup tasks to help ensure that you are ready to tackle any problems that might lie ahead.

- **Install the Configuration Manager 2007 Toolkit**—As I stated earlier, the Configuration Manager 2007 Toolkit comes with Trace32.exe, which helps you interpret log files. It also comes with other useful tools to help troubleshoot common issues with client policies, software distribution, and desired configuration management.

- **Install the Configuration Manager Console**—The Configuration Manager console gets installed by default to the computer where the primary site was installed. You probably don't want to log into this sever, however, to manage your site database. Use the Configuration Manager 2007 setup program to install the Configuration Manger console on your workstation so that you have quick access to the information about your site.

- **Review the Site Status Node**—Configuration Manager 2007 includes a node dedicated to the status of your overall site. Review the messages in this node to verify that all of the components and site systems are working correctly. This is covered in detail in Chapter 3.

Note

As we go through the rest of this book, we'll be using many facets of the Configuration Manager console for things like software distribution, reporting, and configuring options for the overall site. To get a quick overview of the Configuration Manager console and to review its features, see Chapter 1.

The Final Word

This chapter is your first introduction to site installation and configuration. We covered the prerequisites needed to install a primary site server including other external components such as SQL and hardware requirements. Note that we did not delve much into design or advanced installation topics as these will be covered in the next chapter.

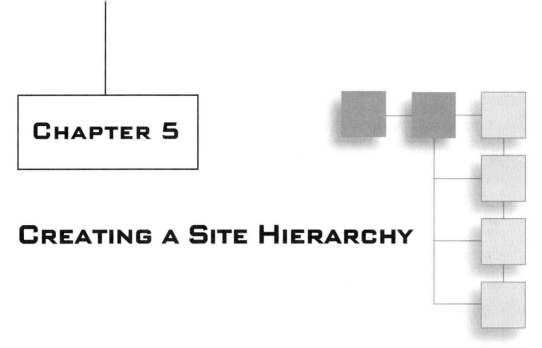

CHAPTER 5

CREATING A SITE HIERARCHY

In Chapter 4, we briefly covered some of the concepts regarding site relationships and hierarchies but didn't go into detail about all of the options available. In this chapter, we'll dig deep into these concepts and go through—step by step—how to build a site hierarchy by creating multiple primary and secondary sites.

UNDERSTANDING SITE RELATIONSHIPS

Configuration Manager 2007 allows for manageability and scalability through a hierarchical and componentized design. Understanding the concept behind this design is somewhat confusing—especially for people who are new to SMS and Configuration Manager 2007. This section is dedicated to helping you understand these concepts.

Types of Sites

As stated in Chapter 4, three types of sites can exist within a Configuration Manager 2007 hierarchy. These are referred to as primary, secondary, and central sites. Each Configuration Manager site must contain one site server and may contain multiple site systems. Depending on the type of site you install will dictate how your Configuration Manager implementation will operate, because they are designed with specific functions, requirements, and limitations. As you design your Configuration Manager structure, you will need to understand the types of sites that are available and what they are capable of. These types of sites are explained below.

Primary Sites

When you initially install Configuration Manager 2007, you must first install a primary site. A primary site is responsible for managing clients that are assigned to it and that fall within its boundaries.

When you install a primary site, the server you install it to is referred to as a site server. Site servers are responsible for many Configuration Manager functions like publishing site information to Active Directory, hosting multiple site settings that are used by other site systems, and receiving data from clients and storing it in the site database. Site servers must be installed to a Microsoft Server class operating system such as Windows Server 2008 R2. A site cannot function without the site server.

If necessary, primary sites may also contain multiple site systems. Site systems can be configured to run on any supported Microsoft operating system including workstation or server class operating systems and are responsible for distributing the load across multiple machines so that no one system is overloaded.

Note

Site servers are also referred to as site systems in Configuration Manager since they too can host roles. The roles that site systems can host are covered in detail in the next chapter.

Primary sites are also responsible for managing sites that fall beneath it. Depending on the complexity of your environment, you may only need one primary site. If this is the case, this type of site is referred to as a central-primary or a standalone site since there are no parent sites or child sites in the hierarchy. If your organization is large and complex, you may need to have multiple primary sites placed in different locations to effectively handle the load of your clients.

Note

Information from child sites such as status messages and inventory data roll up to parent sites where the data is aggregated. This process continues until all data for all child sites exists in the central server's database. This is very important to keep in mind as you design your Configuration Manager hierarchy. If data from thousands of clients is being sent up the hierarchy, a large load may be placed on your server and network infrastructure.

Primary sites have the following attributes:

- **Primary sites are attached to a Microsoft SQL database**—Primary sites require that they be attached to a Microsoft SQL database to store information about its site. If there is only one primary site in the hierarchy (the central-primary site), only one database will exist. If the Configuration Manager implementation is large and complex, there could be multiple primary sites with databases attached to each site

- **Primary sites can be parent or child sites**—Primary sites can be parent sites or child sites in a Configuration Manager 2007 hierarchy. Multiple primary sites configured in a parent/child hierarchy are often used when you need to control things like network bandwidth, administration tasks, or different client settings throughout the environment. If a primary site is configured as a child site, it must be connected to a parent site that is also a primary site.

- **Primary sites can have clients directly attached to them**—Primary sites are the only type of sites that can have clients directly attached to them. When clients are attached to a site, they send and receive information such as policy configurations, client inventory data, and client status messages. Secondary sites can act on behalf of a primary site if configured properly. More about this topic is covered below.

- **Primary site systems (including the primary site server) can host every site system role**—Primary site systems can host all of the site system roles including the site database server role. Site system roles allow site servers to perform specific functions such as hosting software distribution files or responding to PXE requests. For more information on site system roles, see Chapter 6, "Configuring Site System Roles."

- **Primary sites require a Configuration Manager Server license**—Each primary site requires a dedicated Configuration Manager server license. Because of the cost overhead associated with this (and the potential cost of a SQL database license), primary sites are only used when a secondary site or branch distribution point cannot meet the requirements of the organization.

Secondary Sites

Secondary sites are similar to primary sites in that they require at least one site server and can have multiple site systems within the site. They are different in that they can only be configured as child sites and are managed via their parent primary sites. Secondary sites are typically used in offsite locations to organize and ease administration tasks. Secondary sites are also a good choice when needing to conserve network bandwidth between sites with slow links. Data can be sent to the secondary site using rate limits and then sent to clients on the local LAN at an unlimited rate where the secondary site server resides. Secondary sites have pros and cons associated with them when compared to primary sites. Some of these are listed below.

Secondary sites have the following attributes:

- **Secondary sites cannot be attached to a SQL database**—Primary sites are the only types of sites that can be connected to a SQL database. Secondary sites store their information in their parent primary site's SQL database.

- **Secondary sites can only be child sites in a Configuration Manager 2007 hierarchy**—Secondary sites must exist as a child site under a parent primary site. They cannot be administered directly but rather via their parent primary site. This means that when a secondary site is installed, a Configuration Manager console is not installed with it. The Configuration Manager console that is connected to its parent primary site is used to administer the secondary site (Figure 5.1).

- **Secondary sites cannot have clients directly assigned to them**—Because clients cannot be assigned to secondary sites, they cannot be managed by secondary sites. Clients can, however, obtain software packages from secondary sites if the correct server role has been defined.

- **Secondary site systems (including the secondary site server) can only host some of the site system roles**—Secondary site systems can only host some of the site system roles. One of the roles it does not support is the site database server role. Site system roles allow site servers to perform specific functions such as hosting software distribution files or respond to PXE requests. For more information on site system roles, see Chapter 6.

- **Secondary sites do not require a Configuration Manager server license**—One of the benefits of using a secondary site server is that you are not required to pay for an extra Configuration Manager server license. This allows you to use an unlimited amount of secondary site servers without ever increasing cost overhead.

Central Sites

When you install Configuration Manager 2007, you can only install two types of sites: Primary or secondary sites. So you might be wondering what this central site thing is. Central sites are primary sites that sit at the top of the Configuration Manager hierarchy (Figure 5.2). They are designed to store all of the information about the Configuration Manager infrastructure and are typically used for central reporting and management. Central sites adhere to all of the same guidelines as primary sites because they *are* primary sites. In a large and complex hierarchy, central sites typically do not have clients assigned to them but rather to one of their child primary sites. This takes the burden off of the central site since it is often under stress from managing all of the sites below it.

CREATING A CHILD SECONDARY SITE

In Chapter 4, we went through the process of installing a primary site (CHI), including checking for and configuring the necessary software and hardware prerequisites. In this section, we will expand our site using the guidelines outlined in Chapters 2 and 4 to design a Configuration Manager 2007 site hierarchy.

In its current state, the CHI site is considered as a central-primary or a standalone site since it does not have any parent or child sites attached to it. In this step, we will install a child secondary site underneath the CHI standalone/central-primary site, which will convert it into a parent primary site.

Secondary sites are typically used to reduce the load on primary sites and to help conserve network bandwidth between slow links (like WAN connections, for example). Secondary site systems can host many of the same site system roles that systems in a primary site can but don't require as much cost or administration overhead when compared to a primary site. Think about using secondary sites in locations like branch locations when you don't need granular administrative control over the site, but you do need granular control over network bandwidth. Because secondary sites are managed from their parent primary site, all of the settings (including client settings) are inherited from the parent primary site and cannot be changed at the secondary site.

When you are ready to create a secondary site, note that it can be installed in one of two ways. You can install a secondary site manually using the Configuration Manager 2007 installation media or you can install it through the Configuration Manager console. Using the Configuration Manager console to install a secondary site is the preferred method since it automatically creates the necessary site senders and adds the necessary computer objects into the right groups. We'll cover both installation methods below.

Manually Installing a Secondary Site

Manually creating a secondary site is helpful because you get an idea of all of the things that happen automatically when a secondary site is installed via the Configuration Manager console. By experiencing these steps firsthand, you can more easily troubleshoot site problems like communication and security issues.

Secondary Site Step-by-Step Manual Installation

To start the manual installation of a secondary site, obtain the Configuration Manager 2007 SP2 installation media (whether it is on physical media or the network), browse to the root folder, and follow these steps:

Caution

> Before you install your secondary site to the designated site server, make sure the site server meets all of the prerequisites for installation. Step-by-step guides for this process can be found in Chapter 4.

1. After double-clicking on SPLASH.HTA, the installer program starts and displays the initial setup window. Click Configuration Manager 2007 SP2 under the Install section to begin the install.

2. Wait for the Configuration Manager 2007 SP2 Install Wizard window to be displayed and review the information. Click Next to start the wizard.

3. When the Available Setup Options window is displayed, choose the Install a Configuration Manager site server option. Click Next to continue.

4. If you agree to the license terms, click Next on the Microsoft Software License Terms window to continue.

5. At this point, the Installation Settings window is displayed. This is where you can choose to install Configuration Manager with simple or custom settings. Remember that if you choose to install with simple settings, you will not have the ability to configure important aspects of your site. For this example, we'll install Configuration Manager 2007 using the custom settings option.

6. When the Site Type window is displayed, you can choose between a primary site or a secondary site. Because we already have a primary site installed, we can now install a secondary site. This is the option we will choose in this example. Click Next to continue (Figure 5.1).

7. When you are prompted to choose your destination folder, either keep the defaults or enter another location. We'll keep the defaults in this example. Click Next to continue.

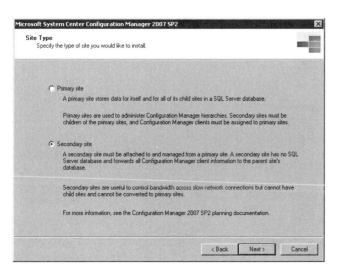

Figure 5.1
Secondary Site Installation

8. At this point, the Site Settings window is displayed. This is where you enter your three-digit site code. When we created our primary site in Chapter 4, we used the site code CHI (for Chicago). In this example, our secondary site will reside in a branch location that is located in Oak Lawn so we will use OAK as our site code. Remember that site codes must be unique and are used to identify each site. The site name is used to further identify the site since a three-character code is very limited in detail, so we will use Oak Lawn Secondary Site in this field. Click Next to continue (Figure 5.2).

9. When the Parent Site Settings screen is displayed, it asks you for the parent site code and the parent site server name. This information is used to link the secondary site to the correct parent primary site in the hierarchy. Remember that this is mandatory since secondary sites must have a parent primary site above them in the hierarchy. For the parent site code, enter the site code of the primary site that will sit directly above this site in the hierarchy. In our example, the parent site code is CHI. For the parent site server name, enter the NetBIOS name of the server where the parent primary site was installed. In our example, the parent site server name is CHI-PRIMARY. Click Next to continue (Figure 5.3).

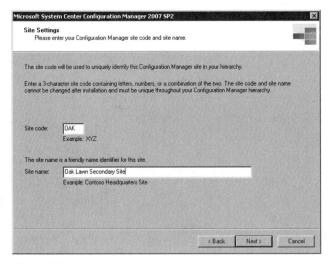

Figure 5.2
Secondary Site Code

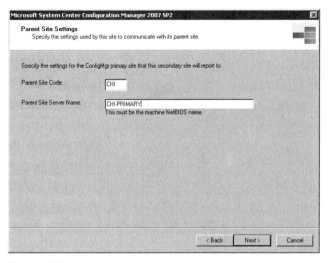

Figure 5.3
Parent Site Settings

Tip

Remember the Site to Site Connection group? The name you enter in the parent site server field will dictate which server name gets added to the Site to Site Connection group on this server.

10. The next window allows you to configure options regarding updated prerequisite components. These prerequisites are for your client systems and are used to update them so that they are ready for the Configuration Manager client. Configuration Manager downloads these components on demand to a path you specify so that setup can continue. Because we already downloaded these files in our last chapter, we can use these predownloaded files instead of having to re-download them from the Internet. Choose The Latest Updates Have Already Been Downloaded to an Alternate Path and click Next to continue (Figure 5.4).

Tip

If you want to download the client prerequisites without having to go through the default Configuration Manager 2007 setup, you can use the command line setup.exe /download <path> to accomplish this.

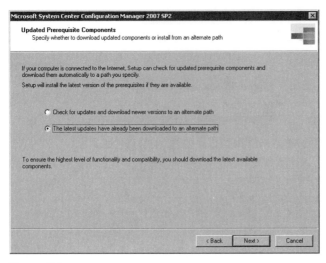

Figure 5.4
Updated Prerequisite Components

11. The Updated Prerequisite Component Path window is now displayed. This window allows you to specify the location to the pre-downloaded prerequisite files. In our example, we downloaded them to C:\downloads on CHI-PRIMARY back in Chapter 4. To access them from this server, we will enter \\chi-primary\c$\downloads. (See Figure 5.5.)

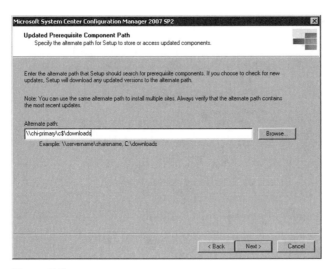

Figure 5.5
Updated Prerequisite Component Path

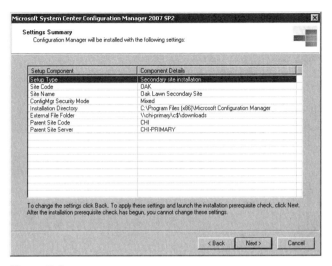

Figure 5.6
Settings Summary Window

Note

You must be logged in with an account that has at least read access to the prerequisite files if they are contained on a remote server.

12. The Settings Summary window is now displayed. This gives you an overview as to what will be installed and where it will be installed. Carefully review this information to make sure that you have not made a mistake. Click Next to start the prerequisite checker (Figure 5.6).

13. The installation prerequisite checker starts automatically after the Installation Summary window. This checks to make sure that the required components and permissions are in place prior to starting the installation and gives you a chance to go back and fix any issues that are found so that your installation can be successful. Click Begin Install to start the installation.

Tip

To see exactly what the prerequisite checker looks for, visit http://technet.microsoft.com/en-us/library/bb680951.aspx.

14. When the installation begins, you are presented with the Setup Action Status Monitoring window. This window shows you the progress of the installation as well as the status of each step. If there is a failure, you are notified about it here. Once the installation completes, click Next to continue.

15. The last window to be displayed shows the results of the installation. If an error was detected, you can view the results of the log file by clicking the View Log button. This window also allows you to start the Configuration Manager console once the wizard is closed. Click Finish to close the wizard.

Adding Site Systems to the Correct Security Groups

During a manual install of a Configuration Manager 2007 secondary site, some of the necessary install steps do not occur and have to be done manually. One of these steps is adding the correct site server computer object to the correct security group that is created by Configuration Manager 2007. This group is designed to give site systems the correct security permissions that are needed by Configuration Manager.

Tip

To see which rights are given to the SMS_SiteSystemToSiteServerConnection group, see this link for details: http://technet.microsoft.com/en-us/library/bb680864.aspx. To see which rights are assigned to the SMS_SiteToSiteConnection group, see this link for details: http://technet.microsoft.com/en-us/library/bb632850.aspx.

Connection Groups   There are two security groups that get created during the Configuration Manager 2007 setup. These groups are as follows:

- **Site System to Site Server Connection group**—During setup, Configuration Manager 2007 creates the SMS_SiteSystemToSiteServerConnection_ sitecode group locally on the site sever where it is installed. This group gives the necessary permissions to remote site systems so that they can communicate to the site server to access registry keys and directories that are necessary for certain Configuration Manager role services to function correctly. The only computer objects that should be added to this group are remote site systems that are configured within the site.

■ **Site to Site Connection group**—During setup, Configuration Manager 2007 creates the SMS_SiteToSiteConnection_sitecode group locally on the site server where it is installed. This group gives the necessary permissions to other site systems that are configured as its parent or child sites. This is the group we need to manually create and configure.

Note

These groups are added as local groups to both primary and secondary site servers during a primary or secondary site installation. If the primary or secondary site server is a domain controller, they will be created as domain local groups.

Connection Groups on the Primary Site Server   In this example, we will be adding the secondary site server's computer account to the Site to Site Connection group on the primary site server.

1. On your primary site server, go to Start > Administrative Tools > Computer Management. In our example, our primary site server is CHI-PRIMARY.

2. Expand the Local Users and Groups node and click on Groups.

3. Note that two Configuration Manager connection groups have already been created by Configuration Manager. These are SMS_Site SystemToSiteServerConnection_sitecode and SMS_SiteToSiteConnection_ sitecode. These groups automatically get created during the installation of a primary or secondary site. You should see these two groups on each of your site servers (or in Active Directory as domain local groups if your primary site servers are domain controllers). In our example, these groups are named SMS_Site SystemToSiteServerConnection_CHI and SMS_SiteToSiteConnection_CHI. (See Figure 5.7.)

4. Double-click on the SMS_SiteToSiteConnection_sitecode group that corresponds to the primary site that will sit above your secondary site in the hierarchy. In our example, this group is called SMS_SiteToSiteConnection_CHI.

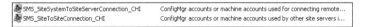

Figure 5.7
Configuration Manager Groups on the Primary Site Server

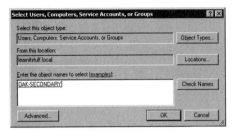

Figure 5.8
Add Secondary Site Server to Group

5. When the Select Users, Computers, Service Accounts, or Groups dialog window comes up, type the name of the server that hosts the secondary site. In our example, OAK-SECONDARY is the site server that hosts the secondary site. Click Check Names to verify that the server name is correct and then click OK to continue. Note that computers must be selected in the object types list for this to work properly (Figure 5.8).

6. Once the secondary site server is listed in the Members field, click the OK button (Figure 5.9).

Connection Groups on the Secondary Site Server   Once the secondary site server has been added to the Site to Site Connection Group on the primary site server, the primary site server has to be added to the Site to Site Connection

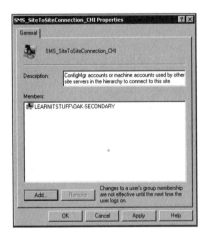

Figure 5.9
Add the Secondary Site Server to the Primary Site to Site Connection Group

group on the secondary site server. The steps to add the primary site server to the secondary site server's Site to Site Connection group is exactly the same as before except they are done on the secondary site server and reference the primary site server. The steps are briefly listed below:

1. On your secondary site server, go to Start > Administrative Tools > Computer Management. In our example, our primary site server is OAK-SECONDARY.

2. Expand the Local Users and Groups node and click on Groups.

3. Note that two Configuration Manager connection groups have already been created by Configuration Manager. These are SMS _Site SystemToSiteServerConnection_sitecode and SMS_SiteToSite Connection_sitecode. In our example, these groups are named SMS _Site SystemToSiteServerConnection_OAK and SMS_SiteToSite Connection_OAK.

4. Double-click on the SMS_SiteToSiteConnection_OAK group.

5. When the Select Users, Computers, Service Accounts, or Groups dialog window comes up, type the name of the server that hosts the primary site. In our example, CHI-PRIMARY is the site server that hosts the primary site. Click Check Names to verify that the server name is correct and then click OK to continue. Note that computers must be selected in the object types list for this to work properly.

6. Once the secondary site server is listed in the Members field, click the OK button.

Connecting the Secondary Site to the Primary Site

Before primary and secondary sites can communicate with each other, a sender and a sender address must be properly set up and configured. Senders and sender addresses are automatically created when a secondary site is installed from the Configuration Manager console but do not get created during a manual setup.

Think of senders and sender addresses as you would the post mail system. Senders are like your mail carriers, whereas addresses are like home or business addresses. The mail carrier takes your mail and delivers it to the correct home or business address using the existing rail, road, or air infrastructure. If the roads are clear, not much is needed to deliver the message. However, if the roads are closed due to a storm, the mail carrier will attempt to re-deliver the message using predefined rules from the post office or by using another route if one is available.

Note

Information about the sender can be seen in the sender.log file and the Component Status node within the Configuration Manager console. We will talk about this log and more in Chapter 21, "Troubleshooting Common Issues."

Configuration Manager 2007 Senders

Senders deliver messages between sites using sender addresses over existing network connections. They can be configured to specify network settings like the number of simultaneous connections a site can have and the number of retries a site will send in the event of a failed communication. Multiple types of senders can be configured depending on the type of network link you are using to communicate with other sites.

Types of Senders   There are six different senders available within Configuration Manager 2007:

- **Standard senders**—Standard senders are installed by default on all primary and secondary site systems. For most well connected sites (such as sites on a LAN), this is typically the only sender that you'll need.

- **Courier senders**—Courier senders are also installed by default but are not managed through the Configuration Manager console like other senders. Courier senders are used when you need to send large amounts of data from one site to another but you don't want to use a network connection to deliver the data. These senders allow you to send data using a physical medium such as a DVD or external hard drive. This physical medium can then be physically sent to the remote location by a courier service, for example.

- **Asynchronous RAS sender**—This sender is used for site to site RAS communications when connected across an asynchronous line.

- **ISDN RAS sender**—This sender is used for site to site RAS communications when connected across an ISDN line.

- **X.25 RAS senders**—This sender is used for site to site RAS communications when connected across an X.25 line.

- **SNA RAS sender**—This sender is used for site to site RAS communications when connected across an SNA link.

Installing a Sender on the Primary Site Server To install a Configuration Manager 2007 sender, do the following:

1. Go to your primary site server and open the Configuration Manager console. In our example, our site server is CHI-PRIMARY.

2. Once the Configuration Manager console is open, expand the Site Database node, expand the Site Management node, and then expand your primary site that is displayed as the three-character site code. In our example, our primary site code is CHI. Once the Site node is expanded, expand the Site Settings node (Figure 5.10).

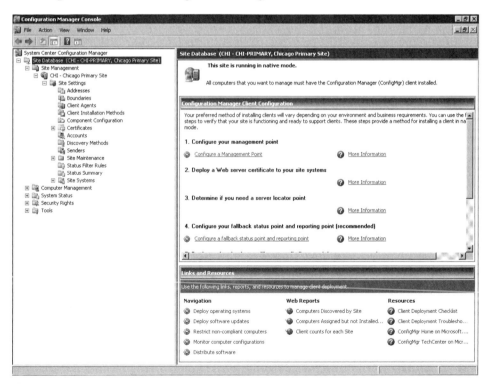

Figure 5.10
Site Settings Node

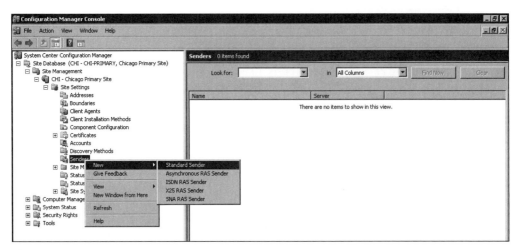

Figure 5.11
Create a New Sender

3. In our example, we will install a standard sender since our site-to-site communications will be over a fast ethernet connection. You may want to install another type of sender based on your communication needs. To install a standard sender, right-click on the Senders node and choose New > Standard Sender (Figure 5.11).

4. The New Standard Sender window is displayed. On the General tab, you can see the server where the standard sender will be created, which is shown in Figure 5.12. In our example, it's being created on CHI-PRIMARY. On the Advanced tab, you can specify limits for concurrent sendings and retry settings that are shown in Figure 5.13. Click OK to complete the creation of a standard sender.

Installing a Sender on the Secondary Site Server When you install a secondary site manually using the Configuration Manager 2007 installation media, the sender is automatically installed on the secondary site. No further configuration is needed unless you wish to install a different type of sender or change the sender settings that are discussed below.

Sender Configuration Settings As shown in Figure 5.13, there are multiple communication settings that can be configured per sender. These settings are very useful when trying to balance the level of throughput versus the level of available bandwidth. Below are the configurable options within a sender:

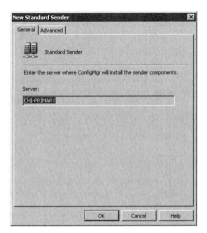

Figure 5.12
Standard Sender General Tab

Figure 5.13
Standard Sender Advanced Tab

- **Maximum concurrent sendings—All sites**—Default is 5. This setting specifies the maximum number of simultaneous connections for the sender. The number of open connections can be to one or multiple sites.

- **Maximum concurrent sendings—Per site**—Default is 3. This setting specifies the maximum number of simultaneous connections per site.

Note

The default value for the maximum concurrent sendings per site is 3 for standard senders but it is restricted to 1 for RAS senders.

- **Retry settings—Number of retries**—Default is 2. This setting specifies how many times a failed communication is retried.

- **Retry settings—Delay before retrying**—Default is 1. This setting specifies the number of minutes to wait before retrying a failed communication.

Caution

Make sure that the maximum concurrent sendings for All Sites is greater than the maximum concurrent sendings Per Site. If the All Sites setting is set as the same number as the Per Site setting, it's possible to use up the total number of connections when trying to connect to an unavailable site. This could potentially stop site-to-site communication to some or all sites.

Configuration Manager 2007 Sender Addresses

Once a Configuration Manager sender has been set up and configured, you then need to configure a sender address so that Configuration Manager sites know how to communicate with other Configuration Manager sites. Senders use sender addresses to find site servers within a Configuration Manager site so that they can send communications between one another. For each Sender Address type, the same sender type must also be installed. If multiple senders are installed, you can use multiple addresses for the purpose of increased data throughput or communication backup links.

One of the more important aspects about sender addresses is that they allow you to configure the amount of network bandwidth that is used during site-to-site communications. This is extremely helpful if you have a remote location that is connected over a slow link and you need to dictate not only how much bandwidth a Configuration Manager site will use when sending data but also *when* the site can send data and at what rate.

Installing a Sender Address on the Primary Site Server   To install a Configuration Manager sender address on the primary site server, do the following:

1. Go to your primary site server and open the Configuration Manager console. In our example, our site server is CHI-PRIMARY.

2. Once the Configuration Manager console is open, expand the Site Database node, expand the Site Management node, and then expand your primary site, which is displayed as the three-character site code. In our example, our primary site code is CHI. Once the Site node is expanded, expand the Site Settings node.

3. In our example, we will install a standard sender address since our site-to-site communications will be over a fast Ethernet connection. You may want to install another type of sender address based on your communication needs. To install a standard sender address, right-click on the Addresses node and choose New > Standard Sender Address (Figure 5.14).

4. The New Standard Sender Address Wizard window is displayed. The settings on the General page define how the primary site will connect to the secondary site and the name of the site server at the secondary site. In our example, we want to connect our primary site (CHI) to our new secondary site (OAK), which has been installed to OAK-SECONDARY. Click Next to continue (Figure 5.15).

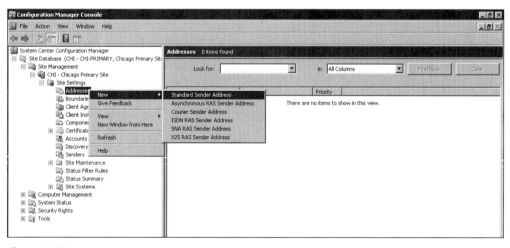

Figure 5.14
Create a New Sender Address

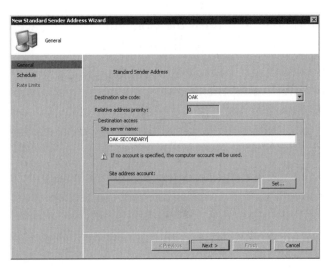

Figure 5.15
General Standard Sender Address Properties

5. The Standard Sender Address Schedule window is displayed. This window allows you to schedule when specific types of data are sent. We will cover this in detail below. In our example, we will leave the defaults and click Next to continue (Figure 5.16).

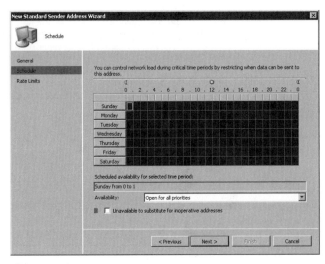

Figure 5.16
Standard Sender Address Scheduling

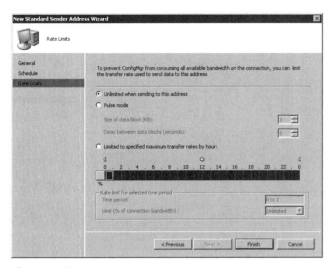

Figure 5.17
Standard Sender Address Rate Limits

6. The last window of the wizard to be displayed is the Rate Limit window. This window allows you to configure how much network bandwidth will be used when transferring data from this site to another site. We will cover this in detail below. In our example, we will leave the defaults and click Finish to complete the wizard (Figure 5.17).

As you saw in the last step, sender addresses have multiple configuration options that allow you to configure options such as how and when to send data to a remote site. These settings are covered below.

Sender Address Properties—General Tab   The General tab on a sender address allows you to configure options that relate to site-to-site communication (Figure 5.18). The options on this tab are as follows:

- **Destination site code**—The destination site code shows you the site that this sender address will send data to. This can be a primary or secondary site. The site code can only be configured during the sender address installation.

- **Relative address priority**—The relative address priority is used when you have two or more sender addresses that connect to the same site. Sender addresses with a lower number (higher priority) are tried first. If

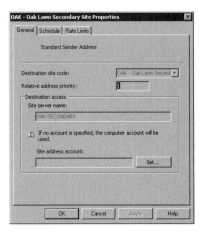

Figure 5.18
Standard Sender Address—General Tab

data cannot be sent over the sender address with the highest priority, the sender address with the next priority is tried.

- **Site server name**—The site server name tells the sender address which site server to connect to at the remote site.

- **Site address acccount**—This field is optional. The site address account is used when you do not want to use the local site server's computer account to connect to the remote site server but rather a specific domain account. This is needed if the computer account does not have the appropriate security permissions on the remote site server.

Note

If you specify a site address account, you cannot switch back to the computer account without deleting the sender address and recreating it.

Sender Address Properties—Schedule Tab   The Schedule tab on a sender address allows you to specify when different data priorities are sent to remote sites (Figure 5.19). The options on this tab are as follows:

- **Sunday—Saturday**—This section allows you to select time periods throughout the week that dictate when specific data priorities are sent. For example, you might only want data that is marked as high priority

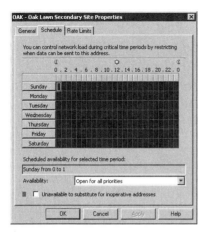

Figure 5.19
Standard Sender Address—Schedule Tab

(such as a critical software update) to be sent every day during production hours while data marked as low priority (such as standard software updates) can be sent on specific days during non-production hours. You can choose from:

- Open for all priorities
- Allow for medium and high priority
- Allow high priority only
- Closed

- **Unavailable to substitute for inoperative addresses**—This option lets you control whether this address can be used as a failover address if another address to the same site fails. This is what we we're talking about above with multiple addresses with different priorities. If for some reason you do not want this address to be used as a failover (or backup) address during specific time periods, you can specify this by checking this box.

Sender Address Properties—Rate Limits Tab   The Rate Limits tab allows you to configure some of the most useful configuration options within a sender address. The options on this tab allow you specify how much bandwidth is consumed when sending data between sites, which can be a major concern if you have slow links between sites (Figure 5.20). The options are discussed below:

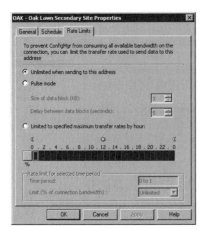

Figure 5.20
Standard Sender Address—Rate Limits Tab

- **Unlimited when sending to this address**—This option specifies that no rate limiting is used when sending data to other sites using this sender address.

- **Pulse mode**—This option lets you control the size of data blocks (in kilobytes) that are sent and the delay (in seconds) at which they are sent. Pulse mode is useful if your site-to-site connection is very low on bandwidth and you need to fine-tune the connection as much as possible.

- **Limited to specified maximum transfer rates by hour**—This option allows you to specify the percentage of available network bandwidth (as calculated by the originating site) so that data transfers by the sender will not consume all of the network bandwidth. These limits are configured per hour and can be set as 10%, 25%, 50%, 75%, 90%, or unlimited. For example, you may only want to allow Configuration Manager to consume 10% of the network bandwidth between the production hours of 8:00 AM to 5:00 PM. After hours, however, you may want to consume an unlimited amount of bandwidth.

Tip

For a comprehensive understanding on how Configuration Manager calculates available network bandwidth between sites, see this link: http://technet.microsoft.com/en-us/library/bb694241.aspx

Automatically Installing a Secondary Site

Now that we've gone through the steps to manually install a secondary site, this section should seem pretty familiar. During this section, we will use the Configuration Manager console to install our secondary site to the site server we specify without having to manually create senders and sender addresses or having to add the correct computer accounts to the correct security groups.

Before You Begin

Before you install your secondary site to the designated site server, make sure the site server meets all of the prerequisites for installation. Step-by-step guides for this process can be found in Chapter 4.

An extra step that is not covered by the guides in Chapter 4 is to add the primary site server's computer account to the local administrators group on the site server where the new secondary site will be installed. The primary site server needs administrative access to the secondary site server for things like copying necessary installation files, creating the Configuration Manager connection groups, and installing components like system services. As an alternative to giving the primary site server administrative access to the secondary site server, a site address account that has sufficient access can be configured. In our example, the CHI-PRIMARY computer account has been added to the local administrators group on OAK-SECONDARY.

Secondary Site Step-by-Step Automatic Installation

To start the automatic installation of a secondary site, open the Configuration Manager console on the primary site server and follow the steps below.

Tip

Although the Configuration Manager console is installed by default on a primary site server, it does not have to be run from the primary site server. The Configuration Manager console can be installed to any supported workstation, which is then configured to communicate with the primary site server. This is the preferred method for running the Configuration Manager console since it does not require access to a potentially critical server.

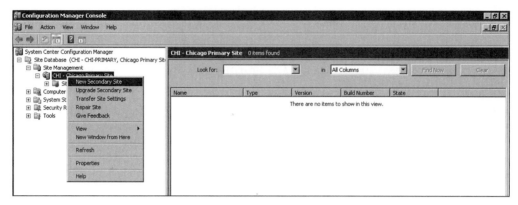

Figure 5.21
Create a New Site from the Configuration Manager console

1. From the Configuration Manager console, right-click on the primary site that will manage your secondary site and choose New Secondary Site (Figure 5.21).

2. The Secondary Site Creation Wizard is displayed. Click Next to continue (Figure 5.22).

3. The Site Identity window is displayed. This is where you need to create the site code and the site name for your secondary site. In our example,

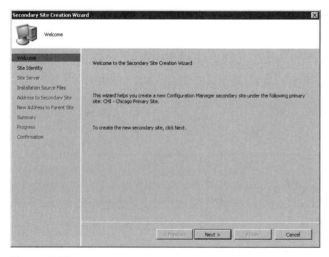

Figure 5.22
Secondary Site Creation Wizard

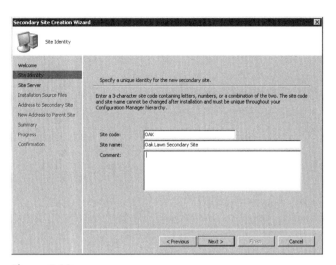

Figure 5.23
Site Identity Window

we'll choose OAK for the site code and Oak Lawn Secondary Site for the site name. You can optionally include a comment as well. Click Next to continue (Figure 5.23).

4. The Site Server window is displayed. Enter the site server where you want the secondary site installation to occur and the remote installation directory for the installation. In our example, we'll use OAK-SECON-DARY for the site server name and C:\Program Files (x86)\Microsoft Configuration Manager for the installation directory since our server is 64 bit. Click Next to continue (Figure 5.24).

5. The Installation Source Files window is displayed. This window lets you choose whether to copy the installation files to the secondary site server from the primary site server or to pre-stage the installation files on the secondary site server before installation begins. Having the option to pre-stage the files on the secondary site server is helpful if you have a slow connection and have someone at the remote site that can place these files on the server directly. In our example, we will copy the installation source files from the primary site server. Click Next to continue (Figure 5.25).

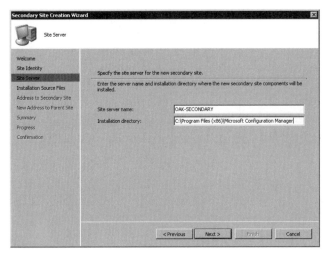

Figure 5.24
Site Server Window

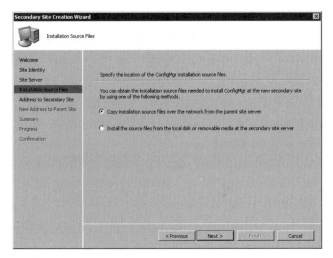

Figure 5.25
Installation Source Files Window

Caution

If you choose to pre-stage the source files on the secondary site server, you must place the install files on the root of the drive where Configuration Manager 2007 will be installed. The files must follow the same folder structure as the original installation media so make sure that the files and folders from the root of the media are copied directly to the root of the drive

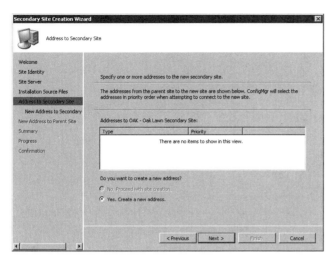

Figure 5.26
Sender Address to Secondary Site Window

where Configuration Manager will be installed. One step that is often forgotten is to include the prerequisite components that we downloaded in Chapter 4 with the installation files. These files must be placed on the root of the drive in a folder called redist in order for Configuration Manager to be installed correctly.

6. The Address to Secondary Site window is displayed. This window lets you create a new sender address on the primary site server that connects to the secondary site server. This is the same step that we did manually in the last section. This window will show you all of the sender addresses that exist for this site. In our example, no sender addresses exist therefore we must choose the "Yes. Create a new address." option. Click Next to continue (Figure 5.26).

7. The New Address to Secondary window is displayed. This window allows you to create the type of address that will be used to contact the site server at the secondary site. Optionally, you can choose to specify a site connection account that will be used instead of the primary site server's computer account. In our example, we'll use a standard sender address and specify OAK-SECONDARY as our secondary site server name. Click Next to continue (Figure 5.27).

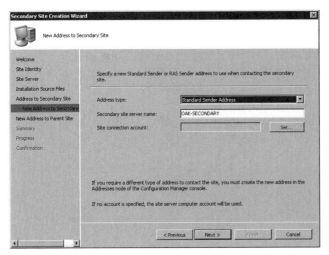

Figure 5.27
New Address to Secondary Site Window

Note

The only types of sender addresses that you can create using the New Address to Secondary window are standard sender addresses or asynchronous RAS sender addresses. If you need to install another type of sender address, you will have to create it using the Configuration Manager console like we did in the previous section.

8. The Address to Parent Site window is displayed. This window lets you create a new sender address on the secondary site server that connects to the primary site server. In our example, we'll choose to create a standard sender address at the secondary site, which will connect to the parent site server (CHI-PRIMARY). Click Next to continue (Figure 5.28).

9. The Summary window is displayed. This window shows the steps that will be taken in the next step. If you have made an error during this wizard, you can go back prior to making any changes. Click Next to start the installation.

10. The Confirmation window is displayed. This shows you the status of the installation. If there was an error in the installation, you would see these errors here. In our example, we had no errors. Click Close to complete the New Secondary Site Wizard.

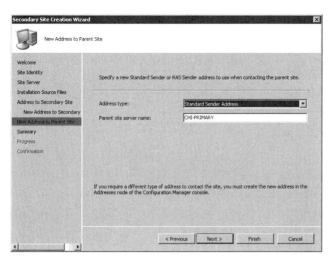

Figure 5.28
New Address to Parent Site Window

Viewing the Secondary Site in the Configuration Manager Console

Once your secondary site has been installed, it will be viewable within the Configuration Manager console. Any child site (including primary and secondary sites) will be listed in the Site Management node directly under its designated parent primary site. Once the secondary site is expanded, a Site Settings node is available with almost the exact same options as the primary site, excluding the Client Agent node. Client agent properties are inherited from the parent primary site and cannot be configured at the secondary site (Figure 5.29).

Tip

If you expand the Addresses and Senders nodes within the new secondary site, you will see addresses and senders that connect this site to its parent primary site. The senders and sender addresses can be configured in the same way that we did for our primary site. The senders and sender addresses must be installed at both sites so that two-way communications can occur.

Connection Groups and Read-Only Domain Controllers

In some of our remote locations, we have servers using Windows Server 2008 R2 as the operating system that hosts multiple roles such as Active Directory Domain Services and DFS. Because these

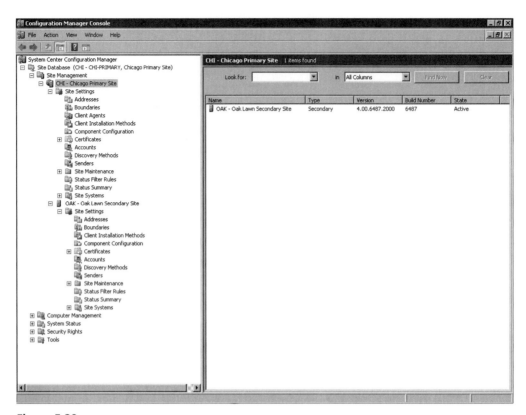

Figure 5.29
Secondary Site within the Configuration Manager Console

locations are unsecured, we chose to make these servers read-only domain controllers. When we started planning for our Configuration Manager 2007 rollout, we decided to also use these servers as secondary site servers since these sites were connected through relatively slow T1 lines. We planned out how our sender addresses would be set up, including rate limits and schedules based on the production hours of each location and got approval from our manager to go ahead with the rollout. Things did not go as planned, however.

We decided to use the Secondary Site Installation Wizard from the Configuration Manager console to deploy our secondary site servers since we have no IT staff at these locations and because it seemed to be the easiest method overall. We made sure that all of the prerequisites had been met (or so we thought) and started the installation. We expected to see these sites show up under our central-primary site in the Configuration Manager console but nothing ever happened. We checked the secondary site servers to see if any Configuration Manager folders had been created during installation but nothing was there. Nothing happened. At all.

After some research, we found a TechNet article that explained the problem.

It turns out that if you are installing a secondary site using the wizard from the Configuration Manager console on a server that is a read-only domain controller, the necessary connection groups do not get created and must be created manually prior to the installation. Because these servers are domain controllers, the connection groups have to be created in Active Directory, not locally on the servers. The connection groups were supposed to give access to the primary site server that was initiating the installation on the secondary site servers, but these groups were never created and rights were never assigned. Because the primary site server didn't have the correct rights on the secondary site server, the necessary files and services could not be created and the installation failed.

CREATING A NEW CENTRAL SITE BY SETTING A NEW PRIMARY SITE

As an IT administrator, change can be one of the hardest things to overcome since it usually requires so much work on the front and backend. When you live in a world where transparency is key for your users, you need a product that can help keep up with these changes while providing tools that allow you to implement change with the least amount of impact. Configuration Manager 2007 was designed with change in mind and includes many options to help with the dynamic world around you.

Imagine, for instance, that you are the IT administrator for a midsized company based out of Chicago. Your company has recently expanded and is now moving their headquarters from Chicago to New York. The Chicago office will stay intact but the new administrators out of the New York office want to be able to manage your site and child sites easily without taking administrative control away from you and your site. Ideally, they would like to be able to check on things such as software update compliance, computer inventory statuses, and software distribution successes/failures all from the New York site without having to connect to the Chicago site every time they want to run a report. Down the road, they would like to add more branch offices in different cities in the same fashion as the Chicago office but have one central location from which to administer and gather data. All of this is possible using Configuration Manager 2007 and central sites.

Configuration Manager allows you to specify a new primary site as your parent site. Once a primary site has been placed at the top of the hierarchy, it is now considered a central-primary or central site. It can administer all sites below it and all of the data from its child sites gets sent to the central site for reporting purposes. Central sites are perfect for scenarios like the one listed above because sites do not have to be destroyed and then re-created even though the hierarchy is undergoing a massive change. This allows you to keep all of your data about your site and configuration settings as well.

Setting a primary site as a parent site is easy and is done from the Configuration Manager console. Once a new or existing primary site is selected to be the parent, it simply needs to be connected to the site that will sit below it in the hierarchy through sender addresses. Once the Sender addresses are configured, you specify which site code should be the parent site and everything else is done automatically.

In our example below, a new primary site has been created with the site code of LIS. We will set LIS to be the new parent site to CHI, which we created in our last chapter. We will go through—step by step—and set LIS as the new parent site for CHI so that you can see all of the necessary configuration options involved.

Caution

In a Configuration Manager hierarchy, client data is replicated and sent up and down the hierarchy. This allows for each parent site to manage and report on information from its child sites all the way up to the central site, which then manages all sites below it. Before creating or expanding your hierarchy, make sure that you have enough bandwidth between sites to accommodate this data exchange. You need to be especially careful if your child sites contain a large number of clients. All of the data from these clients such as inventory and status messages will be sent to its parent site until it reaches the central site at the top. Depending on the type of link connecting these sites, a significant amount of bandwidth may be consumed. Using sender addresses, you can set rules on how and when data is sent from each site to decrease the impact of this data flow.

Resources Managed by Parent Sites

Once you create a Configuration Manager 2007 hierarchy with parent and child sites, you have the ability to manage the child sites from the parent sites. When a configuration item is created at a parent site, such as a new collection, it can be seen in read-only form on the child site(s) but cannot be modified. These objects appear in the Configuration Manager console with lock symbols to represent that they are read-only. This allows administrators at child sites to see an overall view of the hierarchy without giving them the ability to change objects that were created above. They can, however, create objects at their own sites to manage different resources at that site and below. Most of these objects, however, do not get sent up to the parent site(s) and must be managed at the site where they were created. For example, if a collection is created at a child site, it is not viewable at its parent site and must be managed at the child site. Exceptions to this rule are made when talking about boundaries. Boundaries created at child sites are able to be managed at their parent sites but boundaries created at parent sites cannot be seen or managed at child sites. We'll talk more about boundaries later in this chapter.

Step-by-Step for Setting a New Parent Primary Site

Specifying a new parent primary site is quite easy and is accomplished within the Configuration Manager console. As mentioned above, this allows you to change the hierarchy to accommodate for changes in your network design. Take note, however, that there could be a possibility of data corruption if not careful.

Imagine that you've got a Configuration Manager 2007 hierarchy with CEN as your central site and ABC as your child primary site. If software distribution objects were created in the CEN site, their package IDs might have been CEN00003 and CEN00004. After a while, you decide to remove the ABC site from the hierarchy, leaving only the CEN site. Since information such as collections and software packages are replicated to lower level sites, the software distribution objects were sent to the ABC site, keeping their package IDs of CEN00003 and CEN00004 (along with any other packages that might have been created at the ABC site like ABC00004, etc.). Later, you decide to add the ABC site back to the hierarchy, which now contains hundreds of software distribution objects including the original CEN00003 and CEN00004 objects. After ABC was removed from the hierarchy, you modified CEN00003 and CEN00004 at the ABC site for administrative purposes, making them different from the objects that still exist at CEN. Because the objects at CEN and ABC are different versions but have identical package IDs, the two software distribution objects at the CEN site will overwrite the same objects at the ABC site, possibly causing data corruption to occur.

Prerequisites for Connecting Sites

Before a new parent site can be set, we must connect the LIS and CHI site including adding the respective computer accounts to the site-to-site connection groups on both servers as well as creating corresponding sender addresses at both sites. These steps are identical as the ones we completed when we manually installed a secondary site.

To set a new parent site, open the Configuration Manager console that is connected to the soon-to-be primary child site. In our example, we will connect to the CHI site. Follow the steps below to assign a new parent site:

1. From the Configuration Manager console, right-click on the primary site where you want to assign a new parent and choose Properties. In our example, we'll be adding a new parent to the CHI site.

2. The properties for the primary site are displayed. Click on the Set Parent Site button (Figure 5.30).

3. The Set Parent Site window is displayed. Choose the Report to Parent Site option and choose the site code of the new parent's primary site. If it is not available in the drop-down list, simply type the three-character site code and click OK (Figure 5.31).

4. After you choose your new parent site, you will see this change reflected in the site's property page. In our example, the new parent site is LIS (Figure 5.32).

Figure 5.30
Primary Site Properties Page

Figure 5.31
Set Parent Site Window

5. Open the Configuration Manager console on the new parent site and expand the site under the Site Management node. You should now see a new child site that you can manage (CHI in our example) and any child sites under that (OAK) (Figure 5.33). In our example, LIS is at the top of the hierarchy (the central site), CHI is below LIS (the parent child site), and OAK is below CHI (the child secondary site). This introduces the parent, child, grandchild concept, which can be common in Configuration Manager 2007 hierarchies.

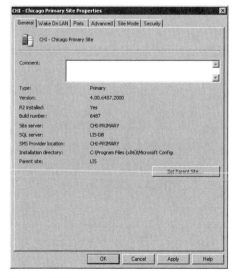

Figure 5.32
New Parent Server

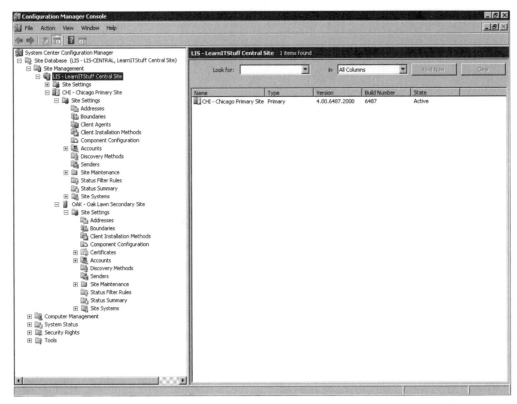

Figure 5.33
Example Configuration Manager 2007 Hierarchy as Seen from the Configuration Manager Console

BOUNDARIES

Larger environments typically employ multiple subnets connected by various types of links such as high-speed fiber optic connections, fast wireless connections, slow ISDN or T1 connections, or even VPN connections across dialup networks. Each of these subnets (or networks) might have as few as a dozen clients (such as a branch location) up to thousands of clients (like at a corporate office). These networks might be designed to separate geographic locations, work functions, wireless connections, or other reasons not listed here. Configuration Manager allows you to identify each network that exists in your organization so that you can define what actions clients will take when connecting from one of these networks.

By default, Configuration Manager does not create any boundaries during the installation of a site. Although you do not have to have boundaries configured to use Configuration Manager 2007, they are very helpful when dealing with multiple clients on multiple networks. Boundaries can be created using IP subnets, Active Directory sites, IPv6 prefixes, and IP address ranges.

Boundaries have multiple advantages such as:

- **Auto site assignment**—Each Configuration Manager site can be configured with multiple boundaries. Boundaries are configured per site in the hierarchy and are published to Active Directory if configured properly. When a client comes online for the first time, it will check to see if its IP address is within one of the configured boundaries by querying Active Directory for site boundary information. If the Active Directory schema was extended, then each site publishes its boundary information to the system management container that we configured in Chapter 4. If a client is joined to the domain and has the Configuration Manager 2007 client installed, it's able to find the boundary information via AD, compare its IP address to those boundaries, and automatically assign itself to the correct site if it is within one of those boundaries. If the Active Directory schema was not extended or if the client is in another forest, it can use a server locator point to determine its site. We will discuss server locator points in Chapter 6.

- **Determining fast vs. slow networks**—When you configure a boundary, you must specify if it is a fast or slow network. This information is used by clients to determine if they should execute potentially bandwidth-intensive tasks such as downloading data for software distributions. If you specify that a boundary is a slow network, you can configure things like software updates and software distributions to not occur when clients are attached to slow networks. This is helpful for laptop users who are connected to the corporate network through a slow VPN connection and you don't want them installing a large package while on the road. This concept is covered in more detail in Chapter 11.

- **Protected distribution points**—When you create a site system (which is hosting a distribution point), you can specify whether it is protected by specifying which boundaries have access to it. If a client is within one of the allowed boundaries, it can pull data from the distribution point. If it is not within one of the allowed boundaries, it must find the data from another distribution point if configured to do so.

A good example of using protected distribution points is if you have a location with multiple departments, each having its own dedicated distribution point. For bandwidth reasons, you only want clients from the appropriate departments to connect to their corresponding distribution points when needing data. Because these distribution points are all on the same IP subnet, any one of them might be used to distribute data to clients. This means a client in the marketing department might be pulling data from the human resources distribution point. To get around this, you could create boundaries based on IP ranges and ensure that each department's client IP address is within these corresponding ranges. Once the boundaries have been defined and the client IP addresses fall within these boundaries, you could then protect each site system with the corresponding boundaries. We will discuss more about protected sites and distribution points in the next chapter.

■ **Client roaming**—Roaming occurs when clients leave their assigned sites and enter new sites by physically changing locations. The most common reason for client roaming is when a user moves a laptop from one location to another. When clients enter a new boundary that is not in their assigned site, they can use the distribution points from these non-assigned sites to pull down data in the event of a software update or software distribution scenario. This is extremely helpful if their assigned site can only be accessed over a slow network connection. Instead of having to "phone home" to access content, it can be accessed locally. There are two types of client roaming:

  ■ **Global roaming**—Global roaming occurs when clients compare their IP address with boundaries published in Active Directory. Once the client determines the site it has roamed into, it contacts that site's management point. This is referred to as the resident management point. The resident management point tells the roaming client which distribution points are available so that it can retrieve content locally. If no content is available locally, the client will contact its default management point and request distribution points that do contain the requested content.

- **Regional roaming**—Regional roaming occurs when clients cannot access boundary information published to Active Directory. If a client cannot access this information, it continues to contact its default management point. Regional roaming clients are not capable of determining which site they have roamed into but they can determine which distribution points are available by requesting this information from their default management point.

Note

Management points can only access information about distribution points when they fall under them in the hierarchy. If distribution points are located in sites that sit above the management point, the management point is not able to access information about these distribution points. This is also the case if the management point is located in a peer site within the hierarchy.

Step-by-Step for Creating a New Boundary

Boundaries can be created at any site in the hierarchy including secondary sites. Boundaries are located under the Site Settings node for each site within the Configuration Manager console. If a boundary is created at a parent site, it can be created for the parent site or any child site beneath it. If a boundary is created at a child-only site, it can only be created for the child site. In our example, we can create boundaries at the LIS site for the LIS site itself, the CHI child primary site beneath it, and the OAK secondary child site that sits under CHI. If we create a boundary at CHI, we can only create it for the CHI site itself or for OAK. If we create it at OAK, we can only create it for the OAK site.

To create a boundary, do the following:

1. Open the Configuration Manager console and expand the site where the boundary will be created. Expand the Site Settings node and then click on the Boundaries node. In our example, we will create the boundary under the LIS since we can create boundaries for all sites beneath it (Figure 5.34).

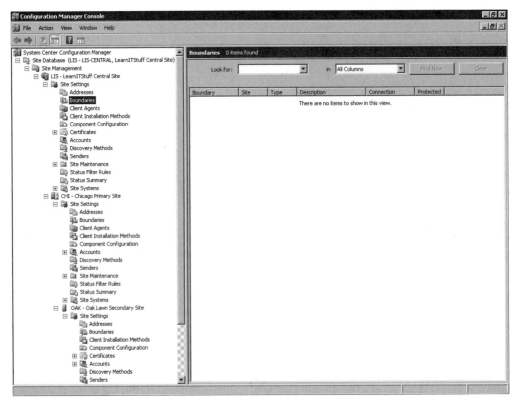

Figure 5.34
The Boundaries Node

2. Right-click on the Boundaries node and choose New Boundary (Figure 5.35).

3. The New Site Boundary window is displayed. This window lets you create a boundary for any site that you can manage (based on your location within the hierarchy) using IP subnets, Active Directory sites, IPv6 prefixes, or IP ranges. You can also designate if this is a slow or fast connection. In our example, we'll create a boundary for the CHI site using an IP subnet with a fast connection (Figure 5.36).

Tip

After a boundary has been created, you can view any protected systems that this boundary is assigned to by going to the Protected tab. We'll talk more about protected systems in the next chapter.

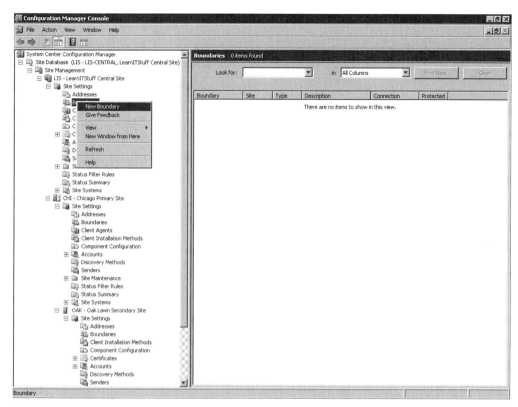

Figure 5.35
Create a New Boundary

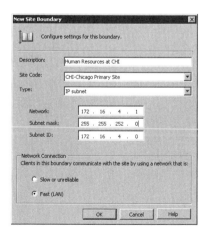

Figure 5.36
New Site Boundary Window

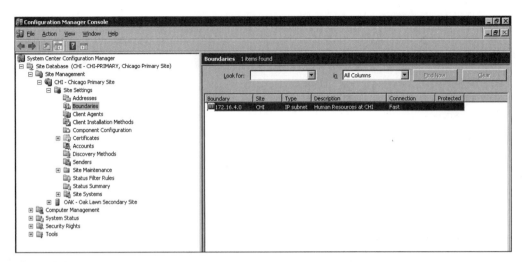

Figure 5.37
Viewing the Boundary from a Child Site

4. Now that the boundary has been created for a child site, it can be viewed and managed from that site directly. In our example, we created a boundary for CHI at the LIS central site. This boundary is viewable and manageable from CHI although it was not created at that site (Figure 5.37).

THE FINAL WORD

This chapter builds on the foundation that was established in the last chapter by covering more advanced site installation options. After reading this chapter, you should understand how and why to install a secondary site and how to modify your hierarchy to include a central site. In the next chapter, we'll cover site systems and the roles that they can host to improve the ability and efficiency of a site.

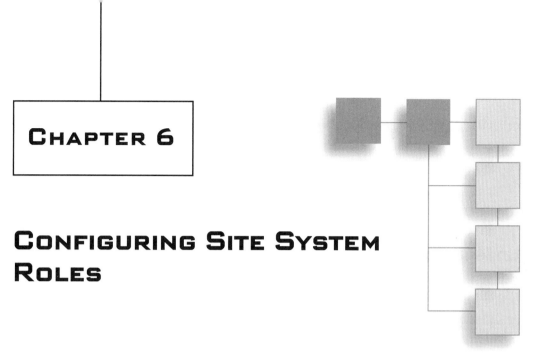

CHAPTER 6

CONFIGURING SITE SYSTEM ROLES

Now that we've got a basic hierarchy built with multiple primary and secondary sites, we can configure systems within these sites to host site system roles. These systems are referred to as site systems. *Site systems* are computers, servers, or server shares that perform functions on behalf of a Configuration Manager 2007 site. These functions are referred to as *roles*. An example of a role might be a PXE service point or a distribution point. We'll talk more about these roles later in this chapter.

Before a site system can host a site system role, it must meet the prerequisites for that role. In this chapter, we will cover the prerequisites needed to install these roles, the installation steps of the roles themselves, and finally, we'll talk about some of the monitoring options to help verify that these roles are working correctly.

SITE SYSTEM ROLES

Site system roles are installed on site systems to perform tasks for each Configuration Manager site. Roles are designed to be distributed throughout multiple systems to provide load balancing in the event that the site contains a large number of resources. Although a site server can host all site system roles, it's not recommended—especially in a large environment—since this could overwhelm the site server, causing the site to become non-responsive. In smaller organizations where hardware resources are limited, it may be appropriate for a single site server to host all of the site system roles as long as you do not exceed capacity. If this is the case, you can always add another site system to help balance the load.

Site system roles are installed through the Configuration Manager console using wizards that provide quick and easy configuration. These wizards are started from the Site Systems node under each site in the console.

Understanding Site System Installation

When a role is installed to a site system, it is installed, by default, to the first NTFS formatted drive with the most free disk space. The default location for the install files is <Install Location>\SMS. If you need more control over the location of the installation files, you can create a file called NO_SMS_ON_DRIVE.SMS and place this file on the root of any drive where you do not want Configuration Manager files to be installed. Note that other folders get created in locations other than <ConfigMgrInstallationDirectory>\SMS and cannot be controlled by the NO_SMS_ON_DRIVE.SMS file.

If a management point role is installed, an SMS_CCM folder is created on the root of the installation drive. If a reporting point role is installed, two folders get created called SMSComponent and SMSReporting_sitecode under the Inetpub\wwwroot\ folder. Other miscellaneous files get placed in %WinDir\System32 as well.

Log Files

Configuration Manager 2007 uses an extensive number of log files (over 170) to help administrators troubleshoot issues with client and server components. Although these logs can sometimes be cryptic and hard to understand, there is a massive Internet community dedicated to helping you understand what these error messages mean and what to do to fix the situation. Internet sites like MyITForum and TechNet are common locations to find just the answers you need. To see a complete list of these log files, go to http://technet.microsoft.com/en-us/library/bb892800.aspx.

In this chapter, we will cover some of the common log files that pertain to the setup and operational aspects of site system roles.

Tip
The Configuration Manager 2007 toolkit is available from Microsoft and includes Trace32.exe. Trace32.exe allows you to read log files in an easy to read format while letting you view them in real-time. I highly recommend that you use this tool when troubleshooting Configuration Manager 2007 issues. To download the Configuration Manager 2007 Toolkit, follow this link: http://www.microsoft.com/downloads/en/details.aspx?FamilyID=5A47B972-95D2-46B1-AB14-5D0CBCE54EB8

Management Points

Management points are used to transfer information between site servers and clients in Configuration Manager 2007. Information that gets sent to clients might include information about newly advertised programs and the location of distribution points that hold the content. Information that is received from clients might include inventory data and status messages. Don't get this confused with a distribution point, however. We will cover distribution points next.

Only one management point can be installed per site. A single management point can support up to 25,000 clients per site. If multiple management points are configured using network load balancing (NLB), the site can support up to 300,000 clients. Note that when multiple management points are configured with NLB, the site only sees one management point but the load is distributed amongst all management points in the NLB cluster. Although there can be only one management point per site in a Configuration Manager 2007 hierarchy, secondary sites can use something called proxy management points to help ease network loads by allowing clients at remote locations to query proxy management points locally. The proxy management point then queries the default management on behalf of its clients, dramatically reducing site-to-site communications since only one system is requesting information. This is even more helpful when sender addresses are configured to limit the amount of data that is sent to and from secondary sites.

The option to install a management point is enabled by default when you install a primary site server but you can opt out of this if you choose to do so.

Caution
Each site must have a management point installed for client communication to occur. If you choose not to install a management point to a site system in your site, you will not be able to manage Configuration Manager clients.

Prerequisites for Management Points

Before a management point can be installed, it must have the following prerequisites installed and configured:

- Internet Information Services (IIS)
- WebDAV
- BITS server

These prerequisites were installed and configured in Chapter 4, "Installing a Primary Site." See this chapter if you have any questions regarding specific setup information for these prerequisites.

Management Point Installation

Imagine that you are the IT administrator for a small company with only a few hundred clients. You have one primary/central site with multiple roles installed to the site server, including the management point. After a year of operation, you are informed that you have to incorporate a new location that contains 5,000 client computers into your hierarchy. You are concerned that this will hinder the performance of your site server since it is hosting the management point and decide to build a new site system that will take over as the management point for your site.

The steps we perform in this section will demonstrate a scenario similar to the one we described above. We have removed the management point role from our primary site server, CHI-PRIMARY, and are going to install it to a new site system, CHI-SITESYSTEM.

In Chapter 4, we installed a management point during the initial setup of our primary site, but we did not cover the installation using the Configuration Manager console. Once our management point has been installed to our new site system, we'll look at the configuration options available for that role.

To install a management point, do the following:

1. Open the Configuration Manager console at the site that will host the management point. In our example, we'll connect the Configuration Manager console to the CHI site.

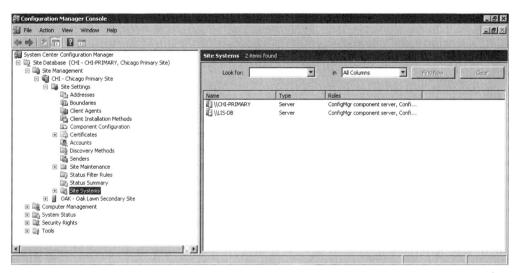

Figure 6.1
Site Systems Node

2. Once the Configuration Manager console is open, go to the Site Systems node under your site. This is the node where you can create, view, modify, and delete site systems for your site (Figure 6.1).

3. Right-click on the Site Systems node and choose New > Server (Figure 6.2).

4. The New Site System Server Wizard window is displayed. This window allows you to configure multiple options regarding the new site system. Once the correct options (listed below) are selected, click Next to continue (Figure 6.3).

- **Name**—This field identifies your server but is not used to contact it within Configuration Manager. This field can contain any name that you wish to use. In our example, we'll choose CHI-SITESYSTEM.

- **Specify a fully qualified domain name (FQDN) for this site system on the intranet checkbox**—This checkbox allows you to specify an FQDN for the site system. This is the recommended practice especially for site systems using native mode since most certificates use the FQDN as the subject name. If this checkbox is enabled, the Intranet FQDN name field will also be enabled.

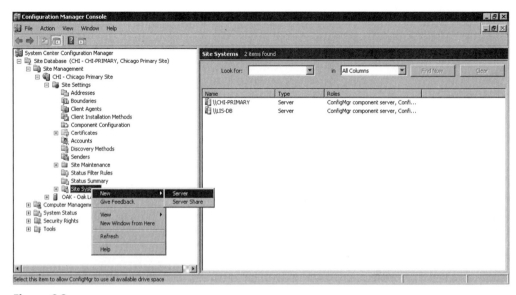

Figure 6.2
New Site System Server

Figure 6.3
New Site System Server Wizard

- **Intranet FQDN name field**—Use this field to type in the FQDN of your site system. In our example, we'll use CHI-SITESYSTEM. LEARNITSTUFF.LOCAL.

- **Specify an internet based fully qualified domain name (FQDN) for this site system checkbox**—This checkbox allows you to use an Internet FQDN, which is used in conjunction with Internet based client management. If this checkbox is enabled, the Internet FQDN field is also enabled.

- **Internet FQDN name field**—Use this field to type in the Internet FQDN of your site system. If this field is used, the address must be registered with Internet DNS servers. This is used when Internet based client management is enabled for your site. For more information about Internet based client management, see Chapter 8, "Managing Clients."

- **Use this site server's computer account to install this site system**—Select this option if the site server's computer account has the necessary permissions to install the management point (or other site roles) to the site system.

- **Use another account for installing this site system**—Select this option if the site server's computer account does not have the necessary permissions to install the selected roles. If this option is enabled, the Site System Installation Account field is also enabled.

- **Site System Installation Account field**—Use this field to specify the domain username and password that has the necessary permissions to install site system roles to the site system. In our example, we'll choose to install the site system as the domain administrator.

- **Enable this site system as a protected site system**—Select this option if you wish to enable this as a protected site by specifying a list of allowed boundaries. We will configure a site as a protected site later in this chapter.

- **Allow only site server initiated data transfers from this site system**—This option is typically used when your site systems are located in a different forest. When this option is checked, the site server will initiate the connection to the site system for data transfers. This option can only be used for management points, distribution points, software update points, and fallback status points. Note that if you use this option, you must choose a site system installation account. Computer accounts will not work.

Figure 6.4
Site System Role Selection

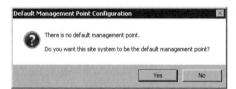

Figure 6.5
Default Management Point Warning

5. The Site System Role Selection window is displayed. This window allows you to choose which roles will be installed to this site system. We will cover all of these roles in this chapter. In this example, we'll install a management point by checking the checkbox. Click Next to continue (Figure 6.4).

6. At this point, you are warned that there is no default management point for your site and have the option to make this the default management point. In our example, we will choose Yes (Figure 6.5).

7. The Management Point configuration window is displayed. This lets you choose which options will be enabled for the management point. In our example, we'll keep the defaults and click Next to continue. The configuration options for a management point are shown in Figure 6.6.

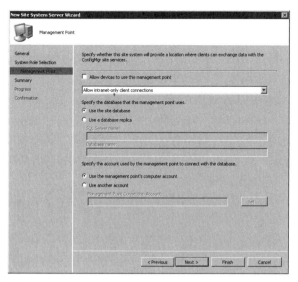

Figure 6.6
Management Point Configuration Options

- **Allow devices to use this management point**—Enabling this option will allow this management point to communicate with mobile devices.
- **Allow intranet-only client connections**—This option only allows clients on the intranet (using the intranet FQDN) to connect to this management point.
- **Allow Internet-only client connections**—This option only allows clients on the Internet (using the Internet FQDN) to connect to this management point. Note that this option is only available if the site is in native mode and if an Internet FQDN has been specified.
- **Allow both intranet and Internet client connections**—This option allows both intranet and Internet client connections. Note that this option is only available if the site is in native mode and if an Internet FQDN has been specified.
- **Use the site database**—This is the default option. This option uses the site database that was configured during site installation.
- **Use a database replica**—Use this option to let the management point use a database replica instead of the default site database. If this option is selected, the SQL Server name and Database name fields are enabled.

- **SQL Server name field**—Use this field to specify the SQL Server that is hosting the database replica.
- **Database name field**—Use this field to specify the database name and instance.
- **Use the management point's computer account**—This option specifies that this server will access the site database using its computer account. Note that if you use this option, Configuration Manager attempts to automatically add the site system's computer account to the smsdbrole_MP on the site database.
- **Use another account**—This option is typically used if the site server (where the management point is being installed) is in a different domain than the site database. If this is selected, you must specify a domain user account and then add that user to the smsdbrole_MP on the site database. If this option is selected, the Management Point Connection Account field is enabled.
- **Management Point Connection Account field**—This fields lets you specify the domain user account that has been added to the smsdbrole_MP on the site database.

8. The Management Point Installation Summary window is displayed next. This lets you review your selections before you actually make any changes. In our example, everything is correct. Click Next to continue.

9. The Management Point Confirmation window is displayed. This shows you the results of the wizard. If any problems were encountered during the wizard, you will be notified here. Click Close to close the wizard (Figure 6.7).

10. Once a new site system is installed, you will be able to see this under the Site Systems node. Verify that your new site system is listed. In our example, we see \\CHI-SITESYSTEM (Figure 6.8).

Management Point Log Files

Management Points can be monitored through multiple log files that are created on the site system hosting the role. Table 6.1 details the management point installation log files.

Table 6.2 details the management point operational log files.

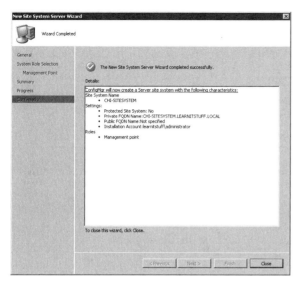

Figure 6.7
Management Point Installation Confirmation

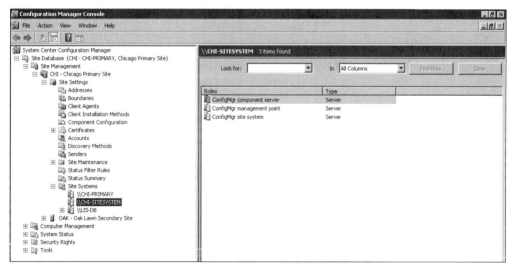

Figure 6.8
New Site System in the Site Systems Node

Verifying Management Point Installation

Once the Management Point Installation Wizard is complete, you should check to see if there were any errors during the management point installation. To see

Table 6.1 Management Point Installation Log Files

Log File	Location	Description
MPSetup.log	<ConfigMgrInstallationDirectory>\SMS\Logs	Details the management point installation wrapper process
MPMSI.log	<ConfigMgrInstallationDirectory>\SMS\Logs	Details the installation of the management point MSI installer

Table 6.2 Management Point Operational Log Files

Log File	Location	Description
Mpcontrol.log	<ConfigMgrInstallationDirectory>\SMS\Logs	Details the management point installation wrapper process
Mpfdm.log	<ConfigMgrInstallationDirectory>\SMS\Logs	Details the installation of the management point MSI installer
MP_Ddr.log	<ConfigMgrInstallationDirectory>\SMS_CCM\Logs	Details the conversion process of XML.ddr records from clients and the process of copying them to the site server
MP_GetAuth.log	<ConfigMgrInstallationDirectory>\SMS_CCM\Logs	Details the management point status
MP_GetPolicy.log	<ConfigMgrInstallationDirectory>\SMS_CCM\Logs	Details policy information
MP_Hinv.log	<ConfigMgrInstallationDirectory>\SMS_CCM\Logs	Details the conversion process of XML hardware inventory records from clients and the process of copying them to the site server
MP_Location.log	<ConfigMgrInstallationDirectory>\SMS_CCM\Logs	Details location manager tasks
MP_Policy.log	<ConfigMgrInstallationDirectory>\SMS_CCM\Logs	Details policy communication
MP_Relay.log	<ConfigMgrInstallationDirectory>\SMS_CCM\Logs	Details the copy process of files that are collected from the client
MP_Retry.log	<ConfigMgrInstallationDirectory>\SMS_CCM\Logs	Details the process of hardware inventory retries
MP_Sinv.log	<ConfigMgrInstallationDirectory>\SMS_CCM\Logs	Details the conversion process of XML hardware inventory records from clients and the process of copying them to the site server
MP_Status.log	<ConfigMgrInstallationDirectory>\SMS_CCM\Logs	Details the conversion process of XML.svf status messages from clients and the process of copying them to the site server

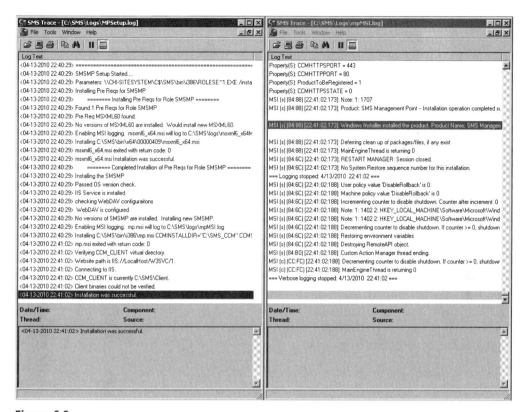

Figure 6.9
Viewing the MPSetup.log and mpMSI.log Files Using Trace32

detailed information about the success or failure of the install, you should review the MPSetup.log and mpMSI.log files. If you are viewing these log files with Trace32.exe, you should see something similar to Figure 6.9.

Study the log files to see if you had any warnings or errors. Warnings are automatically highlighted in yellow, whereas errors are highlighted in red. This gives you the ability to quickly find error messages within large, complex log files.

Caution

If you are installing the management point role to a site that is running in native mode, make sure the site system that will host the management point has a web certificate and that the certificate is correctly bound to the default website in the Internet Information Services Manager console. If the certificate has not been installed or bound to the default website, installation of the management point will fail.

Distribution Points

Distribution points are used to distribute content to Configuration Manager 2007 clients. Since they are typically one of the most relied upon site system roles, many options are available to help you meet the needs of your organization. Configuration Manager 2007 allows for two types of distribution points to be installed: standard distribution points and branch distribution points. Branch distribution points are new to Configuration Manager 2007 and help in situations where a small number of clients need to access content locally instead of traversing a slow WAN connection. Standard and branch Distribution points are covered next.

Distribution Point Content

The type of content that can reside on distribution points include:

- **Software Packages**—Software packages might include software installers like .exe and .msi files, scripts, or any other file that might need to be accessed by a client.

- **Driver Packages**—Driver packages include driver files that are needed by Windows operating systems to operate a device. We'll cover drivers and driver packages in Chapter 13, "Managing Operating System Deployment."

- **Operating System Images**—Operating system images are .wim (Windows Image Format) files that are deployed to clients to install an operating system. Images are made by cloning a master or base computer that has been modified with the settings you need so that you can consistently deploy this image to multiple computers. We'll cover operating system image deployments in Chapter 13.

- **Operating System Packages**—Operating system packages are copies of the source installation media. They are used to set up an operating system for the first time so that a WIM image can be created to make an operating system image.

- **Boot Images**—Boot images are .wim files that include a small version of Windows called the Windows pre-installation environment or WinPE for short. Boot images allow a computer to boot to WinPE where it can execute tasks such as applying an operating system image.

The distribution point role only requires BITS and WebDAV (and IIS) to be enabled when it is configured as a BITS-enabled distribution point. If it will not be BITS enabled, IIS (including BITS and WebDAV) is not required.

Types of Distribution Points

Two types of distribution points are available within Configuration Manager 2007. These are standard distribution points and branch distribution points. The following list describes the pros and cons of each.

Standard Distribution Points

- **Intended for use in mid to large scale environments**—Standard distribution points are designed for locations where a large number of clients put a heavy load on the site system that hosts the distribution point. Because of this, server class hardware is typically chosen to host standard distribution points.

- **Must be installed on a server class operating system**—Standard distribution points can only be installed on computers that have a supported server class operating system installed.

- **Clients can download content using BITS**—Standard distribution points can be BITS enabled, allowing clients to download content only when bandwidth is available. This can dramatically reduce the amount of network traffic from the distribution point to the clients when bandwidth is scarce.

- **Supports mobile device clients**—Standard distribution points can be enabled to support mobile devices such as Windows CE or Windows Mobile. For more information about mobile devices, see Chapter 16, "Managing Mobile Devices."

- **Supports intranet or Internet Based Clients**—Standard distribution points can host content for intranet clients or for Internet based clients when using Internet based client management. For more information on Internet based client management, see Chapter 8.

- **Supports server shares**—Standard distribution points can be hosted on standard server shares if configured to do so. We will talk more about server shares later in this chapter.

Branch Distribution Points

- **Intended for use in branch locations**—Branch distribution points were created for smaller locations such as branch sites that only have a handful of clients. The Branch distribution point role is intended for smaller systems such as client workstations since it will not typically experience a heavy load.

- **Can be installed on multiple classes of operating systems**—Unlike a standard distribution point, branch distribution points can be installed to workstation or server class operating systems. Again, this role is intended for branch locations where a server class operating system may not be available.

Note

If a branch distribution point is installed to a workstation class operating system, only 10 concurrent connections are allowed at one time. This is a limitation of the operating system, not the role itself. If the branch distribution point role is installed to a server class operating system, it can support thousands of clients.

- **Must receive content from a standard distribution point**—Branch distribution points must receive their content from standard BITS-enabled distribution points. If a standard distribution point is not available, branch distribution points will not function.

- **Limited BITS functionality**—Branch distribution points use BITS to initially transfer data from a standard distribution point. This conserves network bandwidth especially if a branch site is connected using a slow link. Once the content has been stored on the branch distribution point, clients can only download it using SMB.

- **Can only host content for computer intranet based clients**—Branch distribution points cannot be used with Internet based client management. They can only host content for clients within the intranet. They also cannot host content for mobile devices.

- **Supports on-demand package distribution**—Packages can be configured to download to the branch distribution point only after a client computer requests the package. This helps keep space requirements down on the branch distribution point as well as bandwidth since not all packages have to be transferred to the branch site until content is requested. We'll cover packages in Chapter 11, "Managing Software Distribution."

Distribution Points and Server Shares   If you would like to have more control over where and how distribution point packages are stored, you have the option to create a distribution point on a server share. Instead of automatically creating a share on the first NTFS drive with the most available free disk space, you can specify that Configuration Manager stores packages on an existing share of your choice. By doing this however, Configuration Manager will not create new shares if drive space is low, it will not monitor the health of the sever share, and it will not support branch distribution points or Internet based clients.

BITS Overview

BITS stands for background intelligent transfer service and is used when a distribution point is BITS enabled. Enabling a distribution point to be BITS enabled can be done during the distribution point setup or after the fact by changing the distribution point's properties.

When data is transferred using BITS, bandwidth is dynamically throttled based on the amount of available bandwidth. BITS also allows clients to resume downloads if the connection was interrupted. Although clients prefer to use BITS to download content, they will fall back to the server message block (SMB) protocol if BITS is not available.

A number of factors go into determining if clients download content using BITS or SMB. Some of these factors include:

- **Content is stored on branch distribution points**—Branch distribution points download content via BITS from a standard distribution point but transfer content to clients using SMB.

- **The advertisement is set to run from the distribution point**—When an advertisement is created, it can be set to run from the distribution point. If this option is enabled, the content is downloaded using SMB.

- **The distribution point is not BITS enabled**—If a standard distribution point is not BITS enabled, it cannot transfer content using BITS.

- **Clients are mobile devices**—Although mobile devices can only receive content from a BITS-enabled distribution point, they don't actually use BITS to download the content.

Branch distribution points are the only type of distribution points that use BITS when initially storing content. Standard distribution points within a site will always use SMB when transferring packages from the site server. Packages that are copied between Configuration Manager sites use sender addresses to limit the amount of bandwidth that is used.

BITS throttling can be configured for branch distribution points or for branch distribution points and clients. These settings are configured within the properties of the computer client agent. When throttling is enabled, you must specify an amount, in kilobytes per second, that can be transferred from the distribution point. You must also specify a throttling window by configuring a start and end time for when BITS downloads are used. If you would like for data to be transferred via BITS outside of the throttling window, you must also specify the amount of data that is transferred during this time period (Figure 6.10).

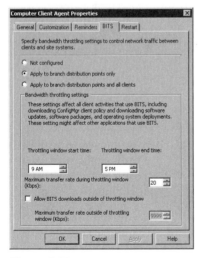

Figure 6.10
Configuring BITS Throttling

Installing a Distribution Point

In this section, we will cover the installation of a standard distribution point and briefly touch on branch distribution points as well as server shares. In our example, we'll install the distribution point role to our Chicago site system, CHI-SITESYSTEM via the Configuration Manager console that is connected to the CHI primary site. To install a distribution point, do the following:

1. Open the Configuration Manager console at the site where the site system is located. In our example, we'll connect the Configuration Manager console to the CHI site.

2. Once the Configuration Manager console is open, go to the Site Systems node under your site.

3. Either right-click on the Site Systems node and choose New > Server if you want to create a new site system that will host the distribution point role or right-click on an existing site system and choose New Roles. In our example, we'll right-click on \\CHI-SITESYSTEM and choose New Roles (Figure 6.11).

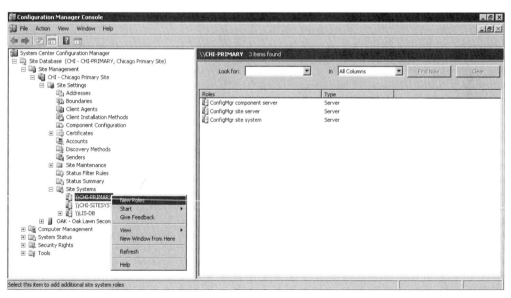

Figure 6.11
Adding Roles to an Existing Site System

4. The New Site System Server Wizard window is displayed. This window allows you to configure multiple options regarding the new site system as shown back in Figure 6.3. If this wizard is started on an existing site system, the options that were used to create it are shown here and can be edited if so desired. Once the correct options are selected, click Next to continue.

5. The Site System Role Selection window is displayed. This window allows you to choose which roles will be installed to this site system. In this example, we'll install a distribution point by checking the checkbox. Because we chose to install the management point role on this site system in the last section, it is no longer listed as an option on this window. Click Next to continue (Figure 6.12).

6. The Distribution Point Configuration window is displayed. This lets you choose which options will be enabled for the distribution point. In our example, we'll enable the Allow Clients to Transfer from this Distribution Point Using BITS, HTTP, and HTTPS option and click Next. The configuration options for a distribution point are discussed below and shown in Figure 6.13.

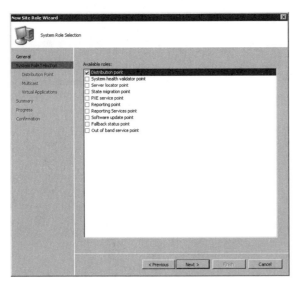

Figure 6.12
Adding the Distribution Point Role

Figure 6.13
Distribution Point Configuration Options

- **Enable as a standard distribution point**—Choose this option if you want to enable this site system as a standard distribution point. This option is only available if the site system has a server class operating system installed.
- **Allow clients to transfer content from this distribution point using BITS, HTTP, and HTTPS**—Checking this box enables this distribution point as a BITS-enabled distribution point. This option is not available if enabled as a branch distribution point.
- **Allow intranet-only client connections**—This option only allows clients on the intranet (using the intranet FQDN) to connect to this distribution point.
- **Allow Internet-only client connections**—This option only allows clients on the Internet (using the Internet FQDN) to connect to this distribution point. Note that this option is only available if the site is in native mode and if an Internet FQDN has been specified.
- **Allow both intranet and Internet client connections**—This option allows both intranet and Internet client connections. Note that this option is only available if the site is in native mode and if an Internet FQDN has been specified.

- **Allow clients to connect anonymously**—This option should be checked if mobile devices will use this distribution point to download packages. This option is not available if the site is in native mode.
- **Enable as a branch distribution point**—Select this option if you want to configure the site system as a branch distribution point. This option is only available if the Configuration Manager client has been installed and the operating system is not Windows 2000.
- **Use specific partition**—This option lets you choose the partition on the branch distribution point that will hold the packages. If no option is chosen, the first largest drive is used.
- **Group membership**—This option allows you to create distribution point groups to which the distribution point can be added. This is useful if you want to copy multiple packages to specific distribution points without having to check each one individually.

7. If R2 or higher is installed, the Multicast configuration window is displayed. This allows you to enable the distribution point to use the multicast feature when deploying packages under certain scenarios. We will cover the properties of this window in Chapter 13. In our example, we'll choose the defaults and click Next to continue (Figure 6.14).

Figure 6.14
Multicast Configuration Window

Figure 6.15
Application Virtualization Streaming Window

8. If R2 or higher is installed, the Virtual Application configuration window is displayed. This window allows you to enable Virtual Application (App-V) Streaming for this distribution point. We will cover App-V in Chapter 11. In our example, we'll choose the defaults and click Next to continue (Figure 6.15).

9. The Distribution Point Installation Summary window is displayed next. This lets you review your selections before you actually make any changes. In our example, everything is correct. Click Next to continue.

10. The Distribution Point Confirmation window is displayed. This shows you the results of the wizard. If any problems were encountered during the wizard, you will be notified here. Click Close to close the wizard (Figure 6.16).

Distribution Point Log Files

Unlike the management point installation in the above section, the distribution point role does not have a dedicated installation log file to review that details the installation process. There is a log file, however, that can be viewed to help with distribution point issues. This file is detailed in Table 6.3.

Figure 6.16
Distribution Point Installation Confirmation

Table 6.3 Distribution Point Log Files

Log File	Location	Description
Distmgr.log	\<ConfigMgrInstallationDirectory\> \SMS\Logs	Details package creation, compression, delta replication, and information processes
Although this log file does not specifically deal with the distribution point system, it can lead you in the right direction when distribution point problems occur.		

Branch Cache Support

Starting with Windows 2008 R2 and Windows 7, a new feature was introduced called branch cache. This feature allows systems on a local network to act as on-demand file servers—keeping content local instead of each system going across a slow network link for copies of the same data. The first time a client requests data from a fileserver, it is downloaded to the local computer and then automatically shared for other clients on the local subnet. This helps reduce network bandwidth consumption by keeping data local.

Configuration Manager 2007 SP2 (and higher) distribution points support the branch cache feature and with BITS version 4.0, Windows Vista SP1 (and higher), and Windows Server 2008 SP1 (and higher) can support this feature as well.

So how does it work?

Let's say you have 15 Configuration Manager 2007 clients at a remote site that is connected over a slow ISDN line. The remote site has no local distribution point so each time a new software package has to be installed, the clients are forced to download it over the slow connection—individually, which sometimes takes hours or days to complete. As you are contemplating how to resolve this problem, the administrator at the remote site informs you that they need Office 2007 installed on all 15 computers ASAP. Because of all the problems they've had with software distribution in the past, this situation has escalated into a political nightmare, causing the higher ups to start questioning your methods and abilities.

Instead of installing a branch distribution point, you decide to give the branch cache feature a try since your distribution point and clients support the feature. Once you're satisfied that everything is enabled correctly, you advertise the program to the 15 clients and wait (nervously) to see the results.

Because no clients have previously downloaded the Office 2007 package, it must be sent across the slow ISDN line one time to the first client. Once the download is complete, other clients start receiving their advertisements and start to download the package. Instead of going to the distribution point, however, they download the content from the client who already has the content in their cache. Because these clients are on the same subnet with a fast LAN, clients 2 through 15 receive the content in a matter of minutes and start installing Office 2007 shortly thereafter. Because of branch cache, your bosses are happy and you get to keep your job!

Configuration Manager 2007 does not require any extra setup to use branch cache other than making sure your distribution points are BITS enabled. If the branch cache feature is enabled on your servers and configured on your clients', Configuration Manager simply uses the feature for its own benefit.

For more information on branch cache, see this link: http://technet.microsoft.com/en-us/library/dd637762(WS.10).aspx

Fallback Status Points

The fallback status point (FSP) role is an optional (but recommend) role that helps you troubleshoot problems with client installation, client site assignment, or clients that cannot be managed because of issues that may arise. FSPs work by receiving state messages from clients and then logging these messages in the database. A state message might be something such as the success or failure of the client installation. If an issue is detected, you can run various pre-canned reports to help identify the issue so that you can be proactive and remedy the situation quickly.

FSPs are especially important when running in native mode because they are able to communicate with unauthenticated clients unlike other roles such as the management point. If FSPs required authenticated communication, clients who cannot be managed because of certificate problems could not send status messages to the fallback status point, leaving you unable to detect these types of errors.

An FSP should be one of the first roles that you install so that you can assign clients to the FSP during the initial deployment of the Configuration Manager client. During the install of the Configuration Manager client, an FSP can be assigned using a command line option:

```
CCMSetup.exe FSP=<Name of Fallback Status Point>
```

This can be set in the Client Push Installation setting under the Client Installation Methods node in the Configuration Manager console. This is covered in Chapter 7, "Deploying Clients."

Note

Multiple FSPs can exist within a site but only one FSP can be assigned to a client.

Installing a Fallback Status Point

The installation of a fallback status point is pretty straightforward and doesn't require a lot of setup. In our example, we'll install the fallback status point role to our Chicago site system, CHI-SITESYSTEM via the Configuration Manager console that is connected to the CHI primary site. To install a fallback status point, do the following:

1. Open the Configuration Manager console at the site where the site system is located. In our example, we'll connect the Configuration Manager console to the CHI site.

2. Once the Configuration Manager console is open, go to the Site Systems node under your site.

3. Either right-click on the Site Systems node and choose New > Server if you want to create a new site system that will host the fallback status point role or right-click on an existing site system and choose New Roles. In our example, we'll right-click on \\CHI-SITESYSTEM and choose New Roles.

4. The New Site System Server Wizard window is displayed. This window allows you to configure multiple options regarding the new site system as shown back in Figure 6.3. If this wizard is started on an existing site system, the options that were used to create it are shown here and can be edited if so desired. Once the correct options are selected, click Next to continue.

5. The Site System Role Selection window is displayed. This window allows you to choose which roles will be installed to this site system. In this example, we'll install a fallback status point by checking the checkbox. Click Next to continue (Figure 6.17).

6. The Fallback Status Point configuration window is displayed. This lets you choose which options will be enabled for the FSP. In our example, we'll choose the defaults and click Next to continue. The configuration options for a fallback status point are discussed next and shown in Figure 6.18.

- **Allow intranet-only client connections**—This option only allows clients on the intranet (using the intranet FQDN) to send state messages to this fallback status point. This is the default option when in mixed mode or when in native mode with no Internet FQDN set.

- **Allow both Internet and intranet client connections**—This option allows both intranet and Internet clients to send state messages to this fallback status point. Note that this option is only available if the site is in native mode and if an Internet FQDN has been specified.

- **Number of messages**—This option lets you specify how many messages get sent to the site server within the time interval specified below.

- **Throttle interval (in seconds)**—This option lets you specify, in seconds, how many messages get sent to the site server. For example, within 3600 seconds, only 10,000 messages can be sent to the site server.

Figure 6.17
Selecting the Fallback Status Point Role

Figure 6.18
Fallback Status Point Configuration Options

7. The Fallback Status Point installation summary window is displayed next. This lets you review your selections before you actually make any changes. In our example, everything is correct. Click Next to continue.

8. The Fallback Status Point confirmation window is displayed. This shows you the results of the wizard. If any problems were encountered during the wizard, you will be notified here. Click Close to close the wizard.

Fallback Status Point Log Files

The installation and operation of fallback status points can be monitored through multiple log files that are created on the site system hosting the role. Table 6.4 details the fallback status point installation log files.

Table 6.5 details the fallback status point operational log files.

Server Locator Points

Server locator points are used when clients cannot retrieve site information from Active Directory because the schema was not extended to support Configuration Manager 2007, site information publishing is disabled, clients are in a different forest from the site server, or clients are only members of a workgroup. If a server locator is not used in any one of these scenarios, automatic site assignment will not be possible.

Configuration Manager 2007 hierarchies only require one server locator point even if you have multiple sites within the hierarchy. If multiple sites exist, the

Table 6.4 Fallback Status Point Installation Log Files

Log File	Location	Description
FSPMSI.log	\<ConfigMgrInstallationDirectory>\SMS\Logs	Details the installation of the fallback status point MSI installer
SMSfspsetup.log	\<ConfigMgrInstallationDirectory>\SMS\Logs	Details messages generated during the installation of the FSP

Table 6.5 Fallback Status Point Operational Log Files

Log File	Location	Description
Fspmgr.log	\<ConfigMgrInstallationDirectory>\SMS\Logs	Details activities of the FSP role
Fspisapi.log	\<ConfigMgrInstallationDirectory>\SMS\Logs	Details communications between clients and mobile device clients

server locator point should be installed at the central site so that it can obtain information about all sites below it.

Installing a Server Locator Point

The installation of a server locator point, like the fallback status point, is a fairly painless process. In our example, we'll install the server locator point role to our central site system, LIS-CENTRAL, via the Configuration Manager console that is connected to the LIS central site. This must occur at the central site for the server locator point to work correctly. In our environment, we have already extended the schema so this is not necessary, but we'll go through the steps anyway. To install a server locator point, do the following:

1. Open the Configuration Manager console at the central site. In our example, we'll connect the Configuration Manager console to the LIS site.

2. Once the Configuration Manager console is open, go to the Site Systems node under your site.

3. Either right-click on the Site Systems node and choose New > Server if you want to create a new site system that will host the server locator point role or right-click on an existing site system and choose New Roles. In our example, we'll right-click on \\LIS-CENTRAL and choose New Roles.

4. The New Site System Server Wizard window is displayed. This window allows you to configure multiple options regarding the new site system as shown back in Figure 6.3. If this wizard is started on an existing site system, the options that were used to create it are shown here and can be edited if so desired. Once the correct options are selected, click Next to continue.

5. The Site System Role Selection window is displayed. This window allows you to choose which roles will be installed to this site system. In this example, we'll install a server locator point by checking the checkbox. Click Next to continue (Figure 6.19).

6. The Server Locator Point configuration window is displayed. In our example, we'll choose the defaults and click Next to continue. The

Figure 6.19
Selecting the Server Locator Point Role

configuration options for a server locator point are discussed next and shown in Figure 6.20.

- **Use the site database**—This is the default option. This option uses the site database that was configured during site installation.

- **Use a database replica**—Use this option to let server locator point use a database replica instead of the default site database. If this option is selected, the SQL Server name and Database name fields are enabled.

- **SQL Server name field**—Use this field to specify the SQL Server that is hosting the database replica.

- **Database name field**—Use this field to specify the database name and instance.

- **Use the server locator point's computer account**—This option specifies that this server will access the site database using its computer account. Note that if you use this option, Configuration Manager attempts to automatically add the site system's computer account to the smsdbrole_SLP role on the site database.

- **Use another account**—This option is typically used if the site server (where the server locator point is being installed) is in a different

Figure 6.20
Server Locator Point Configuration Options

domain than the site database. If this is selected, you must specify a domain user account and then add that user to the smsdbrole_SLP role on the site database. If this option is selected, the Server Locator Point Connection Account field is enabled.

- **Server Locator Point Connection Account field**—This fields lets you specify the domain user account that has been added to the smsdbrole_SLP role on the site database.

7. The Server Locator Point installation summary window is displayed next. This lets you review your selections before you actually make any changes. In our example, everything is correct. Click Next to continue.

8. The Server Locator Point confirmation window is displayed. This shows you the results of the wizard. If any problems were encountered during the wizard, you will be notified here. Click Close to close the wizard (Figure 6.21).

Informing Clients of a Server Locator Point

Once a server locator point is installed, clients need to be told about it so that they can use it to find site information. There are two ways to specify the server locator point for a client. They are as follows:

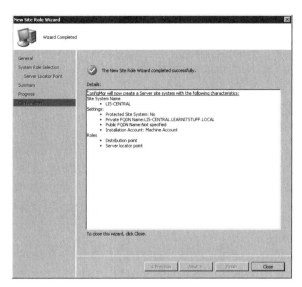

Figure 6.21
Server Locator Point Installation Confirmation

- **Manually publish the server locator point in WINS**—By default, clients automatically search for a server locator point via WINS unless disabled during setup. To disable server locator point WINS lookups, use the following command line option during the install: `Ccmsetup.exe SMSDIRECTORYLOOKUP=NOWINS`

- **Specify the server locator point during client deployment**—To specify the server locator point during client setup, use the following command line option during the install: `Ccmsetup.exe SMSSLP=<Server Locator Point name>`

N o t e

All of the ccmsetup.exe switches are covered in Chapter 7, "Deploying Clients."

Reporting Points

Reporting points allow users to access reporting information from a Configuration Manager database such as client hardware inventory information and software/software update distribution information via a web browser so that no specialized software has to be installed on the requestor's computer. If your organization has a large number of users requesting reporting information, it might be a good idea to set up more reporting points on different site systems to balance the load.

Reporting Point Prerequisites

Reporting points require that IIS with Active Server Pages be installed and enabled. If the site server hosting the reporting point is a Server 2008 class operating system, Windows Authentication must also be manually enabled. If you would like to use graphs in your reports, Office Web Components must be installed as well.

Note

If you are using a 64-bit operating system as your site system that is hosting the reporting point role, you will not be able to use the Office Web Components functionality since it is only compatible with 32-bit operating systems.

Choosing a Location for Your Reporting Point Role

Because a reporting point is attached to each site's database, it only has access to the information within that database. If you install a reporting point to a child primary site, it cannot retrieve reporting information from sites above it in the hierarchy. If you want to access reporting information from all sites in the hierarchy, install the reporting point on the central site.

Installing the Reporting Point Role

After making sure that the site system is in the correct location and meets the prerequisites for the reporting point role, you are ready to begin installation. In our example, we'll install the reporting point role to our central site system, LIS-CENTRAL via the Configuration Manager console that is connected to the LIS central site. This is being done at this location so that we can report on all systems in the hierarchy. To install a reporting point, do the following:

1. Open the Configuration Manager console at the site where the site system is located. In our example, we'll connect the Configuration Manager console to the LIS central site.

2. Once the Configuration Manager console is open, go to the Site Systems node under your site.

3. Either right-click on the Site Systems node and choose New > Server if you want to create a new site system that will host the fallback status point role or right-click on an existing site system and choose New Roles. In our example, we'll right-click on \\LIS-CENTRAL and choose New Roles.

4. The New Site System Server Wizard window is displayed. This window allows you to configure multiple options regarding the new site system, as shown back in Figure 6.3. If this wizard is started on an existing site system, the options that were used to create it are shown here and can be edited if so desired. Once the correct options are selected, click Next to continue.

5. The Site System Role Selection window is displayed. This window allows you to choose which roles will be installed to this site system. In this example, we'll install a reporting point by checking the checkbox. Click Next to continue (Figure 6.22).

Figure 6.22
Selecting the Reporting Point Role

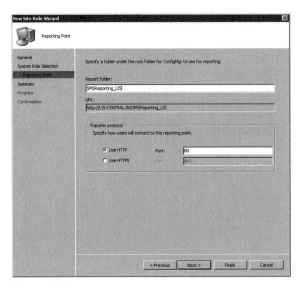

Figure 6.23
Reporting Point Configuration Options

6. The Reporting Point configuration window is displayed. This lets you choose which options will be enabled for the reporting point. In our example, we'll choose the defaults and click Next to continue. The configuration options for a reporting point are discussed below and shown in Figure 6.23.

- **Report Folder**—Enter the name of a folder (256 characters or less) that will be created on the reporting point site system. This folder is created under \Inetpub\wwwroot beneath the site server root. The folder name chosen in this field is also used as the name of the virtual folder.

- **URL**—This field is based on the Report Folder field above and the transfer protocols below. Use this URL to access the report page.

- **Use HTTP**—When this option is specified, an unsecured HTTP connection is used to view Configuration Manager reports. The default port of 80 is used but can be modified in the port field.

- **Use HTTPS**—When this option is specified, a secured HTTPS connection is used to view Configuration Manager reports. The default port of 443 is used but can be modified in the port field.

Figure 6.24
Reporting Point Installation Confirmation

7. The Reporting Point installation summary window is displayed next. This lets you review your selections before you actually make any changes. In our example, everything is correct. Click Next to continue.

8. The Reporting Point confirmation window is displayed. This shows you the results of the wizard. If any problems were encountered during the wizard, you will be notified here. Click Close to close the wizard (Figure 6.24).

Reporting Point Log Files

The installation of reporting points can be monitored through multiple log files that are created on the site system hosting the role. Table 6.6 details the reporting point installation log files.

Note

The reporting point role is now considered the legacy reporting role as of the R2 release of Configuration Manager 2007. A newer, more standardized reporting role is available that uses SQL reporting services as its reporting engine. This is the reporting point that will be used in future releases of Configuration Manager. We'll discuss this new role in the next section.

Table 6.6 Reporting Point Installation Log Files

Log File	Location	Description
RSetup.log	<ConfigMgrInstallationDirectory>\SMS\Logs	Details the reporting point setup process
SMSReportingInstall.log	<ConfigMgrInstallationDirectory>\SMS\Logs	Details the reporting point installation process including installation tasks and configuration changes

Reporting Services Point

Starting with Configuration Manager 2007 R2, the reporting services point is available, which allows Configuration Manager 2007 to use an existing SQL reporting services infrastructure to deliver reports directly from the Configuration Manager console. SQL reporting services is the preferred method of reporting in Configuration Manager since it uses an industry-standard reporting system, offers higher performance over the legacy reporting point, and enables users to subscribe to reports, among other things. SQL reporting services will be used from here on out in Configuration Manager and the legacy reporting point will be phased out.

Reporting Services Point Prerequisites

The reporting services point has multiple prerequisites that must be configured before it can be used. The prerequisites are listed next.

- SQL reporting services server must be installed and configured
- The site server must be running the R2 release of Configuration Manager 2007
- The Configuration Manager console must be upgraded to R2 before it can display the Reporting Services node
- IIS 6 or later must be installed on the site system hosting the reporting services point

Tip

To see more information about how to set up SQL Reporting Services for Configuration Manager 2007, see this link: http://technet.microsoft.com/en-us/library/cc512033.aspx.

Installing the Reporting Services Point Role

Once all of the prerequisites have been met for the reporting services point role, you can begin the installation. To install the reporting services point role, do the following:

1. Open the Configuration Manager console at the site where the site system is located. In our example, we'll connect the Configuration Manager console to the LIS central site.

2. Once the Configuration Manager console is open, go to the Site Systems node under your site.

3. Either right-click on the Site Systems node and choose New > Server if you want to create a new site system that will host the fallback status point role or right-click on an existing site system and choose New Roles. In our example, we'll right-click on \\LIS-CENTRAL and choose New Roles.

4. The New Site System Server Wizard window is displayed. This window allows you to configure multiple options regarding the new site system as shown back in Figure 6.3. If this wizard is started on an existing site system, the options that were used to create it are shown here and can be edited if so desired. Once the correct options are selected, click Next to continue.

5. The Site System Role Selection window is displayed. This window allows you to choose which roles will be installed to this site system. In this example, we'll install a reporting services point by checking the checkbox. Click Next to continue (Figure 6.25).

6. The Reporting Services Point configuration window is displayed. This lets you choose which options will be enabled for the reporting services point. The only option that can be configured for a reporting services point is the Report Folder field. This option lets you specify the name of the reporting services folder that is created on the site system. This folder contains reports that can be accessed from the Configuration Manager console. In our example, we'll choose the defaults and click Next to continue (Figure 6.26).

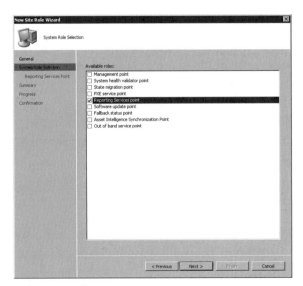

Figure 6.25
Selecting the Reporting Services Point Role

Figure 6.26
Reporting Services Point Configuration Window

7. The Reporting Services Point installation summary window is displayed next. This lets you review your selections before you actually make any changes. In our example, everything is correct. Click Next to continue.

Figure 6.27
Reporting Services Point Installation Confirmation

8. The Reporting Services Point confirmation window is displayed. This shows you the results of the wizard. If any problems were encountered during the wizard, you will be notified here. Click Close to close the wizard (Figure 6.27).

Software Update Points

If you work in an environment with many Windows-based devices such as servers and workstations, you know the headaches associated with keeping these devices patched. When patch Tuesday rolls around, it can be difficult to approve and install multiple updates on multiple systems, especially if you have to do this process manually. Luckily, the folks at Microsoft developed a product called Windows Server Update Services (WSUS) which allows administrators to centrally manage all Microsoft updates and distribute them to your devices via the network. WSUS is a free tool and greatly reduces the overhead that is typically associated with patching multiple systems in diverse environments. Although WSUS works very well, there are some drawbacks such as limited reporting and targeting capabilities. You can use Configuration Manager 2007 to fill in these gaps, however, by using a feature called software update points.

Software update points are used to deploy the same types of updates that WSUS does but can be managed more granularly using settings in the Configuration

Manager console. Clients use their native Windows Update agent to communicate with the software update point to verify that their systems are in compliance according to the rules that you define. If you've ever used WSUS, you'll be familiar with the product families and categories that are available when configuring the software update point since Configuration Manager uses WSUS as the backend for the software update point. Once clients have been updated, they report their compliance to the software update point so that you can run detailed reports using the same reporting mechanisms that we discussed earlier in this chapter. Multiple software update points can be installed in the hierarchy but only one can be enabled as the active software update point.

Understanding How and When to Use Software Update Points

Suppose you have a primary site that sits above a secondary site in the hierarchy. You currently use WSUS 3.0 to manage and deploy software updates but would like to now use Configuration Manager 2007 because of the reporting and deployment options that are available. You also would like to have Configuration Manager 2007 manage this so that you can have a unified management solution.

You install a software update point to a site system in the primary site and configure it as the active software update point so that clients will start using the software update point as their update location. This includes clients at both the primary and secondary sites. After a week, you verify that your clients are updating correctly but start to get complaints from users at the secondary site about high bandwidth consumption that is causing problems for the entire site. You find that the link to the secondary site is too slow to handle the traffic that is being generated by clients while checking for software update compliance. To solve this problem, you decide to install another software update point on a site system at the secondary site that will handle traffic from clients at the secondary site. Because each client at the secondary site no longer has to traverse the slow link, the bandwidth between the primary and secondary site is restored to normal because compliance traffic is now kept locally at the secondary site.

Software Update Point Prerequisites

Because software update points use WSUS to manage software updates, the WSUS 3.0 SDK must be installed on the site system that will host the software update point role so that is can communicate with the WSUS server managing the updates. The WSUS server can be installed on the site system hosting the software update point or it can be installed on another server in the hierarchy. Depending on the version of Configuration Manager 2007, different versions of WSUS 3.0 are required. These versions are detailed next.

- Configuration Manager 2007 SP1 requires WSUS 3.0 SP1 or SP2
- Configuration Manager 2007 SP2 requires WSUS 3.0 SP2

Caution

If you convert your patch management system from WSUS to software update points within Configuration Manager 2007, be sure to let Configuration Manager manage the WSUS settings on the client machines. If you previously used another method such as group policy to deploy settings for WSUS, clients may report to the wrong update server and reporting information may be inaccurate.

Installing a Software Update Point

Before installing a software update point, make sure that the WSUS 3.0 SDK is installed on the site system that will be configured as the active software update point and that a WSUS server is accessible from this server. Again, this can be installed locally to the site server itself or it can be hosted on another accessible server. Once this requirement has been met, do the following:

1. Open the Configuration Manager console at the site where the site system is located. In our example, we'll connect the Configuration Manager console to the CHI site.

2. Once the Configuration Manager console is open, go to the Site Systems node under your site.

3. Right-click on the Site Systems node and choose New > Server if you want to create a new site system that will host the software update point role or right-click on an existing site system and choose New Roles to add roles to an existing site system. In our example, we'll right-click on \\CHI-SITESYSTEM and choose New Roles.

4. The New Site System Server Wizard window is displayed. This window allows you to configure multiple options regarding the new site system

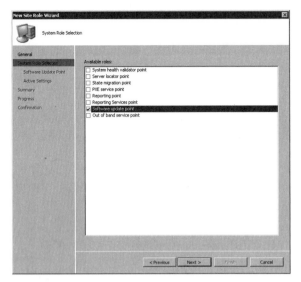

Figure 6.28
Selecting the Software Update Point Role

as shown back in Figure 6.3. If this wizard is started on an existing site system, the options that were used to create it are shown here and can be edited if so desired. Once the correct options are selected, click Next to continue.

5. The Site System Role Selection window is displayed. This window allows you to choose which roles will be installed to this site system. In this example, we'll install a software update point by checking the checkbox. Click Next to continue (Figure 6.28).

6. The Software Update Point configuration window is displayed. In our example, we'll choose the defaults and click Next to continue. The configuration options for the server update point are discussed next and shown in Figure 6.29.

  ▪ **Use a proxy server when synchronizing**—If your software update point will need to connect to a proxy server to get access to the Internet, check this box to enable this setting.

  ▪ **Server name field**—Enter the name of the proxy server that will allow you to gain access to the Internet.

  ▪ **Port field**—Enter the port number that your proxy server uses to connect to the Internet.

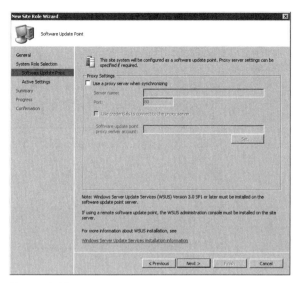

Figure 6.29
Server Locator Point Configuration Options

- **Use credentials to connect to the proxy server**—If your proxy server requires authentication to access the Internet, check this box to enable this feature.
- **Software update point proxy server account**—Enter the name of the proxy server account that will be used to access the Internet.

7. The Software Update Point active settings window is displayed. In our example, we'll check the box that says Use this Server as the Active Software Update Point. Click Next to continue. The options for active settings are displayed and shown in Figure 6.30.

- **Use this server as the active software update point**—If this option is enabled, the site server is configured to be the active software update point for the site.
- **Port number**—This option lets you configure the port that is used for WSUS communication. By default, port 80 is used to connect the site system to the WSUS server when not in native mode. However, if port 80 is already in use by another service (such as a Configuration Manager 2007 management point), you may have to configure WSUS to use another port number to ensure that it does not conflict with one that is already in use.

Figure 6.30
Active Software Update Point Settings

- **SSL port number**—This option lets you configure the port that is used for WSUS secure communication. By default, port 443 is used to connect the site system to the WSUS server when in native mode. However, if port 443 is already in use by another service (such as a Configuration Manager 2007 management point), you may have to configure WSUS to use another port number to ensure that it does not conflict with one that is already in use.

8. The Synchronization Source configuration window is displayed. This window lets you configure how and where the software update point will synchronize Microsoft updates. In our example, we'll choose the defaults and click Next. The options for Synchronization Source settings are shown in Figure 6.31.

   - **Synchronize from Microsoft Update**—This option should be checked for the highest software update point in this hierarchy (such as the central site). This will allow the software update point to synchronize all updates with the Microsoft Update service.

   - **Synchronize from an upstream update server**—This option should be checked for any software update points that sit below another software update point that is already configured to synchronize from

Figure 6.31
Synchronization Source Configuration Window

Microsoft Update. Primary site servers that are configured with the Synchronize from Microsoft Update option are automatically configured as an upstream update server.

- **Do not synchronize from Microsoft Update or an upstream update server**—This option should only be checked if you want to use the WSUS utility to manually synchronize updates by using the import/ export feature.

- **Do not create WSUS reporting events**—Selecting this option will configure the Windows Update agent on the client to not create WSUS reporting events. This is the default setting since Configuration Manager 2007 does not use this data for reporting purposes.

- **Create only WSUS status reporting events**—Selecting this option will configure the Windows Update agent on the client machine to create WSUS status reporting events.

- **Create all WSUS reporting events**—Selecting this option will configure the Windows Update agent on the client machine to create all WSUS status reporting events.

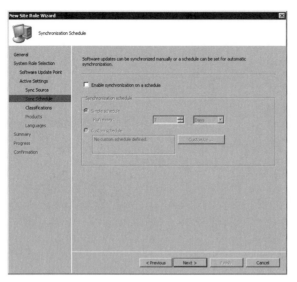

Figure 6.32
Synchronization Schedule Configuration Window

9. The Synchronization Schedule configuration window is displayed. This window lets you configure when the software update point will check for Microsoft updates. Simple and custom schedules can be configured. In our example, we'll choose the defaults and click Next. Note that these configurations can be edited after installation has occurred (Figure 6.32).

10. The Classifications Synchronization window is displayed. This window lets you configure what kinds of updates will be synchronized. These updates are classified by type such as critical updates or service packs. In our example, we'll choose the defaults and click Next. Note that these classifications can be edited after installation has occurred (Figure 6.33).

11. The Product Synchronization window is displayed. This window lets you configure what kinds of updates will be synchronized. The updates in this window are categorized by product such as Office or Windows. In our example, we'll choose the defaults and click Next. Note that these products can be edited after installation has occurred (Figure 6.34).

12. The Languages Synchronization window is displayed. This window lets you configure which updates are downloaded for different types of language. If you only support one language in your environment, you

Figure 6.33
Classification Synchronization Window

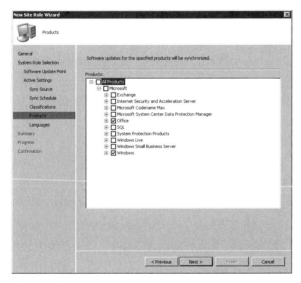

Figure 6.34
Product Synchronization Window

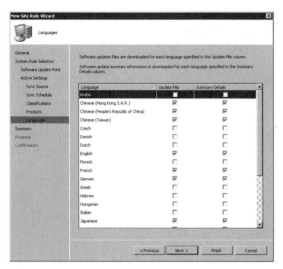

Figure 6.35
Languages Synchronization Window

can de-select the un-used languages to save space on your WSUS server. In our example, we'll choose the defaults and click Next. Note that these languages can be edited after installation has occurred (Figure 6.35).

13. The Software Update Point summary window is displayed next. This lets you review your selections before you actually make any changes. In our example, everything is correct. Click Next to continue.

14. The Software Update Point confirmation window is displayed. This shows you the results of the wizard. If any problems were encountered during the wizard, you will be notified here. Click Close to close the wizard (Figure 6.36).

Using SSL on a WSUS Website

If you decide to use SSL with WSUS, there are five virtual directories that must be configured via the IIS Manager console. These directories are APIRemoting30, ClientWebService, DSSAuthWebService, ServerSyncWebService, and SimpleAuth-WebService. The following steps must be performed on these virtual directories:

1. Open the IIS Manager console on the server that is hosting WSUS.

2. Expand the Server node (name of your server), sites, and then the Default Website node. Note that WSUS may have been installed to a

Figure 6.36
Software Update Point Summary Window

custom website during the initial setup. If this is the case, expand the site node for WSUS.

3. For each virtual directory listed above, highlight the virtual directory and double-click the SSL Settings icon from the features view window.

4. When the SSL Settings window is displayed, check the box that says Require SSL.

5. From the Actions pane, click Apply to save the changes.

6. Close the IIS Manager console.

7. Obtain the WSUS installation files from the installation media or network share.

8. Navigate to the Tools directory, hold down Shift, and right-click in the Tools folder. Choose Open Command Prompt.

9. Navigate to the Tools directory, hold down Shift, and right-click in the Tools folder. Choose Open Command Prompt.

10. Type the following command: `WSUSUtil configuressl <Intranet FQDN of the software update point site system>`

Note

This command configures WSUS health monitoring to use SSL.

Software Update Point Log Files

The installation and operation of software update points can be monitored through multiple log files that are created on the site system hosting the role. Table 6.7 shows the software update point installation log files.

Table 6.7 Software Update Point Installation Log Files

Log File	Location	Description
SUPSetup.log	<ConfigMgrInstallationDirectory>\SMS\Logs	Details the software update point installation process

Table 6.8 details the software update point operational log files.

PXE Service Points

PXE stands for Preboot eXecution Environment and allows you to boot your computers to an image that is delivered over the network. This image is delivered via a site system that is hosting the PXE service point role. This is great for systems that have corrupted Windows installations or computers that are brand new from the factory that do not have your standard image deployed to them. New factory computers are often referred to as bare metal systems and this is how we will refer to them throughout this chapter. When a bare metal system boots to PXE, it receives a small version of Windows called Windows pre-installation environment or Windows PE for short. This image has the necessary boot and network drivers, allowing it to communicate with the Configuration Manager 2007 infrastructure so that is can execute any advertisement that may be advertised to it.

PXE Service Point Prerequisites

The PXE service point has multiple prerequisites that must be followed prior to installation. These are listed below.

Clients   If you want your clients to boot to PXE, their BIOS must support the PXE technology and must be enabled. Typically, a keystroke is needed to bring

Table 6.8 Software Update Point Operational Log Files

Log File	Location	Description
WCM.log	<ConfigMgrInstallationDirectory>\SMS\Logs	Details information regarding the connection status from the software update point to the WSUS component regarding update categories, classifications, and languages
WSUSCtrl.log	<ConfigMgrInstallationDirectory>\SMS\Logs	Details health information regarding the WSUS server for the site
Ciamgr.log	<ConfigMgrInstallationDirectory>\SMS_CCM\Logs	Details information about software update configuration items
distmgr.log	<ConfigMgrInstallationDirectory>\SMS_CCM\Logs	Details information about the replication of software update deployment packages
objreplmgr.log	<ConfigMgrInstallationDirectory>\SMS_CCM\Logs	Details information about notification files from parent to child sites
PatchDownloader.log	<ConfigMgrInstallationDirectory>\SMS_CCM\Logs	Details the process for downloading updates from the update source
replmgr.log	<ConfigMgrInstallationDirectory>\SMS_CCM\Logs	Details the process for replicating files between sites
smsdbmon.log	<ConfigMgrInstallationDirectory>\SMS_CCM\Logs	Details information about software update configuration items in the site server database
wsyncmgr.log	<ConfigMgrInstallationDirectory>\SMS_CCM\Logs	Details the processes around software update synchronization

up a boot menu, which allows you to choose PXE as one of your boot options. See your computer manufacturer's guidelines for help on this topic.

Servers   Before your site system can host the PXE service point role, it must have Windows Deployment Services installed. Configuration Manager uses the Windows Deployment Services service to listen and respond to client PXE requests and to also transfer operating system images during an OS deployment. We'll talk more about WDS and OS Deployment in Chapter 13, "Managing Operating System Distribution."

Caution

It is very important that you do not manually configure WDS after it has been installed. Configuration Manager automatically configures WDS when the PXE service point role is installed and can fail to correctly configure WDS if it has been manually configured by an administrator. This is a common situation because many guidelines on the Internet inform you that you must configure WDS after it has been installed. This is true if you are using WDS as a standalone deployment solution but not if you are using WDS with Configuration Manager 2007.

Network   Let's face it. Configuring PXE to work across complicated networks is often a difficult task. Because so many variables can exist in these types of situations, it's not only hard to implement, but to troubleshoot as well. Generically speaking, if your DHCP server, PXE service point, and clients are all on the same subnet, everything should work as expected. When clients and servers are separated by routers, however, things start to get hairy.

Routers are great. They allow you to connect separate networks together with all kinds of neat options, including access lists, routing protocols, and so on. One of the other great things that routers do is to stop broadcasts. If you have hundreds or thousands of clients on a network, they generate a lot of broadcast traffic that can clog up a network if not configured correctly. One of the ways to prevent broadcasts from flooding a network is to put a router in place so that they do not get forwarded to other networks. Unfortunately, DHCP and PXE requests are broadcasts that get dropped by routers as they try to traverse subnets.

IP Helper Addresses and DHCP   When a computer issues a DHCP request without a DHCP server on the same subnet, the DHCP request (a broadcast) is sent to the router and then dropped before ever reaching the DHCP server. There are some configurations that can be done, however, to help remedy this process. The best way to resolve this issue is to use an IP helper address. IP helper addresses are used on routers and layer 3 switches to forward all DHCP requests to the configured IP helper address. When a client issues a DHCP request, the router sees this and then forwards it on to the IP helper address, which is typically the IP address of your DHCP server. The DHCP server sees the request and responds to the router, which is then forwarded back to the client.

At this point, you are probably asking, what the heck does DHCP have to do with PXE? When a network card issues a PXE request, it's really using a modified DHCPDISCOVER packet with extra PXE options. This means that PXE requests behave like DHCP requests and can be forwarded using the IP helper addresses as well. If a PXE server, like the PXE service point site system, is located on the same subnet as the client but the DHCP server is on another subnet with the correct IP helper address configured in the router, the client will get DHCP from the remote server and PXE options from the local server, merging them into one request that allows the client to boot to PXE correctly. If the PXE server is not on the same subnet as the client, that's where things start to get tricky.

DHCP PXE Server Options   If you are using a Microsoft DHCP server, you can configure options within DHCP that will allow you to direct your PXE clients to things like the PXE boot server and the filename of the boot image that will be transferred from this server. Note that you should only use these options when all other avenues have failed.

There are three DHCP options that exist in regards to PXE. These are as follows:

- **Option 060—PXEClient**—This option should be used if your PXE service point is installed on the same server as your DHCP server. When configured, DHCP tells your clients that the PXE server is on the same server as your DHCP server so that they know where to go to download the PXE boot image.

- **Option 067—Boot Server Host Name**—This option should be used when your PXE Service Point site system is located in a different subnet than your client computer. DHCP tells the client which server to download the boot image from.

- **Option 068—Bootfile Name**—This option is most often used in conjunction with option 067. Once the boot server is specified with option 067, option 068 should be configured to inform clients of the name and location of the boot file.

- **No PXE Options Configured**—Do not configure any options relating to PXE if the PXE service point is located on the same subnet as the client. The client will discover this automatically through standard broadcasts.

Installing a PXE Service Point

For simplicity, PXE service points should be installed to site systems that exist on the same subnet as the clients that need to boot to PXE. If this is the case, no extra setup is needed including extra DHCP and router configurations. In our example, we'll assume that this is the case and install it to a site system that will be on the same subnet as our clients. We will install this to our CHI-SITESYSTEM server. To install a PXE Service Point, do the following:

1. Open the Configuration Manager console at the site where the site system is located. In our example, we'll connect the Configuration Manager console to the CHI site.

2. Once the Configuration Manager console is open, go to the Site Systems node under your site.

3. Right-click on the Site Systems node and choose New > Server if you want to create a new site system that will host the software update point role or right-click on an existing site system and choose New Roles to add roles to an existing site system. In our example, we'll right-click on \\CHI-SITESYSTEM and choose New Roles.

4. The New Site System Server Wizard window is displayed. This window allows you to configure multiple options regarding the new site system as shown back in Figure 6.3. If this wizard is started on an existing site system, the options that were used to create it are shown here and can be edited if so desired. Once the correct options are selected, click Next to continue.

5. The Site System Role Selection window is displayed. This window allows you to choose which roles will be installed to this site system. In this example, we'll install a PXE service point by checking the checkbox. Click Next to continue (Figure 6.37).

6. After you select the PXE service point role, you are notified about the ports that will automatically be opened on the firewall (if enabled) so that PXE requests can be transferred correctly. Click Yes to open these ports and to continue with the installation (Figure 6.38).

7. The General configuration window for the PXE service point is displayed. In our example, we'll make sure that the Allow This PXE Service Point to Respond to Incoming PXE Requests and Require a Password for Computers to Boot Using PXE options are selected and click Next to

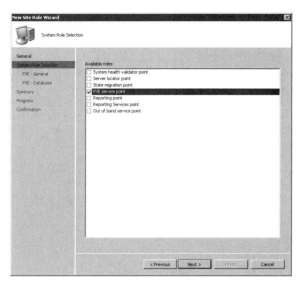

Figure 6.37
Selecting the PXE Service Point Role

Figure 6.38
Open PXE Related Firewall Ports

continue. The configuration options for the General configuration window are shown in Figure 6.39.

- **Allow this PXE service point to respond to incoming PXE requests**—This option enables or disables the PXE service point. This option is good for temporarily disabling the PXE service point.

- **Enable unknown computer support**—Starting with Configuration Manager 2007 R2, unknown computer support is available. This option allows computers that are unknown to the Configuration Manager database to boot from the PXE service point.

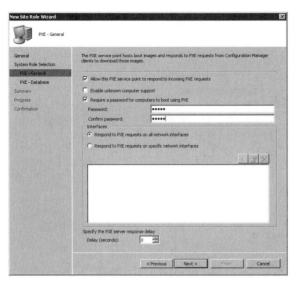

Figure 6.39
PXE Service Point General Options

- **Require a password for computers to boot using PXE**—This option allows you to specify a password that users must enter before the computer will display any available task sequences. This requires user intervention even if a mandatory task sequence has been advertised to the collection.
- **Respond to PXE requests on all network interfaces**—This option specifies that the PXE service point will listen for PXE requests on all network interfaces.
- **Respond to PXE requests on specific network interfaces**—This option specifies that the PXE service point will only listen on the selected network interface.
- **PXE server response delay**—This option lets you specify, in seconds, the amount of time that the PXE service point will wait before it answers PXE requests. This is good if you are dealing with multiple PXE service points and need to adjust timing.

8. The Database configuration window for the PXE service point is displayed. In our example, we'll make sure that the Create Self-Signed PXE Certificate option is selected and click Next to continue. The

Figure 6.40
PXE Service Point Database Options

configuration options for the Database configuration window are shown
in Figure 6.40.

- **Use the PXE service point's computer account**—This option specifies that this server will access the site database using its computer
  account. Note that if you use this option, Configuration Manager
  attempts to automatically add the site system's computer account to
  the smsdbrole_PSP role on the site database.
- **Use another account**—This option is typically used if the site server
  (where the PXE service point is being installed) is in a different
  domain than the site database. If this is selected, you must specify a
  domain user account and then add that user to the smsdbrole_PSP
  role on the site database. If this option is selected, the PXE Service
  Point Connection Account field is enabled.
- **PXE Service Point Connection Account field**—This field lets you
  specify the domain user account that has been added to the
  smsdbrole_PSP role on the site database.

- **Create self-signed PXE certificate**—This option allows you to specify a self-signed certificate that is typically used in mixed-mode environments. When using this option, you must specify an expiration date for the certificate.

- **Import certificate**—This option lets you import a certificate from a trusted root certification authority and is required for sites in native mode. This option requires you to browse to a server and import a certificate. You must also specify the password that is associated to the certificate.

9. The PXE Service Point installation summary window is displayed next. This lets you review your selections before you actually make any changes. In our example, everything is correct. Click Next to continue.

10. The PXE Service Point confirmation window is displayed. This shows you the results of the wizard. If any problems were encountered during the wizard, you will be notified here. Click Close to close the wizard (Figure 6.41).

Figure 6.41
PXE Service Point Installation Confirmation

PXE Service Point Log Files

Table 6.10 details the PXE service point operational log files.

Table 6.9 PXE Service Point Installation Log Files

Log File	Location	Description
PXESetup.log	<ConfigMgrInstallationDirectory>\SMS\Logs	Details the PXE service point installation process
PXEMsi.log	<ConfigMgrInstallationDirectory>\SMS\Logs	Details the PXE service point MSI installer

Table 6.10 PXE Service Point Operational Log Files

Log File	Location	Description
MPClientID.log	<ConfigMgrInstallationDirectory>\SMS_CCM\Logs	Details information about the management point when it responds to client ID requests from PXE
PXEcontrol.log	<ConfigMgrInstallationDirectory>\SMS\Logs	Details health information regarding the PXE control manager
Smspxe.log	<ConfigMgrInstallationDirectory>\SMS_CCM\Logs	Details information about the PXE service point

State Migration Points

State migration points are used during operating system deployments to store user state data from client machines while operating systems are deployed. User states might include files in the local My Documents folder, mapped network drives, or desktop wallpapers. After the OS deployment, the user state is copied from the state migration point back down to the client. State migration points work in conjunction with the User State Migration tool, which must be installed on a client workstation using a task sequence. We'll cover this step in Chapter 13.

State Migration Point Prerequisites

The only prerequisites for the state migration point are that IIS must be installed on the site system that will host the role and the client must have USMT installed as part of a task sequence. USMT 4.0 is available starting with Configuration Manager 2007 SP2 but only works with Windows Vista clients and higher. If you need to restore client state to Windows XP clients, you will need to use USMT 3.01. The state migration point must also have enough space to store the user state files.

Installing a State Migration Point

To install the state migration point, choose a site server that will host the role in your environment and use the New Site Roles Wizard to complete the process. In our example, we will install this to our CHI-SITESYSTEM server. To install a state migration point, do the following:

1. Open the Configuration Manager console where the site system is located. In our example, we'll connect the Configuration Manager console to the CHI site.

2. Once the Configuration Manager console is open, go to the Site Systems node under your site.

3. Right-click on the Site Systems node and choose New > Server if you want to create a new site system that will host the software update point role or right-click on an existing site system and choose New Roles to add roles to an existing site system. In our example, we'll right-click on \\CHI-SITESYSTEM and choose New Roles.

4. The New Site System Server Wizard window is displayed. This window allows you to configure multiple options regarding the new site system as shown back in Figure 6.3. If this wizard is started on an existing site system, the options that were used to create it are shown here and can be edited if so desired. Once the correct options are selected, click Next to continue.

5. The Site System Role Selection window is displayed. This window allows you to choose which roles will be installed to this site system. In this example, we'll install a state migration point by checking the checkbox. Click Next to continue (Figure 6.42).

6. The State Migration Point configuration window is displayed. This window allows you to control settings for the state migration point. The configuration options for the state migration point are shown in Figure 6.43.

   - **State migration folders**—Choose folders on the site system that will store state migration data. The number of maximum clients and free space can be specified when creating folders (Figure 6.44).

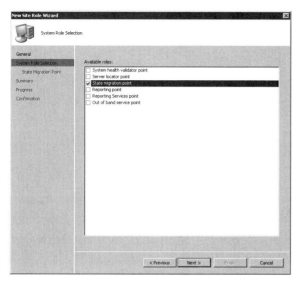

Figure 6.42
Selecting the State Migration Point Role

Figure 6.43
State Migration Point General Options

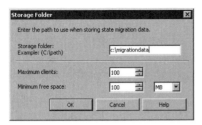

Figure 6.44
Create New State Migration Point Folders

- **Deletion policy—Immediate**—This option will delete user state migration data immediately after it has been restored to the client PC.
- **Deletion policy—Delete After**—This option allows you to specify the amount of time that user state migration data will be stored on the server.
- **Enable restore-only mode**—This option specifies that the state migration point will reject clients that wish to store data on the site server. The server will only be used to restore user state data.

7. The State Migration Point installation summary window is displayed next. This lets you review your selections before you actually make any changes. In our example, everything is correct. Click Next to continue.

8. The State Migration Point confirmation window is displayed. This shows you the results of the wizard. If any problems were encountered during the wizard, you will be notified here. Click Close to close the wizard (Figure 6.45).

State Migration Point Log Files

The installation and operation of state migration points can be monitored through multiple log files that are created on the site system hosting the role. Table 6.11 details the state migration point installation log files.

Table 6.12 details the state migration point operational log files.

System Health Validator Points

The system health validator point is used in conjunction with a site system that is running Server 2008 or Server 2008 R2 and has Network Policy Services

Figure 6.45
State Migration Point Installation Confirmation

Table 6.11 State Migration Point Installation Log Files

Log File	Location	Description
SMSSMPSetup.log	<ConfigMgrInstallationDirectory>\SMS\Logs	Details the state migration point installation process
SMPMsi.log	<ConfigMgrInstallationDirectory>\SMS\Logs	Details the state migration point MSI installer

Table 6.12 State Migration Point Operational Log Files

Log File	Location	Description
SMPisapi.log	<ConfigMgrInstallationDirectory>\SMS\Logs	Details information about the state migration point client request responses
Smpmgr.log	<ConfigMgrInstallationDirectory>\SMS\Logs	Details health information regarding the state migration point

enabled. The system health validator point is the system that checks to see if clients are in a compliant or non compliant state by using health state references. Health state references are published to Active Directory by a Configuration

Manager 2007 site server and are updated when a change to the network access protection policy occurs. When a system health validator point receives a client statement of health, it determines if the clients are in a compliant or non compliant state. Once it has compliancy information, it informs the Network Policy Server about each client's health state. The Network Policy Server can then remediate a client if it is non-compliant or it can restrict its network access until the correct software updates have been installed.

System Health Validator Point Prerequisites

System health validator points only work when installed on a site system with Network Policy Server enabled. This can only be done if the server's operating system is Windows Server 2008 or 2008 R2. Clients also must be using an operating system that works with network access protection. This includes Windows Vista and higher.

Because health state references must be published to Active Directory, the schema must be extended for this feature to work.

Installing a System Health Validator Point

This role is one of the easiest roles to install since there are no options available during setup. To install the system health validator point, choose a site server that will host the role in your environment and use the New Site Roles Wizard to complete the process. In our example, we will install this to our CHI-SITESYSTEM server. To install a system health validator point, do the following:

1. Open the Configuration Manager console where the site system is located. In our example, we'll connect the Configuration Manager console to the CHI site.

2. Once the Configuration Manager console is open, go to the Site Systems node under your site.

3. Right-click on the Site Systems node and choose New > Server if you want to create a new site system that will host the software update point role or right-click on an existing site system and choose New Roles to add roles to an existing site system. In our example, we'll right-click on \\CHI-SITESYSTEM and choose New Roles.

4. The New Site System Server Wizard window is displayed. This window allows you to configure multiple options regarding the new site system as shown back in Figure 6.3. If this wizard is started on an existing site system, the options that were used to create it are shown here and can be edited if so desired. Once the correct options are selected, click Next to continue.

5. The Site System Role Selection window is displayed. This window allows you to choose which roles will be installed to this site system. In this example, we'll install a system health validator point by checking the checkbox. Click Next to continue (Figure 6.46).

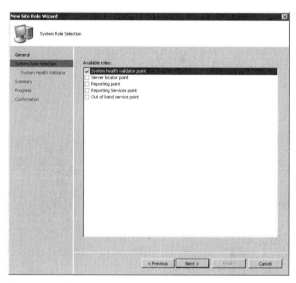

Figure 6.46
Selecting the System Health Validator Point Role

6. The System Health Validator Point configuration window is displayed. Because there are no configurable options for this site system role, nothing is left to do except to click Next to continue (Figure 6.47).

7. The System Health Validator Point installation summary window is displayed next. This lets you review your selections before you actually make any changes. In our example, everything is correct. Click Next to continue.

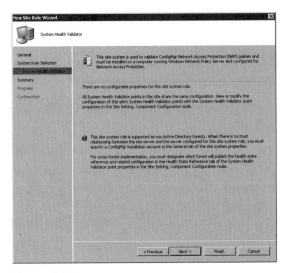

Figure 6.47
System Health Validator Point Installation Window

8. The System Health Validator Point confirmation window is displayed. This shows you the results of the wizard. If any problems were encountered during the wizard, you will be notified here. Click Close to close the wizard (Figure 6.48).

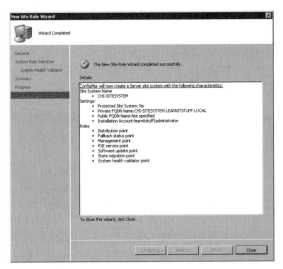

Figure 6.48
System Health Validator Point Installation Confirmation

System Health Validator Point Log Files

The installation and operation of system health validator points can be monitored through multiple log files that are created on the site system hosting the role. Table 6.13 details the system health validator point installation log file.

Table 6.13 System Health Validator Point Installation Log Files

Log File	Location	Description
SMSSHVSetup.log	ConfigMgrInstallationDirectory>\SMS\Logs	Details the installation process for the system health validator point

Table 6.14 details the system health validator point operational log files.

Table 6.14 System Health Validator Point Operational Log Files

Log File	Location	Description
Ccmperf.log	%systemdrive%\SMSSHV\SMS-SHV\Logs	Details the process of initializing the system health validator point performance counters
SMSSHV.log	%systemdrive%\SMSSHV\SMS-SHV\Logs	Details the basic operations of the system health validator point such as the initialization process
SmsSHVADCacheClient.log	%systemdrive%\SMSSHV\SMS-SHV\Logs	Details the process of retrieving health state references from Active Directory
SmsSHVCacheStore.log	%systemdrive%\SMSSHV\SMS-SHV\Logs	Details information about cached health state references
SmsSHVRegistrySettings.log	%systemdrive%\SMSSHV\SMS-SHV\Logs	Details information about the system health validator point while the service is running
SmsSHVQuarValidator.log	%systemdrive%\SMSSHV\SMS-SHV\Logs	Details client statement of health operations

Out of Band Service Points

Out of band service points let you interact with the out of band management controller that is installed with chipsets containing active management technology.

Computers with AMT allow you to manage the computer even if an operating system is not installed correctly or if the computer is turned off. Computers with AMT also support advanced power features, allowing you to reliably wake up computers instead of depending on the old Wake on LAN standard.

Out of Band Service Point Prerequisites

Out of band service points require that you have Configuration Manager 2007 SP1 or higher installed as well as a PKI infrastructure setup in your environment since out of band management requires the use of certificates to communicate with clients. Out of band service points can only be installed on site systems within a primary site. Secondary sites and server shares are not supported.

Installing an Out of Band Service Point

To install the out of band service point, choose a site server that will host the role in your environment and use the New Site Roles Wizard to complete the process. In our example, we will install this to our CHI-SITESYSTEM server. To install a state migration point, do the following:

1. Open the Configuration Manager console where the site system is located. In our example, we'll connect the Configuration Manager console to the CHI site.

2. Once the Configuration Manager console is open, go to the Site Systems node under your site.

3. Right-click on the Site Systems node and choose New > Server if you want to create a new site system that will host the software update point role or right-click on an existing site system and choose New Roles to add roles to an existing site system. In our example, we'll right-click on \\CHI-SITESYSTEM and choose New Roles.

4. The New Site System Server Wizard window is displayed. This window allows you to configure multiple options regarding the new site system as shown back in Figure 6.3. If this wizard is started on an existing site system, the options that were used to create it are shown here and can be edited if so desired. Once the correct options are selected, click Next to continue.

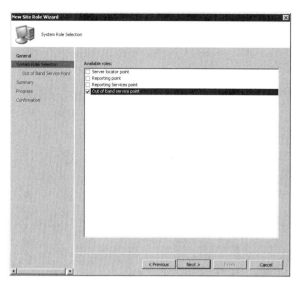

Figure 6.49
Selecting the Out of Band Service Point

5. The Site System Role Selection window is displayed. This window allows you to choose which roles will be installed to this site system. In this example, we'll install an out of band service point by checking the checkbox. Click Next to continue (Figure 6.49).

6. The Out of Band Service Point configuration window is displayed. This window allows you to control settings for the out of band service point. The configuration options for the out of band service point are shown in Figure 6.50.

- **Error—Retries**—This option specifies the number of times that power on commands will be sent to a computer. Power on commands are only resent if the computer failed to respond.

- **Error—Delay**—This option specifies the number of minutes between failed power on transmissions.

- **Transmission—Maximum**—This option specifies the number of power on transmissions that the out of band service point will send to the target computer.

- **Transmission—Wait**—This option specifies the wait period that will be used when sending power on commands to computers. This is used to help avoid saturating the network with power on commands.

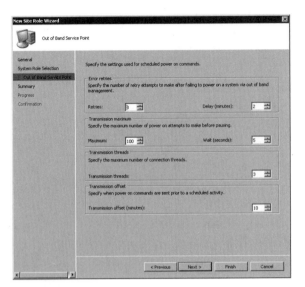

Figure 6.50
Out of Band Service Point Properties

- **Transmission Threads**—This option lets you specify the number of threads that will be used on the out of band service point to send power on commands. The higher number of threads relates to the amount of CPU utilization and bandwidth that is consumed by the out of band service point.
- **Transmission Offset**—This option lets you specify, in minutes, the amount of time that power on commands are sent prior to a task being executed such as software distribution. This ensures that the computer is awake before the advertisement is scheduled to start.

7. The Out of Band Service Point installation summary window is displayed. This lets you review your selections before you actually make any changes. In our example, everything is correct. Click Next to continue.

8. The Out of Band Service Point confirmation window is displayed. This shows you the results of the wizard. If any problems were encountered during the wizard, you will be notified here. Click Close to close the wizard (Figure 6.51).

Figure 6.51
Out of Band Service Point Confirmation

Out of Band Service Point Log Files

The installation and operation of out of band service points can be monitored through multiple log files that are created on the site system hosting the role. Table 6.15 details the out of band service point installation log file.

Table 6.15 Out of Band Service Point Installation Log Files

Log File	Location	Description
AMTSPSetup.log	<ConfigMgrInstallationDirectory>\SMS\Logs	Details the out of band service point installation process

Table 6.16 details the out of band service point operational log files.

Asset Intelligence Synchronization Points

Asset intelligence synchronization points are used to connect to System Center Online to download updated Asset Intelligence (AI) information. This ensures that you have the most up-to-date software catalog, which can help you automatically identify software titles in your organization.

Table 6.16 Out of Band Service Point Operational Log Files

Log File	Location	Description
Amtopmgr.log	<ConfigMgrInstallationDirectory>\SMS\Logs	Details operational aspects of the out of band service point including discovery, provisioning, and power control commands
Amtproxymgr.log	ConfigMgrInstallationDirectory>\SMS\Logs	Details operational aspects of the site server including discovery, provisioning, and power control commands

Asset Intelligence Synchronization Point Prerequisites

Asset intelligence synchronization points have an interesting prerequisite story. Originally, Microsoft only planned to allow software assurance customers the ability to connect to System Center Online to download catalog updates. They did this by requiring a special certificate during install time that had to be used to download the content. At the last minute, however, Microsoft decided to make this available to all customers but did not get the word out sufficiently so there was a lot of confusion on how to obtain the certificate. This caused customers to not install the asset intelligence synchronization points since they could not figure out how to obtain the certificate. Note that synchronization is only available with the SP1 release of Configuration Manager 2007.

After Configuration Manager 2007 SP2, the certificate is optional during setup so that anyone can use asset intelligence synchronization points.

Installing an Asset Intelligence Synchronization Point

The asset intelligence synchronization point must be installed to the top-most primary site in the hierarchy (the central site). In our example, we will install this to our LIS- CENTRAL server. To install an asset intelligence synchronization point, do the following:

1. Open the Configuration Manager console at the central site. In our example, we'll connect the Configuration Manager console to the LIS site.

2. Once the Configuration Manager console is open, go to the Site Systems node under your site.

3. Right-click on the Site Systems node and choose New > Server if you want to create a new site system that will host the software update point

role or right-click on an existing site system and choose New Roles to add roles to an existing site system. In our example, we'll right-click on \\LIS-CENTRAL and choose New Roles.

4. The New Site System Server Wizard window is displayed. This window allows you to configure multiple options regarding the new site system as shown back in Figure 6.3. If this wizard is started on an existing site system, the options that were used to create it are shown here and can be edited if so desired. Once the correct options are selected, click Next to continue.

5. The Site System Role Selection window is displayed. This window allows you to choose which roles will be installed to this site system. In this example, we'll install an asset intelligence synchronization point by checking the checkbox. Click Next to continue (Figure 6.52).

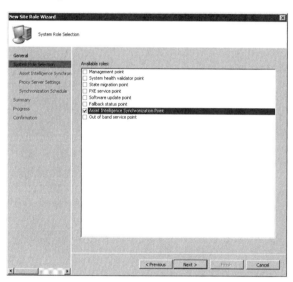

Figure 6.52
Selecting the Asset Intelligence Synchronization Point

6. The Asset Intelligence Synchronization Point configuration window is displayed. This window allows you to control settings for this role. The only configurable option on this window is to specify the System Center Online certificate provided by Microsoft. As stated earlier, this certificate is optional as of Configuration Manager 2007 SP2. In our example, we'll choose the defaults and click Next to continue (Figure 6.53).

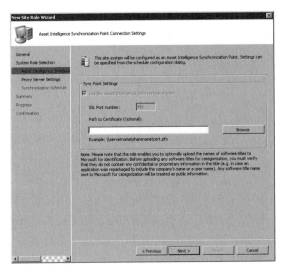

Figure 6.53
Asset Intelligence Synchronization Point Configuration

7. The Proxy Server Settings configuration window for the asset intelligence synchronization point is displayed. In our example, we'll choose the defaults and click Next to continue. The configuration options for the Proxy Server Settings window are shown in Figure 6.54.

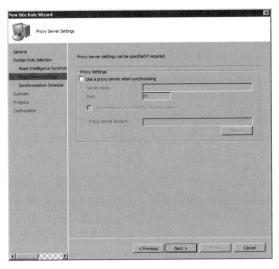

Figure 6.54
Asset Intelligence Synchronization Point Proxy Server Configuration

- **Use a proxy server when synchronizing**—If your asset intelligence synchronization point will need to connect to a proxy server to get access to the Internet, check this box to enable this setting.

- **Server name field**—Enter the name of the proxy server that will allow you to gain access to the Internet.

- **Port field**—Enter the port number that your proxy server uses to connect to the Internet.

- **Use credentials to connect to the proxy server**—If your proxy server requires authentication to access the Internet, check this box to enable this feature.

- **Proxy server account**—Enter the name of the proxy server account that will be used to access the Internet.

8. The synchronization schedule for the asset intelligence synchronization point is displayed. In our example, we'll choose the defaults and click Next to continue. The configuration options for the Synchronization Schedule window are shown in Figure 6.55.

- **Enable synchronization on a schedule**—This option allows you to synchronize the Asset Intelligence catalog with System Center Online using the schedule that you define below.

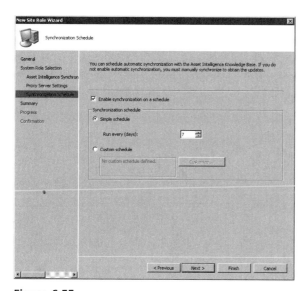

Figure 6.55
Asset Intelligence Synchronization Schedule Configuration

- **Simple schedule**—This option allows you to set up a simple schedule by specifying the number of days in which synchronization occurs.
- **Run every (days)**—This option allows you to specify, in days, how often the catalog is synchronized.
- **Custom schedule**—If you need to specify a custom schedule, such as every third day, you can specify this by selecting this option. Click the Customize button to set up these customized schedules.

9. The Asset Intelligence Synchronization Point installation summary window is displayed next. This lets you review your selections before you actually make any changes. In our example, everything is correct. Click Next to continue.

10. The Asset Intelligence Synchronization Point confirmation window is displayed. This shows you the results of the wizard. If any problems were encountered during the wizard, you will be notified here. Click Close to close the wizard (Figure 6.56).

Figure 6.56
Asset Intelligence Synchronization Confirmation

THE FINAL WORD

This chapter mainly focused on the installation of the site system roles, not on how to use them. As we move forward, we'll discuss most of these roles in detail so that you have a good understanding of how they are used and the gotchas that can occur.

CHAPTER 7

DEPLOYING CLIENTS

To take advantage of all of the management features that Configuration Manager has to offer, you will need to install the client on your Windows servers and workstations. The client is used as the mechanism to communicate with the managed systems. The client is configured to check in with the site's management point and will request the latest policy file. The policy file is based upon the settings that have been configured for the site and tells the client what it is supposed to do. The client will then configure itself according to the settings contained within the policy file.

As you will discover within this chapter, the client can be configured in a number of ways. During the initial install, many of the settings for the client are selected and enforced. After the client is installed, several options exist to manipulate the client settings, either by using the administrator console or by using scripts. Some of the configuration options can only be changed by manually manipulating the client settings, while others can be controlled easily through the console.

We'll start off with a discussion of the console and the many facets of its personality. Once you are familiar with the client components, we will jump into a discussion of the installation methods and all of the settings that can be configured when the client is installed. Finally, we will take a look at the options that exist when managing the client after the installation has succeeded.

Introduction to the Client

System Center Configuration Manager cannot manage Windows servers and workstations without installing a small client component first. The client is like an autopilot. On airplanes, the autopilot controls how the airplane behaves: where it is headed, the speed, altitude, and several other factors. The client controls certain aspects of the system: when the inventory runs, when to report metered software, when to notify if a system is not configured properly, when software needs to be installed, and several other functions. Whereas the autopilot does not control every aspect of an airplane, the client does not control every aspect of a system. Users can still perform tasks, run programs, and manipulate certain settings.

When the client is running on a system it shows up in task manager as the process ccmexec.exe. This process is only part of the picture. The client itself is made up of components known as agents. Agents are designed to control specific aspects of the managed system. There is an agent that is used to control hardware and software inventory, and another that manages software distribution. All of these agents take their orders from settings that are configured within the console.

Agents

In earlier versions of Systems Management Server, the agents were loaded as necessary. Until hardware inventory or software inventory was enabled, the agent was not installed on the managed system. Systems Management Server 2003 changed that. The client is now installed with all of the agents already available, but not enabled. The agents lie dormant until they are needed. Installing the client with all of the agents does consume more bandwidth initially, but managing the bandwidth consumption during that initial download is easier than trying to determine how you are going to deploy a new feature later on.

There are several agents that make up the Configuration Manager 2007 client. You will notice that immediately after the client is installed, the agents appear in an "Installed" state, as seen in Figure 7.1. This state will change shortly after the client has received its first policy. Contained within the policy is a set of instructions for each of the agents that are configured to run. For those that are configured to run, they will change to an "Enabled" state.

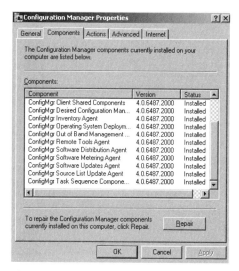

Figure 7.1
Configuration Manager Client Agents

CCM Framework

The CCM Framework is the underlying component that allows all of the other components to perform their functions. The status shows up as Installed and will remain that way. There are not any mechanisms within the console to manage the CCM Framework component.

CCM Policy Agent

The CCM Policy agent is responsible for accessing the policy from the management point. Once the CCM Policy agent has downloaded the policy, other components are notified as to the actions that they are supposed to perform.

CCM Status and Eventing Agent

As the components that make up the client perform actions, the CCM status and eventing agent is responsible for sending the captured information back to the management point. All of the status information that is generated during the typical processing is sent back to be processed by the site server. The site server will then filter the status messages and events based upon rules that are set within the administrative console.

ConfigMgr Client Core Components

As part of the installation of the client, the core components that allow the client to function and access parts of the operating system are installed. This component, just like the CCM framework, CCM policy agent, and eventing agent, does not have any mechanism in place for an administrator to configure.

ConfigMgr Client Shared Components

The ConfigMgr Client shared components comprise the components that are used by the operating system, the client, and other components. These shared components include items such as remote desktop controls, Windows Update agents and other components.

ConfigMgr Desired Configuration Management Agent

After the desired configuration management settings are configured within the console, the ConfigMgr desired configuration management agent is enabled. If the client system is a member of a collection that has a DCM Policy applied to it, the client will be instructed to scan the system for compliance. The rules are downloaded by the CCM policy agent as part of the policy.

ConfigMgr Inventory Agent

The ConfigMgr inventory agent is responsible for processing the software and hardware inventory on the system. The inventory is based upon the rules set within the console. There are two inventory rule types, software and hardware. When either of the inventory agents is turned on, the ConfigMgr inventory agent is enabled. Rules for performing inventory lookups are then included with the policy that is downloaded by the CCM policy agent, and the CCM status and eventing agent is responsible for delivering the generated inventory information back to the management point.

ConfigMgr Operating System Deployment Components

The ConfigMgr operating system deployment component agent is responsible for processing policy settings that are controlled by task sequences. Although we typically think of operating system deployment as a rollout of a new operating system, task sequences can be used without actually installing a new operating system. The ConfigMgr operating system deployment components will pass the task sequence information to the ConfigMgr task sequence components. The tasks that make up a task sequence will process commands and actions outside of the normal Configuration Manager agent processing.

ConfigMgr Out of Band Management Agent

Out of band management, as it applies to the Intel vPro technologies, allows an administrator to remotely access a system even while the operating system is not operational. There are several management options available, including starting a stopped system, checking and updating the BIOS, monitoring system startup, and configuring the boot environment. The ConfigMgr out of band management agent provides additional management functionality to the core vPro technologies. For more information about out of band management, see Chapter 8.

ConfigMgr Remote Tools Agent

As the name implies, the ConfigMgr remote tools agent is used to gain remote access to the system. Depending on the settings configured in the remote tools client agent settings, anyone who has been granted permissions to perform a remote control session will be able to view or interact with a logged on user's session. For more information about remote control tools, see Chapter 8.

ConfigMgr Software Distribution Agent

The ConfigMgr software distribution agent is responsible for making sure that advertised programs are installed properly. When an advertisement becomes available, an entry is placed in the system's policy. Once the policy is accepted by the system, any entries for software distribution are read by the ConfigMgr software distribution agent. The package information, program to be run, and distribution point that is to be used are evaluated and then managed.

ConfigMgr Software Metering Agent

Each program and process that runs on a system is monitored by the operating system. You can see them within the task manager component as they are running. Once the software metering agent is enabled, the ConfigMgr software metering agent becomes responsible for reviewing each process as it starts and stops. If the process matches a software metering rule, it is logged so that the information can be forwarded to the site server. For more information on software metering, see Chapter 9.

ConfigMgr Software Updates Agent

The ConfigMgr software updates agent is responsible for controlling all of the aspects of software updates. Once the software updates agent is configured, the settings are used to control the scanning, evaluation, and installation of updates.

ConfigMgr Source List Update Agent

As systems move from one subnet to another, and even from site to site, the ConfigMgr source list update agent will evaluate the client's location and update the network location where the software installation files are located. If the client moves to a subnet that has a distribution point from which it can get the software files, the ConfigMgr source list update agent will update the location to be the new, nearer distribution point.

ConfigMgr Task Sequence Components

Task sequences are typically configured as part of operating system deployment. Whenever a task sequence is configured and advertised to a system, the ConfigMgr task sequence components are responsible for processing each task sequence. For more information on operating system deployment, see Chapter 13.

Operating system deployment is not the only component that uses task sequences. Task sequences can be used to perform other actions, such as executing a series of actions on an existing system.

Client Configuration Options

The client has other configuration tabs available. Some of these will appear depending upon the features that have been enabled in the site. Two of the configuration tabs that always appear are Actions and Advanced, as seen in Figure 7.2. The Actions tab is used to initiate agent processes. For instance, when you want to run a hardware inventory on a client system, you can open up the control panel, double-click the Configuration Manager icon, select the Actions tab, click on the Hardware Inventory Client Agent, and click the Initiate Action

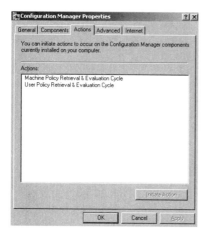

Figure 7.2
Actions Tab

button. At that point, the ConfigMgr inventory agent is notified that it needs to evaluate the hardware inventory and the action will start.

Actions Tab

The agents that appear within the Actions tab depend upon the agents that have been enabled for the site. Two actions always appear: Machine Policy Retrieval And Evaluation Cycle and User Policy Retrieval And Evaluation Cycle. These two actions will retrieve the policy for the client and then configure the other agents to start performing actions. Machine policy retrieval and evaluation cycle runs on a schedule that is configured in the site settings—typically every 60 minutes. The user policy retrieval and evaluation cycle will run if user policy evaluation is configured in the advertised program client agent settings. If it is enabled, the user policy is evaluated on the same schedule as the machine policy.

Advanced Tab

The Advanced tab, seen in Figure 7.3, is used to control the site and cache information for the client. The configuration options on this tab are not always available for editing. When the client is installed, there are switches that can be set that disable editing of these options unless the logged on user is an administrator.

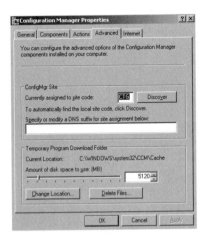

Figure 7.3
Configuration Manager Client Advanced Tab

If you do have the rights to configure the ConfigMgr site settings, you can manually change the site code for the client and force the client to discover the site code if one has not been assigned. To change the site code from an existing site code, enter the new site code into the Currently Assigned To This Site text box and click Apply or OK. The client will then reconfigure itself based upon the information it receives from the management point for the new site. If the client has not been assigned to a site yet, you can click the Discover button and have the client attempt to figure out which site it belongs to.

In the lower section of the Advanced tab, Temporary Program Download folder, you can configure where the client cache is located, the size of the client cache and you can delete any files that are stored in the client cache.

Updates Tab

When the software update client agent is enabled, all of the clients within the site will display the Updates tab, seen in Figure 7.4. The settings that you find on this tab allow the user to configure a schedule as to when updates are installed. If the Configuration Manager administrator configures updates to be deployed, the settings on this tab will control when the updates will be installed. However, if the administrator has configured a mandatory installation time, that time will be used if the time configured on the Updates tab is later than the mandatory installation time.

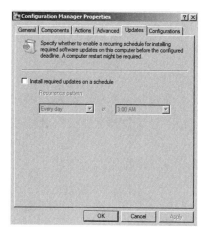

Figure 7.4
Updates Tab

Configurations Tab

When the desired Configuration Management client agent is enabled, all of the clients within the site will display the Configurations tab as seen in Figure 7.5. This tab displays the Desired Configuration Management baselines that are applied to the system. When a baseline is applied, the name of the baseline will appear in the window, along with the last evaluation time and whether the

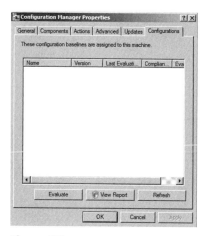

Figure 7.5
Configurations Tab

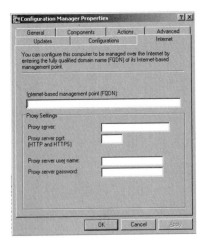

Figure 7.6
Internet Tab

system was in compliance or not. Anyone who has access to the client properties can select a baseline from the list and click Evaluate to re-run the evaluation process for that baseline.

Internet Tab

The Internet tab, as seen in Figure 7.6, appears when the client is installed in a native mode site. When this tab is available, the communication parameters for the client to communicate with the management point can be configured. For more information on managing native mode clients, see Chapter 8.

CLIENT INSTALLATION OPTIONS

Configuration Manager gives you myriad options when managing your infrastructure. Many of the management features are enabled via the client component. The client is controlled by the settings configured within the site settings as well as the installation options that are used when the client is installed. Careful planning of the client installation is required, especially if you have special requirements within your site.

The configuration options that you have when installing the client include the amount of logging that you want to receive, where the log files are located, the size of the client cache, where the client cache is located, and several other options. The CCMSetup.exe program is used to control the client installation. When invoked, CCMSetup will run according to the switches that are applied and then download the Client.msi installer file. As the CCMSetup starts the installation of Client.msi, it passes installation properties to control how Client.msi is installed. The following is a list of the switch options that are available.

- **/source:***PATH*—Typically, CCMSetup.exe downloads Client.msi from the site's management point. This switch can be used to specify a different source location to download the file.

- **/mp:***ComputerName*—This switch is used to identify one or more management points that will be used when downloading the client installation files. When specifying more than one management point, multiple /mp switches can be used, each referencing a different management point. This way, if the first management point is not available, another management point can be used to get the client installation files. One thing to remember when using this switch, it only references the management point to use when retrieving the client installation files, not the management point with which the client will be communicating.

- **/retry:***Minutes*—If CCMSetup cannot download Client.msi, the timeout value specified with this switch will control how long CCMSetup will wait before trying the download again. The default retry timeout is 10 minutes.

- **/downloadtimeout:***Minutes*—This switch will control how long CCMSetup will attempt to download Client.msi. CCMSetup retries downloading on the /retry setting interval until the timeout specified in this switch is reached.

- **/service**—This switch forces CCMSetup to run as a service using the local system account.

- **/noservice**—This switch will prevent CCMSetup from running as a service. Used when the local system account does not have the appropriate permissions to access network resources.

- **/forcereboot**—The default behavior during installation is to have CCMSetup exit after the client installation is complete and wait until the next reboot, even if a reboot is required to complete the installation. If the /forcereboot switch is used, the system will be rebooted if a reboot is required after installation has completed.

- **/logon**—This switch is primarily used with a logon script. When this switch is used, the client installation will check to see if the client is already installed. If it is installed, the current client installation will stop.

- **/BITSPriority:***Priority*—This switch controls the BITS download priority when client installation files are downloaded. The priority levels, from highest to lowest, are: FOREGROUND, HIGH, NORMAL, LOW.

- **/uninstall**—This switch will force the client software to be completely removed from the system.

- **/native:**Option—This switch specifies that the client will use native mode communication when installed. The options that are available:
  - CRL if you want to perform Certificate Revocation List checking
  - FALLBACK enables HTTP communication when roaming or performing initial site assignment
  - CRLANDFALLBACK enables both CRL checking and HTTP communication

- **/config:ConfigFile**—Using this switch, you can use a text file that contains the installation properties that control the installation. If using the /noservice switch, the ConfigFile must be stored in the same directory location as the CCMSetup file.

Other properties can be specified that directly affect the client installation. These properties are placed on the same command line as the CCMSetup properties that we just discussed. These properties are passed to the Client.msi file and will be used to control the setup and configuration of the client. The standard installation parameters are as follows:

- **SMSSITECODE = [AUTO |** *SITECODE*]—The site code can be specified at installation by using this option. Automatically setting the site code when Active Directory has been extended can be performed by using the option AUTO.

- **SMSMP =** *ManagementPointName*—The management point that the client will be assigned can be configured using this property.

- **SMSSLP** = *ServerLocatorPointName*—The server locator point that the client will use when it needs to determine the site's management point is configured using this property.

- **FSP** = *FallBackStatusPointName*—Using this property, the client's fall-back status point can be specified.

- **SMSCONFIGSOURCE** = **[R|P|M|U]**—This property allows you to spec-ify that the client configuration settings can be found in: R—the registry, P—command line properties, M—existing settings when upgrading an older client version, or U—upgrade the client to the latest version. These settings can be used alone, or in conjunction with one another such as SMSCONFIGSOURCE = RPU.

- **CCMINSTALLDIR** = *Dir*—By default the client is installed in the %WINDIR%\Ssytem32\CCM directory. The location can be controlled using this property.

- **DNSSUFFIX** = **DNSSuffix**—When the management point is configured to register DNS domain information, the client can automatically deter-mine the management point that it will be assigned to. Cannot be used in conjunction with SMSSITECODE=AUTO.

- **CCMADMINS** = *Domain\Admin1;Domain\Admin2*—When Configura-tion Manager administrators do not have local administrative rights on the system, this property can be used to grant them administrator rights to the Configuration Manager client. User or Group accounts can be specified and must be separated by semicolons.

- **CCMENABLELOGGING** = **[TRUE|FALSE]**—Client logging is enabled if this property is set to TRUE. By default, logging is enabled and the log files are stored in the %WINDIR%\System32\CCM\Logs directory.

- **CCMLOGLEVEL** = *[0|1|2|3]*—When logging is enabled, this property controls the amount of logging that is performed. By default, the logging level is set to 3. Level 3 logs errors only. Level 2 logs warnings and alerts. Level 1 logs informational, warnings, and errors. Level 0 enables verbose logging used primarily with troubleshooting.

- **CCMLOGMAXHISTORY** = *Number*—This property controls how many log files are kept for historical reporting purposes. The default number of log files is 1. If 0 is used, no log file history is saved.

- **CCMLOGMAXSIZE** = *size*—When used, this switch controls the size of the log files in bytes. Once this maximum size is reached, the log file is saved as a history log file unless the CCMLOGMAXHISTORY is configured at 0.

- **CCMDEBUGLOGGING** = [0|1]—This property can be used to turn debug logging off (0) or on (1). This property can only be used when CCMENABLELOGGING is set to true and should only be used for debug purposes.

- **SMSCACHEDIR** = *Dir*—Using this property, you can specify where the cache directory is located on the system. By default the cache is located in %WINDIR%\System32\CCM\Cache. This property can also be used in conjunction with the SMSCACHEFLAGS property to control where the directory is located based upon partition size or free space.

- **SMSCACHEFLAGS** = **Option**—When used in conjunction with the SMSCACHEDIR and SMSCACHESIZE properties, the location of the cache directory can be based upon partition size or free space and the size of the cache can be controlled. Multiple options can be configured using a single SMSCACHEFLAGS property by separating them with a semicolon. The property options are as follows:

  - **PERCENTDISKSPACE**—Specifies that the size of the cache is based upon a percentage of the partition where the cache is created. Must be used in conjunction with the SMSCACHESIZE property.

  - **PERCENTFREEDISKSPACE**—Specifies that the size of the cache is based upon a percentage of the free space on the partition at the time the client is installed. Must be used in conjunction with the SMSCACHESIZE property.

  - **MAXDRIVE**—Specifies that the cache will be located on the largest partition on the system.

  - **MAXDRIVESPACE**—Specifies that the cache directory will be located on the partition with the most free space.

- **NTFSONLY**—Specifies that the cache directory can only be created on a drive that is formatted as NTFS.

- **COMPRESS**—Specifies that the folder will be created and stored in compressed format.

- **FAILIFNOSPACE**—Specifies that the client software installation will stop and uninstall all of the components if there is not enough space on the client to create the cache directory.

- **SMSCACHESIZE**—Using this property will allow the cache directory to be sized to the specific MB. If the SMSCACHEFLAGS=PERCENTDISK-SPACE is used, the cache size can be defined as a percentage of the drive.

- **DISABLESITEOPT** = [**TRUE** | **FALSE**]—Setting this property to TRUE will restrict users that do not have administrative rights on the system from changing site settings on the Advanced tab of the Configuration Manager properties.

- **DISABLECACHEOPT** = [**TRUE|FALSE**]—Setting this property to TRUE will restrict users that do not have administrative rights on the system from changing cache settings on the Advanced tab of the Configuration Manager properties.

- **CCMALLOWSILENTREBOOT** = [**0|1**]—If a reboot is required following the installation of the client, the reboot will be allowed when this property is set to 1. The default setting is 0, which will wait until the next reboot of the system.

- **SMSDIRECTORYLOOKUP** = **Option**—When using WINS to locate the server locator point or management point, the option NOWINS specifies that WINS will not be used for lookup, WINSSECURE specifies that the client must check the management point's certificate signature and validate the authenticity of the management point before it will allow communication, and WINSPROMISCUOUS allows the client to communicate with the management point that is specified by the WINS server without checking the signature.

The properties that can be configured for native mode are as follows:

- **CCMALWAYSINF = [0|1]**—This property is used to specify whether the client will always be an Internet-based client or not. Setting this option to 1 will configure the client as Internet-based only.

- **CCMCERTCEL = [Subject: | SubjectStr]**—This property controls which certificate will be used when more than one certificate is available.

- **CCMCERTSTORE = StoreName**—This property controls the certificate store in which the certificate will be stored.

- **CCMHOSTNAME = ManagementPointFQDN**—This property defines the Internet based management point with which the client will communicate.

- **CCMHTTPPORT = Port**—This property controls the port that will be used when communicating over HTTP, typically port 80.

- **CCMHTTPSPORT = Port**—This property controls the port that will be used when communicating over HTTPS, typically port 443.

- **SMSPUBLICROOTKEY = Key**—This property specifies the trusted root key when the key cannot be retrieved by querying Active Directory.

- **SMSSIGNCERT = CertPathAndName**—This property specifies the path of the site server signing (public) certificate.

- **SMSROOTKEYPATH = RootKeyPathAndName**—This property is used when the Configuration Manager trusted root key needs to be reinstalled.

- **RESETKEYINFORMATION = [TRUE|FALSE]**—This property can be used when the client has the wrong Configuration Manager trusted root key.

The native mode properties and parameters are further explained in Chapter 8.

Real World—Non-Uniform Client Installations

While evaluating systems at CorporationX, I noticed that the operating system on many of the systems was not installed on the same partition. It was explained to me that over the years, different administrative teams had decided upon their own operating system installation options. Some believed in placing the operating system on the first partition, C:, while others would place the operating system on other partitions, using the excuse that they believed the system performance would be better.

The other problem that was encountered was the system partition size. Some were formatted to use large partitions of more than 100GB, while others were restricted to 20GB or less. Many of the systems with the smaller partitions did not have very much free space, sometimes less than 2GB. Knowing that the client would like to keep the default 5GB cache size, it was determined that the SMSCACHEFLAGS property would be used. The resulting options that were placed in the Client Push Installation properties were:

```
SMSSITECODE=AUTO CCMLOGMAXHISTORY=1 CCMLOGMAXSIZE=250000 DISABLESITEOPT
DISABLECACHEOPT SMSCACHEDIR=CACHE SMSCACHEFLAGS=MAXDRIVESPACE;NTFSONLY
CCMADMINS=DOMAIN\SCCMADMINS
```

CONFIGURING CLIENT INSTALLATION PREREQUISITES

Before the client will function within the site, additional configuration needs to be performed. The client can be installed without these prerequisites being in place, but it will not be able to perform any of the management functions. For everything to work, site boundaries need to be defined, the site system roles need to be created, and client discovery needs to be performed.

Configuring Boundaries

Boundaries play a critical role when it comes to the client. Without boundaries, the client cannot determine which site it is in. This becomes problematic for a few reasons. When the client is first installed, and the site code is not designated during the installation, the client will not be able to automatically determine to which site it belongs. Of course, there are other settings that need to be configured for automatic client installation, but boundaries define the IP addresses that are considered part of the site.

When the client cannot determine its residency, it will not be able to determine with which management point it should communicate. When the client cannot communicate with a management point, it will not be able to receive a policy and thus will not know what actions to perform. Essentially, the client becomes dormant, waiting until it can determine its site membership.

When Active Directory has been extended, site servers will send the boundary information to the nearest domain controller. This information is then recorded in the System Management container. Once the information has been sent, clients will be able to determine their site boundaries by sending a query to a domain controller. This information can then be used to automatically configure the client when it is installed, allow the client to determine if it is in its assigned site or if it is roaming, and determine if the client is considered to be in a fast or slow boundary for software distribution purposes. For more information on extending Active Directory and configuring boundaries, see Chapter 2.

Configuring Site System Roles

There are three site system roles that should be operational to support the client: management point, fallback status point, and server locator point. Of the three, the management point is the only site system that needs to be operational. As you know by now, the management point is responsible for giving the client its policy. The client also delivers status messages, state messages, inventory results, and metering information to the management point. If a management point is not available, the client becomes dormant, waiting for one to come online so that it can start functioning.

The fallback status point and server locator point are not necessary, but may be needed depending upon the site's needs. The fallback status point is a critical component when the site is configured for native mode. It is the system that receives status messages when the client cannot communicate with the management point. It does provide additional functionality during client deployment however. When the client installation starts, the administrator will not have any visibility into what is happening during the install. Only after the install completes, either successfully or unsuccessfully, will the administrator have any information relayed back to the site. The information that is sent by the client is not very verbose however, and it is sometimes difficult to determine the problem when installation fails. When the fallback status point is available, the installation information will be sent from the client installer files back to the fallback status point. This information will then be entered into the database. Administrators can then view the deployment reports to view what problems were encountered during the installation.

The server locator point is more widely used in scenarios where clients are in workgroups or untrusted domains. When the server locator point is available, clients that cannot query Active Directory can query the server locator point for the name of the management point of the site. The server locator point for the site can be included within the installation parameters by using the

SMSSLP=*ServerLocatorPointName* parameter or it can be entered into the WINS server used by clients.

Enabling and configuring the site system roles is further explained in Chapter 6.

Discovering Resources

When performing client installation, especially Client Push Installation, resources need to be "discovered" in order to efficiently push the client to resources. The process of discovering resources includes querying Active Directory for user, computer, and group accounts as well as scanning the network for systems and devices. When a resource is discovered, discovery data is entered into the Configuration Manager database. This information includes the resource name, type of resource it is, and other identifying information. Before a resource can be discovered, at least one discovery method needs to be configured.

There are four discovery methods that use Active Directory to retrieve resource information. Each one needs to be configured separately, but some of the discovery methods rely on others to be able to work correctly.

Active Directory System Discovery and Active Directory User Discovery

Computer accounts in Active Directory are discovered using the Active Directory System Discovery method. User accounts are discovered using the Active Directory User Discovery method. These two discovery methods have the same properties that you can configure. When enabled, the site system will send an LDAP query to the nearest domain controller or global catalog server, requesting a list of computer or user accounts that reside within the OUs and containers specified. The data that is returned with the LDAP response includes the computer or user name, fully qualified domain name, operating system type and version, IP address, and several other attributes. This collected data is then used for organizing the systems and users within collections.

To configure Active Directory System Discovery or Active Directory User Discovery, navigate to Site Settings > Discovery Methods and right-click the appropriate discovery method. Choosing Properties from the context menu will present the property tabs. The first tab, General, allows you to enable this discovery method and define the Active Directory paths that you will use when discovering resources. As seen in Figure 7.7, more than one path can be defined,

Figure 7.7
Configuring Search Paths

allowing you to control how much traffic you generate to the domain controller, as well as the system resources that will be consumed when processing the LDAP query.

By default, the entire domain is used as the query criteria. The advantage to searching through the entire domain is that you may find resources that were added to the domain, but reside within an Organizational Unit or container and you did not know they were there. If you do have good controls in place, and you know where all of the resources reside within Active Directory, you can start configuring the search locations by selecting the New button. The first configuration screen, seen in Figure 7.8, allows you to specify where you want to start the LDAP query. Choosing the option Local Domain will allow you to configure the OU or container that you want to query, based upon the hierarchy of the domain where the site server is a member.

The second option, Local Namespace, will present the domain information from the Forest Root domain, and all subdomains. Using this option will allow you to define a search path based on another domain from the one that site server is a member.

The final option allows you to configure the query to be sent to the nearest global catalog server. The typical queries use an LDAP call, but when you configure the discovery method to use this option, you can change the request to a Global Catalog request, thus bypassing any domain controller that isn't configured as a Global Catalog.

Figure 7.8
Choosing Base LDAP Query Location

At the bottom of the window, you have two options to work with: Recursive and Include Groups. The Recursive option will direct the site server to generate an LDAP query that will request responses that include resources that reside in child organizational units beneath the target organizational unit. The Include Groups option directs the LDAP query to include objects that are members of groups within the LDAP query path.

After clicking OK, you are presented with a screen that looks like Figure 7.9. This selection screen allows you to drill down to the path that you want to use

Figure 7.9
LDAP Search Location Selection

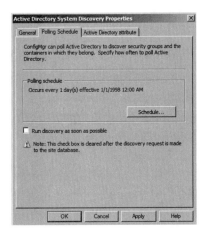

Figure 7.10
Polling Schedule Options

for your query. After you select the target organizational unit, it will appear within the previous windows in the Path text box. Selecting OK at this point will create the entry within the General tab. At this point, changes to the target location cannot be made. You will have to remove the search container from the list and recreate it with the correct path.

The second tab on the two discovery method properties is the Polling Schedule, as seen in Figure 7.10. From here, you can configure how often the LDAP query is sent to the domain controller. Clicking the Schedule button will present the standard Schedule window, as seen in Figure 7.11. The options at the top of the window allow you to set a start date and time. The date and time that is selected

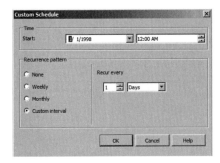

Figure 7.11
Scheduling Options

in this screen can be in the past or the future. Take note of the time however. The time that you select is the time that is used for the schedule. If you select 4:00 AM and the recurrence pattern is set to every Saturday, the LDAP request will be sent at 4:00 AM every Saturday.

The lower portion of the Schedule window allows you to set the recurrence pattern. You can set the recurrence to None, Weekly, Monthly, or Custom. If None is selected, you will have to run the query request manually. Weekly, Monthly, and Custom give you some very granular options as to when the query request will occur. You could set the recurrence pattern to daily by using the Custom option and specifying every day as the criteria.

Back on the Polling Schedule tab, there is a checkbox option labeled Run Discovery as Soon as Possible. When selected, as soon as you click OK or Apply, the LDAP request will be queued on the site server and processed as soon as a thread is available. You can run manual discoveries at any time, no matter how the schedule is set. Of course, this is the only way a discovery will run if you have set the schedule to None.

The final tab, Active Directory Attributes, is used to specify which attributes will be requested when the discovery runs. There is a core set of attributes that are collected when the discovery runs, and these cannot be changed. You can add additional attributes to the list if you would like to gather more information about the system. This can come in very handy for administrators that would rather not put the information in IDMIF files that are read during hardware inventory. The data can be entered within Active Directory and collected during the discovery process instead. For more information on IDMIF files, see Chapter 9.

Active Directory Security Group Discovery

The Active Directory Security Group Discovery is used to find Security Groups within Active Directory. The only caveat to this is that only Security Groups that have discovered resources as members are included. With that in mind, make sure you have run the Active Directory User Discovery at least once so that the user account resources can be evaluated against the security groups found in Active Directory.

Only two tabs appear on the Active Directory Security Group Discovery method: General and Polling Schedule. These two tabs have the same options as the Active Directory System Discovery and Active Directory User Discovery methods.

Active Directory System Group Discovery

The Active Directory System Group Discovery is used to find organizational units, global groups, universal groups, and distribution groups within Active Directory. The only caveat to this is that only organizational units and groups that have discovered resources as members are included. With that in mind, make sure you have run the Active Directory System Discovery at least once so that the computer account resources can be evaluated against the security groups found in Active Directory.

Only two tabs appear on the Active Directory System Group Discovery method: General and Polling Schedule. These two tabs have the same options as the Active Directory System Discovery and Active Directory User Discovery methods.

CLIENT INSTALLATION

There are several options available for installing the client on a server or workstation. Over the years, as System Management Server matured and became System Center Configuration Manager, many different methods of installation were designed. Some are used so that a user can install the client, others are available for administrators to install the client without user intervention. Some are push methods; others use a pull mechanism. There is an installation method that meets every need. With so many different installation methods, an administrator should take care and plan according to the requirements of the situation.

No matter which method is used, the installation steps remain the same. CCMSetup is the master program that controls all aspects of the installation. CCMSetup will start by determining which system is the site's management point. CCMSetup will use Active Directory if the Active Directory extensions have been applied or WINS if Active Directory has not been extended. If neither of these options work, the server locator point for the site, if it exists, will be queried. If all else fails, CCMSetup will search the folder that it was run from to determine if client.msi is also stored in that directory.

Once client.msi is found, the system's BITS service is checked. If BITS is not installed or out of date, BITS will be installed/updated to meet the requirements of Configuration Manager. CCMSetup will then download client.msi and perform the installation according to the properties applied.

Client Push Installation

As the name implies, Client Push Installation allows an administrator to specify the system where the client installation will take place. The site server will then create a connection to the system, copy the installation files, and initiate the installation. The file copy and installation is performed using what is known as the Client Installation Account. This account can be configured in the site settings under Client Installation Methods > Client Push Installation, as seen in Figure 7.12. You are not limited to configuring a single account in this area. Several accounts can be configured. When the installation attempt is performed, each of the accounts listed will be tried in order until a successful connection is made to the system.

The accounts that are configured as installation accounts can be domain accounts or local accounts. This allows organizations to use a local administrator account when installing the client instead of a domain account, especially a domain administrator account. All accounts have to be entered using the

Figure 7.12
Client Push Installation Account

domain\account format, which is easy enough to configure for domain accounts, but when local accounts are to be used, it's not as intuitive. There are actually two formats that can be used when entering a local account: *.\account* and *localhost\account*.

On the third tab of the Client Push Installation Properties, Client, you can enter the properties that control Client.msi. The text box can be used to enter each of the properties and the options that you need to configure the client during installation.

There are two ways to perform a client push. The administrator can initiate the push installation from the console, or it can be configured to automatically occur whenever a new resource is discovered. Both methods have their place when deploying the client to systems. Careful planning of the deployment will enable you to install the client efficiently and not overburden your network.

So when would you want to use each of the methods mentioned? When you are initially deploying the clients within the site, you will probably want to employ a phased approach. That way, not all of the systems will receive the client at the same time. This will allow you to control the amount of network traffic that is consumed. Once the initial phased approach is complete, you will probably want to make sure that all of the systems that are introduced into the organization are also managed. When you reach this point, you can turn on the automatic push installation to newly discovered resources. There will always be "one-off" systems that you will need to perform a different installation method on, such as systems within the perimeter network that have a firewall between them and the site server. For those systems you will need to evaluate the other installation options to see which one fits your needs the best.

If you want to push the client to an individual system, you can open a collection that includes the system, such as All Systems, right-click on the system's name, and select Install Client. This will start the Install Client Wizard as seen in Figure 7.13.

You can use the push install method on several systems at a time by right-clicking a collection and selecting Install Client. Again, the Install Client Wizard will start. This time however, you need to make sure that you want to install the client on all of the systems within the collection. By default, any system that is assigned to the site will be targeted for client installation.

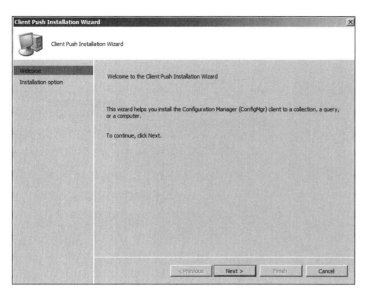

Figure 7.13
Install Client Wizard

As you progress through this wizard, you will be presented with several options that you can use to control how the client is installed. By default, the options that are configured in the Client Push Installation properties are used when installing the client. However, some of the options can be overridden from the wizard options. On the first page of the wizard you will be presented with the options seen in Figure 7.14.

By default, domain controllers are not included in the installation options. By excluding domain controllers, you can make sure that you do not affect the operation of domain controllers and global catalog servers. If you are planning on managing domain controllers, you can select the first checkbox, Include Domain Controllers.

The second option, Only Include Assigned Systems, will restrict the installation to only systems that fall within the site boundaries. This is the only option that is selected by default. When you look at the console information, one of the columns that shows for resources is Assigned. Any system that is assigned to the site will be listed with a Yes in this column. If you right-click a system that is listed as not assigned and start the wizard, you will have to select the checkbox for Only Include Assigned Systems, otherwise the client install will not proceed.

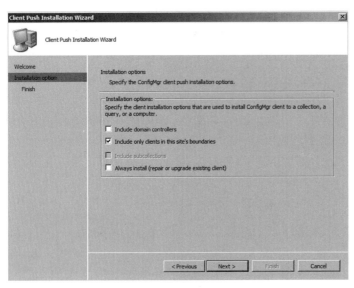

Figure 7.14
Install Client Wizard Installation Options

The third option on this page is Include Subdirectories. If you had selected only one system when starting the Install Client Wizard, this option has no effect. If you had selected a collection and started the wizard, all systems within the collection and any subcollection will be targeted for client installation. Before selecting this option, make sure that you know how many systems are included in the subcollections. You do not want to introduce too much network traffic if you are performing the client installations during production hours. For more information on creating and managing collections and subcollections, see Chapter 11.

Note

Take care when selecting the systems that you want to push the client. If you select multiple systems within the console and select Install Client from the Actions pane, you are actually pushing the client to all of the systems within the collection. If you watch closely, when you select two or more systems in the details pane, the system action for Install Client disappears. The only Install Client option available is in the Collection actions. Right-clicking on one of the selected systems will not show the Install Client option either.

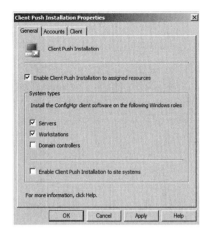

Figure 7.15
Client Push Installation Properties

The client can be automatically deployed to assigned resources by selecting the appropriate options on the General tab of the Client Push Installation Properties, seen in Figure 7.15. The first checkbox, Enable Client Push Installation to Assigned Resources, should include the word "automatically" somewhere in the name. When selected, any system that is discovered using one of the discovery methods that is within the site boundaries will be considered assigned to the site. Once assigned to the site, the client will be deployed to the system. Because you probably don't want to deploy the client to every system in your organization when the site is built, you will probably want to keep this checkbox clear.

There are some deployment methods that do make sense to use this option. You can still perform a phased deployment by selecting this checkbox and then adding in boundaries one at a time. As the discovery runs, any systems that are now seen within the site due to the new boundary entries will have the client installed. This deployment method allows an administrator to configure a boundary during the workday, then letting the discovery method run at night when network utilization is minimal.

Another time this may come in handy is when the site is small and the administrator wants to get all of the system into the database as soon as possible. Automatically deploying the client can come in very handy and reduce some of the administrative overhead associated with running the push installation by hand.

The other checkboxes on the General tab control which system types will have the client installed. You are not required to have all of the systems within the site become clients. You can specify that servers, workstations, domain controllers, and site systems will be targeted for client deployment. If you don't want your domain controllers to have the client installed, simply clear the checkbox. Later, if you want to push the client to them, you can select the checkbox and the client will be installed during the next discovery cycle.

Software Update Client Installation

One of the more interesting methods of installing the client is to use the software update client installation method. When enabled, new metadata is added to the software update point. As a system is scanned for update compliance, the client is detected as a missing update. The client software itself, which is loaded on the software update point as another update, is installed on the system. The nice thing about this method is that it is a pull mechanism, the client software is not "pushed" to the system. If there are firewalls that block a push installation, this method will work to get the client installed. Another benefit is that the system installs the client, and a user account is not required to have administrative rights in order to install the client.

Group Policy Installation Options

Another pull installation method is to use group policy to install the client. The software installation policy settings can be used to enable this. As the system starts up, the group policy is applied. If the client has not been installed, the policy will enforce the installation using settings that are included in the GPO settings. To use this method, you will have to import a special administrative template into the GPO that you are planning on using. The systems will also have to point to an existing software update point as their Windows Server Update Services location. The administrative template, ConfigMgr2007Installation.adm, is located in the TOOLS\ConfigMgrADMTemplates directory of the installation media.

After importing the template into the group policy that you are going to use, you can open the properties of the configure client deployment settings. The options that are available are the enabled radio button and the CCMSetup field. Enter the properties that you want passed to Client.msi within the CCMSetup field.

The entries that are configured within group policy are embedded into the registry of the systems where the group policy is applied. When the client installation begins, CCMSetup will check the registry settings and apply them during the installation. If the CCMSetup command line has any property entries applied to it, those entries will override the entries applied within the group policy.

Logon Script Options

Using a logon script can be an efficient method of installing the client. When a user logs on, the client installation is invoked. This is another pull method, so if there is a firewall blocking any push installation, the client can still be installed. The drawback to this method is that the user needs to have administrative privileges on the system to install the client. There is no mechanism to install the client with another account.

When using the logon script installation options, there is one switch that can be used that will keep the client installation from occurring every time the user logs on. When the /logon switch is used, CCMSetup will check to see if the client is already installed on the system. If it is installed, CCMSetup will stop processing and the client will not be reinstalled. Failure to include the /logon switch will cause the client to reinstall every time the user logs on.

Manual Installation

As the name implies, manual installation requires that a user install the client software on the system. As with the logon script installation option, the user that is performing the installation will need to have administrative rights to install the software. However, for test purposes, individual system build and custom installation needs, the manual installation method is easy to perform. From a command line, you can start the CCMSetup.exe program to begin the installation of the client.

Software Distribution Installation

There are several software distribution methods that compete with System Center Configuration Manager. As organizations move away from the other methods and adopt System Center Configuration Manager, they can package the client software with the current software distribution method they are using.

Once deployed, the client will remain dormant until System Center Configuration Manager is installed and configured.

Computer Imaging

Finally, the last method of installing the client is a "hybrid" version. Including the client in a computer image allows you to easily build a system from a preconfigured image. The initial installation of the client needs to be a manual installation however. Once installed, captured, and deployed, you know that the client is configured correctly for all of the systems that receive the image.

Creating the initial reference image with the client already installed required you to perform some specific actions. First, the client needs to be manually installed on the reference system. During the manual install, the site code should not be specified. By not setting a site code, the client does not receive any information from existing sites. Once installed, the client's process needs to be stopped.

Because the system needs to be unique within the organization, all computer certificates need to be removed. Failure to remove the computer certificates will cause authentication problems within the organization. If the certificates are not removed, all of the systems that receive the image will be seen as the same system as far as any certificate-based authentication is concerned.

Client Approval

After the client has been assigned to a site, it will start attempting to communicate with a management point. The initial communications that occur include some validation between the client and the management point. This validation checks to see if the client is allowed to send data to the management point or not. Otherwise known as "approval," data sent from clients will either be accepted by the management point, or it will be rejected.

In native mode, the client has a certificate that proves its identity. When it attempts to communicate with the management point for the first time, the client's identity is validated and the client is automatically approved to communicate. At that point it will be allowed to receive a policy and start configuring itself to perform the actions specified within the site settings.

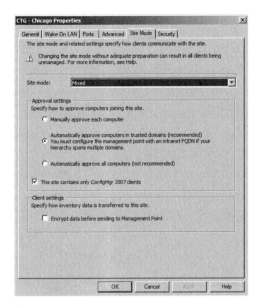

Figure 7.16
Configuring Approval Settings

In mixed mode, things are a little bit different. The client does not have a certificate to prove its identity, so it is up to the administrators to determine whether they want to allow clients to communicate. There are three settings that can be configured to control communication. These settings can be found on the Site Mode tab in the Site properties, as seen in Figure 7.16.

The first setting, Manually Approve Each Computer, forces the administrators to review each of the newly installed clients and manually approve them for communication within the site. Although this is the most administrator intensive option, it is also the most secure. Even if a client is installed on one of the systems within your domain or forest, they cannot be managed, nor can they send status or state messages to the management point. This setting guarantees that you know which systems are approved and will alleviate the potential denial of service attack against your site.

The second setting, although not as secure, is used more often than the other two. This setting, Automatically Approve Computers In Trusted Domains (Recommended), will verify the domain membership of each client system and automatically approve the systems within domain in your forest and all trusted domains. This setting alleviates the administrative overhead associated with approving systems, but does not stop someone from within your domain from causing problems.

The final option, Automatically Approve All Computers (Not Recommended), is the least secure option. This setting will allow any computer that has a client installed and configured for the site to start communicating with the management point. Although the least secure, if you have several systems that are not members of your domain, such as workgroup-based systems or systems from untrusted domains, you can automatically configure them to communicate with the management point.

On the Site Mode tab, you can change between native and mixed modes. When you select native mode from the drop-down, the options change to allow you to configure the certificate that will be used within the site. When you select the mixed mode option, the approval settings appear.

Approving Clients

Clients appear as not approved for two reasons. Either the site is in Manually Approve Each Computer Mode—in which every system will initially appear as not approved, or the site is configured as Automatically Approve Computers In Trusted Domains (Recommended)—in which workgroup systems or systems from untrusted domains are configured for the site. In either case, the systems that are not approved will appear within a collection with the Approved column showing No, as seen in Figure 7.17.

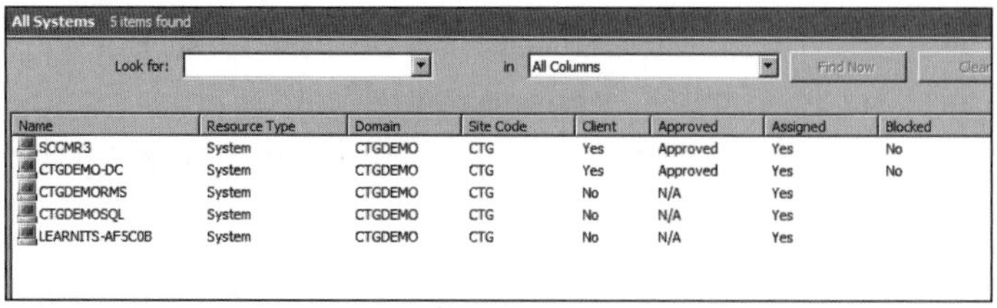

Name	Resource Type	Domain	Site Code	Client	Approved	Assigned	Blocked
SCCMR3	System	CTGDEMO	CTG	Yes	Approved	Yes	No
CTGDEMO-DC	System	CTGDEMO	CTG	Yes	Approved	Yes	No
CTGDEMORMS	System	CTGDEMO	CTG	No	N/A	Yes	
CTGDEMOSQL	System	CTGDEMO	CTG	No	N/A	Yes	
LEARNITS-AF5C0B	System	CTGDEMO	CTG	No	N/A	Yes	

Figure 7.17
Viewing Systems' Approval Settings

To approve a client, it is as simple as selecting the client system within the collection and selecting Approve from the Actions pane or the right-click menu. Once approved, the Approve column will change to Yes and the client will start communicating with the management point.

Disabling Clients

You may notice that clients can be approved, but there is not an option to "unapprove" a client. Instead, you have the option to stop clients from communicating with the management point by selecting the client system within a collection and choosing Disable from the Actions menu or the right-click menu. As you will notice as soon as you perform this action, the Approved column does not change to No. The client is still approved within the site, but by selecting Disable, you have told the management point to ignore all communication from the selected client.

UNINSTALLING THE CLIENT

Previous versions of System Management Server did not have an uninstall option for the client. The only option for uninstalling the client was to run a program from the SMS Toolkit called CCMCLEAN.exe. This caused some frustration for many administrators the first time they wanted to uninstall the client and couldn't find an obvious method to do so.

That all changed with System Center Configuration Manager. If you look in the list of properties that are listed earlier in this chapter, you will notice that one of the switches listed is /uninstall. As you can imagine, the client software will be removed from the targeted system. When the uninstall is performed, there is no user interaction required and there is not any detailed information displayed about what happened during the uninstall. There is a log file left behind in the client installation folder, named CCMSetup.log that does include information as to what happened during the uninstall process.

THE FINAL WORD

Without the client loaded on a system, Configuration Manager cannot perform any of the management functions it is famous for. In this chapter we reviewed the prerequisites needed to support the client, the installation options available for installing the client, and the methods of performing the installation. Now that the client is installed and functioning, we need to take a look at how we can manage the client. In the next chapter, we will evaluate the management options available for mixed and native mode clients, as well as how to perform out of band management and remote control.

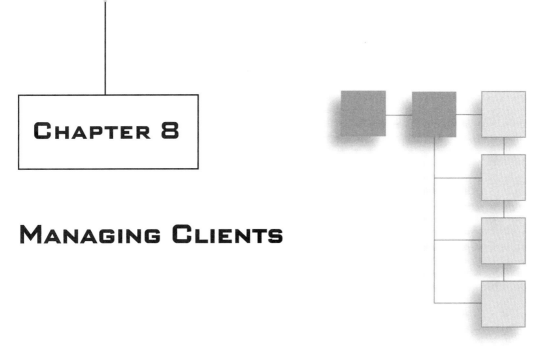

CHAPTER 8

MANAGING CLIENTS

There are special client configurations that are used to manage systems. In this chapter, we will discuss Internet based client management, out of band management, and remote tools. Internet based client management is used to manage systems that are connected to the Internet. Out of band management allows you to work with systems at the BIOS level, starting, stopping, and monitoring how they are running. Remote tools allows an administrator to view the desktop of a managed system, thus enabling the administrator to assist users as they are working.

INTERNET BASED CLIENT MANAGEMENT

Before you can manage clients that are sitting at Starbucks or lounging at home, you need to make a few alterations to your Configuration Manager site. Internet based client management is only supported when a site is in native mode. Of course, native mode is only available when you have a public key infrastructure in place. While it is not required for you to implement a full PKI within your organization, it is typically cheaper to do so. The only drawback to running your own PKI is that you have to make sure you have someone on staff who understands how to manage it. If you don't want to manage your own PKI, you can purchase certificates from a provider. Purchasing certificates for use on all of your client systems can be extremely expensive.

Public Key Infrastructure

As you are planning your move to native mode, you will have to create certificates for use on the site server, all of the site systems, and the clients within the site. In this section, we will discuss the certificate requirements as well as the system configuration needs at the server and workstation levels.

There is a lot of planning that goes into a public key infrastructure. Due to the complexity involved, several companies prefer to allow third-party companies to manage the certificates that are used within their network. Due to the number of certificates that are needed to support Internet based client management, we recommend that you bite the bullet and start investing in supporting your own public key infrastructure. There are several good books on the subject, and you will find guidance on Microsoft's TechNet site to help you get started.

Site Server Signing Certificate

The Site Server Signing Certificate is used to prove the identity of site data. When a client requests a policy from a management point, the management point signs the policy in both mixed and native mode. The client is then guaranteed that the policy is being received from the management point. In native mode, the policy is signed by both the management point and the site server. This additional signing not only proves the identity of the management point, but also the site where the management point resides. Having the site server sign the policy validates that the management point has not been compromised and that it is the management point for the site. This validation becomes extremely important when the management point is exposed to the Internet.

Specific information is required when creating the Site Server Signing Certificate. To correctly identify the site, site server, and management point, the Site Server Signing Certificate has to be created with the appropriate settings in order to work. The Site Server Signing Certificate is primarily a document signing certificate. Whenever a document, such as a client policy, is to be sent to a system, the Site Server Signing Certificate is used to prove the validity of the file.

Creating Site Server Signing Certificate Template To create the Site Server Signing Certificate template that is used to sign files, follow these steps:

1. On Certificate Server, click Start > Programs > Administrative Tools > Certification Authority.

2. Expand the name of your certification authority (CA), and then click Certificate Templates.

3. Right-click Certificate Templates, and click Manage.

4. In the results pane, right-click Computer in the Template Display Name column and select Duplicate Template.

5. In the Properties of New Template dialog box, on the General tab, enter a template name for the Site Server Signing Certificate Template and then select Publish Certificate in Active Directory.

6. Click the Subject Name tab.

7. Click Supply in the request.

8. Click the Extensions tab.

9. Verify that Application Policies is selected and then click Edit.

10. In the Edit Application Policies Extension dialog box, select both Client Authentication and Server Authentication, and then click Remove.

11. In the Edit Application Policies Extension dialog box, click Add.

12. In the Add Application Policy dialog box, select Document Signing as the only application policy and then click OK.

13. Verify Application Policies: Document Signing is the only entry in the Properties of New Template dialog box and click OK.

14. Click the Issuance Requirement tab.

15. Select CA Certificate Manager Approval.

16. Click OK and close the Certificate Templates administrator console, certtmpl – [Certificate Templates].

17. In Certification Authority, right-click Certificate Templates, click New > Certificate Template to Issue.

18. In the Enable Certificate Templates dialog box, select the new template you have just created, SCCM Site Server Signing Certificate, and then click OK.

Requesting the Site Server Signing Certificate   To request the Site Server Signing Certificate, follow these steps:

1. On the site server, load Internet Explorer and connect to the Web enrollment service with the address http://*cert.server.com*/certsrv, where *cert. server.com* is the fully qualified name of your server.

2. On the Welcome page, select Request a Certificate.

3. On the Request a Certificate page, select Advanced Certificate Request.

4. On the Advanced Certificate Request page, select Create and Submit a Request to This CA.

5. On the Advanced Certificate Request page, specify the following:
   - Under the Certificate Template section, select the SCCM Site Server Signing Certificate template.
   - Under the section Identifying Information for Offline Template, in the Name text box, enter the following: The site code of this site server is <xxx>, where <xxx> is the site code of the site. This string needs to be entered exactly as shown with no punctuation of any type.
   - Under the section Key Options, enable Store Certificate in the local computer certificate store.
   - Under the section Additional Options, enter your choice for Friendly Name, such as SCCM Site Server Certificate.

6. Click Submit.

7. On the Certificate Pending page, you will see that your certificate request has been received but requires an administrator to issue the certificate. Make a note of the displayed Request ID.

Approving the Site Server Signing Certificate   To approve the certificate request, follow these steps:

1. On the certificate server, in Certification Authority, click Pending Requests.

2. In the results pane, you will see the requested certificate with the Request ID displayed on the Web enrollment page.

3. Right-click the requested certificate, click All Tasks, and then click Issue.

4. Close Certification Authority.

Installing the Site Server Signing Certificate   To install the Site Server Signing Certificate, follow these steps:

1. On the site server, load Internet Explorer and connect to the Web enrollment service with the address http://*cert.server.com*/certsrv, where *cert. server.com* is the fully qualified name of your server.

2. On the Welcome page, click View the Status of a Pending Certificate Request.

3. On the View the Status of a Pending Certificate Request page, click the hyperlink of the friendly name you supplied for the Site Server Signing Certificate.

4. On the Certificate Issued Web page, click Install this certificate.

5. If you are prompted with a Potential Scripting Violation warning message, click Yes.

6. The results page should display that your new certificate was successfully installed.

Web Server Certificate

Some site systems, such as the management point, require Internet Information Services World Wide Web Service to function. When the site is in native mode, all of the client systems will communicate with the Web server through a secure channel using Secure Socket Layer (SSL) encrypted communication. These systems require a certificate to not only prove their identity, but to also encrypt the data they are sending.

Creating the Web Server Certificate Autoenrollment Group   In smaller environments, all of the site systems that require IIS services may be on the same server. In larger environments, the roles could be distributed among several servers to enhance performance. The easiest way to manage the systems needing a Web Server Certificate is to create a security group and add the site systems to the group. This group will then be granted the ability to automatically enroll and install the Web Server Certificate.

To create the security group for Web Server Certificate Autoenrollment, follow these steps:

1. On the domain controller, click Start > Programs > Administrative Tools > Active Directory Users and Computers.

2. Right-click the domain, click New, and then click Group.

3. In the New Object – Group dialog box, enter SCCM Server Accounts as the Group name and then click OK.

4. In Directory Users and Computers, right-click the group you have just created and then click Properties.

5. Click the Members tab, and then click Add to select the member server.

Creating the Web Server Signing Certificate   To create the Web Server Signing Certificate template, follow these steps:

1. On certificate server, while still running the certification authority management console, right-click Certificate Templates and click Manage to load the certificate templates management console.

2. In the results pane, right-click the entry that displays Web Server in the column Template Display Name, and then click Duplicate Template.

3. In the Properties of New Template dialog box, on the General tab, enter a template name to generate the Web certificates that will be used on Configuration Manager site systems, such as SCCM Web Server Certificate, and select Publish Certificate in Active Directory.

4. Click the Subject Name tab, select Build from this Active Directory Information, and then select the following for the Subject Name format:
   ▪ **Fully distinguished name**—This option is required for Internet based client management.

5. Click the Security tab, and remove the Enroll permission from the security groups Domain Admins and Enterprise Admins.

6. Click Add, enter SCCM Web Server Certificate in the text box, and then click OK.

7. Select the following Allow permissions for this group: Read, Enroll, and Autoenroll.

8. Click OK and close the Certificate Templates management console, certtmpl – [Certificate Templates].

9. In the Certification Authority management console, right-click Certificate Templates, click New, and then click Certificate Template to Issue.

10. In the Enable Certificate Templates dialog box, select the new template you have just created, SCCM Web Server Certificate, and then click OK.

11. Do not close Certification Authority.

Manually Requesting the Web Server Certificate Adding systems to the autoenrollment group will allow systems to request certificates automatically. The only drawback is that the system needs to be rebooted in order for the group membership to take place. If you do not have the luxury of restarting a system to enroll a certificate, you can manually request the certificate. The process is very similar to the process used when requesting the Site Server Signing Certificate.

To manually request the Web Server Certificate, use the following steps:

1. Restart the member server to ensure it can access the certificate template with the configured permission.

2. Click Start, click Run, and type mmc.exe. In the empty console, click File and then click Add/Remove Snap-in.

3. In the Add/Remove Snap-in dialog box, click Add, click Certificates, and then click Add.

4. In the Certificate snap-in dialog box, select Computer account and then click Next.

5. In the Select Computer dialog box, ensure Local computer: (the computer this console is running on) is selected and then click Finish.

6. In the Add Standalone Snap-in dialog box, click Close.

7. In the Add/Remove Snap-in dialog box, click OK.

8. In the console that now displays Certificates (Local Computer), expand Certificates (Local Computer) and then click Personal.

9. Right-click Certificates, click All Tasks, and then click Request New Certificate.

10. On the Welcome to the Certificate Request Wizard page, click Next.

11. On the Certificates Type page, select SCCM Web Server Certificate from the list of displayed certificates and then click Next.

12. On the Certificate Friendly Name and Description page, optionally enter a friendly name and description to help you identify this certificate and then click Next.

13. On the Completing the Certificate Request Wizard page, click Finish.

14. You should see the Certificate Request Wizard dialog box informing you that the certificate request was successful.

15. Close Certificates (Local Computer).

Configuring IIS   Once the Web Server certificate has been created, IIS needs to be configured to use the certificate. The certificate needs to be imported for IIS to use, and Secure Socket Layer settings need to be applied before clients can connect to the site systems.

To configure IIS, perform the following steps:

1. On the member server, start Server Manager.

2. Expand Roles > Web Server > Internet Information Services (IIS) Manager.

3. In the Connections pane, expand Sites, right-click Default Web Site, and then select Edit Bindings.

4. Select https and click the Edit button.

5. In the Edit Site Bindings window, select the web server certificate you just created and click OK.

6. Click Close.

7. Close Server Manager.

Computer Certificate

Every client within a native mode site needs to have a certificate to function correctly. Even in many mid-sized companies, configuring certificates for every client's system can be a daunting task. Client systems can have their computer certificates automatically generated by using Group Policy. Correctly configuring the autoenrollment settings for workstations and servers that will be managed by Configuration Manager will ease the administrative burden of installing certificates on each of the systems.

Configuring Computer Autoenrollment Group Policy   The easiest way to configure autoenrollment is to create a group that has permissions to autoenroll a certificate. Once you add a computer account to the group, the computer will request and install the appropriate certificates when they start up.

To create the group that will be used for autoenrollment, follow these steps:

1. On the domain controller, click Start > Administrative Tools > Group Policy Management.

2. Right-click the domain, and then select Default Domain Policy and click Edit.

3. In the Group Policy Object Editor, navigate to Computer Configuration/ Windows Settings/Security Settings/Public Key Policies.

4. Right-click Automatic Certificate Request Settings, click New, and then click Automatic Certificate Request.

5. In the Welcome to the Automatic Certificate Request Setup Wizard, click Next.

6. On the Certificate Template page, select Computer from the list of available certificate templates and then click Next.

7. On the Completing the Automatic Certificate Request Setup Wizard page, click Finish.

8. Close Group Policy Management.

Verifying Autoenrollment   The process of requesting and installing a certificate will occur in the background as the computer starts up. To verify that the certificate was installed correctly, follow these steps:

1. Open a command prompt with elevated privileges and run the command gpupdate /force.

2. Log on with an account that has administrative privileges.

3. Click Start, click Run, and then type mmc.exe.

4. In the empty management console, click File, and then click Add/Remove Snap-in.

5. In the Add/Remove Snap-in dialog box, click Add > Certificates > Add.

6. In the Certificate Snap-in dialog box, select Computer account and then click Next.

7. In the Select Computer dialog box, ensure Local computer: (the computer this console is running on) is selected and then click Finish.

8. In the Add Standalone Snap-in dialog box, click Close.

9. In the Add/Remove Snap-in dialog box, click OK.

10. In the console that now displays Certificates (Local Computer), expand Certificates (Local Computer) and then click Personal.

11. In the results pane, confirm a certificate is displayed that has Client Authentication displayed in the Intended Purpose field and Computer displayed in the Certificate Template field.

12. Close Certificates (Local Computer).

13. Repeat steps 1 through 12 on the member server that will be configured as the management point to verify that it also has a client certificate.

Native Mode

The site needs to be in native mode before any of the benefits of Internet based client management can occur. After the Site Server Signing Certificate has been issued, the site can be put into native mode. Of course, there is nothing stopping you from creating the appropriate certificates before the site is installed and then installing the site in native mode. As a matter of fact, installing the site in native mode is the default option during the installation of the site server.

When installing the site in native mode, you do have to have the Site Server Signing Certificate already installed on the site server. If it is installed, the certificate will appear within the installation wizard. If there is more than one document signing certificate on the computer, make sure that you choose the correct certificate; otherwise, the site will not function correctly.

Changing the site to native mode is a simple process as long as the certificate is available. The property page that is used to switch the site to native mode is found within the site properties. The Site Mode properties page is used to configure native mode. Using the Site Mode drop-down, the Site Mode properties page changes to display the settings specific to native mode. The first thing you will need to configure is the Site Server Signing Certificate. Click the Browse button and select the appropriate certificate from the certificate store.

Note

When initially installing and configuring your site, use mixed mode. Native mode increases the level of complexity for the site. Introduce native mode once you have the site working as planned so that you do not have to troubleshoot certificate and public key infrastructure problems at the same time.

IBCM Site Systems

Four site system roles are supported for Internet based client management—management point, distribution point, software update point, and fallback status point.

Management Point Configuration

Management point properties are used to control which systems the management point will support. The drop-down within the management point properties controls the clients that can connect. When supporting both Internet and Intranet clients, the Allow Intranet and Internet Client Connections option needs to be selected. When two different management points are used, as in the case where the Internet management point is located in the perimeter network, each management point will have a specific client setting. The management point on the internal network will be configured with the Allow Intranet-Only Client Connections option. The management point within the perimeter network will be configured with the Allow Internet-Only Client Connections option.

Distribution Point Configuration

The distribution point properties that are used to control client communication are very similar to those configured within the management point properties. The settings are the same between the two site systems, but the distribution point settings are found within the Communication Settings section of the General tab of the distribution point properties. The same rules apply for which setting you need to select based upon the client type that the distribution point will support.

Software Update Point Configuration

The software update point can be configured to support Internet and Intranet clients. As with the other roles, the software update point within the internal network does not have to be configured to allow Internet based clients. If this is the case, and the active software update point is configured with the option Do Not Allow Access To Internet Based Clients, additional configuration needs to be performed. The Internet Based tab of the software update point properties can be used to specify the system that will be used to support the Internet-based clients. As with the software update point, the active Internet based software update point can be a standalone software update point or a network load balanced cluster of systems running the software update point role.

Fallback Status Point

The fallback status point is the oddball system when the site is in native mode. It is the only system that is not configured for secured communication. Whereas every other site system that required IIS is configured with a Web Server Certificate, the fallback status point will not be configured with one. The fallback status point is used whenever a client has problems communicating using SSL. If, for instance, the client cannot communicate with the management point, it will send status messages to the fallback status point.

The Allowed Client Connections section is used to specify whether Internet and/ or Intranet connections are allowed. Depending upon your network design, you could have a fallback status point that is used to support your Intranet clients while another supports your Internet clients. You could also have a fallback status point that is used to support both. Configuring this option will control which clients are allowed to send messages to the fallback status point.

The remaining two options are used to throttle the state messages that are sent from the fallback status point to the site server. To keep from overloading the site server and the site database, these settings can be configured to control the amount of data that is sent within a specified timeframe. The default setting of a maximum of 10,000 State Messages within a 3600 second window will usually suffice in many organizations. If your SQL Server and site server can handle the additional load, and the number of state messages are not choking the network, you can increase this number. Decreasing this number does have the undesirable affect of slowing down the state messages as they are sent from the clients to the fallback status point and then forwarded to the site server.

Firewall Considerations

Communication between the site systems within the site is usually allowed within the Intranet. The internal network allows the ports and protocols to be sent and received without any special firewall, router, or switch changes. When you introduce systems that will be within the perimeter network, you may have to configure special rules on the firewalls that separate the perimeter network from the Intranet. The following ports are needed between the site systems that reside in the perimeter network and the site server and site systems in the Intranet.

- **Management Point to Site Database Server**—Port 1433. Communication between the management point and the site database must run on this port. Microsoft does not support changing the port.

- **Management Point to Site Server**—Ports 445, 135 and dynamic RPC ports

- **Distribution Point to Site Server**—Ports 445, 135 and dynamic RPC ports

- **Software Update Point to Site Server**—Ports 445, 80 or 8530, and 443 or 8531 for SSL

- **Upstream Software Update Point**—80 or 8530, and 443 or 8531

- **Fallback Status Point to Site Server**—Ports 445, 135 and dynamic RPC ports

IPSec

Communication between the site systems and site server use several ports, especially when installing site system roles. Whenever RPC ports are required, controlling the dynamic range of ports used can be problematic. Instead of opening several ports on the firewall that separates the perimeter network and the Intranet, you can instead configure IPSec policies to manage the communication between the site systems in the perimeter network and those in the Intranet. The ports required for IPSec are:

- UDP Port 500
- IP Protocol 50
- IP Protocol 51

As you create the IPSec policies, you can use any of the supported security methods, including Kerberos, Certificates, or Pre-Shared Keys. If the systems within the perimeter network are not within the same forest as the internal network, using Kerberos is off the table. Of the two remaining options, Pre-Shared Keys are the easiest to initially implement, but do not grant a high level of security and require manual intervention whenever the keys need to be changed.

Client Installation Options

In Chapter 7, the client installation switches were discussed. As you perused through the available installation switches, you may have noticed that some of the switches are used specifically for Internet based client management. The most important of these client options is the CCMHOSTNAME switch. CCMHOSTNAME is used to specify the name of the Internet based management point. The data that you associate with the CCMHOSTNAME entry is found on the Internet tab of the Configuration Manager properties on the client systems. Let's assume that you need to configure your client systems to communicate with the management point ibcm-mp.cengage.com. The CCMHOSTNAME entry would appear as CCMHOSTNAME=ibcm.cengage.com.

OUT OF BAND MANAGEMENT

Out of band management was introduced in SCCM SP1 to serve the purpose of providing management capabilities for the Intel vPro chipset. Out of band management (OOBM) allows ConfigMgr to connect to a computer's AMT controller without having to go through the SCCM client agent. This allows for the management of computers that are powered off, sleeping, or otherwise unresponsive. SCCM SP1 provides both provisioning as well as management capabilities for machines with the Intel vPro chipset. Once provisioned, SCCM utilizes Windows remote management technology (WS-MAN) to connect to the AMT controller on client machines.

Out of band management includes the following functionality:

- Waking up machines
- Powering off machines
- Restarting machines
- Accessing the BIOS (and bypassing the BIOS password if supported)
- Booting from an external device
- Booting to a command-based DOS like OS to run commands (Serial over Lan)
- Reimaging a machine by booting from a boot image on the network or via a PXE server

With SP2, the management capabilities were extended further. With SP1, the functions listed above were supported over an unauthenticated wired network. With SP2 came support for 802.1X wired connection as well as wireless connections. Additionally, the following functionality was also added:

- Auditing/Logging of AMT features
- Support for different power states
- Ability to save up to 4096 bytes in ASCII in the NVRAM of the management controller

Out of Band Management Point

Before machines can be managed via the OOBM functionality in SCCM, they must be provisioned. SCCM SP1 and beyond provide the framework for provisioning the machines so they can be fully managed using the OOBM functionality. In order to provision vPro machines, the OOBM service point must first be installed at a primary site where the clients will be provisioned.

OOBM Service Point

Out of band management point can be installed on a separate site system server or an existing site system server. However, it cannot be installed on a secondary site server or a server share. Only one OOBM service point can exist per primary site. Before the site system can be defined from within the SCCM console, certain prerequisites must be met:

- Windows Remote Management (WinRM) 1.1 or later must be installed on server(s) to host the OOBM service point role
- AMT Provisioning Certificate
- Server Authentication Certificate
- Out of Band Management OU container

Windows Remote Management (WinRM)

Windows Remote Management (WinRM) is the Microsoft implementation of WS-Management Protocol, a standard Simple Object Access Protocol (SOAP)-based, firewall-friendly protocol that allows operating systems and hardware (from different vendors) to interoperate.

The WS-Management protocol specification provides a standardized way for systems to access and exchange management information across an enterprise. WinRM and *Intelligent Platform Management Interface (IPMI)*, along with the Event Collector are components of Windows Hardware Management. It provides a common way for systems to access and exchange management information across the enterprise.

Certificates

There are two certificates necessary to provision AMT machines using System Center Configuration Manager 2007: The AMT Provisioning Certificate and the Server Authentication Certificate.

These certificates are necessary to install the OOBM service point in your SCCM environment as well as to provision the AMT machines via SCCM.

AMT Provisioning Certificate   The AMT Provisioning Certificate is used by SCCM to provision Intel AMT computers. This certificate can either be purchased from an external certificate authority such as GoDaddy or Verisign, or can be created internally by an enterprise certificate authority. However, in using an internal certificate, the root certificate thumbprint (certificate hash) needs to be input manually on each machine you wish to provision, which makes it a very difficult methodology outside of a lab environment.

The AMT provisioning certificate is configured in the out of band management component, which in turns installs on any OOBM service point site system server.

Server Authentication Certificate   This certificate facilitates the secure communication between provisioned vPro machines and the OOBM console. It therefore resides in the RAM of the AMT controller and is not visible to Windows. During the provisioning process, the OOBM service point facilitates the installation of this certificate. An enterprise certificate authority is necessary to generate this certificate as well as the ability to automatically approve certificate requests from the primary site server where the OOBM service point resides.

Out of Band Management OU Container

Out of band management requires that SCCM publish an Active Directory (AD) object to an Organizational Unit (OU) that will store the AMT machines once provisioned. SCCM will publish an AMT object in the specified OU for each machine provisioned by the OOBM service point. The primary site server for the site the OOBM service point resides in needs to have full rights to this OU for publishing purposes.

Installing the OOBM Service Point

Now that we have an understanding of the components required to install an OOBM service point, let's proceed to the installation of the service point.

Out of Band Management Component Configuration

The first step is to configure the component.

1. In your SCCM console, navigate to Site Settings > Component Configuration > Out of Band Management.

2. Double-click on the Out of Band Management module to get to its properties.

3. On the General tab, under the Provisioning Settings section, input the AD OU previously created to store the provisioned machine objects.

4. Unless changed on all machines, leave the MEBx Account to: Admin. Click Set to input the password for the admin account.

Note

The password set will be used to reset the default password on the MEBx controller, which is set to "admin" by default. If that default password has been changed from admin, this step of the provisioning process will be ignored, and the manually set password will be left.

5. Check the Allow Out of Band Provisioning box, and leave the port default.

6. Next, under the Certificates section, click Browse under the Provisioning Certificate and browse to the .pfx file associated with the third-party provisioning certificate. Input the associated password for the certificate.

7. Click Select for the Certificate Template and enter the Server Authentication template previously created on the Enterprise CA.

8. Go to the AMT Settings tab.

9. Here, add user accounts/groups of users that will be managing the machines via out of band capabilities. These accounts are authenticated via Kerbros during the OOB management sessions.

10. Select the appropriate features/rights for each individual group/user and check off the appropriate boxes.

11. Under the Default IDE-redirect image section, browse to a location where a boot ISO resides. If you don't want to leverage this functionality, leave it blank.

12. For the Manageability is on in the following power state:

Leave default of Always On (S0-S5) unless you want to limit the ability for OOB management to specific power states.

Check off all the boxes below:
- Enable Web interface
- Enable serial over LAN and IDE redirection
- Allow ping responses
- Enable BIOS password bypass for power on and restart commands (requires that the manufacturer has enabled the BIOS password bypass option for AMT)
- Enable Support for Intel WS-MAN translator (this allows OOB service point to communicate with AMT systems with firmware less than version 3.2.1, and requires WS-MAN translator to be installed on the OOB service point)

13. Next, on the Provisioning Settings tab add digest user and password.

Note

If the default admin account/password have not been modified manually on the controller or via another management tool, there is no need to add an account here. SCCM is configured to use the default account/password. In case of a mixed environment where some machines have the default account/password while others have a set of different account passwords, enter all non-default account/passwords in this section to ensure SCCM tries all combinations to access the controller.

14. Next, on the Provisioning Schedule tab, define the provisioning schedule. The default value is set to run every day on a simple schedule.

Now, the out of band management component is properly configured, and the installation of the out of band service point can begin.

Out of Band Service Point Installation

The out of band service point serves as the provisioning tool within SCCM as well as the point through which AMT controllers can be controlled via the SCCM console.

1. Navigate to the Site Systems node under Site Settings, and select a site system onto which you want to install the out of band service point.

2. Right-click on the site system and select New Role.

3. On the General tab of the wizard, ensure the FQDN of the site system is displayed, click Next.

4. Select the out of band service point, and click next.

5. On the Out of Band Service Point tab, leave default settings, click Finish.

The OOB service point is now installed, and will be listed under the roles of the site system it was installed on. The OOB service point is now ready to provision and manage Intel AMT devices.

Provisioning AMT Machines

Once the out of band service point has been installed and configured, SCCM is ready to provision AMT machines. While the vPro machines come with the AMT controller, they need to be provisioned before the management capabilities can be realized. There are various methods available to provision the AMT machines; however, we will focus on SCCM's ability to provision them. Once provisioned, SCCM also provides the capability of managing the provisioned machines via the SCCM console. The management capabilities will be discussed in the next section of this chapter.

Configuring Network Discovery for AMT Controllers

In order to provision AMT machines, SCCM must be able to discover machines with the AMT controller. The out of band service point looks for network devices that are listening on the IANA registered port numbers TCP 16992 and TCP 16993. This is achieved via network discovery. In the SCCM console, under discovery methods, selecting Network Discovery will allow for the discovery of AMT controllers. This option is only available once a site server has been configured as the out of band service point.

Alternatively, you can right-click on a machine or a collection and manually initiate a discovery of AMT controllers.

Creating a Collection to Provision AMT Machines

Once discovery is configured, machines with the AMT controller can be discovered, and the discovery data will be input into the SCCM database. This data not only identifies machines with AMT controllers, but also whether they're provisioned or not. Based on this information, the next step in the provisioning process is to create a collection that identifies all AMT machines that aren't yet provisioned.

1. Create a new collection and name it Unprovisioned AMT Machines.

2. In collection properties, go to the query section.

3. For the criteria, select System Resource—AMT Status, and set the value to 2.

Two (2) represents an unprovisioned machine. Once provisioned, this value will change to 3. This will allow you to have another collection that defines a provisioned machine simply by using the value of 3 as the criteria.

Once the AMT network discovery has occurred, and unprovisioned AMT machines are discovered, this collection will be populated. Once those machines are provisioned, they will automatically be removed from this collection.

Automatically Provisioning the AMT machines

Once the discovery begins to populate the Unprovisioned AMT Machines collection, we can begin the process of automatically provisioning the machines. The process is very simple once the out of band service point has been installed and properly configured. The AMT network discovery identifies machines with AMT controllers, populates the collection we have created with the appropriate query based criteria, and now we're ready to enable automatic provisioning on that collection.

1. Right-click the collection and select Modify Collection Settings.

2. Navigate to the Out of Band tab. Check the box for Enable Automatic Out of Band Management Controller Provisioning.

This enables SCCM to automatically provision machines with the AMT controller. Once they are provisioned, their AMT Status changes to 3. Create another collection named Provisioned AMT Machines. For the criteria for the collection, select System Resource—AMT Status, and set the value to 3.

Monitor the status of this collection. As AMT machines are provisioned, and a discovery cycle has run, their status will change to 3, and will begin to drop out of our Unprovisioned AMT Machines collection and begin to populate the Provisioned AMT Machines collection. At this stage, the provisioning process has been implemented, and all AMT machines that qualify all the prerequisites for provisioning via SCCM will automatically be provisioned as they are introduced to the SCCM environment.

Managing Provisioned Machines

Once an AMT machine has been provisioned, all the out of band functionality described earlier can be realized for that machine directly from the SCCM console. To manage a provisioned resource via the out of band service point, simply right-click on the resource, and select the Out of Band Management option and select Out of Band Management Console. You can also run the console via a command line from the bin folder of the SCCM install location:

```
\bin\oobconsole.exe -s <siteserver> -t <resourceID>
```

You must know the resource ID of the machine you want to manage, making the SCCM console the easier method for management. However, you may have a scenario in which a group of admins do not have access to the SCCM console but still need to manage machines out of band.

Once you launch the OOBM console, a separate console is presented for the specific machine you are managing.

Out of Band Management Console

The console is split into eight separate sections.

- System Status
- System Information
- Power Control
- System Event Log
- IDE-Redirect Log
- System Audit Log
- Serial Connection
- Data Storage

System Status   The System Status section displays some basic system information for the system being managed:

- The power state
- IP address
- Host name

- Domain suffix
- System ID
- Date of last refresh
- Time of last refresh

System Information   The System Information section displays hardware inventory for the AMT controller. This information is not standardized and can vary from manufacturer to manufacturer.

Power Control   This section allows for the control of power states for the managed computer. You can shut down, restart, or power on the managed machine. The remote machine doesn't need to be powered off to be able to be managed via the out of band management console.

In the ability to power on or restart the managed system, there are options for how you want the machine to power on:

- Normal Boot
- IDER (IDE Redirection) Boot from an ISO image defined in the OOB service point configuration
- BIOS
- Force Hard Drive Boot
- Force CD/DVD Boot
- Force PXE Boot

These options are useful when the OS is not responsive, allowing for the reimaging of a machine via out of band capabilities.

System Event Log   This section displays activity for the management controller on the selected computer with the following buttons:

- Clear Log
- Set Log Level

The log level can be set to one of the following:

- Errors

- Warning

- Verbose

IDE-Redirect Log   This section displays activity for any IDE-Redirection sessions initiated for the system. This is only applicable to SCCM SP2 and above, and in SP1, this activity is detailed in the System Audit Log.

System Audit Log   This section displays the audit logging information for any auditable components of the AMT controller. In SCCM SP1, this section also logs the IDE-Redirect activity for the controller. There is the ability to export the system audit log, and also to clear the system audit log via this section.

Serial Connection   This section allows for a serial connection via a terminal emulation session to the managed system, allowing for the execution of commands and character based applications.

Data Storage   This section allows for the viewing and storage of up to 4096 bytes in ASCII in the AMT data store on the controller. This functionality is only available with SCCM SP2 and above.

Process for Acquiring a Third-Party Provisioning Certificate

In order to leverage an internal PKI certificate as the provisioning certificate, the root hash of the CA has to be manually input into the MEBx of each AMT controller. This is a very tedious task that cannot be automated or deployed via a scripting methodology. As such, the easiest way to provision AMT machines is to acquire a third-party certificate. The certificate may be acquired from a multitude of vendors including GoDaddy and Verisign.

The process of acquiring a third-party provisioning certificate is as follows:

- The certificate type must be Deluxe SSL or Premium SSL. Standard SSL will not work.

- The OU has to explicitly be OU=Intel(R) Client Setup Certificate.

- CN = ServerName.domain.com (this must be the FQDN of the Provisioning Server for Remote Configuration generating the CSR).

- Organization = The legal name of your organization that can approve your certificate request.

To generate the CSR for the certificate request from a third-party vendor, the following steps must be executed.

1. On your server, launch IIS Manager. Within IIS manager, select Server Certificates.

2. Within Server Certificates, select Create Certificate Request.

3. In the Request Certificate window, fill in the appropriate information. Click Next.

4. Leave the Cryptographic Service Provider default. Change the bit length to 2046. Click Next.

5. Specify the location and file name for the certificate request. Click Finish.

6. Once saved to file, open the file. This will need to be cut and pasted into a request for third-party provisioning certificate.

Once this information has been provided to GoDaddy or Verisign, a provisioning certificate will be issued which will allow for the provisioning of AMT machines without the need to manually input data into the MEBx BIOS.

REMOTE TOOLS

Imagine that you are an administrator who is responsible for supporting and troubleshooting thousands of computers spanning multiple sites. Your typical computer users are not what you would call tech savvy and frequently call the help desk for basic support. Because you can't interact with their computers, it's very difficult to walk them through basic troubleshooting steps without getting an on-site technician involved. This causes a loss of productivity and frustration for all parties involved. To help with these types of scenarios, Configuration Manager 2007 includes a set of tools—referred to as remote tools—to help ease the pain. The Remote Tools section within Configuration Manager 2007 allows you to remotely view, operate, and log remote events all from the Configuration Manager console.

Note

Client computers must have the Configuration Manager client installed as well as the remote tools client agent enabled for remote operations to work successfully. We will talk about these options in the next section.

Configuring the Client Agent

After the Configuration Manager client has been deployed to the workstations in your site, the remote tools client agent must be enabled for remote operations to succeed. This can be done using the Client Agents node within the Configuration Manager console under the Site Management node. There are five tabs within the remote tools client agent properties that allow you to configure options such as security and notifications. These are listed below:

- General
- Security
- Notification
- Remote Assistance
- Remote Desktop

General Tab

The General tab allows you to enable the remote tools client agent on client computers. If the client agent is enabled, the following options can be set:

- **Users cannot change policy or notification settings in the remote control control panel**—This option specifies that users cannot make changes in the remote control control panel applet that is installed when the Configuration Manager client is installed.

- **Ask for permission when an administrator tries to access clients**—This option specifies that users must grant access to administrators who are trying to remotely connect using the remote tools (remote control) feature.

- **Level of access allowed for Windows 2000 clients**—This option specifies the level of control that is granted to the user initiating the remote connection. You can choose between full control or no access.

- **Level of access allowed for Windows XP or later clients**—This option specifies the level of control that is granted to the user initiating the remote connection. You can choose between full control, view only, or no access.

Security Tab

The Security tab allows you to specify who is allowed to view and control client computers using remote tools and remote assistance by specifying users or groups. The users or groups that you specify in this section are added to the ConfigMgr Remote Control Users local group that is added on each computer when the Configuration Manager client is installed.

Tip

If a global group is nested within a local group and the local group is defined within the permitted users list, the local group is not enumerated causing users within the global group to not have the necessary permissions. Make sure to specify the global groups within the permitted users list to allow appropriate access.

Notification Tab

The Notification tab allows you to specify if visual or sound notifications are enabled on client computers. These notifications are used when a remote control session is active. The options on this tab are:

- **Display a visual indicator**—This option allows you to enable a visual indicator for the user when an administrator is connected to their computer. When enabled, you can choose between a status icon on the taskbar or a status indicator on the desktop.

- **Play a sound**—This option allows you to enable an audio indicator for the user when an administrator is connected to their computer. When enabled, you can play a sound when the session begins and ends or repeatedly during the session.

Note

These settings only apply to the remote tools (remote control) feature, not to remote assistance.

Remote Assistance Tab

The Remote Assistance tab allows you to specify whether Configuration Manager can start a remote assistance session on a remote computer. The groups defined in the permitted viewers list are added to the Offer Remote Assistance Helpers local group on each remote workstation where the Configuration Manager client is installed and the remote tools client agent is enabled. Note that the remote assistance feature always requires permission from users on remote computers.

The options on this tab are:

- **Configure unsolicited remote assistance settings**—This setting enables an administrator to connect to a remote computer using remote assistance even though a user has not requested assistance.

Tip

Enabling this option is the same as enabling the Offer Remote Assistance policy located under Computer Configuration\Administrative Templates\System\Remote Assistance.

- **Configure solicited remote assistance settings**—This setting enables a user to ask for assistance using the remote assistance feature.

Tip

Enabling this option is the same as enabling the Solicited Remote Assistance policy located under Computer Configuration\Administrative Templates\System\Remote Assistance.

- **Level of access allowed**—This option specifies the level of control that is granted to the user initiating the remote assistance connection. You can choose between full control, remote viewing, or no access.

Note

The Remote Assistance feature on the site server must be installed for the remote assistance option to work successfully.

Remote Desktop Tab

The Remote Desktop tab allows you to specify if users defined in the permitted viewers list can initiate remote desktop connections to remote computers via the Configuration Manager console. If enabled, the following settings can be defined:

- **Allow permitted viewers to connect using remote desktop connection**—If this option is selected, users defined in the permitted viewers list can use the Configuration Manager console to initiate a remote desktop connection to remote computers.

- **Require network level authentication on computers running Windows Vista**—If this option is specified, connections will only be granted to computers that support network level authentication (NLA). This includes Windows Vista and Windows 7.

- **Disable remote desktop connection**—If this option is specified, remote desktop connections cannot be initiated from the Configuration Manager console including users defined in the permitted viewers list.

Initiating a Remote Control Session

There are three different methods that can be used to remote control a computer via the remote tools option within Configuration Manager 2007. These are described next.

Remote Tools (Remote Control)

As we discussed briefly in Chapter 1, the remote control feature included with remote tools uses the collaboration technology that was first introduced with Windows Vista to provide a safe, fast, and efficient connection using the RDP protocol. The remote control option differs from normal remote desktop sessions by giving an administrator the ability to remotely view and operate a user's computer while he is actively using it. This means that the remote computer's screen is not locked when you start a remote control session. Unlike the remote control feature that was included in SMS 2003, administrators cannot remote control a user's computer unless they are logged into the computer. In other words, you cannot interact with a remote computer when it is at the logon screen (Ctrl+Alt+Delete).

To start a remote control session using remote tools, right-click on a computer within the Configuration Manager console and choose Start > Remote Tools.

Remote Assistance

Remote assistance is built into Windows XP and higher operating systems and allows a more advanced interaction experience between the remote operator and the user by offering features such as chat. Remote assistance is ideal if you need to talk with the user using chat or if you need added security when connecting to remote computers. If you decide to use remote assistance, this feature must be enabled on the site server in which the Configuration Manager console is connected. Also note that the remote user must accept the remote assistance request before you have the ability to remote view or remote control their computer.

To start a remote assistance session using remote tools, right-click on a computer within the Configuration Manager console and choose Start > Remote Assistance.

Remote Desktop

If a user is not logged into a workstation, the remote control and remote assistance features cannot be used. If you try to connect to a computer using remote tools or remote assistance that is in a logged out state, the remote tools client agent detects that no user is logged in and prompts you to use the standard remote desktop connection (mstsc.exe) instead. Note that this can only occur if the remote desktop feature is enabled within the remote tools client agent.

To start a remote assistance session using remote desktop, right-click on a computer within the Configuration Manager console and choose Start > Remote Desktop Client.

THE FINAL WORD

Managing the Configuration Manager client is rather easy and straightforward when you are managing systems within your network. There are some gaps in coverage with the basic client, however. This chapter introduced management tools that go a long way to fill some of those gaps. Internet based client management allows you to manage many of the client features when the managed system is connecting through the Internet. Out of band management is available to manage Intel systems that are either not turned on, or you need to manage components that are not native to Configuration Manager, and are available through the Intel architecture. Finally, remote tools can be used to access systems and control systems.

In the next chapter we are going to cover the asset collection and management of systems. With tools found in Configuration Manager, you are able to discover hardware configuration, installed software, and the software usage on managed systems. Using this information, administrators can determine usage patterns, software licensing requirements, target software deployment, and even determine unauthorized software installations.'

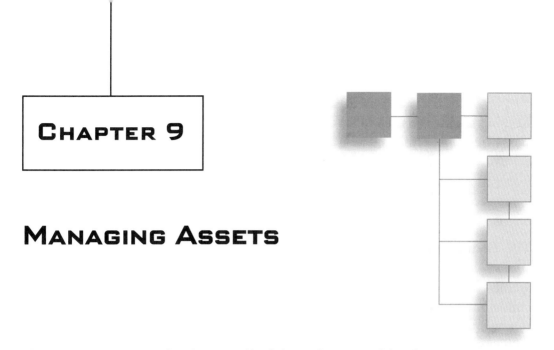

CHAPTER 9

MANAGING ASSETS

Show me a company that knows all of the software and hardware components used within its organization and I will show you a happy, but overworked company. Let's face it, obtaining a full inventory of all of the hardware and software within your organization is no small feat. The hardware that you approved for purchase may be recorded in your hardware spreadsheet or database, but were you informed about the external drive that Susan in Accounting just put on her system so that she can do a quick backup of her files? And even though you probably know the software that makes up your line of business applications, you probably don't know about that handy little app that George just installed on his laptop. And even if you do know what software you have installed in your company, do you know what is actually being used?

System Center Configuration Manager has components built in to assist you with your hardware and software inventory. After the client is installed on a system, it can perform several queries to determine what hardware is installed, and how the hardware is configured. Software can also be discovered. You will be able to record what software is installed, what versions are in place, and what is being used. In this chapter we will look at the components that are used to discover and record that hardware and software inventory, as well as the software usage.

MANAGING HARDWARE INVENTORY

Keeping track of hardware inventory doesn't seem like it will be that hard of a task when you first take it on. However, unless there are some strict change controls and good documentation in place, the installed hardware can change over time. As components such as hard drives and memory fail, or upgrades to components are made, the hardware inventory database can quickly become out of date.

The Configuration Manager client can perform inventory on the managed systems within the site on a periodic basis. It is actually quite amazing the amount of detail that Configuration Manager reports. Any of the hardware configuration information that is stored in the WMI can be reported. You will not want all of the detail that is available however. Most of the information that is contained within the WMI will not do you any good to collect. There are several settings that would just take up valuable space within your database. You just might want some of the information that is not collected by default. At the same time, there might be some information that is collected that you don't need.

Enabling Hardware Inventory

The first thing you will need to do when collecting hardware inventory is to enable and configure the client agent. The client agent is responsible for querying and collecting the inventory information from the system. When you open the properties of the hardware inventory client agent you will find two tabs: General and MIF Collection. On the General tab you can select the Enable button to turn on the hardware inventory collection within the site. Once enabled, all of the clients within the site will start collecting inventory based upon the configured schedule.

The scheduling options allow you to configure when the inventory is collected. There are two primary options to consider: simple schedule and custom schedule. Selecting the former option allows you to set a recurring start time based upon minutes, hours, or days. After the inventory is collected the first time, the schedule goes into effect. If the schedule is set to run once a day, and the inventory was collected at 10:34 PM, it will run every day at 10:34 PM or until a manual inventory is performed. You can perform a manual inventory by running the hardware inventory cycle on the client system. Once you do so, the

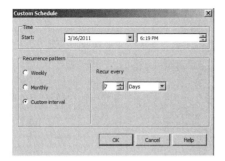

Figure 9.1
Custom Schedule Options

timer will be reset on the client. For instance, if you perform a manual inventory at 8:23, and the schedule is still set for once a day, the inventory schedule will now be set to run every day at 8:23 and not the original 10:34.

The custom schedule allows you to configure a more granular approach when performing the inventory scan. Figure 9.1 shows the configuration screen that appears when you select the Customize button. In the Time section, you can select the start time for the inventory. Unlike the simple schedule, the custom schedule is configured to run at this specific time, and even if you run a manual update, the scheduled time will still be observed and the inventory will process again at that time.

The Recurrence Pattern section is used to configure how often the inventory cycle will run. As seen in Figure 9.2, the weekly options allow you to choose the day of the week that the inventory will be processed. You can choose to run the

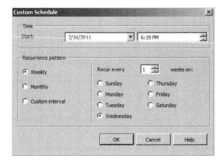

Figure 9.2
Weekly Recurrence Pattern

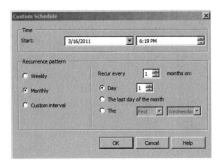

Figure 9.3
Monthly Recurrence Pattern

inventory every week or once every 2, 3, or 4 weeks. If you choose to run the inventory processing on a monthly schedule, you can choose once a month or every 2, 3, 4, 5, 6, 7, 8, 9, 10, 11, or 12 months. You also get to choose which week of the month that the processing will occur, as seen in Figure 9.3.

The last option is to run on a custom schedule. This is similar to the simple schedule, but the start time of the inventory is configured to run at the same time every time the processing starts. With the custom schedule, you can configure the processing to start on a daily, weekly, or monthly basis, and specify the recurrence pattern of each.

The MIF Collection tab settings, seen in Figure 9.4, allow you to specify which type of files you are going to use when the inventory collection starts. Both the IDMIF and NOIDMIF files can be used, but they do not have to be. In more secure environments, it is usually better to leave these two checkboxes deselected. That way, potentially sensitive information that could be collected is not stored within the Configuration Manager database. For more information on MIF files, see the section "Adding Additional Information" later in the chapter.

Configuring Hardware Inventory Client Agent Step-by-Step

In the Configuration Manager console:

1. Expand Site Database > Site Management > Site Name > Site Settings.

2. Select the Client Agents node.

3. Double-click the Hardware Inventory Client Agent.

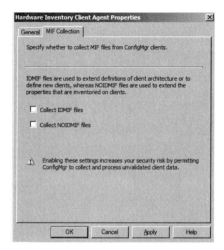

Figure 9.4
MIF Collection Settings

4. Select the Enable Hardware Inventory On Clients checkbox to enable hardware inventory.

5. Select Simple Schedule if you want to "randomize" the inventory collection time.

6. If using simple schedule, configure the recurrence using number of minutes, hours, or days.

7. Select Custom Schedule if you want to control the recurrence time.

8. If using custom schedule, select the Customize button.

9. In the Time section, enter the date and time that you want to start collecting hardware inventory.

10. In the Recurrence Pattern section, select Weekly, Monthly, or Custom Interval to control how often the hardware inventory collection will occur.

11. If Weekly is chosen:

Select the number of weeks for the recurrence. Valid options include every week through every four weeks.

Select the day of the week that the hardware inventory collection will be performed.

12. If Monthly is chosen:

> Select the number of weeks for the recurrence. Valid options include every month to every twelve months.

> Choose the Day option and specify the day number if the inventory collection should run on a specific day each month.

> Choose the The Last Day Of The Month option if the inventory collection should run on the last day.

> Choose the The option and select the recurrence pattern for a specific day of the week such as Second Saturday of the month.

13. If Custom Interval is chosen, enter how often the recurrence should occur. Valid entries are from every 1 to 59 Hours, 1 to 23 Hours, and 1 to 31 Days.

14. Click OK.

15. In the Maximum Custom MIF File Size section, enter the maximum total file size of all of the custom MIF files.

16. Click the MIF Collection tab.

17. If using MIF files, select the checkbox for Collect IDMIF Files, Collect NOIDMIF Files, or both.

18. Click OK.

Configuring Hardware Inventory Options

Enabling and scheduling the hardware inventory client agent is only one part of the Hardware Inventory collection process. And right out of the box, configuring the client settings will allow you to start collecting the default hardware inventory items. Microsoft has done a commendable job of determining what hardware inventory items are typically collected. In most environments, the default settings will suffice. However, there may be times when you would like to collect more or less than the default parameters allow. To change the default settings, we need to leave the administrator console and work with some files on the site server: SMS_def.mof and Configuration.mof. These two files allow you to define the information that is collected and which repositories will be used to get the inventory information.

Configuration.mof

In previous versions of System Management Server (SMS), the Windows Management Instrumentation (WMI) database was queried for hardware configuration settings. The access settings necessary to query WMI were included within SMS. Configuration Manager 2007 allows the client to query more repositories than just the WMI. The Configuration.mof file is used to define the method of accessing a repository. Repositories on a system include the WMI hardware repository and the system's registry. Only existing WMI classes and registry entries can be defined within the Configuration.mof file. If a new repository needs to be defined, it will have to first be defined on the system, and then the entries within the Configuration.mof file can be included.

The Configuration.mof file is kept on the site server within the *CfgMgrInstall-Path*\SMS\Inboxes\clifiles.src\hinv folder. Any changes to the file should be made here. The settings that are configured within this file are included as part of the policy body. Each client will receive the updated entries the next time they perform a policy request. Once the policy is received at the client, the settings are compiled by the client automatically, allowing the client to perform inventory actions against the configured repositories.

Figure 9.5 shows a small portion of the Configuration.mof file. Here you will see registry locations being defined. Creating entries within the Configuration.mof file for all of the repository locations prepares the client so that any required inventory requests can be handled. Once the Cofiguration.mof file is defined, downloaded, and compiled, the SMS_def.mof file is used to filter the components and settings that are inventoried.

SMS_def.mof

Whereas the Configuration.mof file defined where the inventory items were stored within the system, the SMS_def.mof file is used to filter the information that is actually collected within the system. If you think of it in terms of a GPS, the Configuration.mof file defines the parameters, or start, stop, and end points of the trip, while the turn by turn directions would be the SMS_def.mof file's domain.

Figure 9.5
Configuration.mof File

Taking a look at the SMS_def.mof file, a portion of which can be seen in Figure 9.6, you will notice several entries defined. Each object included in the file is configured so that it will either be picked up in an inventory or not. The inventory item is named in the "SMS_Group_Name" line. On the line that

Figure 9.6
SMS_def.mof File

starts with "SMS_Report", the value is either "True" or "False". As you can imagine, if the setting is configured as "True", the item will be inventoried. But that is only the first part of the inventory decision process. The actual hardware component information that you will report in is included within this grouping.

Read further down the file and you will see each individual component and setting for the object. With these individual attributes exposed, you can configure how much inventory data to collect. If you decide that you want to collect information on the video card that is installed within the system, but you don't want to collect every single setting that is accessible from WMI, you can "silence" the collection by using the "False" option.

So with the SMS_def.mof file, you can define the components that will be inventoried within the system, and then define the attribute settings that will be collected. As you start working with this file, remember a couple of suggestions:

- **Back up the SMS_def.mof file**. Before making any changes, save a copy of the default SMS_def.mof file. If the changes that are made cause problems with inventory collection, you can quickly replace the original file.

- **Start with the default settings.** When you enable Hardware Inventory, the items that are configured as True within the SMS_def.mof file are used when querying the system. Review the information that is collected and determine if you want to include additional attribute information. If you decide you do not need specific inventory information, you can turn off the collection of those settings.

- **Do not enable every component and attribute.** It is very easy to use a text editor and perform a mass find and replace that changes every False to True. Doing so will overwhelm your network and database. There is a lot of information contained within the WMI repository and the SMS_def. mof file can be used to collect a massive amount of hardware information.

- **Document the changes to the SMS_def.mof file.** When upgrading Configuration Manager, either by installing a Service Pack or new version, the SMS_def.mof file may be changed. Documenting all of the changes that you have made to the file will make it much easier to replace those changes in the new version.

Editing the SMS_def.mof File

1. Open Windows Explorer.

2. Navigate to C:\Program Files\Microsoft Configuration Manager\inboxes \clifiles.src\hinv.

3. Right-click SMS_def.mof and select Open.

4. Choose Notepad from the program options.

5. In Notepad, find the reporting component that you want to modify, such as operating system.

6. Scroll down to the attribute you want to change and edit the entry from True to False or vice versa.

7. Save the SMS_def.mof file and exit Notepad.

Adding Additional Information

Although there is a lot of information that can be collected by default, there may be times that additional information is required for your organization. For instance, you may want to report on the type of plotter that is connected to a system, or the department where the system is located. This information is not typically included in the default hardware inventory options. For this type of information, there are additional methods of collecting and placing the data into the database.

Managed information format (MIF) files are commonly used to extend the information that is collected for a system. An MIF file is a text file that contains settings that are read during the hardware inventory collection cycle. The settings that are included in these files are usually information that you cannot obtain from the WMI. There are two types of MIF files used with hardware inventory: NOIDMIF and IDMIF.

NOIDMIF Files   When you want to collect additional information about a client system, NOIDMIF files are used. NOIDMIF files contain additional information that is tied to the system and appear as inventory information for the managed system. Let's say you want to associate a system to a specific department, phone extension, or some other identifying information. You can create the NOIDMIF file with all of the relevant information and store it within the %WINDIR% \System32\CCM\Inventory\Noidmifs directory. When the inventory client agent scans the system for hardware inventory, the files within this directory are read and the details are added to the hardware inventory results that are sent to the site server.

IDMIF Files   There are times when you may want to add additional information into the database for devices that are not managed by Configuration Manager. If you want to collect information within the database for a device that is connected to a system, or a network device that does not have a Configuration Manager client loaded on it, you could create an IDMIF file that defines what the device is, and the settings that you want to reflect within your inventory. IDMIF files use the same format as a NOIDMIF file, but they contain additional information that identifies the device. The attributes and settings that are defined within the IDMIF file are then related to the new device object. Once you have defined the IDMIF file, it must be saved in the %WINDIR%\System32 \CCM\Inventory\Idmifs directory so that the hardware inventory client agent can read it and report on it.

MANAGING SOFTWARE INVENTORY

Collecting software inventory is not as straightforward as hardware inventory. With the software inventory components, you have to know what you would like to include within the inventory. Microsoft was nice enough to include the option to scan for all executables, but that is as far it goes. If you want to collect information on any other file type, it is up to you to configure.

The information that you receive from the inventory process is quite extensive. File information, such as version, name, original name, manufacturer, and many other attributes are collected and recorded in the database. Being able to report on the software that is installed within your organization can be of great value, especially when it comes to license validation.

The software inventory client agent is used to define the software inventory scanning options. There are actually two distinct scanning options to configure: inventory and collection. Inventory scanning involves parsing the hard drives on the system in search of software that meets the criteria specified within the configuration properties. When the software is discovered, the details for the files are read and sent back to the management point for inclusion within the database.

File collection is actually copying the files to the site server. This functionality can be configured so that you can copy configuration files to the database for use in troubleshooting at a later time. When configuring file collection settings, you can specify the file or files that you want to collect and then define the total file size that you will allow to be copied to the site server.

Enabling and Configuring Software Inventory

Configuring software inventory options entails configuring settings on the software inventory client agent. In much the same way as you configured the hardware inventory client agent, the properties that are found on the General tab of the properties include the schedule that the agent will run, and the settings that define what software scanning options you want to configure. Notice that there are several other tabs available for configuring the software inventory client agent. Each of these configuration tabs allows you to manage specific aspects of the software inventory so that you don't have an all or none situation. Finding that right balance between getting the inventory that you need and not populating the database with unnecessary information does take a little planning.

Enabling the Software Inventory Client Agent

The most basic configuration option is to enable the client agent. Although this task is a very basic and easy option, you need to think about what you are doing. As with all of the client agents, when you enable the task, you are turning on the software inventory functionality for all of the managed systems within your organization. As soon as they receive their updated machine policy, they are going to begin scanning the hard drive for software based upon the schedule and configuration options that you specify. For this reason alone, you should have a test environment in place so that you can get a baseline on the amount of data that will be included in your database. Once you have tested and determined how much data will be included, you will be able to determine how large your database will grow.

Configuring the software inventory client agent so that it will perform its duties on the schedule that you specify is fairly straightforward. Within the administrator console, navigate to the Client Agents node and open the properties for the software inventory client agent. On the General tab you will find the option

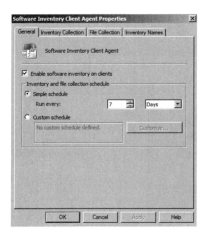

Figure 9.7
Enabling Software Inventory

that allows you to enable the client and the scheduling options, as seen in Figure 9.7. Setting these options is identical to configuring them for the hardware inventory client agent that was discussed earlier in this chapter in the section "Configuring the Hardware Inventory Client Agent."

Controlling Software Inventory Scanning

By default, only executables, those files that have an extension of .exe, have their details included in the site database. If you want to include any other file types or file names within the software inventory, you will have to configure the agent to report the details during the scheduled scan. Typically, file types that are inventoried include .cmd, .bat, vbs, and other file types that you want to report on. And that is really the key. If you have a need to report on a file type, whether it is for determining where the files are installed or for licensing purposes, make sure you include the extension for the file type.

If you want to report on a specific file, you can enter the entire file name within the File Types area of the Inventory Collection tab, seen in Figure 9.8. This configuration option becomes very handy for determining which systems have license files or to determine the file versions installed on each of the managed systems. Choosing to use a file name instead of searching based upon the file extension reduces the amount of information that is stored within the database.

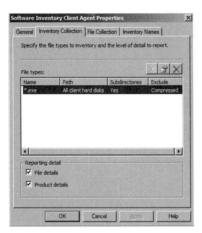

Figure 9.8
Inventory Collection Tab

You can use the wildcard character "*" when entering the new information. For instance, for any file that has uses the "bat" extension, you could enter *.bat. If you want to inventory any file that starts with "config", you could enter "config*". If you are looking for specific file information, you can even specify the entire path to the file or files. For instance, if you determine that you only want to inventory the batch files in the C:\Configuration\Batch directory, you would enter the path as C:\Configuration\Batch*.bat.

On the Inventory Collection tab, you will find all of the software extensions and file names that are used during the inventory collection cycle. It is here that you can modify the inventory collection rules to fit your environment. Clicking the New button presents you with the configuration options to add in settings for inventory rules.

Controlling Software Inventory File Collection

Whereas the software inventory function discovers and reads the files on the local system drive partitions, software collection actually discovers and copies the configured files to the site server. The files that are collected are then stored within the database. The settings that are found on the File Collection tab, seen in Figure 9.9, allow you to control the files that are collected and the total size of the files that are discovered. The size parameter allows you to configure the amount of data that is sent across the network and ultimately entered into the database.

Figure 9.9
File Collection Tab

Managing Software Inventory Names

If you have worked with software distribution and inventory for any time at all, you probably discovered very quickly that the product name information and manufacturer information does not always follow a standard. You typically end up with entries in your inventory for the same manufacturer or product that are spelled differently. If you take a look at the entries for Microsoft already included in the Inventory Names tab, you will find many different naming conventions for Microsoft Corporation. There are entries that you can tell made it through the quality assurance process and were overlooked, and others that were due to changes in the standards that evolved over time.

Microsoft is not the only company that has many different spellings and mistakes in their naming conventions. The first time you look at the inventory reports or entries within the Resource Explorer, you will notice the redundant entries for each company. It is up to you to start determining how you want those entries to appear. You could just leave them the way they are, but then the reports that you generate will not look very nice. Instead, you should review all of the entries that appear in your reports and then configure the Inventory Names tab with the appropriate settings.

If you are manipulating the names that appear for manufacturers, you can start making your entries by selecting the New button. If you want to make changes

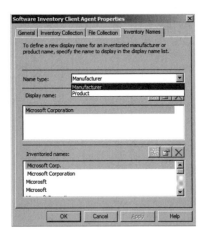

Figure 9.10
Configuring Manufacturer and Product Names

to the product names, you will have to select the option for Products from the Name Type drop-down as seen in Figure 9.10. When entering the names for either the manufacturers or products, click on the New button in the Display Name section and enter the name you want to appear on the reports and in Resource Explorer. Once you have the new display name entered, make sure it is selected and click the New button in the Inventoried Names section. Do this for every name variation that you want to change. It is typically easiest to collect the software inventory and then print out a report of the entire inventory. This will give you an easy list to review as you are configuring your entries.

As you are adding in the names, you can quickly check to see if the entries are working correctly by using Resource Explorer. Because it reads the database information every time you start it, it will display each entry based upon the display name information that is configured. Just make sure that before you check your work, click the Apply button in the software inventory client agent.

Configuring Software Inventory Client Agent Step-by-Step

In the Configuration Manager console:

1. Expand Site Database > Site Management > Site Name > Site Settings.

2. Select the Client Agents node.

3. Double-click the Software Inventory Client Agent.

4. Select the Enable Software Inventory On Clients checkbox to enable Software Inventory.

5. Select Simple Schedule if you want to "randomize" the inventory collection time.

6. If using simple schedule, configure the recurrence using number of minutes, hours, or days.

7. Select Custom Schedule if you want to control the recurrence time.

8. If using custom schedule, select the Customize button.

9. In the Time section, enter the date and time that you want to start collecting inventory.

10. In the Recurrence Pattern section, select Weekly, Monthly, or Custom Interval to control how often the inventory collection will occur.

11. If Weekly is chosen:

Select the number of weeks for the recurrence. Valid options include every week through every four weeks.

Select the day of the week that the hardware inventory collection will be performed.

12. If Monthly is chosen:

Select the number of weeks for the recurrence. Valid options include every month to every twelve months.

Choose the Day option and specify the day number if the inventory collection should run on a specific day each month.

Choose the option The Last Day Of The Month if the inventory collection should run on the last day.

Choose the The option and select the recurrence pattern for a specific day of the week such as Second Saturday of the month.

13. If Custom Interval is chosen, enter how often the recurrence should occur. Valid entries are from every 1 to 59 Hours, 1 to 23 Hours, and 1 to 31 Days.

14. Click OK.

15. In the Maximum Custom MIF File Size section, enter the maximum total file size of all of the custom MIF files.

16. Select the Inventory Collection tab.

17. Review the current inventory rules in the File Types section.

18. To add a new rule, click the New button.

19. Enter the file type, file name, and optionally the file path in the Name text box.

20. In the Path section, click the Set button.

21. In the Path Properties, select whether you want to scan all partitions on a system, or a specific path. The path can be an environment variable or the full path.

22. If you only want to scan the defined path, clear the Search Subdirectories checkbox.

23. Click OK.

24. Clear the Exclude Encrypted and Compressed Files if you want to collect these types of files during the inventory scan. They are excluded by default.

25. Clear the Exclude Files in The Windows Directory if you want to include system files in the scan. They are excluded by default.

26. Click OK.

27. To edit any existing rules, select the rule and click the Properties button.

28. To delete any existing rules, select the rule and click the Delete button.

29. Select the File Collection tab.

30. Review the current collection rules in the File To Be Collected section.

31. To add a new rule, click the New button.

32. Enter the file type, file name, and optionally the file path in the Name text box.

33. In the Path section, click the Set button.

34. In the Path Properties, select whether you want to scan all partitions on a system, or a specific path. The path can be an environment variable or the full path.

35. If you only want to scan the defined path, clear the Search Subdirectories checkbox.

36. Click OK.

37. Clear the Exclude Encrypted And Compressed Files if you want to collect these types of files during the inventory scan. They are excluded by default.

38. In the Maximum Size field, enter the maximum size in KB of all files that are collected. If this total is exceeded, no collection is performed for this rule.

39. Click OK.

40. To edit any existing rules, select the rule and click the Properties button.

41. To delete any existing rules, select the rule and click the Delete button.

42. Select the Inventory Names tab.

43. Select either the Manufacturer or Product options from the Name Type drop-down.

44. To add a new display name entry, click the New button in the Display Name section.

45. Enter the display name as it should appear within reports and Resource Explorer.

46. Click OK.

47. Verify the display name that you want to manage is selected and click the New button in the Inventoried Names section.

48. Enter the name as it appears within the inventory. Perform this action for every variation on the name.

49. Click OK.

50. To edit any existing display names or inventoried names, select the name and click the Properties button.

51. To delete any display names or inventoried names, select the name and click the Delete button.

52. Click OK.

REVIEWING INVENTORY INFORMATION

After you have performed an inventory, hardware or software, the information that you collected is stored in the database, but you need a method of viewing the data. Configuration Manager has a few built-in utilities that allow you to view the inventory information. The first method is using Resource Explorer. Resource Explorer is an inventory viewer that can be started directly from a resource within the console. If you navigate to a collection and right-click on a system resource, you can launch it by selecting Start > Resource Explorer. A new window will start and you will see a view similar to the one seen in Figure 9.11.

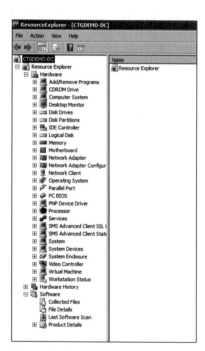

Figure 9.11
Resource Explorer

Expanding the Hardware node will allow you to view the hardware information from the latest hardware inventory scan. When you expand a component, the collected attributes for the component will be displayed. The components and attributes that you see within the Hardware tree reflect the information that was collected by hardware inventory client agent as it queried WMI and read NOIDMIF files.

Moving down one level, the Hardware History hive includes the results of the latest hardware inventory scan as well as the previous inventory scans. If you are performing a hardware inventory once a week, you will see hardware history entries for each of the weeks as far back as you are saving the history data. You can then use this information for troubleshooting purposes, finding out when the hardware configurations changed.

To control how many history entries you have displayed is dependent on two configuration settings. The first is in the hardware inventory client agent settings, as seen in Figure 9.12. Here you can configure the schedule as to when the hardware inventory is collected. The other setting is in the Delete Aged Inventory History properties in the Site Maintenance area, as seen in Figure 9.13. This maintenance task is used to groom the inventory entries from the database. By default, this task runs every Saturday and will groom entries that are older than 90 days.

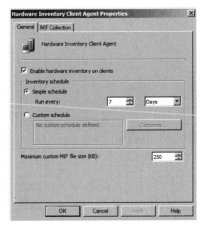

Figure 9.12
Hardware Inventory Client Agent Schedule Properties

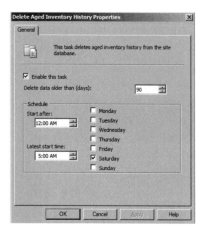

Figure 9.13
Delete Aged Inventory History Task Settings

Viewing software inventory information from within the Resource Explorer will give you a very quick peek into the software that is installed on managed systems. Expanding the Software node will expose four reporting options: Collected Files, File Details, Last Software Scan, and Product Details. The Collected Files section will display all of the files that were collected, based upon the rules that were defined on the Collected Files tab of the software inventory client agent properties. You can use this section to review the files that have been collected, and then compare them against current versions on the managed systems. The Last Software Scan view displays the last time the software inventory was performed.

The File Details section presents every file that was inventoried, along with the inventoried properties on the file. It is here that you can review all of the file information when you are trying to troubleshoot problems or verify that an installed file is the correct version. For a file to appear within this view, you will need to make sure there is a rule configured within the software inventory client agent inventory collection properties.

The Product Details view presents a listing of all of the products that were discovered during the software inventory. Whereas the file details lists each file by file name, the product details presents the installed software based upon the product information that was collected during the inventory. The data that is shown in this view can be very confusing at first, due to the inconsistency in

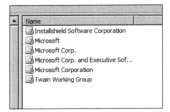

Figure 9.14
Multiple Names for a Product

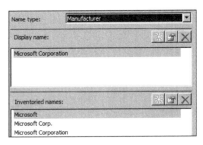

Figure 9.15
Software Inventory Client Agent Inventory Names Properties

Figure 9.16
Monthly Recurrence Pattern

which the developers defined the products' details. If you look at Figure 9.14, you will notice that there are several different naming conventions for Microsoft. To normalize this information, you can create entries within the Inventory Names tab of the software inventory client agent properties, as seen in Figure 9.15. Once the entries have been entered, the query results from the database will present the inventoried items in an easier to read manner, as seen in Figure 9.16.

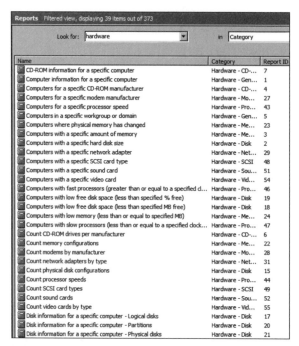

Figure 9.17
Hardware Inventory Reports

The other method of viewing your inventory is through reporting. There are several canned reports that ship with Configuration Manager, with a good portion of them devoted to inventory. There are 39 hardware inventory reports included with the default installation. You will find such reports as Computer Information For A Specific Computer, Computers Where Physical Memory Has Changed, and Disk Information For A Specific Computer—Physical Disks. Figure 9.17 is a screen shot of the Reporting node and some of the reports that are available.

The default reports provide a great deal of insight into the hardware inventory. They are not all-encompassing however. It is very possible that you will need unique reports created for your organization. Chapter 10 discusses the reporting point, reporting services point, and some of the finer points of creating reports.

MANAGING ASSET INTELLIGENCE

Asset intelligence goes beyond the standard software inventory. When you take a look at what can be inventoried by using the software inventory client agent, you will find that only files and file types that you specified are inventoried. Asset intelligence actually goes one step further and queries multiple repositories on the system to discover software that has been installed. The client agent will look for application "fingerprints" within the system. Not only can you receive information about applications that have been installed, you can also find out what type of browser helper objects and screen savers have been installed.

There are actually two services from Microsoft that will give you this type of information. The first is the options built into the asset intelligence components within Configuration Manager, the other is the asset inventory service (AIS) that is available as part of the Microsoft Desktop Optimization Pack (MDOP). There is a distinct difference between the two services. AIS is an online service. A small client is installed on the system and when the inventory is read, it is uploaded to Microsoft's AIS servers for storage and reporting. The asset intelligence components within Configuration Manager are contained within your organization. You don't have to worry about connecting to a web service to run inventory reports and you don't have to worry about your information being stored on somebody else's systems.

Configuring Asset Intelligence Components

There are two components that are used to configure asset intelligence within a site: asset intelligence synchronization point and the asset intelligence configuration settings. Once these two components have been configured, the hardware inventory client agent and the software inventory client agent are used to deliver additional inventory data back to the site server.

Asset Intelligence Synchronization Point

Prior to the release of Configuration Manager 2007 R3, the asset intelligence synchronization point required a certificate that would allow it to authenticate to the asset intelligence repository website. This certificate was only available from Microsoft, and needed to be imported before a synchronization could occur. With the release of Configuration Manager 2007 R3, the certificate is no longer required. Anyone who implements an asset intelligence synchronization point can synchronize the catalog of data.

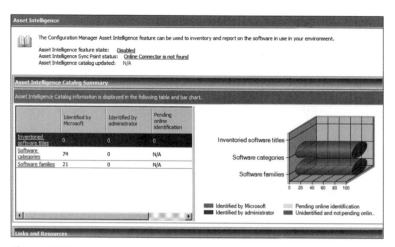

Figure 9.18
Asset Intelligence Home Page

Asset Intelligence Configuration Settings

Once the asset intelligence synchronization point is configured and the initial synchronization with the asset intelligence website is complete, your site database will be populated with all of the asset intelligence inventory criteria. This criteria, known as the catalog, is used when identifying software installed on managed systems. If you look at Figure 9.18, you will see the asset intelligence home page, which is displaying the discovered software, along with the categories and families with which the software belongs.

Categories can be defined as broad groupings for the software. In Figure 9.19, you will see many of the categories that exist within the Software Categories view. Families are the software collection types and used to further define the software usage within categories. Figure 9.20 shows the Software Families view. For instance, the Productivity and Viewers family could be included with the Category of Browsers as well as Multimedia and File Viewers. Multimedia and File Viewers category could also included the Home and Entertainment family. Microsoft has classified software into families and categories. Once inventoried, reports can be run that will display all of the installed software that is included in the Productivity and Viewers family, which would include all of the browsers, multimedia players, and file viewers. For a more granular report, you could view only the software in the Browsers category, which would then omit the entries for the multimedia players and file viewers.

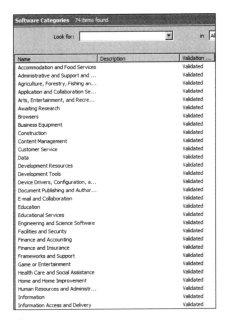

Figure 9.19
Software Categories

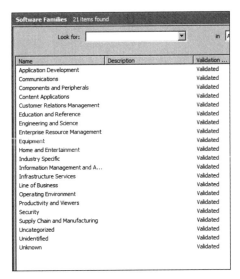

Figure 9.20
Software Families

New families and categories can be created if the included options do not meet the needs of your organization. Right-clicking on either of the views will present the option to create a new object. A wizard will appear that only asks for the object name to be defined. Once defined, any of the inventoried software items can be assigned to the new family or category. Notice that the Validation State column displays User Defined for the new object that you created. This is due to the fact that Microsoft has not performed their validation testing on the object. If you are sending updated information to the asset intelligence website, Microsoft will evaluate the information that you provided, and once they have validated the definition, the entry will be changed to Validated upon the next synchronization.

Moving down one node within the asset intelligence area is the Custom Labels view. This is where you can create additional tags for software, which in turn can be used when running reports and organizing information. Custom Labels are always user-defined and never validated by Microsoft.

Within the Inventoried Software Titles section there are two nodes: Unidentified And Not Pending Online Identification and All Inventoried Software Titles. The latter node lists every software title that was inventoried, whether or not it has been identified by Microsoft and categorized. The Unidentified And Not Pending Online Identification node is used to quickly identify discovered software that has not been categorized by Microsoft. It is here that you can open the properties of the software item and configure its category and family information. If you are participating in the asset intelligence update service, the changes that you make to software criteria, either the category or family information, will be uploaded to Microsoft where they can validate it.

Beneath the Inventoried Software Titles section lies two nodes that allow you to view processor and hardware options for software titles. The Processor Properties node seen in Figure 9.21, is used as a reference for processor options that are available from the asset intelligence database. This information is read-only and meant to assist administrators when they are trying to determine processor types that are used in their environment. The information that is found within this node cannot be modified. Updates to the information are available from the asset intelligence online catalog.

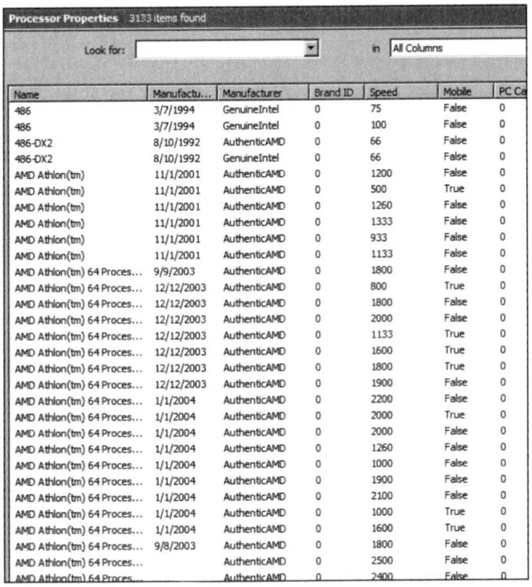

Processor Properties 3133 items found

Look for: in All Columns

Name	Manufactu...	Manufacturer	Brand ID	Speed	Mobile	PC Ca
486	3/7/1994	GenuineIntel	0	75	False	0
486	3/7/1994	GenuineIntel	0	100	False	0
486-DX2	8/10/1992	AuthenticAMD	0	66	False	0
486-DX2	8/10/1992	GenuineIntel	0	66	False	0
AMD Athlon(tm)	11/1/2001	AuthenticAMD	0	1200	False	0
AMD Athlon(tm)	11/1/2001	AuthenticAMD	0	500	True	0
AMD Athlon(tm)	11/1/2001	AuthenticAMD	0	1260	False	0
AMD Athlon(tm)	11/1/2001	AuthenticAMD	0	1333	False	0
AMD Athlon(tm)	11/1/2001	AuthenticAMD	0	933	False	0
AMD Athlon(tm)	11/1/2001	AuthenticAMD	0	1133	False	0
AMD Athlon(tm) 64 Proces...	9/9/2003	AuthenticAMD	0	1800	False	0
AMD Athlon(tm) 64 Proces...	12/12/2003	AuthenticAMD	0	800	True	0
AMD Athlon(tm) 64 Proces...	12/12/2003	AuthenticAMD	0	1800	False	0
AMD Athlon(tm) 64 Proces...	12/12/2003	AuthenticAMD	0	2000	False	0
AMD Athlon(tm) 64 Proces...	12/12/2003	AuthenticAMD	0	1133	True	0
AMD Athlon(tm) 64 Proces...	12/12/2003	AuthenticAMD	0	1600	True	0
AMD Athlon(tm) 64 Proces...	12/12/2003	AuthenticAMD	0	1800	True	0
AMD Athlon(tm) 64 Proces...	12/12/2003	AuthenticAMD	0	1900	False	0
AMD Athlon(tm) 64 Proces...	1/1/2004	AuthenticAMD	0	2200	False	0
AMD Athlon(tm) 64 Proces...	1/1/2004	AuthenticAMD	0	2000	True	0
AMD Athlon(tm) 64 Proces...	1/1/2004	AuthenticAMD	0	2000	False	0
AMD Athlon(tm) 64 Proces...	1/1/2004	AuthenticAMD	0	1260	False	0
AMD Athlon(tm) 64 Proces...	1/1/2004	AuthenticAMD	0	1000	False	0
AMD Athlon(tm) 64 Proces...	1/1/2004	AuthenticAMD	0	1900	False	0
AMD Athlon(tm) 64 Proces...	1/1/2004	AuthenticAMD	0	2100	False	0
AMD Athlon(tm) 64 Proces...	1/1/2004	AuthenticAMD	0	1000	True	0
AMD Athlon(tm) 64 Proces...	1/1/2004	AuthenticAMD	0	1600	True	0
AMD Athlon(tm) 64 Proces...	9/8/2003	AuthenticAMD	0	1800	False	0
AMD Athlon(tm) 64 Proces...		AuthenticAMD	0	2500	False	0
AMD Athlon(tm) 64 Proces...		AuthenticAMD	0	2400	False	0

Figure 9.21
Processor Properties

Hardware Requirements, seen in Figure 9.22, is also used for reference. When an administrator wants to determine the minimum hardware requirements for a software package, this repository can be used. Unlike the Processor Properties section, the Hardware Requirements node is extensible. An administrator can add additional entries into the database, entering requirements for software that is not included in the asset intelligence catalog, such as software developed within the organization.

The final node within the asset intelligence section is Asset Intelligence Reports. Although each of the listed reports seen in Figure 9.23 is also available from the Reporting node, having them accessible from this section is very convenient. You don't have to filter the reporting display to find all of the reports that are used with asset intelligence, you only need to navigate to this node and run the appropriate reports.

Managing Software Metering

When working with licensing, most companies want to know what software they have installed so that they can make sure they are not breaking any rules.

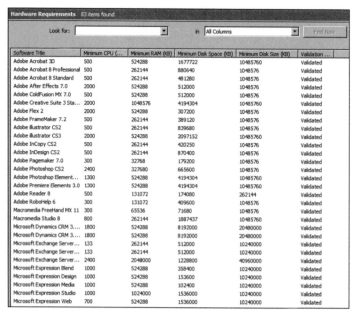

Figure 9.22
Hardware Requirements

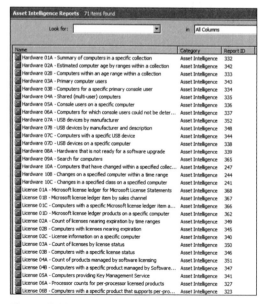

Figure 9.23
Asset Intelligence Reports

Software Inventory and asset intelligence will let you know what you have installed on the managed systems within your organization, which is the first step in maintaining license compliance. And if that is all you were concerned about, you could stop there. However, getting the software inventoried is only the first part of making sure your organization is using its software budget efficiently.

Software metering is a mechanism that allows you to actually see the software that is being used within your organization, and where it is being used. If you have 2,000 systems with a copy of licensed software installed, but only 300 of the users actually run the software, you are paying far too much in licensing for a product that is being under-utilized in your organization.

Configuring Software Metering Components

Two components need to be configured so that software metering functions. The first component is the software metering client agent. The settings found on the properties of this client agent allow you to control whether the agent is enabled and when the collected metering data is uploaded to the site server. The General tab of the software metering client agent properties, seen in Figure 9.24, is used solely to enable or disable the agent. The Schedule tab is used to control the file upload. As you can see in Figure 9.25, the schedule can be set to run one time, at

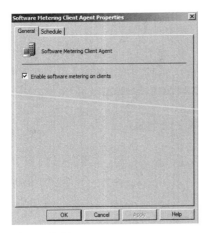

Figure 9.24
Software Metering Client Agent General Properties

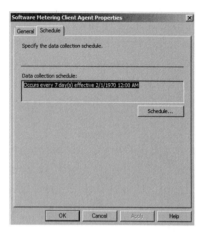

Figure 9.25
Software Metering Client Agent Schedule Properties

the specified date and time, without any recurrence, or to recur on a weekly or custom schedule.

The weekly schedule can be used to control the day of the week that the metering data is uploaded to the site server, along with the weekly recurrence rate. The recurrence can be set to occur every week up to every fourth week. The custom schedule can be used to configure a recurrence rate of minutes, hours, or days.

The second component that needs to be configured is the software metering rules. Without the rules, the client will not be able to determine which software processes need to be logged. Figure 9.26 displays the Software Metering node and some of the rules that are already configured. The rules that you see in this figure have been automatically generated by Configuration Manager. During the

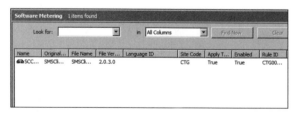

Figure 9.26
Software Metering Rules

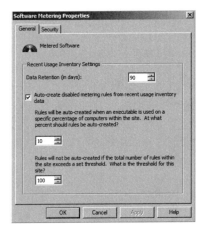

Figure 9.27
Software Metering Rule Automatic Creation Rules

software inventory cycle, the software that was discovered is included automatically within the software metering rules. These rules are not enabled however, so no metering is being performed on them.

Accessing the properties of the Software Metering node, as seen in Figure 9.27, allows you to configure how the auto-generated rules are managed. Within the Auto-create Disabled Metering Rules From Recent Usage Inventory Data section, there are two options. The first option controls the percentage of systems that need to report that a specific software object is used. By default 10% of the managed systems need to have the software installed and accessed before a rule will be generated. That percentage can be modified to fit your needs. If you want to be more aggressive, you can reduce the percentage and have rules generated at a faster rate, or you can increase the value to reduce the number of rules that are automatically created.

The second option controls how many rules will be automatically generated for the site. The default is 100 rules. This keeps the total number of rules at a manageable rate. If you are looking to create many more rules, you can increase this number. Remember that the more you increase the value of this option, the more rules will be created, the more information appears on this screen, and more data is stored within the database.

There is one other option on the software metering properties, and that is data retention. This setting controls how long the software metering recent usage

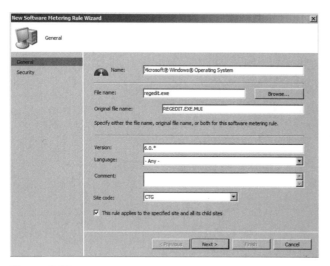

Figure 9.28
Properties of an Automatically Generated Rule

information is stored within the database before it is groomed out. The default of 90 days is appropriate for most organizations. This way, 90 days worth of the current software usage is collected for automatically creating rules.

Creating Software Metering Rules

Although rules can be created automatically for you, there may be times when you want to create rules for specific collection needs. If you take a look at some of the automatically created rules, you will notice that they are based upon generic file versions and the language of the managed system. Figure 9.28 shows the properties of an auto-created rule. The version criteria is using a wildcard to specify that any version of the software that starts with 5.1 is included within the metering collection. If you wanted to only capture usage on a specific version of the software, you would have to modify the version information. The same is true for the Language option. Only the language of the monitored system is included in the rule. If other language versions should be monitored, the language settings will need to be altered.

Creating a new rule involves running a wizard and specifying the software criteria. Navigate to the Software Metering node, right-click, and choose New > Software Metering Rule. The General page, seen in Figure 9.29, appears first,

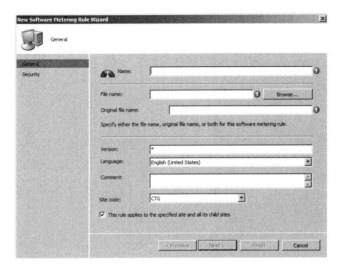

Figure 9.29
Creating a Software Metering Rule

reflecting the options that are available from the properties of a rule. Name the rule something that will define what is being metered.

If you have access to the software component that you are going to meter, you can click the Browse button and navigate to the executable. The nice thing about using this option is that all of the information from the file you are accessing will populate the fields within this page. In Figure 9.30, the executable for the program SCCM Client Center has been selected. The File Name, Original File Name, Version, and Language have all been populated for you. The settings that populate the properties are very specific however. To use this same rule to collect information of different versions of the program, you can wildcard the Version settings. Changing the 2.0.0.0 to 2.* allows you to report on any revision of the "2" version. Changing the setting to just the * character will allow you to report on any version of the program, not just the 2 version.

Notice the checkbox option, This Rule Applies to the Specified Site and all Its Child Sites. When this is selected, and there are child sites beneath the site where the rule is configured, the rule will be copied to the child site. The copied rule will be locked at the child site and cannot be modified by the child site's administrators.

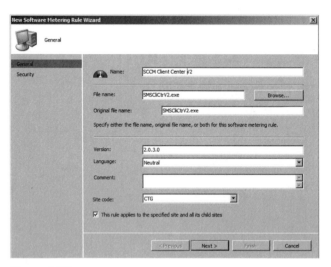

Figure 9.30
Program Properties

The two options for file name allow you to control the monitored program's naming options. Every file has an original file name that is stored in the header of the file. Even if the file is renamed, the original file name sticks with the file. The entry that is listed in the File Name text box is the name of the executable as it is seen on the system. Renaming a file can break the metering of the file. However, if the Original File Name entry is configured, it does not matter what the file name has been changed to; the metering agent will still pick up the file when it runs on a monitored system.

Software Metering Workflow

Once the software metering components have been configured, the policy information for the managed systems is updated. Every managed system within the site will be configured to monitor for when a metered program runs. During the client's machine policy refresh, the new metering rules will be evaluated and the software metering client agent will start monitoring processes. When a monitored program runs, the agent records information within a log file. The details that are recorded are as follows:

1. File Information:
   - File ID
   - File Name
   - File Version
   - File Description
   - File Size

2. Program Information:
   - Company Name
   - Product Name
   - Product Version
   - Product Language

3. Usage Information:
   - Start Time
   - End Time
   - Meter Data ID
   - Resource ID
   - User Name
   - Terminal Services User Session
   - Still Running Flag

For every start and end action, an entry is placed within the log file. When the scheduled upload time occurs, the client sends the log file to the site server. If for some reason the client is unable to contact the site server, the log files are stored on the managed system until communication with the site server is restored. Once communication has been restored, the client will upload the log file immediately.

The site server stores the log file until the summarization tasks run. You can configure when the summarizers run by configuring the properties of two tasks: Summarize Software Metering File Usage Data and Summarize Software Metering Monthly Usage Data. These two tasks are configured to run daily, as seen in Figure 9.31. If you have your schedules set up correctly, the client will send the data to the site server before the summarization tasks run. After the tasks have processed the log files and entered the data into the database, you will be able to run reports and view the software usage for the previous day and for the month.

The summarizers are responsible for converting the raw log data into concise data records within the database. All of the log files that have been uploaded to

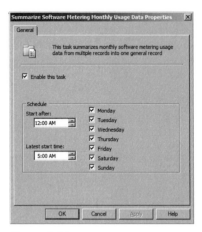

Figure 9.31
Summarization Rules Schedule

the site server are parsed and the usage information for each program is placed in the database. The Summarize Software Metering File Usage Data task is responsible for keeping track of the usage for each individual program over 15 minute and 1 hour intervals. The summarization task takes into account concurrent usage for programs. When a user starts and stops a program such as Microsoft Word, each action is recorded and then summarized. If the user starts and stops Microsoft Word within a 10 minute time frame on the same computer, one usage is recorded. If the same user starts and stops Microsoft Word on two different computers within that timeframe, then two usages are recorded. When you view the summarized data in the software metering reports, you will notice that the information that is summarized includes the program name, version, language, and number of distinct users that ran the program.

The Summarize Software Metering Monthly Usage Data task condenses the log file data into the database. The data is evaluated for the past 30 days and keeps track of the total usage and usage patterns for each metered program. The data that is aggregated for this task includes the program name, version, language, running times, number of usages, last usage, user name, and computer name.

There are two other tasks associated with software metering: Delete Aged Software Metering Data and Delete Aged Software Metering Summary Data. They control the data that needs to be groomed from the database. The former task is set to groom the software metering data that is older than 5 days. If you are not summarizing data on the default schedule of once a day, you may want to increase this value. Summary data is deleted when it ages beyond 270 days by default. If you want to keep a year's worth of summary data, you can increase this number, but just remember, you will also be increasing the amount of data stored within your database.

THE FINAL WORD

The rich inventory options available within Configuration Manager can assist you with several functions. After the inventory has been generated, the resulting information can be used to create collections, thus making it easy to target software to specific systems. You can also use the inventory information to keep track of the software and hardware within your organization. In the next chapter we will introduce queries and reports.

CHAPTER 10

CREATING AND MANAGING QUERIES AND REPORTS

At its very core, System Center is a database. It is a database with a wealth of information about users, hardware and software inventory, software packages and updates, and just about anything else you would ever care to know as a Systems Administrator. Creating queries and reports is your method of asking for and presenting that information. In this chapter, we will discuss what makes up a query and a report, the process of creating and managing each, the differences between these two methods, and some real world examples to get you started.

QUERIES

Queries in Configuration Manager 2007 are used to request information from the site database. While queries are a good way to find information, they are most valuable when you intend to *target* the information they produce with an advertisement. This is what separates queries from reports. Queries can be applied to the membership rules of a collection. For example, say you have users scattered throughout your organization with Logitech webcams—and you would like to target these computers as beta testers for your new internal instant messaging solution. Not a problem. You can create a query for all computers in your organization sporting a QuickCam, associate it with a collection, and then deploy your instant messaging software via an advertisement targeting that collection.

Understanding the Language

Queries in Configuration Manager 2007 are written in WQL (WMI Query Language), a subset of SQL (Structured Query Language). WQL is a retrieval-only, case-insensitive language that does not support deleting, updating, or inserting new information. Unlike SQL, WQL retrieves data from classes rather than tables and returns instances rather than rows. This means queries cannot talk directly to the back-end SQL database. They use something in between, known as the SMS Provider. The SMS Provider is a WMI provider that sits between you and the database. It is important to understand that when you create a query, you are requesting information from the SMS Provider, which then retrieves the data from the site database. This might seem a bit redundant, but the SMS Provider helps enforce object security—preventing the user running the Configuration Manager console from returning site information he is not authorized to view.

Elements of a Query

Queries are made up of four required elements and four optional elements. These elements will spring up during the query creation process, so you should have an understanding of each before you move to the next section of this chapter.

Required Elements of a Query

- **Query name**—This is defined by you. It is best to be as descriptive as possible when naming queries (within the 50-character limit).

- **Object type**—An object type is a set of attributes about an object in Configuration Manager. Think of an object type as a starting point to help you retrieve the information you are looking for. When you call your credit card company to check your account balance, they ask you to "Press 1 for sales, press 2 for customer service, press 3 for account balances." Object types are no different. You select an object type to help narrow down the types of attributes for which you might be looking.

- **Attribute classes**—Attribute classes are groups of related attributes. Attribute classes are mostly synonymous with object types, except when dealing with the System Resource object type (which has several Attribute classes).

- **Attributes**—Attributes are the properties within an Attribute class. For example, under the Attribute class Operating System, you have Attributes such as Version and Install Date.

Optional Elements of a Query

- **Criterion types**—Criterion types are used to identify the form the query expression will take. There are five available criterion types: Simple Value, Null Value, Attribute Reference, SubSelected Values, and List of Values.

- **Logical operators**—Logical operators are part of the WQL syntax and are used to broaden or narrow the scope of the query. In Configuration Manager, AND, OR, and NOT are valid Logical operators.

- **Group parentheses**—Group parentheses are used in more complex queries. Just like in math, these parentheses are used to identify which expression is first evaluated.

- **Attribute class joins**—Attribute class joins allow you to configure or modify a join operation.

Running Queries

To get started, open the Configuration Manager console and go to Site Database > Computer Management > Queries.

When you first pull up queries in the Configuration Manager console, you are presented with three default fields:

- **Name**—This is the Query Name defined in the previous section.

- **Resource class**—This is the object type defined in the previous section.

- **Query ID**—This is the unique identifier Configuration Manager uses to identify each individual query. Default queries will start with SMS; queries you create will start with your three-character site code.

To run a query, simply click it. The results will appear in the result pane on the right (Figure 10.1).

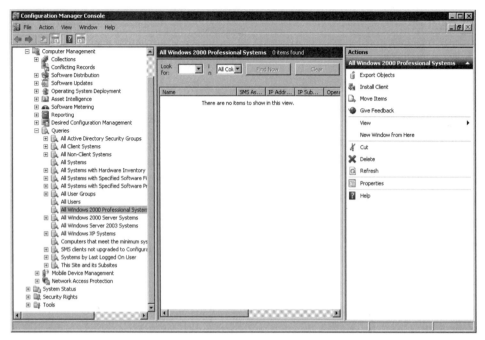

Figure 10.1
Query Results

Default Queries

Creating queries from scratch is simple enough, but it's often unnecessary. Microsoft has provided several default queries within the Configuration Manager console, which often fit the bill for your basic needs. At the very least, these default queries work well as a starting point for creating your own custom queries.

Caution

It is a bad idea to modify default queries. If you intend to use a default query for a starting point, create a new query and import the query statement from the default query.

Creating Custom Queries

Creating custom queries in Configuration Manager is easy. At the very minimum, you just need to know what you're looking for, and where you're looking for it.

In this example, we will create a query for all workstations with Microsoft Office Visio 2003 Professional. We will return the computer name, serial number, and display name of the application.

1. To get started, open the Configuration Manager console and go to Site Database > Computer Management > Queries. Then, right-click Queries, select New > Query. You are presented with the New Query Wizard (see Figure 10.2).

2. Fill out the New Query Wizard, and then click the Edit Query Statement button. You are presented with the Query Statement Properties window (Figure 10.3).

3. Under the General tab, click the New button (Figure 10.4). You are presented with the Result Properties window (Figure 10.5). This is where you set what properties you want the query to return.

4. Click the Select button. You are presented with the Select Attribute window. Match the options shown in Figure 10.6, then click OK. These options will return the computer name.

5. Click OK again on the Result Properties window.

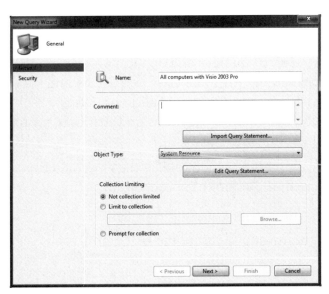

Figure 10.2
New Query Wizard

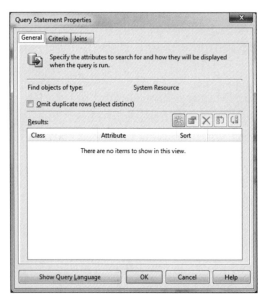

Figure 10.3
Query Statement Properties

Figure 10.4
New Button

6. Repeat steps 3-5 to return the serial number and application display name. For serial number, change the Attribute class to PC Bios and change the Attribute to Serial Number. For the Application Display Name, set Attribute Class to Add/Remove Programs and Attribute set to Display Name. You should end up with Figure 10.7.

7. Under the Query Statement Properties window, click the Criteria tab. This is where you will define the conditions for your query.

8. Click the New button.

9. Under the Criterion Properties window, ensure the Criterion Type is set to Simple Value, then click the Select button.

10. Set the Attribute class to Add/Remove Programs and the Attribute to Display Name, and then click OK.

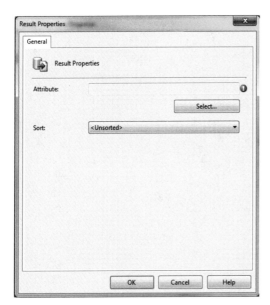

Figure 10.5
Result Properties Window

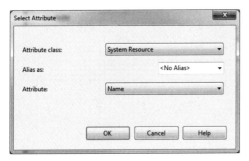

Figure 10.6
Select Attribute Window

11. Back at the Criterion Properties window, set the Operator to "is equal to," then type Microsoft Office Visio Professional 2003 in the Value field. Click OK.

12. You should now see an item listed under the Criteria list box (Figure 10.8).

13. Click OK on the Query Statement Properties window.

14. Click Next, and then Finish on the New Query Wizard.

Figure 10.7
Properties to Return in Query Statement Properties

Figure 10.8
Criteria in Query Statement Properties

Now, simply click the All Computers with Visio 2003 Pro query in the Configuration Manager console to run it. The results should appear in the result pane on the right. If you have no computers running Visio 2003 Pro on your network, don't be surprised if this returns zero records.

Note

When looking for 64-bit applications, you'll need to change the Attribute class to Add/Remove Programs (64).

Modifying Queries

In the previous example, we created a query to find all computers with Microsoft Office Visio 2003 Professional. What if we would like to use that query but modify the parameters a little? Not a problem. In this example, we'll modify the query to look for all computers with Autocad that have less than 2GB of RAM. Instead of using "is equal to," we'll use "is like" and a "%" to designate a wildcard. This will help broaden the search for any version of Autocad.

1. Open the Configuration Manager console and go to Site Database > Computer Management > Queries. Navigate to the All Computers with Visio 2003 Pro query you created in the previous example. Then, right-click the query and choose Properties.

2. Change the name of the query to Autocad Computers with Less Than 2GB RAM. Then, click the Edit Query Statement button.

3. In the Query Statement Properties window, choose the Criteria tab, high-light your criteria, and choose the Modify button (Figure 10.9).

4. In the Criterion Properties window, change the Operator to "is like," then change the Value to %Autocad% and click OK (Figure 10.10).

5. Back at the Query Statement Properties window, click the New button to add an additional piece of criteria.

6. Leave Criterion Type set to Simple Value, then click the Select button.

7. Set the Attribute Class field to Memory and the Attribute field to Total Physical Memory (KB), then click OK.

8. Now, change the Operator to "is less than."

Figure 10.9
Criteria in Query Statement Properties

Figure 10.10
Using "is like" Operator in Criterion Properties Window

9. In the value field below, enter 2000000. Click OK.

10. Click OK again on the Query Statement Properties window.

11. Click OK again.

You have now successfully modified your Microsoft Visio query to look for all computers with Autocad that have less than 2GB of RAM.

Creating a SubSelect Query

Creating queries to look for software is useful. However, sometimes you need to know the exact opposite. Sometimes, you are looking for computers that don't have something. Wouldn't it be nice to know every computer on your network that does not have a webcam? Or more importantly, maybe you'd like to know every computer on your network that does not have an anti-virus client? To do this, you create something called a subselect query. This involves creating two separate queries. First, you create a query looking for every computer that has something (like every computer with your standard anti-virus client). Then, you create a second query (a subselect query), which returns all computers that are not listed in your first query. In this example, we will look for all computers without Symantec Endpoint Protection. If you are running a different anti-virus client, track down the display name it uses and adjust accordingly.

1. To get started, open the Configuration Manager console and go to Site Database > Computer Management > Queries. Then, right-click Queries, select New > Query.

2. Name the query All Computers with Symantec Endpoint (or whatever anti-virus product you use), then click the Edit Query Statement button.

3. Under the General tab, click the New button.

4. In the Result Properties window, click the Select button below the Attribute field.

5. Leave the Attribute class set to System Resource, then set the Attribute to ResourceID and click OK. Click OK again on the Result Properties window.

Note

We are choosing to return the ResourceID because this is a numeric field that is indexed in the Configuration Manager database. This is the field we will use to do our comparisons. You could use something else, but it would likely take a lot longer to retrieve results depending on how big your database is. This will make more sense as you step further through this tutorial.

6. Back at the Query Statement Properties window, select the Criteria tab, then click the New button to add criteria.

7. Leave Criterion Type at Simple Value and click the Select button below the Where field.

8. Under the Select Attribute window, select the Add/Remove Programs Attribute class, then choose Display Name as the Attribute and click OK.

9. Set the Operator to "is equal to" and then fill out the Value field with the Display Name of your anti-virus software. In my case, the Display Name would be Symantec Endpoint Protection.

10. Click OK on the remaining windows and finish creating your query.

You have successfully created a query that looks for all computers on your network running your standard anti-virus client. Go ahead and run the query to ensure the results are accurate.

Next, we will create a subselect query that looks for all computers that do not appear in the results of the query you just created.

1. Start the New Query Wizard and name your query: All Computers without Symantec Endpoint.

2. Leave Object Type set to System Resource, and then click the Edit Query Statement button.

3. Under the General tab, click the New button. Then, click the Select button.

4. In the Select Attribute window, set the Attribute class to System Resource and set the Attribute to Name. Click OK twice.

5. Choose the Criteria tab and then click the New button.

6. Change the Criterion Type to SubSelected values (Figure 10.11), then click the Select button.

7. At the Select Attribute window, set Attribute Class to System Resource and set Attribute to Resource ID. Click OK.

Note

When creating the SubSelect Query, you are setting what attribute to compare itself to in the previous query you created. Since the previous query was set to return the Resource ID attribute, this SubSelect query sets the criteria to compare its Resource ID attribute to the Resource ID returned in the previous query.

8. Under the Criterion Properties window, change the Operator to "is not in," then click the Browse button below to the left.

Figure 10.11
Setting SubSelected Values within Criterion Properties Window

N o t e

We are setting this field to "is not in" because we are looking for all the Resource ID attributes that are not listed in the previous query. If we left this field set to "is in," it would return all matches.

9. The Browse Query window appears. Find and select All Computers with Symantec Endpoint, then click OK.

10. The Criterion Properties window should now have the SubSelect Query code displayed (Figure 10.12).

11. Click OK on the remaining windows and finish walking through the wizard to create the query.

When you run the SubSelect query you just created, the results should show all computers without anti-virus. Hopefully, the number is zero!

N o t e

If there is a computer that is not properly reporting its inventory data to the Configuration Manager database, it might appear in the results of this query even though it may have the software installed. Investigate these machines further if something doesn't look right.

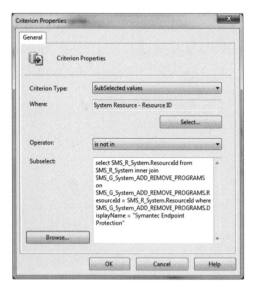

Figure 10.12
SubSelect Query Code in Criterion Properties Window

Status Message Queries

Status message queries can be found in the Configuration Manager console under Site Database > System Status > Status Message Queries. These queries are used to present status information about packages, advertisements, collections, clients, and other components in the SCCM Site Database. This means that the data you are requesting is not live, but rather, a snapshot of the most up-to-date information logged in the database. Using this method retrieves data very quickly, but can sometimes be a bit frustrating if you are trying to get an immediate status of a component after you make a change.

To create a status message query:

1. Open the Configuration Manager console and navigate to Site Database > System Status > Status Message Queries.

2. Right-click on Status Message Queries and choose New Status Message Query.

3. Name the status message query.

4. If you want to create a new query from scratch, click the Edit Query Statement button. If you would like to use an existing status message query as a template for your query, you can click Import Query Statement.

Reports

In Configuration Manager 2007, reports, like queries, are used to request information from the Site Database. Reports are managed through the Configuration Manager console, where you can create, modify, clone, delete, or view a report. Viewing or modifying reports requires appropriate credentials, like all other objects in Configuration Manager.

Unlike queries, reports cannot be targeted. You might wonder why anyone would want to write a report instead of a query. It really boils down to your audience—the people who are going to be looking at and using this information. Reports are great for people like managers and users. While queries are confined to the Configuration Manager console for viewing the results, reports can be viewed through a web browser by anyone with permission. The key is that your target audience does not require the Configuration Manager console. Reports also generate a richer viewing experience, with the ability to build charts, set automatic refresh intervals, and set e-mail triggers.

Types of Reports

Reports in Configuration Manager 2007 come in three flavors: predefined, custom, or supplemental reports. Predefined reports and custom reports are done within the SCCM console, while supplemental reports are more advanced reports created outside of SCCM. In this chapter, we will be focused on predefined and custom reports.

Tip

> If you have rights, it is a good idea to create reports at the central site. Since data flows up in the Configuration Manager hierarchy, the central site contains most of the data you'd be looking for. This is especially important if you're trying to retrieve accurate, global data.

Understanding the Reports Language

Unlike queries, reports are written in SQL (Structured Query Language). In this section, we will identify where this information is stored in the Configuration

Manager database, the basics of the SQL syntax, and how to leverage advanced features of SQL to get the data you are looking for.

SQL Views

When you run a report, an SQL statement runs against a set of SQL views. Think of a view as a dynamic table. Instead of querying the tables directly, you are querying a dynamic table that retrieves its columns and records from multiple tables throughout the Configuration Manager site database. These views help combine related information scattered in tables through the site database, saving you a lot of time.

Fundamentals

SQL can be complicated, but it doesn't have to be. In this section, we'll go over a few basic commands of the SQL syntax and how they are used to retrieve data from Configuration Manager. At this point, you don't need to worry about trying to do this yourself. Just read through this section and learn the basic fundamentals of the SQL syntax. We will walk through creating a report later in this chapter.

At a very basic level, an SQL statement looks like this:

```
SELECT * FROM v_Package
```

In this example, we are asking for every record and every column in the SQL View named v_Package. In Configuration Manager, this would return information about every package. Now, let's add some criteria. Perhaps we only want to select packages that have Microsoft set as the Manufacturer. In this scenario, we add a WHERE clause to do just that.

```
SELECT * FROM v_Package WHERE Manufacturer = 'Microsoft'
```

This returns all records and columns from the v_Package view with 'Microsoft' in the Manufacturer column. However, using an asterisk after your SELECT statement is not always a good idea. Most of the time, you know what columns you need to return. Instead of using an asterisk as a wildcard to return all columns in the view, you should list the columns you would like to return. This makes your query statement much more efficient.

```
SELECT Name,Version,Manufacturer,PackageID FROM V_Package WHERE Manufacturer =
'Microsoft'
```

This statement searches for all packages that have Microsoft as the Manufacturer, and returns the four columns listed in the SELECT statement.

If you understand the syntax up to this point, you're doing great. You have a fundamental understanding of how to request information from a database using SQL. Next, we'll look at some more advanced aspects of the SQL syntax.

SQL JOINS

An SQL JOIN is a clause that combines records based on a common field from multiple tables or views in a database. When creating reports in Configuration Manager 2007, understanding how to use a JOIN is a necessity. For example, if you need to return the computer name and serial number of a machine, these are stored in two separate views in the Configuration Manager site database. These views share a common field (Resource ID) which you can use to create a JOIN.

While there are several different types and subtypes of SQL JOINS, there are two primary types of JOINS you will be using in Configuration Manager reports:

- **INNER JOINS**—An inner join returns rows when there is at least one match in both views. In other words, if you are joining two views on the Resource ID field, a matching value will have to exist in both views. In your SQL syntax, if you simply specify JOIN without designating which type, an inner join is used by default.

- **OUTER JOINS**—An outer join returns all rows regardless of a matching row between the joined views.

Running a Report

When you run a report in SCCM, you are using something called the report viewer. The report viewer is available through the Configuration Manager console or through your web browser.

To run a report from the Configuration Manager console:

1. Open the Configuration Manager console and go to Site Database > Computer Management > Reporting > Reports.

2. Scroll to a report you'd like to run, right-click it, and choose Run.

Note

Depending on how your console is configured, your report results will either appear in the console or in a browser window.

To run a report from a web browser:

1. Open your web browser and navigate to the URL: http://servername/ SMSReporting_site code.

2. On the left, you can navigate through all of the different reports available. Click a report and it will run in the right pane.

Creating a Basic Custom Report

Now that you have a basic understanding of the SQL syntax, it's time to put what you just learned to good use. Creating reports in Configuration Manager can be challenging—so we'll start with something simple. In this first example, we will write a basic report to list the name and ID of all advertisements.

1. To get started, open the Configuration Manager console and go to Site Database > Computer Management > Reporting > Reports. Then, right-click Reports, select New > Report. The New Report Wizard appears (Figure 10.13).

Figure 10.13
New Report Wizard

2. Name the report Names and IDs of all advertisements, then type Learning into the Category field.

Note

Creating new categories is a great way of organizing your custom reports. The Category field is case-sensitive, so make sure to be consistent when trying to put a custom report into a category you had previously created.

3. Click the Edit SQL Statement button. You are presented with the Report SQL Statement window (Figure 10.14).

Tip

On the left, you will see a list of available SQL views. When you select a view, the available columns for that view appear in the right listbox. In this example, we will be working with the v_Advertisement view. You can select that view and see the available columns you might want to return.

4. In the SQL statement textbox, erase the existing contents and type the following command:

```
SELECT AdvertisementName,AdvertisementID FROM v_Advertisement ORDER BY
AdvertisementName
```

Figure 10.14
Report SQL Statement Window

5. Click the OK button. You should return back to the New Report Wizard.

6. Click Next through the remaining pages in the wizard, accepting default settings.

7. Back at the Configuration Manager console, find your report, right-click and select Run.

Tip

An easy way for finding reports is to use the "Look for" field above. You can use this to search all columns or select specific columns you want to search.

You have successfully created a report to list All Advertisements and Advertisement IDs. Notice in the SQL SELECT statement, we added the keyword ORDER BY to sort the results by the Advertisement Name. The ORDER BY keyword sorts records in ascending order by default.

Creating a Reports Search Folder

Search Folders under Configuration Manager Reports allows you to create a dynamic folder that lists reports that meet a specific set of criteria. In the previous example, we created a category for our report called Learning. For the sake of managing these reports and being able to quickly reference them, we will create a search folder that will list all reports that have the Learning category. As we move through this chapter, you will create additional reports that will also use this category.

To create a search folder:

1. Open the Configuration Manager console and go to Site Database > Computer Management > Reporting > Reports.

2. Right-click Reports and choose New > Search Folder. You are presented with the Search Folder Criteria window (Figure 10.15).

3. Check the Category box under the Step 1 list box.

4. In the Step 2 box, choose "items to find" next to Category.

5. Scroll through the list box and find the Learning category, then select it.

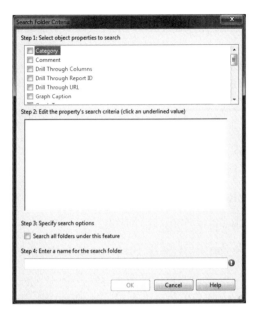

Figure 10.15
Search Folder Criteria

6. Click OK on the Search Text window.

7. Check the Search All Folders under This Feature option under Step 3.

8. Under Step 4, enter a name for your search folder. In this example, we will simply call it Learning.

9. Click OK on the Search Folder Criteria window.

10. The Learning Search folder should now appear under Reports in the Configuration Manager console.

Creating Advanced Custom Report

At many companies, storing music files on your computer is against policy. Of course, if you don't lock down your machines, you are bound to have users with gigabytes of music scattered all over their hard drives. Wouldn't it be nice to have a report for that? In this example, we will create a report to search for all computers with more than ten MP3 files. We'll be working with the v_GS_SoftwareFile view, which contains the file inventory data retrieved with the software inventory client agent.

Note

For this example, you will need to set your software inventory client agent to scan for MP3 files if this is not already configured. To do so, Navigate to Site Database > Site Management > Your Site > Site Settings > Client Agents. Then, choose Software Inventory Client Agent. Under the Inventory Collection tab, create a new entry for *.mp3. Make sure to include subfolders.

1. Open the Configuration Manager console and go to Site Database > Computer Management > Reporting > Reports.

2. Right-click Reports and choose New > Report.

3. Name the report All Computers with Greater than 10 MP3s.

4. Set the Category to Learning, then click the Edit SQL Statement button at the bottom of the wizard.

5. Erase the default contents in the SQL statement textbox at the bottom of the window, then enter the following syntax:
```
SELECT v_R_System.Netbios_Name0 as 'Computer Name', COUNT(distinct
v_GS_SoftwareFile.FileName) as 'Total MP3 Files'
FROM v_GS_SoftwareFile
JOIN v_R_System on v_R_System.ResourceID = v_GS_SoftwareFile.ResourceID
WHERE v_GS_SoftwareFile.FileName LIKE '%.mp3'
GROUP BY v_R_System.Netbios_Name0
HAVING COUNT(distinct v_GS_SoftwareFile.FileName) > 10
ORDER BY 'Total MP3 Files' DESC
```

6. Click OK on the Report SQL Statement window.

7. Click Next through the New Report Wizard until the Report Wizard says it has completed successfully. Then click Close.

8. Below Reports, navigate to the Learning search folder you created. Then, choose the Run All Computers With Greater Than 10 MP3s report to verify your query statement was successful.

Now, let's go line by line and walk through the code behind this report. I've listed the code, numbering each line.
```
[1] SELECT v_R_System.Netbios_Name0 as 'Computer Name', COUNT(distinct v_GS_-
SoftwareFile.FileName) as 'Total MP3 Files'
[2] FROM v_GS_SoftwareFile
```

```
      JOIN v_R_System on v_R_System.ResourceID = v_GS_SoftwareFile.ResourceID
[3] WHERE v_GS_SoftwareFile.FileName LIKE '%.mp3'
[4] GROUP BY v_R_System.Netbios_Name0
[5] HAVING COUNT(distinct v_GS_SoftwareFile.FileName) > 10
[6] ORDER BY 'Total MP3 Files' DESC
```

LINE 1—We are requesting the Computer Name and the Count of Files meeting our criteria.

LINE 2—This line designates where to look. In this example, we are looking in v_GS_SoftwareFile and v_R_System, two SQL views in the Configuration Manager site database. We use a JOIN statement to link these two views by a common field (Resource ID). Since there is no specific JOIN type specified, an inner join will be used.

LINE 3—This is where we set the criteria. In this case, we use LIKE and % as a wildcard to designate any file that ends with '.mp3'.

LINE 4—Because we are using the aggregate function COUNT, we are required to use the GROUP BY clause. This is because aggregate functions return query result sets instead of individual records. Other aggregate functions include SUM, AVG, MAX, and MIN.

LINE 5—The HAVING clause functions much like a WHERE clause, except it applies to groups instead of individual rows. In this example, we are using the HAVING clause to retrieve records where the total number of MP3 files is greater than 10.

LINE 6—This line orders the results by the Total Number of MP3s column. DESC means it is set to descending, that way your biggest MP3 offenders appear at the top of the list.

Creating Report with Prompts

Sometimes it's nice to be able to supply information into a report without having to further modify it. Prompts in Configuration Manager Reports allow you to ask for information while running a report. This is a great way of limiting the number of reports and also a great way of giving the person running the report a little flexibility. In this example, we will use the predefined report All Inventoried Files on a Specific Computer as a starting point. When you run the report, you'll see that it already provides a prompt. We're going to modify the report parameters a little to look just for MP3 files. This will allow us to create a link with the report you created in the previous example. If you don't know what linking reports is for, don't worry. We'll go into that further in the next section.

To get started:

1. Open the Configuration Manager console and go to Site Database > Computer Management > Reporting > Reports.

2. Using the Look for field at the top of the screen, type All Inventoried Files on a Specific Computer and press Enter.

3. Right-click the Report and choose Clone. The Clone Report dialog box appears (Figure 10.16).

Tip

You should never modify the predefined reports in Configuration Manager. Always use the Clone feature and work off of a copy of the original report.

4. In the New Report name field, change the text to All inventoried MP3s on a specific computer, and then click OK.

5. Now, search for the new report you just created. Right-click on it, then choose Properties.

6. Click the Edit SQL Statement button. The Report SQL Statement window appears.

7. Click the Prompts button. The Prompts dialog appears (Figure 10.17).

8. Note that the name of the prompt is "variable," then click OK.

Figure 10.16
Clone Report Dialog Box

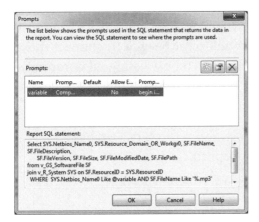

Figure 10.17
Prompts Dialog Box

9. Back at the Report SQL Statement window, toward the bottom of the SQL statement, notice how this statement uses the prompted value:
`WHERE SYS.Netbios_Name0 Like @variable`

10. Since we are looking for only MP3 files, we will use the AND operator to add an additional piece of criteria to this query statement. Change the previous line of code to look like this:
`WHERE SYS.Netbios_Name0 Like @variable AND SF.FileName Like '%.mp3'`

11. Click OK.

12. In the Category drop-down, select Learning. Then click OK. Remember that this field is case-sensitive, so make sure to use the existing Learning category that you have already created.

13. Run the report to ensure it works properly.

Linking Reports

Report links allow you to access more information about the results in your report. With a report link, you can link a specific field in a report to another report entirely. This enables you to limit the amount of information on the original source report, while giving the user a quick way to delve deeper into the report data if needed. In the previous two examples, we created a report that would list all computers with more than 10 MP3 files. Then, we created a report to list all MP3 files on a specific computer. Wouldn't it be nice to connect these reports? With a link in place, you can run the first report listing all computers with MP3 files, then choose the computer name to run the report to list the specific MP3 files on the computer you select. Let's give it a try.

1. Open the Configuration Manager console and go to Site Database > Computer Management > Reporting > Reports.

2. Find the All Computers with Greater Than 10 MP3s Report.

3. Right-click the Report and choose Properties.

4. Click the Links tab (Figure 10.18).

5. Under Link Type, select Link to Another Report.

6. Click the Select button next to report. The Select Report window appears (Figure 10.19).

7. Select the All Inventoried MP3s on a Specific Computer report, then click OK.

Figure 10.18
Report Links Tab

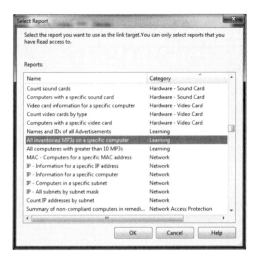

Figure 10.19
Select Report Window

Note

Under the Prompts section, note that the variable name "variable" is linked to Column 1. This means that Column 1 of the report All Computers with Greater Than 10 MP3s will be passed into the prompted value for this report. If you look back at the order of columns, you'll see that Column 1 is the Computer Name.

8. Click OK again to save your changes.

9. Run your All Computers with Greater Than 10 MP3s report.

Note

You will notice a small arrow icon to the left of Computer Name. Select this arrow next to a specific computer and it will pass that computer name as the prompted value for the other report. This will then list all MP3 files for that specific computer.

THE FINAL WORD

Creating queries and reports in Configuration Manager is your method of requesting and presenting information from the site database. Both of these methods have their own niche that makes them unique and useful in their own right. Ask yourself who your audience is—and what you intend to ultimately do with the information you're retrieving. If your audience consists of users and managers, a report might be the better solution. If your results will be used as something you target with an advertisement, a query is likely the way to go. There is no wrong choice if the result is what you need it to be. You don't have to be a database wiz to make useful information out of all of that data in the site database. You just need to know what you're looking for, and where you're looking for it.

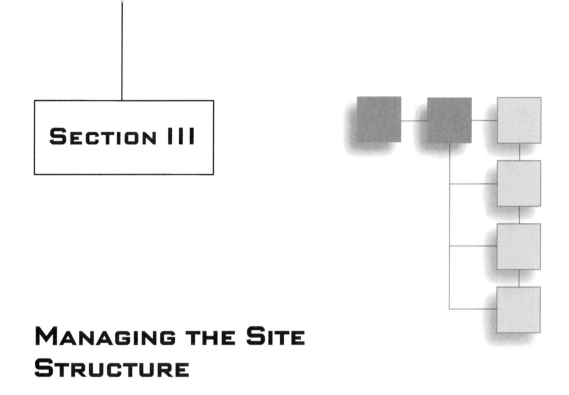

SECTION III

MANAGING THE SITE STRUCTURE

In this section, we will be focusing less on the design and procedural aspects of Configuration Manager and more on concepts and components within the product. Because our Configuration Manager infrastructure is now set up and in place, we can delve into the functionality aspects of Configuration Manager and how to manage these components. This section can be somewhat difficult because of the sheer number of components that are required to make all of this stuff work. Each component can have multiple settings that are located in different sections within Configuration Manager. Trying to find your way through the product and remembering which items are responsible for what will more than likely be tough to conquer. After time, however, configuring these items becomes easier through repetition.

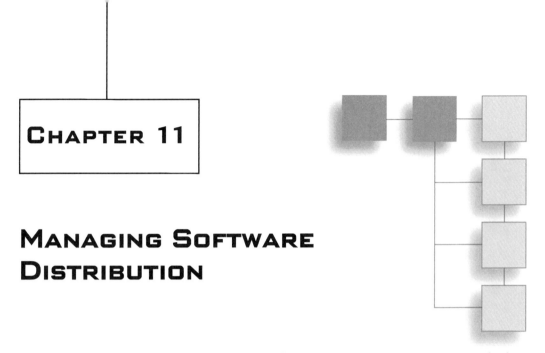

CHAPTER 11

MANAGING SOFTWARE DISTRIBUTION

One of the most common uses of Configuration Manager 2007 is to deploy software to computers within an organization.

Configuration Manager 2007 gives you many options regarding this feature so that you can meet the needs of your environment whether it be small and simple or large and complex. This chapter will familiarize you with the components of software distribution, how to configure and manage these components, and finally, how to use these components to distribute software to the computers or users that you specify.

INTRODUCTION TO SOFTWARE DISTRIBUTION

Software distribution within Configuration Manager 2007 requires many components to be in place and configured before software can start to be installed on a user's computer. Some components are mandatory while others are optional— giving you the ability to customize your environment to meet your needs. The components that are listed next are just some of the items that can be used to optimize your software distribution experience and will be covered in depth throughout the remainder of this chapter.

- Collections
- Packages
- Programs

- Advertisements
- Schedules
- Maintenance Windows
- Wake-On-LAN
- Reports
- Notifications
- Task Sequences
- Distribution Points
- Client Cache

In other words, there are a lot of things that you need to know to successfully distribute software across your organization. As we go through this chapter, we'll demystify these components and give you the confidence and know-how to distribute software to your heart's content.

UNDERSTANDING COLLECTIONS

Okay. Let's talk about collections. Collections are one of the most important aspects within Configuration Manager 2007. In fact, without collections, the product is almost useless.

Collections are objects—kind of like folders—that group Configuration Manager resources together such as computers, users, or groups. These resources can be grouped in one of two ways: direct-based membership or query-based membership. Direct-based collections group together resources based on the resource that you manually specify. For example, if you want computer 1 to be in collection A, you specify that computer 1 is in collection A—end of story. Query-based collections group resources together based on specific criteria that you specify. For example, computers whose names end in 00 will automatically be added to collection B. Query-based collections give Configuration Manager administrators the ability to have a lot of fun and be clever as to how they manage their environment.

PREDEFINED COLLECTIONS

When Configuration Manager 2007 is initially installed, it comes with a set of predefined collections. These collections are query based and group resources together based on common query scenarios such as operating system type or all systems within the Configuration Manager hierarchy. The collections that come predefined are as follows:

- All Active Directory Security Groups
- All Desktops and Servers
- All Systems
- All Unknown Computers
- All User Groups
- All Users
- All Windows 2000 Professional Systems
- All Windows 2000 Server Systems
- All Windows Mobile Devices
- All Windows Mobile Pocket PC 2003 Devices
- All Windows Mobile Pocket PC 5.0 Devices
- All Windows Mobile Smartphone 2003 Devices
- All Windows Mobile Smartphone 5.0 Devices
- All Windows Server 2003 Systems
- All Windows Server Systems
- All Windows Workstation or Professional Systems
- All Windows XP Systems

These collections serve as a starting point so that new Configuration Manager administrators can easily find their resources without having to manually create new collections. The All Systems collection, for instance, is a good example of a collection that helps administrators quickly view all of the computers and servers that exist in their site or even the entire Configuration Manager hierarchy if you are connected to the central site.

Note

Every collection in Configuration Manager 2007 has a collection ID. This ID is how Configuration Manager references its collections and is used for things like custom queries, reports, and scripts. These IDs are generated by the site name and a random hex number. For example, if a collection was created at the LIS site, its collection ID might be LIS00005. The predefined collections, however, have specific collection IDs and are the same in each site. For example, the All Systems collection ID is SMS00001. If you decide to build a Configuration Manager hierarchy with a central site, the predefined collections can only be managed at the central site and are locked at lower sites. This is because the central site and the lower sites all have the same predefined collections with the same collection IDs. Since these are the same throughout the hierarchy, the central site manages these collections. We'll talk a bit more about how different collections behave when in different sites later in this chapter.

Tip

If you're new to Configuration Manager 2007 and skipped over Chapters 7 and 8, you might be wondering why there are no resources in your default collections. If you haven't set up a discovery method or haven't deployed the Configuration Manager 2007 client to your computers, you won't see any resources until these steps have taken place. I highly recommend that you read Chapters 7 and 8 prior to jumping into this section.

CREATING COLLECTIONS

If you're not satisfied with the predefined collections, you can create your own (which I highly recommend!) to help manage your environment. Creating collections can be very tricky since there's not really a right or wrong way to do it. Some administrators organize by geographic location, some by role or function, or some by a mixture of both. Other administrators have a multitude of collections that are organized specifically for software distribution tasks such as the software manufacturer name or program run time. Because collections are so versatile, just about anything can be accomplished by using them—especially in a complex environment. Although there isn't necessarily a right or wrong way to create a collection, there are some best practices to use when creating your collections.

- **Separate workstations from servers**—If you create a collection that contains both workstations and servers, you might accidently install unwanted software to your servers. If the software is configured to restart the machines, this could potentially cause an issue.

- **Separate systems (workstations, servers, etc.) from users**—Collections can hold multiple resources such as workstations, users, and user groups. If you create a collection that contains multiple types of resources, you run the risk of installing software at unintended times or not installing software at all if it is designed to install for a user but no users exist in that collection, for example.

Note

In the next version of Configuration Manager, you will not have the ability to group dissimilar resources together, such as computers and users, in the same collection. Although it may be tempting to organize your environment in this fashion, I recommend against it since it will not be allowed in future releases.

- **Keep the update schedule at the defaults**—When creating a collection, you have the option of creating membership rules which define how resources will be added to the collection and when the collection will query the database to find more resources that may have been added since the last membership query. By default, this is set to recur every day. If you have a large number of collections that contain a large number of resources, and these collections are set to update very frequently, it could put a huge burden on your database, causing the Configuration Manager infrastructure to operate very slowly. Use caution when modifying these settings. If you have R3 installed, use the Dynamically Add New Resources option to achieve collection evaluation updates more frequently. We'll cover that more in depth later in this chapter.

- **If you use direct membership collections, don't use an update schedule**—If your environment demands that you create collections by using direct memberships instead of queries, don't use an update schedule. Direct membership-based collections do not need to be updated since their resources are manually added by an administrator and never change automatically.

■ **Use query-based membership collections whenever possible**—Query-based membership collections are much easier to maintain than direct-based membership collections. The reason for this is that Configuration Manager uses SMS unique identifiers to keep track of its resources rather than resource names. If you manually add a computer to a collection for example, and then you replace that computer at a later date with a new one (using the same name), the resource(s) in the collection(s) will no longer reference the new computer because the SMS unique identifiers will no longer match—even if the new computer has the same name. If that computer was manually added to 500 collections, you'd have to manually remove the old computer 500 times and then re-add it 500 times as well. This is not ideal, to say the least.

■ **When re-using a collection, use a "link to collection" instead of dupli-cating it**—If you work in a complex environment, you may need to create multiple collections in sub-collections that contain the same resources for logistical reasons. If you need to create a collection in another location that is identical to one you've already created, use the New > Link to Collection option when duplicating the collection. This will allow you to create a collection by choosing one that's already been created. When you do this, it not only reduces your workload by not having to re-create the query, but it saves on Configuration Manager resources as well because multiple collections aren't actually querying the database for new resources. The original collection is querying the database but the view that you see in Configuration Manager simply references the original collection.

Creating a New Collection

The process of creating a collection is pretty straightforward. Simply connect the Configuration Manager console to the site where you want to create the collection and follow the steps below. In our example, we'll connect to the CHI primary child site.

1. Expand the Computer Management node.

2. Right-click on the Collections node and choose New Collection. (See Figure 11.1.)

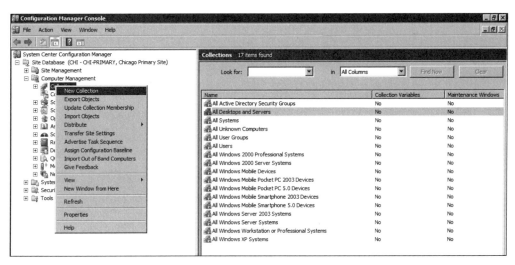

Figure 11.1
Create a New Collection

3. The New Collection Wizard is displayed. Enter a name for the new collection in the Name: field. If you have any comments that you'd like to include with this collection, such as the role of the collection or who created it, enter that in the Comment: field. In our example, we'll name this Chicago. Click Next to continue. (See Figure 11.2.)

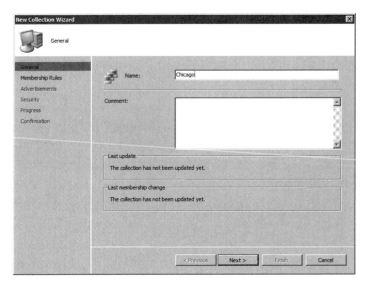

Figure 11.2
New Collection Wizard

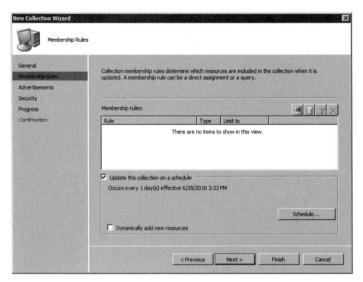

Figure 11.3
Membership Rules

4. The membership rules section of the New Collection Wizard is displayed. This window lets you choose which type of collection this will be. You can make it a direct membership-based collection or a query membership-based collection. You can also choose to skip this step if you wish to create your membership rules later or if this collection will not contain any resources—only other collections (sub-collections) below it. The configuration options for the collection membership rules section are discussed next and shown in Figure 11.3.

   ▪ **Membership rules**—This section allows you to create membership rules for this collection. Membership rules define how resources are added to a collection and can be determined by direct membership or query. We will cover membership rules in depth later in this chapter.

   ▪ **Update this collection on a schedule**—By default, collections update automatically every day at the time the collection was created. Collection updates are necessary because they must query the database for new resources based on the query membership that is defined in the membership rules section. If a new resource is added that meets the criteria of the query, it will be added to the collection when an update occurs. If updates are disabled on a collection, they will never add new resources unless manually done so by direct membership. As stated earlier, refrain from changing this schedule if possible. The Configuration Manager 2007 scalability tests are based on a Configuration Manager infrastructure using the defaults—including the collection update schedule.

- **Schedule**—If you choose to change the update schedule, the Schedule button allows for you to do so.

- **Dynamically add new resources**—This checkbox is only available if Configuration Manager 2007 R3 is installed. This allows for something called Fast Evaluation. It works by first doing a full collection update (evaluation) and then only looking for newly discovered resources. If a new resource is found, only that resource is processed and added to the collection, which makes for less overhead. Because of the overhead decrease, new resources can be added to collections within minutes instead of hours. Prior to R3, administrators were forced to change the collection update schedule because one day was simply too slow to add resources to collections. With R3, you shouldn't have to change the update schedule if Dynamically Add New Resources is checked.

5. The Advertisements section of the New Collection Wizard is displayed. Since this is a new collection, no programs are advertised to this collection. Click Next to continue. (See Figure 11.4.)

6. The Security section of the New Collection Wizard is displayed. If you need to change any security rights that are listed, you can do so for this specific collection. (See Figure 11.5.) For more information about security within Configuration Manager 2007, see Chapter 19, "Using Tools from the Toolkit." Click Next to continue.

7. The Confirmation section of the New Collection Wizard is displayed (see Figure 11.6). Click Close to close the Wizard.

Note

The different steps that we covered in the New Collection Wizard can be seen and modified at a later time by right-clicking on the collection and choosing Properties.

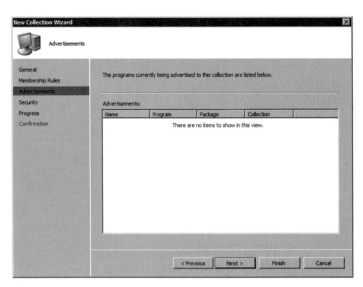

Figure 11.4
Advertisements

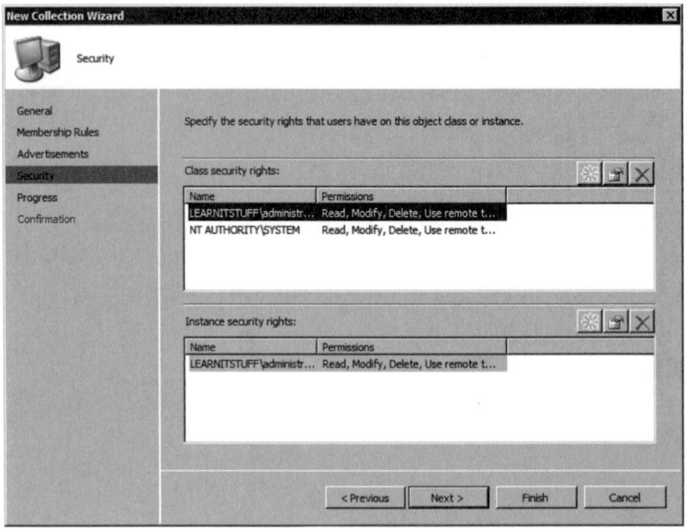

Figure 11.5
Security

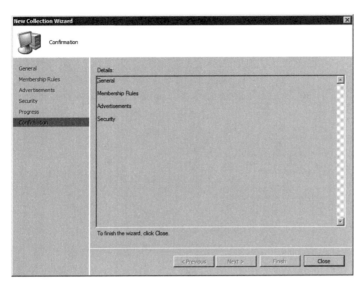

Figure 11.6
Confirmation

Creating a Link to Collection

Another option when creating a collection is to create a link to collection. A link to collection allows you to "create" a collection by simply referencing an already existing collection. This is nice when you need to duplicate a collection for management purposes but don't want to have to re-create the query multiple times and also don't want to burden the database with multiple queries since only one collection actually exists—the collection that you are referencing. Link to collections can only exist underneath existing collections. To create a link to collection, do the following:

1. Expand the Computer Management node.

2. Expand the Collections node, right-click on an existing collection and choose New > Link to Collection. In our example, we'll create the link to collection under the Chicago collection that we created in the last step. (See Figure 11.7.)

3. The Browse Collection dialog box opens. This allows you to choose which collection you will be linking to. Any collection that exists in your site can be chosen. In our example, we'll choose the All Windows XP Systems and click OK to continue. (See Figure 11.8.)

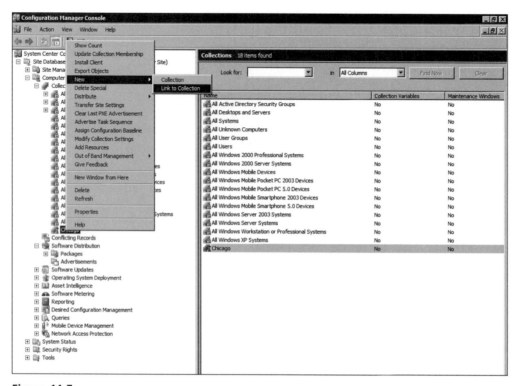

Figure 11.7
Create a New Link to Collection

Figure 11.8
Browse for Collections

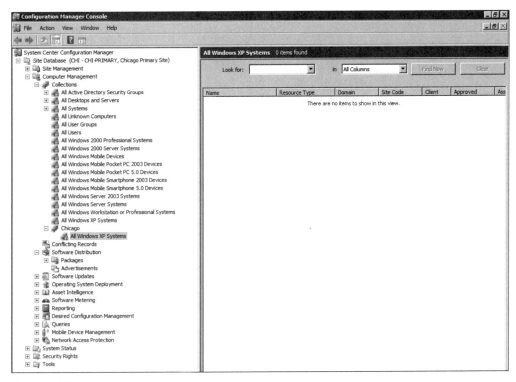

Figure 11.9
Creation of the Link to Collection

4. The link to collection has now been created under the collection that you
   chose in step 1. In our example, we chose a collection that was created at
   a higher level site in the hierarchy. This is useful because you may not
   want to link to collections that you made at your site, rather, you'd like
   to link to collections that another administrator at the central site has
   created. (See Figure 11.9.)

ADDING RESOURCES

Once you have created your collections, you now need to put resources into
these collections. Once the resources have been added, you also need to know
how to manage those resources for day-to-day operations.

Direct Membership

The simplest, yet hardest to manage, way of adding resources to your collections is by using direct membership. Using direct membership, you can add users, user groups, systems, and unknown computers to collections via a manual process. Once these resources are added to a collection, they will remain in that collection until you manually remove them or until the objects are deleted from Configuration Manager. As we talked about earlier in this chapter, direct membership-based collections might cause an issue if you have two or more resources (like computers) with the same name because of a hardware replacement or other reason. If this is the case, the wrong resource might be in the direct membership collection instead of the correct one. Think about using query-based membership collections if this is the case in your environment.

Note

Collections can have multiple membership rules. This means that you can have one or more direct-based membership rules, one or more query-based membership rules, or even a combination of the two. If you have a combination of the two, this is a type of hybrid-based membership collection and can be difficult to manage—especially if you forget how the membership rules were created.

Direct- or query-based membership rules can be created during the collection creation process or after a collection has already been created. Since we went through the process of creating a collection in the last section, we'll use one of our existing collections to create a new membership rule.

To add a membership rule to an existing collection, do the following:

1. Expand the Computer Management node.

2. Expand the Collections node, right-click on an existing collection, and choose Properties. In our example, we'll open the properties on the Chicago collection that we created in the last step. (See Figure 11.10.)

3. The Properties window for the collection is displayed. Click on the Membership Rules tab. (See Figure 11.11.)

4. The Membership Rules tab is displayed. At the top of the page, four icons are visible. These control your membership rules such as creating new memberships, modifying memberships, and deleting memberships.

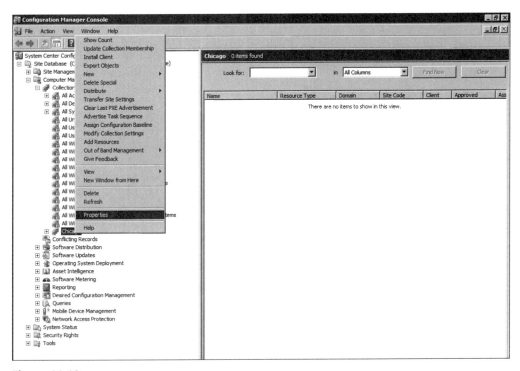

Figure 11.10
Open Properties on an Existing Collection

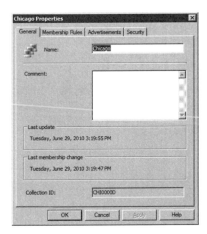

Figure 11.11
Collection Properties

Figure 11.12
Membership Rules Tab

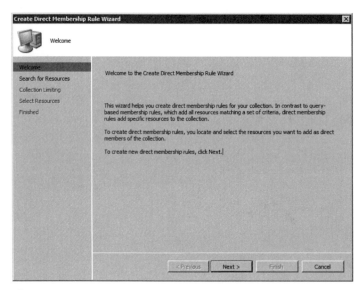

Figure 11.13
Direct Membership Rule Wizard

In this example, we will create a new direct membership rule by clicking on the direct membership rule creation icon. (See Figure 11.12.)

5. The Direct Membership Rule Wizard is displayed. This wizard takes you through the steps of adding a resource to a collection using direct membership rules. Click Next to continue. (See Figure 11.13.)

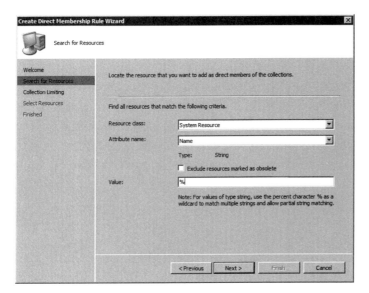

Figure 11.14
Search for Resources Section

6. The Search for Resources section is displayed. This lets you find the resources that you want to add to your collections. Resources can be Systems (Computers), Users, User Groups, or Unknown Computers. These are known as resource classes. Each resource class can have attributes and values as well. This is shown in Figure 11.14. For example, the system resource has an attribute of name—meaning the computer name. The value would be the actual name of the computer. For more information on resource classes, the attributes and possible values they have, refer to Chapter 10, "Creating and Managing Queries and Reports." The configuration options for the Search for Resources section are also shown in Figure 11.14 and are discussed next.

- **Resource class**—A resource class is a type of resource that exists in Configuration Manager 2007. The possible resource classes that exist in Configuration Manager 2007 are system resources, user resources, user resource groups, and unknown computers. In our example, we will search for computers, which fall under the system resource class.

- **Attribute name**—The attribute name varies between each resource class. In our example, we will use the name attribute of the system resource class to find computers based on their computer name.

- **Exclude resources marked as obsolete**—This option excludes obsolete objects from your search results. We will talk more about obsolete objects later in this chapter.

- **Value**—The Value field defines the value of the attribute that you specified above. For instance, if a computer was named SERVER-01, you could use that string value to return results for computers whose name matches that value. In our example, we will use the wildcard, %, to find all system resource classes (computers) whose attribute "name" matches "%" or all.

7. Once you define your search for resources on the Search for Resources section, click Next.

8. The Collection Limiting section of the Direct Membership Rule Wizard is displayed. This lets you search for resources that fall within specific collections. This is helpful when you have thousands of resources and want to limit your search to only one collection. In our example, we will leave this field blank and click Next to continue. (See Figure 11.15.)

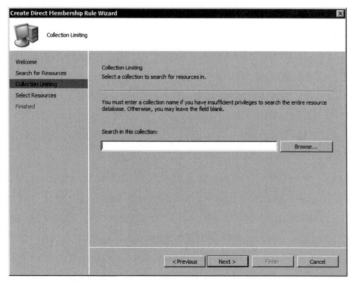

Figure 11.15
Collection Limiting

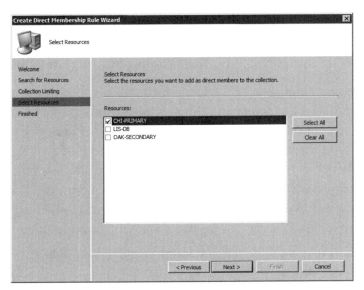

Figure 11.16
Select Resources

Note

If your security rights do not allow you to search the entire resource database, you must specify a collection that you have access to. The search will fail if you do not have the appropriate permissions.

9. The Select Resources section is displayed. This lets you choose all of the matching resources (based on your query) that will be added to this collection. In our example, we'll choose the CHI-PRIMARY resource. Click Next to continue. (See Figure 11.16.)

10. The final page of the wizard is displayed, showing you which resources were added to your collection. Click Finish to close the Wizard.

Query-Based Membership Rules

Query-based membership rules can be simple or very complex depending on what you need to do in your environment. Collections use WMI Query Language (WQL) to construct queries just as standard queries do within Configuration Manager. Because we already covered more of the advanced topics as far as query design and structure back in Chapter 10, we won't get much into that here. We will, however, create some generic queries so that we can show examples of how to populate our collections with more resources.

Query-based membership rules can be created during the collection creation process or after a collection has been created just as with direct-based membership rules. Query-based membership rules, however, can be imported from existing queries that you have already created in the queries node. This is immensely helpful when creating multiple (non-identical) collections that are based on the same query. Instead of having to re-create the query from scratch, you can just import a query and then modify it slightly to meet your needs. We will cover creating queries from scratch and also cover importing a query next.

Since we already have a collection (Chicago) with a direct membership-based rule, we will create a new collection (Central Site) and make a new query-based membership rule from scratch. Follow these steps to complete this process:

1. Create a new collection. In our example, we'll name it Central Site.

2. When you get to the membership rules section of the New Collection Wizard, create a query-based membership collection as shown in Figure 11.12.

3. The Query Rule Properties window is displayed. This window allows you to create a new query membership rule. The configuration options for the Query Rule Properties window is shown in Figure 11.17 and are discussed next.

   ▪ **Name field**—This field is used to name the query. I suggest that you name it something descriptive so you know what it's for in the future. In our example, we'll name this query Find Computers by Name at the Central Site.

   ▪ **Import Query Statement**—This button lets you import existing queries that exist under the Queries node. We will cover this later in this chapter.

   ▪ **Resource class drop-down**—This lets you choose the class that the query will be based upon. In our example, we will be looking for computers so we will choose the System Resource class.

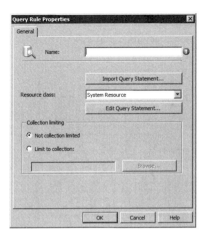

Figure 11.17
Query Rule Properties

- **Edit Query Statement**—This option lets you create a query from scratch or lets you modify one that was imported from an existing query.
- **Collection Limiting**—This section lets you limit the query to a specific collection if you choose to do so. This is helpful if you have a large number of resources and want to limit the search to only a specific collection.

4. Click the Edit Query Statement button to create a new query.

5. The Query Statement Properties window is displayed. This should look familiar to you since it is the same window that we used to create queries back in Chapter 10. In this example, we will create a query to find all computers whose names start with LIS so that they are then added to the Central Site collection.

Tip

To get a complete understanding of how to create a query and all of the options available, please read Chapter 10, "Managing Queries and Reports."

6. Once the query has been created, it will be shown in the Membership Rules section of the New Collection Wizard as shown in Figure 11.18. Click Next to continue.

7. Complete the New Collection Wizard.

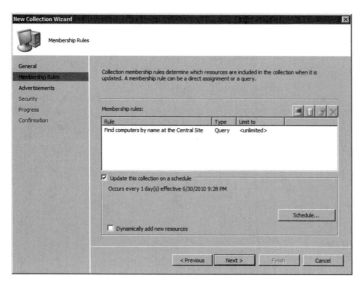

Figure 11.18
Query Rule

Right-Click Menu Option

Prior to Configuration Manager 2007 R3, there were no built-in methods to add a resource to a collection through the ease of a right-click menu. The only options you had were to create or modify a collection membership rule which took time and wasn't very efficient. Third-party developers started creating right-click tools that allowed you to add resources to collections via a right-click menu, but they did not come in the product by default and were not supported by Microsoft in the event of a problem. With R3, that's all changed. You can now either right-click on a collection to add a resource to it or you can right-click on a resource itself and choose which collection it will become a member of. You can also remove a resource from a collection, which is a very nice addition and helps solve an annoying problem that existed up until now. We'll go over that in a bit.

The first method to add a resource to a collection using the new R3 right-click features is by selecting the collection itself. This means that you can right-click on the collection that you want to add resources to and select all of the resources that meet your search criteria instead of having to select multiple resources individually and step through the process multiple times. This method is good when you need to add multiple resources to one collection.

Caution

Using the R3 right-click menu options to add resources to collections does so by direct membership only. If you have a query-based collection membership rule in effect on a collection and you add multiple resources to it using the R3 right-click menu option, you will create direct membership rules on the collection in addition to your query-based membership rule. This might make it more difficult to manage your collections so be aware.

In our example, we will add the rest of the Chicago systems to the Chicago collection by using the R3 right-click menu options. Follow these steps to add multiple resources to a collection via a right-click menu:

1. Right-click on the collection to which you would like to add resources and choose Add Resources as shown in Figure 11.19. In our example, we'll perform these steps on the Chicago collection.

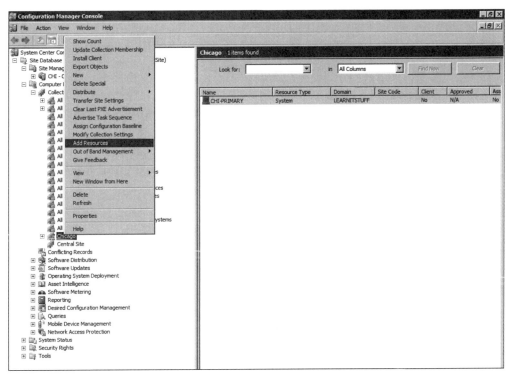

Figure 11.19
Add Resources to Collection (from a collection)

Figure 11.20
Add Resources to Collection Window

2. The Add Resources to Collection window is displayed. This window lets you choose which types of resources to query upon so that you can add them to a collection. The configuration options for the Add Resources to Collection window are shown in Figure 11.20 and are discussed next.

- **Name contains**—This field lets you search for a resource by its name attribute. In our example, we'll look for any system resource that has a value of CHI in the name attribute.

- **Resource Type**—This drop-down box lets you choose which type of resource you are looking for. In our example, we'll choose System Resource since we are looking for computers.

- **Search in collection**—If you would like to limit your search, you can specify a collection to look in instead of searching the entire resource database.

- **Advanced**—The Advanced button lets you search for other attribute values along with the name attribute value at the top of the window.

- **Search**—This button starts the search for resources.

- **Search results**—Any items that matched your search query are returned in the search results list. One or more of the returned resources can be highlighted and added to the collection by clicking the Add button. You can also remove the resource(s) by clicking the

Remove button. In our example, three resources were returned. Since we already added CHI-PRIMARY to the Chicago collection earlier in this chapter, we will deselect that resource and only add CHI-SITE-SYSTEM and CHI-WIN7-01 to the selected resources list.

- **Selected resources**—Once you click the Add button, the resource is moved to the selected resources list. This list shows you which resource will be added to the collection when you press the OK button.

3. The new resources should now be added to your collection.

The other method of adding resources to collections is by using the R3 right-click tools on the resource itself. This allows you to find a resource and quickly add it to an existing collection or new collection. In our example, we'll add a user resource to a new collection using the right-click tools by following these steps:

1. Right-click on the resource that you will add to a collection and choose Manage Collection Membership. In our example, we'll right-click on the Administrator user and create a new collection by choosing New Collection. (See Figure 11.21.)

2. The New Collection Wizard starts just as it did back in Figure 11.2. Create a new collection that your resource will be a member of. In this example, we'll name it Administrators. As you complete the wizard, you'll see that a direct membership has already been created for the new user at the Membership Rules section. Complete the New Collection Wizard by clicking Close.

3. You should now see the new collection that you created with the Administrator user resource as a member.

REMOVING RESOURCES

As time goes by, you might need to remove a resource from a collection—especially if it was added through a direct membership rule. Although this is a fairly simple process, many administrators accidently delete the resource instead of removing the membership rule. For example, if a computer is in multiple collections because of multiple membership rules and an administrator wants to

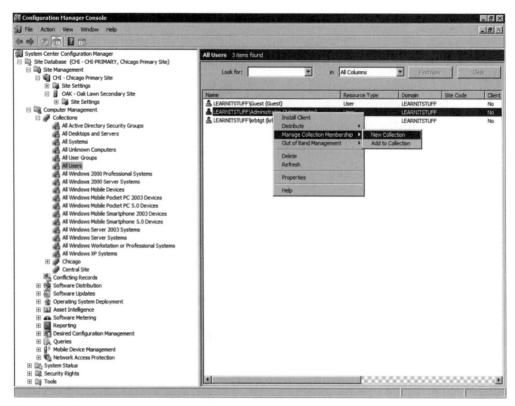

Figure 11.21
Add Resources to Collection (from a resource)

remove the computer from one of the collections, some might right-click on the computer object itself and click Delete. This not only removes it from the collection it was in, but from all collections as well because the object is deleted from the Configuration Manager database. Luckily, R3 helps in situations where a resource was added through a direct membership rule by giving you a right-click menu option to remove it properly. We'll quickly go through the removal of these objects (not deleting them!) via the new R3 right-click tools and by removing a membership rule.

The process to remove a resource by changing a direct membership rule is easy but can be time-consuming if you have to complete the process a large number of times. You simply modify the rule that applies to the resource—just as you did when you created it in the first place. Instead of creating a new rule, you simply delete the one you created previously. Select the rule that applies to the resource that you want to remove from the collection and delete it.

Removing a resource that was added by a query-based membership rule is a little more difficult depending on how the query was set up. If you simply remove the query-based membership rule, all of the resources that were found via that rule will also be removed from the collection. The solution is to modify your query so that it does not include the resource in question.

The last method to remove a resource from a collection is by using the new right-click menu options that were introduced in R3. Simply find the resource that has been added with a direct-based membership rule, right-click on it, and choose Remove from Collection. Although the end goal is the same as manually deleting the direct-based membership rule, it is a much faster process.

MANAGING COLLECTIONS

Once a collection and a membership rule have been created, you should be able to view and manage your resources accordingly. There are some things to understand about collections, however, that directly impact how your resources are managed.

Collection Update Schedules

Earlier in this chapter, we talked about some of the best practices when creating collections. One of these best practices was to keep the update schedule at its default settings so that a large burden would not be (potentially) put on the Configuration Manager infrastructure because of too many queries. However, if you need to change the update schedule for any reason, it can be done by clicking the Schedule button as shown in Figure 11.3. Once you click the Schedule button, you can create your own custom schedule as shown in Figure 11.22.

The schedule can be set up to run in intervals like weekly or monthly, or you can create your own custom interval such as every 1 minute. (Do not do this!)

Dynamically Add New Resources

With the release of Configuration Manager 2007 R3, the Dynamically Add New Resources option is now available in the collection properties, as seen in

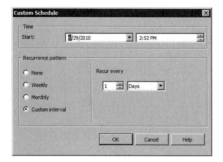

Figure 11.22
Custom Collection Update Schedule

Figure 11.3. When enabled, this turns on something called fast evaluation, which helps pull in new resources much faster without the burden on the infrastructure. This is achieved by the following process:

1. A standard collection update process occurs by querying the resource database for the resources that match a collection membership rule.

2. Once the initial query has been performed, a fast evaluation occurs every five minutes, looking for new resources that are not already in the collection. These results are put into a temporary table.

3. The temporary table is then merged with the master collection results table where the results are compared. If the temporary table contains resources that are not in the master table, only the deltas are processed and are then added to the master results table. If no changes are detected, the master results table is not modified.

In other words, before R3, if you had a collection that needed to be updated very frequently, the only way you could do it was to change the collection update schedule. Although this would have worked, it could have potentially slowed down your Configuration Manager infrastructure depending on how many clients were in the collection and how often it was being updated. With R3, you can keep your collection update schedules at their defaults and simply enable the Dynamically Add New Resources option. Although this may put a small burden on your infrastructure, it will not be nearly as much as a frequent update schedule.

Hierarchical Collections

As we've gone through our Configuration Manager 2007 hierarchy setup, we've hinted at how collections work when in a multi-site environment but we have yet to go into detail about it—until now. Collections are one of the objects within Configuration Manager that flow down the hierarchy—not up. The collections themselves don't actually flow down to child sites; their definitions do. This means that the actual collection only really exists at the site where it was created. The site where the collection was created can be seen by looking at the collection ID in the collection properties. The collection ID will start with the three-character site code from which it originated. Lower level sites can see and interact with these collections, but they cannot be modified. These collections will have a padlock icon meaning that they are locked from modification.

Note

> If a membership rule is created for a collection at a top-level site, it will only flow down the hierarchy if it is a query-based membership rule. Direct-based membership rules will not flow down since the resource they reference may not exist at a lower level site.

So what's the point in having collections that flow down the hierarchy? What advantages are there? Imagine that you are the IT administrator for a company with multiple locations. Each location has a limited number of basic IT administrators who are responsible for distributing software and deploying operating systems at their site only. At your company, you strive for consistency and security so you create standardized query-based membership collections at the central site that flow down to your child primary sites. These collections only add resources that you trust your local site IT administrators to manage. For example, the collections you create only add secretary and lab computers but leave out more critical computers like servers and manager computers. The last thing you want is for a local site IT administrator to accidently deploy a new operating system to the vice president of the company during production hours. You prevent this by not allowing them to create collections or membership rules at their site and let the consistent "good" collections flow down to them. That way, they can still manage the approved resources without having to create non-consistent/non-secure collections.

Moving Collections

If you're like me and want to organize your collections under other collections, you might be looking for the "move collection" option. Unfortunately, this option doesn't exist. However, you can achieve the same results by using the Link to Collection feature. If you want to move a collection, create a link to collection in the desired location, and link it to the original collection that you wanted to originally move. Once you verify that the new link to collection is linked to the original collection, you can delete the original "instance" of the collection. This will not delete your link to collection that you just created and it will be in the desired location. We'll talk more about deleting collections in a bit.

Transfer Site Settings—Collections

The Transfer Site Settings Wizard helps you transfer settings within a site or from one site to another. In the context of collections, you can transfer collection settings, but not the collections themselves. The only collection setting that you can transfer is the collection refresh schedule. This is helpful if you have hundreds of collections that you need to update the refresh schedule on but don't want to have to do it manually—potentially hundreds of times. The Transfer Site Settings Wizard allows you to select a source collection (with the correct refresh schedule) and then transfer those settings to any other collection by simply checking a checkbox. You also have the option of exporting the settings to a file so that they can be imported at a later time. The Transfer Site Settings Wizard can be started from a collection's right-click menu option by clicking Transfer Site Settings. The options in the Transfer Site Settings Wizard are also available from the command line. This tool can be started by executing:

```
<ConfigMgrInstallDir>\AdminUI\Bin\Replstcfg.exe
```

For more information on this command line tool, see the following Technet article: http://technet.microsoft.com/en-us/library/bb680932.aspx

Deleting Collections

Deleting a collection is pretty self-explanatory but there are some points I'd like to cover. When deleting a collection, you have two options: Delete and Delete Special. Delete will start the Delete Collection Wizard, which will walk you through the process of deleting a collection. Within the wizard, you have the option to simply delete the collection by choosing the No. I Know that I Want to Delete this Collection option, or you can choose to see more information about the collection such as the current advertisements, membership rules, etc. that might be associated to the collection. You can opt to see more information by choosing the Yes. I Want to See More Information option.

Note

If you are deleting a collection that has been duplicated by using Link to Collections, you will see a different option when deleting the collection. Instead of asking if you want to delete the collection, the wizard will ask you if you want to delete the instance of the collection. If you delete an instance of a collection, the other instances will not be deleted nor will the resources contained in that instance of the collection.

The Delete Special option lets you remove all of the resources within a collection by actually deleting them from the resource database. This option should be used carefully.

Note

The resources contained within a collection are not removed from the resource database when a collection is deleted. Note that if no other collections contain membership rules to display these resources, they may not be visible until another collection and membership rule are created.

Modifying Collection Settings

Although the previous collection topics can be thought of as "collection settings," they are not technically considered as such since they are not listed under the collection right-click menu option of Modify Collection Settings. This option allows you to configure five different types of collection settings. These are as follows:

- **Maintenance windows**—As stated in Chapter 1, maintenance windows are a new feature in Configuration Manager 2007 and specify when changes can occur. Maintenance windows affect software distribution, software updates, and operating system deployment, and are configured on a per-collection basis. They are designed to keep downtimes to a minimum by not allowing potentially dangerous operations from occurring during production hours. Maintenance windows are cumulative in nature because they can be defined on multiple collections. Since one client can be a member of multiple collections, the client will adhere to all of the rules set by each of the maintenance windows in each collection. Maintenance windows can be ignored, however, if necessary. If you need to push an immediate security update or an urgent piece of software, for example, the advertisement can be configured to ignore the rules in a maintenance window and will occur at the time that is set in the advertisement schedule. We'll talk more about maintenance windows in the advertisements section of this chapter.

▪ **Power Management**—This option is new with Configuration Manager 2007 R3. The settings on this tab allow you to collect power information from your systems and then based on reporting data, you can build a custom power policy that meets your environment's needs. (See Figure 11.23.)

▪ **Collection Variables**—Collection variables are pretty neat. You can set a variable on a collection so that any resource that is a part of the collection can see these variables. This is good for things like operating system deployment because OSD task sequences can make use of these collection variables to help you customize your environment.

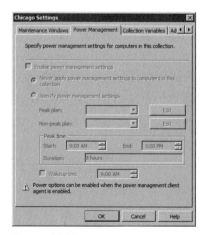

Figure 11.23
Power Management

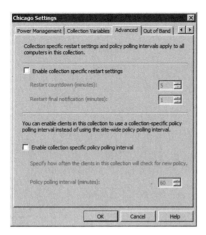

Figure 11.24
Advanced

- **Advanced**—The Advanced tab lets you configure collection specific restart and policy polling settings. If you need your computers in a specific collection to poll their policies more frequently, for example, you can do it on a per-collection basis instead of having to modify it for the entire infrastructure. (See Figure 11.24.)

- **Out of Band**—If you are using out of band management, you can configure all of the capable computers within the collection to be provisioned for out of band management automatically using this tab.

SOFTWARE DISTRIBUTION SITE SETTINGS

Before you can start the process of distributing software with Configuration Manager 2007, you must enable software distribution for the site and optionally change other settings such as notifications and how the computer will behave during this process. These settings are managed through client agents and component settings. We will go over each of these in this section.

As you may remember from Chapters 7 and 8, Configuration Manager controls different client settings through the use of client agents, which are configured per site. These client agents control items such as inventory, software updates, and with R3, power management. The client agents that are used to control behaviors regarding software distribution are the advertised programs client agent and the computer client agent. Client agents are accessed via the Configuration Manager console by going to Site Name > Site Settings > Client Agents.

Advertised Programs Client Agent

The advertised programs client agent is literally where you can "flip the switch" to enable software distribution. This option is not enabled by default so it must be configured before software distribution will be available on your clients. This client agent has two tabs that configure general settings and notification settings. These configuration options are shown in Figures 11.25 and 11.26 and are discussed next.

General Tab

- **Enable software distribution to clients**—This is basically the on/off switch for software distribution in the site. If this is not checked, clients cannot install software via Configuration Manager 2007.

- **Allow user targeted advertisement requests**—This option enables the Configuration Manager client to look for user-targeted advertisements. If this is disabled, only computer targeted advertisements will be successful.

- **New program notification icon opens Add or Remove Programs**— This option allows users to open up the Add or Remove Programs applet

Figure 11.25
General Tab

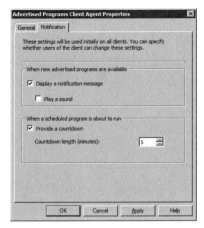

Figure 11.26
Notification Tab

in the control panel by clicking on the notification icon. This will display all of the available advertised programs.

- **Allow virtual application package advertisement**—This option is available if R2 or higher is installed. It allows clients to run virtual application (App-V) advertisements.

Notification Tab

- **Display a notification message**—If this option is selected, a notification balloon will be displayed to users when a new advertised program is available.

- **Play a sound**—If this option is selected, a sound will be played when a new advertised program is available.

- **Provide a countdown**—If a mandatory advertisement is about to run on a computer, a countdown can be shown to users to prepare them for the advertisement. A countdown (in minutes) can be specified in the Countdown Length (minutes) option.

N o t e

The computer client agent provides global restart settings for the client for things like software updates, operating system deployment, or software distribution. If a computer needs to be restarted via one of these items, the restart countdown and final notifications are set via the Restart tab.

Software Distribution Component

The software distribution component is used to configure the location of package source files and advanced distribution point settings. This component is found under Site > Site Settings > Component Configuration > Software Distribution.

General Tab

- **Location of stored packages (Drive on site server)**—This lets you set the location on the site server where compressed package source files are held. Compressed package source files are created if you choose the option "Use a compressed copy of the source directory" in the package properties or if you have a distribution point in a child site See Figure 11.27.

Distribution Point Tab

Concurrent distribution settings:

- **Maximum number of packages**—Specifies how many packages Configuration Manager will copy at once.

- **Maximum threads per package**—Specifies the number of threads that each package can use during distribution to a distribution point.

Figure 11.27
General Tab

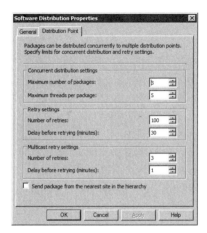

Figure 11.28
Distribution Point Tab

Retry settings/multicast retry settings (See Figure 11.28):

- **Number of retries**—Specifies how many times the distribution manager will attempt to distribute software to distribution points before failing completely. This value can range from 1 to 1000 attempts with the default value being 100 attempts.

- **Delay before retrying (minutes)**—If an attempt to distribute a package to a distribution point fails, this setting specifies the number of times (in minutes) before the distribution manager will try again. This value can be between 1 and 1440 minutes with the default value being 30 minutes.

- **Send package from the nearest site in the hierarchy**—This option specifies that package source files are retrieved from the closest, higher level site in the hierarchy when a distribution point is set to receive a new package. The site server sends its compressed version of the source files to the receiving distribution point rather than having to possibly traverse multiple, slower connections.

UNDERSTANDING PACKAGES

A package in Configuration Manager 2007 is really the sum of many parts. A package is used to distribute software or run executable files on a target system. Although a package may seem like an easy-to-grasp concept compared to collections or some other aspect of Configuration Manager, it consists of many properties and components that can be difficult to remember or to take into consideration when distributing software. We'll cover these properties and components and give examples of how to create packages later in this section.

Types of Packages

Installing software can be complicated because of inconsistency. There are EXE type installers, MSIs, scripts, and now there are even virtual applications such as App-V. To make it even more frustrating, these installers may have custom command line switches that help you install them without user intervention or to even go as far as customizing whether or not an icon is created on the desktop. Others, however, may have no available command line switches whatsoever. Because of all of these inconsistencies, Configuration Manager 2007 helps you ease the pain by giving you the ability to create many different types of packages based on your source installer file(s). Configuration Manager 2007 allows for the following types of packages to be created:

- **Standard (Legacy) Package**—A standard or legacy package is typically used when you have a legacy application installer such as an EXE or script file that needs to be executed on a target computer. These packages require the most upfront work when creating them because you are required to fill out all of the information about the package such as manufacturer, product name, version number, source location, etc.

- **Package from Definition**—Creating a package from a definition file is the easy way to create a package because all or some of the required information is contained in the definition file and is configured automatically at the time of package creation. SMS, PDF (not to be confused with Portable Document Format files), or MSI files are examples of definition files used by Configuration Manager. We'll cover these types of files later in this chapter.

- **Virtual Application Package**—This package type is used for Microsoft Application Virtualization (App-V) Applications. You must purchase the Microsoft Desktop Optimization Pack to obtain the rights to use App-V. You also must configure your Distribution Points to allow for App-V packages. We'll talk about that more in this section.

Packages are created and modified under the Software Distribution node by going to Site Database > Computer Management > Software Distribution > Packages in the Configuration Manager 2007 Console.

CREATING A PACKAGE

This section covers the steps needed to create general (or legacy) packages, packages from definitions, and packages from App-V applications. Because App-V integration requires some additional setup, we'll cover that process at the end of this section as well. During the package creation process, we'll cover all of the available package properties that are available.

Note

Although the three available package types differ slightly in how they are created, they are almost exactly alike under the hood. Properties in a standard or legacy package are the same as a package created from a definition file, for example. The only difference between these packages is that you do not have to manually fill out all of the information when creating a package from a definition file because these properties are pre-configured in the definition file itself. In fact, you could use the general package creation option to create a package that uses an MSI installer (a definition file) instead of the package from definition option. You'd just have to fill in all of the correct information after the package was created for it to function correctly.

General Package Creation

To create a general package (not using a definition file), do the following:

1. Right-click on the Packages node under the Software Distribution node and choose New > Package as shown in Figure 11.29.

2. The New Package Wizard window is displayed. This wizard will walk you through the steps needed to create a basic package. Because this package was created by using a standard package, you have to fill out all of the information about this package. The information collected on the general page will be used to help identify the package from MIF files generated during the product installation and are used when reporting back installation status. We will talk more about this process and MIF files later in this chapter. (See Figure 11.30.)

3. The Data Source section is displayed. This section allows you to define the location of your source files that will be copied to your distribution

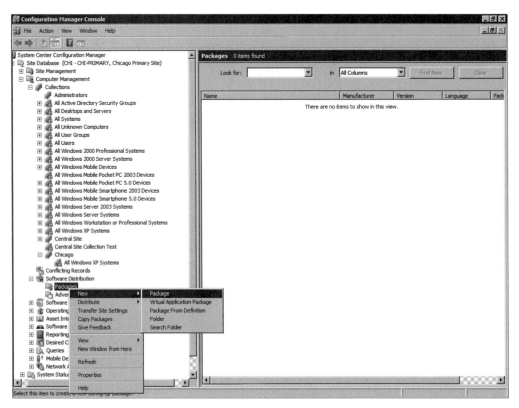

Figure 11.29
New General Package

points. In our example, we will be installing Adobe Air so we need to
tell Configuration Manager where the installation files are located for
Adobe Air. Configuration Manager then copies these files to the distribution point(s) that we choose later in the setup process. In order to tell
Configuration Manager where our source files are located, we need to
check the box that says This Package Contains Source Files. Once that
checkbox is checked, we then need to locate the source directory by
clicking the Set button. These configuration options and more are discussed next and shown in Figure 11.31.

- **This package contains source files**—This option specifies that this
  package contains files needed for execution or installation. In our
  example, we checked this option so that we could tell Configuration

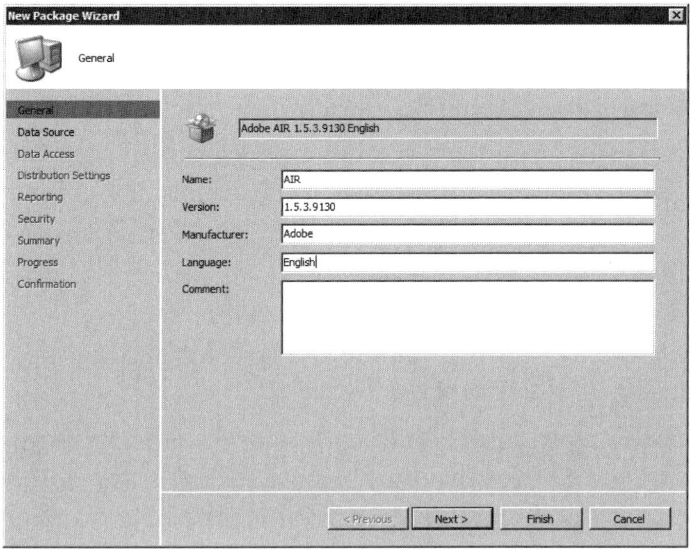

Figure 11.30
General Page

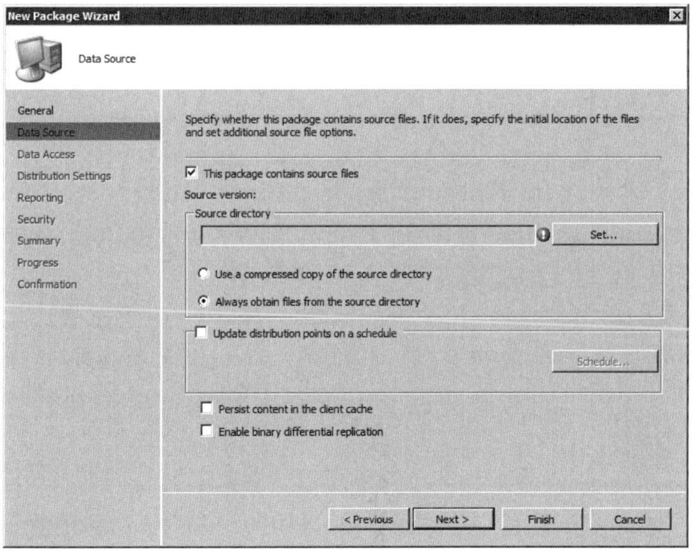

Figure 11.31
Data Source

Manager that we needed to specify the location of the Adobe Air installation files. If you are executing a file that already exists on the local computer or network, you do not have to check this option.

- **Source version**—After you have created a package with source files, you will see the source version number. This number increments each time you specify to update the distribution points it resides on. We will talk more about this in a second.

- **Source directory**—This shows you the source directory containing your source files. This directory can be changed by clicking the Set button.

- **Use a compressed copy of the source directory**—This option is used when your source files may not be available. A situation like this might occur if your source files were originally obtained from a CD that is no longer available. Configuration Manager creates compressed versions of the source location files if this option is checked (which are stored on the site server in the SMSPKG folder) and are used as the original source files when this option is selected.

Note

Configuration Manager 2007 will create compressed versions of each package when the Use a Compressed Copy of the Source Directory option is checked or when a package is copied to a distribution point on a child site.

- **Always obtain files from the source directory**—This option specifies that Configuration Manager will always look in the original source location when updating distribution points.

- **Update distribution points on a schedule**—If the content in your source location is being updated frequently, this option can be used to update distribution points with the latest content automatically.

Caution

If you use this option, make sure that you understand the potential impact it may have on your network and servers. If large packages are being updated frequently and then being pushed to several distribution points many times throughout the day, it may cause a negative impact on your infrastructure.

- **Persist content in the client cache**—This option is used when you want the source files to remain in the client cache on a targeted system. This is useful if the systems will re-run a program frequently and you don't want them to have to re-download the same content over and over again.

- **Enable binary differential replication**—This option is used to update distribution points with the latest version of the package by only updating the parts of files that have changed. If you have large packages, this can help you increase network efficiency by not having to transfer the entire file.

4. After you click the Set button, you then have the option to choose where your source files are located. You can choose to have them located on a network path or on the local site server. The path you choose will be for the entire directory containing your source files, not just the executable file itself. In our example, we'll choose a directory on a network share. (See Figure 11.32.) Click OK to continue.

5. The Data Access section of the New Package Wizard is displayed. This allows you to define how computers will access the data on distribution points. In our example, we'll leave the defaults and click Next to continue. The configuration options for data access are discussed next and shown in Figure 11.33.

   - **Access the distribution folder through common ConfigMgr package share**—This option uses the standard package share folder of

Figure 11.32
Set Source Directory

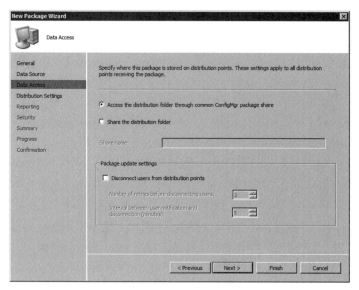

Figure 11.33
Data Access

SMSPKGx$ where x is the drive letter on the site system where the distribution point role is installed. This drive is typically the first formatted NTFS drive with the most space as we discussed back in Chapter 6.

- **Share the distribution folder**—This option lets you choose a custom shared location that already exists in your environment if you need to customize data access for security or other reasons.

Caution

When updating content on a distribution point (including a custom share distribution folder), the content in that folder is deleted and then re-created from the source location that we configured in step 4 of this section. You should not make the custom share distribution folder the same as your source files.

- **Package update settings**—The settings in this section control if Configuration Manager should notify and disconnect users from distribution point shares when a package update occurs. If the Disconnect

Users from Distribution Points option is checked, this option is enabled. The Number of Retries Before Disconnecting Users option specifies how many times Configuration Manager will attempt to update files on the distribution point before it starts to disconnect users. The Interval Between User Notification and Disconnection (minutes) option allows you to specify, in minutes, the amount of time users will have before they are disconnected.

6. The Distribution Settings section is displayed. This section lets you specify how packages are distributed between distribution points and if multicast will be allowed for operating system deployments. In our example, we'll choose the defaults and click Next to continue. The configuration options for distribution settings are discussed next and shown in Figure 11.34.

   ■ **Sending priority**—Specifies how packages are sent from one site to another. High, medium, and low are the three available priorities with medium being the default. Packages are sent across sites in priority order. If two packages have the same priority, they are sent in order of creation.

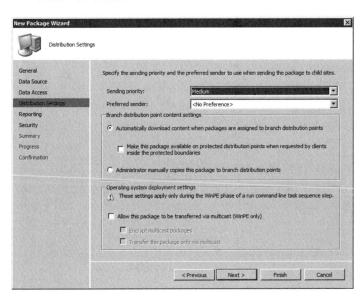

Figure 11.34
Distribution Settings

- **Preferred sender**—Specifies which sender to use when sending packages from site to site. The No Preference option is the default and uses any available sender to send packages.
- **Automatically download content when packages are assigned to branch distribution points**—Specifies that all branch distribution points will automatically download this package if selected as a distribution point for the package. This is the default option.
- **Make this package available on protected distribution points when requested by clients inside the protected boundaries**—This option is available when Automatically Download Content when Packages Are Assigned to Branch Distribution Points is enabled. This option allows clients within protected boundaries to request a package which then triggers the branch distribution point to download the content. Any requests by clients for that package in the future will successfully be able to download it from the branch distribution point.
- **Administrator manually copies this package to branch distribution points**—This option forces administrators to manually copy the package to branch distribution points.
- **Allow this package to be transferred via multicast (WinPE only)**—If Configuration Manager 2007 R2 is installed, this option is available. This option allows operating system images to be transferred via the multicast protocol if the advertisement is setup to do so. This conserves network bandwidth when multiple clients are requesting the same stream of data.
- **Encrypt multicast packages**—This option will encrypt multicast traffic for this package.
- **Transfer this package only via multicast**—This option specifies that this package can only be transmitted using multicast. If this is not enabled but multicast is, it will try using multicast and fall back to unicast if a multicast session cannot be started for some reason.

7. The Reporting section is displayed (see Figure 11.35). This is similar to the general page of the wizard in that it helps Configuration Manager match MIF files for status reporting. If you do not want to use the options configured in the general page, you can use these instead for MIF matching. We'll keep the defaults in our example and click Next to continue.

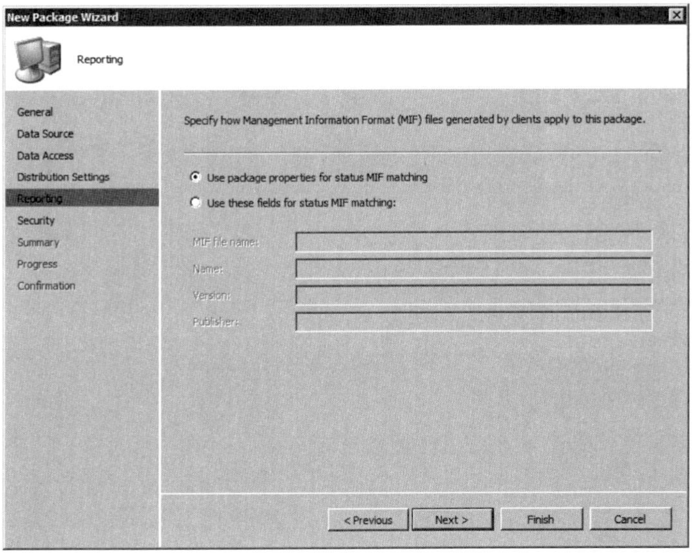

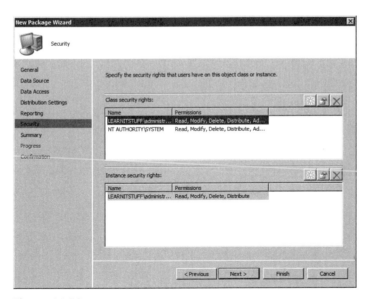

Figure 11.35
Reporting

8. The Security section is displayed (see Figure 11.36). This allows you to modify the security of this package. We'll keep the defaults and click Next to continue.

Figure 11.36
Security

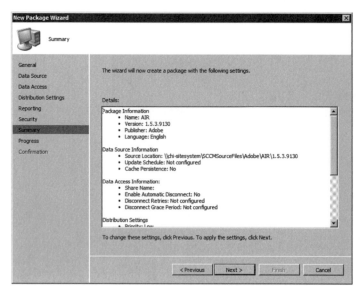

Figure 11.37
Summary

9. The Summary section is displayed as shown in Figure 11.37. This will show you all of the options that you've configured during the wizard so that you can check your settings prior to implementing them. In our example, we'll click Next to continue.

10. The Confirmation section is displayed (see Figure 11.38). This shows you if the package was created successfully. In our example, all was successful. Click Close to close the wizard.

11. The new Adobe Air package can now be seen under the Packages node in the Configuration Manager console as in Figure 11.39.

Definition Package Creation

Creating packages by using definition files is the preferred and easy method to create packages. Definition files help automate the package creation process by automatically including package and program information into the package without user intervention. Package definition files can be .PDF, .SMS, or .MSI files. One of the benefits of using Configuration Manager is that software vendors often provide definition files specifically to support easy package creation in Configuration Manager.

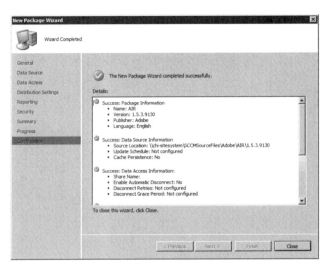

Figure 11.38
Confirmation

In our example, we'll create a new package by using the Package From Definition option and choosing an MSI file.

1. Right-click on the Packages node under the Software Distribution node and choose New > Package from Definition as shown in Figure 11.39.

2. The New Package from Definition Wizard window is displayed. This wizard will walk you through the steps needed to create a package from a definition file. (See Figure 11.40.)

3. The Package Definition section is displayed. This window allows you to choose packages that have already been imported into Configuration Manager 2007 by publisher. If your package is not listed (if it has never been imported in the past), click the Browse button to locate your package definition file. In our example, our package has not been imported so we will click the Browse button to locate it. (See Figure 11.41.)

4. Browse to the package definition file that will be used to create your package.

5. Once the file has been found, click the Open button and wait for your package to be displayed. In our example, we chose an MSI file for Java. Click Next to continue. (See Figure 11.42.)

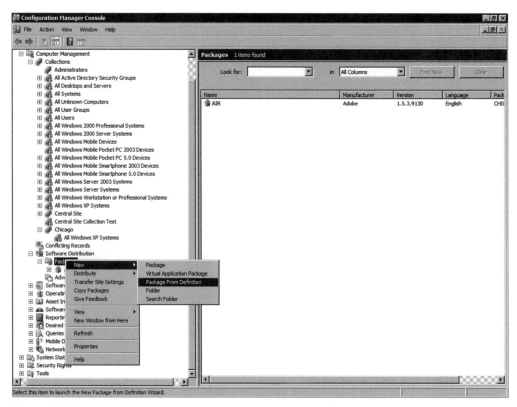

Figure 11.39
New Package from Definition

6. The Source Files section is displayed. This is the same concept as was described in the General Package Creation Wizard. Since our package contains source files, we'll leave the defaults and click Next to continue.

7. The Source Directory section is displayed. The options that are configured in this section were automatically configured by pulling information from the definition file such as the name and the location of the definition file itself. We'll keep the defaults and click Next to continue. (See Figure 11.44.)

8. The Summary section is displayed. This shows you that you have successfully created your package and the details about it. Click Finish to close the wizard. (See Figure 11.45.)

9. The new Java package can now be seen under the Packages node in the Configuration Manager console.

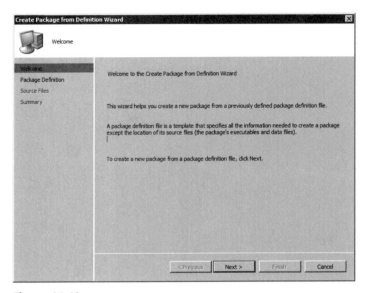

Figure 11.40
Package from Definition Wizard

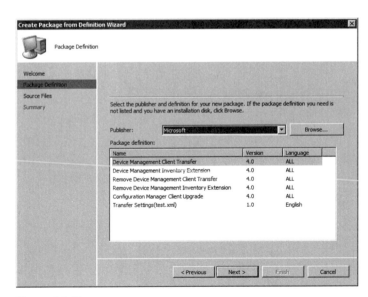

Figure 11.41
Default Package Definitions

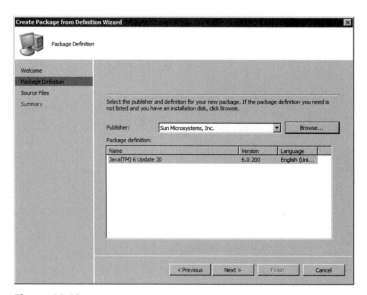

Figure 11.42
Java Package Definition

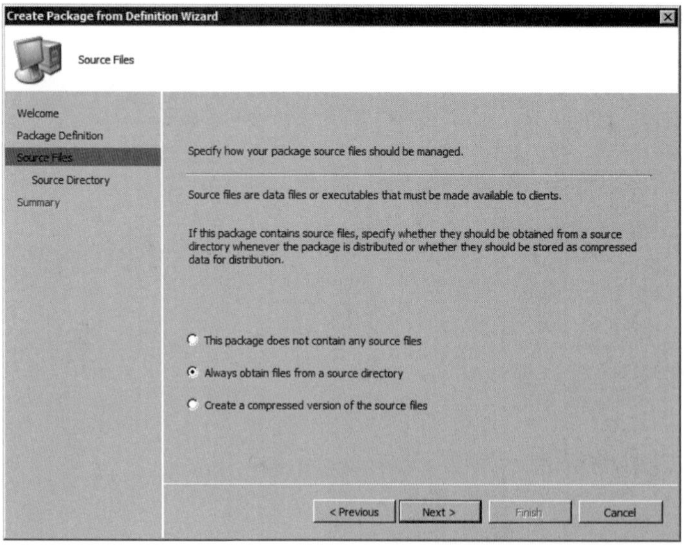

Figure 11.43
Source Files

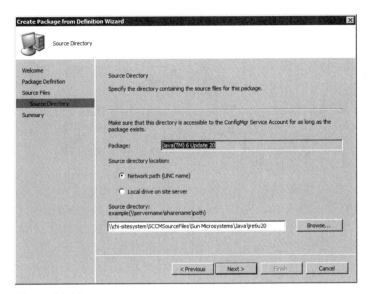

Figure 11.44
Source Files Directory

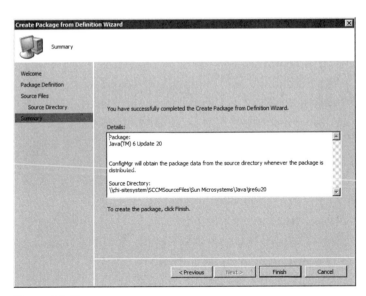

Figure 11.45
Summary

Virtual Applications

Microsoft Application Virtualization or App-V for short is a relatively new technology when compared to EXEs or MSIs. App-V allows you to "install" an application onto a computer without actually installing the application. This works by virtualizing certain aspects of the operating system like the registry or file system so that the application can read and write information to these virtual components without affecting the physical components. When the application starts (with the help of the App-V client), it may expect certain things to be in place such as DLLs that were created during install time or registry entries that hold configuration information. Because the application is not physically installed, these components don't exist on the computer. However, with App-V, these components are brought up in a virtual environment where the application can operate normally without ever knowing otherwise. The App-V client is responsible for bringing up and tearing down these virtual environments so it must be installed on a computer where an App-V application runs.

Some of the benefits of using App-V over traditional installation methods are as follows:

- **Less Time Spent on Application Testing**—Because each program now runs in its own "bubble" of sorts, applications running in one bubble will not typically affect applications running in another "bubble." For example: Application A was installed on Monday and wrote a file—Neat32.DLL—to the System32 directory. The version of the DLL is specific to application A and must remain the same for it to function correctly. On Wednesday, application B was installed that wrote a newer version of Neat32.DLL to the System32 directory—overwriting the one that was created on Monday by application A. Because of this, application A no longer runs correctly. Unfortunately, you did not catch this in your testing and now you have a big problem to deal with. With App-V, this would not be an issue. Because application A runs in its own bubble and has its own virtual file system, it does not get affected by application B. As each application is opened, its file system is opened with the correct files and versions that it was "installed" with.

- **Uses a "Click to Run" Type of Scenario**—App-V applications can use streaming capabilities to transfer themselves onto a client computer via an on-demand process. This means that they can be "installed" and executed just by double-clicking the icon. This helps speed up the process of "installation" compared to traditional software distribution techniques.

- **Automatic Updating**—If an App-V application needs to be updated—to incorporate a service pack for example—it can be updated and then distributed the next time the application is started by a user. App-V will only push out the updated files to clients during this process so the network impact is much lower compared to standard updating techniques. This means that a user could be using Microsoft Office 2007 SP1 in the morning, and after lunch, he has Office 2007 SP2 installed just by re-opening the application.

- **Multiple Instances of One Application**—Because of the way App-V applications run, you could "install" multiple instances of the same program—each configured with different options. You could, for example, run Internet Explorer with Flash version 7 in one instance and run Internet Explorer with Flash version 10 in another—all on the same computer at the same time.

- **Training and Testing**—App-V is also great for training and testing purposes. For instance, if you are running Office 2007 in a non-virtualized fashion and want to test Office 2010, you could virtualize Office 2010 to see if things will work correctly without having to actually install it on each PC.

Unfortunately, App-V is not included with Configuration Manager 2007 and must be purchased separately. It is currently being sold within the Microsoft Desktop Optimization Pack, which is available for Software Assurance customers.

Integrate App-V into Configuration Manager

App-V initially shipped as its own infrastructure and was completely separate from Configuration Manager 2007. With the release of Configuration Manager 2007 R2, you can now integrate App-V into the Configuration Manager infrastructure, which helps ease management tasks. However, there are some steps that have to be taken to enable full App-V integration. These steps are listed next:

1. Install Configuration Manager 2007 R2 as we described in Chapter 1.

2. Enable virtual application streaming on your distribution points in the Configuration Manager console by going to your site > Site Settings > Site Systems > and choosing the site system that has a distribution point role installed. Right-click on the distribution point role and choose Properties. On the General tab, the Allow Clients to Transfer Content from This Distribution Point Using BITS, HTTP, and HTTPS option must be checked. On the Virtual Applications tab, the Enable Virtual Application Streaming option must be checked as well. See Figures 11.46 and 11.47 for details.

3. Ensure that the Allow Virtual Application Package Advertisement option is enabled on the General tab of the advertised programs client agent as shown in Figure 11.25.

App-V Sequencer

Before an application can be imported to Configuration Manager as an App-V package, it must first be converted into an App-V application by using the App-V sequencer. The sequencer watches the installation process and catches all of the changes the application makes to the computer. These changes are captured

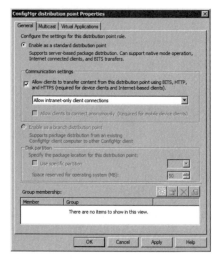

Figure 11.46
BITS-Enabled Distribution Point

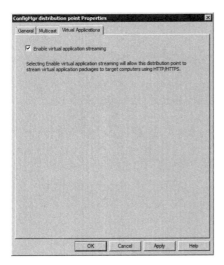

Figure 11.47
Virtual Application Streaming

and converted into a sequenced project that can then be imported into Configuration Manager. Although the sequencing aspect is out of the scope of this book, many resources can be found online regarding this process.

App-V Package Creation

1. Right-click on the Packages node under the Software Distribution node and choose New > Virtual Application Package as shown in Figure 11.48.

2. The New Virtual Application Package Wizard window is displayed. This wizard will walk you through the steps needed to create a virtual application package. The first section of the wizard is the package source section. In this step, you must browse to the XML manifest file that the App-V Sequencer creates when sequencing your application. Once you specify the manifest file, you will be able to see the applications referenced in that manifest file as seen in Figure 11.49. Click Next to continue.

3. The General section is displayed. This section lets you specify properties about your virtual application such as name and version. At the bottom, the option Remove This Package from Clients When It Is No Longer Advertised is checked by default. This deletes the virtual package from

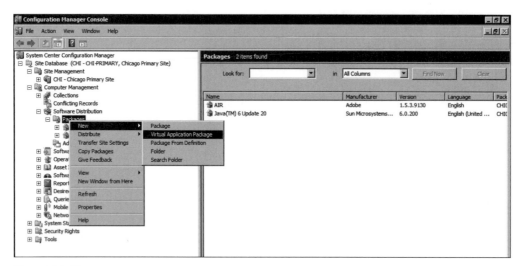

Figure 11.48
New Virtual Application Package

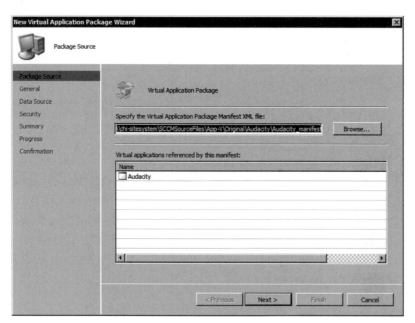

Figure 11.49
Package Source Manifest XML File

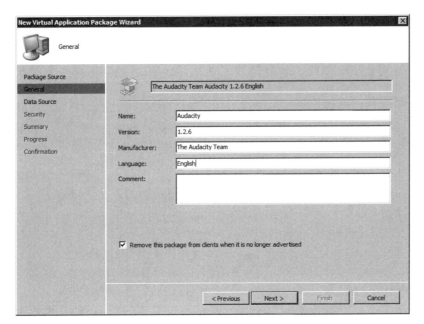

Figure 11.50
General Section

client computers when the advertisement is no longer associated with them. Do not check this option if computers are members of frequently changing collections as this might cause App-V programs to be deleted unintentionally. Click Next to continue. (See Figure 11.50.)

4. The Data Source section is displayed. This section allows you to specify the location of the Configuration Manager App-V modified source directory. In other words, Configuration Manager looks at the un-modified App-V sequencer output files and imports them into Configuration Manager as we did in step 2 above. Configuration Manager then modifies those sequencer files and asks you to put them in a new location (which they call the source or destination directory) where they will remain. The original source files (the ones we chose in step 2) can then be deleted since they are never referenced by Configuration Manager again. Once you have chosen a source location for the Configuration Manager modified version of your App-V sequencer files, click Next to continue. (See Figure 11.51.)

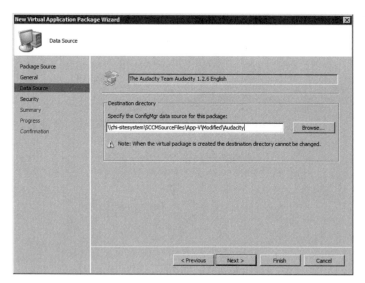

Figure 11.51
Data Source

Tip

The source location or destination directory must exist in order to complete this section of the wizard.

5. The Security section of the wizard is displayed. If you need to modify the security of this package, you can do so from this section. Click Next to continue. (See Figure 11.52.)

6. The Summary section of the wizard is displayed. This will show you the changes that the wizard is about to make. If you are satisfied with these changes, click Next to continue. (See Figure 11.53.)

7. Depending on the size of your package, you may see the progress screen. This is when the data is being copied from the original App-V sequencer output directory to the Configuration Manager modified App-V source location you specified in step 4. When the copy process is done, it automatically moves on to the Confirmation section of the wizard.

8. The Confirmation section of the wizard is displayed. This shows you the changes that were made and if they were successful. Click Close to close the wizard. (See Figure 11.54.)

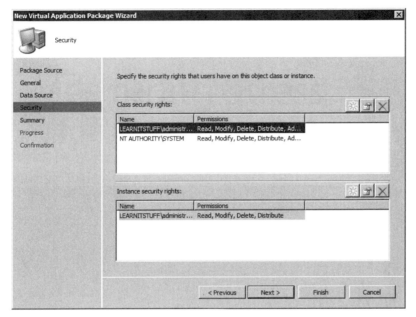

Figure 11.52
Security

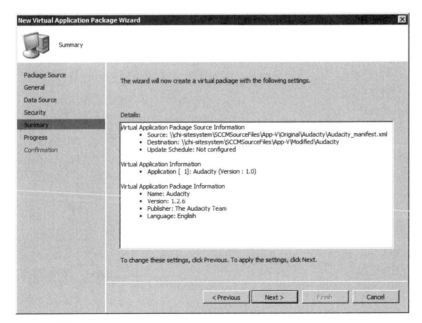

Figure 11.53
Summary

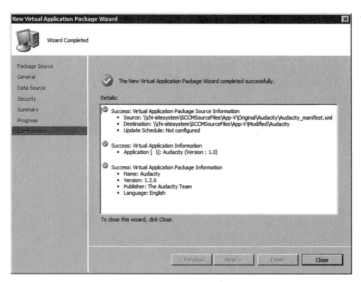

Figure 11.54
Confirmation

9. The new Audacity App-V package can now be seen under the Packages node in the Configuration Manager console.

Updating an App-V Application

All applications need to be updated from time to time. This includes both traditional and App-V applications. The process of updating a traditional application can be done in a number of ways. Some have executable files that update and patch the current installation, some do a complete uninstall of the application and then install a newer, updated version while others simply use scripts to replace older files. With an App-V application, this process is much different. It works like this:

1. Build your original App-V application using the App-V sequencer.

2. Import the App-V application into Configuration Manager.

3. Deploy the App-V application via an advertisement (which we will cover shortly).

Now that the application has been deployed to multiple clients, an update comes out and you must update it. The update process works like this:

1. Open your original (Non Configuration Manager modified) App-V application in the sequencer.

2. Start the sequencing process.

3. Apply the update.

4. Save your updated package and import the updated version into Configuration Manager as an upgrade using the Update Package right-click menu option from the App-V package.

5. Follow the steps in the Virtual Application Package Update Wizard to complete the update process.

COMPONENTS OF A PACKAGE

Each package you create will also have four components listed directly under the Packages node, which is under the Software Distribution node in the Configuration Manager console. These components are as follows:

- Programs
- Distribution Points
- Package Status
- Access Accounts

Programs

Programs are used by packages to execute files on client systems. Multiple programs can exist for one program such as an installer and an un-installer. Because packages can have multiple programs, it makes packages versatile and efficient by having one set of installation files that can be executed in multiple ways via multiple programs.

Creating Programs

Programs are automatically created when packages are created by definition files as long as the definition file has programs defined within it. This makes it easy for an administrator because this step has already been completed. When packages are created manually, however, programs have to be created from

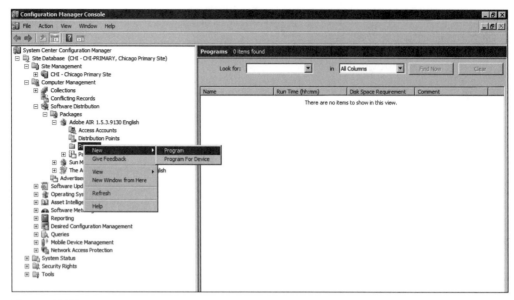

Figure 11.55
New Program

scratch. When we created our first package, Adobe Air, we created it from scratch so it does not have any programs associated to it. Follow these steps to create a program:

1. Right-click on the Programs node under the packages of the main Software Distribution node and choose New > Program as shown in Figure 11.55.

2. The New Program Wizard is displayed. This wizard will walk you through the steps needed to create a program for a package. The first section of the wizard is the general section. In this step, you can configure properties about the program such as the command line parameters it will use when running. The configuration options for general program settings are discussed next and shown in Figure 11.56. Click Next to continue.

   ▪ **Name**—The name of the program. Make this descriptive as it will be used to report on the status of this package.

   ▪ **Comment**—If you would like to make any comments about this program, enter them here.

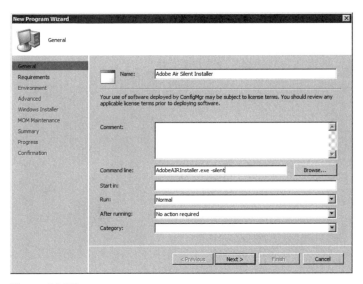

Figure 11.56
General Program Settings

- **Command line**—This field is used to specify the command line that the program will use when running. In our example, we will execute the AdobeAIRInstaller.exe file with the -silent command line option.

- **Start in**—This configures the start in directory.

- **Run**—This drop-down box allows you to choose from Normal, Minimized, Maximized, or Hidden. This is mainly used when wanting to control how the end user experiences the program. If you want to hide the program so that the end user cannot interact with it, choose Hidden. This is not an issue when the program runs and the computer is in a logged off state.

- **After running**—This drop-down box allows you to choose from No Action Required, Program Restarts the Computer, ConfigMgr Restarts the Computer, or ConfigMgr Logs User Off. No action required does nothing and is the default. If you need to log the user off after the program runs, however, you might choose ConfigMgr Logs User Off instead.

- **Category**—If you would like to assign this program to a category, you can do so from this field.

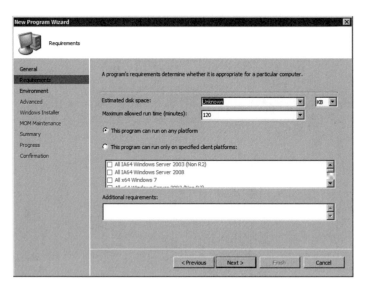

Figure 11.57
Program Requirements

3. The Requirements section of the wizard is displayed. This section gives you the ability to define the requirements on the program. For example, you can specify how much space is required on the hard drive for the program to run. You can choose the operating system that the program can run on as well. In our example, we'll choose the defaults and click Next to continue. (See Figure 11.57.)

4. The Environment section of the wizard is displayed (see Figure 11.58). Where the Requirements section defined if the program could run, this section defines how the program will run. You can specify if the program will run if a user is logged in or not, if it runs with administrative rights vs. the logged in user's rights, if a user can interact with the program, and if it needs to run in a specific fashion such as a UNC path or driver letter. Since we want this program to run in either the logged on or off state, we'll choose Whether or Not a User Is Logged On option and click Next to continue.

5. The Advanced section of the wizard is displayed. This allows you to choose advanced settings about your program. The configuration options for the advanced section are discussed next and shown in Figure 11.59. Click Next to continue.

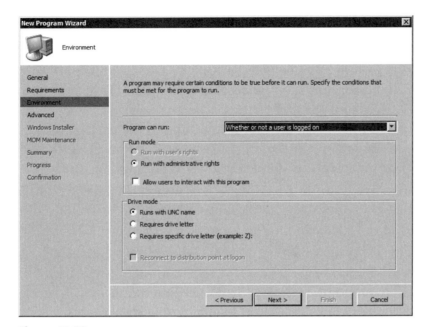

Figure 11.58
Program Environment

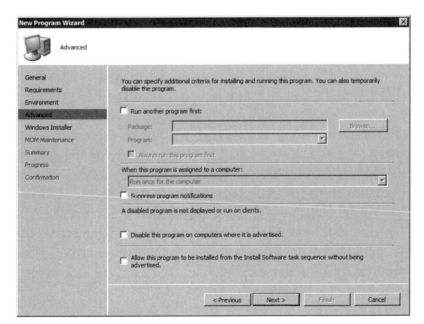

Figure 11.59
Advanced Settings

- **Run another program first**—This option specifies that another program should run before this program. The program can be located in the same package or in another package within Configuration Manager.

- **When this program is assigned to a computer**—This drop-down box is available if the Only When a User is Logged On option is chosen from the Program Can Run setting in the environment section. The options in the drop-down box are Run Once for the Computer or Run Once for Every User Who Logs On.

- **Suppress program notifications**—This option disables the notification balloon popups like notifications and reminders that are displayed in the notification area.

- **Disable this program on computers where it is advertised**—This option disables this program on computers where it has been advertised. The program is disabled from the Run Advertised Programs Control Panel applet as well as mandatory advertisements.

- **Allow this program to be installed from the Install Software task sequence without being advertised**—This option specifies that this program can be run during a task sequence step. If this option is not checked, any task sequence step that references this program will fail to run.

6. The Windows Installer section of the wizard is displayed as shown in Figure 11.60. The options in this section give you a method to dynamically manage Windows Installer installation sources on your clients, which is referred to as installation source management. In the event that a program needs to be repaired or reinstalled, it typically needs the source files to do so. Windows Installer will look to the location that the MSI was originally installed from for these source files. If the original installation source is no longer available, this process may fail. Configuration Manager 2007 gives you the option to redirect these installation sources to distribution points containing the source files by specifying a Windows Installer product code (contained within an MSI file) in this section. This causes the Configuration Manager client to search all available distribution points for MSIs that contain the specified product code. If it finds a match, the source location will be updated automatically to ensure that these locations are valid and available at all times. To enable installation

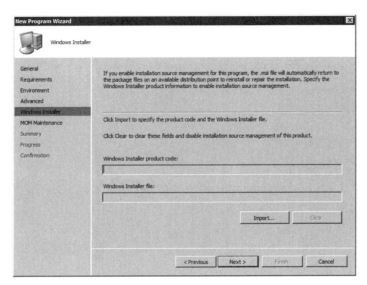

Figure 11.60
Windows Installer (Installation Source Management)

source management for a program, click the Import button and choose the MSI file that is used within this program. The product code will automatically be imported from the MSI. Click Next to continue.

7. The MOM Maintenance section of the wizard is displayed (see Figure 11.61). If you are using Microsoft Operations Manager to monitor your clients, you may get alerts that there is an issue while the software is installed. These options disable MOM alerts while the program is being installed. Configuration Manager uses the "maximum allowed run time" that is specified in the program to decide how long to disable MOM alerts. If the "maximum allowed run time" is set to unknown or greater than 12 hours, Configuration Manager disables MOM alerts for 15 minutes. Click Next to continue.

8. The Summary section of the wizard is displayed. This will show you the changes that the wizard is about to make. If you are satisfied with these changes, click Next to continue. (See Figure 11.62.)

9. The Confirmation section of the wizard is displayed. This shows you the changes that were made and if they were successful. Click Close to close the wizard. (See Figure 11.63.)

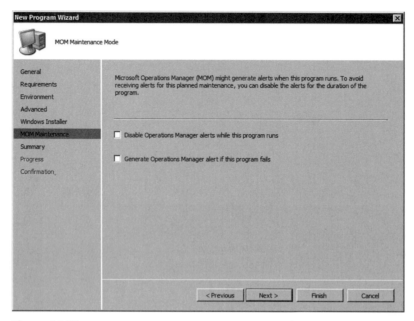

Figure 11.61
MOM Maintenance Mode

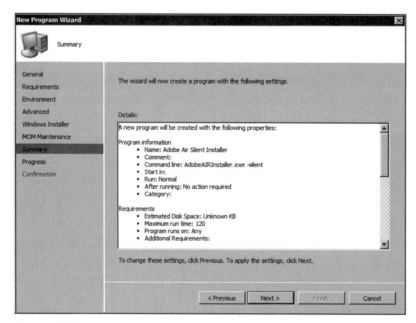

Figure 11.62
Summary

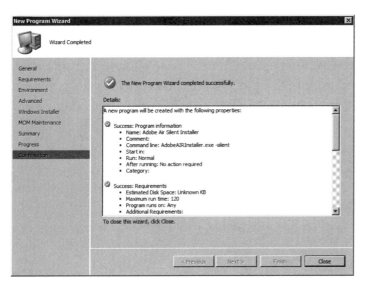

Figure 11.63
Confirmation

Note

App-V packages do not have programs associated to them because they are launched by the App-V client on each computer via a special command line that can be seen in the icon properties of each App-V application. If you use group policy preferences to manage user icons, for example, this command line can be copied and used within the group policy preference icons to launch your App-V applications.

Distribution Points

In Chapter 6, we covered the installation of the distribution point server role and talked in depth about the types of distribution points and options that are available. In this section, we'll cover the different options to get content onto a distribution point from a package perspective and how a distribution point is chosen when multiple distribution points exist.

Distribution points (DPs) are responsible for holding content in regards to software distribution and operating system deployment. On the software distribution side of things, DPs hold files such as the Microsoft Office installation media so that those files can be used by Configuration Manager to install the program. Computers can be configured (via advertisements) to run programs from the distribution points themselves or by downloading the content locally and then running it locally. If the second option is chosen, BITS can be used to transfer this information in a reliable and efficient manner. Distribution points can also be configured to allow virtual application streaming. These options can be found in Chapter 6, "Configuring Site System Roles," and also earlier in this chapter.

Managing Packages on Distribution Points

Before a distribution point can be used for software distribution, packages must be copied to it by an administrator. Once a package has been copied to a distribution point, it may need to be updated or removed depending on if the package has changed or is not needed in a certain location any longer. These topics are covered in this section.

Adding Packages to Distribution Points   After you create and configure your programs, you can then start adding packages to selected distribution points. The method for adding packages to distribution points is easy and is done via the Configuration Manager console. It is done by completing the following steps:

1. Navigate to the Distribution Point node of your package, right-click and choose New > Distribution. In our example, we'll add Adobe Air to our distribution points. (See Figure 11.64.)

2. The New Distribution Point Wizard starts as shown in Figure 11.65. Click Next to continue.

3. The Copy Package section of the wizard is displayed. From here, you can see all of the available distribution points in your hierarchy. Choose which distribution points you want your package to be copied to (from the source location) by checking the box next to the distribution point. If you have created any distribution point groups, you can copy the package to all of the distribution points in that group by clicking on the Select Group button. For more information on distribution point groups, see Chapter 6. In our example, we'll select all of the distribution points in the Chicago site and click Next to continue.

4. The Confirmation section of the wizard is displayed. This shows you the changes that were made and if they were successful. Click Close to close the wizard.

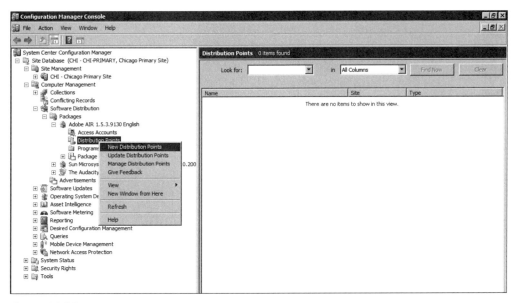

Figure 11.64
Distribution Point node

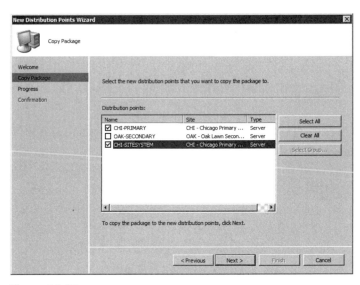

Figure 11.65
Select Distribution Points

Tip

After the wizard is closed, Configuration Manager will start to copy the package from its configured source location to the selected distribution points. To see the progress of this in real time, open the Reliability and Performance Monitor on Vista/Server 2008 distribution points or the Resource Monitor on Windows 7/Server 2008 R2 distribution points to see information such as the speed at which the packages are being transferred over the network. This is a good method for trouble-shooting as well.

Tip

If you need to copy multiple packages onto a single distribution point—such as where a new distribution point has been introduced into the Configuration Manager hierarchy, you can use the Copy Packages option for this purpose. This prevents you from having to go to each package and copy them up to new distribution points individually. This is especially handy if you have hundreds or thousands of packages that need to be copied. The Copy Packages option is available by right-clicking on the Packages node and choosing Copy Packages.

Content Changes Imagine that you have created a package that installs a line of business application that uses customized XML files to point it to different database servers. You deploy the package to all of your business analysts and then later find out that the XML file was not the updated version and management needs you to fix it ASAP. You go out to the source directory for the application and replace the outdated XML file with the new one and re-run your advertisement immediately after the XML file is replaced which then should re-install the application using the new XML file. Unfortunately, you quickly find that the re-installation did not work and that the XML file is still incorrect.

The reason this scenario would not have worked is because although the source location files were updated, the distribution points were not. This causes a couple of problems. First, the new content does not get transferred to the distribution points so the installation will not work as expected. The program will continue to install just as it had before. Secondly, if you have many distribution points and they are connected across slower links, the process of updating these DPs could take some time. If you update your distribution points but don't allow them time to get the new content before a client downloads the now out-of-date package, the package will fail to install due to a hash mismatch.

Hash Mismatches Hash mismatches occur when clients download packages from distribution points that don't match the hash that was originally generated when the package was first imported from the source location. The simple fix for this issue is to update the distribution points with the most current version of the package source files. A new hash will be generated on the source content during the package update and then this content will be sent to all of the selected distribution points. Once the content is updated, your clients should download the most current version of the package so when the hash is checked against the original hash (again—generated at initial import or package update), it should match. Once this is done, re-run your advertisement and all should be well. If an advertisement is set to have clients run files directly from the distribution point, a hash check is not performed even if the files on the DPs don't match the source files. Although the installation may succeed in this case, it may not succeed as expected since it may be using out-of-date content.

Tip

Don't let users in your organization have access to Configuration Manager source files or distribution points by default. If they accidently make a change to these files, hash mismatches may occur as a result.

The Mystery of the Hash Mismatches

A while back, we were having a problem where some of our applications were not getting installed via Configuration Manager 2007. When we looked into the issue, we found that the errors on our clients indicated a hash mismatch. Since only a few people in our organization had access to the Configuration Manager source and DP location files, we quickly found out that no one had knowingly changed any files in these locations. We thought it was an interesting issue but we quickly fixed it by simply updating the distribution points with the newest package version and went on with our day. A few weeks later, we ran into the same issue again but this time on a large scale. We were rolling out a few hundred computers during a building technology upgrade and found that some important programs did not get installed because of the hash mismatch issue. This upset a lot of people because we had to spend extra time finding out which programs failed to install and then re-install them. Because of this incident, we spent some time and found the root cause of the problem. Log files were being created in the distribution point package locations that corresponded to the packages that were failing to install. This was happening because some of our advertisements were set to run from the distribution point (instead of download and execute) and the log files were being created in the same directory that the executable was located in. When the hash check occurred, files in the distribution points were different from the files in the source locations so the hash check failed. Although we found out what was happening, we didn't know why it was happening. We didn't understand why clients had the ability to write files to the distribution points. After looking into it, we found that the network access account (used to access network resources when the computer is not on the domain) was given domain administrator rights—giving them the ability to write files to these locations. This was fixed and the problem was finally resolved.

Updating Distribution Point Content   If you need to update a package on all of the distribution points that it currently resides on, you can use the right-click menu option from the package's Distribution Point node and choose Update Distribution Points. This is the quick and easy method to update your distribution points when package content has changed. There is another method to manage your distribution point content, however, which is also accessed through a right-click menu option called Manage Distribution Points. This launches the Manage Distribution Points Wizard, which allows you to specify which distribution points will be managed and what actions will be taken rather than just updating all of them with a new package version. With this wizard, you get four options. They are shown in Figure 11.66 and discussed next.

- **Copy the packages to new distribution points**—This lets you choose which distribution points will receive the package.

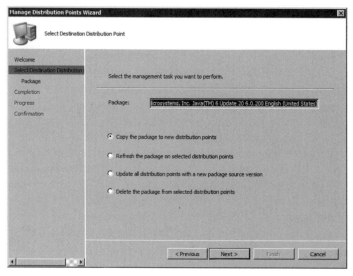

Figure 11.66
Manage Distribution Points Wizard

- **Refresh the package on selected distribution points**—This option should be used when trying to repair a package on a distribution point. This option does not copy files from the package source location, only from the local site server's compressed package.

- **Update all distribution points with a new package source version**— This option builds a new compressed package file and a delta compressed package file. The delta file is sent out to the distribution points where the package resides. The package version is also incremented each time this process occurs.

- **Delete the package from selected distribution points**—This option deletes packages from the selected distribution points.

Package Status

Once you start the process of copying your packages to distribution points, you may need to check on the progress to ensure that the package(s) were successfully copied to each targeted distribution point. Configuration Manager 2007 gives you multiple ways to do this including reports and the Package Status nodes available within each package or globally for the entire site. These nodes let you view many items that quickly help you determine the status of your packages and distribution points.

Getting your packages copied to distribution points can be a slow and sometimes painful task depending on your link speed from site to site. If your link speeds are fast, few issues typically arise. If your link speeds are very slow, you may have issues with packages arriving successfully on some distribution points. Assuming that your package made it successfully to a distribution point can be somewhat risky, especially if your clients depend on that data being there for software distribution or operating system deployment.

Package Status Node—Per Package

The Package Status node lets you quickly identify problems by showing you a list of sites and if the package has successfully made it to those sites or not. In Figure 11.67, you can see that the Java package has been successfully copied to the OAK secondary site since the targeted and installed columns are both "1" and the failed and retrying columns are both "0". This means that there has been

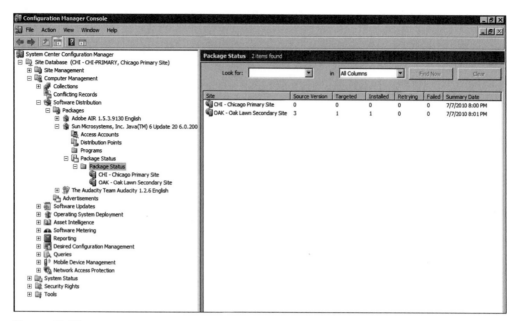

Figure 11.67
Package Status for All Sites

one distribution within the OAK site targeted to receive the package and it has been installed on one distribution point. To see more details about which distribution points received the package, we need to drill down a little further.

If you need to see more detailed information about the status of a package, highlight the site where the targeted distribution point(s) are located. When a site containing targeted distribution points is selected, you can see information such as the distribution point server name, the path where the package is located on that server, and what version of the package has been installed. This is shown in Figure 11.68.

In Figure 11.68, we see that the Java package was successfully copied to the OAK-SECONDARY server and which version of the package was copied. As we talked about earlier, the source version of a package is updated each time you choose to update a distribution point with a new version. This helps you keep track of which package version is on each distribution point. If you have updated your source package four times but only version 2 is on a specific distribution point, you know that distribution point has an outdated version of the package and that something is not working correctly.

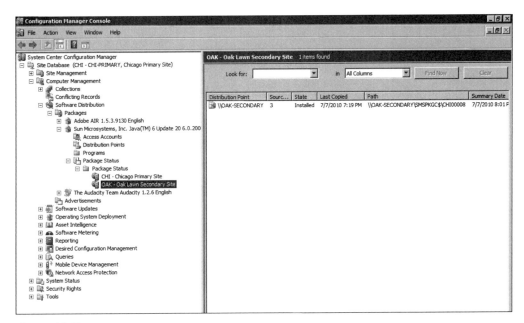

Figure 11.68
Package Status for Distribution Points

If a package cannot be copied to a distribution point for some reason, you may see different results based on the amount of time that has passed. In Figure 11.69, the Adobe Air package was added to the CHI-SITESYSTEM distribution point. This server, however, has lost network connectivity and cannot be reached for an extended period of time. Initially, we would see that the CHI primary site has a package targeted to one distribution point within its site but it has yet to be installed. Also notice that this package has not yet gone into a failed or retry state.

If you drill down further into the package status for this site, you'll see that the status says Install Pending as shown in Figure 11.70. This will remain in this state based on the distribution point settings that we talked about in Figure 11.28.

After the distribution manager has reached the maximum number of retries for a distribution point, it will then go into a failed state. In Figure 11.71, you can see the failed state per site and in Figure 11.72, you can see the failed state per distribution point.

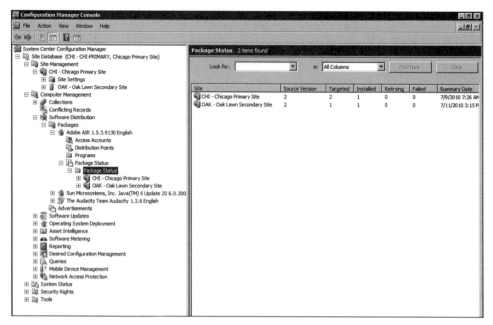

Figure 11.69
Targeted Distribution Point

Package Status Node—Per Site

Reviewing the Package Status node on a per package basis (like we did above) is good if you are trying to get information about a specific package. However, if you are managing thousands of packages on thousands of distribution points, it's good to have a broader view of your package status. This can be achieved from the Package Status node located under Site > System Status as shown in Figure 11.73.

From the Per Site Package Status node, you can see a list of packages and their status like we saw from the Per Package Status node except now we see all of the packages in the site including boot images and operating system images. We will cover those types of packages in the next chapter. As expected, we see that the Adobe Air package was targeted to three distribution points in the CHI site; it was installed on two of those, and it failed on one.

Viewing Status Messages

If you are having an issue with a package and it is showing a state other than installed, you can use the status message viewer to retrieve information about

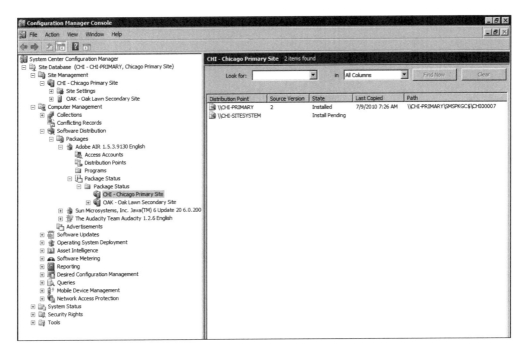

Figure 11.70
Install Pending Status

these errors and then act upon them based on the retrieved message(s). The status message view is covered in detail in Chapter 18, "Using Configuration Manager Console Tools." Quickly, the status message viewer is a component within the Configuration Manager console that allows you to retrieve status messages about the site such as issues related to clients, packages, programs, advertisements, or the overall site health. It is an extremely useful tool and is used quite often in most Configuration Manager implementations. In this section, we'll talk about status messages as they relate to packages and distribution points.

In the last two sections, we dealt with a package that would not transfer successfully to a distribution point. In this section, we'll talk about how to view the messages that have been logged so that we can solve the problem.

The status message viewer is contextual within the Configuration Manager console. This means that you can narrow down the types of retrieved messages to only include ones that pertain to the queried component. For example, if we want to know the status of a specific package in a specific site for a specific site

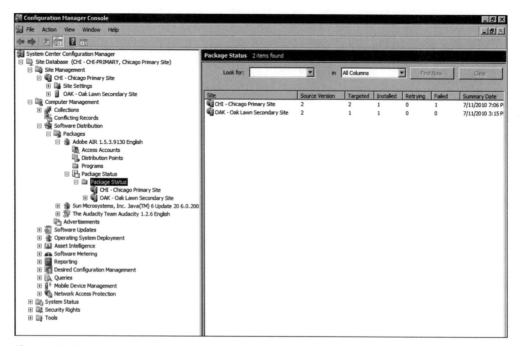

Figure 11.71
Install Failed—Per Site

system, you can filter all of the messages, automatically, just by choosing the correct component within the Configuration Manager console.

In this example, we are going to use the status message viewer to find all status messages for the Adobe Air package. This will include messages pertaining to all of the sites and distribution points that it may or may not be targeted to. To start this process:

1. Right-click on the Package Status node under the package in question and choose Show Messages. You can choose from All, Error, Warning, or Info. In this example, we'll choose All. This is shown in Figure 11.74.

2. The Status Messages: Set Viewing Period window is displayed. This allows you to filter the messages based on a time range. In our example, we'll choose 1 Week Ago and click OK to continue. (See Figure 11.75.)

3. All of the messages for the Adobe Air package are retrieved starting from 1 week ago until now. Because our time period contains a large

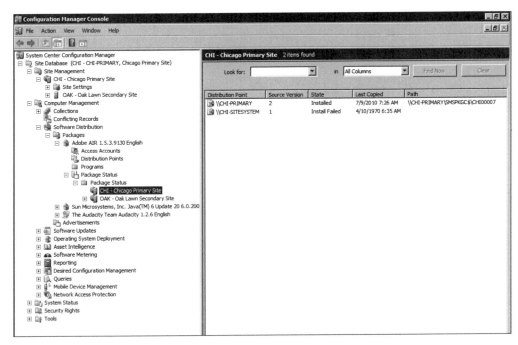

Figure 11.72
Install Failed—Per Distribution Point

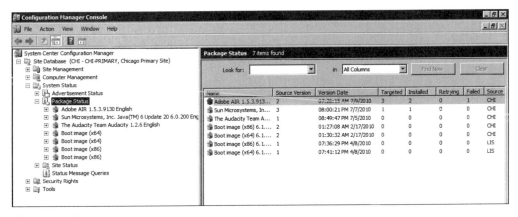

Figure 11.73
Site Package Status Node

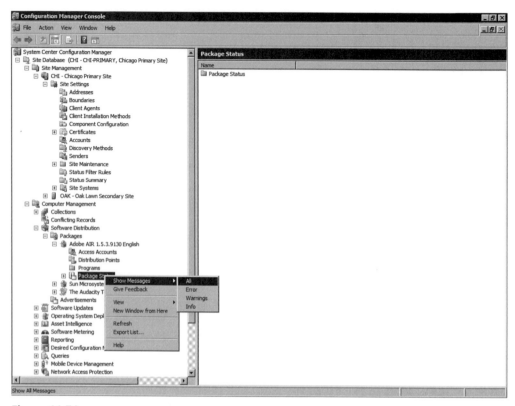

Figure 11.74
Viewing All Status Messages for a Package

Figure 11.75
Set Viewing Period

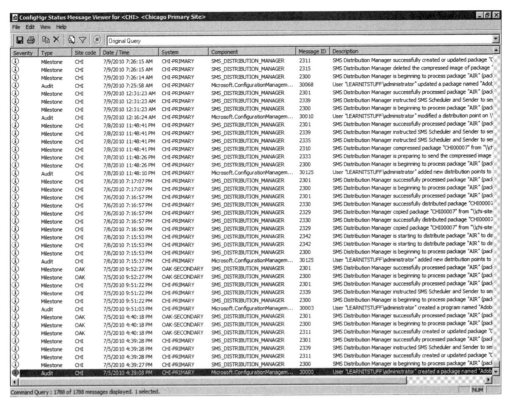

Figure 11.76
Status Messages

number of status messages, we may want to filter it to find only the pertinent information. As you can see in Figure 11.76, we are retrieving messages from multiple systems including CHI-PRIMARY and OAK-SECONDARY.

4. Because we are only concerned with the CHI-SITESYSTEM distribution point, we'll retrieve messages only for this system by retrieving messages from the object itself by right-clicking on the CHI-SITESYSTEM distribution point object and choosing Show Messages > All. (See Figure 11.77.)

5. Once we choose our viewing period like we did in Figure 11.75, we can see all of the messages for only the CHI-SITESYSTEM distribution point as shown in Figure 11.78.

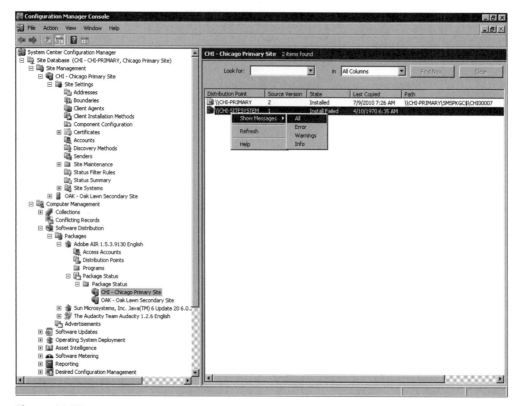

Figure 11.77
View Status Messages for a Specific Component

Note

If you choose to look at the status of a component that cannot communicate back to the site server, it's possible you won't retrieve all of the messages that you need to diagnose the problem since its messages cannot be sent back to the site.

Access Accounts

When packages are added to a distribution point, the local users group is granted read access and the local administrators group is allowed full control to these packages by default. If you need to change these default settings, you can do so through the Access Accounts node under each package, which allows you to modify these access accounts. If you need to create a new access account, you'll have to use the New Access Account Wizard. We'll talk more about access accounts in the next chapter.

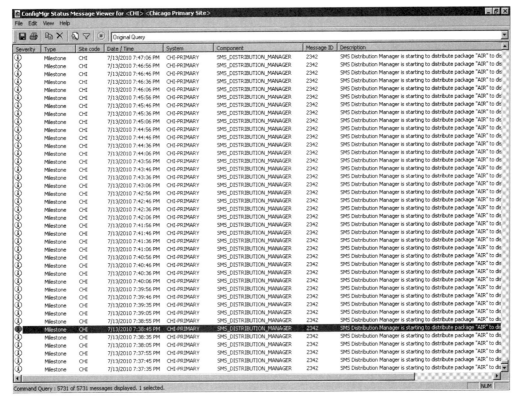

Figure 11.78
Filtered Status Messages

Two types of access accounts exist:

- Generic Access Accounts
- Windows User Access Accounts

Generic access accounts are mapped to a system-specific account on each distribution point. For example, on CHI-PRIMARY, the CHI-PRIMARY \Administrators group has full control to the packages on the distribution point share while the CHI-PRIMARY\Users group has only read access. On the OAK-SECONDARY distribution point, these accounts are mapped to OAK-SECONDARY\Administrators and OAK-SECONDARY\Users.

Windows user access accounts specify a Windows user or group account such as an account in Active Directory.

The following permissions can be set for each account:

- **No Access**—The specified account will not be able to read, write, or delete any files on the distribution point share.

- **Read**—The specified account will be able to view and copy files, change folders within the shared folder, and read extended attributes of files.

- **Change**—The specified account will be able to change the contents and extended attributes of files and to delete files as well.

- **Full Control**—The specified account will have the same permissions as read and change combined.

ADVERTISEMENTS

Now that you've heard the term "advertisement" over and over again throughout this book, let's actually talk about them and what they do. Put simply, advertisements put your programs and task sequences to work. They allow you to target programs and task sequences to collections so that you can execute tasks such as installing software, running scripts, or deploying operating systems to the resources within those collections. They allow you to configure very specific options regarding the execution of an action such as if a program runs locally or from the distribution point or if a program runs once or on a recurring schedule. Advertisements are created and managed under the Advertisements node which is located under Site > Computer Management > Software Distribution.

Multiple types of advertisements can be created:

- **Standard Advertisement**—This type of advertisement lets you advertise programs to resources that will affect Windows computers such as workstations or servers.

- **Device Advertisement**—This type of advertisement lets you advertise programs to resources that will affect mobile devices such as mobile phones running the Windows Mobile operating system.

- **Task Sequence Advertisement**—This type of advertisement lets you advertise task sequences to resources that will affect Windows computers such as workstations or servers.

Creating a Standard Advertisement

Creating an advertisement is very similar to the previous objects we've created within Configuration Manager 2007 in that it, too, is done through a wizard. The New Advertisement Wizard walks you through all of the options that can be configured for an advertisement to ensure that you don't miss a step. These options can be modified at a later time via multiple tabs on the advertisement property page if necessary. To create a new advertisement, follow these steps:

1. Right-click on the Advertisements node under Site > Computer Management > Software Distribution and choose New > Advertisement. (See Figure 11.79.)

2. The New Advertisement Wizard is displayed. This wizard allows you to create a standard advertisement for a program that has already been

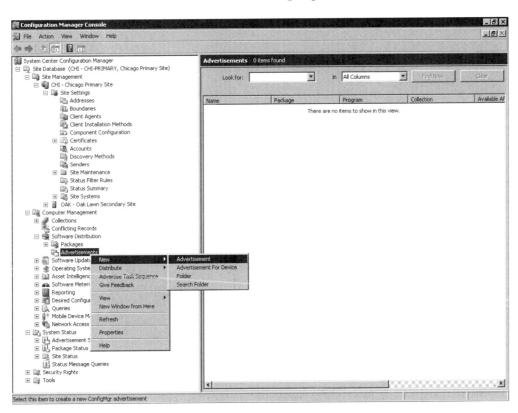

Figure 11.79
New Standard Advertisement

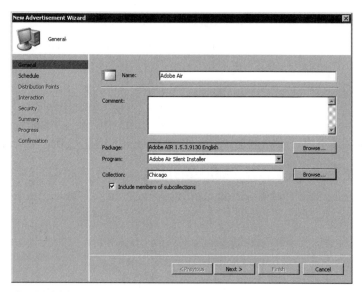

Figure 11.80
General Settings

defined within a package. The configuration options for the general section are discussed next and shown in Figure 11.80. In our example, we'll advertise the Adobe Air package to our Chicago collection and then click Next to continue.

- **Name**—The Name field allows you to name the advertisement.
- **Comment**—If you choose, you can use the Comment field to add more information to the advertisement such as creation date, purpose, and creator.
- **Package**—The Package field allows you to search for the package that you want to advertise. Use the Browse button to locate the correct package.
- **Program**—Once a package has been chosen, you can choose any program that has been defined within the package. The program is what will be executed on the targeted computer.
- **Collection**—The Collection field allows you to target a collection where the advertisement will be executed.
- **Include members of subcollections**—This option specifies that any subcollections (collections under a collection) will also receive the advertisement.

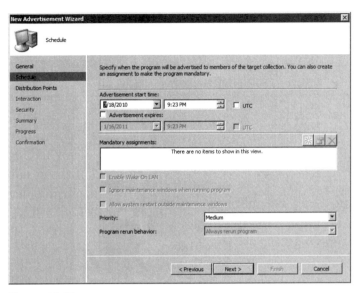

Figure 11.81
Schedule Settings

Note

If you create a package that does not have a program associated with it, you will not be able to select the package in the general section of the New Advertisement Wizard. The package will not be visible until a program is created.

3. The Schedule section of the wizard is displayed. The configuration options for the schedule section are discussed next and shown in Figure 11.81. In our example, we'll choose the defaults and click Next to continue.

- **Advertisement start time**—Lets you choose the start date and time for when an advertisement becomes available to a computer. The time will be calculated by the computer's local time unless the UTC checkbox is selected. If UTC is selected, coordinated universal time is used. Once an advertisement becomes available, end users have the ability to run these advertisements if configured correctly.

- **Advertisement expires**—Lets you choose an end date and time for when the advertisement expires. This is useful if you only want the advertisement to be available during a specific time period and you don't want to delete the advertisement completely.

Tip

Deleting an advertisement also deletes all reporting information about the advertisement such as if a computer ran the advertisement successfully or not. If you wish to keep this reporting information, I suggest expiring the advertisement instead of deleting it.

- **Mandatory assignments**—Lets you choose the date and time or event for when an advertisement runs. Mandatory assignments cannot be declined by an end user and will run at the time or event specified. This is useful if you want to deploy a software package or security update to a large number of computers without burdening the end users to initiate the installation.

- **Enable Wake On LAN**—Lets you choose whether to send out Wake On LAN packets to targeted computers so that they will be powered on when it comes time to run the advertisement. We'll talk more about Wake On LAN later in this chapter. This option is only available if a mandatory assignment has been configured.

- **Ignore maintenance windows when running program**—Lets you choose to ignore any maintenance windows that may be configured for a collection or set of collections. This option is useful if you need to start the advertisement immediately. This option is only available if a mandatory assignment has been configured.

- **Allow system restart outside maintenance windows**—Lets you choose whether or not the computer will be restarted even if the advertisement is run outside of a configured maintenance window. This option is only available if a mandatory assignment has been configured.

Caution

This setting only applies to programs that have the ConfigMgr Restarts Computer option enabled. If the program itself automatically restarts the computer (such as an MSI with the /forcerestart or REBOOT=Force options configured), and the Allow System Restart Outside Maintenance Windows option is checked, the computer will restart in accordance with the program's settings.

- **Priority**—Lets you choose how the advertisement will be replicated to child sites. You can choose Low, Medium, or High. Medium is the default setting.

- **Program rerun behavior**—This option allows you to configure how a program will run if it has been run in the past. The options are Never Rerun Advertised Program, Always Rerun Program, Rerun if Failed Previous Attempt, and Rerun if Succeeded on Previous Attempt. The default setting for standard advertisements is Rerun if Failed on Previous Attempt. The default setting for task sequence advertisements is Never Rerun Advertised Program.

4. The Distribution Points section of the wizard is displayed. This section lets you define how and if a program runs depending on if the client is connected to a fast or slow boundary. Boundaries are covered in detail in Chapter 5, "Creating a Site Hierarchy." The configuration options for the Distribution Points section are discussed next and shown in Figure 11.82. In our example, we'll choose the defaults and click Next to continue.

When a client is connected within a fast (LAN) network boundary:

- **Run program from distribution point**—This option forces the client to run the program directly from the distribution point without downloading any content locally to the client cache.

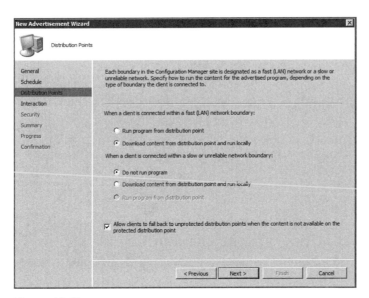

Figure 11.82
Distribution Points

Note

Because no content is being downloaded to the client cache when this option is enabled, no hash check is performed on the package content.

- **Download content from distribution point and run locally**—This option forces the client to download the package content to the client cache and then run the program from there. Once the content is downloaded, a hash check is performed on the content and then compared to that within the source location. If the hash check fails, the program is not installed. This is the default option.

Note

If you choose this option and your distribution points are BITS enabled, package content is downloaded using BITS to ensure a network efficient and fault tolerant download.

Caution

If the size of the package is larger than the client cache, the program will fail to install. The size of the client cache is 5GB by default but can be changed depending on how large the computer's hard drive is. More information about the client cache can be found in Chapter 7.

When a client is connected within a slow or unreliable network boundary:

- **Do not run program**—When this option is enabled, the client will not run the program. This is where the usefulness of boundaries really comes into play. If a client is connected through a VPN connection that is identified by a slow boundary, for example, any advertisements assigned to clients within that boundary will not run when this option is selected.
- **Download content from distribution point and run locally**—This option forces the client to behave in exactly the same way as described above. Content will be downloaded to the client cache and then executed from there.
- **Run program from distribution point**—This option is not available for clients in slow boundaries and is grayed out.

- **Allow clients to fall back to unprotected distribution points when the content is not available on the protected distribution point**— This option allows a client to use an unprotected distribution point if package content is not available on a protected distribution point. If there are multiple protected and unprotected distribution points and this option is unchecked, only protected distribution points are used to access the package content.

5. The Interaction section of the wizard is displayed. This section allows you to specify how users are notified and interact with advertised programs. The configuration options for the Interaction section are discussed next and shown in Figure 11.83. In our example, we'll choose the defaults and click Next to continue.

- **Allow users to run the program independently of assignments**— This setting allows users to not only see the program in the Run Advertised Programs Control Panel applet, but allows them to run it as well. This setting is checked (and grayed out) if no mandatory assignments have been created. If a mandatory assignment has been

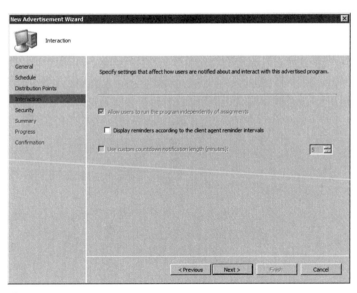

Figure 11.83
Interaction

created, this option is unchecked by default which also disallows users to see or run the program. If a mandatory advertisement has been created and this box is checked, users can see and run the advertised program. If the advertised program's mandatory start date is set for a future date, users can start the program early but they cannot stop the mandatory assignment from running at its scheduled time.

▪ **Display reminders according to the client agent reminder intervals**—If the previous option is checked, this option is available. This option specifies that the client displays reminders to users about a program's mandatory start time.

Note

Reminders are different from notifications. Notifications inform you when new programs are available while reminders inform you of a program's mandatory start time. Reminders can be important for users especially when a mandatory assignment restarts the computer. Reminders and notifications are discussed later in this chapter.

▪ **Use custom countdown notification length (minutes)**—This option is available only if the program has a mandatory assignment configured. This option lets you override the system-wide countdown notification setting by letting you specify a custom countdown notification. This notification is displayed to users before a mandatory assignment occurs.

6. The Security section of the wizard is displayed. If you need to modify the security of this package, you can do so from this section. Click Next to continue.

7. The Summary section of the wizard is displayed. This will show you the changes that the wizard is about to make. If you are satisfied with these changes, click Next to continue.

8. The Confirmation section of the wizard is displayed. This lets you review all of the changes that the wizard made. Click Close to close the wizard.

Wake On LAN

One new and powerful feature that is included with Configuration Manager 2007 is the ability to turn on or wake up computers using Wake On LAN. Wake

On LAN (WOL) is an industry standard that most computer and network card manufacturers support and can be typically enabled via settings in the BIOS. Once WOL is enabled on a computer, you can configure an advertisement to send WOL packets to the targeted machines to ensure that they are powered on prior to running the advertisement. We talked earlier about the WOL setting in the advertisement but there are more global options that you should be aware of as well.

Wake ON LAN Transmission Types

Configuration Manager gives you three types of WOL transmission types to use when waking up computers. These are as follows:

- **Subnet-directed broadcast transmissions**—Using subnet-directed broadcasts is the traditional and often the most reliable method of sending Wake On LAN packets to computers. Subnet-directed broadcasts need the MAC address and the IP address of a targeted computer to successfully send wake-up packets. This information is obtained from the hardware inventory scan so this must be completed at least once for this to succeed. Once a computer is targeted for WOL, Configuration Manager uses the computer's last known IP address to send wake-up packets to its corresponding subnet. Once the wake-up packets reach the destined subnet, it then uses the computer's MAC address to wake up the specific computer. This works well when the primary site server is on the same subnet as the targeted computer but this is not always the case. If the client's primary site server is on a different subnet than the client computer that is targeted for WOL, routers must be configured to send and receive directed broadcasts to and from the correct subnets using a specified port number. If you do not have the ability to change these router configurations, you might have more success using unicast transmissions.

- **Unicast transmissions**—Unicast transmissions are superior to subnet-broadcasts in many ways but also have some cons that make this method less than appealing in some situations. On the up side of things, unicast transmissions are IPv6 compatible, they consume less bandwidth than subnet-directed broadcasts, and they require little to no router re-configuration, which means they are often more secure than subnet-directed broadcasts as well. Unicast transmissions are different from subnet-directed broadcasts in that they send wake-up packets directly to the targeted computer by mapping its IP address to its MAC address (a standard ARP request). The problem with this method is that the MAC address cannot always be found because the primary site server's ARP cache may not contain the appropriate entry nor might the router's ARP cache. If the primary site server cannot resolve the MAC address from the IP address using cached information, it will then send an ARP request to the computer targeted for WOL. If the computer is in an off or sleep state, it cannot respond back with its MAC address and the WOL task may fail. Although the MAC address may be available in the Configuration Manager database (from a hardware inventory scan), Configuration Manager does not seem to use this information when sending unicast WOL transmissions.

▪ **Power on commands**—Power on commands only work if your computers have AMT chipsets (like vPro) and they have been provisioned within Configuration Manager 2007's Out of Band Management feature. If you have an infrastructure that supports this technology, use power on commands since they are more reliable than WOL packets.

Enabling Wake On LAN for a Site

Wake On LAN is enabled on a per-site basis and is disabled by default. To enable WOL for a site, do the following:

1. From the Site Management node, right-click on the site where you wish to enable Wake On LAN and click Properties. In our example, we'll enable WOL for the CHI site. (See Figure 11.84.)

2. The Site Properties window is displayed. This window allows you to change different site properties including Wake On LAN. Click on the Wake on LAN tab to configure WOL settings. Once the WOL tab is displayed, you can enable WOL for the site by clicking the checkbox next to the Enable Wake On LAN for This Site option. Once WOL is enabled, you can then choose whether to use both power on commands and wake-up packets, only power on commands, or only wake-up packets. Below that, you can choose whether to send subnet-directed broadcasts

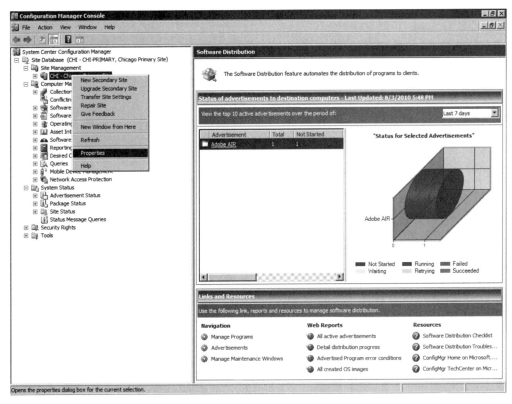

Figure 11.84
Open Site Settings to Enable WOL

or unicasts for the transmission method. In our example, we'll choose wake-up packets only and subnet-directed broadcasts. (See Figure 11.85.)

3. If you need to change advanced WOL settings, you can do so by clicking the Advanced button as seen in Figure 11.85. This opens the Wake On LAN Advanced Properties window, which lets you configure Transmission retries, transmission maximum wake-up packets, transmission threads, and transmission offset. One setting to keep in mind is the transmission offset. This allows you to configure when wake-up packets are sent to computers prior to a scheduled activity. If your computers need more time to boot, for example, you could increase this setting to meet your needs. (See Figure 11.86.)

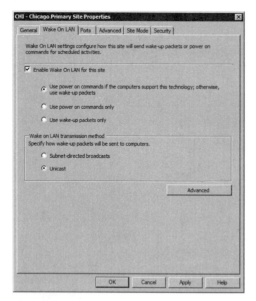

Figure 11.85
Choosing Wake On LAN Options

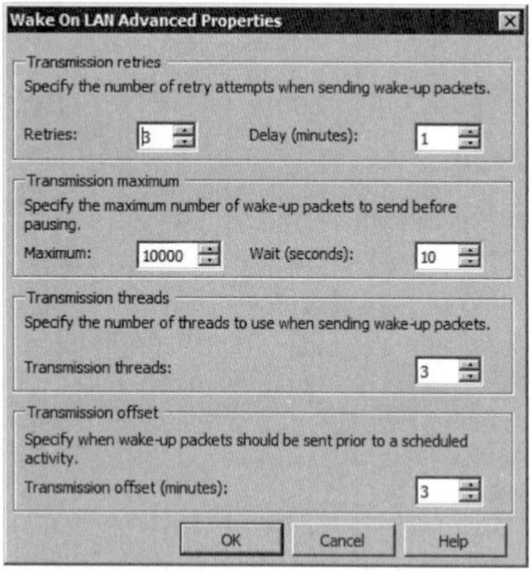

Figure 11.86
Wake On LAN Advanced Properties

Sleep States and WOL

If your computers have been configured to wake up from a sleep or hibernate state with wake-up (magic) packets, you might want to increase the Unattended

Sleep Timeout setting so that they do not go back into a sleep state before the scheduled activity can run. By default, if Windows wakes up from an unattended event and no user intervention is detected, Windows will transition back into a sleep state after two minutes—possibly causing the scheduled activity to fail. The Unattended Sleep Timeout setting can be configured via group policy for Windows 7 machines but not for Windows Vista Machines. In Windows Vista, this had to be configured using registry keys. The registry key locations and functions are described next:

Start by locating this registry key:

```
HKEY_LOCAL_MACHINE\SYSTEM\CurrentControlSet\Control\Power\PowerSettings\
238C9FA8-0AAD-41ED-83F4-97BE242C8F20\7bc4a2f9-d8fc-4469-b07b-33eb785aaca0\
DefaultPowerSchemeValues
```

Under that key, you'll see three more keys. These keys correspond to the default power plans built into Vista. These are as follows:

- **Balanced**—381b4222-f694-41f0-9685-ff5bb260df2e

- **High Performance**—8c5e7fda-e8bf-4a96-9a85-a6e23a8c635c

- **Power Saver**—a1841308-3541-4fab-bc81-f71556f20b4a

After you have identified which power plan you wish to modify, go to the corresponding registry key and locate the ACSettingIndex and DCSettingIndex DWORD values under that key. These settings control how long the unattended sleep timeout period is while running on AC or DC power. Change the decimal value data (in seconds) to your new preferred timeout value in one or both DWORD settings to complete this process. Note that this can be done manually, through a script from Configuration Manager 2007, through a group policy registry preference item, or other means.

RECEIVING SOFTWARE

Once a package (and a program) has been created, copied to a distribution point, and advertised to a collection, users can finally receive the package and run the program. Programs can be started automatically, such as when an advertisement has a mandatory assignment, or they can be started manually, through a special Control Panel applet that gets installed with the Configuration Manager 2007

Client. Notifications can also be broadcasted to users letting them know when new programs are available or when they are about to run—such as when a mandatory assignment is created.

Run Advertised Programs

When the Configuration Manager Client is installed, new Control Panel applets are also installed. One of these applets is called Run Advertised Programs and can be found within the Control Panel. Depending on how the advertisement was configured, this applet lets you run both non-mandatory and mandatory assignments in an on-demand fashion. This is very handy if you need to run assigned programs before their mandatory start dates or if your IT policy states that only approved and tested software is allowed to be installed. If this is the case, you can use the Run Advertised Programs Control Panel applet to act as a software catalog that contains tested and approved software. This way, software is installed in a manageable and consistent way while giving you valuable reporting data such as when the software was installed and if it was successful or not. Depending on how your environment is configured, you can allow all users to have access to Run Advertised Programs or only allow access to approved users. The Run Advertised Programs Control Panel applet is shown in Figure 11.87.

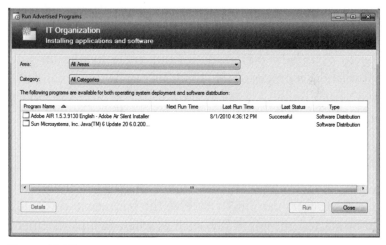

Figure 11.87
Run Advertised Programs

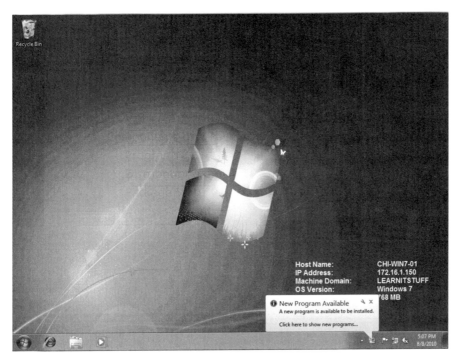

Figure 11.88
New Program Notification

Notifications

As new advertisements are created and made available to computers or users, notifications are broadcasted, by default, informing logged on users that new programs are available. An example of a notification is shown in Figure 11.88.

Reminders

If a mandatory assignment is created with the Allow Users to Run the Program Independently of Assignments and Display Reminders According to the Client Agent Reminder Intervals options set, users will be reminded that a program is about to run. This is shown in Figure 11.89.

Countdown Notifications

After a user is notified and reminded (according to the reminder schedule) about a mandatory program, the program will then install according to the

Figure 11.89
New Mandatory Program Reminder

assignment schedule. Before the installation, however, a countdown notification will be displayed—giving the user a final warning and countdown. The user can optionally install the program before the scheduled time if they choose to do so. These options are shown in Figures 11.90 and 11.91.

Global Notification and Reminder Settings

As discussed earlier in this chapter, notifications are controlled globally in the advertised programs client agent while reminders are controlled globally in the computer client agent. Countdown notifications are also controlled within the advertised programs client agent. Additionally, all notifications and reminders can be controlled per program by selecting the Suppress Program Notifications option on the program's Property page in the Advanced tab.

Figure 11.90
Countdown Notification Balloon

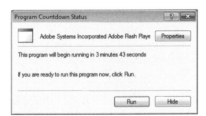

Figure 11.91
Countdown Notification Properties

Tip

All Windows balloon notifications can be controlled via a group policy setting, which is not configurable within Configuration Manager. If an administrator enables the Turn Off All Balloon Notifications group policy setting, this affects all balloon notifications, including the ones initiated by Configuration Manager 2007.

MONITORING SOFTWARE DISTRIBUTION

One of the great things about Configuration Manager 2007 is its ability to give you up-to-date information on almost any client activity. This information can be obtained from reporting information, queries, and log files. In this section, we'll talk about the information we can collect pertaining to software distribution.

Reports

As we discussed in Chapter 10, reports are a very powerful tool to use when needing to collect data about a specific subject. Configuration Manager 2007 comes with 24 canned reports specifically pertaining to software distribution. These reports are listed next:

- Advertisement status messages for a client being upgraded to the Advanced Client
- Advertisement status messages for a particular client and advertisement
- All active package distributions
- All advertisements
- All advertisements for a specific collection
- All advertisements for a specific computer
- All advertisements for a specific package
- All collections
- All distribution points
- All distribution points with virtual application streaming enabled
- All packages
- All packages on a specific distribution point
- All resources in a specific collection
- All status messages for a specific package on a specific distribution point
- All system resource advertisements with status
- All system resources for a specific advanced client distribution in a specific state

- All system resources for a specific advertisement in a specific state

- All virtual application packages in the streaming store of a distribution point

- Chart—Hourly advertisement completion status

- Distribution status of a specific advertisement

- Maintenance Windows available to a particular client

- Status of a specific advertisement

- Status of an advanced client distribution

- Streaming store distribution status of a specific virtual application package

For example, a very useful report is the "Status of a specific advertisement" report. In this example, I ran this report against an advertisement to find out the status. The success result is displayed in Figure 11.92.

In this example, I ran the same report on a different advertisement that returned a failure result as shown in Figure 11.93.

As you can see, the report not only showed that the advertisement failed but why it failed. With this information, I can quickly identify and resolve the problem without much effort. Although this is just an example, this shows you how useful Configuration Manager can be in troubleshooting your software deployments on a small or large scale.

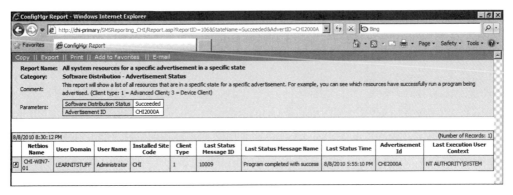

Figure 11.92
Advertisement Status Report—Success

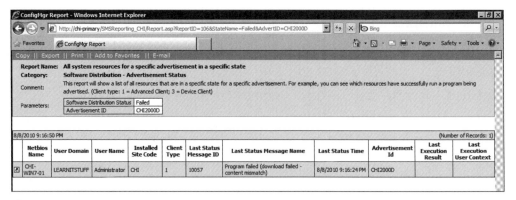

Figure 11.93
Advertisement Status Report—Failure

Tip

I was able to generate the hash mismatch error by changing the content in the distribution point so that it would not match the content in the source location just as we discussed earlier in this chapter.

MIF Matching

Newer installer technologies, like MSI or InstallShield for example, include support for creating MIF files during an install. MIF stands for management information format and is used by Configuration Manager 2007 to give detailed information about the installation status of a program. This is useful because you can get specific information as to why a program failed, for example, when performing troubleshooting steps.

Once a program has finished an installation process, it typically writes its MIF file to either the Windows directory or the Temp directory. Configuration Manager then looks in these directories and searches for any MIF files that have been created. If it finds any MIF files, it parses these files and attempts to match them to a program (defined within Configuration Manager) using the data in the Reporting tab of the package property page. If the package was created using an MSI, the MIF information is extracted from the MSI and is automatically entered into the fields in the Reporting tab. If the package was created using a simple package, the information in the General tab is used by default. Remember that this is the information that you manually enter when creating a generic package. If these fields match the information that was found in a MIF file, that file is used to extend the status reporting information for a program. If no MIF file can be found, only the exit code is used for installation status.

Log Files

Listed next are some of the log files that can be used when troubleshooting software distribution issues. Remember to use Trace32.exe from the Configuration Manager 2007 toolkit for easy log reading!

Note

There are many other log files that Configuration Manager 2007 creates that might help troubleshoot a software distribution problem. To see all of the log files that each site system role creates, refer to Chapter 6.

Table 11.1 Client Log Files for Software Distribution Troubleshooting

Log File	Location	Description
CAS.log	%Windir%\System32\CCM\Logs[1]	Monitors the Content Access service which maintains the local package cache
ContentTransferManager.log	%Windir%\System32\CCM\Logs[1]	Instructs BITS or SMB to download or access packages
DataTransferService.log	%Windir%\System32\CCM\Logs[1]	Monitors all BITS communication for policy or package access
Execmgr.log	%Windir%\System32\CCM\Logs[1]	Monitors advertisements that run on the client system
FileBITS.log	%Windir%\System32\CCM\Logs[1]	Monitors all SMB access to packages
LocationServices.log	%Windir%\System32\CCM\Logs[1]	Monitors the location of management points and distribution points
PolicyAgent.log	%Windir%\System32\CCM\Logs[1]	Monitors requests for policies by the Data Transfer Service
PolicyAgentProvider.log	%Windir%\System32\CCM\Logs[1]	Monitors policy changes
PolicyEvaluator.log	%Windir%\System32\CCM\Logs[1]	Monitors new policy settings
Scheduler.log	%Windir%\System32\CCM\Logs[1]	Monitors scheduled tasks for the client
StatusAgent.log	%Windir%\System32\CCM\Logs[1]	Details status messages that are generated by client components

[1]For x64 installations, the log files are located at %Windir%\SysWOW64\CCM\Logs

Table 11.2 Site Server Log Files for Software Distribution Troubleshooting

Log File	Location	Description
Distmgr.log	<ConfigMgrInstallationDirectory>\SMS\Logs	Details package creation, compression, delta replication, and information processes
Offermgr.log	<ConfigMgrInstallationDirectory>\SMS\Logs	Monitors advertisement updates
Policypv.log	<ConfigMgrInstallationDirectory>\SMS\Logs	Monitors updates to client policies in regards to changes in client settings or advertisements
Replmgr.log	<ConfigMgrInstallationDirectory>\SMS\Logs	Monitors file replication between site server components and the Scheduler component
Sched.log	<ConfigMgrInstallationDirectory>\SMS\Logs	Monitors site-to-site job and package replication
Sender.log	<ConfigMgrInstallationDirectory>\SMS\Logs	Monitors files sent from the site server to other child and parent sites

Table 11.3 Site Server Log Files for Software Distribution Troubleshooting

Log File	Location	Description
Distmgr.log	<ConfigMgrInstallationDirectory>\SMS\Logs	Monitors package creation, compression, delta replication, and information processes
Offermgr.log	<ConfigMgrInstallationDirectory>\SMS\Logs	Monitors advertisement updates
Wolmgr.log	<ConfigMgrInstallationDirectory>\SMS\Logs	Monitors wake-up procedures for advertisements or OS deployments
WolCmgr.log	<ConfigMgrInstallationDirectory>\SMS\Logs	Monitors wake-up events for advertisements or OS deployments

THE FINAL WORD

This chapter introduced many concepts such as collections, packages, and advertisements that you will need to understand before you move forward. If you do not fully grasp these concepts, please consider re-reading these sections before you go on. The next chapter explains how to utilize these concepts to deploy software updates using Configuration Manager 2007.

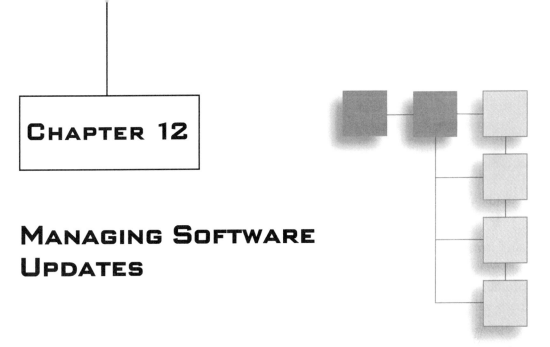

CHAPTER 12

MANAGING SOFTWARE UPDATES

If you have worked any time at all in the IT field, you know what Patch Tuesday is. If you have worked with any computer system for any time at all, you know what patches and updates are. Unfortunately, there are two types of problems when it comes to writing applications and operating systems. First you have the programmers that are lazy and don't follow best practices when writing their applications, and secondly, there are those individuals who try to exploit every weakness within software. Of course, there are other reasons that we need to patch our systems, including incompatibility between components and improvements to existing code.

No matter what the reason for the update or patch, we need to make sure that we can apply them as efficiently as possible so that we reduce our vulnerability and improve how our systems perform. System Center Configuration Manager leverages the efficient scanning mechanism of Windows Server Update Services and the distributed deployment mechanisms of Configuration Manager 2007. With the enhanced reporting capabilities and change management functionality of Configuration Manager, organizations can manage their update processes more efficiently.

OVERVIEW OF THE SOFTWARE UPDATE PROCESS

As with any service, there are several steps that make up the entire software update process. The entire process spans many different systems, including the site server, site database server, The software update point, management point, distribution points, and managed systems. Although complex, once configured correctly, maintaining and deploying the updates can become a very efficient process.

Synchronizing Updates

The active software update point is responsible for synchronizing the update metadata with Windows Server Update Services. All of the update information that is stored in the Windows Server Update Services database needs to be included in the site database. If the two databases are not kept in sync, the clients will not update correctly. Typically, the synchronization process runs automatically and you don't have to worry about starting a sync, but you can also initiate a manual synchronization whenever you choose.

The settings that you specify within the software update point component properties dictate how the synchronization process will be performed. You have the ability to configure if the synchronization occurs on a schedule or if it is a manual process, and which products, languages, and criticality levels of metadata will be synced. You also have the option to synchronize the updates from the Microsoft Updates website, from an upstream Windows Server Update Services server, or performing an import of the update metadata from a file. No matter which method is used, the Windows Server Update Services server needs to add the metadata to its database.

Once the updates have been stored within the Windows Server Update Services database, the same information needs to be added to the site database. Luckily, this does not involve performing another synchronization to the location where you obtained the metadata the first time. Instead, the site server requests a list of all metadata that was just synchronized. The site database will then be updated with the same update information that the software update point has, guaranteeing that when a managed system performs a scan, it can report on which updates are required.

Scanning Systems

After the update metadata has been synchronized, you will need to determine which updates are needed by the managed systems within your site. Each client will need to perform a software update scan that will compare the metadata on the software update point to the installed updates and current versions of operating system and application files on the managed system. The client will start the Windows Update agent, which in turn will contact the software update point identified within the client's policy file. The software update point, leveraging the scanning components of Windows Server Update Services answers the client's request for metadata information. Once the client has the metadata, it begins a scan of the components installed on the system and will record the status of every update. The requirements of each update, whether the update is required, installed, or not applicable is contained within a state message. These state messages are held for a predetermined amount of time before being sent en-masse to the management point. The schedule for sending state messages can be configured on the General tab of the computer client agent. The longer you hold the messages on the client system, the longer it will take to update the database with the information collected during the scan, but the more efficient the transmission of the state messages will be. If you don't need to have immediate response from the clients because you are performing the scans well ahead of the time that you are creating the deployments, you can increase this value.

As the state messages are received by the management point, the management point will forward the state messages to the site server. The site server is responsible for summarizing the data contained within the state messages and storing the results in the site database.

Approving Updates

Once the scan has been performed and the update status has been added to the site database, you are ready to evaluate the required updates. Each update that is needed by at least one managed system will appear with a value of 1 or higher within the Required column in the Software Updates folders.

Selecting the updates that are required, you can download the files that are used to install the updates. During the approval process, the updates are downloaded to a network location that is used as the source location for the update files. Deployment packages are then used to group the updates that will be deployed together. The deployment packages are copied to distribution points within the site. The files that were downloaded are then copied from the source location to the distribution points. Once the deployment packages are made available, the client can then download and install the updates.

Deploying Updates

When the deployment packages become available, the client is notified via its policy that it retrieves from the management point. If the deployment package is available, but not yet mandatory, the updates are not installed unless the user of the system performs a manual installation. Once the deployment package is mandatory, the installation is performed by the system.

When the installation of the updates is initiated, the client system will scan to determine its update requirements. Once the requirements are determined, the client will download only the updates that it requires from the distribution point. The entire deployment package does not have to be downloaded to the client. This is very beneficial, especially when the client is attempting to update over a slower network link. As the updates are downloaded and installed, the client again sends state messages to the management point. As the state messages are received by the management point, the management point forwards the state messages to the site server. The site server summarizes the data contained within the state messages and stores the results in the site database.

Periodically, on the schedule set by the Software Updates Client Agent Properties Deployment Re-evaluation tab, the client will scan again to determine if it is still compliant. If any updates have been backed off of the system, the client will reinstall the update to remain compliant.

OVERVIEW OF THE SOFTWARE UPDATE COMPONENTS

Before deploying updates, there are components and settings that need to be configured. Before you can install a software update point, Windows Server Update Services needs to be installed. The Windows Server Update Services administrative snap-in needs to be installed wherever the Configuration Manager administrator console is installed. These settings and others are critical to a fully functional software update deployment infrastructure. In this section, we will discuss the components that need to be configured and how to configure them.

Windows Server Update Services

The Configuration Manager team decided that they didn't need to re-create the wheel when it came to scanning client systems. Microsoft already had a proven scanning methodology with the Windows Server Update Services server.

Windows Server Update Services proved that it was very efficient and accurate when determining the updates that were required on systems, but it was not as efficient at deploying the updates in large organizations. It also lacked in detailed reporting. The Configuration Manager team made the decision to leverage the best components of Windows Server Update Services, the synchronization and scanning components, and then decided the delivery system and reporting options afforded by Configuration Manager were better utilized in most organizations using Configuration Manager.

N o t e

If you already had a Windows Server Update Services infrastructure in place and are moving to a Configuration Manager supported update process, make sure you remove the group policy settings that specify the Windows Server Update Services systems that the clients will use. When the group policy settings are in place, they will override the local policy settings that are applied on the client when the Configuration Manager policy is applied.

Installing Windows Server Update Services

On Windows Server 2008 R2, Windows Server Update Services is one of the roles that you can add to your server. The installation files are not included with the server installation however. When you start installing the role, the server will contact the download location and retrieve the latest installation files. To begin the installation, open Server Manager and select the Roles node if necessary. Clicking the Add Roles link will present you with the Add Roles Wizard. If the Before You Begin page appears, click Next to move to the wizard.

On the Select Server Roles Wizard, select the checkbox for Windows Server Update Services. Depending on the roles that you have already installed on the server, you may be presented with a dialog that will let you know that additional features and services are required to support Windows Server Update Services on the system. Review the services listed to make sure that you want to allow them to run on the system. If the system is used for other purposes, you need to weigh the risk of having a larger attack surface. If you want to continue installing the Windows Server Update Services role, click Add Required Role Services and then click Next.

Once you click Next, the additional role services that were required will be presented to you. It is here that you can add in any additional role services that you may need to have on the system. If you only want to install the role services required by Windows Server Update Services, you can click Next. Otherwise, select the checkbox for the role services you want to add and then click Next to continue with the Windows Server Update Services installation. Clicking Next and then Install will start the download of the Windows Server Update Services installation files. Once downloaded, the Windows Server Update Services installation package will launch, allowing you to configure Windows Server Update Services.

There is not much that you need to configure on a standard installation of Windows Server Update Services that will be used as the software update point. Most of the configuration settings are configured within the Configuration Manager console. There are a couple of settings that you should configure as the installation wizard starts. The first is the setting Store Updates Locally. This setting should be selected and a file location defined. Although you will not typically store updates on the Windows Server Update Services server, there are updates that require administrator approval of the End User License Agreement. When you accept the license agreement, the acceptance information is stored within the location that you specify. This is also the location where the client installation files are stored when you use the software update point client installation method.

The other option that needs to be specified is the port number option. Typically, Windows Server Update Services is installed as the only application on the server that uses IIS. If this is the case in your organization, you can leave the default setting to use the standard IIS ports of 80 for HTTP traffic and 443 for HTTPS traffic. If you are sharing the IIS server with any other process that needs to use these ports, you do have the option to use custom ports for Windows Server Update Services. Due to the way the Windows Update agent is designed, if you use custom ports for your Windows Server Update Services implementation, you will have to use port 8530 for HTTP requests, and HTTPS requests will have to be configured for port 8531. In most organizations, the latter configuration option is the norm. A typical installation of the software update point role is usually shared with other roles. In large organizations, where the roles are installed on different systems, it is not required to change the ISS ports.

Once Windows Server Update Services has been installed, cancel the Configuration Wizard. The remaining configuration settings will be set from within the

Configuration Manager administrator console. All of the settings will be stored within the site database and the software update point will query the database for configuration settings.

Software Update Point

The software update point is another site system role. This site system role is used when managed systems perform scans to determine which updates are applicable. Before you can successfully define a software update point, you need to have a system that has Windows Server Update Services installed.

Configuring the Software Update Point Component

After installing the Windows Server Update Services role, the system is ready to accept the software update point role. As with any other Configuration Manager site system role, you need to perform the installation from the Configuration Manager console. Navigate to the Site Systems node within the site settings of the site where you are installing the software update point. If the software update point will reside on a system that already has another site system role installed, right-click the appropriate system and select New Roles. If the software update point will be installed on a new site system, right-click the Site System node and select New Server.

Once the role wizard starts, the installation options appear nearly the same. The General page is used to identify the system that has Windows Server Update Services installed and is going to be used as the software update point and the settings for installing the new role. The following page of the wizard, System Role Selection, is used to specify the role that will be installed. Once the software update point option is selected, the remaining options specific to a software update point become available.

Note

For a full explanation of all of the settings that can be applied, see Chapter 6, "Configuring Site System Roles."

The first of the configuration screens, Software Update Point, is used to identify the proxy server to be used during synchronization. Entering the proxy server address, port, and credentials on this page will allow the software update point to connect to Microsoft Update or an upstream Windows Server Update Services server when requesting the metadata.

The second page of settings is used to identify whether the site system being installed is the Active software update point. If it is, selecting the checkbox will present you with additional options to configure. On the Active Settings page, the port numbers in use by Windows Server Update Services will appear. If you are using the default settings within Windows Server Update Services, you can leave the default port settings as is. If you did select to use a custom website for Windows Server Update Services, you will need to configure the settings for the two port numbers to 8530 for HTTP traffic and the SSL port 8531 for HTTPS traffic.

Specifying that the site system will be the active software update point presents five more configuration pages within the wizard. These are used to identify the synchronization options. The configuration pages that appear are as follows:

- **Sync Source**—Used to identify the synchronization source. The options are as follows:
  - Synchronize from Microsoft Update.
  - Synchronize from an upstream update server.
  - Do not synchronize from Microsoft Update or an upstream update server. Select this option only if the export/import function is used to obtain software update definitions.
- **Sync Schedule**—Used to define the schedule that will be used when synchronizing from Microsoft Update or an upstream update server.
- **Classifications**—Used to define the update classifications that will be synchronized. The available update classifications are as follows:
  - **Critical Updates**—Fixes for specific problems addressing critical, non-security related problems.
  - **Definition Updates**—Updates for antivirus and malware protection.
  - **Drivers**—Software components used to manage hardware.
  - **Feature Packs**—New product functionality.
  - **Security Updates**—Fixes for products, addressing security problems.

- **Service Packs**—Cumulative package of released since the release of the product.
- **Tools**—Utilities.
- **Update Rollups**—Cumulative set of hotfixes, security updates, critical updates, and updates packaged together.
- **Updates**—Fixes for a specific problem addressing non-critical, non-security related problems.

- **Products**—Used to define the updates that will be synchronized for products that are installed within your organization. In order to reduce the amount of data that is stored in the database and downloaded to distribution points, make sure you only define the products that you need to support. This list changes as new products and new versions of products are introduced.

- **Languages**—Used to define the languages that are supported within your organization. As with the products option, only select the language requirements for your organization.

Update Repository

The update repository is the container that holds all of the updates that have been synchronized within the site. Once software updates have been enabled in the site by enabling the software update client agent and configuring a software update point, the option to synchronize updates becomes available. As updates are synchronized, subfolders are created for each of the configured products and classifications. It is within the update repository that you will determine which updates need to be deployed, create update lists, and control the downloading of the update files.

Synchronizing Updates

When you installed the software update point, you configured the synchronization settings, which included an option for setting a synchronization schedule. If you enabled this option, the active software update point will contact either Microsoft Update or an upstream update server to retrieve the latest metadata catalog. If you did not configure the scheduling option, you will have to perform a manual synchronization when you want to update the software update point and the site database.

Changing the schedule is performed within the console by opening the software update point component properties within the Component Configuration node of the site settings. The Sync Schedule tab is used to alter the schedule.

A manual synchronization can be performed at any time, whether or not a schedule has been defined. Selecting the Update Repository node within the Software Updates section of Computer Management will present the Run Synchronization action within the Actions pane. Alternately, you can select Run Synchronization from the context menu when you right-click the Update Repository. Once selected, you will be presented with a dialog warning you that you are about to run a synchronization. This dialog also informs you of the component that is used for the synchronization of the databases once the metadata has been received by the software update point.

As the synchronization is performed, you can monitor the progress by viewing the wsyncmgr.log log file. Initially, you will see the line "Performing sync on local request". Once the synchronization starts, you will see the number of categories processed, and then the updates that are being synchronized will appear. Make sure you are viewing the log file with the SMS Trace utility so that you will have dynamic updates whenever something changes within the log.

After a synchronization has completed, the update metadata that was stored within the database will appear as available updates within the console. Refresh the Update Repository and expand the folders that appear within. You should find folders for each of the classifications that were selected when you modified the Classifications tab of the software update point component properties. Expanding the folders will present you with additional folders containing the updates that were synchronized. Each classification folder will contain an All Updates folder. This folder is handy to have if you want to view the specifications of all of the updates within the classification, but most of the time it will contain too many entries to be of much use. Instead, you will find the other folders easier to use and manipulate.

Each of the products that were defined within the software update point component properties will have a search folder created when the first update for that product is synchronized. There will be several folders broken out underneath the Microsoft folder within critical updates. Breaking out the products and classifications in this manner makes it much easier to manage the updates. For instance, if you are preparing to roll out updates for Windows 7, you can simply click the Windows 7 updates folder and only updates that apply to Windows 7 will appear. You can then review the updates that are listed as required for systems within your organization.

Update Lists

An update list is just what it sounds like—a list of updates. The primary purpose of an update list is compliance reporting. There are some other nice features wrapped around update lists however. As you are creating update lists and defining the updates that will be included, you have the option to download the files associated with the update. You can also create a deployment based upon the updates that have been added to an update list. And while all of these things are nice to have, the compliance component is the most important aspect of an update list.

There are three reports included with Configuration Manager that take advantage of update lists. Two of the reports are compliance reports and one is for update management. Of the two compliance reports, the Compliance 8, Computers In A Specific Compliance State For An Update List is the most useful. This report will compare all of the systems within the specified collection against the selected update lists and return the systems that meet the chosen compliance state. If you want to view all of the Windows 7 systems within the All Windows 7 Systems collection that are in a Non-Compliant state for an update list, this report would generate that information for you.

When creating update lists, make sure you create them according to how you roll out your updates. You should only include updates that are deployed together, targeted at systems that have like needs. You should not include updates for Windows 7 and Windows XP systems within the same update list. The compliance reports would not be very useful if you do so.

Creating Update Lists

You have to have at least one update selected to create an update list. If you try to create an update list by right-clicking on the Update List folder, you will quickly notice that you don't get the option to create one. Instead, you will have to select an update that you want to be included within the update list, then right-click the update and select Update List. The wizard allows you to add the selected updates to an existing update list or create a new update list. After defining the update list in which the update will be included, you also have the option to download the update file.

Deployment Templates

Deployment templates are meant to make deploying updates easier on administrators. There are several configuration options that are going to be the same as you create new deployment packages. These settings can be defined within a deployment template, and then when you create a new deployment package, you can specify a deployment template that will be used to automatically fill in many of the configuration options. You can create as many deployment templates as necessary to define the different deployment methods that you need to support update deployments.

Creating Deployment Templates

You can create a deployment template as you are deploying your updates, or you can precreate deployment templates for later use. It is up to you how you want to create them, either way works well. Many administrators prefer to create the templates ahead of time so that they have them ready to go when it is time to deploy the updates. Others take the approach of creating them as needed when the updates are ready to be deployed.

To create a deployment template prior to update deployment, right-click the Deployment Template node and select New Deployment Template. To create one during deployment package creation, select the Create a New Deployment Definition option on the Deployment Template page of the Deploy Software Updates Wizard. Either way, the wizard that appears allows you to configure all of the default settings for the deployment template.

- On the Template Name page, enter the name of the deployment template. Optionally, enter more information in the Description field for documentation purposes.

- On the Collection page, select the collection that contains the managed systems that will receive the updates. Clear the checkbox for Include Members of Subcollections if you only want to target the collection specified and none of the subcollections.

- On the Display/Time Settings page, there are three options to work with:
  - Select Allow Display Notification on Clients if you want your users to know that there are updates available to install. Select Suppress Display Notifications on Clients if you do not want clients informed of update availability.
  - The deployment schedule section allows you to control the time when the updates are available to install and when they become mandatory installs. The two options you can set control whether the time will be based upon the time zone of the client system or Coordinated Universal Time (UTC). If you want the update to be installed at the same time, no matter where in the world the client is located, choose the UTC option.
  - The Duration section is used to specify a default amount of time that the update will become available but not made mandatory. The amount of time specified here can be overridden when creating a deployment package.

- On the Restart Settings page, you can specify which systems will not reboot after the updates are applied and if maintenance windows will be respected. At the top of the page, the checkboxes can be selected to specify that you do not want to restart servers, workstations, or both. At the bottom of the page, you can specify that maintenance windows will not stop a system from rebooting if one of the updates requires a reboot after installation.

- On the Event Generation page, you can integrate the installation of the updates with Operations Manager monitoring systems. The first checkbox, when selected, will effectively place the managed system in maintenance mode as the updates are installed. When the second checkbox is selected, any installation failures will be reported to the Operations Manager system. For either of these options to work, the managed system needs to have the Operations Manager client installed.

- On the Download Settings page, you can control how the client downloads the updates. The top section controls the downloading of the updates when the client is in a slow or unreliable boundary, or outside of the site's boundaries. The lower section controls how clients will access the updates if they cannot retrieve the updates from their protected distribution points.

- Select the first Do Not Install Software Updates option to keep the client from installing any of the updates in the deployment package until they are on a reliable network connection within the site boundaries.

- Select Download Software Updates from Distribution Point and Install if you want to make sure that the updates are installed no matter where the client is located.

- Select the second Do Not Install Software Update option to restrict the client from falling back to an unprotected distribution point when attempting to download and install updates.

- Select Download Software Updates from Unprotected Distribution Point and Install to allow the client to retrieve the updates from an unprotected distribution point.

The SMS 2003 Setting page is used to control how the existing SMS 2003 clients will process update packages. SMS 2003 clients have a different software update methodology than Configuration Manager clients. To report the updates that are required and those that have been installed, a hardware inventory needs to be performed. The client can be forced to perform a hardware inventory as soon as the updates have been installed by selecting the Collect Hardware Inventory Immediately checkbox. If left clear, the client will report hardware inventory on its next hardware inventory schedule. The remaining options control how the client will run the update package. These settings are the same as seen within Chapter 11, "Software Distribution."

Deployment Packages

Deployment packages contain the updates that are deployed to specific clients. Akin to software distribution packages, deployment packages are copied to distribution points, where the clients can download required updates. The Configuration nodes resemble a software distribution package. The Access Accounts node is used to control who is able to access the files on the selected distribution points. The Distribution Points node is used to identify and control the distribution points where the update files will be copied. The SMS 2003 Programs node is used to manage the installation of updates on systems with SMS 2003 clients. The Software Updates node is used to manage the updates that are included within the deployment package. The Package Status node is used to view and troubleshoot the distribution of deployment packages to the distribution points.

Creating Deployment Packages

You can start the Deployment Wizard from a few locations within the Software Updates node of the console. You can right-click an update or several selected updates, or you can right-click an update list and select the Deploy Software Updates Wizard. You can also launch the wizard by dragging and dropping one or more updates onto a deployment template, or you can drag and drop an update list onto a deployment template.

No matter how you launch the Deploy Software Updates Wizard, you will be presented with the same options. Many of the settings should look familiar if you have read Chapter 11, "Software Distribution." You are essentially creating a package that will be distributed to distribution points within the site hierarchy.

The first page of the wizard, General, is used to identify the deployment package and enter additional information that can be used to describe the updates and the systems that they apply to.

The Deployment Package page is used to specify the package that the updates will be added to, or the settings that will be used to create a new deployment package. As mentioned earlier, when managed systems apply required updates, they will download only the necessary updates from the deployment packages on the distribution points. This behavior allows you to manage fewer deployment packages while using an efficient delivery mechanism to the managed systems. With this in mind, you can add updates to existing deployment packages by selecting the first radio button and browsing for the deployment package to use.

Note

When creating a new deployment package, the deployment date and time can be configured. This allows you to specify when the client will install the updates. If you add updates to an existing package, and the deployment date and time have already passed, the client will install the new patches during the next scheduled deployment installation time.

Note

If you have systems that should not be installing updates until approved times, make sure to create maintenance windows for them. Until the maintenance window is open, the updates will not install.

Selecting the second radio button gives you the ability to define a new deployment package. The Name and Description fields can be used to identify the package and its usage. The Package Source field is used to define where the update files are stored on the network. This source location is used when copying the update files to distribution points. You must use a UNC path to the package source files location. Verify that the site server has at least read permissions.

The Sending Priority option controls the priority that is used when delivering packages to distribution points in other sites. High priority packages will be sent before Medium and Low priority messages. Medium packages will be sent before Low priority messages. Verify the settings on the Address to the sites to validate that the sending priority is allowed during the time that you need to send the deployment packages to distribution points.

Selecting Enable Binary Differential Replication is very important for deployment packages. If you are adding files into deployment packages, only the new and updated files are copied to the deployment packages stored on distribution points. This will reduce the amount of traffic on the network, and more importantly, across slower WAN links within the organization.

On the Distribution Point page, you can specify the distribution points that will store the deployment package. Those familiar with sending software distribution packages to distribution points will notice that the distribution point page appears a little different. You have to click the Browse button in order to select the distribution points. From the Add Distribution Points dialog, you can select distribution points from any of the sites within the site hierarchy.

The Download Location page is used to specify where the updates originate—Microsoft Updates or on the local network. The default selection, Download Software Updates from the Internet, will download the updates from Microsoft Update. If you have downloaded the updates to the local network already, either when you created an update list or by choosing to download the updates from the update properties, you can specify the path to the updates.

The Language Selection page allows you to define a subset of languages, or all of the languages, that you have synchronized.

The Schedule page is used to define when the updates are available to install and when they become a mandatory advertisement. The first section is used to define when the updates are available to install. The default is As Soon As Possible, but if you want to delay the availability of the update, you can select Date and Time and enter the date and time when the update is available to clients.

The lower section is used to identify when the updates become mandatory deployments. If you don't want to make the updates mandatory, you can select the Do Not Set a Deadline for Software Update Installation. Mandatory deployments can be defined by using the default setting of Set a Deadline for Software Update Installation. Notice that the date and time that is already entered is set to the amount of time defined within the deployment template. If you had set the Duration option to 7 days, the date and time shown on this page will be one week from the current date and time.

When you set the deployment package with a mandatory installation time, you also get to other options to configure. The Enable Wake on LAN option can be set if you want to attempt to wake up the managed systems within your network. The Ignore Maintenance Windows and Install Immediately at Deadline can be used on critical updates that have to be installed immediately and you do not want to wait until the next maintenance window. For either of these options to be effective, you will have to configure the appropriate components. Wake On LAN and Maintenance Windows are discussed in Chapter 11.

Deployment Management

The culmination of the entire update deployment configuration ends up in one component—the Deployment Management objects. These objects are created automatically when you use the Deploy Software Updates Wizard. In many respects, these could be considered the advertisements for a deployment package. The information contained in the deployment object specifies how the update will be installed, to which collection it is targeted, and the parameters that will be used during the deployment.

Opening the properties of a deployment object will allow you to see how the updates will be applied, and also allow you to make changes to how the deployment package is configured. The General tab can be used to identify the deployment object's name. Make sure to change this to something that is descriptive for what it is used for. Most of the remaining tabs reflect settings that were applied during the deployment.

- **Collections**—Specifies the collection that is targeted for the update deployment.

- **Software Updates**—Includes all of the updates that are in the deployment. This list reflects the updates that are included in the deployment package. Remove updates from this list before removing them from the deployment package.

- **SMS 2003 Settings**—Defines how SMS 2003 clients handle the update deployments.

- **Schedule**—Controls when the updates become available to install and when they become mandatory updates.

- **Download Settings**—Controls how clients download updates when they are on an unreliable or slow boundary and how they request updates when the updates are not available on the protected distribution points.

- **Display/Time Settings**—Controls whether the update availability is made known to users and the time zone settings that are used during the deployment.

- **Restart Settings**—Controls suppression of reboots on workstations and servers and maintenance window acknowledgement.

- **Event Generation**—Controls how the client works with operations manager alerts during update deployment.

Software Updates Client Agent

The final component resides on the managed systems within the site—the software updates client agent. This agent is responsible for scanning the client computer and managing the update installation. Once this agent is enabled, all of the managed systems within the site will start processing updates according to the settings applied. As with all other client agents, if there are any systems that need different settings than those applied within the site, they will need to be moved to another site where the settings apply to them.

The software updates client agent is enabled on the General tab. This is also where you configure the schedule that the client will use when scanning for updates. When using a simple schedule, the client will scan once during the timeframe specified. If the simple schedule option is configured to run once a day, and the first scan is performed at 3:28 PM, the client will scan every day at 3:28 unless a manual scan is initiated at a different time.

If the schedule is set as a custom schedule, the client will scan according to the settings applied within the schedule settings. With a custom schedule, all of the clients will scan at approximately the same time. To keep from having the network flooded with state messages, there is a random offset of up to 2 hours from the configured time. Each client will generate a random time offset and start scanning at that time. If the custom schedule is set to run a scan at 12:00 PM, a client could scan anywhere between the hours of 12:00PM and 2:00 PM.

On the Update Installation tab, there are two settings that apply to how the updates are managed on the client. The first option, Enforce All Mandatory Deployments, is used to control how far into the future the client should evaluate updates and install any that are mandatory within that configured timeframe. For instance, if there are update deployments that are configured as a mandatory install on Sunday, the client is installing updates on Friday, and the client is configured to include any mandatory deployments within the next 7 days, all mandatory updates from Friday and Sunday would be applied at the same time. When configured, this option can reduce the number of reboots and service interruptions caused by multiple updates set with different mandatory installation times.

The other option, Hide All Deployments from End Users, will block notifications that users typically receive when update deployments are available. Using this option, you can keep the users from knowing that updates are ready to install, making it so the updates will only be installed when the mandatory installation time arrives.

The final tab, Deployment Re-evaluation, is used to control when the client will perform a compliance scan to determine if the updates that were applied are still installed. This option is available because the site server is not notified when updates are manually uninstalled from a system. And in this age of virtualization, systems can be reverted to a previous version very quickly. The site database will still have record of the update being installed even though the system is back to a state where the update was not installed. The scan that is performed during the deployment re-evaluation cycle will validate the updates and reinstall any missing updates.

DEVELOPING A SOFTWARE UPDATE PROCESS

So let's put all of these components together into a cohesive software update process. Once the site components are configured and you have proven that you can synchronize the metadata and have access to the update files, you need to determine which updates are required within your organization, which updates you are going to deploy, when you will deploy them, and the managed systems that will receive them.

To start with, review how you currently apply updates to systems. You more than likely have a process for updating workstations and another for updating servers. In many organizations the update process for workstations is not as complex as the process that covers the server environment. We seem to be moving away from the distributed application model where application process and data storage is at the workstation level. And while not every company is there yet, there are many who do not store any company data on user's workstations. With the latest advances in application management, many of the applications are not even installed on a workstation. So for workstations, there is not the same level of testing that is required before updating.

Servers pose a different level of risk. For most servers, you cannot afford to have them become unavailable due to a conflict when updating them. And because most servers fall into the mission critical level, you cannot simply roll updates out to them whenever you feel like it. There are specific timeframes where you are allowed to perform maintenance on servers. It is within those maintenance windows that you are allowed to update the machine, which means all of your testing needs to be completed and validated before the maintenance window, or else you are waiting until the next maintenance window.

Determining Patch Requirements

Before jumping in and creating update lists and deployment packages, you should determine which updates are actually required within your organization.

All of the managed systems should report back the results of the scans that were performed. The state messages that were returned will include information on every patch that is required, installed, or not needed. The status of the updates can be seen in several locations. Anywhere an update is listed, you will find columns that specify how many systems already have the update installed, how many still require the update, the number of systems where the update is not required, and how many systems have not reported back and the status is still unknown. Using this information you can quickly determine which updates you need to package for deployment. Clicking the Required column will sort the rows so that you can group the updates that are required from those that are not.

One additional feature of the Software Updates node is the ability to create search folders. Search folders allow you to define the update properties that you want to find. They come in very handy when you are preparing to deploy updates. You can create search folders for updates that were released in the last week, the updates that are critical updates for Exchange release in the last month, all superseded updates, and many other options.

Right-clicking the Search Folders node will allow you to launch the Search Folder Criteria window. All of the options that are searchable are presented within this pane. If you are familiar with creating Outlook rules, you will be comfortable creating search folders. When you select the checkboxes for the options that you want to use for your search criteria, the criteria search options appear in the Step 2 pane. In this example, the critical Windows 7 updates that have been released within the last month are displayed within the results pane. You can create as many search folders as necessary and use them to deploy updates.

The software updates home page is another way to determine which updates are required. For example, the home page can be configured to show critical updates that were issued during November 2010. Using the search criteria, you can change the vendor, update classification, and timeframe that are displayed on the home page. Once the results appear on the home page, the updates that are applicable to the defined timeframe will appear. As with updates elsewhere in the Software Updates node, the Required column will detail the updates that the systems have reported as needing. From the home page, you can select the updates that you want to deploy and either start the Deploy Software Updates

Wizard, create and update lists, or download the files for the updates by simply selecting the appropriate updates, right-clicking, and choosing the appropriate action from the context menu.

One added benefit of using the software updates home page is the additional functionality built into the home page. Updates are listed with their article ID. The article IDs are linked to the knowledge base articles on Microsoft's TechNet website. If you want to get more information on an update, you can click the article ID link and read the information from the website instead of downloading the update to ready the included help file. The other feature of the home page is the report listings at the bottom of the page. The most commonly used reports are listed for easy access.

The final option to use when determining the updates that are needed is to use reporting. The built-in Management 1—Updates Required But Not Deployed report can be used to review updates that systems have reported as required, but you have not created a deployment package targeted to them yet. The report parameters are used to filter Collection ID and Vendor. Using those two options, you will receive a report that details all of the required updates for the systems within the collection. The third filter criteria, Update Class, is used to reduce the number of results to a specific update classification. Once selected, the resulting report will not contain as many entries and will be easier to use.

Testing Patches

Once the required patches have been identified, you need to verify that they are going to work within your environment without causing any problems. Verifying patches against all of the systems and services can be a daunting task. Trying to account for all of the combinations of applications and services running on any system may be impossible in some organizations. Within recent years, virtualization technologies have matured to the point that they are a viable candidate, not only for testing purposes, but also for production systems. Because the price point on many virtualization technologies has become very affordable, we now have the luxury of virtualizing systems. Using physical to virtual (P2V) technologies, we can create identical copies of our production systems and have them running within a test network. These test systems can then be used to test the updates before we approve the update within our production environment. Having a test environment can alleviate many of the compatibility problems that may arise when installing updates in production.

Note

Although creating an identical copy of a system by using P2V technologies allows you to test against operating system, application, and service configurations, the device drivers for many devices will not be the same in a virtual environment as they were on the physical system.

There are two schools of thought when it comes to testing patches—use the same site systems when testing or use a completely different site in the test environment. Using the first option, you have the luxury of creating deployment packages that will be the same ones used in production once the deployment package has been approved. All of the settings are essentially the same, and you simply need to point the deployment object to the appropriate collection when moving to production. The drawback to this scenario is that you need to have the test systems within a boundary that is accessible to the Configuration Manager site systems thus making the test/development network accessible to the production network. Many companies work in such a manner and have a link between networks. While completely valid, additional security measures need to be taken in case something happens in the test network that could adversely affect production.

If your test/development network is isolated and no communication is allowed between the production and test networks, you will need to replicate the Configuration Manager infrastructure within the test network. Although this may not seem like a big deal, you are essentially configuring and running two separate organizations and trying to keep each one configured and running identically. Again, virtualization technologies are very useful in this scenario. You can "snapshot," or save the systems at a specific configuration, before making any changes. The organizations that are best at this will snapshot their systems, make the appropriate configuration changes, and then revert back to the snapshot if the configuration changes do not work correctly. Once the testing is complete, the test network will be configured the way the production network needs to be configured. Once the changes have been applied to the production network, both networks should be in sync and another snapshot of the test network can be taken.

With that in mind, the process for rolling out updates will follow these steps:

1. Synchronize the updates from the synchronization source (Microsoft Update, Upstream Update Server, Manual Import).

2. Scan the managed system for update compliance.

3. Review the updates and decide on which will be deployed.

4. Create an update list for the updates to be deployed (optionally download the updates at the same time).

5. Deploy the updates using the Deploy Software Updates Wizard (optionally download the updates at the same time).

6. Verify that the updates installed on the managed systems.

7. Verify that the managed systems were not adversely affected by the update deployment.

Production Rollout

Once you have tested the updates that you are going to apply on your managed systems, you need to perform the same actions on the production systems. If you have done your homework, the updates that you deploy into production should not cause any problems with the production systems where they are installed. There are some additional considerations when working in a production environment however. These considerations are due to the nature of a production environment, and are meant to protect the systems from accidental configuration changes.

Maintenance Windows

The first thing you will need to take into consideration is maintenance windows. Maintenance windows stop the installation of updates and the reboots that are associated with them. Maintenance windows are intended to aid in keeping your systems running when they are supposed to be running and allow updating and rebooting during the service windows that are defined within service level agreements.

There are times that maintenance windows become a hindrance however. For instance, when an update is released that fixes a zero-day exploit, you may need to deploy the update as soon as possible. The maintenance window that protects the affected systems may not allow update installation during the time that you are planning to deploy the update. If this is the case, there is an option associated with the update deployment that allows for an override of the maintenance window. When you override the maintenance window, you can override it for the installation of the update, the restart of the system, or both.

Pilot Rollout

The production rollout should have at least two phases. The first phase is known as the Pilot and the second phase is the full rollout. Pilot systems are typically a representative community of systems that are tested before the remaining systems are affected by the updates. Sometimes affectionately called the "Production Test," these systems are used to verify that there were not any differences between the test systems and the production systems. For workstations, you can select a representative group of workstations that span many different users and departments so that you can get feedback before you affect the entire organization. Servers are trickier, however. You may want to select a few systems that represent the entire group, but in the case of an update that only applies to SQL servers, you may not have many that need the update and therefore won't have a true pilot group.

Collections

Within the production sites, you will need to create collections that will represent the systems that have the same update needs. These base collections will then be used to roll out the updates efficiently to the systems and also control the maintenance windows. When you sit down to plan out the collections that you will use, try to cover the types of updating that you will perform. You will have an easy time creating collections based upon applications and operating systems, but that may not meet the needs of your organization. As mentioned earlier, you will need to revisit the update deployment methodology that you currently use and then reflect that methodology within the site hierarchy. Do not be afraid to ask yourself some hard questions, such as "is there a better way to do this" when you are evaluating your deployment strategy.

We caution against creating maintenance windows on the same collections that you use for update deployment. This is due to the fact that a system can be included in more than one collection. If a system has a service window every Sunday from 5:00 PM to 11:00 PM and it is added to a collection that has a maintenance window from 5:00 PM to 11:00 PM on Saturday, you could cause the system to apply the updates and reboot outside of the correct service window.

Your best bet when creating collections for software updates is to create two empty collections that act as containers. Do not add any resources to these collections. You should also never create a deployment that uses these two top-level collections. The first collection should be named something akin to "maintenance windows." The second—Software Updates. Beneath each of these collections you can create the subcollections that will be used for the purpose stated in their names. The Maintenance Windows subcollections should be created based upon the service windows that you have identified. When populating the collections, try to limit each managed system's collection membership to one collection. This will make it much easier for you to manage the maintenance window for each system.

The subcollections beneath software updates should reflect the groups of systems that are typically updated in the same manner. This can be accomplished by compiling a list of servers that you manage. Most commonly you will find collections created for exchange servers, SQL servers, ISA servers, file servers, etc. You will also find collections based on these servers installed on specific platforms. As companies migrate off of Windows Server 2000 or Windows Server 2003, collections may be created based upon the server/operating system combination. Thus you may have Exchange 2007 servers on Windows Server 2008 or Exchange 2010 servers on Windows Server 2008. The organizational aspect of Configuration Manager makes developing an update deployment process both flexible and complex at the same time. You are able to design it to meet your needs, but it can also be over-engineered, creating more complexity than is truly needed. Take your time when developing the collections to make sure they will work efficiently.

Deployment Templates

Pre-creating the deployment templates is also recommended so that you can easily deploy updates as soon as they become available. As you are planning the collections that will contain the managed systems that you are updating, keep in mind the deployment templates and how they will be designed. If designed correctly, the templates should only be used intermittently. When you create a deployment package the first time, the deployment template is used. Any time you need to make a new deployment package using the same settings, the template can be used. Such is the case if you want to set a new mandatory deployment time for updates, and thus you create a new deployment package to host the new updates. However, for any new updates that are going to be delivered to systems that already have a deployment package and you are not concerned about waiting for the update to be installed, you also have the option of simply adding the update to the deployment package.

Maintaining Deployment Packages

From time to time you will need to clean out stale updates from the deployment packages. Updates become superseded or are expired and end up consuming space in the deployment packages. Removing these files from the deployment packages does take time. You have to review the updates and find the updates that have been superseded. You also need to make sure that the updates that take the place of the superseded updates have been deployed before you remove them. Once you have validated that the updates do need to be removed, the actual process for removing them is not difficult—again, just time consuming.

1. Navigate to the deployment package.

2. Expand the deployment package and select the Software Updates folder.

3. Review the updates in the details pane. Select the updates marked as Superseded.

4. In the properties of the update, select the Supersedence Information tab to find the update Article ID.

5. From the Reports node, run the report Management 5—Deployments that contain a specific update.

6. Enter the update's article ID on the Update (Required) text field and click Values.

7. Select the update from the list.

8. Click Display.

9. Verify the update has been included in a deployment.

10. If the update has been deployed, open the deployment within the Deployment Management folder and select Software Updates.

11. Delete the update from the deployment.

12. Navigate to the Software Updates folder within the deployment package.

13. Delete the update from the deployment.

14. Verify the checkbox for Refresh Distribution Points is selected and click OK.

Log Files

There are several log files that aid in the troubleshooting of software updates. You will find the log files on both the servers that support software updates and on the clients where they are deployed. As with other log files, using SMS Trace to read the logs is recommended. The log files can be found:

- On the site server in %SCCMInstallationDir%\Logs.

- On the Windows Server Update Services server in %ProgramFiles%\ Update Services\Logfiles.

- On the client in %windir%\System32\CCM\Logs or %windir%\ SysWOW64\CCM\Logs on x64 systems.

The log files available on the site server:

- **WCM.log**—Provides information about the connection between the site server and the Windows Server Update Services server. Details the connection status as well as the changes to the subscribed information for categories, classifications, and languages.

- **WSUSCtrl.log**—Provides information about the Windows Server Update Services server's connection to the site database server and the health of the Windows Server Update Services system.

- **wsyncmgr.log**—Provides information about the update synchronizations.

The log file available on the Windows Server Update Services server are as follows:

- **SoftwareDistribution.log**—Provides information about the updates that were synchronized from the synchronization source.

The log files available on the client computers are as follows:

- **ScanAgent.log**—Provides information about scan requests and the tools that requested the scan.

- **SmsWusHandler.log**—Provides information about the scanning process on SMS 2003 client systems when the inventory tool for Microsoft Updates is used.

- **WUAHandler.log**—Provides information on the Windows Update agent when it is searching for software updates on client systems.

- **WUSSyncXML.log**—Provides information about the inventory tool for Microsoft Updates sync process on SMS 2003 clients.

- **WindowsUpdate.log**—Provides information about connections to the Windows Server Update Services server and the compliance scans performed by the Windows Update agent.

- **UpdatesHandler.log**—Provides information about the software update compliance scan, download, and installation.

- **UpdatesStore.log**—Provides information about update compliance during the compliance scan.

- **UpdatesDeployment.log**—Provides information about software update activation, evaluation, and enforcement.

There is one other log, the PatchDownloader.log, that is found on the system that initiated the update download process. The PatchDownloader.log file presents information about the updates that were downloaded, including the source location of the patch file and the destination location.

THE FINAL WORD

Every organization needs to make sure that all of their systems have the latest updates installed. Failure to do so can result in breaches in security and poor system performance. Configuration Manager integrates with Windows Server

Update Services to create an enterprise level update deployment mechanism. A properly configured and managed software update infrastructure can alleviate many of the headaches associated with deploying software updates.

In the next chapter, we are going to look at the final version of software distribution, but this time we will cover operating system deployment.

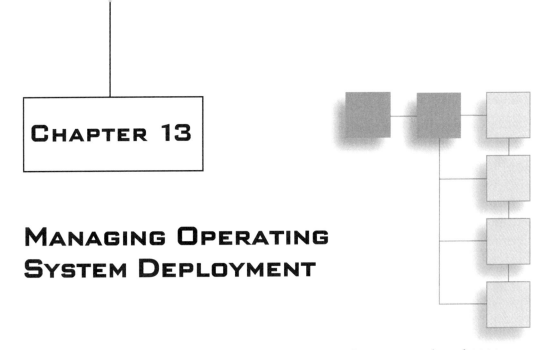

CHAPTER 13

MANAGING OPERATING SYSTEM DEPLOYMENT

You're an IT administrator for a large organization that just purchased 2000 new computers company wide. Your team is tasked with getting these computers set up and deployed within a month's time. You decide to use Configuration Manager 2007's operating system deployment (OSD) feature to meet this goal. During the initial phase, you create and capture your reference image and deploy it to the necessary distribution points in your organization so that it is readily available to you and your team when the time comes to start the imaging phase. Once this has been completed, you then import the correct drivers for the new systems into Configuration Manager 2007 and create driver packages for each system. A task sequence is then built that applies the operating system, installs the correct drivers based on the computer model, installs the correct software for the system, and then installs all of the Windows Updates that have been published since the reference image was built. After the task sequence has been built, all your team has to do is boot the computers to the network via PXE, choose the correct task sequence from a list, and click OK. After the PCs have finished running the task sequence, they will be joined to the domain and ready for use.

Think this is too good to be true? Well, it's not! If configured properly, Configuration Manager 2007 can do all of these tasks and more all through its operating system deployment features.

Introduction to Operating System Deployment

Configuration Manager 2007 provides the ability to deploy operating systems to targeted computers without the headaches that older imaging technologies faced, like having to constantly update the reference image to keep up with the latest drivers and software updates. Operating system deployment (OSD) within Configuration Manager 2007 utilizes task sequences to give you the flexibility that is needed when performing complicated tasks such as distributing operating systems or software. Task sequences are used to execute predefined or custom tasks in the order that you specify. They can optionally include logic so that some tasks only execute in specific scenarios based on criteria obtained through different methods such as WMI queries. The OSD feature can be used to deploy images to both new and existing computers so that you can manage multiple deployment scenarios all through one console. Configuration Manager 2007 supports operating deployment to like and unlike systems simultaneously and can even use newer deployment technologies such as multicast to help with performance and scalability. We'll talk about the different components of OSD such as boot images, task sequences, driver packages, and more, later in this chapter.

You can access the OSD feature from the Configuration Manager console under Computer Configuration > Operating System Deployment.

Operating System Deployment Features

Let's face it. Deploying operating systems can be a difficult task. Some of the common issues that tend to plague operating system deployments include stop errors due to incorrect drivers or conflicting HAL types, images becoming outdated due to old drivers or software, network bandwidth issues due to the number of computers being imaged at the same time, and trying to back up users' files before the imaging process begins. Configuration Manager 2007 includes many features that help with these scenarios right out of the box. Some of the major features of OSD are mentioned next.

Windows Imaging Format (WIM) Technology

When you capture an image with Configuration Manager 2007, it is stored within a WIM file and is referred to as a WIM image. WIM technology is

Microsoft's newest deployment technology and is used in many scenarios, including the Windows installation DVDs themselves. Starting with Windows Vista and Server 2008, every Windows installation DVD that you purchase uses WIM technology to install the operating system to your computer. Because the operating system image is directly applied to your hard drive, the installation time is dramatically reduced compared to the installation methods used in previous versions of Windows. One of the greatest benefits of the WIM technology is that it is file based instead of sector based, which allows you to create hardware agnostic images. Hardware agnostic images can be deployed to multiple computer types with different hardware abstraction layers (HALs), which allow you to cut down on the number of images needed to support your environment. Another benefit of the WIM technology and file-based imaging is that it allows you to store multiple images within a single WIM file using single instancing. With single instancing, you can capture two images, for example, and store them both within a single WIM file without doubling the size of the file. If both images contain the same files, these files are only stored once, and are simply referred to by both images. The advantages of this can be seen when using the Windows Server 2008 R2 installation media. When you set up Windows Server 2008 R2, you are asked to choose which edition you would like to install. Each edition is stored within the install.wim file, located in the sources directory off the root of the installation media. This can be verified using the ImageX utility with the /info switch as shown in Figure 13.1.

Figure 13.1
Multiple Images within a WIM File

As you can see, there are actually eight images stored within the install.wim file that correspond to all of the Windows Server editions available. Because of single instancing, the install.wim file is just under 2.5GB instead of a whopping 20GB—a huge savings! If you have multiple images in your environment, you could combine all of them into a single WIM file, potentially saving valuable disk space while simplifying management at the same time.

Windows Automated Installation Kit (WAIK)

Now that you understand a little bit about the WIM technology, let's talk about the tools that make use of this technology.

If you recall from Chapter 1, the Windows Automated Installation Kit (WAIK) is installed to each primary site server and is what Configuration Manager 2007 uses to capture and modify WIM images including operating system images and Windows pre-installation Environment (Windows PE) images. Note that the WIM technology is not exclusive to Configuration Manager. Configuration Manager simply uses WAIK and ImageX so that you never have to manually edit WIM images. Other third-party developers can also make use of the WIM technology by using the WIM API (wimgapi.dll) to perform tasks similar to that of Configuration Manager 2007. This can already be seen in many products on the market today.

Although Configuration Manager 2007 allows you to create and modify WIM images natively, you may find that these options are not enough, especially if you need to perform advanced WIM configurations in your environment. If this is the case, you may need to use the ImageX utility that comes installed with WAIK to perform the configurations that you need. Three different versions of ImageX get installed by default with WAIK, each corresponding to the three supported architectures: x86, x64, and IA64. These versions can be found in the following folders on machines where WAIK is installed:

- **x86**—C:\Program Files\Windows AIK\Tools\PETools\x86\imagex.exe
- **x64**—C:\Program Files\Windows AIK\Tools\PETools\x64\imagex.exe
- **IA64**—C:\Program Files\Windows AIK\Tools\PETools\IA64\imagex.exe

Tip

For more information on the ImageX utility and how it's used, use the ImageX /? command line option or visit http://technet.microsoft.com/en-us/library/cc749447(WS.10).aspx.

Task Sequences

Task sequences make operating system deployment possible in Configuration Manager 2007. They allow you to chain together multiple tasks (or actions) and start them in specific orders or situations, helping solve many of the problems that take place during an OS deployment. The task sequencer within Configuration Manager 2007 allows you to create tasks such as formatting drives or installing software that are conditional, based on the criteria that you define. We briefly discussed task sequences in Chapter 1 but be sure to read about them in detail later in this chapter.

Driver Management

One of the major issues that many people face when deploying operating systems is trying to figure out how to install the multitude of drivers that are needed for your machines to function correctly. Configuration Manager solves this problem by allowing you to import, categorize, and deploy drivers to your machines without ever having to modify the master image. This allows you to add and update drivers quickly, saving time when compared to traditional methods. We'll discuss the different driver management options later in this chapter.

User State Migration

Another tool included with WAIK is the User State Migration Tool (USMT), which allows you to migrate application settings and user files during an operating system deployment. This can be an invaluable tool if your users are saving files to their local drives and have customized settings such as desktop backgrounds or mapped network drives that need to be restored on the newly installed operating system. These files and settings are stored securely on a server where the state migration point role has been installed and configured. Turning on USMT is as easy as adding an action to the task sequence. We'll go through, step by step, how to configure USMT later in this chapter. For more information on adding the state migration point site system role, see Chapter 6, "Configuring Site System Roles."

CONSIDERATIONS FOR OPERATING SYSTEM DEPLOYMENT

Before you can start deploying operating systems with Configuration Manager 2007, it's important that you follow the recommended guidelines for setting up your Configuration Manager 2007 infrastructure. Some of these guidelines help ensure that you have the proper prerequisites in place while others are suggestions to help with OSD in your environment. We'll go through these guidelines and prerequisites and go over any steps that have not been covered previously in this book. The guidelines and prerequisites that we will cover are as follows:

- Supported Operating Systems
- Disk Space Considerations
- Disk Configuration Considerations
- Windows Deployment Services
- PXE Service Point Site System Role
- User State Migration Point Site System Role
- Distribution Point Site System Role
- Network Access Protection Considerations
- Native Mode Considerations

Supported Operating Systems

Configuration Manager 2007 can deploy both client and server operating systems as long as they are supported by the version of Configuration Manager 2007 that you have installed in your environment. Although Configuration Manager 2007 supports client and server operating systems for deployment, only server class operating systems can support the installation of Configuration Manager's roles such as standard distribution points or PXE service points. Table 13.1 lists the operating systems supported by Configuration Manager 2007 SP2.

Table 13.1 Configuration Manager 2007 SP2 Operating System Support

Operating System	Version[1]	Service Pack	Architecture
Windows 2000	Professional, Advanced Server, Datacenter[2]	SP4	x86
Windows XP	Professional	SP2 or SP3	x86 or x64
Windows XP Tablet PC	N/A	SP2	x86
Windows Embedded Standard 2009	N/A	N/A	x86
Windows Fundamentals for Legacy PCs	N/A	N/A	x86
Windows Vista	Business, Enterprise, Ultimate	SP1 or SP2	x86 or x64
Windows 7	Professional, Enterprise, Ultimate	No SP	x86 or x64
Windows Server 2003	Web	SP1 or SP2	x86
Windows Server 2003	Standard	SP1 or SP2	x86 or x64
Windows Server 2003	Enterprise, Datacenter, Storage Server	SP1 or SP2	x86, x64
Windows Server 2003 R2	Standard Edition	N/A	x86 or x64
Windows Server 2003 R2	Enterprise, Datacenter	N/A	x86 or x64 or IA64
Windows Server 2008	Standard, Enterprise, Datacenter	SP1 or SP2	x86, x64
Windows Server 2008 R2	Standard, Enterprise, Datacenter	No SP	x64

[1] Operating System Deployment not supported on clients that use the mobile device client.
[2] Configuration Manager 2007 supports Datacenter versions but are not certified.

Space Considerations

OS images, OS installation packs, disk images, and driver packages tend to take up a lot of disk space on distribution points in which they are stored. It is important to make sure that you have enough space on these distribution points to ensure that your Configuration Manager infrastructure remains healthy. If you recall from Chapter 11, packages are sent to distribution points in a number of ways, depending on how the hierarchy is configured and how your packages are configured. Use the following guidelines as a general rule. Note that this is not specific to operating system deployment. These guidelines apply to all packages including software distribution.

- **Single site with no child sites**—If you have a single site with no child sites, your distribution points need to have enough free equaling the size of your packages.

- **Multiple sites with child sites**—If you have multiple sites and packages are being sent to child sites, the site server automatically compresses the package, requiring .5 times the space of the package since the compressed version is stored on the site server itself. If your site server also hosts the distribution point role, it may need 1 to 2.5 times the size of the original package source files to remain in a healthy state.

- **Delta signatures**—Because Configuration Manager 2007 uses delta signatures to only copy the bits that have changed, these delta signatures must be stored on the distribution points along with the package itself. This requires 1.1 times the size of the uncompressed package.

- **Package configurations**—If your packages are configured to use a compressed version of the source files, the site server needs 1.5 times the size of the original package.

Disk Configuration Considerations

Once you have verified that you have enough space to store your packages and related content, you must think about your client disks and how they are configured. Configuration Manager 2007 only supports specific capturing and deployment scenarios, which are described next. Note that we will go over the capture and restore steps later in this chapter.

Capturing Images

Configuration Manager 2007 only supports capturing images from the following types of Windows disks:

- Basic disks
- Simple volumes on dynamic disks

It is not supported to capture images from dynamic disks that have spanned, striped (RAID 0), mirrored (RAID 1), or parity (RAID 5) volumes.

Tip

If you are using RAID volumes without the use of dynamic disks, such as with a RAID controller, this is transparent to Configuration Manager 2007. As long as the Windows disk is of a supported type, you should be able to capture images using Configuration Manager 2007.

Restoring Images

Configuration Manager 2007 only supports capturing and restoring images to drives that have the same configuration. If you capture an image from a computer configured with a basic disk, for example, you can only restore it to a computer that has a basic disk configuration. Although other scenarios might be possible, they are not supported.

Windows Deployment Services

Windows Deployment Services (WDS) is Microsoft's technology for deploying operating systems in large deployment scenarios. WDS is responsible for delivering the WIM images that we talked about earlier in this chapter to the machines that you specify. WDS eliminates the need for users to manually install operating systems from CDs or DVDs by delivering this content via the network in an image format unlike its predecessor, Remote Installation Services (RIS), which was only capable of installing operating systems through installation automation. WDS is available as a server role starting in Windows Server 2008 and can be optionally installed to Windows Server 2003 SP2 systems.

Users who are new to Microsoft's deployment technologies and Configuration Manager 2007 often think that WDS is a Configuration Manager 2007-specific technology. This is not the case. WDS can be used without Configuration Manager 2007 for deploying operating systems in a small- to medium-sized organization with the help of the (free) Microsoft Deployment Toolkit (MDT). MDT is often referred to as a lite-touch deployment technology, meaning that little user interaction is needed, whereas Configuration Manager 2007 is referred to as a zero-touch deployment technology—or no user interaction. Although the MDT and Configuration Manager 2007 are separate products, some of the features of the MDT can be installed and combined with Configuration Manager 2007 so that you get the best of both worlds.

Installing WDS

Before you can deploy operating systems to systems not managed by Configuration Manger 2007, you must install WDS. We will cover the installation of WDS on a Windows Server 2008 R2 platform. To install WDS, do the following:

1. Open the Server Manager by going to Start, right-clicking on Computer, and left-clicking on Manage (Figure 13.2).

2. Once the Server Manager opens, left-click on the Roles node.

3. The Roles Summary window is displayed. Click on Add Roles to continue (Figure 13.3).

4. The Before You Begin window is displayed. Click Next to continue (Figure 13.4).

5. The Server Roles window is displayed. Click the checkbox next to Windows Deployment Services and click Next to continue (Figure 13.5).

6. The Windows Deployment Services introduction window is displayed. Click Next to continue (Figure 13.6).

7. When the WDS Role Services window is displayed, check Deployment Server and Transport Server then click Next to continue (Figure 13.7).

8. When the WDS Confirmation window is displayed, click Install.

9. When the WDS Results window is displayed, click Close.

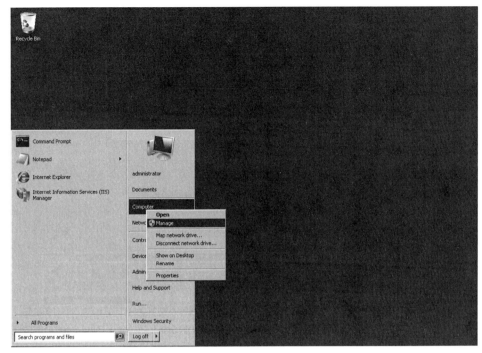

Figure 13.2
Start > Computer > Right Click > Manage

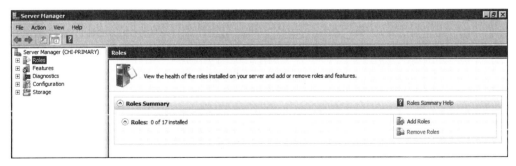

Figure 13.3
Roles Summary Window

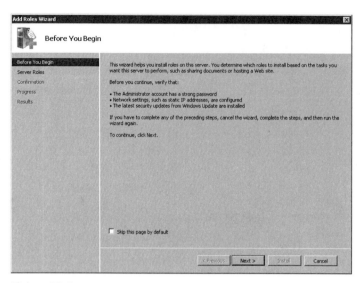

Figure 13.4
Before You Begin Window

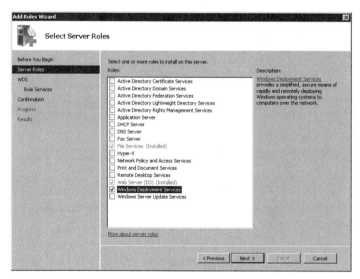

Figure 13.5
Add Server Roles Window

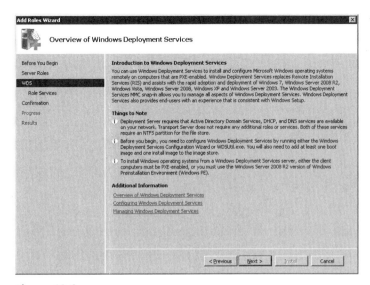

Figure 13.6
WDS Introduction Window

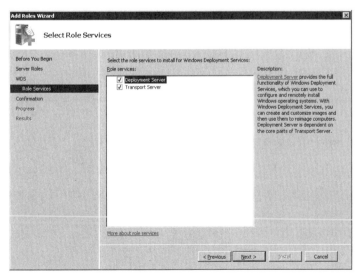

Figure 13.7
WDS Role Services Window

Caution

There's a general rule of thumb when it comes to installing WDS in a Configuration Manager 2007 environment: Install it but don't touch it. Once WDS is installed, Configuration Manager 2007 automatically configures the necessary settings so that you never have to touch any WDS configuration settings unless absolutely necessary. Users who decide to manually configure WDS in a Configuration Manager 2007 environment often find that problems arise and have to uninstall and reinstall WDS to resolve the issues.

PXE Service Point Site System Role

The PXE service point role allows you to boot a system to the network using PXE, which then allows you to start an operating system deployment task sequence. This is ideal for unmanaged computers like bare metal systems or systems with a corrupted Windows installation that cannot boot correctly. We covered the installation of the PXE service point role back in Chapter 6, "Configuring Site System Roles." I highly recommend that you read that chapter before moving forward in this chapter to ensure that you have the basic concepts under your belt.

Note

The PXE service point is not required to use the OSD feature within Configuration Manager 2007. However, if you intend to boot computers to the network via PXE, you must have at least one PXE service point set up and configured for this feature to work correctly.

User State Migration Point Site System Role

The user state migration point is used in conjunction with the User State Migration Tool (USMT) to back up and restore the user state when deploying an operating system. The only time the user state migration point is needed is when you are backing up and restoring the user state with the USMT. For further information on installing the user state migration point site system role, see Chapter 6.

Note

We will discuss the USMT later in this chapter.

Distribution Point Site System Role

The operating system deployment feature in Configuration Manager 2007 has many components that often require you to generate packages such as operating system images, boot images, driver packages, etc. After these packages have been created, they must be placed on distribution points so that your clients can access this data throughout the organization. We installed the distribution point role back in Chapter 6 where we discussed the steps and features of this site system role.

Network Access Protection Considerations

Configuration Manager 2007 includes a feature called Network Access Protection (NAP), which is used to restrict network access to computers that do not meet the security guidelines set forth by the IT administrator. If the NAP client is not installed or set up correctly on your client computers, they may be unable to access network resources once an operating system has been deployed. In order for your clients to function within a NAP-enabled environment, the following configurations must be in place:

- The NAP client must be installed

- The appropriate NAP enforcement clients must be enabled

- The NAP service must be configured to start automatically

- The system may need to be restarted if the NAP client was not configured on the reference image

Note

We will discuss these steps and other features of network access protection in Chapter 15.

Native Mode Considerations

If your site is functioning in Native mode, your clients must have the site server signing certificate installed in order to communicate with the Configuration Manager 2007 infrastructure. There are three supported ways to deploy this certificate:

- Automatically via Active Directory
- Manually when the Configuration Manager 2007 client is installed
- Automatically via the management point

Automatically via Active Directory

If your computers are a member of the domain and the schema has been extended for Configuration Manager 2007, it is recommended to use Active Directory to obtain the site server signing certificate because it is more secure and requires less management overhead. However, if your computers belong to a different forest than your site server, are members of a workgroup, or managed via the Internet, you will not be able to use Active Directory to obtain the certificate.

Manually when the Configuration Manager 2007 Client is Installed

If you need to install the site server signing certificate when the Configuration Manager 2007 client is installed, use the SMSSIGNCERT option to specify the path to the exported certificate. This will install the certificate to the local machine so that it is ready for use.

Automatically via the Management Point

If the Configuration Manager client cannot find the site server signing certificate via Active Directory and it is not installed locally, it will try to download it from the management point. If your clients are managed on the Internet, this is considered the least secure method. If your management point only accepts intranet clients, however, this is more secure simply because the certificate is not being deployed via the Internet.

WALKING THROUGH THE PROCESS

Before we get into the depths of OSD, it might be helpful to take some time to understand the order of events that need to occur to capture and deploy a basic operating system image to your machines. Because Configuration Manager 2007 offers such a high level of customization, the steps listed only show the bare essentials needed to accomplish this task.

1. Import boot images for PXE.

2. Import operating system install packages for reference image creation.

3. Import drivers for your machines.

4. Create driver packages for your machines.

5. Create build and capture task sequence to build and capture your reference image.

6. Import reference image as an operating system image.

7. Create task sequence to deploy reference image along with driver packages to your machines.

We cover these steps in detail in the next section.

CONFIGURING OSD COMPONENTS

Now that we've gone over some of the features and considerations of OSD, it's time to talk about the components that need to be configured for OSD. Some of these components are pretty self-explanatory but others contain many settings that you need to understand before you attempt to deploy operating systems to your computers. If you fail to configure these components correctly, you might not be able to use the OSD feature as intended. We'll go over the OSD components in detail next.

Driver Catalog (Drivers Node)

One of the unique features that Configuration Manager 2007 offers is the ability to import device drivers and then deploy those drivers to boot images or operating systems during install time. This allows you to add, remove, or update drivers without ever having to modify the master image. This saves time and headaches by giving you the ability to deploy and test drivers much faster than ever before. Drivers are first imported into Configuration Manager 2007 and then can be included in driver packages if necessary. We'll go over drivers in this section and driver packages in the next section.

Importing Drivers

The Drivers node that exists below the Computer Management > Operating System Deployment node in Configuration Manager 2007 is where you manage your individual device drivers and is referred to as the driver catalog. Drivers must first be imported into Configuration Manager's driver catalog before you can manage them. Some vendors such as Dell create driver packs specifically for configuration management systems like Configuration Manager 2007. These driver packs include all of the drivers pertaining to a specific system model and operating system so that you do not have to manually download every driver individually. This is very handy and can save a lot of time—especially if you have multiple operating systems and multiple machine types.

Tip

> It might be helpful to organize your drivers into folders or categories based on a common criteria such as computer model or vendor. See the managing drivers section for more information.

In the following example, we'll import the drivers for a Dell OptiPlex 980 workstation and talk about the different options available.

1. Open the Configuration Manager 2007 console and navigate to Computer Management > Operating System Deployment > Drivers. Right-click on the Drivers node and choose Import (Figure 13.8).

2. The Import New Driver Wizard starts. The first page of the wizard allows you to import multiple drivers that exist in a directory or a specific driver by specifying the .inf or txtsetup.oem file. In our example, we'll import all of the drivers for the OptiPlex 980 by choosing the correct folder and clicking Next to continue (Figure 13.9).

3. The Driver Details section of the wizard is displayed. This page shows you all of the device drivers that were found in the folder that you specified in the last step. This page also gives you the option to enable or disable these drivers by checking the "Enable these drivers and allow computers to install them" checkbox. If you would like to assign the drivers to a category for filtering purposes, you can do that as well. In our example, we'll keep the defaults and click Next to continue (Figure 13.10).

4. The Add Driver to Packages section of the wizard is displayed. This allows you to add drivers to existing driver packages or also allows you to create new driver packages. We'll go over driver packages in the next section

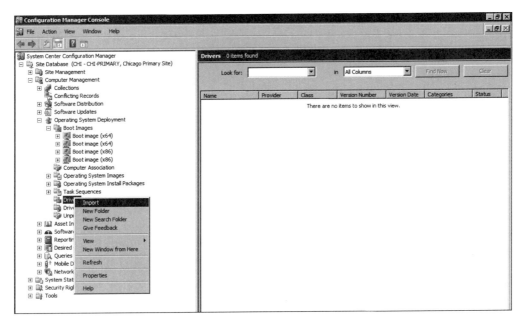

Figure 13.8
Import Drivers

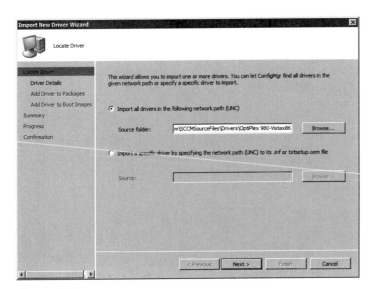

Figure 13.9
Importing Multiple Drivers

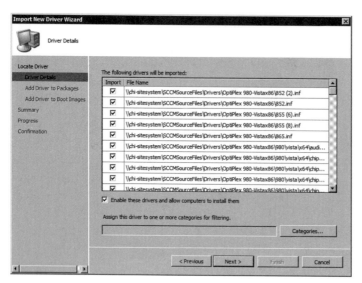

Figure 13.10
Driver Details

of this chapter. In our example, we'll choose the defaults and click Next to continue (Figure 13.11).

5. The Add Driver to Boot Images section of the wizard is displayed. This allows you to add drivers to existing boot images. This is typically used when needing to add mass storage drivers or network drivers to boot images. We'll go over boot images and how to add drivers to them later in this chapter. In our example, we'll choose the defaults and click Next to continue (Figure 13.12).

6. The Summary section of the wizard is displayed. This shows you the drivers that are about to be imported to Configuration Manager 2007. In our example, all of these settings look correct so we'll click Next to continue (Figure 13.13).

7. The Progress section of the wizard is displayed. This shows you the progress of the driver import. Note that this could take a few minutes depending on the number of drivers being imported.

8. The Confirmation section of the wizard is displayed. This shows you if any errors were detected during the driver import process. Click Close to close the wizard.

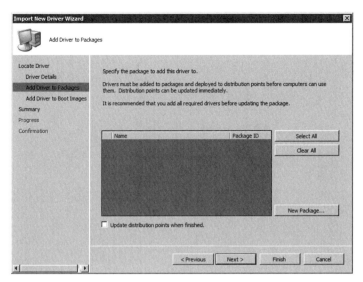

Figure 13.11
Add Driver to Packages

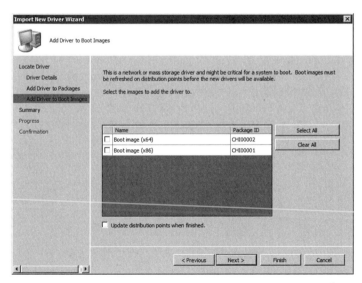

Figure 13.12
Add Driver to Boot Images

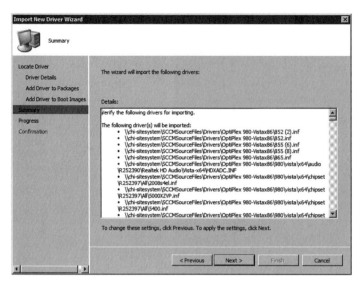

Figure 13.13
Summary

Tip

When you import drivers, Configuration Manager 2007 automatically checks the hash of each driver and compares it to other drivers that have already been imported to the database to prevent duplicate drivers. This is good in that it prevents duplicate drivers, but if you specifically want to create duplicate drivers because of your driver management method, this presents a big problem. To get around this, simply create a text file (or other file/folder of your choice) in the same folder that the .inf file resides. This will trick Configuration Manager 2007 into thinking that the drivers are unique and will allow you to import the same driver more than once. We'll talk about why this might be important later in this chapter.

After all of your drivers have been imported, you can see them in the Drivers node as seen in Figure 13.14.

Managing Drivers

Once your drivers have been imported, you then have the ability to manage these drivers. Managing drivers can be a challenging task because of the number of drivers that are typically needed for one system. In our example, 269 drivers were imported for the OptiPlex 980. If you have multiple machines with multiple operating systems, you could easily have a thousand or more drivers

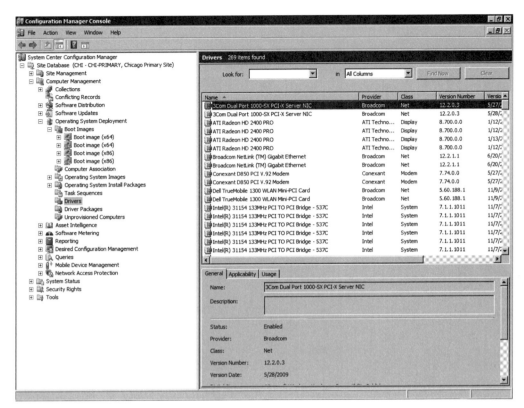

Figure 13.14
Viewing Drivers

in Configuration Manager 2007. To help manage these drivers, Configuration Manager 2007 gives you the ability to create categories and search folders for these drivers. Your category and search folder names can be anything that makes sense to you. There is no wrong or right way to manage your drivers as long as it works for you.

Categorizing Drivers   You can categorize drivers during the import process like we discussed earlier or you can do it after the fact, as described in the following steps. We will add all of our drivers to the Dell OptiPlex 980—Vista x86 category next:

1. Highlight all of the drivers you wish to include in your new category, right-click on a selected driver, and choose Categories. (Figure 13.15).

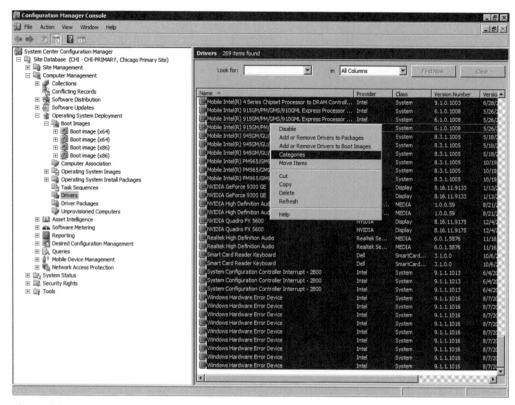

Figure 13.15
Creating a Device Driver Category

2. The Categories window is displayed. This allows you to create new categories and lists all of the existing categories (Figure 13.16).

3. Type in the name of your new category and click Add. The new category will show up in the Available categories section as shown in Figure 13.17. Once you are finished adding categories, click OK to continue.

Tip

Drivers can be members of one or more driver categories.

4. Once your drivers have been categorized, you can filter drivers based on this category. This can be seen in the Categories column and can be searched for using the Look for: box at the top of the window.

Figure 13.16
Categories Window

Figure 13.17
Adding a Category

Tip

The Look for: search box can find drivers in other ways than just category membership. Any column or part of the driver name can be used as a search criterion.

Creating Search Folders   Search folders allow you to create dynamic queries based on specific criteria to help you organize your content. Search folders are not limited to drivers and can be created for many other types of content such as advertisements and packages. The following object properties can be included in a driver search folder:

- Boot Critical
- Categories
- Category Unique IDs
- CI ID
- CI Unique ID
- Class
- Content Source Path
- Created By
- Created Date
- Description
- INF File
- Informative URL
- Last Updated By
- Late Updated Date
- Locale ID
- Name (property is not searchable)
- Provider
- SDM Package Version
- Signed
- Signed By
- Source Site
- Status
- Type
- Version

- Version Date (property is not searchable)
- Version Number

To create a driver search folder, do the following:

1. Right-click on the Drivers node in the Configuration Manager 2007 console and choose New Search Folder (Figure 13.18).

2. Choose an object property to search on. In our example, we'll choose Boot Critical by placing a check in the checkbox next to that value as in Figure 13.19. Once you have selected all of the object properties that you wish to query upon, you must then edit the property's search criteria. In our example, we'll specify that all boot critical drivers are set to true. We'll choose to search all folders under this feature and name the search folder OptiPlex 980 Boot Drivers and click OK to continue.

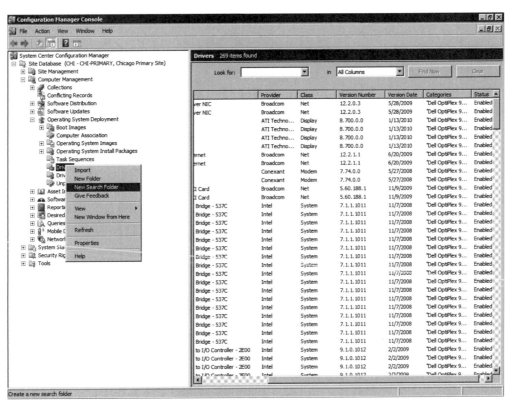

Figure 13.18
Create a New Search Folder

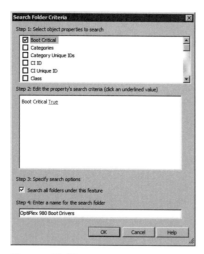

Figure 13.19
Specifying Search Criteria

3. The new search folder should now exist under the Drivers node. As you add and remove drivers, this search folder will automatically display the results corresponding to these changes.

Driver Packages

Driver packages contain the drivers that were imported within the Drivers node. Driver packages typically correspond to the different machine types that you have in your environment and are used during the Apply Driver Packages task sequence step. Although you do not have to create driver packages, you should know that you will not be able to apply a driver package during an OS task sequence if one has not been created and stored on a distribution point. We'll talk more about the Apply Driver Package task sequence step later in this chapter.

Creating a Driver Package

After you import your drivers, you can then add them to a driver package. This process can be done while importing drivers or it can be done after the drivers have already been imported. In this example, we'll create a driver package after the drivers have already been imported. Perform the following steps to create a driver package:

1. Navigate to the Driver Packages node within the Configuration Manager 2007 console, which is located under Computer Management > Operating System Deployment.

2. Right-click on the Driver Packages node and choose New > Driver Package (Figure 13.20).

3. The New Driver Package window is displayed. This window allows you to specify information about the driver package such as the name, comments, and the driver package source. The driver package source should point to an empty folder on the network. This folder will be automatically populated with the correct contents during the creation of the driver package. In our example, we'll call this driver package OptiPlex 980—Vista x86 and point it to a network path in our source location. Click OK to continue (Figure 13.21).

Note

The source location that you choose in this step will automatically be populated with subfolders that correspond to each driver within the driver package. Each subfolder is uniquely named using a globally unique identifier (GUID). This can be seen by navigating to the driver package source folder location that you specified in this step.

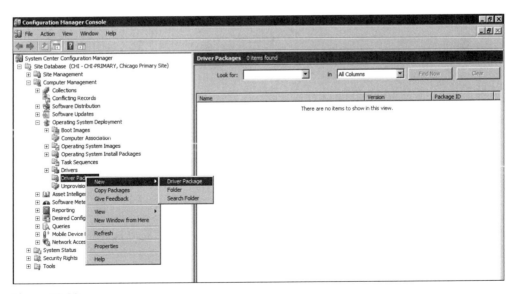

Figure 13.20
New Driver Package

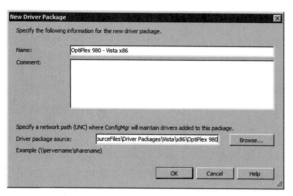

Figure 13.21
Creating a Driver Package

4. After the driver package has been created, you can see it under the Driver Packages node within the Configuration Manager 2007 console.

Adding Drivers to a Driver Package

Once your driver package have been created, you then need to add drivers to the driver packages. Again, this step can be performed automatically when initially importing the drivers, but we'll take you through the manual process so that you know what is going on behind the scenes.

To add a driver to a driver package, do the following:

1. Navigate to the Drivers node within the Configuration Manager 2007 console, which is located under Computer Management > Operating System Deployment.

2. Highlight the drivers that you want to add to the corresponding driver package. Once the correct drivers have been highlighted, right-click on a highlighted driver and choose Add or Remove Drivers to Packages. In our example, we'll highlight all of the drivers and choose this option (Figure 13.22).

3. The Add or Remove Drivers to Packages window is displayed. This window allows you to add the drivers that were selected in the last step to any existing driver packages. If you selected to add your driver package to any distribution points, you can update your driver package

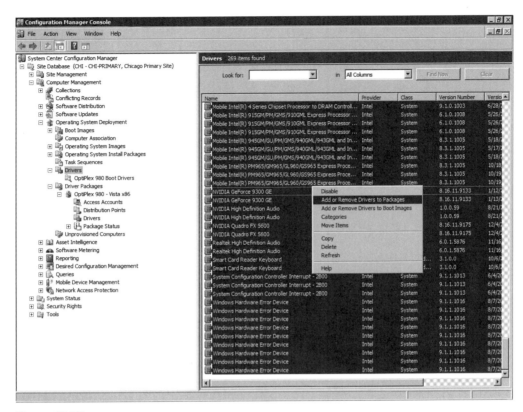

Figure 13.22
Selecting Drivers for Driver Packages

on selected distribution points from here as well. In our example, we'll select the OptiPlex 980—Vista x86 driver package and click OK to continue (Figure 13.23).

Note

The process for removing a driver from a driver package is the same as adding a driver except that you de-select the driver package that the driver should be removed from.

4. After the selected drivers have been added to your driver package, you can verify that this step was successful by navigating to your driver package and clicking on the Drivers node that exists beneath it. All of the drivers that were added in the last step should now show up in this node (Figure 13.24).

Figure 13.23
Add Drivers to Driver Packages

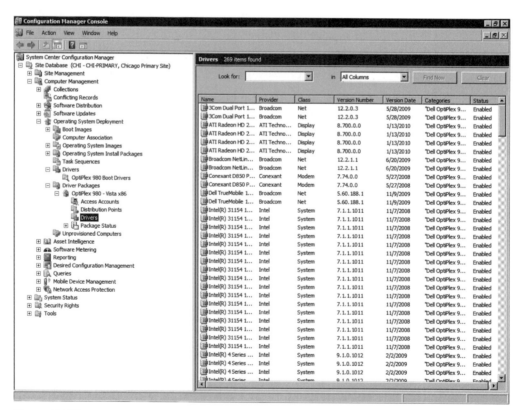

Figure 13.24
Verifying the Drivers in the Driver Package

Adding Driver Packages to Distribution Points

After your driver package have been created, you must distribute these driver packages to your distribution points so that clients can access them. Note that each time a driver is added or removed from a driver package, any distribution point that holds these driver packages will need to be updated accordingly. If you read Chapter 11, "Managing Software Distribution," you should already be familiar with these steps since this process to add driver packages to distribution points is very similar to adding software distribution packages to distribution points.

To add a driver package to a distribution point, complete the following steps:

1. Navigate to the Distribution Point node of your driver package, right-click and choose New > Distribution Point. In our example, we'll add the OptiPlex 980—Vista x86 driver package to our distribution points (Figure 13.25).

2. The New Distribution Point Wizard starts. Click Next to continue.

3. The Copy Package section of the wizard is displayed. From here, you can see all of the available distribution points in your hierarchy. Choose

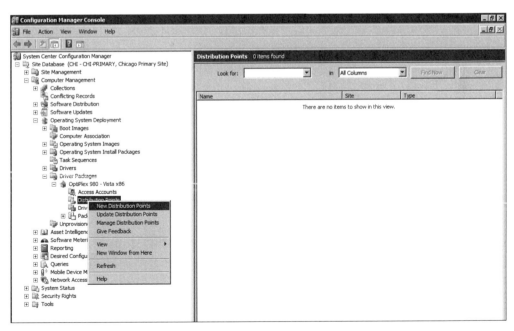

Figure 13.25
New Distribution Point for a Driver Package

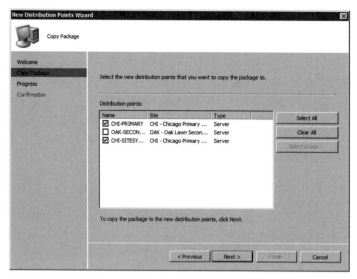

Figure 13.26
Select Distribution Points

which distribution points you want your driver package to be copied to (from the source location) by checking the box next to the distribution point. If you have created any distribution point groups, you can copy the package to all of the distribution points in that group by clicking on the Select Group button. For more information on distribution point groups, see Chapter 6. In our example, we'll select all of the distribution points in the Chicago site and click Next to continue (Figure 13.26).

4. The confirmation section of the wizard is displayed. This shows you the changes that were made and if they were successful. Click Close to close the wizard.

Boot Images

Boot images are used by managed and unmanaged clients and contain a small operating system called the Windows pre-installation environment (Windows PE). When a client boots into Windows PE, it is able to talk to the Configuration Manager infrastructure to complete actions that are not possible when the client is running in a normal Windows environment, such as partitioning the system drive or applying an operating system. Configuration Manager 2007 comes with

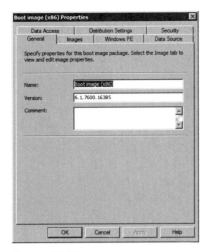

Figure 13.27
Boot Image General Tab

an x86 and an x64 Windows PE boot image as well as giving you the option to add your own. Once the boot images are imported to Configuration Manager 2007, you may need to add additional drivers such as mass storage drivers and NIC drivers so that your computers can boot and talk to the network. After your boot images have the correct drivers added, you can then deploy these images to your distribution points so that your clients can access them as necessary.

Properties of a Boot Image

Before we get into the different steps needed to manage a boot image, it's good to have an understanding of the general properties of a boot image. These property tabs can be accessed by right-clicking on a boot image and choosing Properties (Figure 13.27).

General Tab   The General tab allows you to set and view information about the boot image such as the name, version, or any comments that you wish to include.

Images Tab   The Images tab (Figure 13.28) allows you to view image property values such as the OS version, architecture, creation date, language, size, and description. If the image properties were changed using a tool other than Configuration Manager 2007, like ImageX, you can click the Reload button to refresh these properties.

Windows PE Tab   The Windows PE tab (Figure 13.29) allows you to include different options in your boot image such as drivers, command line support, and

Figure 13.28
Images Tab

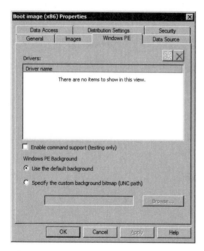

Figure 13.29
Windows PE Tab

user-defined backgrounds. This is one of the most used tabs since it's where you review all of the drives that have been added to your boot image. We will go over this step later in the chapter.

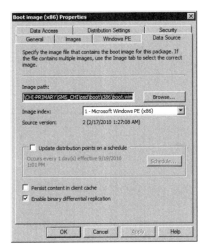

Figure 13.30
Data Source Tab

Caution

Be careful when enabling the command line support option in your boot images. This option can be helpful for troubleshooting purposes because it allows you to access the command prompt simply by pressing F8 when your clients have booted into the Windows PE environment. However, this can be a security risk because some secure information such as the network access account username and password are potentially viewable (in clear text) from this environment. If you are in an environment that is potentially unsecure, do not enable this option.

Data Source Tab   The Data Source tab (Figure 13.30) allows you to specify the image location. If the image file contains multiple images, you can use the image index drop-down box to select the correct image. This tab also allows you to update the specified distribution points on a schedule, keep the image in the client cache, and enable/disable binary differential replication.

Data Access Tab   The Data Access tab (Figure 13.31) is identical to that of a standard package as we covered in Chapter 11. This allows you to change how the package is stored on specified distribution points.

Distribution Settings   The Distribution Settings tab (Figure 13.32) is identical to that of a standard package as we covered in Chapter 11. This allows you to change how the package is sent to child sites and how branch distribution points receive the package. Refer to Chapter 11 for detailed information.

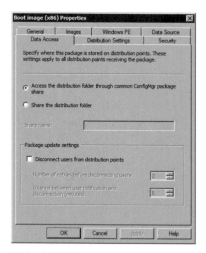

Figure 13.31
Data Access Tab

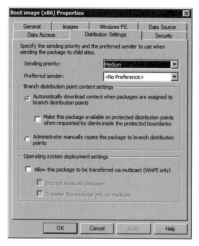

Figure 13.32
Distribution Settings Tab

Security Tab   The Security tab (Figure 13.33) allows you to specify the security rights that users have on the object class or instance.

Adding Drivers to Boot Images

As your clients boot to the boot images within Configuration Manager 2007, you might find that your systems cannot start correctly or that they have no network

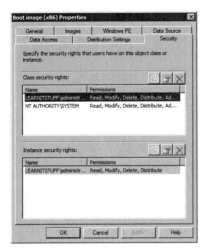

Figure 13.33
Security Tab

access due to the correct drivers not being installed. If this is the case, you may need to add the correct mass storage drivers or network card drivers to your boot images.

Adding drivers to a boot image is much like adding a driver to a driver package. To add drivers to a boot image, follow these steps:

1. Navigate to the Drivers node within the Configuration Manager 2007 console, which is located under Computer Management > Operating System Deployment.

2. Highlight the drivers that you want to add to your boot image. Once the correct drivers have been highlighted, right-click on a highlighted driver and choose Add or Remove Drivers to Boot Images. In our example, we'll highlight all of the boot drivers that we specified when we created our driver search folder (Figure 13.34).

3. The Add or Remove Drivers to Boot Images window is displayed. This window allows you to add the drivers that were selected in the last step to any existing boot images. If you selected to add your boot image to any distribution points, you can update your boot image on selected distribution points from here as well. In our example, we'll select the

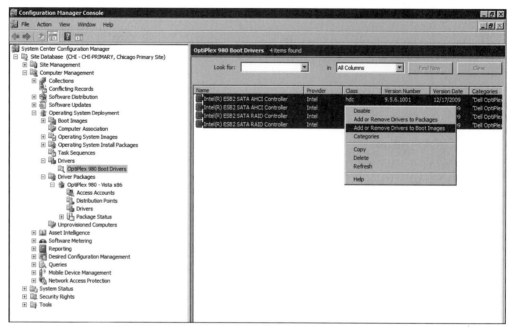

Figure 13.34
Selecting Drivers for Boot Images

"Boot image (x86)" boot image since the architecture of our drivers are x86. Click OK to continue (Figure 13.35).

4. After the selected drivers have been added to your boot image, you can verify that this step was successful by looking at the Windows PE tab as shown in Figure 13.29.

Note

Note that drivers can be added to boot images from the Windows PE tab within the boot image's properties. However, if you are adding drivers from this tab, you are not able to see potentially important information such as driver categories or driver folders that you may have created earlier. This makes it tricky to specify the correct driver, especially when multiple drivers have the same name but are of different architectures or versions.

Adding Boot Images to Distribution Points and PXE Service Points

At this point in the book, we've gone through the process of adding software distribution packages and driver packages to distribution points. As I stated

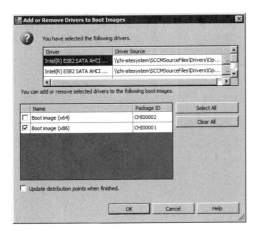

Figure 13.35
Add Drivers to Boot Images

earlier, this process is nearly identical for both of these types of packages. Boot images, however, are slightly different because of the way Configuration Manager 2007 works with WDS to distribute these boot images to client machines.

Choosing a Distribution Point Share for your Boot Images   After WDS and the PXE service point roles have been installed on a site system, a new share is created called SMSPXEIMAGES$. The actual location of this shared folder is on the first NTFS formatted drive with the most free disk space in a folder called RemoteInstall\SMSIMAGES. This folder is used by WDS and the PXE service point to hold boot images, which are then distributed to client computers when they boot to PXE. Configuration Manager 2007 allows you to place boot images in this folder by automatically creating a server share, SMSPXEIMAGES$, which then shows up during the New Distribution Point Wizard. When you go through the process of adding a boot image to a distribution point, you will see that you have two options: The standard distribution point share or the SMSPXEIMAGES$ share. This can be seen in Figure 13.36.

At this point you may be wondering which share you should add your boot images to. That's a good question. The answer is both and here's why.

As you may recall from earlier, WDS is not dependent on Configuration Manager 2007 and can be used independently to distribute images to client machines. Again, this is not meant as an enterprise solution, but it does work well in small- to medium-size environments, especially if you are using the

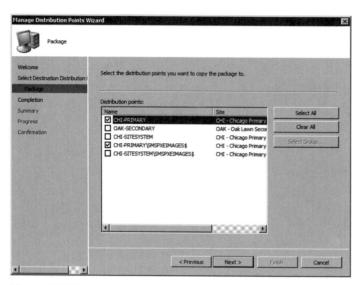

Figure 13.36
Multiple Shares for Boot Images

Microsoft Deployment Toolkit. Because WDS is an independent technology, it is not privy to the distribution point shares that Configuration Manager 2007 creates and uses its own deployment share by default. When WDS and the PXE service point role work in conjunction, a new distribution share, the SMSPXEI-MAGES$ share, is created. When clients boot to PXE, WDS looks in the distribution shares for boot images to deploy. WDS does not look in the standard Configuration Manager 2007 distribution point shares to deploy boot images when clients boot to PXE.

Note

Adding boot images to the SMSPXEIMAGES$ share is also known as adding boot images to the PXE service point.

Why the Distribution Point Share is Necessary for Boot Images Once you've added your boot image to the PXE service point, you must also add it to a standard distribution point share just as you would with any other package. This is necessary if your clients wish to download the boot image as part of a task sequence within Windows. If your boot images are only stored on the PXE service point, only administrators within your environment will have the ability

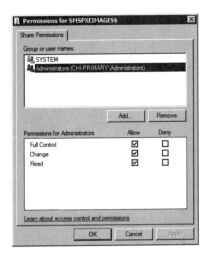

Figure 13.37
SMSPXEIMAGES$ Share Permissions

to access these images. Figure 13.37 shows the default share permissions of the SMSPXEIMAGES$ share.

When a computer starts an operating system task sequence, it uses a special account called the network access account to access content that is stored on distribution points. As a good security practice, the network access account should only have limited access to your environment so that it can only access the Configuration Manager 2007 distribution points to read and download content. If your boot images are only added to a PXE service point and not to a Configuration Manager 2007 distribution point, any operating system task sequences that are executed within Windows will fail because your network access account will not have the necessary access to the SMSPXEIMAGES$ share.

Choosing a Boot Image

Configuration Manager 2007 comes by default with x86 and x64 boot images. Each boot image has specific rules that specify how they must be used. If you don't follow or understand these rules, you could run into problems depending on your environment. These rules are listed next.

x86 Boot Images
- Can deploy 32 bit OS images
- Can deploy 64 bit OS images

- Can deploy 32 bit OS install packages

- Cannot deploy 64 bit OS install packages

x64 Boot Images
- Cannot deploy 32 bit OS images

- Can deploy 64 bit OS images

- Cannot deploy 32 bit OS install packages

- Can deploy 64 bit OS install packages

As you can see, the x86 boot image is the most versatile image as long as you are not deploying 64-bit operating systems using install packages. I recommend using x86 boot images whenever possible to help simplify your environment. The boot image that gets downloaded to each PC will be the one specified in the last OS task sequence that is advertised to the client.

Specifying a Boot Image   Once you've decided which boot image is best for your environment, you have to make sure that boot image is delivered to your clients when they PXE boot. If you've got multiple images, how do you specify which boot image will get delivered? The answer lies in the OS task sequence.

When you create an OS task sequence, you must specify the boot image that will be delivered to your clients. The method in which these images are delivered to your clients depends on how the task sequence was started. If you use the run advertised programs control panel applet to start the task sequence, the image that was specified in the task sequence gets downloaded and staged on the client computer. Once the computer restarts, it boots to the pre-staged boot image and kicks off the task sequence as expected. If you plan on starting a task sequence by booting to PXE, things get a little more complicated.

To specify which boot image is delivered to PXE clients, you must advertise an OS task sequence (with a specified boot image) to a collection that your client is a member of. Because multiple OS task sequences (with different boot images) can be advertised to the same collection, it can be difficult to predict which boot image will be delivered. In the end, the last task sequence that was advertised wins and the boot image specified in that task sequence is delivered. Again, this can get very complicated if you are using multiple boot images in your environment. My recommendation is to use one boot image in all of your OS task sequences so that you do not run into this situation.

N o t e

We will talk about OS install packages and task sequences later in this chapter.

Understanding the PXE Boot Process

Before we move on to the next section, it's important that we go over the basics of what happens during a PXE boot. Note that this process has been simplified but the information can still be helpful when troubleshooting errors related to PXE.

1. A computer boots to the network using PXE.

2. A PXE service point responds to the request and delivers wdsnbp.com from the RemoteInstall\SMSBoot\x86 folder. This file is called the network boot program and is responsible for many tasks such as detecting the computer's architecture.

3. Once the computer's architecture has been discovered, it then downloads files from the appropriate architecture folders located under RemoteInstall\SMSBoot. Typically, three files can be downloaded by the client. These are as follows:

   - **PXEboot.com**—This file gets downloaded by computers if it is targeted for an OS deployment (an advertisement exists) but is not mandatory. PXEboot.com forces the user to press F12 for the network boot to continue.

   - **PXEboot.n12**—This file gets downloaded by computers if it is targeted for an OS deployment (an advertisement exists) and it is mandatory. PXEboot.n12 bypasses the F12 requirement and automatically begins a network boot.

   - **AbortPXE.com**—This file gets downloaded by computers if they are not targeted for an OS deployment (an advertisement does not exist).

4. PXEboot.com and PXEboot.n12 download bootmgr.exe as well as the BCD store.

5. Bootmgr.exe reads the BCD store and then downloads boot.sdi as well as the correct boot image as specified in the last advertised task sequence.

Operating System Install Packages

Operating system install packages are designed to automate the build and capture of a reference system with little to no user interaction, helping keep images clean and consistent. This is done within a predefined task sequence called a build and capture task sequence. This task sequence uses the files from the original installation media to build the reference image and then captures this image into a WIM file. The captured WIM file can then be used within the Operating System Image node for OS client deployments.

When and Why to Use an Operating System Install Package

Operating system install packages are used to help create an ideal world. In this ideal world, not only are your client deployments completely automated, but your reference image builds are completely automated as well. The advantage of automating your reference image builds is that you can keep the reference image in a clean state so that any potential user mistakes made within the reference image aren't deployed to your clients. Any unnecessary changes to the reference image, no matter how small, can cause unforeseen issues and are discouraged whenever possible. Using operating system image install packages and automation, you can create a hands off approach to building and capturing your reference image—making it as clean and reliable as possible. Another advantage of automating the build and capture process is that all of your tasks are documented and configured within Configuration Manager 2007, allowing them to be reproduced with a high degree of confidence. Those of you who have created a reference image know that it can often be difficult because of the number of steps that are involved. If your organization requires that you document these steps, you then have to spend time explaining these steps in detail, which can be very time-consuming. If you forget to document a step or don't describe a task properly, a step could be missed when rebuilding the image, causing unforeseen issues. Using the build and capture task sequence, you can not only document your steps, but you can reproduce them in exactly the same fashion—every time—helping create consistently reliable images.

Although operating system install packages help create an ideal world, it's not often that we are able to live in one. Because of this, you can modify the build and capture task sequence so that you can manually configure options that are not configurable during a task sequence step. If your build and capture step cannot be completely automated, please make sure to document your manual steps, in detail, so that you can reproduce them as best as possible.

N o t e

Note that it is possible to deploy operating system images to your clients using only operating system install packages. Using this process, you do not create an operating system image and simply use the original installation media as your source. The disadvantage to this method is that it can take much longer to deploy operating systems when compared to using a captured WIM image. I do not recommend that you deploy operating systems to your clients using this method if possible.

Creating an Operating System Install Package

To create an operating system install package, follow these steps:

1. Navigate to the Operating System Install Packages node within the Configuration Manager 2007 console, which is located under Computer Management > Operating System Deployment.

2. Right-click on the Operating System Install Packages node and choose Add Operating System Install Package (Figure 13.38).

3. The Add Operating Image Install Package Wizard is displayed. The first page of this wizard allows you to choose the installation source for the operating system installation files. In our example, we'll point to the location where the Windows 7 Professional files have been extracted, and click Next to continue (Figure 13.39).

4. The general section of the wizard is displayed. This page allows you to specify the name, version, and any comments related to the OS install package. In our example, we'll change the name to Windows 7 Professional and add RTM to the version field. Click Next to continue (Figure 13.40).

5. The summary section of the wizard is displayed. If the information looks correct, click Next to continue.

6. The confirmation section of the wizard is displayed. If any errors were encountered during the wizard, they will be displayed here. Click Close to close the wizard.

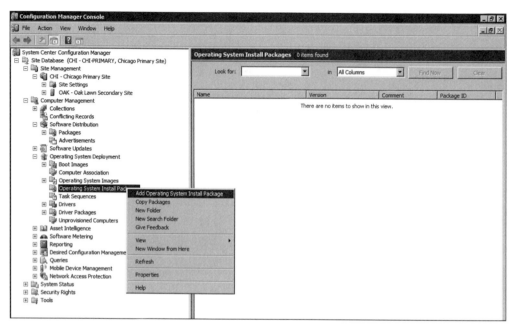

Figure 13.38
Add Operating System Install Package

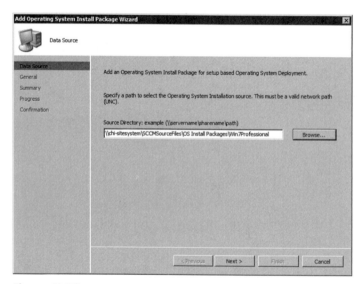

Figure 13.39
Choose Data Source for OS Install Package

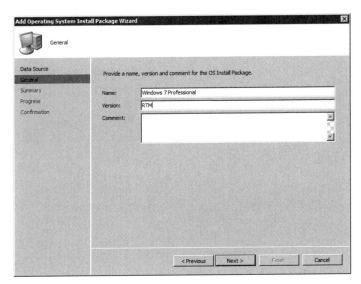

Figure 13.40
Specify Properties for the OS Install Package

Adding the Operating System Install Package to a Distribution Point

Just like with any other Configuration Manager 2007 package, it must be added to distribution points for client access. Remember that OS install packages are large in size so plan accordingly when distributing these packages across your organization. If your Configuration Manager 2007 infrastructure has not been planned out properly, you might have issues while transferring or storing these packages due to their size.

Operating System Images

Operating system images are created by capturing the reference image that we talked about in the last section. Operating system images are in the WIM file format and are distributed to client machines during an OS task sequence. Configuration Manager 2007 makes use of predefined task sequences to capture reference images that include build and capture task sequences and capture media task sequences. We will cover all aspects of task sequences in the next section.

Adding the Operating System Image to Configuration Manager 2007

This section depends upon having a captured operating system image available. At this point, we have not covered the process of capturing an operating system image since it is described in detail in the next section. Because the process of adding an operating system image to Configuration Manager 2007 is much like adding an operating system install package, we will only cover the steps of adding a WIM image so that you are familiar with the process. Again, we will capture the operating system image (WIM file) in the next section.

To add an operating system image (WIM file) to Configuration Manager 2007, follow these steps:

1. Navigate to the Operating System Images node within the Configuration Manager 2007 console, which is located under Computer Management > Operating System Deployment.

2. Right-click on the Operating System Images node and choose Add Operating System Image (Figure 13.41).

3. The Add Operating Image Wizard is displayed. The first page of this wizard allows you to choose the captured reference WIM image. In our example, we'll point to the location of the captured WIM image and click Next to continue (Figure 13.42).

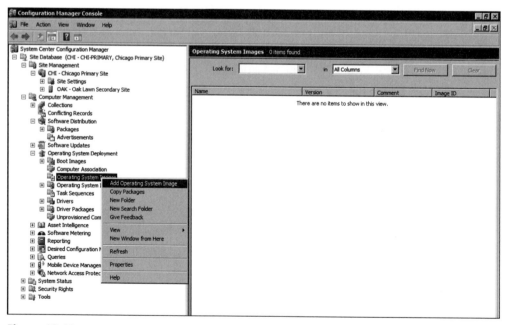

Figure 13.41
Add Operating System Image

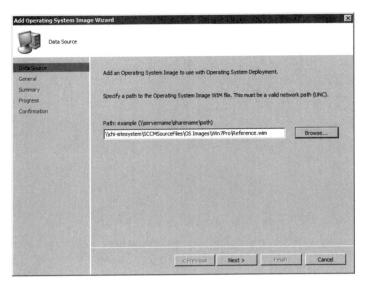

Figure 13.42
Choose Data Source for OS Image

4. The general section of the wizard is displayed. This page allows you to specify the name, version, and any comments related to the OS install package. In our example, we'll change the name to Windows 7 Professional and add RTM to the version field. Click Next to continue (Figure 13.43).

5. The summary section of the wizard is displayed. If the information looks correct, click Next to continue.

6. The confirmation section of the wizard is displayed. If any errors were encountered during the wizard, they will be displayed here. Click Close to close the wizard.

N o t e

Add your OS images to the necessary distribution points so that your clients have the necessary access.

Task Sequences

Task sequences are one of the features that really separate Configuration Manager 2007 from the competition. Task sequences allow you to be creative

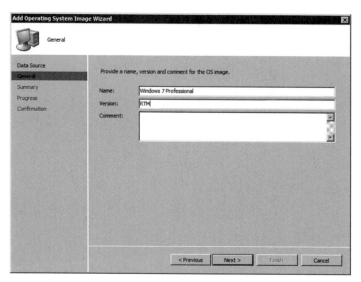

Figure 13.43
Specify Properties for the OS Image

and get things done by thinking outside of the box. They were designed so that newcomers could easily create and configure tasks while giving gurus the ability to manipulate and innovate using the same tools. Task sequences can be used to execute many complicated tasks on multiple systems by chaining these tasks together in the order that you prefer. Task sequences can be used to deploy operating systems, install device drivers, install software, or simply restart a computer. Task sequences contain many components, most of which we will cover in just a bit. Task sequences are created and organized in the task sequence editor which can be found by going to Operating System Deployment > Task Sequences within the Configuration Manager 2007 console.

The Task Sequence Editor

The task sequence editor allows you to create tasks that are executed in a top to bottom order as seen in the task sequence editor. This makes it possible to execute tasks in the order that you prefer since tasks can be moved around easily within the task sequence editor. As you add new tasks, you will find that they have their own properties and option tabs which configure how and when the task executes. The Properties tab is responsible for configuring the overall settings for each task while the Options tab is responsible for configuring conditions related to each task. These conditions are evaluated prior to task execution and determine whether or not the task will run. The task sequencer also allows you to create groups to help organize your task sequence. Groups have the same Properties and Options tabs as tasks, giving you the ability to execute entire groups of tasks based on a single (or multiple) condition. This comes in handy especially if your task sequence contains many tasks. The task sequence editor is good about showing you tasks that have not been properly or completely configured by displaying a red X next to the task (or group). Once all of the information has been filled in, the red X turns into a green checkmark. This allows you to quickly scan through multiple tasks to find out which one might be improperly configured.

Predefined Task Sequences

Task sequences can become complicated very quickly—especially when deploying operating systems—because of the types of tasks that have to be included and the order in which they must be configured. Although this information is available through help documents within the product and on the Internet, it can be difficult for new users to figure this out from scratch. To help with this, Configuration Manager 2007 has three predefined task sequences that help with tricky scenarios such as operating system deployment. These predefined task sequences can be created by right-clicking on the Task Sequences node, choosing New > Task Sequence. This starts the New Task Sequence Wizard. The options that are available within this wizard are:

- Install an existing image package
- Build and capture a reference operating system image
- Create a new custom task sequence

Install an Existing Image Package   This option allows you to create a task sequence that deploys an operating system image along with commonly used options. This wizard completes the following task sequence steps in this order:

- Select the appropriate boot image
- Select the appropriate OS image
- Whether or not to partition and format the hard drive

- Enter the Windows product key
- Select the server licensing mode along with the number of server connections
- Enable or disable the administrator account
- Select a password for the administrator account
- Join a workgroup or domain
- Select an account within AD that has permissions to join the domain
- Install the Configuration Manager 2007 client
- Capture state settings as well as network and Window settings
- Install software updates
- Install software packages

Build and Capture a Reference Operating System Image This option allows you to automate the build and capture of the reference image for the purposes of creating an operating system image. This wizard completes the following task sequence steps in the order listed here:

- Select the appropriate boot image
- Select the appropriate OS install package
- Enter the Windows product key
- Select the server licensing mode along with the number of server connections
- Enable or disable the administrator account
- Select a password for the administrator account
- Join a workgroup or domain
- Select an account within AD that has permissions to join the domain
- Install the Configuration Manager 2007 client
- Install software updates
- Install software packages
- Select the appropriate Sysprep package

- Select the necessary OS image properties

- Select the appropriate image storage path

- Select an account within AD that has write permissions to store the image

Create a New Custom Task Sequence   This option lets you create your own empty task sequence that you can later configure with as many steps as necessary. This wizard completes the following task sequence steps in this order:

- Select the appropriate boot image

Note

Task sequences can be used for operating system deployment or software distribution. If a boot image is not specified when creating a task sequence, the task sequence is considered as a software distribution task sequence. These types of task sequences are designed to install software distribution packages in the order that you specify in the task sequence editor.

Task and Group Options

As stated above, each task and group has a Properties and Options tab, which configures how and when they will run. This section focuses on the Options tab, which allows you to define conditions that determine whether or not the task or group will run.

The Options tab contains the following settings:

- **Disable this step**—This option disables the task or group from running. This is helpful if you need to disable the step within the task sequence but do not wish to remove it completely. This is often used in trouble-shooting situations.

- **Continue on error**—This option lets the task sequence continue even if an error occurs in the task or group. If this option is not checked and a non-fatal error occurs within a task, the entire task sequence will fail.

Within the Options tab is also an Add Condition button. This allows you to add one or multiple conditions to your task or group. You can add the following conditions:

- Task Sequence Variable

- Operating System Version

- File Properties
- Folder Properties
- Registry Setting
- Query WMI
- Installed Software

Note

You can use the if statement to combine multiple conditions.

Tasks and Properties

Task sequences contain many components (or tasks) that can be included to help you manage your environment. These range from installing software to capturing the user state of a computer. They are accessed by the Add tab at the top of the task sequence editor (Figure 13.44) and are categorized into the following groups:

- General
- Disks

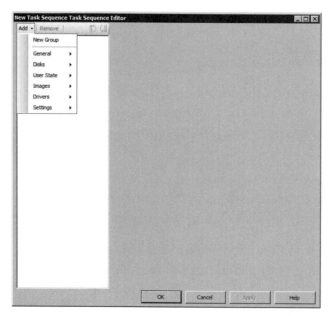

Figure 13.44
Task Categories

- User State

- Images

- Drivers

- Settings

Tip

If you are unsure about how to create a custom task sequence, use the predefined task sequences as a template. These are designed with the necessary steps in the correct orders. If two task sequence editor windows are open side by side, you can copy and paste task sequence steps and groups from one window to the other. This will help you build a custom task sequence from the ground up using supported and recommended task sequence steps/groups.

General Tasks   The tasks listed under the General tab are for day to day operations such as installing software or running scripts. The tasks that exist under the general category are:

- Run Command Line

- Install Software

- Install Software Updates

- Join Domain or Workgroup

- Connect to Network Folder

- Restart Computer

- Set Task Sequence Variable

Run Command Line   The run command line task allows you to run a command such as an executable or a batch script. This is done without having to create a software package and runs directly from the task sequence step itself. This makes it simple to run a script without having to worry about overhead such as distribution points and packages. The options within the run command line task are shown in Figure 13.45 and are described next.

- **Type**—The Type field displays the type of task that has been selected.

- **Name**—The Name field allows you to specify the name of the task. Name the task something descriptive. This can be helpful when trying to organize multiple tasks.

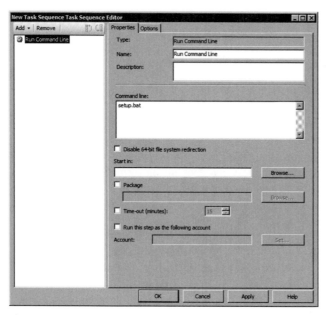

Figure 13.45
Run Command Line Properties

- **Description**—The Description field lets you describe the task. This can be used for documentation purposes.

- **Command line**—The command line field lets you specify which command will be executed on the target computer. If a file extension is used, Configuration Manager 2007 uses the associated program to open the file. If no extension is used, Configuration Manager 2007 tries .com, .exe, and .bat.

- **Disable 64-bit file system redirection**—This option only takes effect when running inside of a 64-bit operating system. This option disables the WOW64 file system redirector so that native 64-bit executables and DLLs are used instead of the 32-bit versions.

- **Start in**—The start in field lets you specify the location for the executable folder. By default, the start in location points to the distribution point folder where the executable exists. If the package has been downloaded during the task sequence, the local cache folder is used.

- **Package**—The package option lets you specify a Configuration Manager 2007 package that contains the files that are specified in the command line field. This is useful when the files that you wish to execute are not already on the target computer.

- **Time-out (minutes)**—The time-out option lets you specify how long the package will run before being terminated by Configuration Manager 2007. The values can be from 10 to 999 minutes.

- **Run this step as the following account**—The account field lets you specify a user account that will run the specified command line. This is useful if you do not (or cannot) run the program under the default local system account.

Note

The command line task sequence step is the only task that has a different Options tab from the rest of the tasks. The Options tab on this task has an additional field for success codes. Because command line tasks can return different success codes, you can specify which codes are considered successful. By default, 0 and 3010 are considered successful codes, but this can be modified to accept anything—including failure codes. If a code is returned that is not listed in the successful codes field, the Configuration Manager 2007 will consider the task to have failed.

Install Software   The install software task allows you to install a software distribution package that has already been created within Configuration Manager 2007. As long as the software package has been created successfully, a program has been created, and has been added to the correct distribution points, this task should install the specified package successfully. The options within the install software task are shown in Figure 13.46 and are described next.

- **Type**—The Type field displays the type of task that has been selected.

- **Name**—The Name field allows you to specify the name of the task. Name the task something descriptive. This can be helpful when trying to organize multiple tasks.

- **Description**—The Description field lets you describe the task. This can be used for documentation purposes.

- **Install single application**—This option specifies that only one application is installed. The correct software distribution package can be located by using the Browse button.

Figure 13.46
Install Software Properties

Note

The only programs that can run within a task sequence are ones that: have been specified to run whether or not a user is logged in, run with administrative rights, and do not allow user interaction. Also, the Allow This Program to Be Installed from the Install Software Task Sequence without Being Advertised option must be checked under the Advanced tab. Only the programs that meet these criteria will be available during a task sequence step.

▪ **Install multiple applications**—This option works by making use of task sequence variables that specify package IDs and program names. When you specify the base variable name, Configuration Manager 2007 goes up sequentially until no more variables exist, causing the task to exit. The task sequence variables that define the packages (and programs) must be manually added to the task sequence editor prior to this task. They should be entered with the <packageID:program name> syntax, separated by a colon. For example, a task sequence variable name might be ABC001 and its variable value might be CHI00005:Silent Install. Another task sequence variable name might be ABC002 and its variable value might be CHI00006:Persystem unattended. In this example, ABC001 would be the base variable name and should be entered into the base variable name field. Configuration Manager 2007 would start with the CHI00005 package and run the Silent Install program and then move onto ABC002, which would start the CHI00006 package and run the per-system unattended program. Because no more variables exist, the task would then be complete and exit.

Note

The base variable value is case sensitive.

Install Software Updates   The install software updates task allows you to install software updates that have been configured in the Software Updates node. Note that this task will only work while running in a standard operating system. The options within the run install software updates tasks are shown in Figure 13.47 and are described next.

- **Type**—The Type field displays the type of task that has been selected.

- **Name**—The Name field allows you to specify the name of the task. Try to name the task something descriptive. This can be helpful when trying to organize multiple tasks.

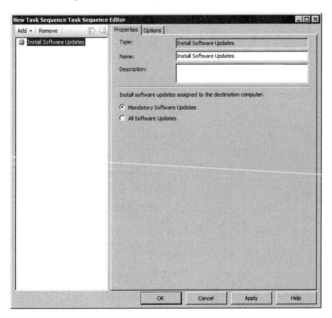

Figure 13.47
Install Software Updates Properties

- **Description**—The Description field lets you describe the task. This can be used for documentation purposes.

- **Mandatory software updates**—This option installs software updates configured as mandatory to the targeted system.

- **All software updates**—This option installs all of the software updates to the targeted system. This includes both mandatory and non-mandatory updates.

Join Domain or Workgroup   The join domain or workgroup task allows you to automatically configure your client's workgroup/domain memberships. The options within join domain or workgroup task are shown in Figure 13.48 and are described here:

- **Type**—The Type field displays the type of task that has been selected.

- **Name**—The Name field allows you to specify the name of the task. Try to name the task something descriptive. This can be helpful when trying to organize multiple tasks.

- **Description**—The Description field lets you describe the task. This can be used for documentation purposes.

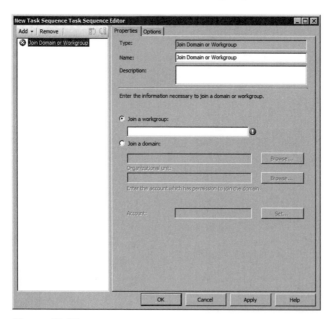

Figure 13.48
Join Domain or Workgroup Properties

- **Join a workgroup**—The Join a Workgroup field lets you specify the name of the workgroup that the computer should join.

- **Join a domain**—The Join a Domain fields let you specify the domain to join, the OU to which the computer object should be placed, and an account in Active Directory that has permissions to join the domain. If no OU is specified, the computer objects are placed in the default computers container.

Connect to Network Folder   The connect to network folder task lets you create a connection to a network folder. The options within the connect to network folder task are shown in Figure 13.49 and are described here:

- **Type**—The Type field displays the type of task that has been selected.

- **Name**—The Name field allows you to specify the name of the task. Try to name the task something descriptive. This can be helpful when trying to organize multiple tasks.

- **Description**—The Description field lets you describe the task. This can be used for documentation purposes.

- **Path**—The Path field lets you specify the location to the network share. This should be in the form of a UNC path.

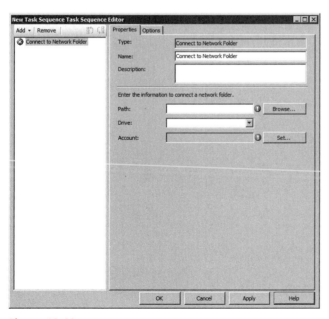

Figure 13.49
Connect to Network Folder Properties

- **Drive**—The Drive field lets you specify a drive letter that is mapped to the UNC path specified above. This is not a required field.

- **Account**—The Account field lets you specify the account that will be used to authenticate to the network share. This creates the network folder connection account if one has not already been created.

Restart Computer   The restart computer task allows you to gracefully restart a computer during a task sequence. The options within the restart computer task are shown in Figure 13.50 and are described next.

- **Type**—The Type field displays the type of task that has been selected.

- **Name**—The Name field allows you to specify the name of the task. Try to name the task something descriptive. This can be helpful when trying to organize multiple tasks.

- **Description**—The Description field lets you describe the task. This can be used for documentation purposes.

- **The boot image assigned to the task sequence**—This option specifies that the computer will restart to the boot image that is assigned to the

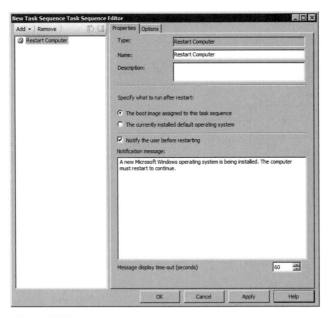

Figure 13.50
Restart Computer Properties

task sequence. This is used if steps defined later in the task sequence need to be run in Windows PE.

- **The currently installed default operating system**—This option specifies that the computer will restart to the default operating system.

- **Notify the user before restarting**—This option notifies the user that the computer is about to restart using the information next.

- **Notification message**—This field lets you specify the message that is delivered to users when the restart task executes.

- **Message display time-out (seconds)**—This option lets you specify the number of seconds that the notification message is displayed to users.

Set Task Sequence Variable   The set task sequence variable task allows you to specify variable names and properties that can be used throughout the task sequence. A good example of a task sequence variable is when you use the install multiple applications option in the install software task. The options within the set task sequence variable task are shown in Figure 13.51 and are described next.

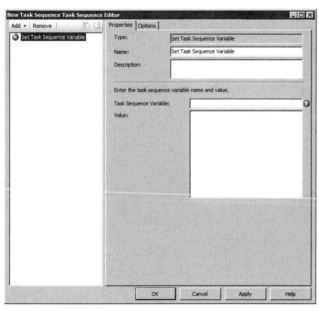

Figure 13.51
Set Task Sequence Variable Properties

- **Type**—The Type field displays the type of task that has been selected.

- **Name**—The Name field allows you to specify the name of the task. Try to name the task something descriptive. This can be helpful when trying to organize multiple tasks.

- **Description**—The Description field lets you describe the task. This can be used for documentation purposes.

- **Task Sequence Variable**—This field lets you specify the task sequence variable name. This name can be called upon and used in other tasks within the task sequence.

- **Value**—This field lets you specify the value of the task sequence variable.

Disk Tasks   The tasks listed under the Disks tab are specifically related to disk activities such as formatting and partitioning a disk. The tasks that appear under the disks category are:

- Format and Partition Disk

- Convert Disk to Dynamic

- Enable BitLocker

- Disable BitLocker

Format and Partition Disk   The format and partition disk task allows you to format and partition disks based on their disk number. If you need to partition and format multiple disks, multiple tasks can be added to the task sequence. The options within the run command line task are shown in Figures 13.52 and 13.53 and are described next.

- **Type**—The Type field displays the type of task that has been selected.

- **Name**—The Name field allows you to specify the name of the task. Try to name the task something descriptive. This can be helpful when trying to organize multiple tasks.

- **Description**—The Description field lets you describe the task. This can be used for documentation purposes.

- **Disk number**—This option lets you specify which disk will be partitioned and formatted during this task.

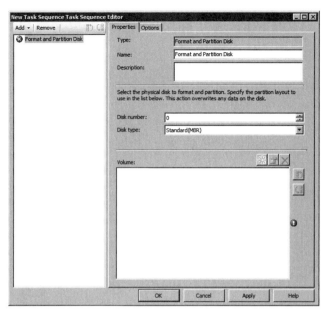

Figure 13.52
Set Task Sequence Variable Properties

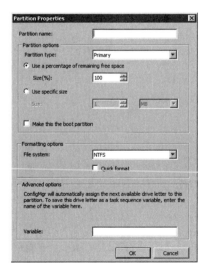

Figure 13.53
Partition Properties

- **Disk type**—This option lets you specify the disk type. You can choose between MBR and GPT types.

- **Volume**—The volume section lets you specify how the disk will be partitioned and which file system will be used. When you specify a new volume, you have many options to choose from. These options are shown in Figure 13.53.

- **Partition name**—The Partition name field lets you specify the name of the partition. This can be seen in the disk properties within Windows.

- **Partition type**—This option lets you specify the partition type. You can choose between primary, extended, and hidden partitions.

- **Use a percentage of remaining free space**—This option lets you specify the size of the partition by using a percentage of free space. If you choose 100%, for example, all of the available free space will be used to create the partition.

- **Use a specific size**—This option lets you specify the size of the partition by using specific sizes. You can choose sizes in megabytes or gigabytes.

- **Make this the boot partition**—This option lets you specify that this partition is the boot partition.

- **File system**—This option lets you specify the file system of the partition. You can choose between none, NTFS, and FAT32. Note that the quick format option is not checked by default when creating this task. If not checked, this task may run for extended periods of time depending on the size of your hard drives.

- **Variable**—The Variable field is used to store the drive letter that Configuration Manager 2007 assigned to the partition during Windows PE. This is helpful if you need to configure something later in the task sequence that references this drive. Note that this does not allow you to specify which drive letter that is assigned in Windows. This is not supported by Configuration Manager 2007.

Convert to Dynamic Disk   The convert to dynamic disk task lets you convert basic disks to dynamic disks based on the disk number. The options within convert to dynamic disk task are shown in Figure 13.54 and are described next.

Figure 13.54
Convert Disk to Dynamic Properties

- **Type**—The Type field displays the type of task that has been selected.

- **Name**—The Name field allows you to specify the name of the task. Name the task something descriptive. This can be helpful when trying to organize multiple tasks.

- **Description**—The Description field lets you describe the task. This can be used for documentation purposes.

- **Disk number**—This option lets you specify which disk will be converted into a dynamic disk. This option is not supported on Windows 2000 systems because of the lack of diskpart.exe.

Enable BitLocker   The enable BitLocker task allows you to enable BitLocker encryption on a selected disk. BitLocker is available in Windows Vista and later operating systems and uses the trusted platform technology (TPM) to store keys that can unlock a drive when needed. If a computer comes with a TPM device, you can save the key in that location. If a TPM device is not available, you have the option to use a USB drive to store the key. If the drive is taken to another computer without the correct TPM device or USB drive (which means the key is

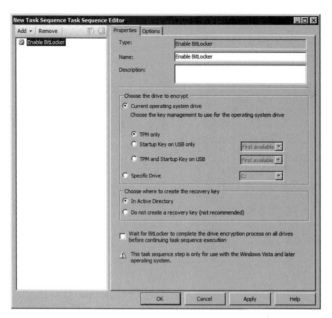

Figure 13.55
Enable BitLocker Properties

also not available), users are prompted to enter the correct startup password. If
the password is not entered correctly, the computer will not boot. The options
within the enable BitLocker task are shown in Figure 13.55 and are discussed
next.

- **Type**—The Type field displays the type of task that has been selected.

- **Name**—The Name field allows you to specify the name of the task.
  Name the task something descriptive. This can be helpful when trying to
  organize multiple tasks.

- **Description**—The Description field lets you describe the task. This can
  be used for documentation purposes.

- **Current operating system drive**—This option allows you to encrypt the
  current operating system drive. If this option is selected, the TPM only,
  Startup Key on USB only, and TPM and Startup Key on USB options
  are enabled.

- **TPM only**—This option specifies that the startup encryption key will be
  stored on the TPM device only.

- **Startup Key on USB only**—This option specifies that the startup encryption key is only stored on a USB disk. If this option is selected, you can choose which USB drive will hold the startup key.

- **TPM and Startup Key on USB**—This option specifies that the startup key is stored on both the TPM device and a USB drive. If this option is selected, you can choose which USB drive will hold the startup key.

- **Specific Drive**—This option allows you to specify which data drive is encrypted with BitLocker. If this option is selected, the system drive must already be encrypted with BitLocker.

- **In Active Directory**—This option lets you store the recovery key in Active Directory if it has been extended for BitLocker.

- **Do not create a recovery key (not recommended)**—This option allows you to not store a recovery password.

- **Wait for BitLocker to complete the drive encryption process on all drives before continuing task sequence execution**—This option prevents the task from finishing until all selected drives have been encrypted. This is not required since BitLocker can encrypt drives in the background but is required if you choose to encrypt the operating system disk and then a data disk during the same task. Because the operating system disk must be BitLocker enabled prior to a data disk being BitLocker enabled, this option must be checked so that the task does not fail.

Disable BitLocker   The disable BitLocker task removes BitLocker encryption from a drive. The options within the disable BitLocker task are shown in Figure 13.56 and are discussed next.

- **Type**—The Type field displays the type of task that has been selected.

- **Name**—The Name field allows you to specify the name of the task. Name the task something descriptive. This can be helpful when trying to organize multiple tasks.

- **Description**—The Description field lets you describe the task. This can be used for documentation purposes.

- **Current operating system drive**—This option allows you to decrypt the current operating system drive. Data drives must be decrypted

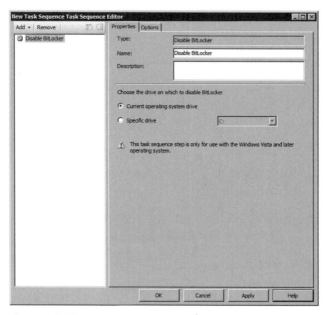

Figure 13.56
Disable BitLocker Properties

before decrypting the operating system drive since the startup key is stored on the operating system drive when BitLocker is enabled.

■ **Specific Drive**—This option allows you to specify which data drive is decrypted.

User State Tasks The tasks listed under the user state section are used to backup and restore user state settings on a computer during an operating system deployment. These options make use of the user state migration tool, which must exist as a software distribution package within Configuration Manager 2007. The tasks that appear under the user state category are as follows:

■ Request State Store

■ Capture User State

■ Restore User State

■ Release State Store

Figure 13.57
Request State Store Properties

Request State Store   The request state store task is used to locate a state migration point that can be used to capture or restore a user state. If capturing a user state, Configuration Manager 2007 queries the management point for a list of state migration points. It goes through the list and queries each state migration point until it finds one that has enough available client connections and enough available free disk space to store the data. If restoring a user state, the state migration point that captured the user state for the selected computer is used. The options within the request state store task are shown in Figure 13.57 and are described next.

- **Type**—The Type field displays the type of task that has been selected.
- **Name**—The Name field allows you to specify the name of the task. Name the task something descriptive. This can be helpful when trying to organize multiple tasks.
- **Description**—The Description field lets you describe the task. This can be used for documentation purposes.

- **Capture state from the computer**—This option allows you to capture the user state from the computer and evaluates all available state migration points to find one that can be used.

- **Restore state from another computer**—This option allows you to restore the user state from the state migration point and queries the state migration point that holds the data for this computer.

- **Number of retries**—This option specifies the number of retry attempts that is made if requesting a state store fails.

- **Retry delay (in seconds)**—This option specifies the number of seconds between each retry attempt.

- **If computer account fails to connect to state store, use the Network Access account**—If the computer is not a member of the domain, the network access account must be used to connect to the state store since a corresponding computer account is not available.

Capture User State   The capture user state task uses the user state migration tool to capture user profiles prior to deploying a new operating system. Once the user profile has been captured, it is then sent to the state migration point where it will be stored until a restore user state task is executed. The user state migration tool must already exist as a software distribution package for this task to work. The options within the capture user state task are shown in Figure 13.58 and are described next.

- **Type**—The Type field displays the type of task that has been selected.

- **Name**—The Name field allows you to specify the name of the task. Name the task something descriptive. This can be helpful when trying to organize multiple tasks.

- **Description**—The Description field lets you describe the task. This can be used for documentation purposes.

- **User state migration tool package**—This option lets you specify the package that contains the user state migration tool. Versions 2.6.1 and 3.0 are supported with Configuration Manager 2007.

- **Capture all user profiles with standard options**—This option captures all of the user profiles that exist on the machine. This includes domain

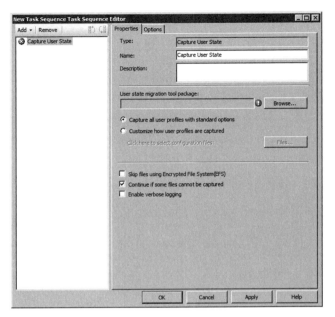

Figure 13.58
Capture User State Properties

and non-domain accounts. If non-domain accounts are captured, they must be assigned a new password during the restore task sequence. We'll talk about that in a second.

- **Customize how user profiles are captured**—This option lets you specify a custom XML file that defines which user profile files are migrated. The XML files specified in this step should reference configuration files that are included within the user state migration tool package.

- **Skip file using Encrypted File System (EFS)**—This option specifies that any files using EFS are not captured. Depending on the OS and USMT version, these files may not be readable after they are restored.

- **Continue if some files cannot be captured**—This option specifies that the task should continue even if a file (or files) cannot be captured. If this option is not selected and a file is not captured, the task fails.

- **Enable verbose logging**—This option specifies that detailed logging will occur during the task. This log is written to the \Windows\System32 \CCM\logs folder and is called Scanstate.log.

Restore User State   The restore user state task uses the user state migration tool to restore user profiles after deploying a new operating system. Once the user profile has been captured, it is then sent to the state migration point where it will be stored until the restore user state task is executed. The restore user state task finds the state migration point that has the correct user state data and uses it to restore files to the machine. The user state migration tool must already exist as a software distribution package for this task to work. The options within the restore user state task are shown in Figure 13.59 and are described next.

- **Type**—The Type field displays the type of task that has been selected.

- **Name**—The Name field allows you to specify the name of the task. Name the task something descriptive. This can be helpful when trying to organize multiple tasks.

- **Description**—The Description field lets you describe the task. This can be used for documentation purposes.

- **User state migration tool package**—This option lets you specify the package that contains the user state migration tool. Versions 2.6.1 and 3.0 are supported with Configuration Manager 2007.

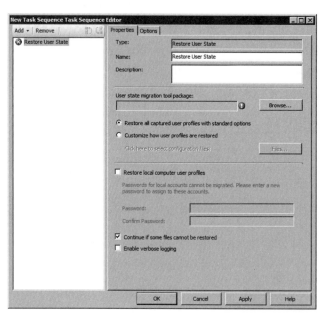

Figure 13.59
Restore User State Properties

- **Restore all user profiles with standard options**—This option restores all of the user profiles that were captured in the capture user state task. This includes domain and non-domain accounts. If a non-domain account was captured, a new password must be assigned to the corresponding account(s) during this task.

- **Customize how user profiles are restored**—This option lets you specify a custom XML file that defines which user profile files are migrated. The XML files specified in this step should reference configuration files that are included within the user state migration tool package.

- **Restore local computer user profiles**—This option restores non-domain (local) user profiles. If a non-domain user profile was captured in the store user state task and this option is not selected, the task will fail. You must specify a new password to assign to these accounts.

- **Continue if some files cannot be restored**—This option specifies that the task should continue even if a file (or files) cannot be restored. If this option is not selected and a file is not restored, the task fails.

- **Enable verbose logging**—This option specifies that detailed logging will occur during the task. This log is written to the \Windows\System32 \CCM\logs folder and is called Loadstate.log.

Release State Store   The release state store task notifies the state migration point that a capture or restore task is complete. If used in conjunction with a capture task, the state migration point is notified that the capture step has completed and allows a restore step to occur. Once the capture is complete, the state migration point changes the file permissions so only the restoring computer has access (read-only). If used in conjunction with a restore task, the state migration point is notified that the restore step has completed, which then initiates the retention settings that were configured on the state migration point. For more information on how to setup the state migration point and its retention settings, refer to Chapter 6. The options within the release state store task are shown in Figure 13.60 and are described next.

- **Type**—The Type field displays the type of task that has been selected.

- **Name**—The Name field allows you to specify the name of the task. Name the task something descriptive. This can be helpful when trying to organize multiple tasks.

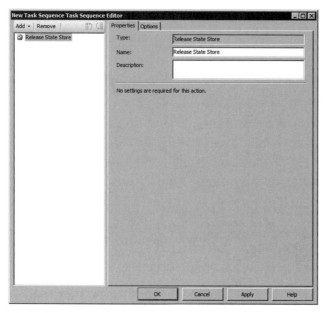

Figure 13.60
Release State Store Properties

- **Description**—The Description field lets you describe the task. This can be used for documentation purposes.

Image Tasks The tasks listed under the images section are used to apply, configure, and capture images to and from client machines. The tasks that appear under the images category are:

- Apply Operating System Image
- Apply Data Image
- Setup Windows and ConfigMgr
- Install Deployment Tools
- Prepare ConfigMgr Client for Capture
- Prepare Windows for Capture
- Capture Operating System Image

Apply Operating System Image   This option allows you to specify the operating system image from a captured image or an install package and denote how it

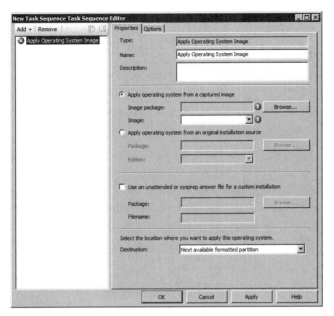

Figure 13.61
Apply Operating System Image Properties

will be applied to the selected drive. The options within the apply operating system image task are shown in Figure 13.61 and are described next.

- **Type**—The Type field displays the type of task that has been selected.

- **Name**—The Name field allows you to specify the name of the task. Name the task something descriptive. This can be helpful when trying to organize multiple tasks.

- **Description**—The Description field lets you describe the task. This can be used for documentation purposes.

- **Apply operating system from a captured image**—This option allows you to specify an operating system image that has previously been added to Configuration Manager 2007. Once the image package has been specified, you are then able to select the image itself by index number. This is useful if the WIM file contains more than one image.

- **Apply operating system from an original installation source**—This option allows you to specify an operating system install package that has previously been added to Configuration Manager 2007. Once the operating system has been specified, you are then able to select the edition by name. This is useful if your operating system install package has more than one edition such as with Windows Server media.

- **Use an unattended or Sysprep answer file for a custom installation**— By default, this option is not checked since it is not needed to complete this task. If an answer file is not specified, one will be generated automatically using information from other tasks, such as the apply windows settings or apply network settings task sequence steps. However, because only basic Windows information is collected in these task sequence steps, it may be necessary to create your own custom answer file. If you choose to include your own answer file, it must be added as a software distribution package and specified here. Note that a program is not required for an answer file.

- **Destination**—This option allows you to specify which disk and partition the operating system will be installed to. The options are next available partition, specific disk and partition, specific logical drive letter, and logical drive letter stored in a variable.

Note

If this task is used with a drive that has already been formatted, the image is applied without deleting any data. If data exists on the drive, the drive is wiped prior to applying the image. This is useful if you do not want to use the format and partition disk task but want to delete all information from the partition.

Apply Data Image   This option allows you to specify a data image from a captured image and determine how it will be applied to the selected drive. The options within the apply data image task are shown in Figure 13.62 and are described next.

- **Type**—The Type field displays the type of task that has been selected.

- **Name**—The Name field allows you to specify the name of the task. Name the task something descriptive. This can be helpful when trying to organize multiple tasks.

- **Description**—The Description field lets you describe the task. This can be used for documentation purposes.

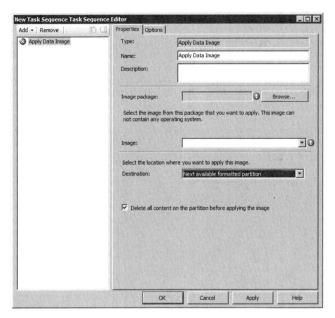

Figure 13.62
Apply Data Image Properties

- **Image Package**—This option allows you to specify a data image that has previously been added to Configuration Manager 2007. Once the image package has been specified, you are then able to select the image itself by index number. This is useful if the WIM file contains more than one image. Note that this image should not contain an operating system.

- **Destination**—This option allows you to specify which disk and partition the operating system will be installed to. The options are next available partition, specific disk and partition, specific logical drive letter, and logical drive letter stored in a variable.

- **Delete all content on the partition before applying the image**—This option specifies that all of the content will be deleted on the selected partition before applying the data image. This is useful if you do not want to use the format and partition disk task but want to delete all information from the partition.

Setup Windows and ConfigMgr   Although there aren't many configurable settings within this task, it performs many necessary steps that are important to a successful operating system image deployment. This step is a key transition

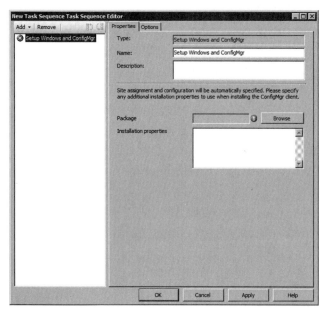

Figure 13.63
Setup Windows and ConfigMgr Properties

step that moves the task sequence out of the Windows PE environment into the newly installed operating system. If this step is not performed successfully during an image task sequence, your deployment will not work as expected. This task can only be started within Windows PE but it does continue to perform steps within the newly deployed operating system. The options within this task are shown in Figure 13.63. These options and the steps that are performed within this task are described next.

- **Type**—The Type field displays the type of task that has been selected.

- **Name**—The Name field allows you to specify the name of the task. Name the task something descriptive. This can be helpful when trying to organize multiple tasks.

- **Description**—The Description field lets you describe the task. This can be used for documentation purposes.

- **Package**—The package option lets you specify the Configuration Manager 2007 client package that has previously been added to Configuration

Manager 2007. This will be used to install the Configuration Manager 2007 client on the client computer(s).

- **Installation properties**—This field lets you specify optional installation properties for the client. These options are described in detail in Chapter 7. A good example of this field is to specify the server locator point in the event that you are installing the Configuration Manager 2007 client to machines that are part of a workgroup.

This task first executes while in the Windows PE environment. It starts by replacing directory environment variables that exist in the Sysprep.inf or unattend.xml answer files with WinPE environment variables. After this, the Configuration Manager 2007 client is downloaded from the package (that we specified above) and placed in the newly deployed image. If an OS image was used to deploy the operating system, the Configuration Manager 2007 client is disabled and the registry is updated so that the new OS will boot with the same drive letter that was used in the OS image. If an OS install package was used, these two steps are skipped.

The computer then reboots into the newly deployed operating system where mini-setup runs using the specified unattend.xml or Sysprep.inf files. After mini-setup finishes, the local administrator account is configured according to the settings specified in the apply windows settings step, which we will describe later in this chapter. The Configuration Manager 2007 client is then installed using the options within this task sequence and is setup in "provisioning mode," which prevents it from executing Configuration Manager 2007 policies until the task sequence completes successfully. If network access protection is enabled, required software updates are installed before moving onto the next task sequence step.

Install Deployment Tools The install deployment tools task sequence step allows you to specify the package that contains the appropriate Sysprep files. These files are only needed on pre Vista/Server 2008 machines during an operating system task.

Caution

Different versions of Windows need different versions of Sysprep. Make sure that you specify the correct version of Sysprep for the operating system that you are using.

Figure 13.64
Install Deployment Tools Properties

- **Type**—The Type field displays the type of task that has been selected.

- **Name**—The Name field allows you to specify the name of the task. Name the task something descriptive. This can be helpful when trying to organize multiple tasks.

- **Description**—The Description field lets you describe the task. This can be used for documentation purposes.

- **Sysprep Package**—This option lets you specify the Sysprep software distribution package that has been previously added to Configuration Manager 2007.

Prepare ConfigMgr Client for Capture   The prepare ConfigMgr client for capture task sequence step is used only when capturing an image that has the Configuration Manager 2007 client installed. This task sequence step has no configurable options but does a number of steps automatically. These steps are described next.

- Deletes Configuration Manager 2007 client-specific information from the smscfg.ini file

- Deletes Configuration Manager 2007 machine certificates

- Deletes the Configuration Manager 2007 client cache

- Deletes the Configuration Manager 2007 assigned site variable

- Deletes all Configuration Manager 2007 policies

- Deletes the Configuration Manager 2007 root key

Prepare Windows for Capture   The prepare Windows for capture task sequence step is used only when capturing an image. This allows you to specify options that take place during the Sysprep process without having to include a customized Sysprep.inf or unattend.xml answer file. The options within this task are shown in Figure 13.65 and are described next.

- **Type**—The Type field displays the type of task that has been selected.

- **Name**—The Name field allows you to specify the name of the task. Name the task something descriptive. This can be helpful when trying to organize multiple tasks.

- **Description**—The Description field lets you describe the task. This can be used for documentation purposes.

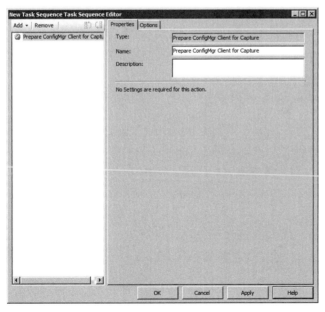

Figure 13.65
Prepare Windows for Capture Properties

■ **Automatically build mass storage driver list**—This option builds a list of mass storage drivers from the reference computer during the Sysprep process. This process basically maps Plug and Play hardware identifiers to the drivers and their locations so that the computer knows how to boot on a system with these mass storage devices. However, because Configuration Manager 2007 allows you to inject and specify which mass storage drivers will be used, this option is not mandatory. Advanced Sysprep users may want the ability to include this option for other non-typical tasks.

■ **Do not reset activation flag**—This option allows Sysprep to skip product activation in Windows Vista and Server 2008 (or higher) systems. Again, this is more for advanced users and should not typically be set.

Capture Operating System Image   The capture operating system image task is directly responsible for capturing and storing an image from a reference computer. The options within this task are shown in Figure 13.66 and are described next.

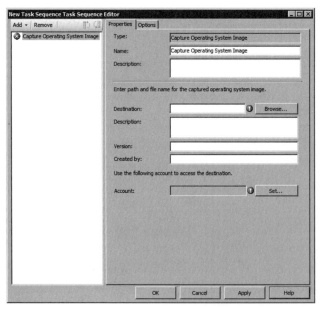

Figure 13.66
Capture Operating System Image Properties

- **Type**—The Type field displays the type of task that has been selected.

- **Name**—The Name field allows you to specify the name of the task. Name the task something descriptive. This can be helpful when trying to organize multiple tasks.

- **Description**—The Description field lets you describe the task. This can be used for documentation purposes.

- **Destination**—The Destination field lets you specify where the reference image will be stored. This field typically points to a UNC network share that has enough space to hold the image.

- **Version**—The Version field allows you to give your image a version number for identification purposes.

- **Created by**—The created by field lets you specify the creator of the image.

- **Account**—This option lets you specify an account that has the appropriate permissions to add the image to the network share that was identified in the Destination field. This creates a capture operating system image account if one has not already been created.

Driver Tasks   The tasks listed under the drivers section are used to apply the correct device drivers to the target machine. The tasks that appear under the images category are:

- Auto Apply Drivers
- Apply Driver Package

Auto Apply Drivers   The auto apply drivers task sequence step is used to stage compatible device drivers on targeted systems using drivers that have been imported to the driver catalog. When this task sequence step runs, it downloads drivers for every device that is present on the system by matching their plug n play hardware IDs to those found in the driver catalog. As long as a matching driver has been added to a driver package that exists on a distribution point, the driver can be downloaded successfully. On operating systems prior to Windows Vista/Server 2008, the drivers are downloaded to the system drive to a folder called "drivers." The devicepath value in the registry is updated to point to each driver in the drivers folder so that Windows will know where to find the correct drivers during the installation phase. For Windows Vista systems and higher, the drivers are placed into the driver store. Note that drivers are not installed until the mini-setup phase of Sysprep, which occurs during the Setup Windows and ConfigMgr task sequence step.

The auto apply drivers task sequence step is nice because driver matching happens automatically without having to worry about specific driver packages that apply to specific systems. This works well as long as you have tested each system and verified that the driver installation occurred successfully. Unfortunately, there are situations where this task sequence step does not work correctly, causing major issues while deploying operating systems. The issues that can cause an auto apply driver task sequence step to fail are listed next.

- **Task sequence media**—If the Configuration Manager 2007 infrastructure is not available, the auto apply drivers task sequence will fail. If you are using this task sequence step with task sequence media, the step will fail due to the lack of network connectivity to the site. We will discuss task sequence media later in this chapter.

- **Driver matching uncertainty**—Although the auto apply driver task sequence step is responsible for determining which drivers should be staged locally, it does not actually apply the drivers. Windows does this during the Sysprep mini-setup phase by matching the best drivers for the device. If multiple network card drivers from the same manufacturer have been imported to the driver catalog, for example, multiple versions may be downloaded to a computer with similar hardware. Unfortunately, Windows may not be able to determine the "correct" driver and may install a driver that has not been certified for the device. Although the driver may work, it might not perform as expected due to the wrong driver being installed.

- **Driver additions**—Once you have tested and verified that your systems install the correct drivers using the auto apply drivers task sequence step, you may need to add additional drivers for new systems. Once a new driver has been imported to the driver catalog, you will have to verify and test each driver for each system all over again since you don't necessarily know which driver will be used. This can get very tedious especially if multiple drivers are added to the driver catalog frequently.

- **Device issues**—The auto apply drivers task sequence step will only download drivers if a matching device can be found on the system. If a device is not installed properly or does not respond to normal Plug and Play hardware enumerations, a driver may not be downloaded even though the device actually exists (or will exist) on the system. A good example of this would be a printer that has been turned off or disconnected from the system during the auto apply drivers task sequence step. In this scenario, a driver would never get downloaded since the device did not exist on the system during this step.

The options within this task are shown in Figure 13.67 and are described next.

- **Type**—The Type field displays the type of task that has been selected.

- **Name**—The Name field allows you to specify the name of the task. Name the task something descriptive. This can be helpful when trying to organize multiple tasks.

- **Description**—The Description field lets you describe the task. This can be used for documentation purposes.

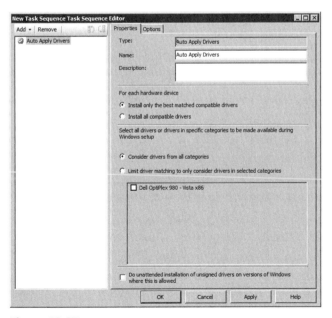

Figure 13.67
Auto Apply Drivers Properties

- **Install only the best matched compatible drivers**—This option instructs Configuration Manager 2007 to only download the best matched drivers to the targeted computer. This is done by ranking the drivers based on specific criteria in their INF files. This option only downloads drivers with a high ranking.

- **Install all compatible drivers**—This option instructs Configuration Manager 2007 to download all compatible drivers to the targeted computer regardless of the driver's ranking. Although more bandwidth may be used when selecting this option, Windows may be able to better determine the correct driver during installation time because more options are available to choose from.

- **Consider drivers from all categories**—This option instructs Configuration Manager 2007 to install all drivers from all user created categories.

- **Limit driver matching to only consider drivers in selected categories**— This option instructs Configuration Manager 2007 to only install drivers from a specific user created category.

- **Do unattended installation of unsigned drivers on versions of Windows where this is allowed**—This option specifies that drivers that have not been digitally signed will be installed silently in supported versions of Windows. Note that starting with Windows Vista 64-bit, unsigned drivers cannot be installed in a supported method. This is true for Windows 7 64-bit as well.

Apply Driver Package   The apply driver package task sequence step is used to stage specific drivers on targeted systems so that the correct drivers can be installed during an operating system deployment. There has been much confusion in the past regarding the differences between the auto apply driver task and the apply driver package task. The auto apply driver task sequence step is used to automatically download and stage drivers based on their Plug and Play hardware IDs while the apply driver package task sequence step is used to download and stage drivers based on criteria that an administrator defines. Many people prefer to use the apply driver package task sequence step because of the limitations that are put in place by the auto apply drivers step such as the ones listed above. Using driver packages, you can group drivers together based on specific criteria such as computer model. This allows you to stage only the tested and approved drivers

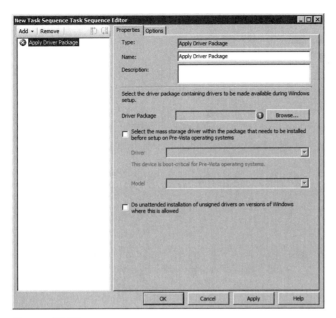

Figure 13.68
Apply Driver Package Properties

for the system to ensure the correct drivers are installed. Another benefit to driver packages is that you can pre-stage drivers for devices that have yet to be installed. This is helpful if you have many approved devices in your environment that only get installed to a limited number of computers. This allows the computer to be ready for the device so that the driver is automatically installed as soon as the device is plugged in. The apply driver package task sequence step is also necessary when using task sequence media to deploy operating systems since the Configuration Manager 2007 infrastructure is unreachable. The options within this task are shown in Figure 13.68 and are described next.

- **Type**—The Type field displays the type of task that has been selected.

- **Name**—The Name field allows you to specify the name of the task. Name the task something descriptive. This can be helpful when trying to organize multiple tasks.

- **Description**—The Description field lets you describe the task. This can be used for documentation purposes.

- **Driver Package**—This option allows you to specify the driver package that will be applied to the system.

Figure 13.69
Capture Network Settings Properties

- **Select the mass storage driver within the package that needs to be installed before setup on Pre-Vista operating systems**—This option allows you to specify the mass storage driver that will be used to boot the operating system on pre-Vista/7 systems. Not selecting the correct driver in this option will likely result in a blue screen of death.

- **Do unattended installation of unsigned drivers on versions of Windows where this is allowed**—This option specifies that drivers that have not been digitally signed will be installed silently in supported versions of Windows. Note that starting with Windows Vista 64-bit, unsigned drivers cannot be installed in a supported method. This is true for Windows 7 64-bit as well.

Settings Tasks   The tasks listed under the settings section are used to gather and apply the correct Windows and network settings to the target machine. The tasks that appear under the settings category are:

- Capture Network Settings
- Capture Windows Settings

- Apply Network Settings
- Apply Windows Settings

Capture Network Settings   The capture network settings task sequence step is used to capture network information during an operating system refresh. This allows settings such as domain and workgroup membership to be re-applied to the computer after a new operating system has been installed. The options within this task are shown in Figure 13.69 and are described next.

- **Type**—The Type field displays the type of task that has been selected.

- **Name**—The Name field allows you to specify the name of the task. Name the task something descriptive. This can be helpful when trying to organize multiple tasks.

- **Description**—The Description field lets you describe the task. This can be used for documentation purposes.

- **Migrate domain and workgroup membership**—This option captures the domain or workgroup membership information from a targeted computer so that is can be restored during the apply network settings task sequence step.

- **Migrate network adapter configuration**—This option captures the network adapter information from a targeted computer so that is can be restored during the apply network settings task sequence step. This information includes DNS, WINS, IP Addresses, and port filter information.

Capture Windows Settings   The capture windows settings task sequence step is used to capture Windows specific information during an operating system refresh. This allows settings such as the computer name and time zone information to be re-applied to the computer after a new operating system has been installed. The options within this task are shown in Figure 13.70 and are described next.

- **Type**—The Type field displays the type of task that has been selected.

- **Name**—The Name field allows you to specify the name of the task. Name the task something descriptive. This can be helpful when trying to organize multiple tasks.

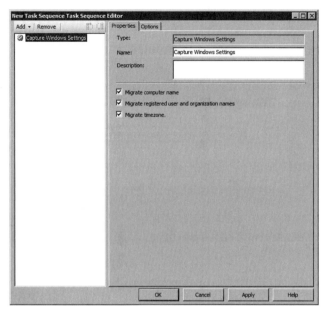

Figure 13.70
Capture Windows Settings Properties

- **Description**—The Description field lets you describe the task. This can be used for documentation purposes.

- **Migrate computer name**—This option captures the computer name from the targeted system and is re-applied during the apply Windows settings task sequence step.

- **Migrate registered user and organization names**—This option captures the user and organization names from the targeted system and is re-applied during the apply Windows settings task sequence step.

- **Migrate timezone**—This option captures the timezone information from the targeted system and is re-applied during the apply Windows settings task sequence step.

Apply Network Settings   The apply network settings task sequence step is used to join a newly deployed operating system to a domain or workgroup. If used in conjunction with the capture network settings task sequence step, the information captured within that step is applied in this step, overriding any options that may be specified. The information specified in this section is used to create the

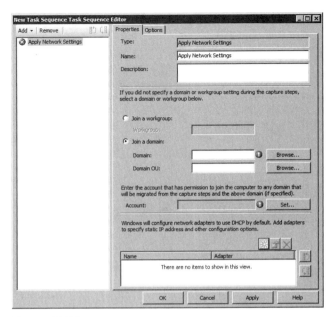

Figure 13.71
Apply Network Settings Properties

Sysprep.inf or unattend.xml answer files used during sysprep. The options within this task are shown in Figure 13.71 and are described next.

- **Type**—The Type field displays the type of task that has been selected.

- **Name**—The Name field allows you to specify the name of the task. Name the task something descriptive. This can be helpful when trying to organize multiple tasks.

- **Description**—The Description field lets you describe the task. This can be used for documentation purposes.

- **Join a workgroup**—This option specifies the workgroup that the targeted computer should join. If the capture network settings task sequence step was used, this option is ignored and the information collected in that task is used instead.

- **Join a domain**—This option specifies the domain that the targeted computer should join. You can choose the domain and the domain OU for the computer account. If the capture network settings task sequence step

Figure 13.72
Network Settings

was used, this option is ignored and the information collected in that task is used instead.

- **Account**—This option specifies the account that will be used to join the computer to the domain. This creates the domain joining account if one has not already been created.

- **Network adapter settings**—The options defined within this section define the properties for the network adapter(s) within the targeted computer. These options include IP/Subnet mask, DNS, WINS, and TCP/IP filtering. See Figure 13.72 for more information.

Apply Windows Settings   The apply windows settings task sequence step is used to configure Windows with general setup information such as the product key and time zone. If used in conjunction with the capture Windows settings task sequence step, the captured information is applied in this step, which may override the user, organization, and time zone options. The information specified in this section is used to create the Sysprep.inf or unattend.xml answer files used during sysprep. The options within this task are shown in Figure 13.73 and are described next.

- **Type**—The Type field displays the type of task that has been selected.

- **Name**—The Name field allows you to specify the name of the task. Name the task something descriptive. This can be helpful when trying to organize multiple tasks.

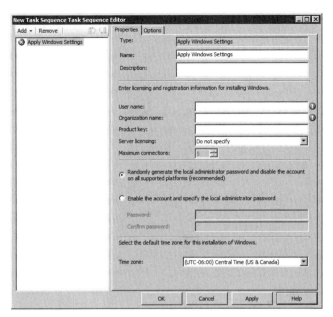

Figure 13.73
Apply Windows Settings Properties

- **Description**—The Description field lets you describe the task. This can be used for documentation purposes.

- **User name**—This option specifies the user name associated with the targeted computer.

- **Organization name**—This option specifies the organization name associated with the targeted computer.

- **Product key**—This option specifies the product key used on the targeted operating system. This is typically a volume license product key for pre-Vista systems and can be left blank if using a KMS licensing server and Vista or higher operating systems.

- **Server licensing**—This option specifies the server licensing mode if the targeted computer will be using a server class operating system. You can choose between per server or per user licensing. If per server is selected, the maximum connections option is enabled.

- **Maximum connections**—This option specifies the maximum number of connections that are allowed per your licensing agreement.

- **Randomly generate the local administrator password and disable the account on all supported platforms (recommended)**—This option randomly generates a password for the local administrator account and then disables it.

- **Enable the account and specify the local administrator password**—This option allows you to specify a password for the local administrator account and enables it. This can be useful on Vista and higher systems since the local administrator account is disabled by default.

- **Time zone**—This option lets you specify the time zone for the targeted computer.

Task Sequence Media

Task sequence media is used to create CD, DVD, or USB media that allows you to deploy or capture operating systems. Although the term "task sequence" is used in the name, task sequence media does not necessarily involve task sequences. Task sequence media can be used in situations where the Configuration Manager 2007 site cannot be reached (such as in an offsite location) or in situations where you need to contact the Configuration Manager 2007 site but cannot boot to PXE. There are four predefined task sequence media types that can be created by right-clicking on the Task Sequences node and choosing Create Task Sequence Media. This starts the New Task Sequence Media Wizard. The options that are available within this wizard are shown in Figure 13.74 and are described next:

- **Stand-alone media**—This option allows you to execute an entire task sequence by using media such as CDs, DVDs, or USB flash drives. All of the content from the distribution point(s) is copied to the media so that the entire task sequence can run in an offline fashion.

- **Bootable media**—This option allows you to create bootable media such as CDs, DVDs, or USB flash drives that simply boot the computer to the boot image. Once the computer boots, it then communicates with the correct Configuration Manager 2007 site to run advertised task sequences just as you would if the computer booted to PXE. This prevents you from having to use a PXE service point.

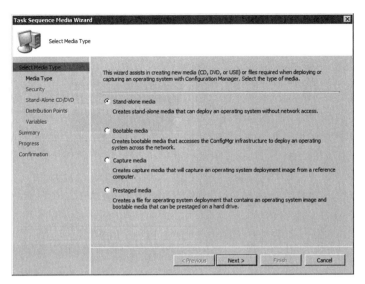

Figure 13.74
Create Task Sequence Media Wizard

- **Capture media**—This option allows you to create media such as CDs, DVDs, or USB flash drives that are designed to capture and create an image from a reference computer without having to use a task sequence capture task.

- **Prestaged media**—This option is new to R3 and is used to prestage boot images and operating systems on computers to help ease deployment. The file generated in this step can be given to computer manufacturers to ensure that the proper OS image and boot image are prestaged on the hard drives even before the computers arrive to your location. When a computer is booted that contains prestaged media, it automatically connects to your Configuration Manager 2007 environment and finishes the task sequence.

Computer Associations

The Computer Association node is located under the Computer Management > Operating System Deployment node within the Configuration Manager 2007 console and allows you to create mappings between systems for the purpose of migrating user state settings from one system to another. Once a mapping has been created, the USMT is used to capture user state data from the source system, which is then restored on the destination system. The associations created in this node keep track of paired systems so that user state data is captured and restored automatically to and from the correct systems.

This node is also responsible for creating manual machine entries. Manual machine entries are created using information such as the computer name, MAC address, and SMBIOS GUID of a new machine that is not yet managed by Configuration Manager 2007. These entries are designed to re-provision new, bare meal systems so that they can be managed by Configuration Manager 2007. Prior to R2, this was the only method to deploy operating systems to bare metal computers since the unknown computers collection did not exist. With R2 and higher, you now have the ability to choose how bare metal systems are managed.

Migration Types

Before you start creating computer associations, you need to understand how and why they are created. There are some situations that do not require a computer association so this section is important to understand.

Side-by-Side Migrations Side-by-side migrations occur when you have a source and destination computer. The source computer is the computer that is currently being used by a user and contains all of their files and settings (user state data). The destination computer is the user's new computer that does not have any of their user state data.

Once the computer association has been created, the following task sequence steps must be executed on the source computer in the following order:

- Request State Store
- Capture User State
- Release State Store

Once these task sequence steps have been executed on the source computer, the user state data is captured and held on a state migration point within the site. At this point, the destination computer is ready to receive the user state data by executing the following task sequence steps in the following order:

- Request State Store

- Restore User State

- Release State Store

The USMT task sequence settings and requirements that we covered in the previous section apply to these steps as well. If these requirements are not met, the user state restore and capture process may fail.

Note

Although these steps can be combined into an OSD task sequence to help automate the OSD process, they are not a requirement of the user state capture and restore process. As long as these steps are executed inside the Windows operating system and not WinPE, user state data can be captured and restored at any time. This helps if the destination computer already has an operating system installed and you simply want to restore user state data from another computer.

In-Place Migrations   In-place migrations occur when only a single computer is involved such as during an operating system upgrade. This is sometimes referred to as a wipe-and-load. In this type of migration, an OSD task sequence is executed within Windows that first captures the user state data and stores it on a state migration point. When the computer reboots into WinPE, the old operating system is removed and replaced with the new one. After the computer boots into the new operating system, the user state data is restored from the state migration point and is ready for use at the end of the OSD task sequence.

Note

When a task sequence contains a set of USMT capture task sequence steps as we talked about above, a computer association is automatically created with the source and destination being set as itself.

Creating a Computer Association

Now that you understand what a computer association is and when it's used, it's time to learn how to manually create the association. To create a computer association, follow the steps next:

1. Right-click on the Computer Association node located under Computer Management > Operating System Deployment and choose New > Computer Association. (Figure 13.75.)

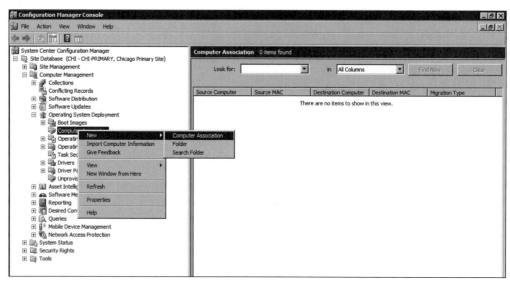

Figure 13.75
New Computer Association

2. The new computer association window is displayed. On the Computer Association tab, choose a source and a destination computer from the available computer objects already in the Configuration Manager 2007 database. If the destination computer is a bare metal computer and has not yet been created in the database, one will have to be manually entered. This is covered in detail next. In our example, we'll choose CHI-WIN7-01 as the source computer and CHI-WIN7-02 as the destination (Figure 13.76).

3. On the User Accounts tab of the New Computer Association window, you have the ability to specify which user accounts are migrated from the source to the destination computer. If no user accounts are specified in this step, all of the user accounts will be migrated. In our example, we won't specify any user accounts and click OK to continue (Figure 13.77).

4. After the computer association has been created, it will show up in the Computer Association node, which then creates the mapping between the source and destination computer. Once a capture and restore user state task sequence has been executed, the data on the source should then be migrated to the destination.

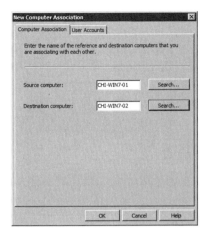

Figure 13.76
Source and Destination Computers

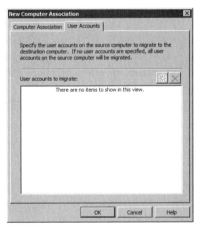

Figure 13.77
User Accounts to Migrate

Importing Computer Information (Manual Machine Entries)

Manual machine entries are used to manage new, bare metal systems with Configuration Manager 2007 and are created using the Import Computer

Information Wizard. As you may recall from previous chapters, a computer object does not get created until a discovery method is used. Unfortunately, new systems aren't easily discovered because they typically have no operating systems installed. This is where manual machine entries come into play. To manage new systems, you must manually create machine entries that represent them within the Configuration Manager 2007 database. These entries must contain the computer name and either the MAC address or SMBIOS GUID of the new machine. Once these machines have been added to a collection, you can then advertise operating systems to that collection, allowing you to PXE the new systems and start an OSD task sequence. This is fairly easy to manage when you have a handful of new systems, but what if you have thousands of new systems? To help with this, there is an option to import multiple systems using a CSV file containing this information. In some situations, it's possible to get a list of this information from your system manufacturer to help out with this but it can still be difficult if dealing with a large number of systems.

Note

This process was made much easier with the addition of the unknown computers collection in the R2 release. We will discuss this after this section.

To create a new manual machine entry, complete the following steps:

1. Right-click on the Computer Association node located under Computer Management > Operating System Deployment and choose Import Computer Information (Figure 13.78).

2. The Import Computer Information Wizard is displayed. You can choose to import computers using a file or import a single computer. In our example, we'll choose the Import a Single Computer option and click Next to continue (Figure 13.79).

3. The single computer information section of the wizard is displayed. In this section, you can enter a computer name, MAC address, and SMBIOS GUID. You also have the ability to create a computer association by choosing a source computer if this system will be used to hold user state data as we described in the last section. In our example, we'll enter CHI-WIN7-03 as the computer name and the MAC address of

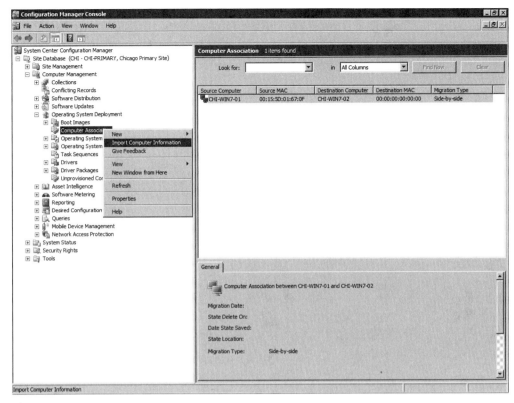

Figure 13.78
Import Computer Information

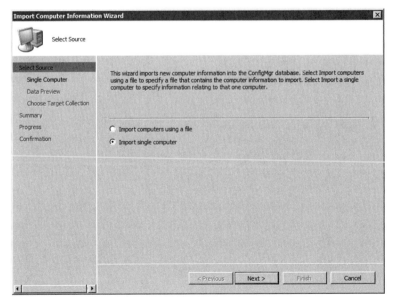

Figure 13.79
Import Single Computer

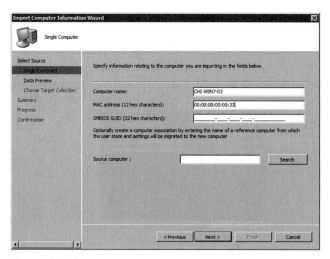

Figure 13.80
Single Computer Information

00:00:00:00:00:00:00:33. We will not create a computer association so the source computer field will be left blank. Click Next to continue (Figure 13.80).

Note

Note that you can use the SMBIOS GUID instead of the MAC address if you choose.

4. The data preview section of the wizard is displayed. It shows you the information that was specified in the previous step for verification. In our example, we'll click Next to continue.

5. The choose target collection section of the wizard is displayed. This allows you to choose the collection in which the new manual machine entry will be added. You can choose between the all systems collection or you can specify another existing collection. In our example, we'll choose the all systems collection and click Next to continue (Figure 13.81).

6. The summary section of the wizard is displayed. If the information looks correct, click Next to continue.

7. The progress section of the wizard is displayed. This shows you the progress of the new systems as they are added to the specified collection.

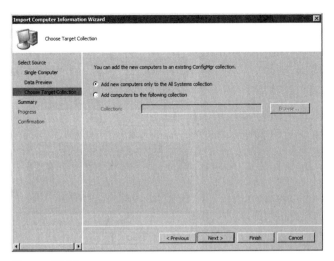

Figure 13.81
Choose Target Collection

Note that this could take a few minutes depending on the number of systems being imported.

8. The confirmation section of the wizard is displayed. If any errors were encountered during the wizard, they will be displayed here. Click Close to close the wizard.

Unprovisioned (Unknown) Computers

The Unprovisioned Computers node and the all unknown computers collection were introduced with Configuration Manager 2007 R2 and allow you to manage unprovisioned systems (such as bare metal systems) without having to create manual machine entries as we discussed in the last section. This process works by enabling unknown computer support on your PXE service points or task sequence media and booting an unprovisioned computer via one of these methods. As the computer initially communicates with the Configuration Manager 2007 site, it determines whether or not the computer is an unknown computer by looking for it in the database. If it is not located in the database, it is flagged as unknown and then looks for any task sequences that may be advertised to the all unknown computers collection. If an OSD task sequence is advertised, the computer displays the available task sequences. If a mandatory task sequence is advertised to the all unknown computers collection and the

Configuration Manager 2007 infrastructure is set up properly, any computer that boots to PXE (or bootable task sequence media) will automatically start the task sequence without user intervention. If the task sequence finishes successfully, the computer is classified as provisioned and is able to be managed.

Caution

Be careful about advertising operating system task sequences using mandatory assignments on the unknown computers collection. If an unknown machine boots to PXE while a mandatory assignment is in effect, the machine might start an OSD task sequence causing possible data loss. If the machine happens to be a production server, this could cause major problems.

Enabling Unknown Computer Support

Before you can utilize unknown computer support, you have to enable it for your PXE service points and your task sequence media (Figure 13.82).

PXE Service Points   As we discussed in Chapter 6, unknown computer support can be enabled when creating the PXE service point role or after the fact via the property page. Step by step directions on how to install and configure the PXE service point role are covered in Chapter 6. If the role has already been installed, you can modify the properties by going to the Site Settings > Site Systems node and choosing the site system that houses your PXE service point. Double-click on the ConfigMgr PXE service point role to open the properties page and ensure that the checkbox for Enable unknown computer support has been checked and click OK to save the changes.

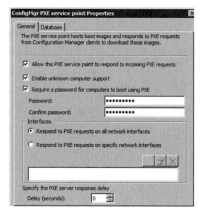

Figure 13.82
Enabling Unknown Computer Support in the PXE Service Point

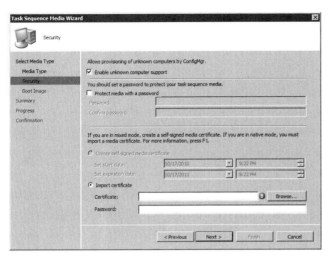

Figure 13.83
Enabling Unknown Computer Support in Task Sequence Media

Bootable Task Sequence Media   Earlier in this chapter, we briefly went over the different types of task sequence media that can be created. When using the bootable task sequence media option, you must check Enable Unknown Computer Support to enable this option as seen in Figure 13.83.

Understanding the Unknown Computer Process

The following scenario is an example of how the unknown computer support works in Configuration Manager 2007.

1. An unprovisioned system boots to PXE or bootable task sequence media with unknown computer support enabled.

2. When the unprovisioned computer boots into Windows PE, it creates multiple task sequence variables including _SMSTSx86UnknownMachine-GUID and _SMSTSx64UnknownMachineGUID. These variables contain the SMS unique identifiers that are defined in the x86 and x64 unknown computer resource objects. These objects are located under the all unknown computers collection and are used as placeholders for systems that have not yet been provisioned with Configuration Manager 2007. In our example, our unprovisioned system is using an x64 architecture so the SMS unique identifier for the x64 unknown computer resource object will be used as shown in Figure 13.84.

Figure 13.84
The x64 Unknown Computer Resource Object

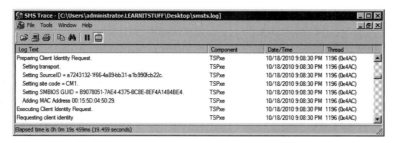

Figure 13.85
Client Identity Request

Note

The SMS unique identifiers for the x86 and x64 computer resource objects may be different in each Configuration Manager 2007 installation.

3. The SMBIOS GUID is set (B9078051-7AE4-4375-BC8E-8EF4A1484BE4) using the unique identifier found in the computer's BIOS. This information is then sent to the management point to try to identify the unprovisioned client. This can be seen in the smsts.log file on the unprovisioned system, as shown in Figure 13.85.

4. The management point receives the client identity request and scans the database for an SMS unique identifier that corresponds to the unprovisioned system's SMBIOS GUID (B9078051-7AE4-4375-BC8E-

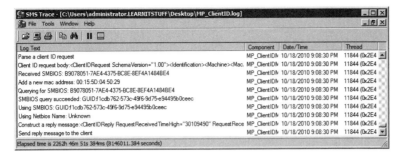

Figure 13.86
Client Identity Reply

8EF4A1484BE4). Because this is a new system, no SMS unique identifier is found so Configuration Manager 2007 creates a new SMS unique identifier for the unprovisioned system (f1cdb762-573c-49f6-9d75-e94495b0ceec). This information is then sent back as a reply to the initial client identity request. This can be seen in the MP_CliendID.log file from the management point and is shown in Figure 13.86.

Note

Debug logging was enabled to show detailed information in the MP_ClientID.log file.

5. When the unprovisioned system receives the reply from the management point, it then knows that it has been identified as an unprovisioned (unknown) system since the newly assigned SMS unique identifier (f1cdb762-573c-49f6-9d75-e94495b0ceec) is not in the database. Because the unprovisioned system is now considered unknown, it uses the unknown machine GUID that is stored in either the _SMSTSx86UnknownMachine-GUID or the _SMSTSx64UnknownMachineGUID variable (based on the unprovisioned system's architecture) instead of the SMS unique identifier that was assigned in step 4. In our example, the x64 unknown computer resource object's SMS unique identifier (c3f3a13f-a672-4f33-a929-e9d64d733073) is used instead of the SMS unique identifier that was assigned to the unprovisioned system (f1cdb762-573c-49f6-9d75-e94495b0ceec). The unprovisioned system is now able to retrieve policy information including any task sequences that might be advertised to the all unknown computers collection. This can be seen in the smsts.log file on the unprovisioned system and is shown in Figure 13.87.

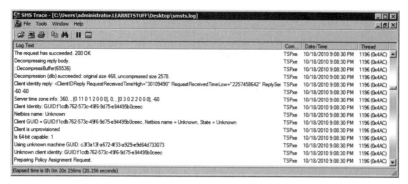

Figure 13.87
Client Identity Set as Unknown

TASK SEQUENCE REPORTS

Configuration Manager 2007 comes with 28 canned reports specifically pertaining to task sequences. These reports are listed next.

■ All system resources currently in a specific group/phase of a specific task sequence advertisement

■ All system resources for a specific task sequence advertisement in a specific state

■ All system resources in a specific state for a specific task sequence advertisement available to unknown computers

■ All system resources that failed in a specific group/phase of a specific task sequence advertisement

■ All task sequence advertisements

■ All task sequence advertisements available to unknown computers

■ Chart—Progress of a task sequence

■ Chart—Weekly progress of a task sequence

■ Count of failures in each phase/group of a specific task sequence

■ Count of failures in each phase/group of a specific task sequence advertisement

- Count of system resources that have task sequence advertisements assigned but not yet run
- Deployment status of all task sequence advertisements
- History—Specific task sequence advertisements run on a specific computer
- List of computers that took longer than the specified length of time to run a task sequence advertisement
- Packages referenced by a specific task sequence
- Progress of a running task sequence
- Progress of a running task sequence advertisement
- Progress of all advertisements for a specific task sequence
- Progress of all task sequences
- Progress of OS deployment task sequences
- Run time for a specific task sequence advertisement on a specific target computer
- Run time for each step of a specific task sequence advertisement on a specific computer
- Status for a specific computer of a task sequence advertisement available to unknown computers
- Status of a specific task sequence advertisement for a specific computer
- Status of all unknown computers
- Status summary of a specific task sequence advertisement
- Status summary of a specific task sequence advertisement available to unknown computers
- Summary report for a task sequence advertisement

Log Files

Listed next are some of the log files that can be used when troubleshooting operating system deployment issues. Remember to use Trace32.exe from the Configuration Manager 2007 Toolkit for easy log reading!

Table 13.2 Log Files for Operating System Deployment Troubleshooting

Log File	Location	Description
CCMSetup.log	%Windir%\System32\ccmsetup	Monitors the setup of the Configuration Manager 2007 client
CreateTSMedia.log	<ConfigMgrConsoleInstallPath>\AdminUI\AdminUILog	Monitors the creation of task sequence media
Dism.log	%Temp%\SMSTSLOG	Monitors driver installation during operating system deployment
DriverCatalog.log	<ConfigMgrInstallationDirectory>\SMSLogs	Monitors the status of drivers as they are imported into the driver catalog
MP_ClientID.log	<ConfigMgrInstallationDirectory>\SMS_CCMLogs	Monitors client identity requests from clients when booting to PXE or boot media
MP_DriverMgr.log	<ConfigMgrInstallationDirectory>\SMS_CCMLogs	Monitors client requests when running the auto apply driver task sequence step
MP_Location.log	<ConfigMgrInstallationDirectory>\SMS_CCMLogs	Monitors location of the management point
PkgMgr.log	%Temp%\SMSTSLOG\pkgmgr.log	Monitors driver installation during an operating system deployment task sequence
Setupact.log	%Windir%	Monitors setup and Sysprep information
Setupapi.log	%Windir%	Monitors setup and Sysprep information
Setuperr.log	%Windir%	Monitors setup and Sysprep information
Smsprov.log	<ConfigMgrInstallationDirectory>\Logs	Monitors the SMS provider
Smsts.log	%Windir%\system32\CCMLogs[1]	Monitors operating system deployment and task sequences
TaskSequenceProvider.log	<ConfigMgrInstallationDirectory>\Logs	Monitors tasks sequences such as when they are imported, exported, or edited

[1]For x64 installations, the log files are located at %Windir%\SysWOW64\CCMLogs

Note

There are many other log files that Configuration Manager 2007 creates that might help troubleshoot operating system deployment problems. To see all of the log files that each site system role creates, refer to Chapter 6, "Configuring Site System Roles."

THE FINAL WORD

Operating system deployment is a huge component of Configuration Manager 2007 and can take a while to grasp, especially if you are new to enterprise deployment scenarios. If you find that your understanding of these concepts is on shaky ground, re-read this chapter and set up an isolated test environment so that you can play with the different components. Keep doing this until you have a good understanding of the processes needed to successfully deploy an operating system. Remember, practice makes perfect!

In the next chapter, we'll talk about a new addition to Configuration Manager 2007 called Desired Configuration Management.

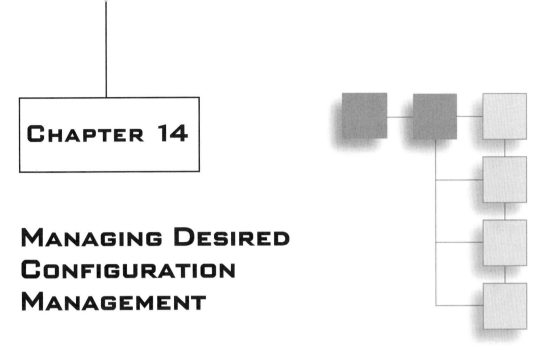

CHAPTER 14

MANAGING DESIRED CONFIGURATION MANAGEMENT

How many times have you configured a server or workstation just the way you want it, and then a few months later wondered if those configuration settings were still in place? As we all know, server configuration settings have a tendency to "drift" over time. That drift may be due to operator error, changing application requirements, or malicious attacks. Being proactive and checking the settings to make sure they are still viable, optimal, and correct takes time—usually time that we don't have. Too many other responsibilities seem to take precedence.

Desired Configuration Management (DCM) was designed to assist with the monitoring of key components on your systems. When you use DCM, you can see when something is amiss on one of your systems. There are some limitations however. You will not automatically receive a notification that there is a problem; that is the responsibility of the System Center Operations Manager. There are some pretty nifty things you can do with DCM however. And that is what we are going to explore within this chapter.

JUST WHAT IS DCM?

At its core, DCM is a tool that is used to review specific configuration items, verifying that they are configured correctly. Any time a system is not configured according to the specified criteria, DCM will place a non-compliant entry into the database. This entry can then be used to determine which systems need to be "repaired." Within Configuration Manager, DCM settings are configured and converted into part of the client policy. The DCM client agent, which is part of the Configuration Manager client, will then scan the system, looking for configuration settings that do not meet the defined criteria.

Most of the organizations that are taking advantage of DCM are doing so because they have systems that need to meet specific regulatory compliance needs. Having an improperly configured system can cost the company a certification during an audit, cost them money if they are fined during a review, or damage their reputation if the system is breached during an attack. Others are using DCM to make sure that critical systems are not incorrectly configured. Some of the other uses of DCM include:

- Validating configuration settings match best practices that have been identified by the vendor.

- Validating systems are configured appropriately before and after software or updates have been applied.

- Assessing security setting to validate a system meets specific security requirements.

- Validating operating system post installation configuration settings.

- Acting as the primary scanning engine for monitoring configuration items, generating the events that can be picked up by a monitoring solution.

Simply enabling DCM and configuring the settings that will be used to determine compliance is not usually enough however. As mentioned in the introduction to this chapter, DCM by itself will only flag a service as compliant or non-compliant in the database. Automatic notification and remediation are not part of the default configuration. Luckily, there are other mechanisms that you can use that will allow you to perform some of these actions.

DCM COMPONENTS

DCM has requirements on both the server and client. On the server side, DCM relies on configuration baselines, configuration items, and collections to function. On the client side, you will need to make sure all systems that will be monitored have Microsoft .NET 2.0 installed and the Configuration Manager 2007 client with the DCM client agent enabled. DCM does not support SMS 2003 clients in a Configuration Manager 2007 site.

DCM Client Agent

As with any of the other client agents that we have discussed throughout this book, the DCM client agent is used to facilitate the monitoring of items on a computer system. The client is also responsible for sending data back to the management point. Upon opening the properties of the DCM client agent, you will notice that there are very few configuration options. Figure 14.1 shows the General tab, which contains only the option to enable DCM and the scheduling options. The standard scheduling options are available: Simple and Custom. The simple schedule option allows you to control the recurrence pattern. As you can see in Figure 14.1, the evaluation will occur every 7 days by default. This value can be configured to any value that works for your organization.

Take note of the custom schedule. Even though you can configure the time that you want the evaluation to occur, the evaluation may not initiate at that time. There is a randomizer built in that will perform the evaluation anywhere up to

Figure 14.1
DCM Client Agent General Properties Tab

two hours after the designated time. This is to keep from having all of the systems perform a scan at the same time, sending all of the resulting information to the management point, congesting the network.

Of course the schedule that you set in the DCM client properties is the default setting. Each baseline that you create can have its own evaluation schedule. For some of the baselines you may need to evaluate more frequently, while others may not need to be evaluated nearly as often. You will have to determine what each baseline's schedule should be. When you are defining these schedules, make sure to consult with the stakeholders for the services, systems, and components that you are monitoring.

Configuration Items

A configuration item is the most discreet component of DCM. Each configuration item defines what you will be evaluating, and the settings that should be applied to the object. There are three types of configuration items that you can create within the Configuration Manager console:

- **Application Configuration Item**—used to evaluate settings on a system, but only if a specific application is installed on that system. Typically, the configuration item will only be evaluated on systems that have the application installed—although that is not a hard and fast rule. You can create an application configuration item that does not evaluate for any specific application, which essentially turns the configuration item into a general configuration item.

- **Operating System Configuration Item**—used to evaluate settings on specific systems, based upon the operating system that is installed on the system. You can choose the operating system you want to target from a list, or you can specify the version details if the operating system is not included in the list. The included operating systems are:
  - Windows 2000 original release
  - Windows 2000 Service Pack 1
  - Windows 2000 Service Pack 2
  - Windows 2000 Service Pack 3
  - Windows 2000 Service Pack 4

- Windows XP Professional original release
- x86 Windows XP Professional Service Pack 1
- x64 Windows XP Professional Service Pack 1
- x86 Windows XP Professional Service Pack 2
- x64 Windows XP Professional Service Pack 2
- x86 Windows XP Professional Service Pack 3
- x64 Windows XP Professional Service Pack 3
- Windows Server 2003 original release
- Windows Server 2003 Service Pack 1
- Windows Server 2003 Service Pack 2
- Windows Server 2003 R2
- Windows Vista
- Windows Vista SP1
- Windows Vista SP2
- Windows Server 2008
- Windows Server 2008 SP2
- Windows Server 2008 R2
- Windows 7

- **General Configuration Item**—used when the configuration item does not align with any particular operating system or application. Can be used to define evaluation criteria when the setting to be evaluated may appear on several operating systems, or is a generic setting on several applications.

Creating Configuration Items

After navigating to the Desired Configuration Management node within the Computer Management section of the Configuration Manager console, you will be presented with the Configuration Baselines and Configuration Items nodes. Right-clicking the Configuration Items node will present you with a menu where you can select one of the configuration item types. You can also create two other object types, folders and search folders.

A folder is simply an organizational construct that will allow you to organize the configuration items logically into containers that make it easier for you to manage. It is completely up to you how you would like to organize the configuration items. You can create a folder that will hold the three different types of configuration items, and then create subfolders to further organize each configuration item type into business unit containers or containers for each administrator to save their own configuration items.

Search folders come in very handy when you have many configuration items within the site. Using a search folder, you enter the search criteria that you want to use when populating the folder. The search criteria are based upon specific properties defined on configuration items. Figure 14.2 shows some of the object properties that you can use when defining the search folder. The object properties are as follows:

- **Categories**—Each configuration item can be associated with one or more categories when created. Categories include Client, IT Infrastructure, Line of Business, and Server by default. Other categories can be defined as needed.

- **Category Instance Unique ID**—Each category has a unique identifier within the site. Because each site can have its categories named the same

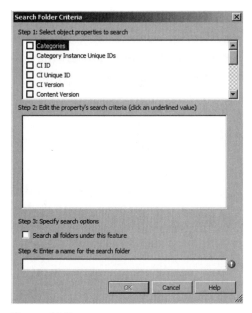

Figure 14.2
Search Folder Object Properties

as categories within parent or child sites, this option can be used to identify the unique category.

- **CI ID**—Each configuration item has an identifier that is assigned when the configuration item is created. These numbers are sequential, so you can very easily tell the order in which configuration items were built.

- **CI Unique ID**—Each configuration item has a unique identifier that is assigned by Configuration Manager when the configuration item is created.

- **CI Version**—As changes are made to existing object and setting options within the configuration item, the version number is incremented by 1. Primarily used in change control to determine how many changes are made.

- **Content Version**—As object and setting options are created or removed from the configuration item, the content version is incremented. Primarily used in change control to determine how many changes are made.

- **Created (UTC)**—Defines the creation date and time of the configuration items.

- **Created By**—The account that was used to create the configuration item is stored in this attribute.

- **Description**—This field is used to store additional descriptive information about the configuration item.

- **Last Modified (UTC)**—After the configuration item is updated, this field is used to store the date and time that the modification was made.

- **Last Modified By**—After the configuration item is updated, this field is used to store the account name of the user that made the configuration change.

- **Model Name**—When the configuration item is based upon a driver, this field stores the model of the hardware.

- **Name**—This field stores the display name of the configuration item.

- **Site Code**—This field stores the site code of the site where the configuration item was created.

- **Status**—Used to specify whether the configuration item is enabled or disabled.

- **Type**—Used to determine the configuration item type, such as application, configuration baseline, driver, operating system, etc.

So what can you monitor with a configuration item? Actually, just about anything. If you have a method of detecting a setting or a way of verifying the existence of an object, you can probably use that method within a configuration item. At the most basic, you can verify that a file, folder, registry key, or assembly exists on a system. At its most complex, you can use a series of scripts to validate configuration settings on services and applications loaded on a system. The full extent of a configuration item's power is up to you. You may be lucky in that your organization does not need very complex compliance checking, but there are organizations that have to perform regulatory compliance checks that use some very complex scripts to validate settings.

There are several options and settings that are available when creating a configuration item. Nearly all of the settings within the three types of configuration items are identical; however, there are some interesting settings that do set them apart from one another. Let's start off by looking at the settings of a general configuration item:

General Configuration Item

The first step is to initialize the creation wizard by right-clicking Configuration Items and select New > General Configuration Item. When the wizard starts, type a name that describes what the configuration item is testing for compliance. For instance, if you are testing to make sure that a folder within the file system has not been altered or deleted, you could name the configuration item "FolderX Validation Test." Optionally, you can enter a longer description within the Description field to further define what the configuration item is doing.

The last option on the first page of the wizard, seen in Figure 14.3, is the Categories section. It is here that you can define topics that the configuration item fits in to. Categories can be based upon any criteria that you choose. You can create categories for server and workstation classes, application types, compliance rules, etc. There are already four categories included within the default installation—Client, IT Infrastructure, Line of Business, and Server. You

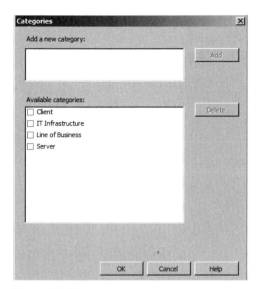

Figure 14.3
Configuration Item Categories

can create additional categories by clicking the Categories button and entering the name of the category. You can choose one or more categories for any configuration item. After making your selections, Search Folders can be created that use the categories as criteria.

Objects

The next page of the wizard allows you to define the objects that you want to test. The tests that you perform here can be used to determine if an object exists, or that the properties of the object have not changed. The object types that are included are File, Folder, Registry Key, and Assembly, seen in Figure 14.4.

Assembly Object An assembly is defined as a file of object code and any additional information that is used to prevent version mismatches. Assemblies are compiled into either an executable file (EXE) or a Dynamic Link Library (DLL). Using the information included within an assembly, you can validate that the object has not changed, thus increasing the object's security.

When selecting Assembly from the New menu of the Object page, you are presented with the New Assembly Properties window, seen in Figure 14.5. On the General tab, you need to specify the name of the assembly as it appears within the Global Assembly Cache (GAC). To view all of the assemblies

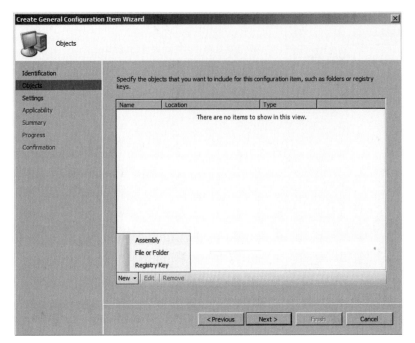

Figure 14.4
Configuration Item Object Types

contained in the GAC, navigate to %WINDIR%\Assembly. The assembly viewer interface will present each of the assemblies along with the Version, Culture, Public Key Token, and Processor Architecture of each assembly.

After entering the name of the assembly, the Validation tab, seen in Figure 14.6, is then used to check for the compliance of the assembly. Clicking the New button will present the three options that you have for compliance validation— Version, Culture, and Public Key Token. Notice that these are three of the four options that you find on the default display of the assembly viewer. If you have a system that you know has not been compromised, and the assembly resides on that system, you can use the information from that system to create the validation rule.

When using the Version option, the version of the assembly can be validated for an exact match, that it falls into a specific version range, or that it does not match specific versions. The Operator values that you can use are as follows:

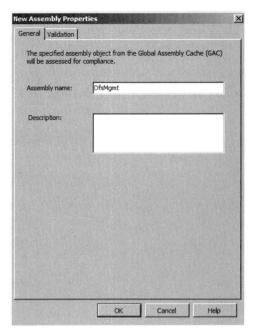

Figure 14.5
Assembly Properties

- Between
- Equals
- Greater Than
- Greater Than or Equal To
- Less Than
- Less Than or Equal To
- None Of
- Not Equals
- One Of

For instance, if you want to make sure the Microsoft.Jscript assembly on the Windows 7 systems has not changed, you can choose the Equals operator and enter 8.0.0.0 in the Value field.

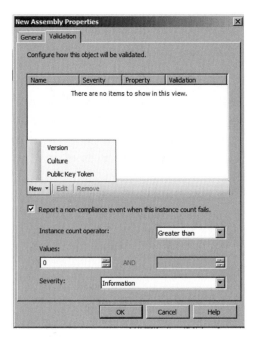

Figure 14.6
Assembly Validation Options

Note

Be aware that the settings that you apply to any configuration item may need to be updated whenever a hotfix, Service Pack, or Feature Release is applied to a system. Non-compliance states may start appearing as soon as any of these items are added to a system.

Culture and Public Key Token validation operators can be evaluated on different criteria than Version. Each of these validation types can be evaluated based upon string-based queries. Equals, Not Equals, None Of, and One Of are all valid operators, but other operators have been replaced with:

- All Of
- Begins With
- Contains
- Does Not Begin With
- Does Not Contain
- Does Not End With

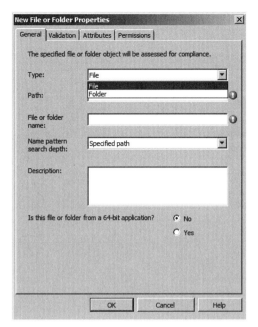

Figure 14.7
File or Folder Object General Properties Tab

- Does Not Match

- Ends With

- Matches

File or Folder Object   The second object compliance type is to check files or folder properties. On the General tab, seen in Figure 14.7, after specifying whether you are going to validate a file or folder by using the Type drop-down, you will need to enter the path to the object you are validating. Make sure you enter the path to the object within the Path text field, and then the name of the folder or file in the File Or Folder Name text field.

The Validation tab works in the same manner as it did in the Assembly object type, but there are different validation tests that you can perform on a file or folder. The options that can be validated against are as follows:

- Size

- Product Name

- File Version

- Date Modified
- Date Created
- Company
- SHA-1 Hash

You will find that the operators that are associated with these validation criteria are the same as those associated with the assembly objects that we discussed prior to this section. Using combinations of these validation options, you can create a very impressive check against a file or folder, validating that none of the basic properties have been altered.

File and folder validation can be extended beyond that which is found on the validation tab however. The other two tabs, Attributes and Permissions, allow you to define additional criteria for validation checking. The Attributes tab, seen in Figure 14.8, is used to verify that specific attributes on the object have not been altered. Here you will find options for the following attributes:

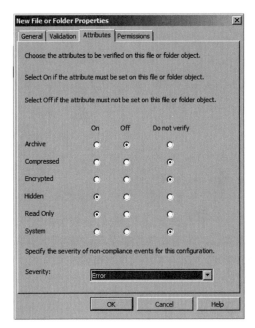

Figure 14.8
File or Folder Attributes tab

- Archive

- Compressed

- Encrypted

- Hidden

- Read Only

- System

For each of these attributes you can make sure the attribute value is turned on or off, or you can ignore the state of the attribute. So if you want to make sure that the Hidden and Read Only attributes are turned on, but the file has not been modified and is ready to be backed up, you would select the On option for the Hidden and Read Only attributes, Off for Archive, and leave the other attributes set to the default value of Do Not Verify.

The Permissions tab, seen in Figure 14.9, is used to verify the permissions granted to specific accounts have not been altered. When enabling permission

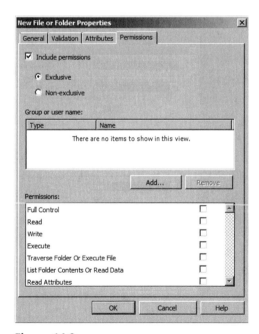

Figure 14.9
File or Folder Permissions Tab

checking, there are two types of validation checks that can be performed against the object—exclusive and non-exclusive permissions. When verifying exclusive permissions, you are verifying that the permissions granted on the object include only the accounts that have been specified within the Group Or User Name field and Permissions list. If the Access Control list associated with the object contains any additional accounts, any accounts are missing, or any of the permissions are different than those specified, the object will be non-compliant.

Non-exclusive permissions are used to verify that the accounts listed have the appropriate permissions. Any additional accounts that are included within the object's Access Control list are not validated, and do not generate a non-compliant state. Using this option, you are essentially saying that you do not care about any other account that has permissions; you only want to make sure that the accounts specified in the configuration item have not had their permissions altered.

Registry Key Object

Registry key validation is akin to file and folder validation. Although there are not as many options, when verifying registry settings, you can define the registry key that should exist on a system, and the permissions that should be assigned to the registry key. The five hives can be used for key validation. Select the hive where the key exists, as seen in Figure 14.10 and then type in the path to the key in the Key field. On the Permissions tab, enter the accounts that need permission verification, either by entering the exclusive or non-exclusive entries within the access control list on the key.

Settings

Once the Objects properties have been defined, the next page of the wizard allows you to configure settings that you would like to validate. The Settings properties that you define here allow you to check to make sure that the settings applied to a component have not changed or been modified. Whereas the configuration settings that you entered in the Object properties test to make sure an object exists and/or the properties of the object have not changed, the Settings properties are used to validate that the component's configuration settings are still in compliance.

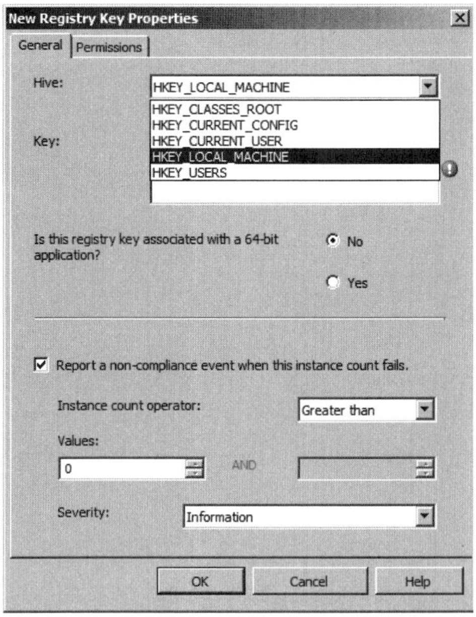

Figure 14.10
Registry Properties

As you start looking through all of the settings that you can configure, you will notice that some of the settings look redundant. This is due to the fact that you can configure object properties and settings properties separately from one another. You don't have to include Object compliance settings along with the Settings compliance settings and vice versa. The two items are autonomous to one another.

Just as you did with the Objects properties, clicking the New button will present you with the options that you have when configuring Settings. Notice that there are more configuration items that you can select from this list than you had with Objects. The items that you can configure are as follows:

- Active Directory Domain Services
- IIS Metabase
- Registry
- Script
- SQL Query

- WQL Query

- XML

Active Directory Domain Services To validate that critical Active Directory accounts or objects have not changed, you can create an LDAP query that checks values on the object. If you know how to create the LDAP query to access a property, you can validate nearly any setting with Active Directory.

After selecting the option to create an Active Directory setting, the Properties page appears with two tabs, General and Validation. The General page is used to define the LDAP query that specifies which property you are checking. As you can see in Figure 14.11, the top section of the General tab is used to create a display name for the configuration item and any additional descriptive information that you want to enter.

The lower section is where the LDAP query is defined. In the LDAP:// prefix section, the query prefix can be entered, either LDAP://, which can be used to

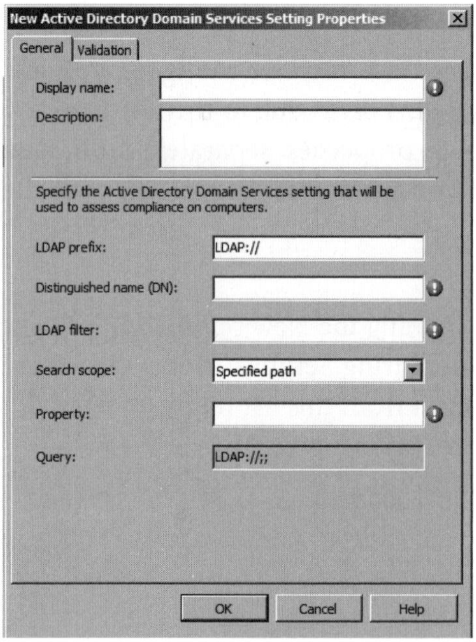

Figure 14.11
Active Directory General Properties Tab

query any domain controller, or GC://, which is used to query Global Catalog servers. The remainder of the query is defined in the rest of the text fields.

- **Distinguished Name (DN)**—Specifies the name of the Active Directory container to be queried.
- **LDAP Filter**—Used to define how the objects within the container will be selected.
- **Property**—Defines the property that will be assessed for compliance.

The Search Scope drop-down is used to control how the query will be executed. You can limit the depth of the search by selecting the appropriate option:

- **Specified Path**—The path defined in the Distinguished Name field is queried, but the query is not recursive.
- **Specified Path and the First Level of Subfolders**—The query will be executed against the path defined in the Distinguished Name text field, and will be recursive through the first level of subfolders beneath the path.
- **Specified Path and All Subfolders**—The query will be executed against the path defined in the Distinguished Name text field, and will be recursive through all subfolders.

On the Validation tab, seen in Figure 14.12, you will find the settings that are used to validate the LDAP query. Anything entered on this tab is evaluated for compliance. The first thing you should do is define the data type by using the drop-down. The standard data types are listed—String, Date/Time, Integer, Floating Point, and Version.

Once you have selected the data type, it is a matter of creating the validation rules for the key. The rules that you create can reflect different alerting levels, based on the value of the setting. Remember that the existence of the object is not validated at this point, only the setting itself. If the setting does not match the criteria that you designate, an entry can be placed in the event log.

The actual validation test is then configured within the Details section. Clicking the New button will bring up a properties page that can be used to specify the value that needs to be set within Active Directory. Clicking the New button

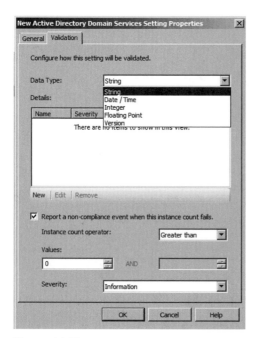

Figure 14.12
Active Directory Validation Tab

brings up the Configure Validation dialog where you can specify the settings that you want to check. Make sure you enter a name that helps describe the validation setting. Doing so will make it easier to determine the compliance setting that is generating the compliant or non-compliant state. Adding additional detail in the Description field will make it easier on anyone that is editing the validation criteria.

The Data Type selection determines the operators that become available. For instance, when you select String as the Data Type, string-based operators such as Begins With, Ends With, Equals, etc. will appear in the drop-down. The Date/Time selection will present options such as Between, Greater Than, Less Than, etc. Make sure you understand the value that you are checking for compliance. Configuring the wrong value or operator will cause the DCM agent to send invalid data back to the site server.

The options that appear in the Operator drop-down are dependent upon the data type that was selected on the Validation tab. Just as you saw in the Objects properties, there are different options that appear when you select String or Date/Time options. As you make your operator selection and enter the value for the key validation, notice that the expression that will be evaluated is displayed in the Expression field. Verify the expression is built exactly the way you want it and then select the severity level for the validation.

You can continue to create validation. The validation criteria that you create can be configured so that you have a setting for Information, Warning, and Error levels, depending upon what is stored in the registry key value.

IIS Metabase   The IIS Metabase Setting properties are used to validate settings within the IIS Metabase—which is the configuration repository for Internet Information Services. This Configuration Item option does not have as many options to configure as the Active Directory settings. The Display Name and Description fields are still used, but there are only two text fields to configure, seen in Figure 14.13:

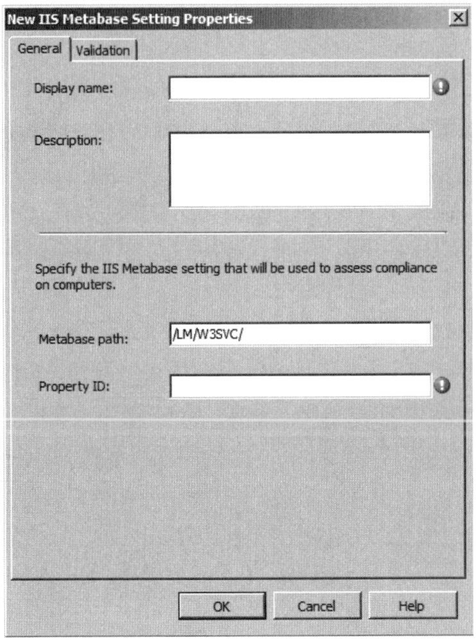

Figure 14.13
IIS Metabase properties

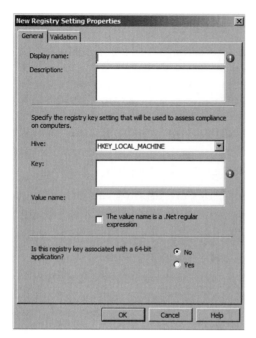

Figure 14.14
Registry Key Properties

- **Metabase Path**—Path to the IIS Metabase property that will be validated
- **Property ID**—Property that will be evaluated for compliance

The Validation tab includes the same options that were available within the Active Directory settings.

Registry   The Registry options that you can configure within the New Registry Setting properties probably look very familiar if you have already worked with Objects properties. The General tab, seen in Figure 14.14, is nearly identical between the two components. You should remember that the settings that have been applied at the Objects properties level are not reflected within the Settings properties. If you are using the same key in both properties, you can copy and paste the key entry from one to the other, but the properties are independent of each other.

The General tab includes only one additional text field that was not part of the Objects properties—Value Name. The data that you enter into the Value Name field is used for the validation criteria. Make sure that you type the value name

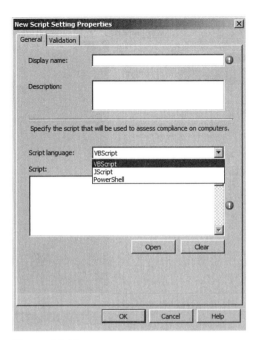

Figure 14.15
Script Properties

exactly as it is used within the registry. Failure to do so will give you improper results.

The Validation tab includes the same options that were available within the Active Directory settings.

Script   When creating the script validation, the results of a script are used as the validation criteria. On the General page, seen in Figure 14.15, you select the scripting language for the script, and enter the script in the Script text window. Unless the script is very basic, chances are you are not going to type it within this window. Instead, the more efficient method is to copy and paste the script from a script editor after you have tested that it works. If you have saved the script, you can click the Open button and navigate the location where the script is stored, saving the time of copying and pasting the text of the script.

The Validation tab includes the same options that were available within the Active Directory settings.

SQL Query   The General tab of the SQL Query, seen in Figure 14.16, is used to define which database will be checked for compliance, and the T-SQL statement

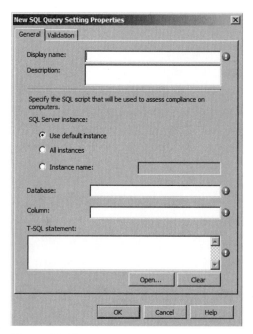

Figure 14.16
SQL Query Properties

that will be used for the compliance testing. You have the option of testing the default database server instance, a specific database server instance, or all database server instances. If you choose the Instance Name option, you must supply the instance name. With all of the options, you will need to specify the database and column that will be used in the compliance check. Finally, you will need to enter the T-SQL statement that will be used to query the database and select the data for validation. As with the script validation test, it is easier to copy and paste the statement in this text window than it is to type it in. Additionally you can select the file that has the SQL query in it by clicking the Open button.

The Validation tab includes the same options that were available within the Active Directory settings.

WQL Query   As with the SQL Query, WQL Query validation checks to make sure that the results of the query are valid. Unlike the SQL Query, you can only enter the criteria based upon a WQL Where clause. You start by defining the namespace, class, and property that you are going to query, seen in Figure 14.17, then enter the Where clause definition within the text window.

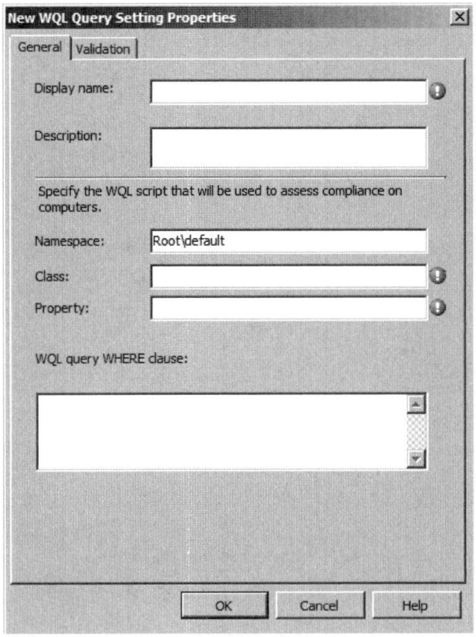

Figure 14.17
WQL Query Properties

The Validation tab includes the same options that were available within the Active Directory settings.

XML   The XML validation resembles the file and folder options that were available from the Objects properties. To use this validation type, you need to enter the path to the file, the name of the file, and whether the file is stored in the specified path, or whether the query should be recursive, locating the file in subdirectories. Once the file is defined, the XPath query can be entered into the text window. As with the script validation, you can click the Open button to locate the file and import it into the validation.

There is also a new button, Namespaces, that can be used to define the namespace or namespaces that will be used within the validation, seen in Figure 14.18. The window that appears when you click the New button is used to quickly create prefix and namespace combinations for your validation.

The Validation tab includes the same options that were available within the Active Directory settings.

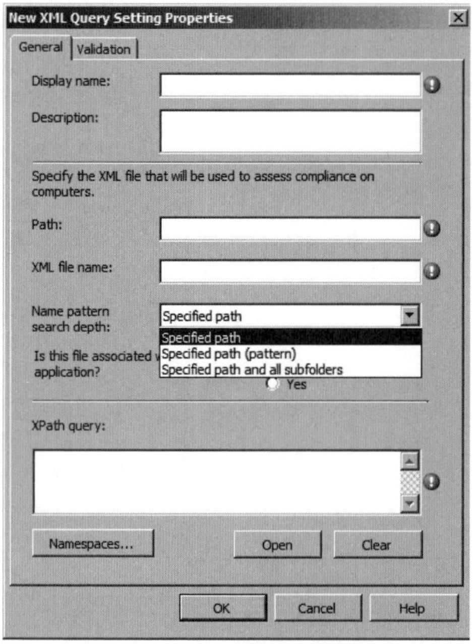

Figure 14.18
XML Query Properties

After configuring all of the Object and Settings properties, you are presented with the Applicability page. This is where you can specify the Windows operating system versions that the configuration item will be used to validate. This list is akin to the list of operating systems found in the Operating System Configuration Item properties. If you need to limit the operating system scope for the configuration item, select the Specified Windows platforms, as seen in Figure 14.19, and then select the checkboxes next to the applicable operating system versions.

Application Configuration Item

The settings that were presented for general configuration item are all contained within the application configuration item. The additional configuration option is the detection method, as seen in Figure 14.20. The detection method is used to determine whether or not the application is actually installed on the system. If it is installed, the configuration item will be evaluated.

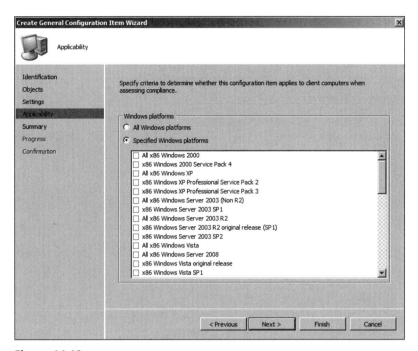

Figure 14.19
Operating System Applicability

There are three options that you can use for application detection—always assume the application is installed, search for the Windows Installer product code and version, or use a script to determine if the application is installed. If you choose the first option, Always Assume Application Is Installed, every system covered by the baseline will be evaluated. This may not always be prudent however. The application may not be installed on all systems within your organization and the baseline may be applied against systems that do not have the application.

The two other methods are preferred. Using the Use Windows Installer (MSI) Detection option will allow you to specify exactly which application is required. Instead of typing in the product code and version of the MSI, you can click the Open button and navigate to the MSI installer file. Once you select it, the fields will be populated automatically.

If the application was not installed using a Windows installer file, or there is another method that you would like to use when detecting whether or not an

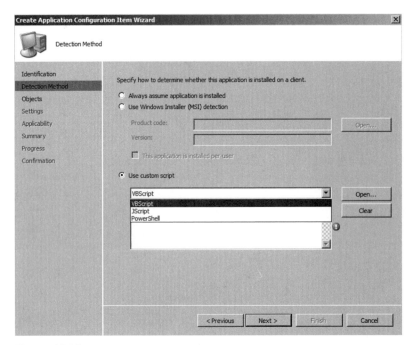

Figure 14.20
Application detection methods

application is installed, you can use a script to detect the application. After selecting the scripting language—VBScript, Jscript, or PowerShell—you can either type the script into the text box, or click the Open button to select the appropriate script.

Operating System Configuration Item

Whereas you can create a general configuration item and select the operating systems where the configuration item will evaluated, the operating system configuration item is used to designate a specific operating system version that the configuration item will target. As you can see in Figure 14.21, the list of operating systems that you can choose when you select Specify Windows Version By Description is limited to specific operating systems. This list is updated when a new service pack is installed on the site server. If there is a new operating system or there has been an update to an existing operating system, you may need to manually designate the version to be evaluated. Figure 14.22 shows the options that are available from the Specify Windows Version By

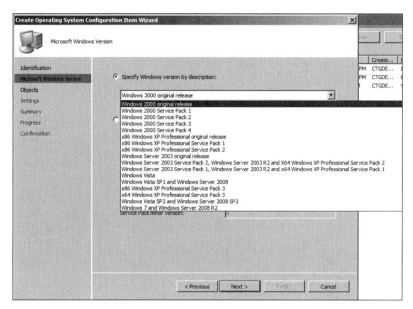

Figure 14.21
Operating Systems List

Details option. If you want to automatically fill in the fields with an operating system version, select it from the Specify Windows Version By Description drop-down and then select the Specify Windows Version By Details button. You can then change the version number that matches the full operating system version.

Configuration Baselines

Baselines contain one or more configuration items that need to be evaluated against systems within your site. When you create a baseline, you need to determine which configuration items will make up the baseline. Once created, all of the configuration items within the baseline will be evaluated according to the baseline's settings. Baselines are associated with collections, and every system within the collection will be evaluated accordingly. Baselines can contain several configuration items and a configuration item can be associated with one or more baselines. You are not required to create unique configuration items for each baseline.

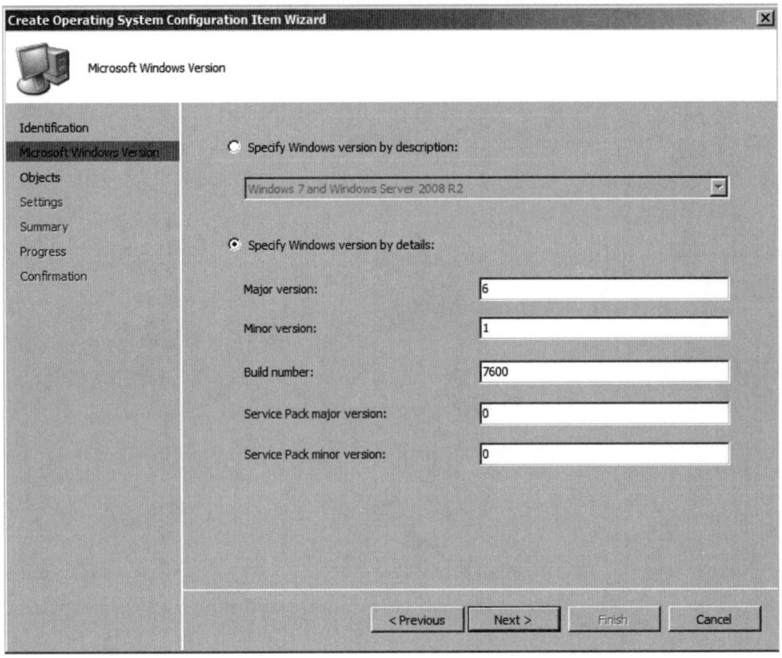

Figure 14.22
Windows Versions

If you look at Figure 14.23, you will see a configuration baseline that contains configuration items that need to be evaluated on a system. Once the configuration baseline has been defined, it can be assigned to a collection. Collection assignment is very easy and can be performed in a couple of ways. From the Configuration Baselines node, you can right-click a baseline and select the option Assign to a Collection. If you right-click on a collection, one of the options you will find is Assign Configuration Baseline.

Both methods of assigning a baseline to a collection allow you to select one or more baselines that will be assigned to a single collection; they just do it with different configuration options. Figure 14.24 displays the wizard that appears when you assign a baseline from the Configuration Baselines node. This is the traditional wizard that you will see in many different Configuration Manager configuration options. The first page of the wizard allows you to select other baselines that you want to assign along with the baseline that you right-clicked

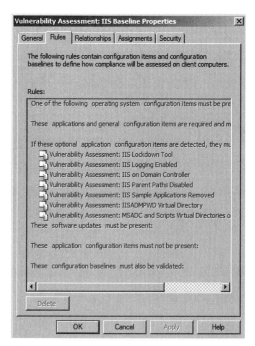

Figure 14.23
Configuration Baseline

to start the wizard. The next page, seen in Figure 14.25, has you select the collection that you are going to assign the baseline(s). The final configuration page allows you to specify the evaluation schedule for the baseline/collection. Each baseline can have a different schedule for each collection that is it assigned to. So you could have a baseline that is assigned to two different collections. The schedule for the first collection could run daily at 7:00 AM and the second collection evaluation schedule could be set to run every three hours.

Role of Collections

Collections perform essentially the same function for DCM as they do for software distribution. Client systems that need to be evaluated are added to the collection where a baseline is assigned. Once added to the collection, the client system will be evaluated on the schedule that is set for the baseline or baselines that are assigned to the collection. You can create collections to contain all of the different baseline evaluations you need for your organization.

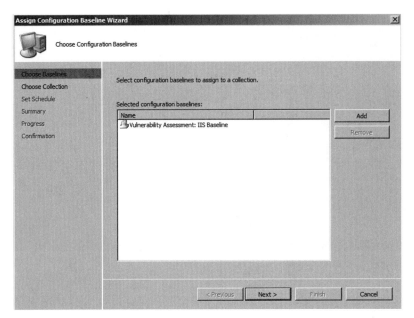

Figure 14.24
Baseline Assignment Wizard

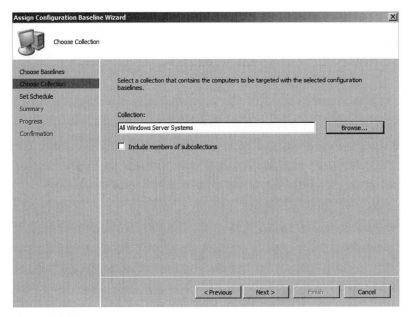

Figure 14.25
Selecting Collection for Assignment Status

Figure 14.26
DCM Collection Hierarchy

Because collections are used as the organizational object for DCM, creating collections specifically for DCM should be considered. Chances are, the systems that you need to evaluate won't fit neatly into the same groupings as software distribution, operating system deployment, or software updates. Building a hierarchy of collections will allow you to define each collection's membership and isolate the collections from being used for any of these other purposes. One option for creating collections for this purpose is to create an empty collection named Desired Configuration Management Collections. Then create subcollections for each of the system types that you need to evaluate. You can also create collections based on the evaluation that is performed and not on a specific server or operating system type. Figure 14.26 shows an example of collections created for DCM purposes.

Once the collections are created, systems that need to be evaluated for compliance will have to be added as members to the collections. As with any collection, the members can be added to the collection based upon direct membership rules or by using a query. Queries are preferred due to the fact that as systems are added to your network, the systems will be dynamically added and removed from the collection. However, there is merit to using direct membership; once a system is added to the membership of the collection, it will not fall out of the collection until someone manually removes it. Using direct membership guarantees that a system will not be removed from the collection when an invalid configuration change occurs.

Which brings us to another point—when using queries to manage the collection membership, make sure that you do not base the collection membership query on anything that is evaluated by a configuration item. As you can probably imagine, doing so could cause the system to be removed from the collection before the evaluation takes place. You would not be notified of a non-compliant situation if that happens. For example, let's say you are basing your collection on systems that have a specific file resident in a specific folder, and at the same time a configuration item is monitoring for the existence of the file. If the file is accidentally removed, there is a good chance that the system will be removed from the collection before the compliance evaluation occurs.

Preconfigured Baselines

There are several preconfigured DCM baselines and configuration items available from Microsoft and third-party companies. Most of these can be found on the Microsoft corporate website at http://pinpoint.microsoft.com/en-US/systemcenter/managementpackcatalog. You can look through the catalog by filtering the search criteria to only display configuration packs. Take time to peruse these configuration packs as you might find one that will meet your needs. You will find several that are good starting points for compliance monitoring, including configuration packs for HIPAA, FISMA, Graham-Leach-Bliley, and SOX compliance monitoring. Do take note that these are good starting points for compliance monitoring, but they are not comprehensive. You will still need to "tune" them for your individual needs.

DCM Reports

There are several reports that are included with Configuration Manager. These reports make it easy for you to determine the compliance status for systems within your site. Some reports are very detailed, whereas others display summary information.

- All compliance evaluation failures for a specified computer
- Compliance details for a configuration baseline
- Compliance details for a configuration baseline by configuration item
- Compliance details for a configuration baseline for a specified computer
- Compliance evaluation errors for a configuration baseline by configuration item on a computer
- Compliance evaluation errors for a configuration baseline on a computer
- Compliance evaluation errors for a configuration item on a computer
- Compliance for a computer by configuration baseline

- Compliance for a computer by configuration item
- Compliance history for a configuration item on a computer
- Computers reporting non-compliance for a specific configuration item validation criteria
- Computers with compliance evaluation failures
- Computers with compliance evaluation failures for a specific configuration baseline
- Computers with compliance evaluation failures for a specific configuration item
- Configuration baseline assignments by collection
- Configuration baseline assignments for a computer
- Non-compliance details for a configuration item on a computer
- Summary compliance by configuration baseline
- Summary compliance by configuration item
- Summary compliance for a collection by computer
- Summary compliance for a collection by configuration baseline
- Summary compliance for a collection by configuration item
- Summary compliance for a configuration item by computer
- Summary non-compliance for a configuration baseline by validation criteria
- Summary non-compliance for a configuration item by validation criteria

THE FINAL WORD

Making sure you know when critical systems are no longer configured correctly is vital to many organizations. The overall health of the systems within the organization can be adversely affected if settings are changed or misconfigured. Desired Configuration Management allows administrators to detect when systems are no longer compliant by monitoring many of the settings on the systems. The Configuration Manager client will check the specified settings at a predetermined schedule and then send a compliant or non-compliant message to the site server.

In the next chapter, we will discuss another method of making sure systems are configured correctly. Network Access Protection is used to validate a system before it can communicate with systems on the production network. Configuration Manager 2007 can be used in conjunction with Network Access Protection to remediate the systems that are non-compliant.

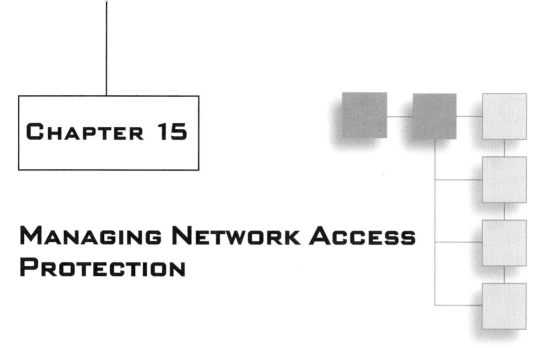

CHAPTER 15

MANAGING NETWORK ACCESS PROTECTION

Let's be honest. If you're a systems administrator, you're more than likely a control freak. If so, you'll love the Network Access Protection (NAP) component included with Configuration Manager 2007. NAP is a free component that is built into Windows Server 2008 (and higher) class operating systems and is available across multiple platforms including Windows, Linux, and Mac. In addition to being available on multiple platforms, third-party software vendors can write their products to work with NAP to detect specific settings within their software to extend the default capabilities of NAP. If NAP is in an enforcement mode, non-compliant systems are denied access to the full network until they can be remediated. If NAP is in reporting mode, non-compliant systems only send reporting information and do not restrict access to the network. If automatic remediation is enabled, clients attempt to fix the problem, automatically, by changing settings or downloading files such as required software updates or antivirus signatures. The concept behind this technology is fairly easy to understand but can be a little confusing to implement because of the number of components involved. In this chapter, we'll create a basic NAP infrastructure and finally integrate Configuration Manager 2007 with NAP and demonstrate how this component works.

NAP AND CONFIGURATION MANAGER 2007

One of the biggest areas of confusion in regards to NAP is understanding where Configuration Manager fits into the puzzle. What most people fail to realize is that NAP is not a Configuration Manager specific technology. In fact, different versions of this technology have been around for years such as the Network Access Quarantine Control (NAQC) component that was introduced with Windows Server 2003. This feature required that remote computers connecting to the corporate network using VPN or dial-up connections met specific requirements before being allowed in to the internal network. Starting with Windows Server 2008, Microsoft replaced NAQC with NAP, which expanded on the original premise of NAQC by restricting network access to both external and internal systems. Because of the huge interest in NAP, the Configuration Manager team decided to allow Configuration Manager 2007 to integrate into NAP so that administrators could even further expand on the types of requirements that had to be met prior to allowing network access.

Benefits of NAP with Configuration Manager 2007

Now that we've explained that NAP is its own separate technology, you might be wondering, if NAP is separate from Configuration Manager 2007, what benefits do you gain by integrating NAP with Configuration Manager? That's a very good question. The answer is that you can require specific software updates to be installed before a computer is allowed on the network. Although you can enforce similar restrictions using built-in NAP components, you can only restrict network access to computers that do not have automatic updating enabled or "all available security updates installed." When Configuration Manager 2007 is integrated with NAP, you can choose the specific software update(s) that must be installed before the computer is allowed on the network.

Note

Before integrating Configuration Manager 2007 with NAP, a basic NAP infrastructure must first be in place. I highly recommend that you slowly implement NAP using a phased in approach to prevent possible problems. Once the basic infrastructure is in place, you can then begin to expand on NAP by integrating third-party NAP components such as the one included with Configuration Manager 2007. Using this phased-in approach, you can narrow down issues to NAP or Configuration Manager 2007.

NAP Fundamentals

NAP is implemented by using multiple servers and components to validate, enforce, and remediate clients. Understanding the basic functions of these components and servers will help you better understand how to implement NAP so that you can eventually use the NAP component of Configuration Manager 2007.

NAP Components and Terminology

This section briefly describes the major components used within a NAP infrastructure.

NAP Agent

The NAP client agent is installed on supported client systems and must be enabled so that one or more system health agents can send their state of health to their corresponding system health validators. This is implemented as a system service called the network access protection agent. This service can be enabled manually on the client image or via group policy settings.

State of Health

A system's state of health (SoH) is used to verify if the client is in a compliant state. System health agents evaluate clients and generate a SoH based on their findings. The SoH is then passed onto a system health validator, which checks for compliancy based on predefined policies.

System Health Agents

System health agents (SHAs) are installed locally on client systems and are used to determine and generate a client's SoH. Multiple SHAs can be installed on a single client, each one designed to evaluate specific settings.

Note

Typically, software vendors create SHAs to monitor different aspects about their software such as if an antivirus client has up-to-date definitions.

The Windows Security health agent (WSHA), which is included by default in Windows Vista/7, monitors the Windows Security Center for issues and generates a SoH based on these results. Although the WSHA is the only one provided by default, other software vendors can create custom SHAs to gather specific information about their products. Microsoft, for example, has created SHAs for some of their other products such as Forefront Client Security and Configuration Manager 2007. When the Configuration Manager 2007 client is installed, the Configuration Manager health agent (SCCM SHA) is installed as well.

System Health Validators

System health validators (SHVs) are installed on server class operating systems and are configured within the network policy server (NPS) console. Since the NPS role is only available to Windows Server 2008 and higher, older operating systems cannot be used to implement NAP. Included by default with the NPS role is the Windows Security health validator, which is used to validate SoH information as reported by its corresponding SHA (the WSHA). When the system health validator point is added to a site system via Configuration Manager 2007, it also installs the Configuration Manager system health validator.

Health Registration Authority

A health registration authority is a component of NAP that is needed when using the IPsec enforcement method. Health registration authorities are used to verify client credentials and request certificates on behalf of the NAP client. Health registration authorities are servers that run Windows Server 2008 (or higher) with the NPS role installed.

Network Policy Server Role

The network policy server (NPS) role is added through the Server Manager and contains multiple components including a RADIUS and NAP health evaluation server. The NAP health evaluation server contains policies and SHVs that are used to evaluate a client's SoH.

System Health Validator Point

The system health validator point is a role within Configuration Manager 2007 that is used to integrate Configuration Manager 2007 into NAP. This role must be added to a site system that already is configured with the NPS role for the integration to be successful. Once this site system role is added, the Configuration Manager system health validator is added within the NPS console.

NAP Server Roles

NAP uses different servers within its architecture to validate, enforce, and remediate client computers using the components described above. The following servers are used within NAP.

Enforcement Servers

Enforcement servers are designed to allow or disallow network access based on the response from a NAP health policy server. NAP clients first send their SoH to enforcement servers, which then forward these messages to health policy servers. Based on the client's SoH and the health policies defined, the NAP client is typically granted or denied network access. In most cases, NAP clients are not completely denied access but are instead placed on a restricted network so that remediation can occur. The type of NAP enforcement dictates the type of enforcement server that must be used. For example, if you are using DHCP enforcement, the DHCP server itself acts as the enforcement server. If you use the 802.1x enforcement method, a switch or access point might be the enforcement server. In this case, these devices are referred to as NAP enforcement points.

Health Policy Servers

NAP health policy servers are Windows Server 2008 or Windows Server 2008 R2 servers with the NPS role installed. They use system health validators and NAP policies to determine a client's compliancy. Health policy servers typically need to be able to communicate with NAP clients on the restricted network as well as unrestricted services such as domain controllers or health requirement servers that may reside on the corporate network. This is especially true if they must perform user authentication for VPN or 802.1x enforcement methods.

Health Requirement Server

Health requirement servers are optional to NAP and are only required when SHVs need to obtain health requirements that are defined outside of the health policy server. Configuration Manager 2007 creates health state references that are stored in Active Directory, which are used by the Configuration Manager SHV to check health requirements. In this case, domain controllers would be considered as health requirement servers.

Remediation Servers

Remediation servers are used to provide basic networking services to non-compliant computers so that they can be remediated and allowed access to the network. Depending on the enforcement method, remediation servers might include domain controllers, DNS servers, DHCP servers, antivirus definition servers, WSUS servers, Configuration Manager 2007 distribution points, and more. When using NAP with Configuration Manager 2007, distribution points must be configured as remediation servers so that clients can gain access to the necessary software updates while on the restricted network.

METHODS OF ENFORCEMENT

When an SHA reports a client's SoH to its corresponding SHV, the client is evaluated against NAP policies for compliancy. If the client is in a non-compliant state, it may be restricted from accessing the network if enforcement is enabled. NAP supports five methods to restrict a non-compliant computer from accessing the network.

DHCP

Although DHCP enforcement is the easiest to implement, it's also the easiest to bypass. DHCP enforcement is achieved when a system renews its IP address from a NAP-enabled DHCP server (enforcement server). If the client is in a non-compliant state, the DHCP server sets the client's subnet mask as 255.255.255.255. If you don't have much experience with subnetting, this basically means that only one host can be a part of the network. In other words, the client PC is the only node allowed on the network. To obtain access to remediation servers, remediation server groups can be used. When a server is added to a remediation server group, the DHCP enforcement method defines static routes on client PCs to direct traffic to these servers.

Caution

Setting a static IP address on the client can bypass the DHCP enforcement method.

802.1x

If you have 802.1x compatible network devices, you can restrict network access to non-compliant systems by placing them on restricted VLANs or by using ACLs. To obtain access to remediation servers, these servers must be on the same restricted VLAN or must be permitted in the ACL. Multi-homed or trunked NICs can be used to permit access to both the restricted and unrestricted networks if necessary.

RD Gateway

If you need to access internal systems from the Internet, an RD Gateway server can be used instead of a traditional VPN server. NAP makes use of RD Gateway servers to restrict access to non-compliant computers by denying connections to the internal network. To obtain access to remediation servers, they must be accessible from the Internet.

Note

> TS Gateway was renamed to RD Gateway in Windows Server 2008 R2. Prior to R2, remediation was not available using this enforcement method.

IPsec

If you use IPsec to secure communications within your organization, you can use NAP to allow access only to clients that have successfully obtained the required client certificate. To obtain access to remediation servers, NAP exemption certificates are issued to non-compliant computers and remediation servers. This is the most secure enforcement method of NAP.

VPN

If you use remote access VPN connections to gain access to the internal network, NAP can deny these connections if clients are in a non-compliant state. To obtain access to remediation servers, IP filters or remediation server groups can be used.

NAP ENFORCEMENT MODES

NAP includes three enforcement modes that dictate how the client acts when it is deemed non-compliant. These three modes are as follows:

- **Reporting Mode**—This mode enables you to collect information about non-compliant computers without presenting end users with notifications or restricting them from the network.

- **Deferred Enforcement Mode**—This mode enables you to restrict network access for non-compliant computers by defining a deadline of when remediation must occur. End users can be notified about the computer's non-compliant state and can manually remediate their computer via the NAP UI. If the computer is not remediated by the defined deadline, the computer will be put into a restricted network. If auto remediation is enabled, remediation can occur automatically.

- **Full Enforcement**—This mode enables you to restrict network access for computers as soon as they enter a non-compliant state. End users can be notified about the computer's non-complaint state and can manually remediate their computer via the NAP UI. If auto remediation is enabled, remediation can occur automatically.

Note

Users must have administrative access to manually remediate the client.

When you first implement NAP, it is recommended to start with reporting mode so that you can get an idea of the impact that NAP will have on your environment. After evaluating these results, you can then enable deferred or full enforcement mode.

CONFIGURING NAP

Because a functioning NAP environment must be in place before it can be integrated with Configuration Manager 2007, we'll quickly setup NAP using the DHCP enforcement method. Once all of the components have been configured, we'll test a client to make sure that NAP is working as expected.

For simplicity's sake, our test environment will use a single server to host both the NPS and DHCP roles. Because these roles are on the same server, this server will be our enforcement server (implemented within the DHCP role) as well as our health policy server (implemented within the NPS role). In a production environment, these roles may need to be separated and setup for redundancy. Please make sure to follow Microsoft's guidelines on designing a proper NAP infrastructure.

Installing the NPS Role

To start our NAP infrastructure setup, we must first install the NPS role. Adding this role enables us to use this server as our health policy server, which is responsible for evaluating a client's SoH. In our example, we'll use CHI-SITESYSTEM to host the NPS role. To install and configure the NPS role, do the following:

1. Open the Server Manager by going to Start, right-clicking on Computer, and left-clicking on Manage.

2. Once the Server Manager opens, left-click on the Roles node.

3. The Roles Summary window is displayed. Click on Add Roles to continue.

4. The Before You Begin window is displayed. Click Next to continue.

5. The Server Roles window is displayed. Click the checkbox next to Network Policy and Access Services and click Next to continue (Figure 15.1).

6. The Network Policy and Access Services introduction window is displayed. Click Next to continue (Figure 15.2).

7. When the Network Policy and Access Services Role Services window is displayed, check the Network Policy Server option, then click Next to continue (Figure 15.3).

8. When the Network Policy and Access Confirmation window is displayed, click Install.

9. When the Network Policy and Access Results window is displayed, click Close.

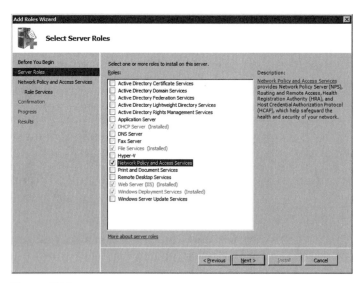

Figure 15.1
Add Server Roles Window

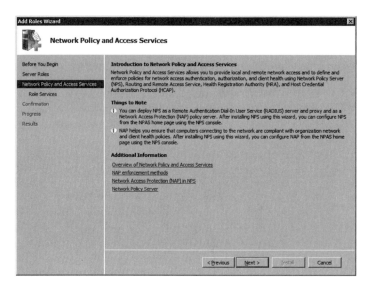

Figure 15.2
Network Policy and Access Services Introduction Window

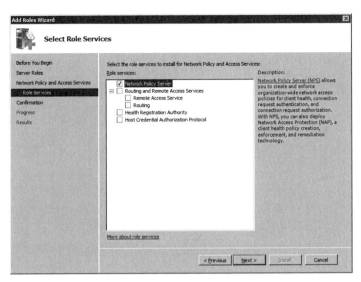

Figure 15.3
Add NPS Option

Configuring the Health Policy Server for DHCP Enforcement

Now that the NPS role has been installed, it needs to be configured as a health policy server for DHCP enforcement. Follow the steps below to configure the health policy server.

1. Open NPS console by going to Start > Administrative Tools > Network Policy Server (Figure 15.4).

2. On the Getting Started page, click the Configure NAP link (Figure 15.5).

3. The Configure NAP Wizard is displayed. Under the Network connection method drop-down box, choose Dynamic Host Configuration Protocol (DHCP) and click Next to continue (Figure 15.6).

4. The Specify NAP Enforcement Servers Running DHCP section of the wizard is displayed. This allows you to specify the DHCP server(s) that will be used as NAP enforcement servers. Since we are running DHCP on this server, we do not need to specify remote DHCP servers in this example. Click Next to continue (Figure 15.7).

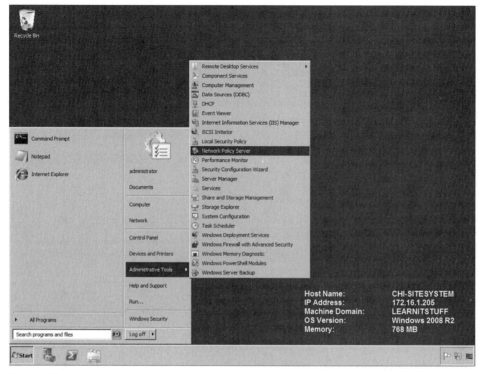

Figure 15.4
Starting the NAP Console

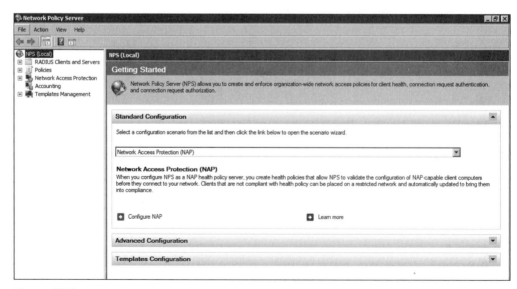

Figure 15.5
Configure NAP within the NPS Console

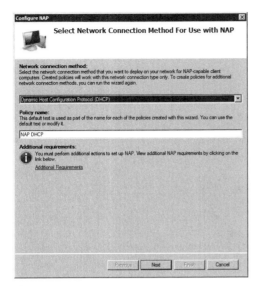

Figure 15.6
Use DHCP Connection Method

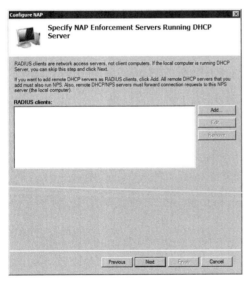

Figure 15.7
Specify Remote DHCP Enforcement Servers

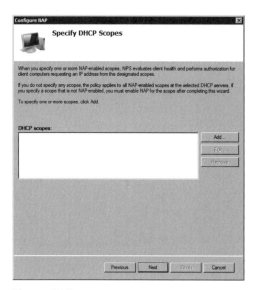

Figure 15.8
Specify DHCP Scopes

5. The Specify DHCP Scopes section of the wizard is displayed. This allows you to specify one or more NAP-enabled DHCP scopes that will be used to restrict network access. If you don't choose any scopes, all scopes will be used. Since we only have one scope defined, we'll simply click Next to continue (Figure 15.8).

6. The Configure Machine Groups section of the wizard is displayed. This allows you to specify predefined machine groups that this policy will apply to. Since we want this policy to apply to all computers, we'll leave this set as the default and click Next to continue (Figure 15.9).

7. The Specify a NAP Remediation Server Group and URL section of the wizard is displayed. This is where you specify your remediation servers and troubleshooting URL for your clients. In our example, we'll add our domain controller/DNS server as a remediation server so that clients on the restricted network can access basic domain services. Click New Group to configure a remediation server group (Figure 15.10).

8. The New Remediation Server Group window is displayed. In the Group Name field, type a name for your remediation server group. In our

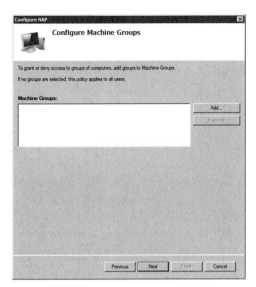

Figure 15.9
Specify Machine Groups

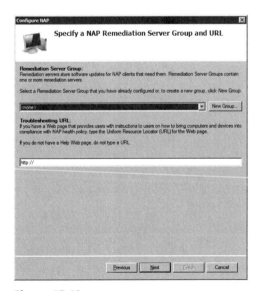

Figure 15.10
Specify Remediation Server Group

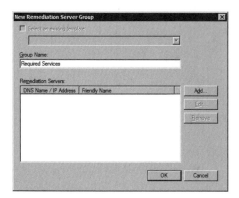

Figure 15.11
New Remediation Server Group

Figure 15.12
Create Remediation Server Group

example, we'll use Required Services. Click Add to specify your remediation servers (Figure 15.11).

9. The Add New Server window is displayed. This allows you to add specified remediation servers to your remediation server group. In the Friendly name field, type a name to identify your remediation server. In our example, we'll choose DC/DNS. In the IP address or DNS name, type in the IP address or DNS name of your remediation server. In our example, we'll choose LIS-DC. Repeat this process for each remediation server that you wish to add to the group. Click OK to close the Add New Server window, click OK to close the New Remediation Server Group window, and then click Next to continue (Figure 15.12).

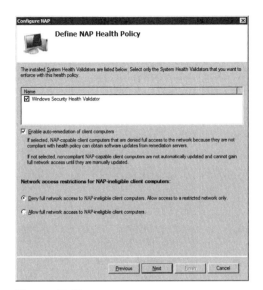

Figure 15.13
Define NAP Health Policy

10. The Define NAP Health Policy window is displayed. This allows you to specify one or more SHVs to use for enforcement. You can also specify whether auto-remediation is enabled for your clients and how to handle clients that are not NAP capable. Note that because the system health validator point role has not yet been added to this server, the Configuration Manager SHV is not listed. In our example, we'll keep the defaults and click Next to continue (Figure 15.13).

11. The NAP Enforcement Policy Completion and Summary section of the wizard is displayed. This gives you an overview of what was configured using the wizard. If all looks correct, click Finish to close the wizard.

Configuring the Windows Security Health Validator

Now that the health policy has been defined to use the Windows Security health validator, we need to configure the WSHV. In our environment, we'll specify that the Windows firewall must be enabled to be considered compliant. To configure these options, follow the steps below.

1. Open NPS console by going to Start > Administrative Tools > Network Policy Server.

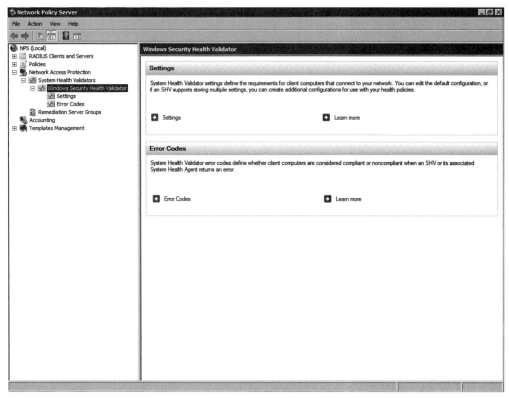

Figure 15.14
WSHV Settings

2. Expand the Network Access Protection node, expand the System Health Validators node, and highlight the Windows Security Health Validator node (Figure 15.14).

3. The options for the WSHV are displayed including settings and error codes. In our example, we'll only worry about the Settings node. Under the Settings node, a list of all configurations for the SHV is shown. By default, only the default configuration is listed. We will modify the default configuration for our environment. To modify the default configuration, right-click and choose Properties.

4. The settings for the WSHV are displayed. In our example, we'll uncheck all options except for the A Firewall Is Enabled for All Network Connections option for demonstration purposes. Click OK to save these changes (Figure 15.15).

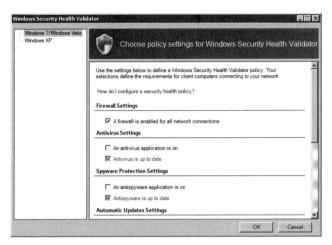

Figure 15.15
WSHV Settings

Configuring DHCP for NAP

Now that the NPS role has been installed and the WSHV policy has been configured, we must enable our DHCP scope for NAP by following the steps below. Note that in this example, the DHCP role has already been installed and configured with an active IPv4 scope. To enable the scope for NAP, follow the instructions below:

1. Open DHCP console by going to Start > Administrative Tools > DHCP (Figure 15.16).

2. Expand the Server node and highlight the scope that you want to enable for NAP. Right-click the scope and choose Properties (Figure 15.17).

3. The Scope Properties window is displayed. Click the Network Access Protection tab and enable NAP for this scope by selecting Enable for This Scope. Click OK to continue (Figure 15.18).

4. Expand the NAP-enabled scope and highlight the Scope Options node. Notice that three options (003 Router, 006 DNS Servers, and 015 DNS Name) were defined during the initial scope setup and their class is defined as none (Figure 15.19).

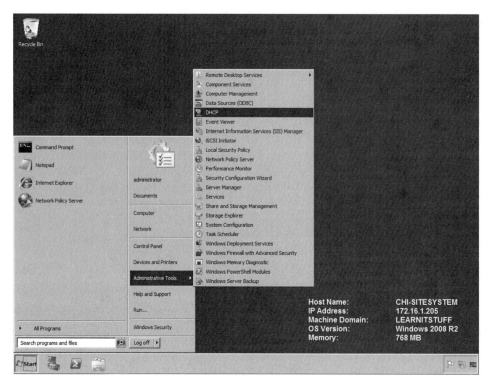

Figure 15.16
Starting the DHCP Console

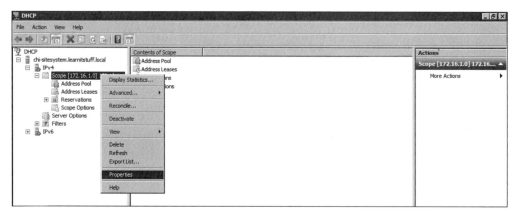

Figure 15.17
Open the Properties of a Scope

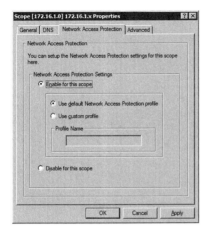

Figure 15.18
Enable NAP for a Scope

Figure 15.19
Standard Scope Options

Note

These options are used for DHCP-enabled clients that meet the health policy requirements and that are deemed compliant.

5. To specify the options that will be delivered to non-compliant computers, we must create new options using the Network Access Protection Class. To do this, right-click on the Scope Options node and choose Configure Options. When the Scope Option window is displayed, click the Advanced tab and select Network Access Protection Class from the User Class drop-down menu (Figure 15.20).

6. Now that the Network Access Protection Class has been selected, the options that were configured under the user class (Router, DNS Servers, DNS Name) are no longer configured. In our example, we will configure

Figure 15.20
Change from User Class to Network Access Protection Class

Figure 15.21
Configuring NAP Class Options

the NAP class with the same options that were defined in the user class. In the DNS Name, however, we will use restricted.learnitstuff.local as shown in Figure 15.21. Once these options are set, click OK. Both user class and NAP options are displayed in the scope as shown in Figure 15.22.

Option Name	Vendor	Value	Class
003 Router	Standard	172.16.1.254	Default Network Access Protection Class
003 Router	Standard	172.16.1.254	None
006 DNS Servers	Standard	172.16.1.200	Default Network Access Protection Class
015 DNS Domain Name	Standard	restricted.learnitstuff.local	Default Network Access Protection Class
006 DNS Servers	Standard	172.16.1.200	None
015 DNS Domain Name	Standard	learnitstuff.local	None

Figure 15.22
User and NAP Classes

NAP in Action

Now that we have the server side of NAP configured, we can see what happens to a client when used in a NAP-enabled environment. There are three primary categories of NAP clients:

- Compliant clients
- Non-compliant clients
- NAP-ineligible clients

We've talked a lot about how a client is determined to be compliant or non-compliant, but what about clients that simply don't support NAP? Clients classified as NAP-ineligible can be granted or denied full network access as defined in the NAP health policy as shown earlier in Figure 15.13. NAP-ineligible clients might be network devices such as print servers, clients using legacy operating systems, or clients using NAP-eligible operating systems that have not been configured for NAP. We'll talk about these scenarios next.

Behavior of NAP-Ineligible Clients

Although Windows Vista and Windows 7 natively support NAP, these clients are seen as NAP-ineligible when the NAP agent (the NAP service) is not enabled. By default, this service is set to disabled and does not start automatically. Because the service cannot send information to the NAP infrastructure, these clients are deemed NAP-ineligible and are potentially placed on a restricted network as defined by the NAP health policy. In our example, the NAP health policy is configured to deny full network access to NAP-ineligible clients. Figure 15.23 shows the result of a Windows 7 client when the NAP service is in a disabled state:

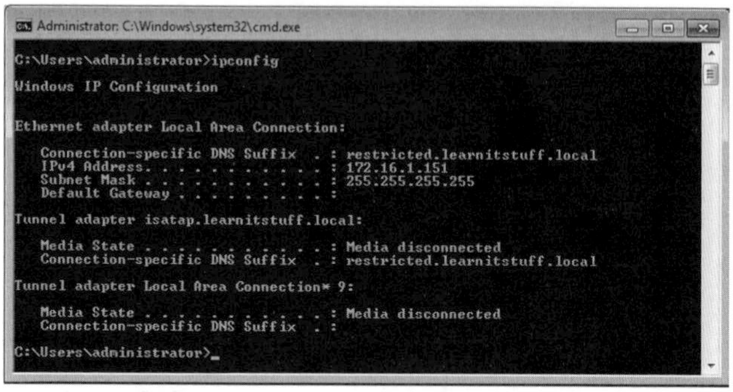

Figure 15.23
DHCP NAP Enforcement

Figure 15.24
Static Routes

Tip

To help simplify NAP client configurations, use group policy to enable the NAP client service.

Even if the requirements of the policy are met, the client will be placed on the restricted network until the NAP service starts. We talked a little about this in Chapter 13 regarding the setup of the client image. If the image is setup with the NAP service as disabled, it might not be able to access the network. In Figure 15.23, we see that even though the client has a valid IP address, the subnet mask is set to 255.255.255.255, which prevents access to other devices on the network. In Figure 15.24, we see the output of the route print -4 command.

Figure 15.24 shows that 172.16.1.205 (CHI-SITESYSTEM) is the only server that has been configured with a static route. This is because CHI-SITESYSTEM is the enforcement server that the client will always have access to. We'll talk more about static routes with DHCP NAP enforcement in a bit.

Behavior of Non-Compliant Clients

When a NAP-eligible client is deemed non-compliant and the NAP health policy dictates that it be placed on a restricted network, the same results that we saw in Figure 15.23 take place on the non-compliant client. This time, however, the end user is notified and can potentially remediate the computer so that it can be re-evaluated and allowed full access to the network. When a user is initially notified about a non-compliant NAP status, they see it as a standard system notification, as seen in Figure 15.25.

When a client is in a non-compliant state and the route print -4 command is issued, the static routes shown in Figure 15.26 are displayed.

Note that along with 172.16.1.205 (CHI-SITESYSTEM), 172.16.1.200 is now listed as well. This is LIS-DC, our DNS and domain controller that we defined as a remediation server back in Figure 15.12. This is how the DHCP NAP enforcement method provides access to remediation servers.

Note

Because auto-remediation is enabled within our health policy, the firewall is automatically enabled and the client is allowed access to the network. Because this change does not require the client to download files, no remediation servers are needed.

INTEGRATE CONFIGURATION MANAGER 2007 WITH NAP

Now that the native NAP components have been configured, let's integrate Configuration Manager 2007 so that we can use its custom SHV and SHA to

Figure 15.25
NAP End User Notification

Figure 15.26
New Static Routes

report on software update compliancy. This is done by installing and enabling several components within the Configuration Manager infrastructure. If you already have a working NAP infrastructure with multiple health policies, SHAs, and SHVs, you may also need to add or modify these items for Configuration Manager to work correctly.

System Health Validator Point

Only one system health validator point needs to be installed for a Configuration Manager hierarchy. It is recommended to install this role in the central site because the policies that are defined flow down to all clients in lower sites. For the sake of consistency, we'll install this role in the CHI primary site instead of the LIS central site by installing this to CHI-SITESYSTEM. For detailed information on the prerequisites and configuration steps, see Chapter 6, "Configuring Site System Roles."

Site servers publish something called the health state reference to the system management container in Active Directory. The health state reference is used to identify the Configuration Manager's site code and the date of the Configuration Manager NAP policy. The system health validator point periodically downloads and caches the health state reference to identify if the client is in a compliant state. Because the state of reference is published to Active Directory, the schema must be extended for this to occur.

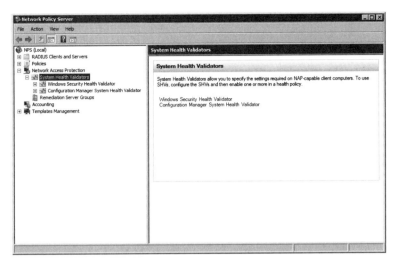

Figure 15.27
Configuration Manager SHV

Using the Configuration Manager System Health Validator

Once the system health validator point is installed, the Configuration Manager system health validator (CMSHV) can be seen within the NPS console, as shown in Figure 15.27.

Unlike the Windows security health validator (WSHV), no options can be configured within the CMSHV. The compliancy settings that you define for your clients are done via the Configuration Manager console in the Network Access Protection node. Before you can use the CMSHV, you have to specify that it be used in the existing DHCP NAP policies instead of the WHSV. To do this, follow the steps below:

1. Open NPS console by going to Start > Administrative Tools > Network Policy Server.

2. Expand the Policies node and highlight Health Policies. The configured health policies are shown. In our example, the configured health policies are NAP DHCP Compliant and NAP DHCP Noncompliant (Figure 15.28).

3. Right-click on the NAP DHCP Compliant health policy and choose Properties. The Settings tab for the health policy is displayed. Uncheck

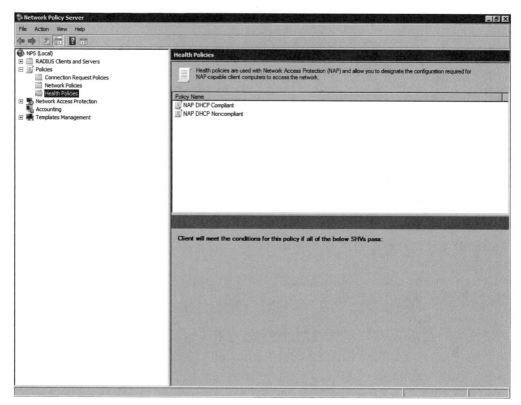

Figure 15.28
NAP Health Policies

the Windows Security health validator and check the Configuration Manager system health validator. Repeat these steps for the NAP DHCP Noncompliant health policy. Click OK to continue (Figure 15.29).

Note

In a production environment, there could be multiple health policies that use multiple SHVs to check compliancy. Remember that this example is simplified and is configured for demonstration purposes only.

Configuration Manager System Health Validator Component Properties

Depending on your environment, you may need to change the properties of the CMSHV, which is done via the Configuration Manager console by going to Site Settings > Component Configuration > System Health Validator Component.

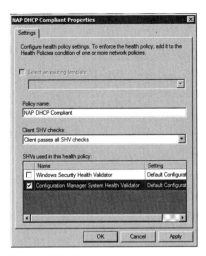

Figure 15.29
Enabling the Configuration Manager System Health Validator

The settings on the General and Health State Reference tabs are shown in Figures 15.30 and 15.31 and are described next:

General Tab

- **Active Directory query interval**—This option specifies how often (in minutes) that the system health validator point downloads and caches the health state reference from Active Directory. The recommended value for this option is to be twice the value of the policy polling interval, which is 60 minutes by default. Because of this, this option is set as 120 minutes by default.

- **Statement of health time validation period**—This option specifies the amount of time that a client's cached SoH is considered valid. If this setting is too low, clients may be forced to re-evaluate their compliancy status and send a new SoH. This means that the client could take a longer time to become compliant, causing user frustration. However, if this setting is too high, you risk your computers being seen as compliant when they are actually non-compliant.

- **Date created must be after (UTC)**—This option specifies that the client's SoH is created after a specified time. This option should only be used when it is necessary for clients to be up-to-date with the latest NAP policies.

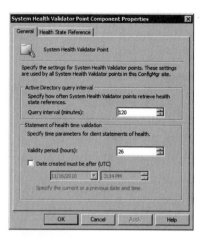

Figure 15.30
General Tab

Figure 15.31
Health State Reference Tab

Health State Reference Tab

- **Use the same Active Directory forest**—By default, the site server will publish the health state reference to the Active Directory forest that it belongs to. This option is the default.

- **Designate an Active Directory forest**—This option allows you to specify the Active Directory forest that the health state reference is published to.

- **Domain suffix**— This option allows you to specify the fully qualified domain name of the Active Directory forest where the health state reference is published.

- **Health state reference publishing account**—If the computer account of the site server does not have appropriate access rights to the specified Active Directory forest, use this option to specify an account that does. Must be in the domain\user format.

- **Health state reference querying account**—If the computer account of the site server does not have appropriate access to read from the specified Active Directory forest, use this option to specify an account that does. Must be in the domain\user format.

Configuration Manager NAP Remediation Servers

As part of the Configuration Manager 2007 integration with NAP, make sure that your site systems hosting roles such as management points and distribution points are configured as remediation servers so that clients can access them when on the restricted network. To add or modify remediation servers, open the NPS console and navigate to Network Access Protection > Remediation Server Groups.

Enable the Configuration Manager 2007 NAP Client Agent

Before clients can use the Configuration Manager NAP client agent (the SCCM SHA), it must be enabled in the Configuration Manager console. This is done by navigating to Site Settings > Client Agents > Network Access Protection Client Agent. Once enabled, you can start configuring your Configuration Manager NAP policies.

CONFIGURATION MANAGER NAP POLICIES

Configuration Manager 2007 NAP policies are configured within the Configuration Manager console in a site that has been enabled for NAP. A site that has been enabled for NAP contains a site system with the system health validator point role installed and the NAP client agent enabled. Once these settings have been enabled, the Policies node under the Network Access Protection node is displayed and can be used to create policies.

Note

Because the NAP functionality within Configuration Manager 2007 is specifically designed to check for and install software updates on NAP-enabled clients, the software update component must be configured with at least one deployment package that contains software updates pertaining to NAP clients.

To create a Configuration Manager 2007 NAP policy, open the Configuration Manager console at a NAP-enabled site and do the following:

1. Navigate to Computer Configuration > Network Access Protection > Policies.

2. Right-click the Policies node and choose New Policies (Figure 15.32).

3. The New Policies Wizard is displayed. This allows you to choose specific software updates (from predefined deployment packages) that must be installed on your NAP-enabled clients for them to pass compliancy checks. In our example, we'll choose all Windows 7 x86 updates and click Next to continue (Figure 15.33).

4. The set NAP Evaluation section of the wizard is displayed. This allows you to specify when the policy becomes effective. After the policy

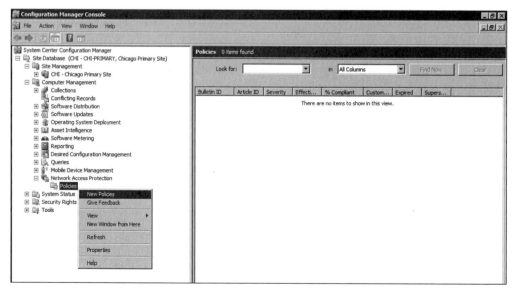

Figure 15.32
Create NAP Policies

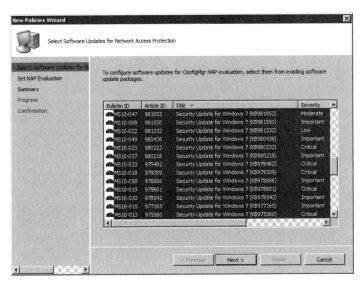

Figure 15.33
Specifying Software Updates for NAP

becomes effective, the software updates specified in the last step must be installed or the client may be denied full network access. In our example, we'll choose "As soon as possible" and click Next to continue (Figure 15.34).

5. The Summary section of the wizard is displayed. If the information looks correct, click Next to continue.

6. The Confirmation section of the wizard is displayed. If any errors were encountered during the wizard, they will be displayed here. Click Close to close the wizard.

Tip

Remember that Configuration Manager NAP policies flow down to all child sites within the hierarchy. This is why it is recommended to NAP enable the central site.

CONFIGURATION MANAGER NAP CLIENT BEHAVIOR

Now that we have the Configuration Manager NAP infrastructure configured, we can see what happens to a NAP-enabled Configuration Manager client when the required software updates are not installed.

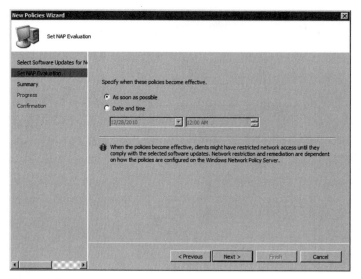

Figure 15.34
Specify NAP Evaluation

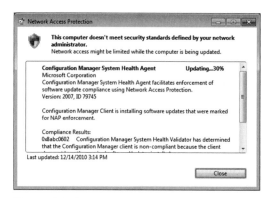

Figure 15.35
Remediation Progress

Like we showed earlier in Figure 15.25, the end-user can be notified when the computer is not in a compliant state. If auto-remediation is enabled, the client will attempt to download and install the required software updates from the configured remediation servers. If auto-remediation is not enabled, the user has the ability to remediate the client manually. When remediation takes place, the end user is able to see the window as shown in Figure 15.35.

After the required software updates are installed, the client then may restart depending on the settings defined.

THE FINAL WORD

As you can see from this chapter, Configuration Manager 2007's NAP integration feature can be very useful in protecting your environment from unauthorized client access as long as you have the proper NAP infrastructure in place and have created a well-defined plan of execution. If you make sure to follow the guidelines set forth in this chapter, you should be on your way to a more secure environment. In the next chapter, we'll discuss mobile devices and how they can be managed using Configuration Manager 2007.

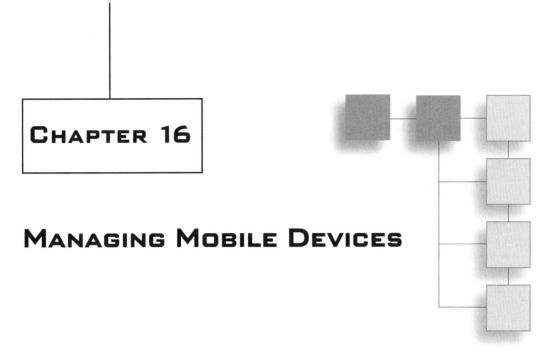

CHAPTER 16

MANAGING MOBILE DEVICES

You have three options for managing Windows mobile devices. You can use System Center Mobile Device Manager, Exchange Server, or System Center Configuration Manager. Each of these solutions provides the ability to manage your mobile devices efficiently. System Center Mobile Device Manager is meant to only manage mobile devices. It is a standalone product that gives you control over the mobile devices in your organization. It can provide you with inventory and policy control of Windows mobile devices. Microsoft Exchange provides control over your Windows mobile devices also, but only controls policies on the phones.

System Center Configuration Manager provides the ability to manage Windows mobile devices also. You get inventory and policy control over the mobile devices, but you also get the ability to distribute software. If you want a single tool to manage your workstations, servers, and mobile devices, you should consider using the mobile device management features of Configuration Manager.

SUPPORTED PLATFORMS

Before you start building your mobile device management platform, check to make sure you have supported clients. Configuration Manager only supports Windows mobile devices natively. To support other platforms, such as iPhone, Blackberry, or Android-based mobile devices, you will need to install a third-party utility. As for the Windows devices that are supported:

- Windows Mobile Smartphone 2003

- Windows Mobile Smartphone 5.0

- Windows Mobile Smartphone 6 Standard

- Windows Mobile Smartphone 6 Professional

- Windows Mobile Smartphone 6 Classic

- Windows Mobile 6.1

- Windows Mobile 6.5

- Windows Mobile for Pocket PC 2003

- Windows Mobile for Pocket PC 2003 Second Edition

- Windows Mobile for Pocket PC Phone Edition 2003

- Windows Mobile for Pocket PC Phone Edition 2003 Second Edition

- Windows Mobile for Pocket PC 5.0

- Windows Mobile for Pocket PC Phone Edition 5.0

- Windows CE 4.2 (ARM Processor only) (Not supported in Native Mode)

- Windows CE 5.0 (ARM and x86 Processors)

- Windows CE 6.0 (ARM and x86 Processors) (Configuration Manager 2007 SP2 with Hotfix 977384)

CONFIGURING DEVICE MANAGEMENT SUPPORT

As with most of the features within Configuration Manager, there are configuration settings within the Site Settings and Computer Management nodes that are required before you will be able to manage devices. Within the Site Settings, the client agent needs to be enabled and configured, and the Site Systems that will support device management have to be configured to do so.

The Mobile Device Client Agent is used to control the actions on the mobile device. If you look at the properties of the Mobile Device Client Agent, as seen in Figure 16.1, the first thing you will probably notice is that all of the tabs relate to other client agents. The other client agents within the site do not affect mobile devices. Only the settings within the Mobile Device Client Agent are used for

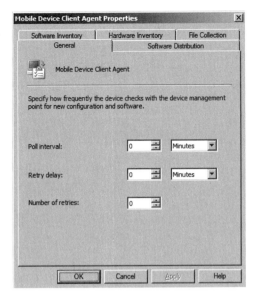

Figure 16.1
Mobile Device Client Agent

mobile device management. You can have different settings for mobile devices than you have configured for all other clients within the site.

Figure 16.1 displays the settings found on the General tab of the Mobile Device Client Agent properties. These settings are used to control the polling interval that is used by the mobile device. The Poll Interval setting controls how often the client attempts to download the policy from the Management Point that is configured to allow connections from devices. This setting should be configured so that the policy download is often enough that the client can retrieve the policy and update the actions it needs to perform. You do not want to check too often however, depending on the data plan used with the device. Typically, the default of every 30 minutes is usually sufficient. If the client cannot retrieve the policy, it will go into a retry state and attempt to retrieve the policy on the retry settings schedule.

If you are planning on sending software installation programs or using packages to push files onto a device, you will need to enable the software distribution component of the agent. Figure 16.2 shows the checkbox used to enable software distribution to mobile devices within the site.

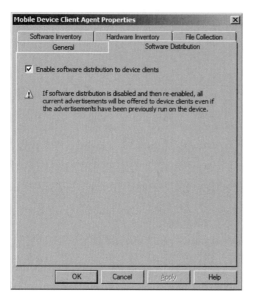

Figure 16.2
Enable Software Distribution

The Software Inventory tab, seen in Figure 16.3, is used to discover and report on files found on the mobile devices within the site. The software inventory settings configured for standard clients are not included within the mobile device settings, so if you want the same file types to be inventoried, you will have to configure them on this property tab. Figure 16.4 shows the configuration settings for files that will be inventoried. The configuration options in this window should appear familiar, they are nearly identical to the settings found in Chapter 9.

The Hardware Inventory tab, seen in Figure 16.5, is used to enable hardware inventory collection and control how often a hardware inventory is performed.

The File Collection tab, seen in Figure 16.6, shares some common options with the File Collection settings found on the Software Inventory Client Agent. Once enabled, the frequency of file collection and the files to be collected can be defined. As with the file collection for any other managed system, use this feature with caution. Collecting too many files or performing the collection too often will cause an increase in data usage. If you have data plans that do not offer unlimited data, you may want to limit the usage of the File Collection feature.

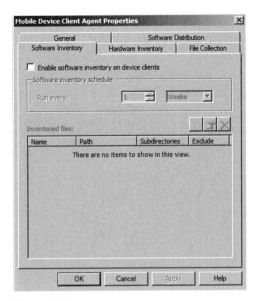

Figure 16.3
Software Inventory Settings

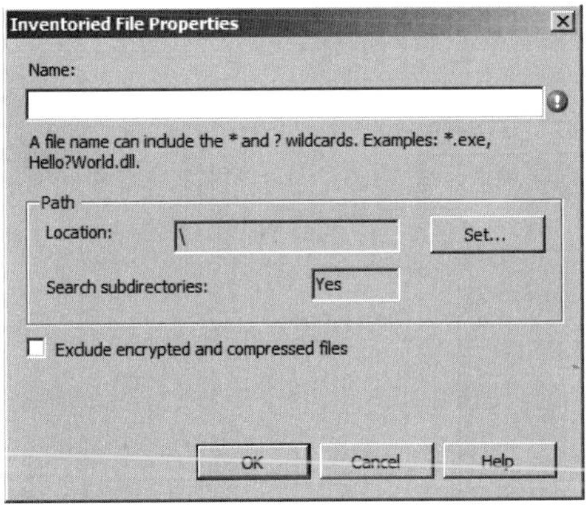

Figure 16.4
Configuring Inventory File Types

MOBILE DEVICE MANAGEMENT SETTINGS

The Mobile Device client settings will control what the client will do on the managed device. The settings provided on the client property tabs only provide a portion of the functionality of what you can do when managing a mobile device.

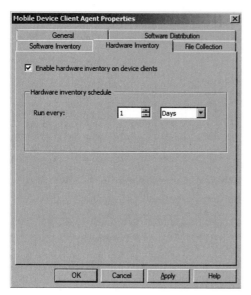

Figure 16.5
Hardware Inventory Settings

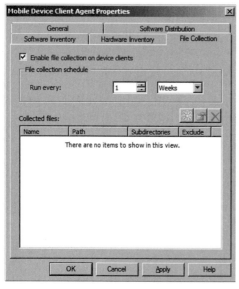

Figure 16.6
File Collection Settings

You can optionally configure additional settings that control how the device will function. These settings are known as the configuration items. You can create configuration items that perform functions such as controlling password policies to installing certificates on your devices.

Configuration Items

Configuration items are discreet components that you can configure that will provide additional control over the managed mobile devices within your organization. Depending on the platform that you are managing, the configuration items can be used to restrict specific functions and safeguard the device. The following sections identify each of the configuration items that are available within Configuration Manager and the platforms that support the configuration item.

Browser Favorite

Figure 16.7 displays the settings that you can configure for a browser favorite. These settings can apply to Windows Mobile 3, Windows Mobile 5, Windows Mobile with Messaging and Security Feature Pack, and Windows Mobile 6. This

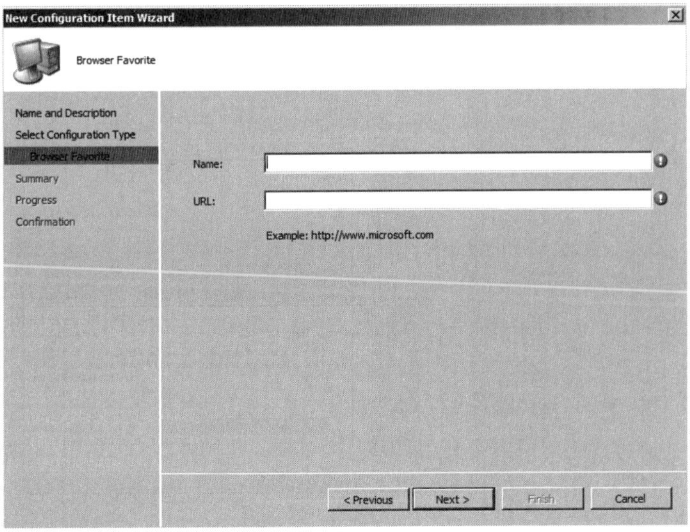

Figure 16.7
Browser Favorites configuration item

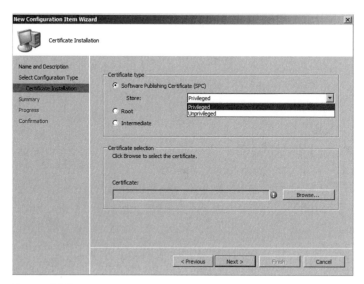

Figure 16.8
Certificate Installation configuration item

configuration item is very basic; the only setting necessary is to name the favorite and identify the URL that the favorite corresponds to.

When configuring Browser Favorite configuration items, you can define as many favorites as you need. You can then specify which configuration items will be used within a configuration package. The most common Browser Favorite settings are usually links to corporate websites, and webmail.

Certificate Installation

The Certificate Installation Configuration Item properties are shown in Figure 16.8. When specifying how the certificates are stored within the certificate store, you have the option of specifying the certificate is stored in the execution store with privileged or unprivileged rights, stored in the Root certificate store or the Intermediate certificate store. When storing certificates within the execution store, applications that are signed with a certificate that is deemed to have privileged rights have full access to the mobile device settings, including registry and system files. Those certificates that are configured as unprivileged do not have access to critical system components, but are allowed to run. Once the store has been selected, the certificate that will be stored needs to be identified. Clicking the

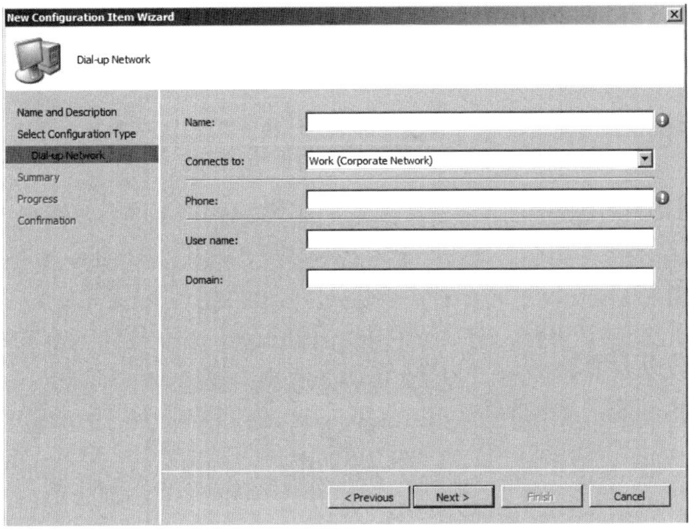

Figure 16.9
Dial-up Network configuration item

Browse button allows you to select the certificate. These settings can apply to Windows Mobile 3, Windows Mobile 5, Windows Mobile with Messaging and Security Feature Pack, and Windows Mobile 6.

Dial-up Network

The Dial-up Network configuration item can be used to distribute connection settings to the mobile devices you are managing. You can configure the settings at the Configuration Manager Console and then distribute them to all of the appropriate devices easily. The settings found in Figure 16.9 are used to define the connection and the account information used to make the connection. These settings can apply to Windows Mobile 3, Windows Mobile 5, Windows Mobile with Messaging and Security Feature Pack, and Windows Mobile 6. These settings include:

- **Name**—The name of the dial-up connection as it will be seen by the owner of the mobile device.

- **Connects To**—Used to define whether the corporate network or the Internet is used to make the connection.

- **Phone**—Specifies the number that is used to connect.

- **User**—The account used to authenticate to the dial-up network.

- **Domain**—The domain used to authenticate to the dial-up network.

Exchange ActiveSync (WM03 mode)

Exchange ActiveSync is used to synchronize data between Exchange Servers and mobile devices. Due to limited memory, not all of the data stored within a user's mailbox can be stored within the mobile devices. These settings apply to Windows Mobile 3 only. The settings that you can configure for the Windows Mobile 3 version of the Exchange ActiveSync Configuration tab, seen in Figure 16.10, are as follows:

- **Server**—Name of the ActiveSync server.

- **This Server Uses An SSL Connection**—When selected, all communication to the ActiveSync server is encrypted using SSL encryption.

- **Synchronize**—When selected, over-the-air (OTA) synchronization will occur at the specified interval—5, 15, 30, 60, 120, or 240 minutes.

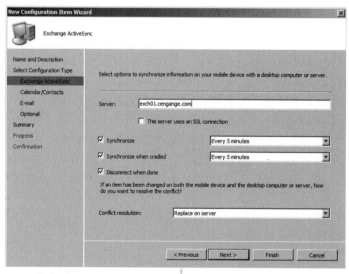

Figure 16.10
Exchange ActiveSync (WM03 Mode) configuration item

- **Synchronize When Cradled**—When selected, cradled devices will be synchronized at the specified interval—5, 15, 30, 60, 120, or 240 minutes.

- **Disconnect When Done**—When selected, the device will disconnect from the ActiveSync server.

- **Conflict Resolution**—Defines how conflicting records are handled. If the record is found on the device and the Exchange Server, you can specify that the data on the server will be replaced or the data on the device will be replaced.

Synchronization settings for Calendar and Contacts information is seen in Figure 16.11:

- **Calendar—Enable Calendar Synchronization**—When selected, the calendar items in the user's mailbox are copied to the mobile device.

- **Calendar: Age Filter**—Used to control how much calendar data is synchronized on the mobile device.

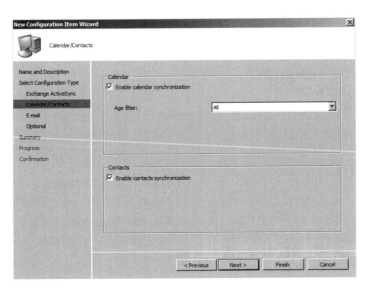

Figure 16.11
Calendar and Contact Settings

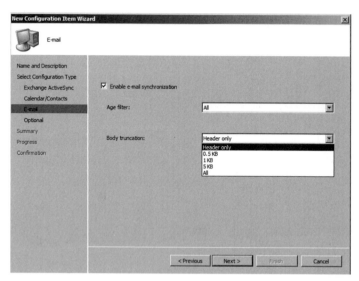

Figure 16.12
E-mail Synchronization Settings

- **Contacts: —Enable Contacts Synchronization**—When selected, the user's contacts are synchronized between the Exchange Server and the mobile device.

E-mail synchronization settings, seen in Figure 16.12, control how much information is stored on the mobile device.

- **Enable E-mail Synchronization**—When selected, e-mail items are synchronized on the mobile device.

- **Age Filter**—Controls how much data is kept on the mobile device. Can be configured to store 1 or 3 days, 1 or 2 weeks, or 1 month worth of data.

- **Body Truncation**—Controls how much of a message is downloaded to the device. Using this setting, you can control the data that is sent to the device, which helps on limited data plans, as well as the amount of device storage that is consumed. The options include downloading the header only, .5, 1, or 5 KB of the message, or all of the message.

Figure 16.13 shows the settings from the Optional tab. These are used for authentication to the Exchange Server:

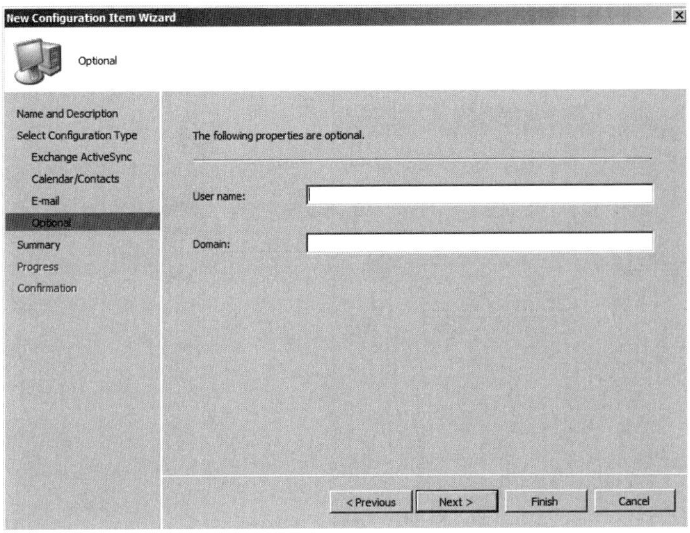

Figure 16.13
Optional Settings

- **User Name**—Account used to connect to the Exchange Server and access the user's mailbox.

- **Domain**—Specifies the Active Directory domain of the user connecting to the Exchange Server.

Exchange ActiveSync (WM05 mode)

Windows Mobile 5 has many of the same configuration settings as its Windows Mobile 3 counterpart, but as you can see in Figure 16.14, there are fewer options on the Exchange ActiveSync tab. This is due to Windows Mobile 5 having more efficient synchronization and conflict resolution methods. These settings can apply to Windows Mobile 5, Windows Mobile with Messaging and Security Feature Pack, and Windows Mobile 6. The settings that you can configure for the Windows Mobile 5 version of the Exchange ActiveSync Configuration tab are as follows:

- **Server**—Name of the ActiveSync server.

- **This Server Uses An SSL Connection**—When selected, all communication to the ActiveSync server is encrypted using SSL encryption.

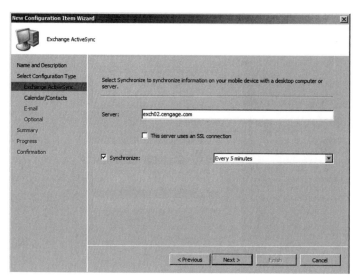

Figure 16.14
Exchange ActiveSync (WM05 Mode) Settings

- **Synchronize**—When selected, over-the-air (OTA) synchronization will occur at the specified interval—5, 15, 30, 60, 120, or 240 minutes.

GPRS Network

When General Packet Radio Service (GPRS) services are used by the mobile device, the GPRS Network configuration item can be used to distribute the GPRS settings to the device. As with other configuration items, these settings can be managed centrally from the Configuration Manager Console and deployed to the appropriate devices. These settings can apply to Windows Mobile 3, Windows Mobile 5, Windows Mobile with Messaging and Security Feature Pack, and Windows Mobile 6. The settings that you can configure, seen in Figure 16.15, are as follows:

- **Description**—Information displayed on the mobile device.

- **Access Point Name**—Specifies the GPRS Network configuration name.

- **Connect To**—Used to specify whether the client connects to the corporate network or the Internet.

- **User Name**—Optional; if used, specifies the name of the account for GPRS Network connection authentication.

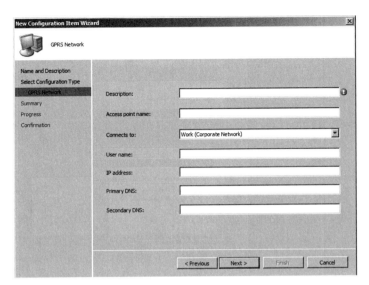

Figure 16.15
GPRS Network configuration item

- **IP Address**—Optional; if used, specifies the IP address used with the GPRS Network connection.

- **Primary DNS**—Optional; if used, specifies the primary DNS server used when connecting to the GPRS Network.

- **Secondary DNS**—Optional; if used, specifies the secondary DNS server when connecting to the GPRS Network.

Internet E-mail

The Internet E-mail configuration item is used to manage the settings used to allow the mobile device to connect to an e-mail server if you are not using Exchange Server, or there is a secondary e-mail server besides the corporate Exchange Server. These settings can apply to Windows Mobile 3, Windows Mobile 5, Windows Mobile with Messaging and Security Feature Pack, and Windows Mobile 6. The settings found in Figure 16.16 are as follows:

- **E-mail Type**—Used to specify an IMAP4 or POP3 connection.

- **Service Name**—Used to display the name of the e-mail services on the mobile device.

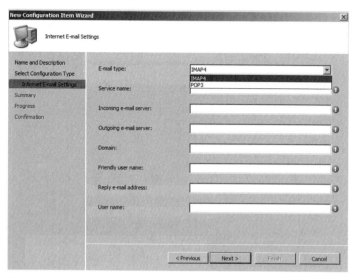

Figure 16.16
Internet E-mail configuration item

- **Incoming E-mail Server**—Specifies the name of the server the mobile device will use to retrieve e-mail.

- **Outgoing E-Mail Server**—Specifies the name of the SMTP server the mobile device will use to send e-mail.

- **Domain**—Specifies the name of the user's domain.

- **Friendly User Name**—Specifies the display name of the e-mail settings.

- **User**—Specifies the account used to send and receive e-mail.

Network Proxy

If the mobile device needs to use a proxy server when connecting to resources, the Network Proxy configuration item is used to define the appropriate settings. These settings can apply to Windows Mobile 3, Windows Mobile 5, Windows Mobile with Messaging and Security Feature Pack, and Windows Mobile 6. Figure 16.17 displays the available settings:

- **Description**—Used to display a description of the proxy settings on the mobile device.

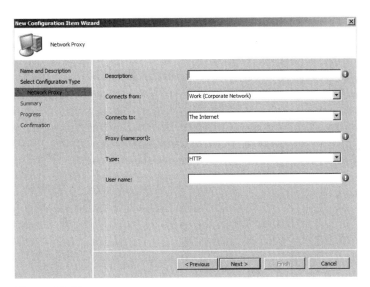

Figure 16.17
Network Proxy configuration item

- **Connects From**—Specifies whether the mobile device is connecting from the corporate network or Internet.

- **Connects To**—Specifies whether the mobile device is connecting to the corporate network or Internet.

- **Proxy**—Used to define the name of the proxy server and the port used to connect.

- **Type**—Used to control the connection protocol for the proxy server. Options are HTTP, WAP, SOCKS4, and SOCKS5.

- **User Name**—Specifies the account used to connect to the proxy server.

Password Policy for MSFP

Password policies are used to control access to devices. Without a password policy, the mobile device can be accessed by anyone who picks up the device. When configuring the password options, make sure you do not make the policies too restrictive or the user may not be able to quickly answer an incoming call. These settings only apply to Windows Mobile with Messaging and Security Feature Pack. Figure 16.18 shows the options available within the Password Policy for the MSFP configuration item:

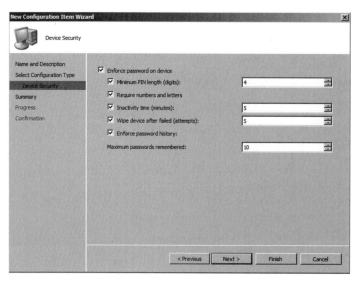

Figure 16.18
Password Policy for MSFP configuration item

- **Enforce Password On Device**—Enables the password policies.

- **Minimum PIN Length (Digits)**—Specifies the minimum number of digits required for the password.

- **Require Both Numbers And Letters**—Specifies that the password must contain a combination of alphanumeric characters.

- **Inactivity Time**—Used to define the amount of time the device can remain idle before requiring a password to access the device.

- **Wipe Device After Failed (Attempts)**—Used to define the number of failed password entries that will be allowed before all data is removed from the mobile device.

- **Enforce Password History**—Used to enable the password history on the device. When enabled, the user cannot use the same password for the number of password changes specified within the Maximum Passwords Remembered option.

- **Maximum Passwords Remembered**—Used to define how many old passwords are remembered when the Enforce Password History option is selected.

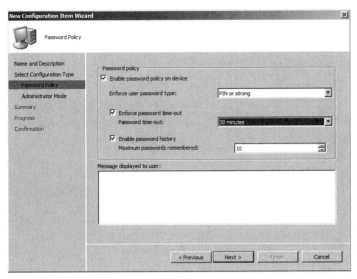

Figure 16.19
Password Policy for Pocket PC 2003 configuration item

Password Policy for Pocket PC 2003

The Password Policy for Pocket PC 2003 configuration item has different options than those found in the Password Policy for MSFP configuration item. These settings only apply to Pocket PC 2003. Figure 16.19 shows the options available:

- **Enable Password Policy On Device**—Enables password policies on devices where the configuration item is used.

- **Enforce User Password Type**—Specifies the type of password used on the device. Options are None Specified, PIN Only, PIN Or Strong. When using a PIN, a minimum of 4 numbers must be used. When using PIN Or Strong, a minimum of 4 numbers or 7 alphanumeric characters, including one number, one uppercase, one lowercase character.

- **Enforce Password Timeout**—Specifies the number of minutes or hours the password remains active. After the timeout is exceeded, the password needs to be reentered.

- **Password Timeout**—Specifies the amount of time for the timeout. Options include 0 Minutes (forever), 1, 5, 15, 30, and 90 minutes, 1 and 2 hours.

- **Enforce Password History**—Used to enable the password history on the device. When enabled, the user cannot use the same password for the number of password changes specified within the Maximum Passwords Remembered option.

- **Maximum Passwords Remembered**—Used to define how many old passwords are remembered when the Enforce Password History option is selected.

- **Message Displayed To User**—Used to define the message that is presented to users.

Figure 16.20 shows the settings available on the Administrator Mode tab. Administrator mode is used to unlock the account when the user has failed entering the correct password. Administrator mode does not allow a user to access any device options, only reset the locked out account.

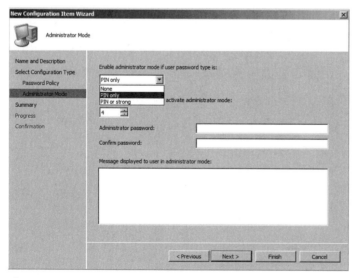

Figure 16.20
Administrator Mode

- **Enable Administrator Mode If User Password Type Is**—Used to control what password type the Administrator mode is allowed to unlock. Options are None, PIN Only, and PIN Or Strong.

- **Number Of Failed Attempts To Activate Administrator Mode**—Used to define the number of failed password attempts before the Administrator mode will appear.

- **Administrator Password**—Specifies the password to use to access Administrator mode.

- **Confirm Password**—Used to confirm that the password is entered correctly.

- **Message Displayed To User In Administrator Mode**—Message that is displayed to the user when Administrator mode is accessed.

Registry

Registry keys can be added or manipulated by using the Registry configuration item. If you have a specific Registry Key that you need to add or change a value, you can use this configuration item to deploy the Registry Key to the appropriate managed mobile devices. These settings can apply to Windows Mobile 5, Windows Mobile with Messaging and Security Feature Pack, and Windows Mobile 6. Figure 16.21 shows the settings:

- **Registry Key**—Used to define the path to the Registry Key.

- **Value Name**—Used to define the value that will be manipulated within the Registry Key.

- **Data Type**—Used to define the type of data that will be used within the Registry Key. Options available are Binary, Boolean, Date And Time, Float, Integer, Multiple Strings, and String.

- **Value**—Specifies the value that is used in the Registry Key. Data entered is dependent upon the Data Type option.

Security Policies

To secure the mobile device from potentially dangerous installation file types, you can configure security policies that will allow or block specific files. The

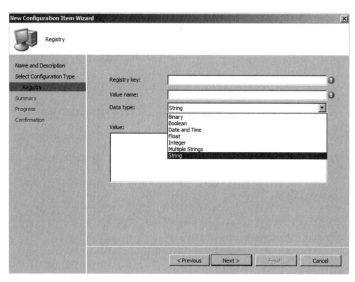

Figure 16.21
Registry configuration item

settings defined within the Security Policies configuration item have three options—Not Managed, Enabled, and Disabled. When set to Not Managed, the policy does not override any settings on the device. Enabled will override the setting on the device and enforce the policy option. Disabled will override the settings on the device, turning the policy setting off. These settings can apply to Windows Mobile 5, Windows Mobile with Messaging and Security Feature Pack, and Windows Mobile 6. Figure 16.22 shows the options that are available:

- **Install Unsigned .cab Files**—Used to control whether the application installer files need to be signed before the user can install them.

- **Prompt For Unsigned .cab Installation**—Defines whether the user will be prompted to install unsigned applications.

- **Run Unsigned Applications**—Defines whether the application needs to be signed before a user is allowed to launch it.

- **Install Unsigned Theme Files**—Defines whether themes need to be signed before the user is allowed to install them.

- **Auto Run Applications From A Memory Card**—Defines whether an application can launch immediately after the SD card it is on is inserted into the device.

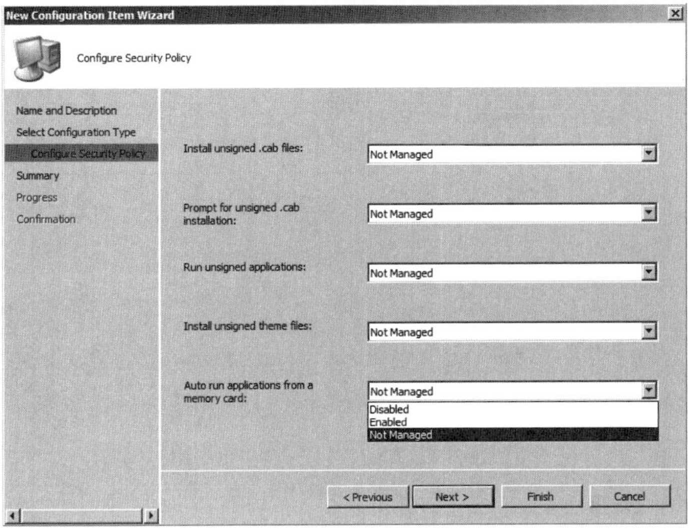

Figure 16.22
Security Policies configuration item

VPN

The VPN configuration item is used in much the same way the Network Proxy configuration item is used. You can specify the settings that will be used when the device connects to a VPN server for secure connections to the corporate network. These settings can apply to Windows Mobile 3, Windows Mobile 5, Windows Mobile with Messaging and Security Feature Pack, and Windows Mobile 6. Figure 16.23 shows the available options:

- **Name**—Used to display a description of the VPN settings on the mobile device.

- **Connects From**—Specifies whether the mobile device is connecting from the corporate network or Internet.

- **Connects To**—Specifies whether the mobile device is connecting to the corporate network or Internet.

- **Host Name**—Defines the name of the VPN server that the client connects.

- **User Name**—Specifies the account used to connect to the VPN server.

- **Domain**—Specifies the name of the domain the user account is in.

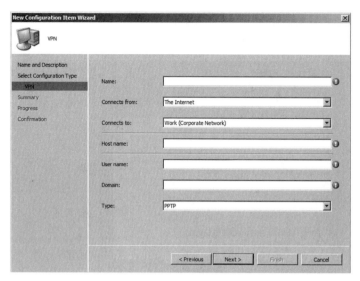

Figure 16.23
VPN configuration item

■ **Type**—Used to define the type of VPN connection. Options are Point-to-Point Tunneling Protocol (PPTP) or IP Security/Layer 2 Tunneling Protocol (IPSec/L2TP).

WiFi Settings

If the mobile device has the option to connect to WiFi hotspots, you can configure the WiFi settings that will be used to make the connection. These settings can apply to Windows Mobile 5, Windows Mobile with Messaging and Security Feature Pack, and Windows Mobile 6. Figure 16.24 shows the options that are available on the Wireless Network tab:

■ **Network Name (SSID)**—Used to define the name of the wireless network.

■ **Connects To (DestID)**—Used to define whether the connection properties connect to the corporate network or the Internet.

■ **This Is A Device-to-Device (Ad-Hoc) Connection**—Used to define the types of wireless networks to which a mobile device can connect. When selected, the device can connect to another system that is not a wireless router.

The Authentication tab, seen in Figure 16.25, shows the connection criteria that will be used when connecting to the wireless network:

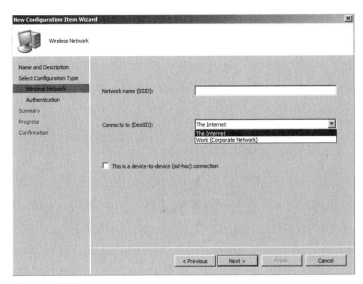

Figure 16.24
WiFi Settings configuration item

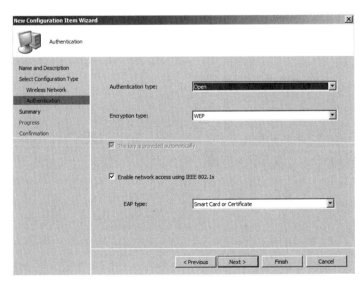

Figure 16.25
Authentication Settings

- **Authentication Type**—Defines the type of connection that will be made to the wireless network. Options include Open, Shared, WPA, and WPA PSK.

- **Encryption Type**—Defines the encryption method that is used when connecting to the wireless network. Options include WEP and Disabled.

- **This Key Is Provided Automatically**—When selected, the authentication key is sent to the device automatically when needed.

- **Enable Network Access Using IEEE 802.1x**—Specifies whether port-based, network access control standards are enforced for authentication.

- **EAP Type**—Used to define whether Smart Card/Certificate or Protected Extensible Authentication Protocol is used when connecting to the wireless network. Options include Smart Card Or Certificate and Protected EAP.

CONFIGURATION PACKAGES

Once the configuration items have been created, they need to be added to configuration packages. Configuration packages are then assigned to mobile devices through an Advertisement, much the same way applications are advertised to systems or devices. A Configuration package can contain one or more configuration items and a configuration item can be added to one or more configuration packages.

Creating Configuration Packages

When creating configuration packages, you should make sure that the configuration items that are added are supported by the target operating system platforms. The process for creating a configuration package is rather straightforward:

1. Expand Computer Management > Mobile Device Management.

2. Right-click Configuration Packages and select New Configuration Package.

3. Enter a name for the configuration package in the Name text field.

4. Optionally, enter a description of the configuration package in the Description field and click Next.

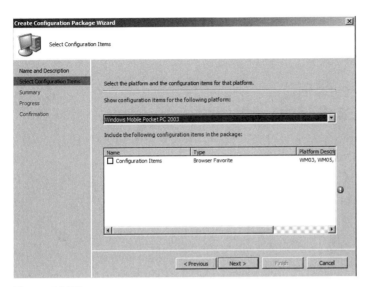

Figure 16.26
Select Configuration Items page

5. On the Select Configuration Items page, see Figure 16.26, select the appropriate platform from the Show Configuration Items For The Following Platform drop-down.

6. Select the checkboxes for the configuration items that should be added to the configuration package and click Next.

7. Review the settings and click Next and Close.

Advertising Packages

Configuration packages have to be advertised to a collection that contains the managed mobile devices. Once the advertisement is created, the mobile devices that are members of the targeted collection will start using the settings defined in the configuration items that are included in the configuration package. The settings will not be applied immediately however. The client will need to refresh its policy. The frequency that the client refreshed the policy will dictate how quickly all of the devices will be compliant with the new configuration settings. To advertise the configuration package:

1. Expand Computer Management > Mobile Device Management > Configuration Packages.

2. Right-click the configuration package to advertise.

3. Click Next when the wizard starts.

4. On the Distribution Points page, Figure 16.27, select the appropriate distribution points and click Next.

5. To advertise a program, verify Yes is selected on the Advertise Program page, Figure 16.28, and click Next.

6. On the Select Program page, Figure 16.29, select the program in the Programs field and click Next.

7. On the Advertisement Target page, Figure 16.30, select a collection to target the advertisement by clicking Browse to find the collection, or select the Create A New Collection And Advertise This Program To It button, then click Next.

8. On the Advertisement Name page, Figure 16.31, enter a name for the advertisement in the Name field.

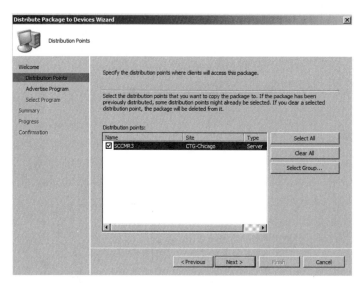

Figure 16.27
Distribution Points page

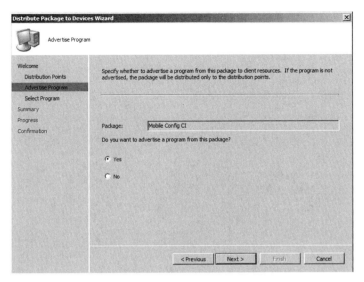

Figure 16.28
Advertise Programs page

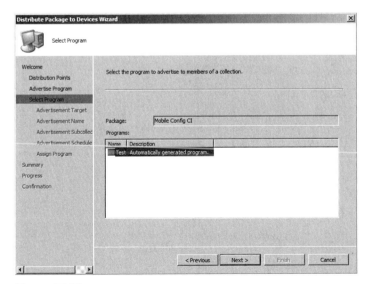

Figure 16.29
Select Programs page

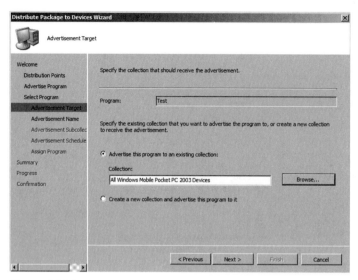

Figure 16.30
Advertisements Target page

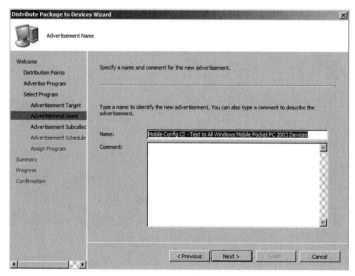

Figure 16.31
Advertisement Name page

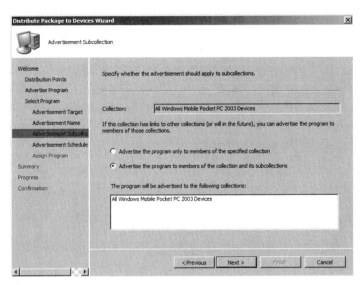

Figure 16.32
Advertisement Subcollection page

9. Optionally, enter a description of the advertisement in the Comment field and click Next.

10. On the Advertisement Subcollection page, Figure 16.32, select the appropriate option on whether the advertisement will target the selected collection or the subcollections also, then click Next.

11. On the Advertisement Schedule page, Figure 16.33, enter the date and time that the advertisement will become available to the device and click Next.

12. On the Assign Program page, Figure 16.34, select whether the advertised program will be assigned to the client. Assigned programs are run on the device when the advertisement becomes available.

13. Select the recurrence pattern for the program. When set to Interval, the program will run on the device according to the interval provided.

14. Select the Rerun This Advertisement When The Program Or Advertisement Details Change if the program should rerun and update the device with the latest configuration settings.

15. Click Next.

16. Review the summary and click Next and Close.

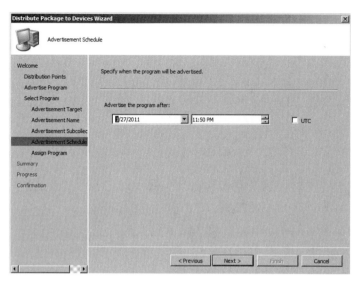

Figure 16.33
Advertisement Schedule page

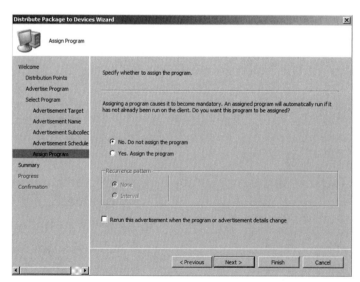

Figure 16.34
Assign Program page

Installing the Client

Managing a mobile device requires a client component, much the same as any other managed system. Installing the client on a mobile device is not as easy as pushing the client to a system. The initial client install needs to be performed manually on the device. The manual installation can either take the form of an installation folder on the systems where the device synchronizes or removable media. After the client has been installed, an upgrade of the client can be performed over the air.

The installation files are included with the Configuration Manager installation folder. Expanding the installation folder you will find the DeviceClientDeployment folder. Depending on how you want to distribute the files, you will need to copy files from this folder into a distribution folder. The distribution folder can then be deployed to the systems where mobile devices sync. To make deployment easier, you can use the software distribution components within Configuration Manager to copy the deployment folder to the appropriate systems.

Creating the Deployment Folder

To start the deployment process, create a folder that will be used as the source folder for the device client installation files. There are two installation options to consider. The first is to create a deployment folder that will contain the installation files of all the supported platforms. When using this option, the platform is detected during the installation. The appropriate installer will then be used. The second option is to include only the platform files that are necessary for the device. This makes for a much smaller amount of data in the deployment folder and lends itself well to being copied to removable media.

After creating the deployment folder, copy the following files into the folder:

> \DeviceClientDeployment\ClientTransfer*Language*
>
> \DeviceClientDeployment\ClientTransfer\DMClientXfer.exe
>
> \DeviceClientDeployment\ClientTransfer\DMCommonInstaller.exe
>
> \DeviceClientDeployment\ClientTransfer\DMCommonInstaller.ini

If the site is in Native Mode, copy all relevant certificates to the deployment folder. For more information about certificates and Native Mode, see Chapter 8.

If you are planning on copying only the platform specific files to the deployment folder, you will need to identify the files that are needed based upon the platform. These files are located within the DeviceClientDeployment\ ClientTransfer*Language* folder. There are three files associated with each platform:

- DeviceClient_*platform*.cab
- DMClientSetup_*platform*.exe
- DMInstaller_*platform*.exe
- Pocket PC 2003 devices will have one additional file included in the deployment folder—SMSPassword_ce4.2_arm.cab
- From the DeviceClientDeployment\ClientTransfer folder, copy the ClientSettings.ini file

The enroller file will need to be copied. Depending on the platform, you will need to copy the following file to the deployment folder:

- **Windows Mobile devices**—Enroll_ARM.exe
- **Windows CE x86**—Enroll_WinCE5.0_x86.exe or Enroll_WinCE6.0_X86. exe
- **Windows CE ARM**—Enroll_WinCE5.0_ARM.exe or Enroll_Win-CE6.0_ARM.exe

Configuring the Client Installation Files

If you are creating a deployment folder that will be used for any platform, you will have to modify the installation files for use on a device. The deployment folder is used to install the client from a system where the device sync needs to have the DMCommonInstaller.ini and ClientSettings.ini files modified. Either of these files can be opened and edited with Notepad or any other text editor.

The DMCommonInstaller.ini file has several sections. There is a section for each of the supported platforms as well as a section named Common that includes the settings found in all of the platforms. Modify the settings in the Common section and then edit the settings for every platform that you will support within your organization. In the Common section, you will find the following settings:

- **CertEnrollServer**—Specifies the name of the Certificate Server that is used to enroll the certificates used on the client.

- **CertEnrollServerPort**—Specifies the port that is used to connect to the Certificate Server when enrolling.

- **CertRequestPage**—Specifies the web enrollment web page for the Certificate Server.

- **CertDownloadPage**—Specifies the web page used to download issued certificates.

- **CertChainDownloadPage**—Specifies the web page used to download certificate chains.

Within each of the platform sections, you will find the following configuration settings:

- **Installer**—The name of the platform-specific device management installer program in the format DMInstaller_platform.exe.

- **ClientSetup**—The name of the platform-specific mobile device client setup program in the format DMClientSetup_platform.exe.

- **Client**—The name of the platform-specific client cabinet file required for mobile device client installation in the format DeviceClient_platform.exe.

- **ClientVersion**—The version of the mobile device client being installed.

- **BaseOSMinVersion**—The minimum version number of the platform's operating system required to support the client.

- **BaseOSMaxVersion**—The maximum version number of the platform's operating system required to support the client.

- **DeviceType**—The type of mobile device supported by the mobile device client.

- **ProcessorType**—The type of processor supported by the mobile device client.

- **EnableVerboseLogging**—Enables verbose logging on the mobile device. The default is False.

- **ClientInstallAction**—Specifies the action to be taken by the installer. The supported values are:
  - **None**—Makes no change to the mobile device client state.
  - **Install**—Install the mobile device client distributed with the installation package onto the mobile device. (Default)
  - **Uninstall**—Removes the mobile device client from the mobile device.
  - **InstallType**—Specifies the type of installation. The supported values are:
    - Clean to remove program database. (Default)
    - Preserve to keep the record of installed programs.

- **Pre-InstallCommandLine**—Specifies the command line to be run before the installation of the mobile device client.

- **Post-InstallCommandLine**—Specifies the command line to be run after the installation of the mobile device client.

- **AdditionalFileX**—Specifies additional files that will be copied to the \temp\dminstall folder on the mobile device when the install program is run.

- **DMServerName**—Specifies the server name of the Device Management Point that the mobile device connects. This setting must be defined.

- **ServerPort**—Specifies the port that the mobile device client communicates. The default ports are 80 (HTTP) or 443 (HTTPS). Uncomment and set this line if the Configuration Manager 2007 environment uses a custom port configuration.

- **SiteCode**—The three character alphanumeric site code of the site.

- **FSPServerName**—The server name of the Fallback Status Point.

- **FSPPort**—The http port on that the mobile device client communicates to the Fallback Status Point Server. The default port is 80.

- **FSPAlternatePort**—The alternate http port that the mobile device client communicates with the Fallback Status Point Server. The default port is 80.

- **SecurityMode**—Specifies the security mode of the mobile device client authentication. The default value is None. The supported values are:
  - **None**—No server or client authentication is required.
  - **SSLServerAuth**—Secure HTTP (HTTPS) server authentication is required. A server certificate is required.
  - **NativeMode**—Secure HTTP (HTTPS) mutual authentication is required. A client Auth Certificate is required.

- **CreateConnection**—Specifies when a connection is created. The default value is USER. The supported values are:
  - **ALL**—Allows the mobile device client to create a connection for any action.
  - **USER**—Allows the mobile device client to invoke a connection only for a user-invoked action.
  - **NEVER**—Prevents the mobile device client from invoking connections for any operations. Manual connection is required.

- **InternetConnected**—Specifies whether the device client will connect to the device management point from the Internet. The default value is False. The supported values are:
  - **True**—The mobile device client connects to the device management point from the Internet.
  - **False**—The mobile device client does not connect to the device management point from the Internet.

- **EnforceConfig**—Specifies that the mobile device configuration user interface is disabled for certain options. The user cannot change the Configuration Manager 2007 mobile device configuration settings. The default value is ServerName. The supported values are:
  - **None**—Allows the user to change server name, security mode, and auto connect options.
  - **ServerName**—Prevents users from editing the server name and security mode options.
  - **All**—Prevents users from editing the server name, security mode, and auto connect options.

- **CertEnrollAction**—Specifies whether a certificate is enrolled during mobile device client installation. The default value is Enroll. The supported values are:
  - **None**—No certificate is enrolled.
  - **Enroll**—Enrolls a client authentication certificate and add server certificate to the ROOT certificate store of the mobile device if the existing certificate cannot be used for device registration. The user will be prompted for their credentials to enroll the certificate.
  - **ForceEnroll**—Enrolls a client authentication certificate and adds a server certificate to the ROOT certificate store of the mobile device regardless of the current state of the existing enrolled certificate. The user will be prompted for their credentials to enroll the certificate.

- **CertEnrollServer**—Specifies the name of the Internet Information Services (IIS) web server of the certification authority (CA).

- **CertEnrollServerPort**—Specifies the port number of the Internet Information Services (IIS) web server of the certification authority (CA).

- **CertSubjectName**—Specifies which certificate in the user store is used for registering the mobile device. The mobile device management client tries all the certificates where the subject name contains the valid CertSubjectName criteria. If the value is None, all valid client authentication certificates in the user store will be tried. The default value is None. The format is: CertSubjectName = *sitecode*.

- **CertRequestPage**—Specifies the web page on a web server that will receive the certificate request.

- **CertDownloadPage**—Specifies the web page on the web server that is used for downloading the certificate.

- **CertChainDownloadPage**—Specifies the web page on the web server that is used for downloading the certificate chain.

- **ImportCerts**—Specifies that certificate files will be imported to the certificate store on the mobile device. The certificate files must be included in the mobile device client deployment folder. Certificates to be imported must be in distinguished encoding rules (DER) encoded binary X.509

format. Base-64 encoded X.509 certificates are not supported. The default value is False. The supported values are:

- **True**—Import certificates.
- **False**—Do not import certificates.

- **EnableSSSCRenewal**—Specifies whether a site server signing certificate is renewed when it expires.
  - **True**—Enable site server signing certificate renewal.
  - **False**—Do not enable site server signing certificate renewal.

THE FINAL WORD

Although managing Windows mobile devices is not an overly common practice, there are those organizations that want to have control over the Windows Mobile devices within their organization. Configuration Manager allows an administrator to inventory and control these devices from a central console, the same console that is used to manage all of the other Windows systems within the organization.

In the next chapter, we are going to review the options that are available for backing up and restoring the Configuration Manager site.

SECTION IV

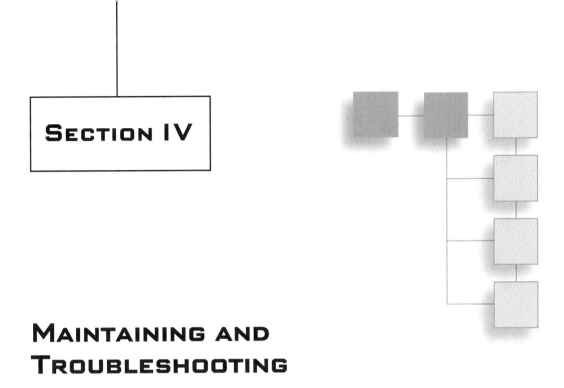

MAINTAINING AND TROUBLESHOOTING

After the site hierarchy is created and configured, the day-to-day operations take over. It is during the day-to-day operations that you will find yourself using some of the tools that are built into Configuration Manager, and those that are used to extend the native functionality. In this section you will find chapters that cover the backup and restore procedures for the site, ways to leverage tools that Microsoft has made available, methods of extending the functionality of Configuration Manager, and some handy troubleshooting tips.

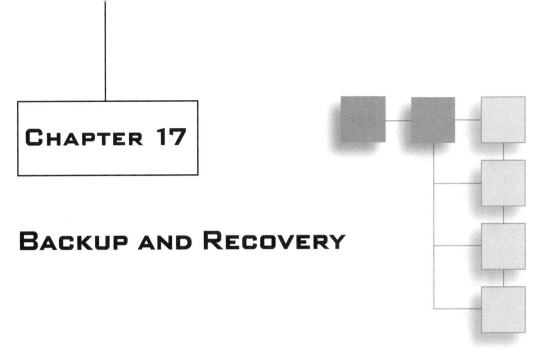

CHAPTER 17

BACKUP AND RECOVERY

No one likes to think about the problems that can arise within a site, but invariably, something will happen that will cause a system crash. And no matter how reliable the hardware is, how well the site was architected, or how well maintained a system is, Murphy's Law will prove to be right once again. To prepare for the problems that occur, the site should be backed up regularly. If there is more than one site, each site should be backed up separately. Once backed up, the site can be restored efficiently in case there is a catastrophe. Of course there is more than one definition for catastrophe. A natural disaster that destroys a building, a fire that consumes a branch office, or a drive failure in a system all fit the description. Having contingency plans to mitigate the downtime is essential to recovering your site.

BACKUP OPTIONS

The Backup ConfigMgr Site Server task is used to back up the site settings and site database. By default, the Backup ConfigMgr Site Server task is not enabled. The Configuration Manager team made the decision to leave it disabled because there are a few different configuration options for the site server and the site database server. Also, the team did not want to configure a default location for the backup files. Instead, they decided the task should remain disabled until the site administrator configures and enables it.

When backing up the site settings and database, the supported backup process is using the Backup ConfigMgr Site Server task. Using the SQL Server backup utility is not supported due to the fact that the site server configuration settings and the site database backup might not be synchronized. If the site server configuration files and the site database are not synchronized, the restore may prove to be problematic.

As mentioned, there are different configurations that you can use when setting up your site. The site database can reside on the same server as your site server, or it can reside on a dedicated database server. The site database server can be installed on a single system, or it can reside on a failover cluster. The Backup ConfigMgr Site Server task has different setting options that can be used for all of these different configuration options.

Opening the Backup ConfigMgr Site Server task from Site Settings > Site Maintenance > Tasks, you are presented with the configuration settings seen in Figure 17.1. As with many of the tasks, there are scheduling options available on this configuration page, as well as the option to configure the path where the backup files will be stored. When you enable the task, you are not able to enter

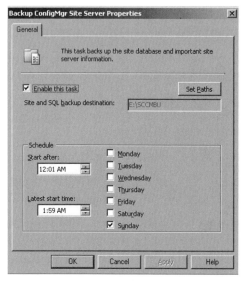

Figure 17.1
Backup ConfigMgr Site Server Task Options

the path, the path field is grayed out. Instead, you will have to click the Set Paths button to configure the path.

When you configure the schedule for the backup, make sure you take into account the schedule for other processes. The backup task stops the Executive and Site Component Manager during the backup process. With the Executive stopped, the Configuration Manager components will not be able to run during the backup process. The backup task captures the Inboxes and Logs directories, which means anything in either of those directories will be saved with the backup. If the site server is in the process of distributing software to distribution points, you will back up all of the files contained in the inboxes related to software distribution. Within a site, the distmgr.box folder will have files that are being sent. If the package is being sent to other sites, the despooler.box, replmgr. box, and schedule.box will contain files that will be backed up. This can increase the size of the data stored in the backup and impact the recovery time for the site. If possible, try to time the backup before any automatic updating of the distribution points.

N o t e

If you want to start the backup outside of the configured schedule, all you have to do is start the SMS_SITE_BACKUP service in the Services control panel.

The Set Backup Paths page that is presented when you click the Set Paths button is seen in Figure 17.2. There are three settings within the Destination Options section that will either be available or grayed out depending on how the site database is configured. If the site database server is co-located with the site server, the first two options appear—Local Drive On Site Server For Site Data And Database and Network Path (UNC Name) For Site Data And Database. The first option, Local Drive On Site Server For Site Data And Database allows you to configure a path on the site server for both the configuration settings and files from the site server, as well as the database backup. The path that you define using this option is a fully qualified path such as E:\SCCMBackup.

With the second option, Network Path (UNC Name) For Site Data And Database, you can configure the backup location to be a share on a file server. This is typically the preferred option due to the fact that you are storing the backup in a location that can be accessed from a rebuilt system if your site server fails.

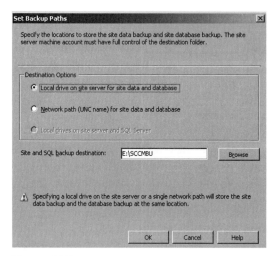

Figure 17.2
Set Backup Paths

Backup Control File

When the scheduled time for the backup arrives, there are two services that are started on a primary site, the SMS_SITE_BACKUP and SMS_SITE_SQL_BACKUP. The SMS_SITE_BACKUP is a service on the site server and the SMS_SITE_SQL_BACKUP is a service on the site database server. Both of these are controlled by the Backup ConfigMgr Site Server task. When the task initiates, it reads the information stored in the backup control file. The configuration information within this file directs the task what services need to be stopped, which systems are running the services, and what information needs to be backed up. The backup control file, appropriately named smsbkup. ctl, is found within the Inboxes\smsbkup.box directory. If your site server is running on a 64-bit platform, there is a 64-bit specific version of the smsbkup.ctl file that can be found in the x64 subdirectory.

To review or edit the smsbkup.ctl file, open it in Notepad. The file starts with warnings about editing. Notice in Figure 17.3, the details list that editing is allowed, but only in specific sections of the file. As you move down the file, you will find that there are sections listed with the title Editing Allowed. Make sure you heed the warning and only edit the sections specified, otherwise you run the risk of causing the backup task to fail.

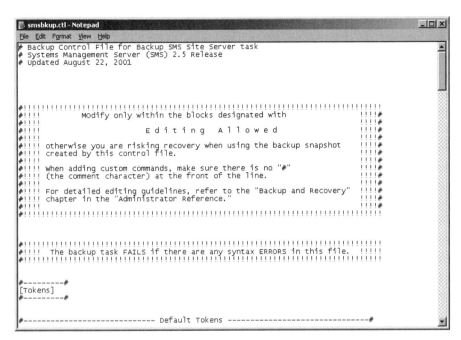

Figure 17.3
smsbkup.ctl File

Each section of the file controls how the backup task performs. In order, the sections are Tokens, Stop, Tasks, and Start. The Tokens section is used to identify the variables that the backup task will use. The Tokens section starts by identifying the default token and its values. The default token information is gleaned from site information stored in the site database and the site server registry. These include:

- **SITE_CODE**—Used to identify the 3 character site code of the site.

- **SITE_SERVER**—Used to identify the name of the system that is the site server for the site.

- **SITE_DB_SERVER**—Used to identify the name of the system that hosts the site database site system role.

- **PROVIDER_SERVER**—Used to identify the name of the system that hosts the provider service.

- **SITE_SERVER_ROOT_DIR**—Used to identify the installation path for the site server.

- **SITE_DB_SERVER_ROOT_DIR**—Used to identify the installation path of the site database.

- **SITE_DB_NAME**—Used to identify the name of the site database.

- **SITE_BACKUP_DESTINATION**—Used to identify the backup location configured in the Backup ConfigMgr Site Server task.

There are three additional tokens defined in this section. These tokens are used to control where the backup files will be located within the backup location configured within the Backup ConfigMgr Site Server task. When the backup task starts, these entries will be read from the smsbkup.ctl file and the directories will be created. The three tokens and their values are as follows:

SITE_SERVER_DEST = %SITE_BACKUP_DESTINATION%\SiteServer

SITE_DB_SERVER_DEST = %SITE_BACKUP_DESTINATION%\ SiteDBServer

PROVIDER_SERVER_DEST = %SITE_BACKUP_DESTINATION%\ProviderServer

The Tasks section is used to control what is backed up during the backup task. There are five entries defined within the first part of the Tasks section. Using the variables defined in the Tokens section, these five entries are used to control the directories that are backed up. The first part of each entry defines the location where the directory exists on the site server and the second part defines the location where the directories and files will be stored. The word "file" at the beginning of each line denotes that entries from the file system are to be backed up. The entries are as follows:

file %SITE_SERVER_ROOT_DIR%\bin \SMSServer\bin	%SITE_SERVER_DEST%
file %SITE_SERVER_ROOT_DIR%\inboxes DEST%\SMSServer\inboxes	%SITE_SERVER_
file %SITE_SERVER_ROOT_DIR%\Logs SMSServer\Logs	%SITE_SERVER_DEST%\
file %SITE_SERVER_ROOT_DIR%\data SMSServer\data	%SITE_SERVER_DEST%\

file %SITE_SERVER_ROOT_DIR%\svracct   %SITE_SERVER_DEST
%\SMSServer\srvacct

The second part of the Tasks section is used to identify the registry keys to back
up. As with the first section, variables are used to define where the registry keys
are located and where they are to be backed up. The word "reg" at the beginning
of each line denotes that registry entries are to be copied during the backup. The
two entries are:

reg \\SITE_SERVER\HKEY_LOCAL_MACHINE\Software\Microsoft\
NAL   %SITE_SERVER_DEST%\SMSbkSiteRegNAL.dat

reg \\SITE_SERVER\HKEY_LOCAL_MACHINE\Software\Microsoft\
SMS   %SITE_SERVER_DEST%\SMSbkSiteRegSMS.dat

On a site server that is installed on a 64-bit operating system these entries are:

reg \\SITE_SERVER\HKEY_LOCAL_MACHINE\Software\wow6432Node\
Microsoft\NAL   %SITE_SERVER_DEST%\SMSbkSiteRegNAL.dat

reg \\SITE_SERVER\HKEY_LOCAL_MACHINE\Software\wow6432Node\
Microsoft\SMS   %SITE_SERVER_DEST%\SMSbkSiteRegSMS.dat

The final part of the Tasks section is used to define how the site database files are
backed up. There is only one entry within this section. The word "sitedbdump"
at the beginning of the line denotes that the database file is to be copied during
the backup task. The entry is:

Sitedbdump %SITE_DB_NAME%   %SITE_DB_SERVER_DEST%\
SMSbkSQLDBsite.dat

The Stop and Start sections of the file are used to stop services before the
backup begins, and then start the services after the backup has completed. The
default services that are affected by these two sections are the SMS_Site_
Component_Manager, SMS_SQL_Monitor, and the SMS_Executive. When
you read through the smsbkup.ctl file, you will notice that the entries for these
services are missing. The Backup ConfigMgr Site Server task already has these
services hard-coded to stop and start, so they are not needed within the
smsbkup.ctl file.

Modifying smsbkup.ctl

If there are any additional features that need to be backed up during the site backup, you can add them to the smsbkup.ctl file. As mentioned earlier, make sure that you only edit the sections where allowed. If you are careful and edit the file correctly, you can capture any additional components that have been added into your Configuration Manager site configuration, including third-party application data.

Within the Tokens section, you can set a token's value by defining the token as *TOKEN_NAME = TOKEN_VALUE*. The other sections rely on a keyword to denote the action that is being taken. Within the Stop and Start sections, you can identify the services or applications that should be stopped or started by using the service or exec command. As you can probably tell, service is used to stop or start a system service and exec is used to stop or start an executable. When using the service command, the syntax is:

```
service \\server_name\service_name
```

When using the exec command, the syntax is:

```
exec executable_name
```

Within the Tasks section, you can define additional files to back up by using the file command. Following the command, you need to identify the folder location where the files reside, and the destination location where they will be stored. When folders are specified, the folder is backed up recursively, capturing all files and subfolders. Wildcard characters are also allowed, where the * is used to denote variable length matches and the ? is used to replace individual characters. You can use the default entries as an example, but the syntax that you will have to use is:

```
file file_path\folder_name Destination_Path\Destination_Folder
```

The registry entries that will be captured during the backup are identified by using the reg command. All keys and values under the specified path will be backed up. The syntax for the reg command is:

```
reg \\Site_Server_Name\Registry_Path\Registry_Key Destination_Path\
Destination_Folder
```

Afterbackup.bat

If you find that you want to perform additional action outside of the actions that are provided during the backup task, or the backup task does not provide the capabilities that you need, you do have one additional feature that you can use for controlling the backup—the afterbackup.bat file. While afterbackup.bat file is an optional component, it is used to perform actions after the backup task has completed. When you create the afterbackup.bat file, you need to save it in the same location as the smsbkup.ctl file—SCCM_Install_Dir\Inboxes\smsbkup.box. Probably the most common use is to copy the backup file to another location for redundant storage. You can create the backup file on the site server during the backup task, and then copy the file to a file server or remote system for safe storage. Anything that you can script can be called from the afterbackup.bat file.

Note

The afterbackup.bat file only runs when there has been a successful completion of the backup task. If the backup task fails for any reason, afterbackup.bat will not be called.

Once the backup has completed, you can find detailed backup information within the smsbkup.log file. It is here, as seen in Figure 17.4, that you will find information on what parts of the backup completed correctly, and where problems occurred. This log is especially useful when you are configuring the backup the first time and are troubleshooting problems that may arise.

RECOVERY OPTIONS

We go through all of the work to set up a viable backup process so that we will have the data that we need if we lose a critical component within our site, or the entire site itself. There are a few components that can be configured as highly available, such as the site database server that can be clustered and the Management Point that can be part of a network load balanced cluster. But there are some components that are effectively a single point of failure. The site server is the perfect example of this, and the one component that is not easily brought back online. Management points, server locator points, reporting points, etc., can be brought back online by installing their functionality on another system. The site server components and configuration settings are not as easy to restore. The site database server, if it does fail, is also not as easy to bring back online.

The Configuration Manager team has provided a solution that minimizes the complexity of restoring a site server, the site database server, or both. The tool

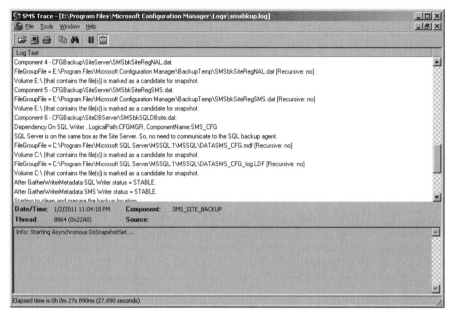

Figure 17.4
smsbackup.log File

that is provided with Configuration Manager is called the ConfigMgr Site Repair Wizard. The ConfigMgr Site Repair Wizard is installed by default on the site server. As its name implies, it has a simple wizard-driven interface that can be used to bring a site back online.

ConfigMgr Site Repair Wizard

To use the ConfigMgr Site Repair Wizard, log on to the site server and click Start > All Programs > Microsoft System Center > Configuration Manager 2007 > ConfigMgr Site Repair Wizard.

Restoring a Failed Site

Restoring a failed site begins with rebuilding servers that will host the site server and site database roles. The new systems should be built to the same specifications as the original systems.

1. Install the appropriate operating system on the site server system.

2. Install the service packs, hotfixes, and updates that were installed on the original site server system.

3. Install the appropriate operating system on the site database system.

4. Install the service packs, hotfixes, and updates that were installed on the original site database system.

5. On the site server system, install and configure all of the prerequisite components for Configuration Manager 2007 R3.

6. Install the same version of SQL Server that was originally installed on the site database system.

7. Install all of the SQL Server service packs, hotfixes, and updates to bring the SQL Server to the same level as the failed SQL Server.

8. Install Configuration Manager 2007 using the same site code as the original site.

9. Install all of the Configuration Manager 2007 service packs, hotfixes, updates, and feature releases to the same levels as the failed site server system.

Once the site server and site database system are installed and up-to-date with all service packs, hotfixes, updates, and feature releases, start the ConfigMgr Site Repair Wizard on the site server. The first page of the wizard reflects the name of the site server that is to be repaired, as seen in Figure 17.5. Verify the name is correct for your site server and click Next.

On the Backup File Location page, seen in Figure 17.6, click the Browse button to locate the backup file used to restore the site. The backup file can be selected from a local system drive or a network location.

If the site database has been lost, leave the Do Not Restore Database checkbox cleared. If the database has not been compromised, select the checkbox to restore only the site server. Verify the settings are correct. Once you click Next, the restore will commence. No additional warnings will be given beforehand. As the restore progresses, you will see a progress screen such as the one shown in Figure 17.7. When complete, click Next.

A new set of parameters appears within the wizard once the restore has completed successfully. The first new page of parameters is used to define where within the site hierarchy the repaired site server resides. You have two choices, as seen in Figure 17.8. Selecting the This Is A Central Site option is used

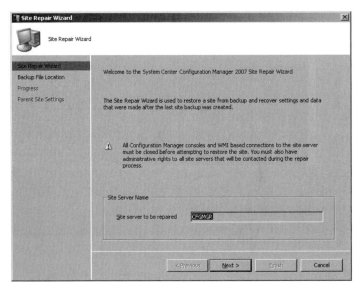

Figure 17.5
ConfigMgr Site Repair Wizard

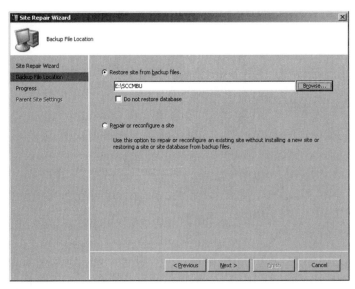

Figure 17.6
Backup File Location

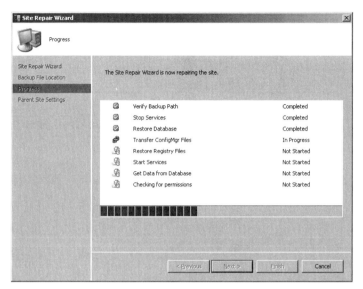

Figure 17.7
Restore Progress

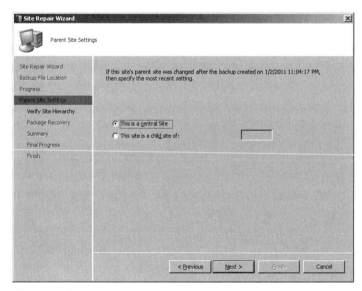

Figure 17.8
Parent Site Settings for Central Site

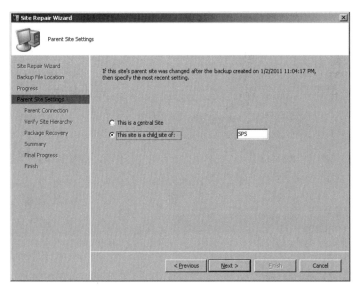

Figure 17.9
Parent Site Settings for Parent Site

when the site is the top-most site in the hierarchy. The second option, This Is A Child Site Of is used to define the parent site of the repaired site. When you select this option, you will need to enter the site code of the parent site.

If the restored site is a child of another site, identify the parent site as shown in Figure 17.9. The address for the parent site will appear within the Parent Connection page. If it does not, or if the information is incorrect, you can enter the address information by clicking the New button and entering the correct data in the Address Properties page seen in Figure 17.10. If the original data in the Addresses section is incorrect, make sure you delete it.

To ensure that any changes that were made to the parent site are replicated back to the restored site, you can select the Recover Data From Parent Site checkbox. Selecting this option will force the Repair Wizard to read the data from the parent site and configure any effective changes to the restored site. If you are sure that there have not been any configuration changes since the last backup, clear the checkbox and the restore will be faster.

If the site is the central site, or the parent site information has been configured, the next wizard page presented is the site hierarchy, seen in Figure 17.11. Any

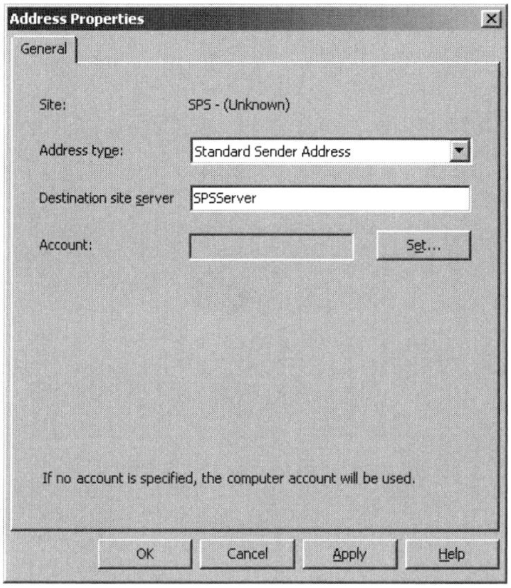

Figure 17.10
Address Properties

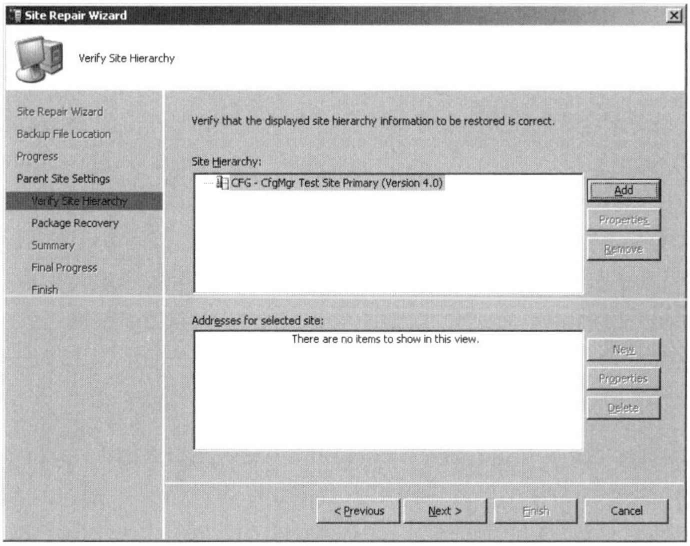

Figure 17.11
Site Hierarchy

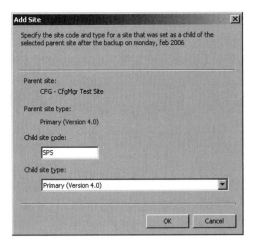

Figure 17.12
Add Site

sites that were added to the hierarchy after the backup was created need to be identified. Clicking the Add button will display the Add Site window, as seen in Figure 17.12. Here you can identify the site code of the child site, and specify whether the site was a primary or secondary site.

The final configuration page of the wizard, Package Recovery, seen in Figure 17.13, is used to guarantee that all of the software distribution, operating system deployment, and software update packages are accessible from the distribution points within the site. The default selection, Verify That All Package Source Files Are Accessible, will check the source data for all packages within the site. Selecting the Update The Distribution Point On This Site Server checkbox is used to update any of the packages that have changed since the last backup was performed. Alternatively, if you know that none of the packages have been updated since the backup was performed, you can select the Skip Package Verification and the restore will be faster.

Before the final restore steps are completed, the Summary page is presented. You can review your criteria before moving on. Once you click Next, the progress page will show whether the steps completed correctly or not. Review the information and then click Next and Close.

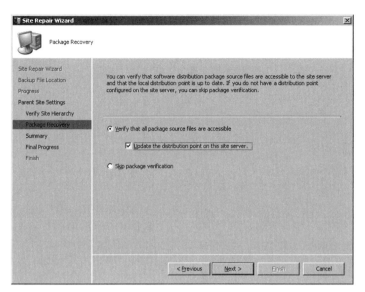

Figure 17.13
Package Recovery

During the site restore process the following tasks are performed:

- Save the svracct folder
- Stop Configuration Manager services on the site server
- Disable Configuration Manager services on the site server
- Restore the site database to the site database server
- Restore Configuration Manager files to the site server
- Restore the SMS and NAL registry keys to the site server
- Restore the svracct folder to the site server
- Increment the Hierarchy Manager Transaction ID
- Increment the DDM serial number
- Synchronize the client policy with the site database
- Increment the serial numbers within the site database
- Reset status message counters to 0
- Read and configure the site according to the latest site control file

- Start the Windows Management Instrumentation service on the site database server

- Reconfigure the child sites with the data restored to the site

- Reconfigure senders to the child sites

- Reconfigure site systems with the latest site control file information

- Restart the site service services

- Reset Access Control List objects on the restored folders and registry keys

- Resynchronize the parent and child sites

- Create appropriate addresses for new sites

- Change the parent site assignment if applicable

- Synchronize with the other sites

- Delete "phantom" child sites

- Regenerate collections, packages, and advertisements that were created after the backup had been created

Repairing a Site

There may be times when a site may have problems that are caused by corrupted settings and a full restore of the site is not necessary. You may also encounter a case where the site backup is not accessible or corrupt. In either of these cases, you can use the ConfigMgr Site Repair Wizard to perform a repair of the site without the backup files. The wizard performs very similar as when you have a backup file, but the database, registry, and configuration files are not copied back to the site server. Instead, the services are stopped and the configuration settings in the database are used to repair the site. Although this is not a recommended option, as a last resort, you can use this option to attempt to repair the site in question.

Log Files

When reviewing the backup task and its progress, the smsbkup.log file can come in very handy. All backup steps are recorded within the smsbkup.log file. Any

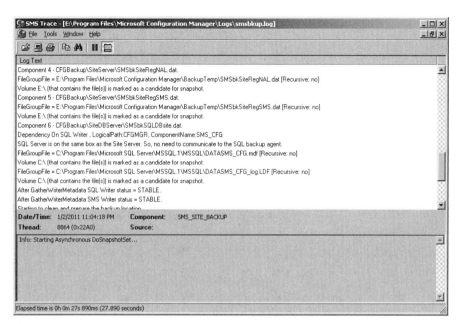

Figure 17.14
smsbkup.log File in SMS Trace

errors that occur can then be identified and used to correct issues with the backup task. As you are reviewing the smsbkup.log file, you will probably notice that the entries reflect the actions that are defined within the smsbkup.ctl file. Figure 17.14 shows a small section of the log. Notice the registry key and database backup entries that were logged.

The other log files that are used during backup and restore procedures are:

- **smswriter.log**—Used to record details of the SMS Writer Volume Shadow Copy Service tasks.

- **smssqlbkup.log**—Used to record the details of the SQL Server backup agent Volume Shadow Copy Service tasks. Only used when the site database is on a separate server than the site server.

- **repairwizard.log**—Used to record the tasks performed by the ConfigMgr Site Repair Wizard during a restore or repair process.

- **recoverymanager.log**—Used to record the tasks performed by the ConfigMgr Site Repair Wizard during the recovery phase of a restore or repair process.

Crash Cart

The term "crash cart" was historically used in the medical field. A crash cart contains all of the items needed to save the life of a person who has gone into cardiac arrest. These mobile carts are stored in inconspicuous locations, but are easily moved when needed. Medical personnel have all of the tools they need at their disposal instead of having to run around and find them when needed. If the medical facility has done a proper job of making sure the crash cart has all of the tools required, the likelihood of saving someone's life is increased.

In a data center, a crash cart takes on the same meaning; just this time the crash cart contains the tools to bring a system back online quickly. These tools include hardware and software components. In the case of a Configuration Manager site server, there needs to be specific software available to bring the system back to its pre-crash state. You should include the following items in your crash cart:

- Keyboard
- Mouse
- Monitor
- Portable DVD drive (if necessary)
- Portable Hard Drive (optional)
- The following software on DVD or the portable hard drive:
- Windows Server 2003 or Windows Server 2008
- SQL Server 2005 or SQL Server 2008
- Configuration Manager 2007
- Appropriate Windows Server Service Packs
- Appropriate SQL Server Service Packs
- Appropriate Configuration Manager 2007 Service Packs
- Appropriate Software Updates for Windows Server version
- Appropriate Software Updates for SQL Server version
- Appropriate Software Updates for Configuration Manager 2007
- Configuration Manager 2007 R3
- Any additional third-party software used within the site

Before you start restoring your site, make sure that all of the Configuration Manager console connections have been closed. Also make sure that you don't have any utilities running that make WMI calls. The ConfigMgr Site Repair Wizard makes connections to the WMI and will fail if any of the repositories are locked by another process.

Before you start restoring the site, verify that you have administrator rights on the site server system, and the site database server. The account that you are logged on with is the account that is used to restore the site settings and the site database.

Event Log

The backup and restore processes, and all of the services used during a backup and restore, record entries into the Application event log of the systems where they run. When it comes to troubleshooting problems, or verifying that a backup completed correctly, you can check the event logs for the appropriate entries. If you are running System Center Operations Manager within your organization and the Configuration Manager management pack has been imported in to the management group, these entries are monitored for you.

- 5505—Site backup has started
- 6829—SMS Writer is stopping the Configuration Manager services
- 3197—I/O operations are frozen on the site database
- 3198—I/O operations are resumed on the site database
- 18264—Database backup is complete
- 6830—SMS Writer has created the snapshots of the site server
- 6831—SMS Writer has started the Configuration Manager services
- 5056—Site Backup started copying snapshot files
- 5057—Site Backup has completed copying snapshot files
- 6833—Site Backup task has completed successfully

THE FINAL WORD

Protecting systems within your organization is critical to the long-term functionality of the organization. It is imperative that you not only back up the systems, including Configuration Manager, but that you also have a plan for restoring the data. Configuration Manager has a built-in backup process that backs up all of the critical data for the site and stores it so that the site can be rebuilt quickly. The restoration tools are tied to the backup utility and will restore the site server as well as the site database when necessary.

In the next chapter, we are going to review the tools that are included within the Configuration Manager administrator's console. These tools will become close friends as you manage the day-to-day activities of your Configuration Manager site.

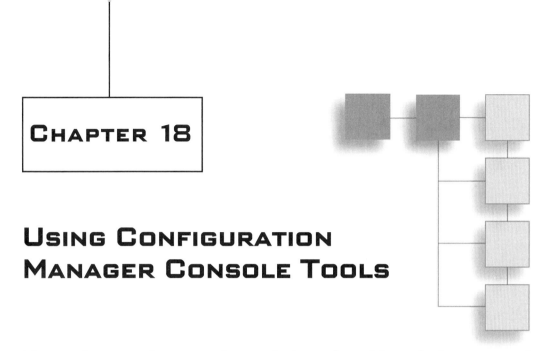

CHAPTER 18

USING CONFIGURATION MANAGER CONSOLE TOOLS

It's time that we took a comprehensive look at a few of the tools that are part of the Administrator console. These tools are touched on in several of the chapters that we have already looked at, but there is a lot more that you can do with some of them. Using these tools can make a Configuration Manager administrator's job easier. We will present the Resource Explorer, status message viewer, and service manager, and detail the full potential of each of these tools.

RESOURCE EXPLORER

In its simplest terms, Resource Explorer is a gateway into the inventory stored within the database. Whenever hardware or software inventory is enabled, the collected information is stored within the site database. As we discussed in Chapter 9, "Managing Assets," all of this collected inventory information can be used for a variety of purposes: building collections, viewing installed hardware, determining software licensing needs, etc. And even though you have the ability to run reports to determine a systems hardware configuration and installed software, using Resource Explorer is more efficient when you want to get a quick look into a specific computer's inventory.

The most common way to open up Resource Explorer is to navigate to a collection, right-click on a system and select Start > Resource Explorer. Doing so will open the Resource Explorer console as seen in Figure 18.1. If you have read through the inventory chapter, you should be familiar with the options that are

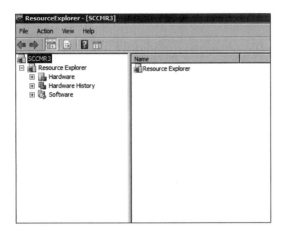

Figure 18.1
Resource Explorer

presented to you. At the top of the navigation pane you will find Hardware. This is where you will find the latest hardware inventory information. Directly beneath Hardware is the Hardware History node, which includes all of the past hardware inventory. The Hardware History will only show the system's history that is still contained in the database. Because we like to keep the database small and efficient, there is a grooming task that deletes old hardware history.

The final node in the navigation pane is the Software Inventory. Expanding this node will present additional information about the inventory that was scanned. As seen in Figure 18.2, you are able to view the product, file, and manufacturer information, as well as the collected files tied to the inventory stored within the database.

Figure 18.2
Viewing Software Inventory Information

Managing Hardware History

After opening Resource Explorer, you can expand the Hardware Inventory node to review the hardware information that was collected during the latest Hardware Inventory scan. All of the data that appears here was collected based upon the settings within the SMS_DEF.mof file. Modifications to this file can enhance or decrease the amount of configuration information that appears here. The Hardware History node will show the same data that you see within the Hardware Inventory node, but it will contain the previous data scans.

Your hardware inventory process probably includes a scheduled inventory scan. Depending on your organization's needs, the inventory scan is probably performed on a weekly or monthly basis. As each of these scans is performed, the prior inventory data is moved into the hardware history. As you can see in Figure 18.3, there are several entries within the Hardware History section, each of which is denoted by the date that the inventory was processed. Each of these entries becomes useful when you are troubleshooting problems or trying to determine when the hardware configuration on a system changed. You don't want to keep every hardware scan for the life of the system. Typically a couple months worth of data is sufficient.

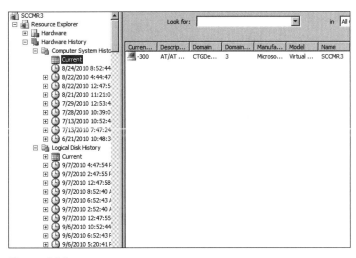

Figure 18.3
Hardware Inventory Scan History

To control the amount of inventory data that is stored within the database, you will need to configure a few settings within the Administrator's console. The first of these settings is the inventory schedule. As mentioned in Chapter 9, the Hardware Inventory client agent is used to configure when the hardware inventory is performed. When determining the schedule, remember that the custom schedule forces all of the systems within the site to scan and upload their inventory at the same time. This can be very network intensive, and SQL Server intensive, when the inventory is processed.

The simple schedule may not seem like the proper method of performing an inventory scan, but it does allow for a staggered inventory collection process. You will incur less network traffic and less SQL Server resource utilization as each of the systems scan and report inventory, but you lose the ability to control exactly when the inventory is ready to use. It is entirely up to your organization's needs as to when the inventory scan cycle is initiated. In Chapter 2, we weighed the benefits and drawbacks to each of the methods.

Once the inventory has been collected, it is only viable for a certain period of time. You don't want to keep the hardware history for too long a period of time because you will have unnecessary data in the database. At the same time, you don't want to purge the information too quickly; if you do, you will not have good reporting.

Within the Tasks section in Site Settings, you will find a task named Delete Aged Inventory History. As the name suggests, this task is used to remove all of the old inventory data from the database. By default the task will run once a week on Saturday morning between midnight and 5:00 AM. If you look at Figure 18.4, you can see the options that are available when you open the properties for the task. The key option here is the Delete Data Older Than (days) option. You are typically safe using the default of 90 days, but you can change it if you want to reduce or extend the retention time. As with any of the grooming tasks that are available, if you reduce the timeframe, you will run the risk of removing information that could be used for troubleshooting purposes. However, keeping the data for too long of a period of time can cause you to have too much data held within the database, resulting in larger backups and non-essential information.

Reviewing Software Inventory Information

Although the Software Inventory section of Resource Explorer does not contain a History section like the Hardware Inventory section does, there is plenty of

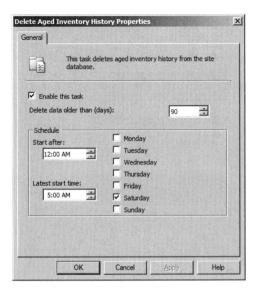

Figure 18.4
Delete Aged Inventory History Task Properties

information to review. When you first open the Software Inventory node, you are presented with four top-level nodes. The first of these, Collected Files, is where you will find all of the files that were actually "captured" and copied from managed systems to the Site Server. These files can then be used for troubleshooting purposes later on.

The second node is File Details. This is where you will find all of the software entities that were found while performing a software inventory scan. These entries should match up to the settings that you chose when you configured the software inventory client agent. As you can see in Figure 18.5, there may be many files with the same name displayed. If the files are named the same, but reside in different directories and partitions, they will all be shown.

The Last Software Scan simply displays the date and time when the last software inventory scan was performed on the system. This information is especially useful when you want to know how stale the inventory information is. The information that you see here displays both the software inventory scan and the file collection time.

The final node within Resource Explorer displays the software inventory based upon the product information. Here you will find all of the files that were

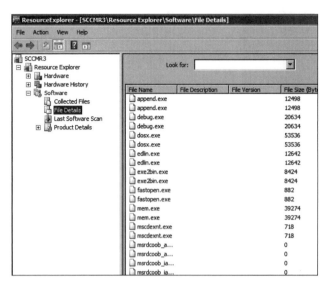

Figure 18.5
Software Inventory Displaying Multiple Entries for the Same File

scanned, sorted by the manufacturer information. This is where the results of the Inventory Names tab of the software inventory client agent, discussed in the next section, is most easily seen. When you create an inventory name, either a manufacturer or product name, and then associate different spellings of the name, the entries will appear in this list as a single item. Figure 18.6 shows the results of creating entries for both manufacturer and product names. Manufacturer names are then used to organize the software details under a single object, and the product names are used to reduce the number of file entries that should be seen as a single entry.

Managing Inventory Names

One of the most irritating parts of running inventory reports is the sheer number of entries that appear when you reconcile software inventory. If you have ever generated a software inventory report, you know what I mean. It seems that every software manufacturer uses different naming conventions for every piece of software. If they are not misspelling the product or manufacturer name, they are entering different names for each product or revision.

Let's assume that you work for the company XYZ Software Distributors, LLC. Although you have standards in place that dictate that the developers use your

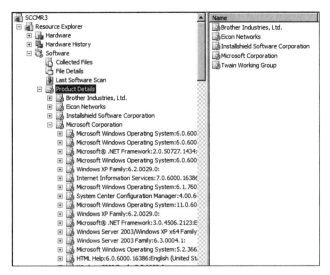

Figure 18.6
Manufacturer and Product Entries after Inventory Names Have Been Created

full name in the software, there are times when the developers mistype the name, or are too tired at 3 AM and use the wrong name. You now have three different manufacturer names associated with your software: XYZ Software Distributors; YXZ Software Distributors, LLC; and XYZ Software Distributors, LLC. These entries reside within the Configuration Manager database as three different manufacturers. To get these three entries to appear in reports and the Resource Explorer as a single manufacturer, you need to create entries within the Inventory Names tab of the software inventory client agent component.

Figure 18.7 shows the Inventory Names tab with the drop-down displaying the two options—Manufacturer and Product. If you want to create concise entries for either of these two options, you can select the appropriate option and then click the New button within the Display Name area. The Display Name option allows you to enter the name that you would like to appear in Resource Explorer. For our fictitious company, we are going to enter XYZ Software Distributors, LLC.

The lower area, Inventory Names, will include all of the disparate names that have been erroneously, and correctly, entered into the software when it was compiled. Although it can be tedious work, make sure that you review the

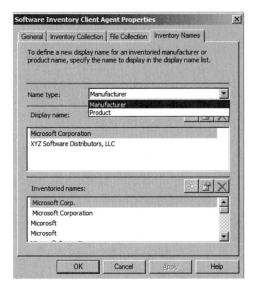

Figure 18.7
Inventory Names tab of the Software Inventory Client Agent

entries in Resource Explorer so that you know all of the different naming schemes that were used for the software. You will also want to periodically check reports or the Resource Explorer to make sure that you have not missed any new names that appear during subsequent inventory collection cycles. As you can see in Figure 18.8, the entries have been added in so that only one display name should appear with Resource Explorer.

Status Message Viewer

As you work with Configuration Manager you will find that it is essential to know what is going on with each of the components running within the site. If you have been reading the other chapters of this book, you know that the Configuration Manager developers were kind enough to design the system so that every component would send status messages and log information. The status messages that are sent from each component are stored within the database. These status messages contain some good information, but there is usually so much information being reported that it can get extremely confusing trying to determine what is critical.

Figure 18.8
Completed Inventory Names Entries

That is where the status message viewer comes in. This tool, which is part of the Configuration Manager console, allows you to view status messages as they pertain to each of the components. As you can see in Figure 18.9, you can also determine very quickly whether a component is having problems by quickly scanning for yellow caution and red critical icons.

Configuring your site so that it reports the information in a manner that is relevant to your organization is vital to your troubleshooting. Over the life of the site, the status settings that you can control will probably change, but not very often. Such is the case with a component such as the data discovery manager. As you perform your initial discoveries, you may want to change how many warnings and errors are received before the component shows a critical state. After all of the resources have been discovered and the agent installed, you can change the settings to a more strict level.

When making changes to the status levels, you will need to navigate to site settings and select Status Summary. You will find three options: Component Status Summarizer, Site System Summarizer, and Advertisement Summarizer. The component status summarizer controls the reporting of status messages from all of the components running within the site. This includes all of the individual components that make up each site system and the site server.

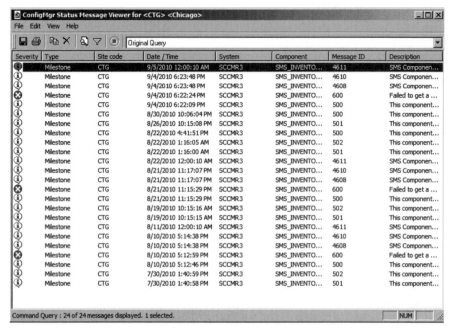

Figure 18.9
Status Messages in the Status Message Viewer

Opening the properties of the component status summarizer presents two tabs, as seen in Figure 18.10.

The General tab allows you to control whether or not status summarization is performed within the site. If enabled, the site server will process and evaluate the status messages, changing the status as necessary. This is also the location where you can control the replication priority and the threshold priority. The replication priority is used to manage what is sent from child sites to parent sites. Because the parent sites store information for each of the child sites, the status messages that are collected at the child site are sent to the parent. To guarantee that the status of the components are reflected in both sites, you may need to change the replication priority, seen in Figure 18.11. For instance, if you have changed the sender settings between sites to only allow high priority data to be sent from the child to the parent during specific hours, and you want to make sure that status messages are being delivered during that time frame, you need to change the replication priority to High. Otherwise you run the risk of not displaying the correct information in the parent site.

Figure 18.10
Component Status Summarizer Properties

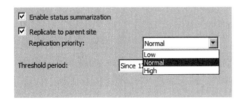

Figure 18.11
Component Status Message Replication Priority

The threshold period dictates which status messages are used when evaluating the status of the components. The default setting is to only use messages that have been received since midnight. As you can see in Figure 18.12, you have several options to choose from when deciding on the evaluation period. If you want to display the site's status on a weekly basis, displaying how the site is performing since the work week began, you can select Since Monday from the list. Take note that doing something like this will cause the summarizer to evaluate more and more information as the week progresses and may not reflect how the site systems have been performing lately.

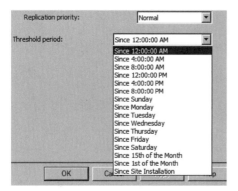

Figure 18.12
Configuring the Threshold Evaluation Period

The Thresholds tab is used to control the status displayed within the System Status node. Looking at Figure 18.13, you will notice that you can control the limits for informational, warning, and error messages. If you select Error Status Messages from the Message Type drop-down, you will see that the warning threshold is configured to 1 and the critical threshold level is set to 5 by default. This means that whenever 1 or more error messages are received, the status will

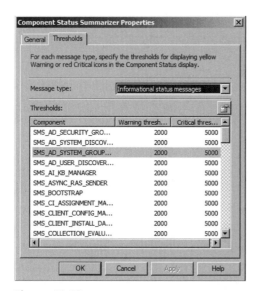

Figure 18.13
Status Message Type Options

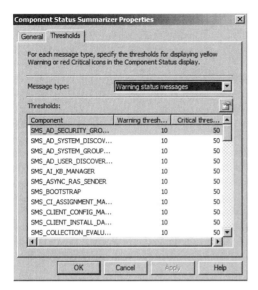

Figure 18.14
Warning Status Message Levels

be changed to a warning state. Whenever 5 or more error messages arrive, the status will show as Critical. Each one of the components can be configured to have unique settings. All you have to do is double-click the appropriate component within the Thresholds selection pane and set the value that you deem appropriate for the component. Note that you have to configure the warning level lower than the Critical level.

Figure 18.14 shows the default levels for warning status messages, and Figure 18.15 displays the levels for error status messages. Note that the levels for informational status messages are primarily a courtesy so that you know when a component is going a little crazy and spitting out too many status messages. This could be a sign of the component having a problem, but only sending out messages that appear to be benign, but in actuality, there is something amiss and you are sending a lot of data across the network to fill up your database.

The site system status summarizer, seen in Figure 18.16, appears to be very similar to the component status summarizer, but upon reviewing the properties you will see there are a few differences. The first difference between the two is shown on the General tab. There is a Schedule option that is used to control when the status summarization is performed on each of the site systems. This is

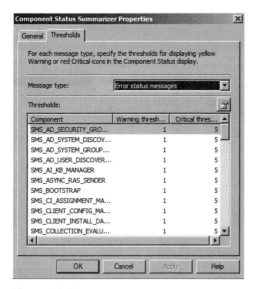

Figure 18.15
Error Status Message Levels

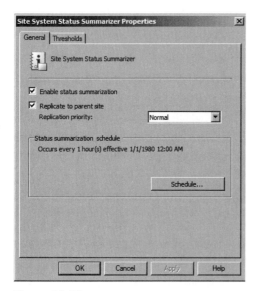

Figure 18.16
Site System Status Summarizer Properties

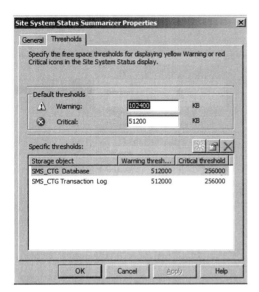

Figure 18.17
Free Space Threshold Levels

the same type of schedule dialog that you will find in many of the property options within Configuration Manager. Once configured, each site system's status will be updated accordingly.

The other difference is found within the Thresholds tab. Here you will find free space thresholds for the database and transactions logs. You can also configure free space thresholds for the partitions that host Configuration Manager components. As seen in Figure 18.17, the thresholds that are set allow you to monitor when the partition that the database and transaction logs becomes dangerously full. You have the option to configure different thresholds of course, and you should determine your comfort level when it comes to free space on these partitions.

Adding in additional thresholds is as simple as clicking the New button and selecting the partition or path that you want to monitor. Notice that you do not get the option to configure your own paths, only paths where Configuration Manager components are installed are reflected in the Storage Object drop-down. Once you have selected the object, enter the KB amounts that you want to use for warning and critical levels.

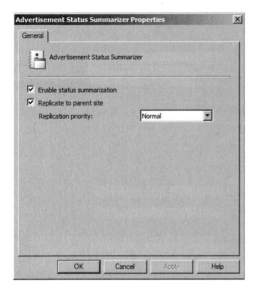

Figure 18.18
Advertisement Status Summarizer Properties

The final option within the Status Summarizer node is the Advertisement Status Summarizer. As you can see in Figure 18.18, you do not have much control over this summarizer. Configuring whether or not the summarizer is enabled and the replication priority are the only two configuration options. Advertisement status messages are continually summarized so that you get pertinent feedback during software distribution.

Once you have the components configured for the appropriate thresholds, you can view the thresholds and threshold period by double-clicking the component within the Site Status container. The property page that appears does not grant you the ability to make changes to the settings, but you can very quickly determine what those settings are.

One thing to note when working with the site status information; when you change the display interval, you are not changing the threshold period. The threshold period determines the time frame that is used when displaying changes in the status state. The display interval only affects how much data is displayed when viewing status messaging from the components. Therefore, if the Threshold Period is configured as Since 12:00 AM and the Display Interval is configured as Since Sunday, it does not matter how many warning and critical status messages are displayed within that time frame, only the messages received after midnight will affect the criticality that is displayed.

SERVICE MANAGER

Configuration Manager can be a little misleading when it comes to working with the services that make up the product. If you take a look at the services that appear within the Services Control Panel option, you will find only a handful of services. The services that do appear are:

SMS_EXECUTIVE

SMS_REPORTING

SMS_SERVER_LOCATOR_POINT

SMS_SITE_BACKUP

SMS_SITE_COMPONENT_MANAGER

SMS_SITE_VSS_WRITER

There are other services that run within Configuration Manager, but they are not exposed as the previous services are. These services actually run as threads within the Configuration Manager system. The only way to control these threads is to use the Service Manager console. It is here that you can view whether a service is running or not, stop and start services, and control the logging for each of the services.

To open Service Manager, navigate to the Tools node at the very bottom of the Configuration Manager Console navigation pane. Clicking on the ConfigMgr Service Manager component will not do anything. You have to right-click the component and select Start ConfigMgr Service Manager. A new console window will appear once you do so.

The first thing you will probably notice about the ConfigMgr Service Manager console is the Components and Servers options. There are two ways that you can view the Configuration Manager components: You can expand the Components node to view all of the components that are installed within the site, or you can expand the Servers node and view each of the servers that are acting as site

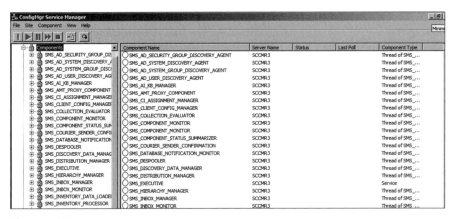

Figure 18.19
Services and Threads

systems. Let's take a look at the Components node first. If you select the Components node, you will see each of the components listed within the details pane. For each component, you will find a listing for the servers that the component is installed on, the status of the component, the last time the component was queried to see if it was running or not, and whether the component is running as a Windows service or a Configuration Manager thread, as seen in Figure 18.19.

After collapsing the Components node and expanding the Servers node, you will find all of the site servers listed. When you expand a server's name, you will be presented with a list of the services running on that site system, as seen in Figure 18.20. Selecting the site server's name will present the same view of components that you were presented in Figure 18.19, except this time you will only see the services running on that specific system instead of all of the services installed within the site.

So what can you do with this information besides determine which services are installed? First off, you can determine whether a service is running or not by issuing a query to see if the thread or service is active. To do so, select the service that you want to check and click the Query button, which is the button that has the exclamation point as its icon. Alternately, you can right-click the component and select Query. Once you click the Query button you will see the circle beside the component name change. It will either be a green arrow, if the component is running, or a red square, if the component is stopped. You should also note that

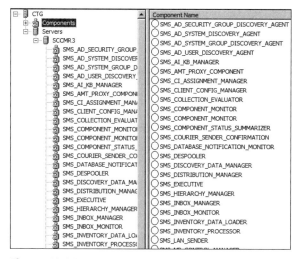

Figure 18.20
Viewing Site System's Components

the status will show the state of the component and the Last Poll column will now be populated with the date and time that you issued the query.

The other buttons allow you to stop, pause, resume, and start the components. For the components that run as Windows services, you have the option of stopping and starting them from the Services control panel option or from ConfigMgr Service Manager. Threads however, have to be controlled from the ConfigMgr Service Manager. Take note that when you change the state of a component, the component's state is not automatically refreshed within the console. Each time you press one of the Start, Stop, Pause, or Resume buttons, you will have to click the Query button to refresh the view to reflect the current state. You can select multiple components and control them all at the same time. Doing so allows you to query, or manipulate, the running state of several components at the same time.

Managing the log files that are used with each of the components is also performed from Service Manager. If you want to manage a specific log file on several systems, expand the Components node, expand the component, and then you can manage each site system. If you are wanting to manage several log files on a specific site server, use the Servers node. Right-click the component and then select the Logging option. You will be presented with a dialog box that will allow you to specify the path to the log file and the maximum size of the log file. Note that if you select multiple components, you are presented with an additional option, Use Same File For All Selected Components. As it implies, all of the selected components will use the same log file.

Configuration Manager reports a lot of data into the log files. This aids in troubleshooting and tracing the flow of processing. It is recommended that you do not combine the logging information from multiple components. Not only will you reach the log file's capacity faster, you will also intermingle the logged data, making troubleshooting a little more difficult. Also note the path to which you are saving the log file information. The default path will be the Log directory within the installation directory for Configuration Manager. Any directory within the installation directory will be backed up by the Configuration Manager backup service. If you store your log files in a different directory, outside of the installation path, you will run the risk of not saving the logged data.

The following log files are controlled through components that appear within Service Manager:

- **adsgdis.log**—SMS_AD_SECURITY_GROUP_DISCOVERY_AGENT
- **adsysdis.log**—SMS_AD_SYSTEM_DISCOVERY_AGENT
- **adsysgrp.log**—SMS_AD_SYSTEM_GROUP_DISCOVERY_AGENT
- **adusrdis.log**—SMS_AD_USER_DISCOVERY_AGENT
- **aikbmgr.log**—SMS_AI_KB_MANAGER
- **atmproxymgr.log**—SMS_AMT_PROXY_COMPONENT
- **ciamgr.log**—SMS_CI_ASSIGNMENT_MANAGER
- **ccm.log**—SMS_CLIENT_CONFIG_MANAGER
- **colleval.log**—SMS_COLLECTION_EVALUATOR
- **compmon.log**—SMS_COMPONENT_MONITOR
- **compsumm.log**—SMS_COMPONENT_STATUS_SUMMARIZER
- **cscnfsvc.log**—SMS_COURIER_SENDER_CONFIRMATION
- **smsdbmon.log**—SMS_DATABASE_NOTIFICATION_MONITOR
- **despool.log**—SMS_DESPOOLER

- **ddm.log**—SMS_DISCOVERY_DATA_MANAGER
- **distmgr.log**—SMS_DISTRIBUTION_MANAGER
- **smsexec.log**—SMS_EXECUTIVE
- **hman.log**—SMS_HIERARCHY_MANAGER
- **inboxmgr.log**—SMS_INBOX_MANAGER
- **inboxmon.log**—SMS_INBOX_MONITOR
- **dataldr.log**—SMS_INVENTORY_DATA_LOADER
- **invproc.log**—SMS_INVENTORY_PROCESSOR
- **sender.log**—SMS_LAN_SENDER
- **mpcontrol.log**—SMS_MP_CONTROL_MANAGER
- **mpfdm.log**—SMS_MP_FILE_DISPATCH_MANAGER
- **netdisc.log**—SMS_NETWORK_DISCOVERY
- **objreplmgr.log**—SMS_OBJECT_REPLICATION_MANAGER
- **offermgr.log**—SMS_OFFER_MANAGER
- **offersum.log**—SMS_OFFER_STATUS_SUMMARIZER
- **outboxmon.log**—SMS_OUTBOX_MONITOR
- **policypv.log**—SMS_POLICY_PROVIDER
- **replmgr.log**—SMS_REPLICATION_MANAGER
- **schedule.log**—SMS_SCHEDULER
- **smsbkup.log**—SMS_SITE_BACKUP
- **sitecomp.log**—SMS_SITE_COMPONENT_MANAGER
- **sitectrl.log**—SMS_SITE_CONTROL_MANAGER
- **smssqlbkup.log**—SMS_SITE_SQL_BACKUP
- **sitestat.log**—SMS_SITE_SYSTEM_STATUS_SUMMARIZER
- **smswriter.log**—SMS_SITE_VSS_WRITER
- **sinvproc.log**—SMS_SOFTWARE_INVENTORY_PROCESSOR
- **swmproc.log**—SMS_SOFTWARE_METERING_PROCESSOR

- **statesys.log**—SMS_STATE_SYSTEM
- **statmgr.log**—SMS_STATUS_MANAGER
- **ntsvrdis.log**—SMS_WINNT_SERVER_DISCOVERY_AGENT
- **WCM.log**—SMS_WSUS_CONFIGURATION_MANAGER
- **wsyncmgr.log**—SMS_WSUS_SYNC_MANAGER

All of the aforementioned log files are initially configured as 2 MB files. If you so desire, you can increase the log file size to 1 GB. I wouldn't recommend that you do so however. Even though SMSTrace is a very nice program and will show you the contents of log files in an easy to read fashion, it will take quite a bit of time for the log file to be read. If you do need to increase the log file size for troubleshooting purposes, make sure you make the file size manageable.

Once you have configured the appropriate size for the log files, each component will write information into the log file until it becomes full. At that point, Configuration Manager will automatically rename the log file using an extension lo_. A new log file will be created. As each new log file becomes full, the previous lo_ version of the file will be deleted to make room for the newly filled file.

THE FINAL WORD

Having these tools built into the console is a definite benefit to any Configuration Manager administrator. Troubleshooting is easier. Inventory information is at your fingertips. Grooming and summarization tasks can be enabled and disabled quickly without having to create those jobs on the SQL Server. Without these tools, you would have to create your own tasks, develop your own SQL queries to get the data from the database, or rely on third-party utilities.

There are times when the built-in tools are not enough though. That is when you may find yourself wishing there was a way to perform actions that are not available to you. Luckily, the Configuration Manager console is extensible. If you are able to script the action that you want to perform, there is usually a method of incorporating that action into the console. The next chapter will show you some of the fun things you can do with the Configuration Manager SDK.

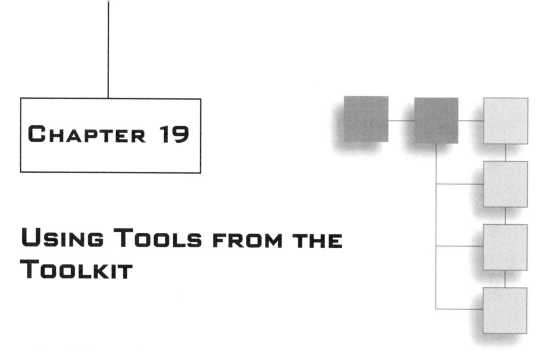

CHAPTER 19

USING TOOLS FROM THE TOOLKIT

Although the Configuration Manager console provides a well-rounded look into the site structure, configuration, and status, it does not provide all of the information that you need to view how an individual client is working. Of course you can look at the settings that are applied to the client from within the console, but if you want to view policy or configuration settings that the client is actually using, you need to visit the managed system.

To make it easier on you as the Configuration Manager administrator, Microsoft has provided a set of client tools. These tools are included within a package known as the Toolkit. The Toolkit includes three client utilities that you can use, and probably will use when you are trying to figure out what is going on with the managed system. These three tools are: SMS Trace, Policy Spy, and Client Spy. You can obtain the Toolkit from http://www.microsoft.com/downloads/en/details.aspx?FamilyID=5A47B972-95D2-46B1-AB14-5D0CBCE54EB8.

WORKING WITH SMS TRACE

Of all of the tools that you have at your disposal, SMS Trace will probably be the one tool that you will use more than any other. At its simplest, SMS Trace is just another log reader. You can open a log file and review its contents when you are troubleshooting problems or viewing components as they process data. To call SMS Trace just another log file reader is not doing it justice however. There are some very nice features that will keep you coming back to continue using it whenever you want to look at a log file.

When you open SMS Trace for the first time it will prompt you to enable it as the default application to be associated with files that have a .log extension. Allowing this behavior will come in very handy later on as you open log files and they appear within SMS Trace. Of course you can always change the association at a later time if you so desire.

One of the benefits of using SMS Trace is the automatic updating feature. As new lines are written to the log, they are presented within SMS Trace. The log file that you are reviewing can be left open and every time an entry is written to the log file, the entry will be displayed along with the details presented in an easy to read fashion. No longer do you have to keep closing and reopening the log files to see what has been appended. SMS Trace is not actually holding the file open and displaying the information in real-time; it is continually reading the file and displaying new lines as they are appended. By default, SMS Trace checks the log file once every 500 milliseconds–much faster than we can close and reopen the file.

With the association set to open log files, you can simply double-click a log file and it will spring open in SMS Trace, but there are advantages to launching SMS Trace and then using the Open command to open a file. Figure 19.1 shows the Open dialog that appears when you click File > Open or click the Open icon. You can select a log file and click open, but take notice of the two options at the bottom of the dialog. The first checkbox, Ignore Existing Lines, can be used to display only new lines as they are written to the log. This comes in very handy with large log files. You don't have to wait for all of the lines to be read and presented. Instead, it scans the file and then only displays the new lines as they appear.

The second option, Merge Selected Files, can be used to display two or more related files at the same time within one SMS Trace window. Consider using this option when you are troubleshooting a problem with related components. For instance, when you are troubleshooting the distribution of packages sent to distribution points in child sites, you can select the distmgr.log, replmgr.log, scheduler.log, and sender.log files to have a real-time view as the Distribution Manager packages the software for delivery, the sender evaluates the sites to

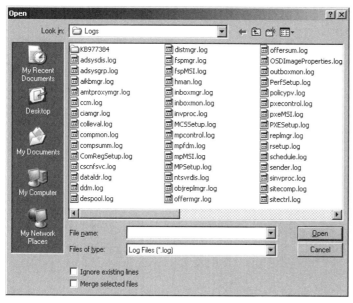

Figure 19.1
Open Dialog Options

distribute the software, the scheduler evaluates the available addresses, and the replication manager delivers the packets.

In the File menu there is another option for opening log files—Open On Server. When you select this option, systems within the site will appear in the selection window, as seen in Figure 19.2. If the selected system is a Configuration Manager site system, the console will connect to it through the SMS-*sitecode* share to access the Logs directory. If the system that you select is not a site system, you will receive an error. Using this feature, you can quickly connect to site systems and not have to worry about remembering in which drive the log files are located.

The Preferences option is used to control how SMS Trace behaves. The General tab, seen in Figure 19.3, controls how often SMS Trace evaluates new lines within the log file. The default is to check and display new lines every 500 milliseconds. If you want to decrease the amount of time that elapses between log file evaluations, you can change this value, although decreasing the elapsed time is not recommended, especially if you are reading log files on a remote system. The longer the evaluation time, the less real-time the log file evaluation becomes.

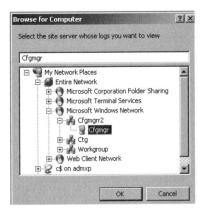

Figure 19.2
Open On Server Dialog

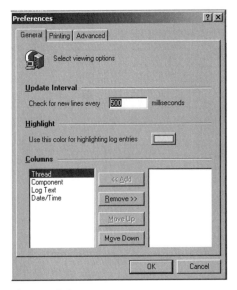

Figure 19.3
Preferences Options

The other options on the General tab allow you to control the color that is used when highlighting the lines that contain search criteria. The default color is yellow, which is also the same color that is used when highlighting any warning log entries. The Columns section controls the data that is displayed from the log files. By default all of the log data is displayed. You can remove columns that you

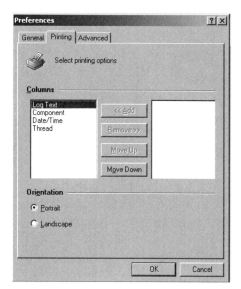

Figure 19.4
Printing Options

do not want to display by selecting the column name and clicking the Remove button. They can be restored by selecting the column name and selecting the Add button.

The Printing tab, seen in Figure 19.4, is used to control the data that is displayed on printouts of the log files, as well as the page orientation. Selecting columns for printing works the same way as configuring the columns for display on the General tab. The options for Portrait or Landscape printing come in very handy when you want to display more of the log file details.

The Advanced tab, seen in Figure 19.5, is used to control how often the screen is refreshed. This option is the most viable when the Ignore Existing Lines option is selected when opening a log file. When used, the display of the log file will clear and only new entries will appear. Set this value to the number of lines that you want to have shown at any time. When the log file reaches this maximum number, the display will clear and new lines will start displaying. If you use this option when you open a log file without using the Ignore Existing Lines, the log file will be re-evaluated and the display will be re-enumerated.

On the Tools menu you will find options that are used to control how you view the log file data that is displayed within SMS Trace. As you can see in Figure 19.6,

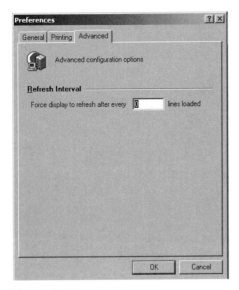

Figure 19.5
Advanced Tab

Figure 19.6
Tools Menu

the Tools menu is divided into three sections. The first section is used to find lines that contain specific criteria and copy lines to the clipboard. When you select Find, or press CTRL-F, the Find dialog presents you with the options to type in the text that you want to search for, whether the search will continue up or down the log file, and if the search should be performed against the log file in the same case that was entered in the search dialog. You can continue searching through the log file using the same search criteria by using the F3 key or selecting

Find Next from the Tools menu. If at any time you need to save the contents of the log file, you can highlight the lines you want to copy and then either select the Copy To Clipboard option or press the CTRL-C key combination. Once copied you can paste the saved information to a Text file or into an email.

The second section of the Tools menu holds some advanced searching features. Highlight is used to identify text that you want to monitor. When the selected text appears within a line of the log file, the line will appear highlighted with the color that was selected on the General tab of the Preferences. If you want to quickly identify lines of text that contain specific text strings, and see them as they appear within the log file, enter the text in the Highlight dialog and specify whether the highlighted text is case sensitive.

The Filter dialog gives you very fine granular control over what appears within the SMS Trace display. Log files can contain large amounts of text data. To limit the data that is displayed, you can define what information is displayed by using the options seen in Figure 19.7. These options can be used independently or in combination with one another to define what appears. The options available include:

- **Filter When The Entry Text**—used to search the details of the log file line. Can be any alphanumeric combination. Search criteria operators include:

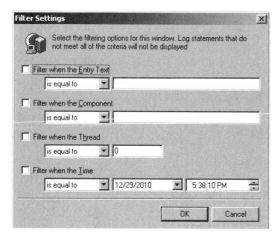

Figure 19.7
Filtering the Display

- Is Equal To
- Is Not Equal To
- Contains
- Does Not Contain

- **Filter When The Component**—Used to display lines that are generated by specific components. Can be any alphanumeric combination. Search criteria includes:

  - Is Equal To
  - Is Not Equal To
  - Contains
  - Does Not Contain

- **Filter When The Thread**—Used to display specific threads during processing. Only numeric thread values are allowed. Search criteria includes:

  - Is Equal To
  - Is Not Equal To

- **Filter When The Time**—Used to limit the timeframe within the log file. Uses date and time parameters. Search criteria includes:

  - Is Equal To
  - Is Not Equal To
  - Is Before
  - Is After

Although these options can be used with any log file, they are most powerful when used with merged log files. For instance, you can merge three log files, and during the processing you can use the option Filter When The Component Is Equal To to limit the display to a specific component. Then clear the filter to view all merged logs together. Using the Filter When The Thread option to display only the information from a specific thread can help you trace a specific process as it is running, such as a single package distribution. Limiting to the individual thread will allow you to view only the one package as it is copied to distribution points.

If you are unfamiliar with the error codes that are generated during processing, you can use the Error Lookup option, seen in Figure 19.8, to quickly list the details of an error code.

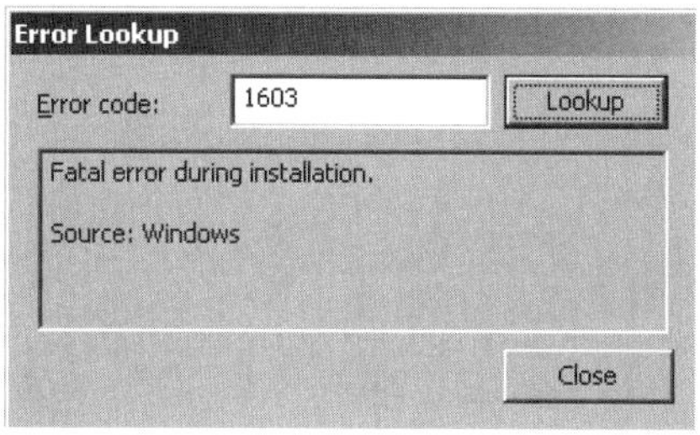

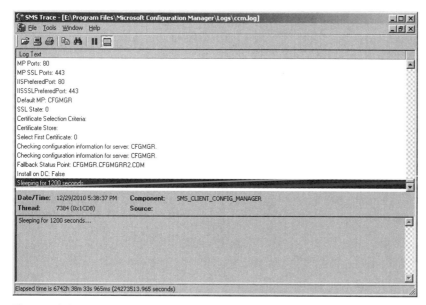

Figure 19.8
Error Lookup

The final third of the Tools menu controls how much information is displayed within SMS Trace. The Pause option is self-explanatory, as it stops the display of any additional lines that appear within the log file. The Hide Details option is used to control whether the additional column detail is displayed. Typically, most users see SMS Trace as seen in Figure 19.9. If you expand the size of the window, additional detail appears, as seen in Figure 19.10. On lower resolution monitors, you may want to restrict the amount of information that is displayed. Using Hide Details, only the Log Text Column appears within the display.

Figure 19.9
Typical SMS Trace View

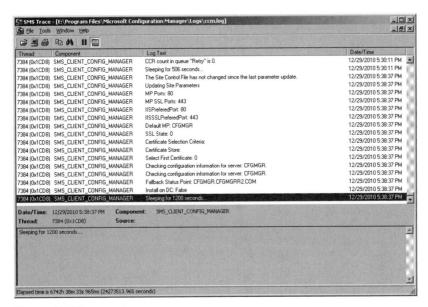

Figure 19.10
Expanded SMS Trace View

Selecting Hide Info Pane will remove the lower information section and display only the log details.

WORKING WITH POLICY SPY

Policy Spy is used to view the settings that the client is using from the policies that it has downloaded. As you know, the client will contact a management point to request the latest policy. The settings that are included within the policy are used to control how the client agents perform. Because policy settings are not stored in a file within the file system, it is very difficult to review the settings. Many of the settings are stored within the WMI, but accessing the settings can be difficult. Policy Spy does the work of culling the setting together into one cohesive view.

For a quick at-a-glance view of the client configuration settings, you can look at the Client Info pane on the lower left of Policy Spy. It is here that you will find the following information:

- **Name**—Computer name of the managed system.
- **ID**—The Configuration Manager unique identifier of the client.

- **Version**—The version number of the client.

- **Site**—The client's assigned site.

- **Assigned MP**—The client's assigned management point.

- **Resident MP**—The client's resident, or local, management point.

- **Proxy MP**—The client's proxy management point when it is within a secondary site.

- **Proxy State**—The state of the client's proxy management point; Active or Pending.

If you open Policy Spy while logged onto a managed system, you will be presented with a display that appears much like the one seen in Figure 19.11. The four tabs that appear on the top of the Results pane are used to view the policy information on the managed system. The Actual tab presents the current policy settings that are applied to the managed system. The policy settings are stored within policy trees, one for the managed system, and one for each user

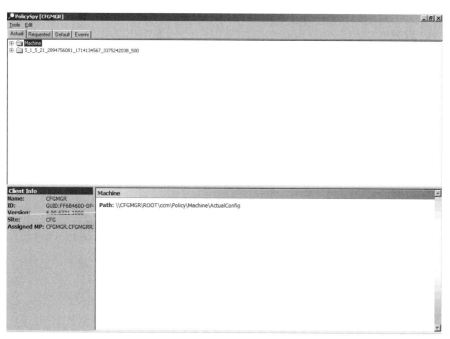

Figure 19.11
Policy Spy

policy that is applied. Expanding any of the policy trees will display the settings applied by the current policy.

The Requested tab appears very similar to the Actual tab. Again, there are policy setting trees shown, but the settings shown on the Requested tab are the settings within the last policy that was retrieved from the management point. The settings found here should be the same as those found on the Actual tab, as long as the last policy received has been applied.

Settings found in the Default tab are those that are applied to a system when it is first installed, and when a client repair is performed.

The Events tab is used to view what is happening with the client as it retrieves and evaluates policy data.

At the top of the Policy Spy window you will find two menu items—Tools and Edit. Tools is used to manage policies, and Edit is used to control the data shown. The options within the Edit menu are as follows:

- **Delete**—Used to delete selected instances within the Results pane.
- **Refresh**—Refreshes the information displayed within the Results and Details panes.
- **Clear Events**—Clears the events displayed within the Events tab.

The Tools menu provides more functionality. As seen in Figure 19.12, the menu is divided into five sections. The first section is used to access policies; the

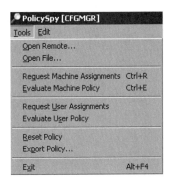

Figure 19.12
Tools Menu Options

second section manages machine policies; the third manages user policies; the fourth manipulates policies; the fifth closes the program. The menu options are as follows:

- **Open Remote**—Used to access policy information on a remote managed system.

- **Open File**—Used to open an exported policy file.

- **Request Machine Assignments**—Used to query the management point for the latest machine policy.

- **Evaluate Machine Policy**—Used to apply the downloaded machine policy on the managed system.

- **Request User Assignments**—Used to query the management point for the latest user policy.

- **Evaluate Machine Policy**—Used to apply the downloaded user policy on the managed system.

- **Reset Policy**—Deletes all policy settings applied to the machine and users.

- **Export Policy**—Used to create an XML file of the policies applied on the managed system.

- **Exit**—Closes Policy Spy.

Using Policy Spy

When problems arise on a managed system, Policy Spy can be used to evaluate the current settings on the managed system. For instance, if you think a component is not working correctly within the client, such as the software metering client agent, you can delete the instance that controls the agent—CCM_SoftwareMeteringClientConfig > SiteSettingsKey="1", seen in Figure 19.13. After selecting the settings line, click Edit > Delete. Not only will the entry be deleted from the Policy Spy interface, you can validate the deletion was effective by opening the Configuration Manager properties within the managed system's control panel. Figure 19.14 shows that the deletion worked—the ConfigMgr Software metering client agent appears as Installed instead of Enabled.

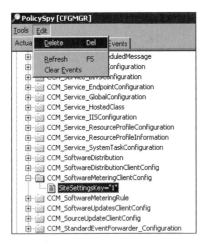

Figure 19.13
Deleting Instances

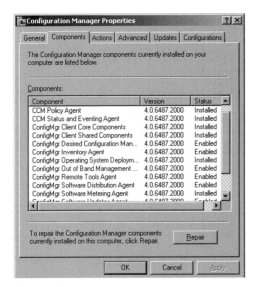

Figure 19.14
Reviewing Client Settings After Deletion

After deleting the instance, you can force a retrieval and evaluation of the policy. Clicking Tools > Request Machine Assignments will force the client to retrieve the latest policy from the management point. To finish the process, you will have to click Tools > Evaluate Machine Policy to force the client to re-evaluate the policy file and reconfigure the components according to the policy settings.

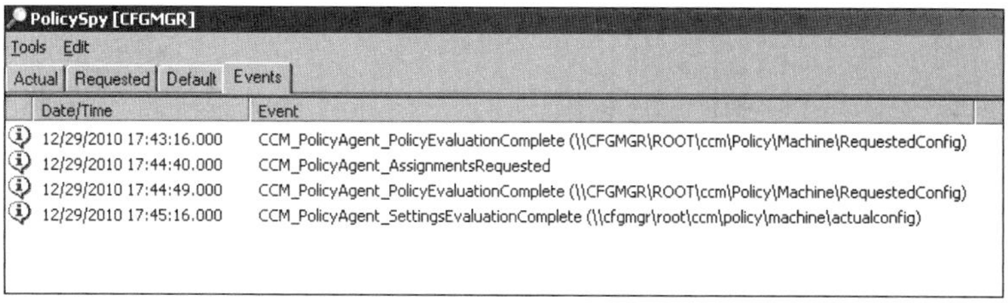

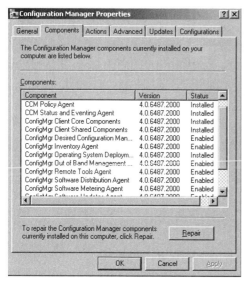

Figure 19.15
Monitoring Events

Switch over to the Events tab and you can monitor the events that occur as the client processes the information. After a minute or so from the time that you forced the machine policy evaluation, you should see an event specifying that the actual machine policy has been updated, as seen in Figure 19.15. After you see the event appear, refresh the Actual tab of Policy Spy to see if the settings were reapplied. Once reapplied, you should also see the ConfigMgr Software metering client agent appears in an Enabled state, as seen in Figure 19.16.

If you want to make sure the client is performing correctly, and applying the policy correctly, you can compare the settings found on the Requested tab to

Figure 19.16
Reviewing Client Settings After Policy Evaluation

those found within the Actual tab. Start off by forcing the policy retrieval and evaluation. Then watch the Events tab for the indication that the actual policy has been updated. Navigate back to the Requested tab and expand the setting or settings that you want to check. The Requested tab contains the information from the policy that was just retrieved from the management point. Verify the setting is configured the way that you expected, based upon the settings that you have configured at the site. Then navigate to the Actual tab and expand the same settings tree to review what was applied to the client. The settings found on the Actual and Requested tab should be the same. If they are not, attempt to reconfigure the settings by deleting the settings tree and then forcing a new evaluation of the policy.

If you cannot get the policy to apply, use the Tools > Reset Policy to reset the policy back to the default settings. You can find the settings that are applied by default by perusing the information found on the Default tab. Notice that the only client actions available from the default policy are the User and Machine policy retrieval and evaluation functions. You can force the retrieval and evaluation actions from the Tools menu and then verify the settings applied correctly.

WORKING WITH CLIENT SPY

Client Spy is also known as the SMS Advanced Client Troubleshooting Tool. Client Spy can be used to review software distribution processes, inventory processes, and software metering processes. To start, use the Tools menu to connect to a managed system. Once connected, you can review the information for the managed system by selecting the type of information that you want to work with. The options from the Tools menu are as follows:

- **Connect**—Used to connect to a managed system.
- **Software Distribution**—When selected, the details pane displays four tabs to assist in troubleshooting software distribution problems.
- **Inventory**—When selected, the details pane displays the current inventory information.
- **Software Metering**—When selected the details pane displays the current software metering information.

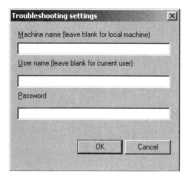

Figure 19.17
Connecting to a System Using Troubleshooting Settings

- **Save current tab to file**—Used to convert the information found in the selected tab to a file. The file can then be sent to another person for review, or can be used for documentation purposes.

- **Save all tabs to file**—Used to convert the information found in all of the available tabs to a file.

- **Exit**—Closes Client Spy.

When connecting to a managed system, the Troubleshooting Settings window, seen in Figure 19.17, appears. If your account has administrative privileges on the managed system that you are connecting, you can simply enter the computer name in the Machine Name field, and click OK. If you need to authenticate with different credentials, you can enter them in the User Name and Password fields before connecting. Once connected, select the Software Distribution, Inventory, or Software Metering options.

Software Distribution

Selecting Software Distribution will present you with four tabs that you can use for troubleshooting. The first tab is Software Distribution Execution Requests. It is here that you will find the software executions for the managed system. Figure 19.18 shows an execution event for the managed system as it appears in the Software Distribution Execution Requests tab. From this information you can determine the following:

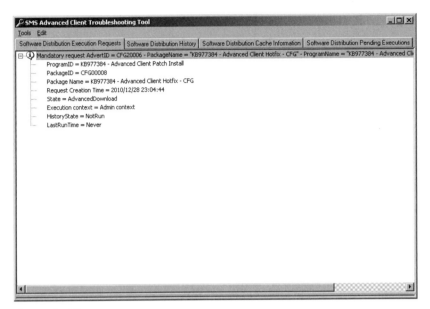

Figure 19.18
Software Distribution Execution Requests

- **ProgramID**—The program associated with the package that will be executed. In this case the program is KB977384—Advanced Client Patch Install.

- **Package ID**—The Configuration Manager identifier for the package. In this case, the identifier is CFG00008.

- **Package Name**—Name assigned to the package. In this case, the package name is KB977384—Advanced Client Hotfix—CFG.

- **Request Creation Time**—Date and time that the advertisement was created.

- **State**—Specifies how the files associated with the package will be accessed. In this case, Advanced Download specifies that the files will be downloaded to the client's cache.

- **Execution Context**—Specifies whether the program will run as the user or with elevated administrative credentials. The current setting Admin Context specifies the client's service account will be used to install the application.

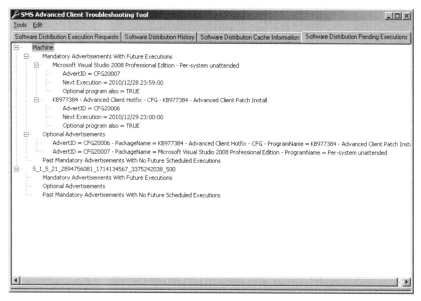

Figure 19.19
Software Distribution Pending Executions Tab

- **History State**—Specifies whether the program has executed in the past.

- **LastRunTime**—If the program has executed, this entry will specify the time the program ran.

If you navigate to the Software Distribution Pending Executions tab, as seen in Figure 19.19, you can see that the mandatory and optional advertisements are listed. If you expand the Machine or user listings, you will see the advertisements that have been targeted are listed within the three nodes:

- **Mandatory Advertisements With Future Executions**—Any advertisement listed in this node has been accepted by the managed system, but the mandatory execution time has not arrived. Each advertisement will be listed with the Advertisement ID, the mandatory execution time, and whether or not the application is also available for the user to run manually.

- **Optional Advertisement**—Advertisements that are not configured as mandatory advertisements, or have been configured to allow the user to run the advertisement before the mandatory execution time.

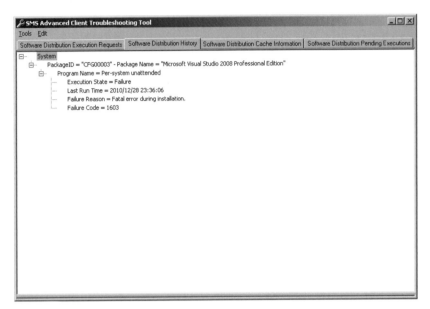

Figure 19.20
Software Distribution History Tab

- **Past Mandatory Advertisements With No Future Scheduled Executions**—Advertisements that have already run and were scheduled for a one-time execution.

Any advertisement that is targeted to a managed system should appear within the Software Distribution Pending Executions tab. If you do not see an advertisement listed that you think should be there, evaluate the policy for the client. If the policy does not reflect that the client should be receiving the advertisement, review the client's membership within the collection where the advertisement is targeted.

The Software Distribution History tab, seen in Figure 19.20, displays the details of all software distribution attempts. Expanding the tree structure for a package will display what happened during the execution of the program. The details that are given include the Execution State—Success or Failure, the last time the program ran, and if the program failed, the failure reason and code are displayed.

The Software Distribution Cache Information tab, seen in Figure 19.21, is used to view the configuration settings and contents of the client cache. Three nodes

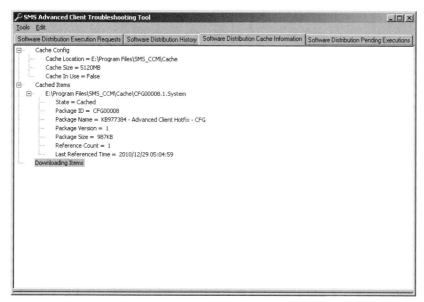

Figure 19.21
Software Distribution Cache Information Tab

appear in the results pane; Cache Config, Cached Items, and Downloading Items. Expanding the Cache Config tree exposes the location of the client's cache, the current size, and whether the cache is in use. The Cached Items tree will have a subtree for every application that appears within the Software Distribution Execution Requests tab, as long as the advertisement has been configured to download the package and run locally. The Downloading Items tree displays any packages that are currently downloading to the managed system's cache.

Inventory

After clicking Tools > Inventory, the Inventory Information tab appears. The information found on this tab, as seen in Figure 19.22, includes the details of the last software inventory, file collection, hardware inventory, and heartbeat. All four of the trees display when the process started, when the details were reported, and the report version that was used. As changes to the components are made, the report version numbers are incremented. If you have a system that is not at the latest report level, try refreshing the policy before the next inventory cycle.

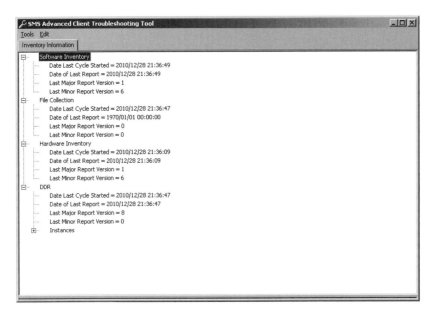

Figure 19.22
Inventory Information Tab

The DDR tree, which is used to report the client's heartbeat information, contains an additional subtree—Instances. The Instances subtree contains information about the components that make up the Data Discovery Record (DDR). If you expand any of the items, you will be presented with the data that is used to update the client's discovery data within the database. Using this information, you can see if the heartbeat is working on the system, when the last heartbeat was sent, and the data that was sent to be included within the database. If any of the data is different between the client's DDR information and the database, you will need to determine why the update did not occur.

Software Metering

The Software Metering tab, seen in Figure 19.23, displays all of the enabled software metering rules for the site. These are shown in a list, sorted by the rule ID. Because all of the rules within the site will be the same for every managed system, you can quickly compare two systems to make sure that they match. Each rule that appears within the tab will contain the File Version, language version, and original file name of the file.

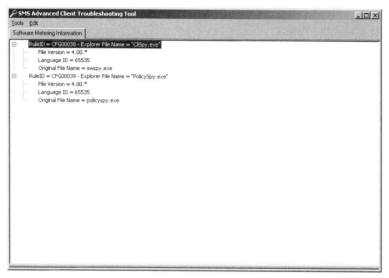

Figure 19.23
Software Metering Tab

THE FINAL WORD

As you have come to find out, Configuration Manager is a rather large suite of tools, all meant to help manage your systems. Managing Configuration Manager can be a rather daunting task. The tools that we have reviewed within this chapter are meant to make managing Configuration Manager a little bit easier. Getting to know these tools will benefit you as you perform your day-to-day activities and troubleshooting.

In the next chapter we are going to take a look at extending the toolsets that have been provided with Configuration Manager. With the Software Development Kit, you can create new interfaces, extend the functionality of the administrator's console, add new components to web interfaces and so much more. Once you have a good understanding of the SDK, you can start managing your systems nearly any way you want.

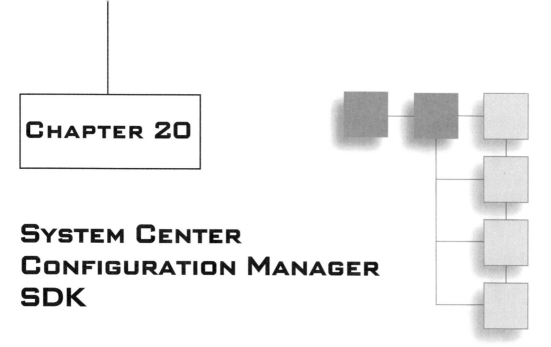

CHAPTER 20

SYSTEM CENTER CONFIGURATION MANAGER SDK

Over the last 19 chapters, this book has covered what System Center Configuration Manager was *designed* to do. Unfortunately, no matter how powerful the Configuration Manager console may be, many companies have unique processes that demand something fully customized to suit their needs. For this purpose, Microsoft has created the Configuration Manager SDK. With a little creativity, a little know-how, and a little ambition, this SDK can seriously help streamline processes.

In this chapter, we will be focused on one specific aspect of the Configuration Manager SDK: programming the SMS provider with managed code. We will go over the fundamentals and get you started writing some basic code to talk to your SCCM infrastructure.

WHO IS THIS CHAPTER FOR?

Do you like to simplify things? Do you spend a lot of time writing scripts that do your job for you? If your answer is yes, then this chapter is for you. Of course, you will need to have a fundamental understanding of programming languages, as this chapter will focus mostly on the Configuration Manager SDK. You do not need to be an expert programmer by any means, but having a basic understanding of variables, data types, subs, functions, and objects will be necessary to follow along in these examples.

PROGRAMMING LANGUAGE

In this chapter, all code examples will be provided in Visual Basic .NET. As far as programming languages go, VB.NET is one of the easiest to follow. Microsoft's MSDN site does not currently offer VB.NET examples for the Configuration Manager SDK, so this will be a nice addition. Even though we will be focused on Visual Basic, the Configuration Manager SDK also supports other .NET languages like C#.

Tip

Microsoft's MSDN site has some great C# examples. You can access the MSDN site at http://msdn. microsoft.com.

DEVELOPMENT REQUIREMENTS

Here are the requirements for developing the SMS provider with managed code:

- Microsoft Visual Studio 2005, 2008, or 2010
- .NET Framework 2.0
- Configuration Manager site server running Windows Server 2003 SP1 or higher

SDK FUNDAMENTALS

To begin, let's cover the SDK fundamentals.

SMS Provider

Any time you access Configuration Manager 2007 with the SDK, you use the SMS provider. The SMS provider is a WMI provider, which can be accessed through WMI or with managed classes.

Interfaces and Classes

Most of the code examples in this chapter use these three interfaces and classes:

- **WqlConnectionManager**—This is the class used to connect to Configuration Manager using WMI. The WqlConnectionManager class is also used for creating and querying object instances in Configuration

Manager. You will see this class used in every code example provided in this chapter.

- **QueryProcessor**—QueryProcessor contains the methods used to perform and cancel queries against the SMS provider. It supports both synchronous and asynchronous queries. In this chapter, we will be focused on synchronous queries.

Tip

Asynchronous queries deal with querying the SMS provider using a background worker. Asynchronous queries can be very useful if you are pulling a lot of information from Configuration Manager. If you are not using an asynchronous query, your application may go to a state of Not Responding for the duration of the query.

- **IResultObject**—This is the interface used to create objects in Configuration Manager and to return results of a query.

Assemblies

An assembly refers to a compiled collection of code typically in DLL format. There are two required assemblies when programming the SMS provider:

- adminui.wqlqueryengine
- microsoft.configurationmanagement.managementprovider

These assemblies can be found on any computer that has the Configuration Manager console installed. With a default installation of the console, the path would be C:\Program Files\Microsoft Configuration Manager Console\AdminUI\ bin. You will add these assemblies as references in the Visual Basic project later in this chapter.

GETTING STARTED

Now it's time to get started. We'll start with installing the software.

Install Required Software

For the examples in this chapter, you will need to download and install the System Center Configuration Manager 2007 SDK v4.0 from www.microsoft.com.

You will also need to download and install Microsoft Visual Basic .NET 2008 Express. You can download this from Microsoft's website at http://www.microsoft.com/express/downloads.

Setup Service Account in Active Directory

The code examples later in this chapter will require a domain username and password statically defined within the code. It is best practice to create an Active Directory service account for this function. All code examples in this chapter will use this service account to query and execute tasks.

To get started:

1. From Control Panel > Administrative Tools, open Active Directory Users and Computers (see Figure 20.1).

2. Right-click on your domain and choose New > User.

3. Set Full Name and User Logon Name to sa0001 (see Figure 20.2).

4. Set the password to Sccm@pps, uncheck User Must Change Password at Next Logon, and check Password Never Expires (see Figure 20.3).

5. Click Next, then click Finish.

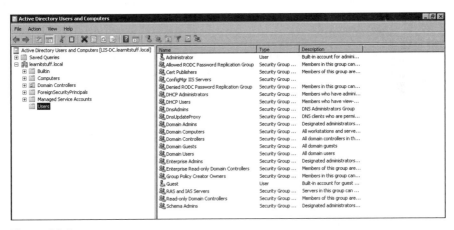

Figure 20.1
Active Directory Users and Computers

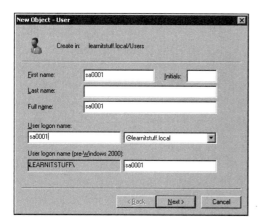

Figure 20.2
New User Dialog Box

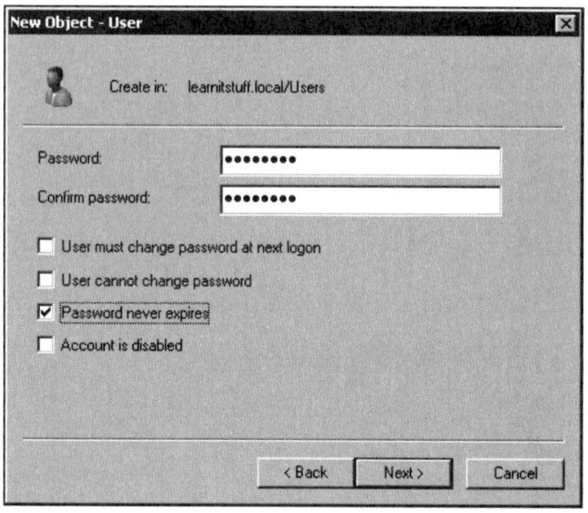

Figure 20.3
New User Password Settings

Now that we have a service account, we need to give that account rights to the system center site. For the purposes of this book, we will grant this service account full privileges to our central primary site.

Caution

This is only for testing and demonstration purposes. It is not good practice to give your service account full rights to the site server. In production, you will want to create a service account that is locked down to the specific components it needs access to.

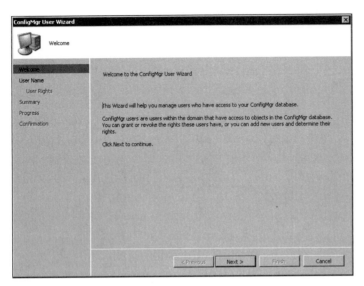

Figure 20.4
ConfigMgr User Wizard Welcome Screen

To get started with permissions:

1. Open the Configuration Manager console.

2. Expand Security Rights > Users.

3. Right-click Users and choose Manage ConfigMgrUsers. You are presented with the ConfigMgr User Wizard (see Figure 20.4).

4. Click Next at the Welcome screen.

5. Choose Add a New User. Then click Browse.

6. In the Select User, Computer, or Group dialog box, enter the service account you just created. If you followed along in these instructions, you should enter SA0001.

7. Click Check Names to confirm a user name resolves, then click OK.

8. Click Next. Choose Copy Rights from an Existing ConfigMgr User or User Group and then click Next again.

9. At the Source User drop-down menu, select your administrator account as seen in Figure 20.5. This will ensure that the service account has full rights to this site database.

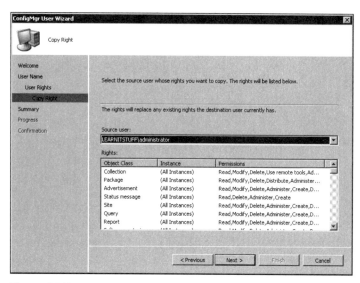

Figure 20.5
ConfigMgr User Wizard Copy User Rights

10. Click Next.

11. Ensure that The Listed Rights Are Sufficient is selected, then click Next.

12. A Summary will appear listing all the rights that have been granted to our service account. Click Next to continue.

13. After a few seconds, the wizard should complete successfully. Click Close.

If you have gotten this far, you have successfully created a domain service account with full rights to your Configuration Manager site. Now comes the fun part. In the next section, we will create a simple Visual Basic project and begin writing code to connect to the Configuration Manager infrastructure.

PROGRAMMING THE SMS PROVIDER WITH MANAGED CODE

Now that we have Visual Basic 2008 Express installed and an active directory service account, it's time to start programming. We need to create a Visual Basic project to get started.

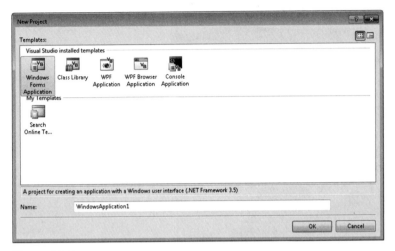

Figure 20.6
New Project Wizard

Create Your Visual Basic Project

Open Visual Basic and then follow these steps:

1. In Visual Basic 2008 Express, choose File > New Project. The New Project window will appear as in Figure 20.6.

2. Ensure that Windows Forms Application is selected, name your project SccmLearning, and then click OK.

3. You are presented with a blank form labeled Form1 as seen in Figure 20.7.

Figure 20.7
Blank Visual Basic Form

Add Required References

At this point, we need to add a couple references to our project that are required to connect to System Center Configuration Manager. These "references" are DLL files (assemblies) provided by Microsoft that come installed with the Configuration Manager console.

To add the required references:

1. In Visual Basic Express, make sure your new project is open. Then, go to Project > Add Reference.

2. Select the Browse tab and then navigate to C:\Program Files\Microsoft Configuration Manager Console\AdminUI\bin.

3. Select the following two files then click OK.
   - adminui.wqlqueryengine.dll
   - microsoft.configurationmanagement.managementprovider.dll

4. To verify these references have been added, choose Project > Show All Files. Then, under the Solution Explorer, expand References. The two DLL files should be listed there along with some default References, as shown in Figure 20.8.

Form Layout

In this application, we are going to execute a few different tasks to learn how to create, delete, and return objects from Configuration Manager. In order to do

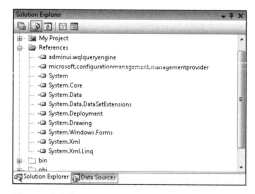

Figure 20.8
References in Solution Explorer

Figure 20.9
Toolbox Menu in Visual Basic Express

this, we will add eight buttons to our form. Each button will perform a different task. We will also add a ListBox off to the side, which will be used to display items returned.

To get started:

1. In the VB Project, choose View > Toolbox. The Toolbox menu should appear on the left as seen in Figure 20.9.

2. Under the Common Controls category, select and drag the button onto your form.

3. On the form, select the button that was just added and choose Edit > Copy.

4. Choose Edit > Paste. Repeat five times until you have six total buttons.

5. Drag the buttons on the form to arrange them so that they are aligned and not overlapping as seen in Figure 20.10.

6. Choose Edit > Select All. All of the buttons should now be selected.

7. Use the mouse to resize the buttons wider. Make the buttons fill about three-fourths the width of the form, as seen in Figure 20.11.

8. Select the title bar of the Form labeled Form1.

9. In the bottom-right corner of the screen, you should see the Properties menu. Make sure the Properties menu lists Form1 as the item selected, then scroll down through the menu to find the Size property.

Figure 20.10
Form with All Buttons Arranged Accordingly

Figure 20.11
Buttons Resized Accordingly

10. Modify the size to 450,300. This makes the form 450 pixels in width by 300 pixels in height.

11. Open the Toolbox again and drag the ListBox onto the form. Align and resize the control to fill up the right side of the form as seen in Figure 20.12.

12. Click on Button1 to select it. In the Properties menu on the right, change the Text property from Button1 to List All Collections. Repeat this step for the remaining five buttons. Match the text property accordingly.
     Button1 text = List all collections
     Button2 text = Create a collection
     Button3 text = Modify an existing collection
     Button4 text = List all packages
     Button5 text = List Package Programs
     Button6 text = Create an advertisement

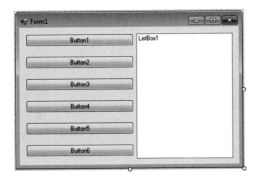

Figure 20.12
Form with all Buttons and a ListBox

13. Choose File > Save All. Leave the name as it is. If you need to change the location, do so now. Then click Save.

Interfacing with Code

In this section, we will build a basic framework for connecting to Configuration Manager with managed code. These code snippets can be reused for almost any SCCM development scenario.

Adding SCCM.vb Class File

Now that we have our form designed, it is time to add some code to connect to Configuration Manager programmatically. A base class has been provided to you for this functionality. You can download the SCCM.vb class file at www.courseptr.com/downloads.

Once the file has been downloaded and saved somewhere on your local machine:

1. In the Visual Basic project, navigate to the Solution Explorer menu on the right and select your project name SccmLearning.

2. Right-click on SccmLearning and choose Add > Existing item.

3. Navigate to the path where you saved the SCCM.vb file, select the file, then click Add.

4. The SCCM.vb file should now be listed in Solution Explorer as seen in Figure 20.13.

Figure 20.13
Visual Basic Project with SCCM.vb Class File Added

Breaking Down SCCM.vb

Double-click on the SCCM.vb file in Solution Explorer so that we can examine the code shown next.

```
Imports Microsoft.ConfigurationManagement.ManagementProvider
Imports Microsoft.ConfigurationManagement.ManagementProvider.WqlQueryEngine


Public Class SCCM
 Public Function CreateConnection(ByVal SERVER_NAME As String, _
 ByVal USER As String, _
 ByVal PASSWORD As String) As WqlConnectionManager
  Try
  Dim wqlConnection As New WqlConnectionManager(New SmsNamedValuesDictionary)
  If USER <> "" And PASSWORD <> "" Then 'User and password provided
     wqlConnection.Connect(SERVER_NAME, USER, PASSWORD)
  Else 'No credentials specified, use logged on credentials
     wqlConnection.Connect(SERVER_NAME)
  End If
      Return wqlConnection
  Catch ex As SmsException
      MsgBox(ex.Message)
      Return Nothing
```

```
      Catch ex As UnauthorizedAccessException
          MsgBox("Authentication Failed: " & ex.Message)
          Return Nothing
      End Try
    End Function
End Class
```

The code has been broken down next to explain each section separately.

The first two lines of code are Imports statements, which are used as a convenience to shorten lines of code. Without these statements, objects such as WqlConnectionManager would have to be qualified with its entire namespace each time it is called. For example, WqlConnectionManager would be referred to as Microsoft.ConfigurationManagement.ManagementProvider.WqlQueryEngine. WqlConnectionManager instead.

```
Imports Microsoft.ConfigurationManagement.ManagementProvider
Imports Microsoft.ConfigurationManagement.ManagementProvider.WqlQueryEngine
```

Next, we create a class called SCCM. You could name this class anything you want; I just thought SCCM made sense.

```
Public Class SCCM
```

We create a function called CreateConnection, which will be called later in this chapter. This function receives the SCCM server name and domain credentials. Later when we call this function, we will pass our service account credentials.

```
    Public Function CreateConnection(ByVal SERVER_NAME As String, _
    ByVal USER As String, _
    ByVal PASSWORD As String) As WqlConnectionManager
```

In VB.NET, the Try statement is used to try to execute a block of code. This is good for error handling. We create a variable called wqlConnection, which instantiates WqlConnectionManager.

```
Try
  Dim wqlConnection As New WqlConnectionManager(New SmsNamedValuesDictionary)
```

The Connect method accepts server name, user name, and password or just simply the server name. If the user name and password are not provided, it will use your existing logged on domain credentials.

```
    If USER <> "" And PASSWORD <> "" Then 'User and password provided
        wqlConnection.Connect(SERVER_NAME, USER, PASSWORD)
```

```
Else 'No credentials specified, use logged on credentials
    wqlConnection.Connect(SERVER_NAME)
End If
    Return wqlConnection
```

The remainder of the code deals with error handling. If the Try statement can't successfully execute the code, these statements are used to "catch" the exception so that the application does not crash.

```
Catch ex As SmsException
    MsgBox(ex.Message)
    Return Nothing
Catch ex As UnauthorizedAccessException
    MsgBox("Authentication Failed: " & ex.Message)
    Return Nothing
End Try
End Function
End Class
```

Now that we've created our domain service account, laid out our Visual Basic form, and added the SCCM.vb class file to our project, we are ready to start programming each button.

Caution

If you have not completed these three steps, you must do so before you can continue. Your program will not work if the previous steps have not been completed.

Button 1: List All Collections

The first button on our form is pretty self-explanatory. This button will be used to list all of the collections in our site. The results will appear in the list box off to the right.

Code It   On your Visual Basic form, double-click on the first button labeled List all Collections. When you double-click on a control in VB, the default event for that control is automatically generated. In this case, the default event for a button is the Click event, as seen in Figure 20.14.

Above the first line of code, add the following two Imports statements:

```
Imports Microsoft.ConfigurationManagement.ManagementProvider.WqlQueryEngine
Imports Microsoft.ConfigurationManagement.ManagementProvider
```

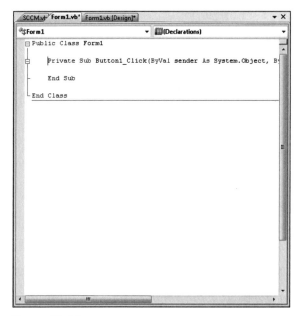

Figure 20.14
Code Generated for Button1.Click

Your code should now resemble Figure 20.15.

These are the same two Imports statements found in SCCM.vb.

Tip

In VB.NET, when you use Imports statements, they only apply to the file where they are contained. Since the SCCM class is part of the SCCM.vb file and the Form1 class is part of the Form1.vb file, you have to put the same Imports statements into both files. In a production application, you might want to move the SCCM class into your Form1.vb file so that the Imports statements are only used once.

Under Public Class Form1, add the following three lines of code to supply your connection information to your primary site.

```
Public sccmServer As String = "CHI-PRIMARY"
Public sccmUser As String = "LEARNITSTUFF\SA0001"
Public sccmPassword As String = "Sccm@pps"
```

Your Form1.vb code should now resemble Figure 20.16.

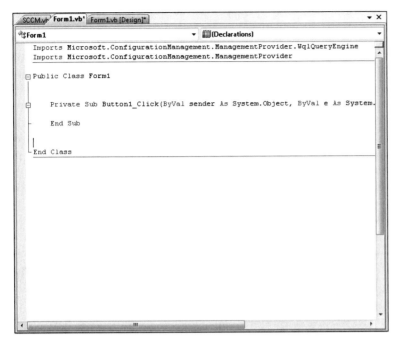

Figure 20.15
Imports Statements Added to Code on Form

The majority of our code will go under the Button1_Click sub. Download the Button1.txt file at www.courseptr.com/downloads. Copy and paste this code into the Button1_Click sub in Form1.vb. Your code should now look like this:

```
Private Sub Button1_Click(ByVal sender As System.Object, ByVal e As
System.EventArgs) Handles Button1.Click
    ListBox1.Items.Clear()
    Dim sccmConnection As New SCCM
    Dim wqlConnection As WqlConnectionManager = _
    sccmConnection.CreateConnection(sccmServer, sccmUser, sccmPassword)
    If wqlConnection IsNot Nothing Then
      Try
        Dim queryStatement As String = "SELECT * FROM SMS_Collection"
        Dim listOfCollections As IResultObject = _
        wqlConnection.QueryProcessor.ExecuteQuery(queryStatement)

        For Each collectionResult As IResultObject In listOfCollections
          ListBox1.Items.Add(collectionResult("NAME").StringValue)
        Next
```

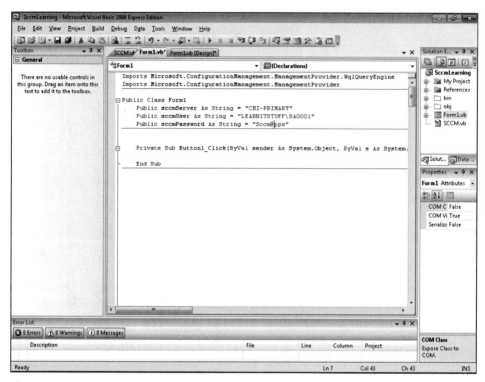

Figure 20.16
Form1.vb with Primary Site Connection Credentials

```
        wqlConnection.Close()
      Catch eX As SmsException
        MsgBox(eX.Message, MsgBoxStyle.Critical)
        Throw
      End Try
    End If
End Sub
```

Break It Down Now let's go over what each section of this code is doing. The first line inside the sub clears the ListBox on your form. If you don't do this, each time you click the button, it will append additional results to this list box. This could lead to confusing duplicate information.

```
      ListBox1.Items.Clear()
```

Next, we declare the variable sccmConnection, which instantiates a new instance of our SCCM class. Remember that our SCCM class contains a function called CreateConnection. That function requests the server, user name, and password, then returns a wqlConnectionManager object if it completes successfully. In this code example, we call sccmConnection.CreateConnection, we pass our primary site server credentials, and wqlConnection becomes the wqlConnectionManager object returned.

```
Dim sccmConnection As New SCCM
Dim wqlConnection As WqlConnectionManager = _
sccmConnection.CreateConnection(sccmServer, sccmUser, sccmPassword)
```

In the SCCM class, the CreateConnection function only returns an object if it successfully connects to the server. If it fails, then nothing is returned. We use an If statement to ensure that a successful connection was made before the code continues.

```
If wqlConnection IsNot Nothing Then
```

The rest of the code is within a Try statement for error handling. We declare queryStatement as a string containing a WQL query. Then, we declare listOf-Collections as an IResultObject containing the results of that query. IResultObject was explained earlier in the SDK Fundamentals section of this chapter.

```
Try
    Dim queryStatement As String = "SELECT Name FROM SMS_Collection"
    Dim listOfCollections As IResultObject = _
    wqlConnection.QueryProcessor.ExecuteQuery(queryStatement)
```

After listOfCollections has been populated with the results from our WQL query statement, we loop through the results and add the name of each collection to our ListBox.

```
For Each collectionResult As IResultObject In listOfCollections
    ListBox1.Items.Add(collectionResult("NAME").StringValue)
Next
```

Tip

In this code example, we only return the Name property from SMS_Collection. However, you could just as easily return any combination of properties you might be looking for. You could also provide a WHERE statement to filter your query down by specific criteria.

Once we are done querying for information, we close our connection to the SMS provider.

```
wqlConnection.Close()
```

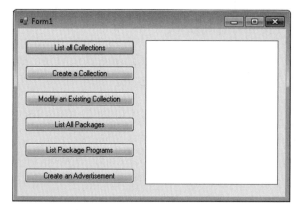

Figure 20.17
Debugging Application

The remainder of the code seen below is just for error handling. We use the catch statement to catch any exceptions within our code.

```
Catch eX As SmsException
    MsgBox(eX.Message, MsgBoxStyle.Critical)
    Throw
End Try
```

Test It　Now that all of our code is in place, we need to test it.

1. In the VB Project, choose Debug > Start Debugging. Your form should appear on the screen, as shown in Figure 20.17.

2. Click on the List All Collections button. The listbox on the right side of the form should populate with all of the collections in your site.

3. When you're done, close the form and it will bring you back to the code of your Visual Basic project. Make sure to save your work.

Button 2: Create a Collection

The second button on our form will be used to create a new collection. When you are programmatically creating a collection, there are a few important concepts to understand.

Important Concepts

1. When you first create a collection programmatically, that collection is not visible through the console. This is because all collections viewed from the console must belong under the COLLROOT collection. By

default, when a collection is created with code, this does not happen. The collection is basically sitting out in no man's land. After the collection is created, you have to use a second set of code to move that collection under the COLLROOT umbrella. This will become more apparent in our code.

2. One of the properties that you will need to define for a new collection is OwnedByThisSite. This is a Boolean property (meaning true or false). If this property is set to false, then the collection will be locked in the console. It will be treated as if it belongs to another site in your hierarchy.

Code It   To get started, download the Button2.txt file at www.courseptr.com/downloads. Double-click on the Create a Collection button on your form. Copy and paste this code into the Button2_Click sub in Form1.vb. Your code should now look like this:

```
Private Sub Button2_Click(ByVal sender As System.Object, _
             ByVal e As System.EventArgs) _
             Handles Button2.Click
  Dim sccmCollectionName As String = InputBox _
  ("Please enter a name for your collection")
  Dim sccmCollectionComment As String = InputBox _
  ("Please enter a comment for this collection")

  Dim sccmConnection As New SCCM
  Dim wqlConnection As WqlConnectionManager = _
  sccmConnection.CreateConnection(sccmServer, sccmUser, sccmPassword)

  If wqlConnection IsNot Nothing Then
    Try
      Dim sccmCollection As IResultObject = _
      wqlConnection.CreateInstance("SMS_Collection")
      sccmCollection("Name").StringValue = sccmCollectionName
      sccmCollection("Comment").StringValue = sccmCollectionComment
      sccmCollection("OwnedByThisSite").BooleanValue = True
      sccmCollection.Put()
      sccmCollection.Get()

      Dim sccmParentCollection As IResultObject = _
      wqlConnection.CreateInstance("SMS_CollectToSubCollect")
```

```
            sccmParentCollection("parentCollectionID").StringValue = _
            "COLLROOT"

            sccmParentCollection("subCollectionID").StringValue = _
            sccmCollection("CollectionID").StringValue

            sccmParentCollection.Put()

            MsgBox("Successfully created " & sccmCollectionName)
        Catch ex As SmsException
            MsgBox(ex.Message, MsgBoxStyle.Critical)
        End Try
    End If
End Sub
```

Break It Down   The first few lines of code set up two string variables that receive their values from input boxes. These input boxes ask you for the collection name and collection comment. This information is stored inside these two variables and used later in this code.

```
Dim sccmCollectionName As String = InputBox _
("Please enter a name for your collection")
Dim sccmCollectionComment As String = InputBox _
("Please enter a comment for this collection")
```

Next, we make our connection to SCCM, verify a connection was established, and begin a Try statement for error handling purposes. This is the same as our previous code example where we list all collections.

```
Dim sccmConnection As New SCCM
Dim wqlConnection As WqlConnectionManager = _
sccmConnection.CreateConnection(sccmServer, sccmUser, sccmPassword)

If wqlConnection IsNot Nothing Then
    Try
```

The rest of the code in this sub is where things really start to happen. First, we create an instance of SMS_Collection and call it sccmCollection.

```
            Dim sccmCollection As IResultObject = _
            wqlConnection.CreateInstance("SMS_Collection")
```

Since sccmCollection is actually an instance of a collection, it has the same requirements as a collection. When creating a collection in Configuration Manager, a name is required. The same rules apply here. Also note that we set the OwnedByThisSite property to True. As I mentioned earlier in this section, if this is set to False, the collection will be treated like it originated from another site and will be locked in the console.

```
sccmCollection("Name").StringValue = sccmCollectionName
sccmCollection("Comment").StringValue = sccmCollectionComment
sccmCollection("OwnedByThisSite").BooleanValue = True
```

We use the Put and Get methods to put the collection in Configuration Manager and then get the collection that we just created. Since the Collection ID is not something you define when you create a collection, this information is not available to you until the Collection has been created. Further down this code example, we will need to reference the Collection ID which is why the Get method is necessary.

```
sccmCollection.Put()
sccmCollection.Get()
```

The rest of our code deals with moving our collection under COLLROOT. We create an instance of SMS_CollectToSubCollect and call it sccmParentCollection.

```
Dim sccmParentCollection As IResultObject = _
wqlConnection.CreateInstance("SMS_CollectToSubCollect")
sccmParentCollection("parentCollectionID").StringValue = _
"COLLROOT"

sccmParentCollection("subCollectionID").StringValue = _
sccmCollection("CollectionID").StringValue
sccmParentCollection.Put()
```

Test It   Now we have two buttons on our form programmed and ready to go. In the first example, we tested the List All Collections button to ensure it was working properly. It is important that we test each button before we move on. Our code examples will build on each other. If a previous example does not function correctly, you may have problems moving forward.

1. In the VB Project, choose Debug > Start Debugging.

2. Click on the Create a Collection button. A sequence of input boxes will appear.

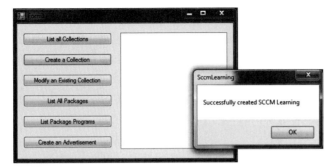

Figure 20.18
Collection Created Successfully

3. At the first input box requesting the collection name, input "SCCM Learning", then click OK.

4. When the second input box appears, input "test", then click OK again.

5. You should receive a message box indicating the collection was successfully created, as seen in Figure 20.18.

6. Click OK to dismiss the message box. Then, click the List All Collections button on your form.

7. Confirm in the list box on the right that the SCCM Learning collection exists.

Button 3: Modify an Existing Collection

The third button on our form will be used to rename the collection we created in the previous example. This example shows how to change the name, but we could have just as easily modified the Comment field or pretty much any other field.

Code It   To get started, download the Button3.txt file at www.courseptr.com/downloads. Double-click on the Modify an Existing Collection button on your form. Copy and paste this code into the Button3_Click sub in Form1.vb. Your code should now look like this:

```
Private Sub Button3_Click(ByVal sender As System.Object, _
    ByVal e As System.EventArgs) Handles Button3.Click

  Dim sccmConnection As New SCCM
  Dim wqlConnection As WqlConnectionManager = _
  sccmConnection.CreateConnection(sccmServer, sccmUser, sccmPassword)
```

```vbnet
    Dim sccmCollectionName As String = _
      InputBox("What is the name of the collection you want to modify?")

    Dim sccmCollectionNewName As String = _
      InputBox("What what would you like to rename this collection?")

    If wqlConnection IsNot Nothing Then
      Try
        Dim queryStatement As String = _
        "SELECT * FROM SMS_Collection WHERE Name = '" _
        & sccmCollectionName & "'"

        Dim listOfCollections As IResultObject = _
        wqlConnection.QueryProcessor.ExecuteQuery(queryStatement)

        For Each collectionResult As IResultObject In listOfCollections
          Try

            Dim sccmCollection As IResultObject = _
             wqlConnection.GetInstance _
             ("SMS_Collection.CollectionID='" & _
             collectionResult("CollectionID").StringValue & "'")

            sccmCollection _
            ("Name").StringValue = sccmCollectionNewName

            sccmCollection.Put()

            MsgBox("Successfully renamed collection.")
          Catch ex As SmsException
            MsgBox(ex.Message)
          End Try
        Next
        wqlConnection.Close()
      Catch eX As SmsException
        MsgBox(eX.Message, MsgBoxStyle.Critical)
      End Try
    End If

End Sub
```

Break It Down   If you haven't already noticed, most of our examples use a lot of similar code. As we make our way through the rest of the examples, I will explain less about the code we have already gone over so that we can focus on what is new and different.

The first ten or so lines of code listed below are really nothing new. We make a connection to SCCM and set up a couple input boxes to find and rename the collection.

```
Dim sccmConnection As New SCCM
Dim wqlConnection As WqlConnectionManager = _
sccmConnection.CreateConnection(sccmServer, sccmUser, sccmPassword)

Dim sccmCollectionName As String = _
  InputBox("What is the name of the collection you want to modify?")

Dim sccmCollectionNewName As String = _
  InputBox("What what would you like to rename this collection?")

If wqlConnection IsNot Nothing Then
  Try
Dim sccmCollectionName As String = InputBox _
("Please enter a name for your collection")
Dim sccmCollectionComment As String = InputBox _
("Please enter a comment for this collection")
```

Next, we query SMS_Collection to find the collection with the same name as what was typed into our first input box.

```
Dim queryStatement As String = _
"SELECT * FROM SMS_Collection WHERE Name = '" _
& sccmCollectionName & "'"

Dim listOfCollections As IResultObject = _
wqlConnection.QueryProcessor.ExecuteQuery(queryStatement)

For Each collectionResult As IResultObject In listOfCollections
  Try
```

Once the collection is found, we change the Name property to the value of our second input box. Then, we use the Put method to update the collection in Configuration Manager.

```
Dim sccmCollection As IResultObject = _
 wqlConnection.GetInstance _
 ("SMS_Collection.CollectionID='" & _
 collectionResult("CollectionID").StringValue & "'")

sccmCollection _
 ("Name").StringValue = sccmCollectionNewName

sccmCollection.Put()
```

Test It

1. In the VB Project, choose Debug > Start Debugging.

2. Click on the Modify an Existing Collection button. A sequence of input boxes will appear.

3. At the first input box requesting the collection name, input "SCCM Learning", then click OK.

4. When the second input box appears, input "SCCM Learning Renamed", then click OK again.

5. You should receive a message box indicating the collection was successfully renamed, as seen in Figure 20.19.

6. Click OK to dismiss the message box. Then, click the List All Collections button on your form.

7. Confirm in the list box on the right that the SCCM Learning Renamed collection exists.

Figure 20.19
Collection Renamed Successfully

Button 4: List All Packages

Listing all packages is really a stepping stone in our overall project. Later in this chapter, we will create an advertisement that will target the collection that we have created programmatically. We will need to provide a Package ID for the advertisement to use.

Code It   To get started, download the Button4.txt file at www.courseptr.com/downloads. Double-click on the List All Packages button on your form. Copy and paste this code into the Button4_Click sub in Form1.vb. Your code should now look like this:

```
    Private Sub Button5_Click(ByVal sender As System.Object, _
                ByVal e As System.EventArgs) _
                Handles Button5.Click
      ListBox1.Items.Clear()
      Dim sccmConnection As New SCCM
      Dim wqlConnection As WqlConnectionManager = _
      sccmConnection.CreateConnection(sccmServer, sccmUser, sccmPassword)
      If wqlConnection IsNot Nothing Then
        Try
          Dim queryStatement As String = "SELECT * FROM SMS_Package"
          Dim listOfCollections As IResultObject = _
          wqlConnection.QueryProcessor.ExecuteQuery(queryStatement)

          For Each collectionResult As IResultObject In listOfCollections
            ListBox1.Items.Add(collectionResult("Name").StringValue _
            & " - " & collectionResult("PackageID").StringValue)
          Next
          wqlConnection.Close()
        Catch eX As SmsException
          MsgBox(eX.Message, MsgBoxStyle.Critical)
        End Try
      End If
    End Sub
```

Break It Down   As you review this code, you might want to go back and examine our first button that lists all collections. You will notice that the code is almost identical. We will go over this example very quickly before we move on.

First, we clear our list box so that it does not append the list of packages to any previous results already contained within the list box. Then, we make a connection, and query SMS_Package.

```
ListBox1.Items.Clear()
Dim sccmConnection As New SCCM
Dim wqlConnection As WqlConnectionManager = _
sccmConnection.CreateConnection(sccmServer, sccmUser, sccmPassword)
If wqlConnection IsNot Nothing Then
  Try
    Dim queryStatement As String = "SELECT * FROM SMS_Package"
    Dim listOfCollections As IResultObject = _
    wqlConnection.QueryProcessor.ExecuteQuery(queryStatement)
```

For each package found in SMS_Package, we combine Package Name and Package ID and append the results to our list box off to the right. Then, we close our connection to Configuration Manager.

```
    For Each collectionResult As IResultObject In listOfCollections
      ListBox1.Items.Add(collectionResult("Name").StringValue _
      & " - " & collectionResult("PackageID").StringValue)
    Next
    wqlConnection.Close()
  Catch eX As SmsException
    MsgBox(eX.Message, MsgBoxStyle.Critical)
  End Try
End If
End Sub
```

Test It

1. In the VB Project, choose Debug > Start Debugging.

2. Click on the List All Packages button. A list of all packages should appear in the list box off to the right.

3. If you have followed along in previous chapters, you should have an Adobe Air package listed. Make a note of the Package ID as we will use it later in this chapter. If you do not have this package, just make a note of a different Package ID that is listed.

4. Once you have verified the button works, close the window to return to your code.

Button 5: List Package Programs

In this example, we will list all program names for one of our packages. In the previous code example, you were asked to make a note of the Package ID for one of your packages. In this example, we will use an input box to prompt for that Package ID, then all program names associated with that package will be delivered to our list box on the right. When we create an advertisement in the next example, we will need a Package ID and associated Program Name, along with a Collection ID to target.

Code It To get started, download the Button5.txt file at www.courseptr.com/ downloads. Double-click on the List Package Programs button on your form. Copy and paste this code into the Button5_Click sub in Form1.vb. Your code should now look like this:

```vb
Private Sub Button5_Click(ByVal sender As System.Object, _
            ByVal e As System.EventArgs) _
            Handles Button5.Click
    ListBox1.Items.Clear()
    Dim sccmPackageID As String = InputBox _
    ("Please enter a PackageID to continue.")

    Dim sccmConnection As New SCCM
    Dim wqlConnection As WqlConnectionManager = _
    sccmConnection.CreateConnection(sccmServer, sccmUser, sccmPassword)
    If wqlConnection IsNot Nothing Then
      Try
        Dim queryStatement As String _
        = "SELECT * FROM SMS_Program WHERE PackageID = '" _
        & sccmPackageID & "'"

        Dim listOfCollections As IResultObject = _
        wqlConnection.QueryProcessor.ExecuteQuery(queryStatement)

        For Each collectionResult As IResultObject In listOfCollections
        ListBox1.Items.Add(collectionResult("ProgramName").StringValue)
        Next
        wqlConnection.Close()

      Catch eX As SmsException
        MsgBox(eX.Message, MsgBoxStyle.Critical)
      End Try
    End If
  End Sub
```

We don't bother breaking down this code, as there is really nothing new here. We create an input box which requests the Package ID, and then we search for all program names associated with that Package ID. We append the Program Name results to our list box.

Test It

1. In the VB Project, choose Debug > Start Debugging.

2. Click on the List Package Programs button. You will be prompted to enter a Package ID.

Note

Remember in the previous example, I told you to make a note of one of the Package IDs listed. You will provide that Package ID here.

3. You should now be presented with a list of all program names associated with that package. Make sure to write down one of the program names exactly as it is listed. We will use this in our Advertisement code example.

Button 6: Create an Advertisement

All of our hard work and preparation has brought us to this moment... the culmination of all we have learned. In this example, we will create an advertisement that will target the collection we created in our Create a Collection example earlier in this chapter. This advertisement will also use one of the packages that we discovered in our List All Packages example. Make sure you have written down the Collection ID, Package ID, and Program Name you wish to use before you continue, as they will be required.

The final button on our form will be used to create an advertisement, but there are a few important concepts I would like to explain before we continue.

Important Concepts

1. One of the required properties when creating an advertisement is AdvertFlags. This is an integer value property, known as a bit flag, which contains different options associated with an advertisement. Bit flags are used in many languages as a way to enumerate a series of values within a small integer value. Bit flags are a complicated subject and could probably be their own chapter entirely. In this example, we will specify an AdvertFlags value of 0, which will not specify any special options.

Tip

For more information on bit flags, visit Microsoft MSDN site at http://msdn.microsoft.com.

2. You will need to have the Collection ID, Package ID, and Program
   Name ready to execute this example code. Without this information, you
   will not be able to successfully create an advertisement programmatically.

Code It   To get started, download the Button6.txt file at www.courseptr.com/
downloads. Double-click on the List Package Programs button on your form.
Copy and paste this code into the Button6_Click sub in Form1.vb. Your code
should now look like this:

```
Private Sub Button6_Click(ByVal sender As System.Object, _
            ByVal e As System.EventArgs) _
            Handles Button6.Click
    Dim sccmConnection As New SCCM
    Dim wqlConnection As WqlConnectionManager = _
    sccmConnection.CreateConnection(sccmServer, sccmUser, sccmPassword)
    If wqlConnection IsNot Nothing Then

        Try

            Dim sccmAdvertisementName As String = InputBox _
            ("Enter a name for your advertisement")
            Dim sccmCollectionID As String = InputBox _
            ("Enter the Collection ID to target")
            Dim sccmPackageID As String = InputBox _
            ("Enter the Package ID for this advertisement")
            Dim sccmProgramName As String = InputBox _
            ("Enter the Program Name associated with PackageID " & _
             sccmPackageID)

            Dim sccmAdvertisement As IResultObject = _
            wqlConnection.CreateInstance("SMS_Advertisement")

            sccmAdvertisement("AdvertFlags").IntegerValue = 0
            sccmAdvertisement("AdvertisementName").StringValue = _
            sccmAdvertisementName
            sccmAdvertisement("CollectionID").StringValue = _
            sccmCollectionID
            sccmAdvertisement("PackageID").StringValue = sccmPackageID
```

```
            sccmAdvertisement("PresentTimeEnabled").BooleanValue = True
            sccmAdvertisement("ProgramName").StringValue = sccmProgramName
            sccmAdvertisement.Put()
            MsgBox("Successfully created advertisement: " _
                & sccmAdvertisement("AdvertisementName").StringValue)
        Catch ex As SmsException
            MsgBox(ex.Message, MsgBoxStyle.Critical)
        End Try
    End If
End Sub
```

Break It Down   In our final example, we reuse a lot of code but also introduce a few new items. First, we set up our connection to our Configuration Manager site.

```
    Dim sccmConnection As New SCCM
    Dim wqlConnection As WqlConnectionManager = _
    sccmConnection.CreateConnection(sccmServer, sccmUser, sccmPassword)
    If wqlConnection IsNot Nothing Then
        Try
```

Next, we create four input boxes that will request the Advertisement Name, Collection ID to target, Package ID, and Program Name.

```
            Dim sccmAdvertisementName As String = InputBox _
            ("Enter a name for your advertisement")
            Dim sccmCollectionID As String = InputBox _
            ("Enter the Collection ID to target")
            Dim sccmPackageID As String = InputBox _
            ("Enter the Package ID for this advertisement")
            Dim sccmProgramName As String = InputBox _
            ("Enter the Program Name associated with PackageID " & _
              sccmPackageID)
```

After our input boxes have been populated, we create an IResultObject called sccmAdvertisement. Then, we use the string value returned from each inbox to set the properties for our advertisement.

```
            Dim sccmAdvertisement As IResultObject = _
            wqlConnection.CreateInstance("SMS_Advertisement")

            sccmAdvertisement("AdvertFlags").IntegerValue = 0
            sccmAdvertisement("AdvertisementName").StringValue = _
            sccmAdvertisementName
```

```
sccmAdvertisement("CollectionID").StringValue = _
sccmCollectionID
sccmAdvertisement("PackageID").StringValue = sccmPackageID
sccmAdvertisement("PresentTimeEnabled").BooleanValue = True
sccmAdvertisement("ProgramName").StringValue = sccmProgramName
```

Finally, we use the Put method to create our advertisement in Configuration Manager, and then send a message box to the screen to indicate success.

```
sccmAdvertisement.Put()
MsgBox("Successfully created advertisement: " _
    & sccmAdvertisement("AdvertisementName").StringValue)
```

Test It

1. In the VB Project, choose Debug > Start Debugging.

2. Click on the List Package Programs button. You will be prompted with four consecutive InputBoxes.

3. At the input box requesting Advertisement Name, input "SCCM Learning".

4. Follow the next three input boxes and populate them with the information you obtained in the previous examples.

5. A message box should appear indicating the advertisement was completed successfully!

6. To verify, open the SCCM console, navigate to Software Distribution > Advertisements.

7. Confirm your SCCM Learning advertisement exists. You're done!

THE FINAL WORD

With this SDK, you can make Configuration Manager whatever you need it to be. This chapter has provided you with the basics to get started, and some great online material to make your life a little easier. Now it's up to you. Whether you're trying to automate some internal admin tasks or developing a self-service portal for end-users, this SDK can help you accomplish it. You just need a little creativity, a little know-how, and a little ambition. Of course, a little programming background might help as well.

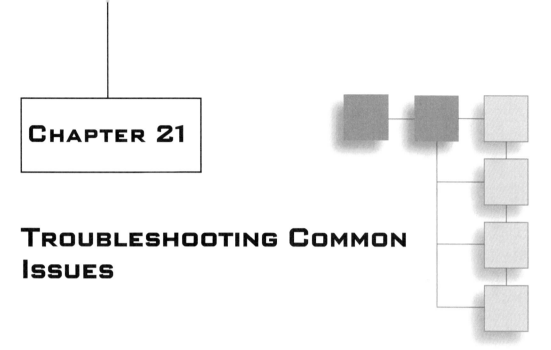

CHAPTER 21

TROUBLESHOOTING COMMON ISSUES

Throughout this book, we've covered a lot of topics ranging from basic framework technologies to in-depth processes about specific components. The previous 20 chapters are excellent for system admins to design and implement a new Configuration Manager 2007 environment, but for organizations with Configuration Manager 2007 already in place, reading through 800 or so pages to find the gotchas can be quite a tall order. This chapter is dedicated to pointing out some of the common issues that can occur when using Configuration Manager 2007 and showing you how to solve them. In some cases, we will discuss specific problems and resolutions in this chapter, but if some of these issues have been pointed out in previous chapters, only references will be made for the sake of not being redundant.

Remember that Configuration Manager is a huge and complex product. Trying to point out all of the possible issues in one chapter, or one book for that matter, is nearly impossible. There are many websites out there dedicated to Configuration Manager 2007 where you can ask and answer questions to and from Configuration Manager experts such as `http://social.technet.microsoft.com/ Forums/en-US/category/configurationmanager` or `http://www.myitforum.com`. Using this book and other resources, you should be able to quickly identify and troubleshoot the most common Configuration Manager 2007 problems.

Tip

Be sure to download the Configuration Manager 2007 toolkit that we mentioned back in Chapter 4 which will help you in your troubleshooting efforts. This can be downloaded from the following URL: http://www.microsoft.com/downloads/en/details.aspx?FamilyID=5A47B972-95D2-46B1-AB14-5D0CBCE54EB8.

Identifying Issues

Identifying Configuration Manager 2007 problems requires a more proactive approach than other products because it's not as widely used by standard users as it is by IT staff. Take a product like Active Directory, for example. If a domain controller goes down during the night, it's possible that affected users won't be able to logon in the morning, prompting lots of calls to the help desk. Since Active Directory is such an integral part of the organization, lots of people know when it's not working. If a PXE service point goes down on the other hand, this will not typically affect users thus not producing large amounts of help desk calls. Although this is a good thing, it can be bad if you are never notified that a problem exists. Using the Site Status node, you can quickly check the health of your site(s) so that you can fix possible issues before they get out of control. We covered the Site Status node in Chapters 1 and 18.

The Site Status node not only helps you identify when a problem has occurred, but it specifies which component is having the issue. More often than not, this allows you to quickly look at each component and fix problems based on the error message received, such as the one listed below in Figure 21.1.

Unfortunately, there might be cases when status messages aren't enough to help you identify the problem. That's when the fun begins!

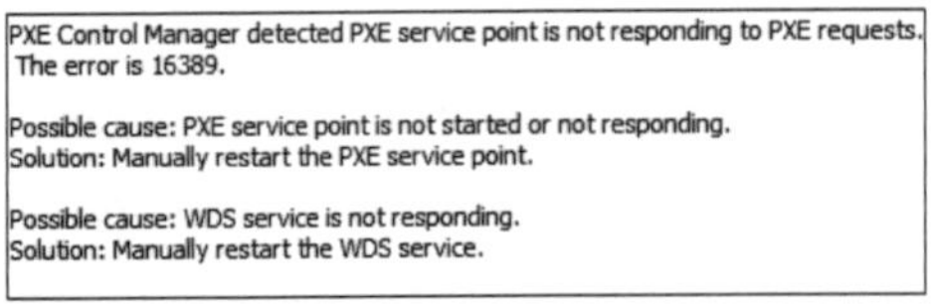

Figure 21.1
Status Messages

Site Issues

Back in Chapter 4, we covered the installation of a primary site including the prerequisites that must be installed for it to be successful. In Chapter 5, we covered the installation of secondary and central sites and the prerequisites for those systems. Use the information covered in those chapters plus the information detailed here to solve common site issues.

Symptom: Communication Failures

From time to time, you'll receive status messages that indicate site communication issues. Use the information below to help troubleshoot these types of issues.

Resolution: Restore Network Communication

If a site system cannot communicate because the network link is down, the site system will report errors until the link is reestablished. These errors can also occur when a site server has lost contact due to a hardware failure or simple server restart. Make sure the site system is up and running and that your firewalls are configured correctly if enabled. For more information about Configuration Manager 2007 port settings, see this URL: http://technet. microsoft.com/en-us/library/bb632618.aspx.

Resolution: Add Security Rights

Configuration Manager 2007 site systems must have specific security access to different parts of each system. This is done by adding the appropriate site system computer account to the correct Configuration Manager security groups (connection groups). If these accounts do not have the appropriate access rights, communication cannot occur. This scenario can be seen between a primary and secondary site when the secondary site is manually installed. During a manual install, these accounts are not automatically added to the correct security groups. This process is detailed in Chapter 5.

Resolution: Manually Copy Public Keys

To transfer public keys between sites, Configuration Manager 2007 makes use of Active Directory schema extensions to publish this information to Active Directory. This allows other Configuration Manager sites to automatically retrieve public keys from other sites, which enables communication. If Active Directory has not been extended for Configuration Manager 2007 or if Configuration Manager has site publishing disabled, public keys must be manually transferred to each site server by placing them in the <install directory>\inboxes\hman.box directory.

Symptom: Installation Failures on RODC Systems

If you find that you cannot install secondary sites to read-only domain controllers, read the following section.

Resolution: Add Security Rights

As we discussed earlier, Configuration Manager 2007 site systems must have appropriate security rights to other site systems for communication to occur successfully. This is also the case for a successful site installation. When using the Secondary Site Installation Wizard to install secondary sites on read-only domain controllers, the installation could fail due to the fact that the primary site server might not have the appropriate rights to initiate the installation. This happens because the necessary connection groups are never created and must be created manually. This is covered in detail in Chapter 5.

Symptom: Cannot Run R3 Power Management Reports

If you try to run the new R3 power management reports from the Configuration Manager Console, it may fail and crash the console.

Resolution: Add Database Rights

The user that is configured to run the power management reports must be added to the smsschm_users database role under the SMS_SITECODE database. Add these rights and try running the power reports again.

CLIENT DEPLOYMENT

Once a Configuration Manager 2007 site has been installed, you must then deploy the client agent to the systems that you wish to manage. This can be done as part of a task sequence during OSD or by using other client installation methods such as client push or software update point client installation. If there is a failure during the client installation, you need to first identify the reason for the failure. A great way to identify installation problems is to use a fallback status point (FSP). Using an FSP, you can collect information about installation failures using built-in reports. Once you have identified the installation issue, you can then start troubleshooting how to fix the issue. We talked about client deployments and the use of an FSP in Chapters 6 and 7. Using the troubleshooting below, you should be able to solve most common client deployment issues.

Symptom: Client Installation Not Successful

If the client agent is not being successfully installed, use the information below to help you troubleshoot possible issues.

Tip

See the ccmsetup.log file located on the client at %Windir%\System32\Ccmsetup to help troubleshoot client installation issues.

Resolution: Disable the Firewall

If a firewall is enabled on the targeted clients, the client agent may fail to install. For a list of ports that are required for client installation, see the following URL: `http://technet.microsoft.com/en-us/library/ff189805.aspx`.

Resolution: Verify Correct Configuration of the Software Update Point

If you are using the software update point client installation method, the software update point must be configured correctly. If there is a problem with the software update point, installation may fail. Check to make sure that your software update point is configured correctly and try the installation again.

If you currently have a WSUS server in place and are deploying these settings to your clients via group policy, it's possible that your clients are pointing to the wrong update server. Disable your group policy and try the installation again.

Resolution: Configure WebDAV

If the client can be manually installed but fails during a client push installation, check to make sure that WebDAV is properly configured on the site server that is initiating the installation. The ccmsetup.log file on the client may indicate

"Failed to correctly receive a WEBDAV HTTP request" if this is the case. Verify that your WebDAV settings are correct and try the installation again. WebDAV configuration steps can be found in Chapter 4.

Resolution: Define Client Push Account

If the client push installation account is not defined, the client agent may fail to install on client systems due to the lack of rights. When a client push installation account is not defined, the computer account of the site server issuing the installation will be used. If the site server computer account does not have appropriate access to client systems, the installation will fail. To ensure that the installation is successful, be sure to define a client push installation account that has administrative rights on client systems. The client push installation account was discussed in Chapter 7.

Symptom: Auto Site Assignment Issues

Once the client agent has been successfully installed, auto site assignment may occur depending on how you've configured your environment. If auto site assignment is not working correctly, follow the steps below to help resolve the issue.

Tip

See the clientlocation.log file located on the client at %windir%\system32\CCM\Logs to help troubleshoot site assignment issues.

Resolution: Extend Active Directory Schema

As we discussed briefly in Chapter 5, clients can be automatically assigned to a site by checking to see if its IP address is within one of the configured boundaries by querying Active Directory for site boundary information. If the client's IP address falls within a configured boundary, it can then assign itself to the correct site. If the Active Directory schema was not extended for Configuration Manager 2007, clients cannot locate site information using this method and must use a server locator point. See Chapters 4 and 5 about extending the schema and about auto client assignment.

Resolution: Use a Server Locator Point

If a client cannot access Active Directory or if the schema was not extended for Configuration Manager 2007, clients can use a server locator point to access boundary information for auto site assignment. Server locator points can be configured during the client agent installation or they can be found using WINS. For more information on server locator points, see Chapter 6.

Resolution: Configure Boundaries

If the Active Directory schema has been extended or a server locator point has been defined but auto site assignment still isn't working, make sure that you have your boundaries configured correctly. If a client's IP address does not match a configured boundary, auto site assignment will not occur. For more information on boundaries, see Chapter 5.

Software Updates

Troubleshooting software updates can be difficult since it uses multiple components of the Configuration Manager infrastructure to check, deploy, and install updates. Make sure you read Chapter 12, "Managing Software Updates" to ensure that you have a good understanding of the software update process.

Symptom: Incorrect Reporting Data

If your compliance reports sometimes show computers with an unknown status or show updates as pending, use the information below to help solve these issues.

Resolution: Do Not Allow Software Updates to Be Installed Outside of Configuration Manager

If users are manually installing software updates using another method, compliance reports may show updates in a pending status. Make sure that users do not have access to manually install software updates using other methods such as Microsoft Update.

Resolution: Disable Group Policy

As discussed previously, if you currently have a WSUS server in place and are deploying these settings to your clients via group policy, it's possible that your clients are pointing to the wrong update server. Not only can this cause issues with software update installation, it can also cause updates to show as unknown. Set the policy as "not configured" or move the workstation object to a new OU outside of the scope of the group policy.

Symptom: WSUS Sync Issues Reported

If you are receiving errors from the WSUS Synchronization Manager (shown as SMS_WSUS_SYNC_MANAGER in the Component Status node), use the information below to help solve your issues.

Tip

See the wsyncmgr.log file located on the site server located at <InstallPath>\Logs to help troubleshoot WSUS Synchronization issues.

Resolution: Install the WSUS Administration Console

If the software update point is installed on a server other than the site server, the WSUS administration console must be installed on the site server for WSUS synchronizations to be successful. Refer to Chapter 4 for more information on this topic.

Resolution: Configure WSUS for SSL Operation

If the site is in Native Mode or if you've configured WSUS to use SSL, WSUS must be configured for SSL operation. We covered this step in Chapter 6.

Resolution: Define Correct Port Numbers

Make sure that the software update point is using the correct port numbers as configured in the IIS WSUS website. These are typically 80 and 443 or 8520 and 8521. See Chapter 6 for more information on setting up the software update point.

Symptom: Clients Not Updating

If your clients are not applying software updates correctly, use the information below to help solve your issues.

Resolution: Check Windows Update Agent Version

Client computers require version 3.0 or higher of the Windows Update Agent (WUA) to work with Configuration Manager 2007. Make sure that the WUA can self-update or manually install version 3 of the WUA using software distribution.

Resolution: Disable Group Policy

If your clients aren't installing software updates correctly, check to make sure that no group policies are in effect that point to another WSUS server. If clients are using the wrong WSUS server, installation and reporting of software updates may fail.

SOFTWARE DISTRIBUTION

The software distribution component within Configuration Manager 2007 is a complicated beast that requires a lot of research and experience to fully master. Read Chapter 11, "Managing Software Distribution," before continuing with this section. Because of the number of issues that can come up with software distribution, make sure to utilize all of the available resources for trouble-shooting such as the Internet as well as this section of the book.

Symptom: Clients Will Not Download Software from Distribution Points

Even if your programs and advertisements are configured correctly, other issues may prevent clients from successfully downloading software from distribution points. Use the items below to help troubleshoot these types of issues.

Tip

See the DataTransferService.log and FileBITS.log files located on the client at %windir%\system32\ CCM\Logs to help troubleshoot package transfer issues.

Resolution: Boundaries not Defined

Although Configuration Manager 2007 does not require you to define boundaries, unexpected behavior might result if none are configured. If no boundaries are configured and an advertisement is created using the default settings, software will not be downloaded from distribution points because clients are evaluated as being connected to slow LANs. Because the default settings of an advertisement dictate that software not be downloaded when clients are connected to slow LANs, the software distribution process will hang until a boundary is created or until the advertisement is modified to allow downloads to occur on slow LANs. It is highly recommended to create and classify boundaries for each network (slow or fast) in your organization. See Chapter 5 for detailed instructions on setting up boundaries.

Resolution: Configure Request Filtering on Each BITS Enabled Distribution Point

If you are using IIS version 7 or higher, a new security feature called request filtering is enabled to help secure the site. This can cause unwanted issues, however, if not configured correctly. Because request filtering blocks specific file types, access to these files is restricted when using a BITS enabled distribution point. If a distribution point contains a software package that contains a restricted file type, access to this file will be blocked and the software distribution process will fail. To fix this, you must configure request filtering to allow for unrestricted access to these files. To configure request filtering, see Chapter 4.

Resolution: Check BITS Status

If you are using a BITS enabled distribution point to access your packages, it's possible that a BITS job may be stuck on the client, preventing other BITS jobs from starting. To check the status (and modify) BITS jobs on the client, download the BITSAdmin tool. More information about this tool can be found at `http://msdn.microsoft.com/en-us/library/aa362813(v=vs.85).aspx`.

Symptom: Wake On LAN Not Waking Computers

Configuration Manager 2007 includes the ability to initiate Wake on LAN packets to computers prior to scheduled activities such as software distribution or operating system deployments. Use the items below to help troubleshoot issues related to WOL.

Tip

See the wolmgr.log and wolcmgr.log files located on the site server at <InstallPath>\Logs to help troubleshoot WOL issues.

Resolution: Enable WOL

Wake on LAN (WOL) must be enabled for each Configuration Manager site before WOL packets can be sent to wake remote computers. WOL can be enabled by going to each site's properties within the Configuration Manager console. This process is covered in Chapter 11.

Resolution: Enable Hardware Inventory

WOL uses properties about a computer such as its IP address and MAC address to send wake up packets. If hardware inventory is not enabled, these properties cannot be collected, which prevents WOL from working correctly. Make sure that hardware inventory is enabled and that clients are reporting this information back to the database before issuing WOL commands.

Resolution: Configure Routers for Directed Broadcasts

Because WOL packets are typically sent as broadcasts and routers discard broadcasts by default, your routers may have to be configured to forward directed broadcasts to enable WOL to work across subnets. Although configuring routers and layer 3 switches are out of the scope of this chapter, more information about these can be found in Chapter 11.

Symptom: Clients Not Executing Software Downloaded from Distribution Points

If your clients are downloading packages from distribution points but are not executing the programs associated with these packages, use the information below to help solve this problem.

Resolution: Check Package Version

If your distribution points do not match your source files, hash mismatches may occur when using the download and execute advertisement option. If a hash mismatch occurs, the software distribution process will fail before executing the program. This can be seen in the CAS.log file located in the %windir%\system32 \CCM\Logs directory on the client system. To fix this, make sure that you update your distribution points with the most current version of the package source files. For more information on this, see Chapter 11.

Symptom: Advertisements Not Available

If you advertise a program to a computer but the computer does not run or list the advertisement in the run advertised programs Control Panel applet, use the information below to help solve this problem.

Resolution: Verify Collection Membership

If a package has been advertised to a collection, make sure the targeted client is a member of the collection. If the client doesn't meet the criteria for a query-based collection, change the query so that it includes the client. If the client has been added to a collection using direct membership, make sure that the SMS GUID of the actual client matches the SMS GUID of the client in the collection. If the SMS GUID changes due to hardware modifications or re-imaging, the computer in the collection may actually be an obsolete object.

Resolution: Be Patient

If a client system has been targeted by a collection using a query-based membership rule, it's possible that the evaluation cycle has not yet completed for the collection. If this is the case, the client will not receive any advertisements until it becomes a member of the collection. To resolve this issue, manually update the collection membership or wait for the evaluation cycle to occur.

Resolution: Check the Approval Status

If your client is a member of a different domain than that of the site server, your client might be classified as not approved. If a client is classified as not approved, no communication will occur between the client and the site server so any updates such as inventory or even computer name changes will not be processed at the site. Make sure that your client has been approved so that communication can occur.

OPERATING SYSTEM DEPLOYMENT

Like software distribution, operating system deployment (OSD) is a huge component within Configuration Manager 2007, which takes some time, patience, and experience to master. Read Chapter 13, "Managing Operating System Deployment" before troubleshooting OSD related issues. Use the items below to help in troubleshooting this topic.

Tip

Enable command line support in the boot image to help troubleshoot OSD issues. These processes as well as the different OSD logs are covered in Chapter 13.

Symptom: Can't Boot to PXE

PXE issues are common with OSD and can be tricky to troubleshoot. Follow the steps below to help with PXE related issues.

Resolution: Verify Subnet Prerequisites

If your PXE service point is on a different subnet than your client machines, these machines will not receive the WinPE image from the PXE service point by default. Because of the way routers are configured by default, the PXE requests from clients are never forwarded to the correct PXE service point. To solve this issue, use workarounds such as IP helper addresses in your routers or add scope options in your DHCP server to locate the correct server. These items are covered in Chapter 6.

Resolution: Define Proper Boot Image

Clients can only boot to the WinPE image via PXE if a proper WinPE boot image has been specified in the OSD task sequence. If no boot image is specified, clients will not see the task sequence as an OSD task sequence and will never download the boot image. Make sure to specify the boot image when creating your OSD task sequence. See Chapter 13 for more information.

Resolution: Configure Advertisement Correctly

If an OSD task sequence has been advertised to a collection of which the client is not a member, the client will not boot via PXE. There must be an active OSD task sequence advertised to at least one collection to which the client is a member. See Chapter 13 for more information.

Resolution: Verify that both x86 and x64 Boot Images Are Deployed

Even if you only have x86 clients, an x64 boot image must be deployed to your distribution points for PXE to work correctly. Because clients use components of both the x86 and x64 boot images regardless of architecture, both of these boot images must be available. See Chapter 13 for more information.

Resolution: Clear the Last PXE Advertisement

When a mandatory advertisement is created for an OSD task sequence, the clients in the targeted collection will automatically reboot and start the OSD task sequence. If an error occurs and the computer does not successfully complete the task sequence, the computer may not boot to PXE thereafter. To prevent possible PXE loops, Configuration Manager implements a method that prevents PXE boots once a failure has occurred. To fix this, you must clear the last PXE advertisement for the affected machine(s). This can be done per machine or for all machines in a collection by using the Configuration Manager console. Right-click on the affected machine or collection object and choose "Clear Last PXE Advertisement".

Resolution: Verify that the WDS Service is Started

If all of the prerequisites have been followed but clients still won't boot at the PXE stage, it's possible that the Windows Deployment Service did not start on the PXE service point. The PXE service point uses Windows Deployment Services (WDS) to listen and respond to PXE requests so this service must be enabled to function properly.

Symptom: Clients Automatically Reboot in WinPE

If your clients reboot during the PXE boot process, read the section below.

Resolution: Define Correct Boot and Network Drivers

If your clients are able to download the PXE boot image but restart unexpectedly during the boot process, it's possible that the correct network or mass storage drivers have not been added to the boot image. Make sure you test each hardware model that will use the PXE boot image(s) to ensure that the correct drivers are installed. See Chapter 13 for more information.

Symptom: Software Not Installed During OSD

If your clients apply the operating system during PXE but do not install software as defined in the task sequence, see the items below to help aid troubleshooting.

Resolution: Define Driver Packages or Auto Apply Drivers During the Task Sequence

If you've added the correct drivers to the WinPE boot image, you still need to define the drivers that should be installed to the full operating system image once applied. If network access is disabled due to a driver issue, all further task sequence steps (including software installation) will fail. Ensure that a driver package or auto apply drivers task sequence step has been defined for your hardware devices.

Resolution: Verify Task Sequence Steps

If you've verified that all of your drivers are installed correctly but software is still not being installed, make sure that the task sequence step is configured properly. Some things to check might be the order of the software installation, conditions not being met, or programs not set up to run in a task sequence step. All of these items were covered in Chapter 13.

Symptom: Errors When Running a Task Sequence

If you receive error messages when starting your task sequence, see the steps below for more information.

Resolution: Verify that Referenced Packages Exist on Distribution Points

If a task sequence contains a step that references a package that has been deleted or removed from distribution points, you might receive an error during the start of the task sequence. Using the task sequence editor within the Configuration Manager console, check each task sequence step to verify that all packages are available. Unavailable packages are typically shown in the task sequence editor with a red X.

Resolution: Check the Date and Time

If you can boot to the PXE boot image but get an error prior to selecting a task sequence, it's possible that the date and time on your client is incorrect. Check the date and time and try again.

DESIRED CONFIGURATION MANAGEMENT

Desired Configuration Management (DCM) was covered in Chapter 14, which outlines the setup and configuration of DCM. Please be sure to read through Chapter 14 to fully understand DCM.

Tip

See the dcmagent.log, ciagent.log, sdmagent.log, sdmdiscagent.log, and discovery.log files located on the client at %windir%\system32\CCM\Logs to help troubleshoot desired configuration management issues.

Symptom: Configurations Are Locked

If configuration baselines and items are locked (showing a padlock) in the Configuration Manager console, use the following items to help resolve your issues.

Resolution: Create Configurations at the Same Site

DCM configuration items or baselines that were created at a parent site are inherited to child sites and appear as locked. Create configuration items at the same site so that you can edit these items.

Resolution: Create Duplicates of Original Configurations

If DCM configurations were imported, or if they were created at a parent site, you can duplicate these items, which then allows you to edit them.

Symptom: Unreliable Compliance Information

If your DCM reports show no data or "unknown" statuses for clients, use the information below to help troubleshoot.

Resolution: Wait for Baseline Evaluation to Complete

If the DCM evaluation cycle has not yet been completed, baseline reports will show a value of unknown. Wait until computers have completed their evaluation cycle or manually update the machine policy by initiating the machine policy retrieval and evaluation cycle from the actions tab in the Configuration Manager control panel applet. Once the machine policy has been evaluated, go to the configurations tab and click the refresh button to download configuration baselines.

Resolution: Install .NET Framework

DCM requires that clients have .NET Framework version 2.0 or later installed on client machines. If not, compliance reports will show invalid data. Install the .NET Framework on client machines to fix this issue.

Resolution: Wait for Caching Compliance Period to Expire

When a client's DCM compliance is evaluated, these results are cached locally for 15 minutes. If you re-evaluate compliance status within 15 minutes of the last evaluation, the cached results will be used. Let the 15-minute caching period expire before re-evaluating compliance.

NETWORK ACCESS PROTECTION

Network access protection (NAP) is a component of Configuration Manager 2007 and requires an external implementation of NAP before it can be integrated into the infrastructure. Because of this prerequisite, many of the troubleshooting steps require that you have knowledge of the basic NAP infrastructure. This section covers the basic Configuration Manager related issues, not overall NAP issues. Refer to Chapter 15, "Managing Network Access Protection" for more information on NAP. For the log files associated with NAP, read Chapter 6, "Configuring Site System Roles."

Symptom: NAP Policies Cannot Be Created

If NAP policies cannot be created within the Configuration Manager console, use the following options to help troubleshoot these issues.

Resolution: Enable NAP

If you do not have the ability to create Configuration Manager NAP policies within the Configuration Manager console, NAP may not be enabled for the site. The process of enabling NAP is covered in detail in Chapter 15.

Resolution: Create NAP Policies at the NAP Enabled Site

NAP policies can only be created at the site where NAP is enabled. If you try to configure NAP policies at a secondary site or at a child primary site, these options are not available. Be sure to configure NAP policies at the site in which it was enabled.

Resolution: Enable Software Updates

NAP requires the software update component to be enabled and configured. Be sure that your site meets this prerequisite prior to configuring NAP policies.

Symptom: The Network Policy Server Component Cannot Be Installed

If you are having issues with the network policy server component, use the information below to help troubleshoot these issues.

Resolution: Use a Windows Server 2008 or higher Operating System

NAP requires that you use a Windows Server 2008 or higher class operating system. The network policy server (NPS) component cannot be installed to servers that do not meet this criterion. Ensure that you are using a Windows Server 2008 or higher operating system when using NAP.

Symptom: Network Access Issues

If your clients are using either the restricted or non-restricted networks at incorrect times, use the information below to help troubleshoot these issues.

Resolution: Enable the NAP Client Service

Depending on your setup, clients may enter a restricted network when NAP ineligible clients connect to the network. If the NAP service is not started, the client is seen as NAP ineligible and might be forced to use a restricted network connection. Ensure that you have a method for starting the NAP client service such as a group policy as described in Chapter 15.

Resolution: Use a NAP Capable Operating System

If the client operating system does not support NAP, it is seen as NAP ineligible and might be forced to use a restricted network connection. Make sure that you are using one of the following client operating systems when using NAP:

- Windows XP SP3
- Windows Vista
- Windows 7

Resolution: Ensure Requirements are Met

When using NAP, system health agents monitor the status of the client and report agent status back to its corresponding system health validator. If the status of the agent does not meet the requirements set forth in the policy, network access may be restricted. This is working as designed. Make sure your clients meet the requirements that are defined in the policy (in some cases, the system health validator) and try again. Check Chapter 15 for details.

Resolution: Extend the Active Directory Schema for Configuration Manager 2007

NAP requires that the Active Directory schema be extended so that health state references can be published and retrieved by the Configuration Manager system health validator. If the schema is not extended, NAP will not function correctly and clients may have restricted network access as a result. Make sure that you extend the Active Directory schema if you are planning on using NAP. Instructions for extending the schema are located in Chapter 4.

THE FINAL WORD

As we stated at the beginning, this chapter is designed to help you troubleshoot some of the basic problems that can occur in a Configuration Manager 2007 environment. If you don't find the answers to your questions in this chapter, hopefully it will help you rule out the issue or point you in the right direction using the other resources listed above. If a problem does arise, remember to be calm and patient. There's almost always a simple solution to the problem!

This is the final chapter of our book! We worked very hard to ensure that we provided an all-inclusive guide for administrators interested in the planning, installation, management, and troubleshooting phases of a Configuration Manager 2007 infrastructure. We used step-by-step walkthroughs and real-world experiences from the trenches to help in the day-to-day management of this large and complicated product. Thank you for taking the time to read this book and we sincerely hope you enjoyed it!

INDEX

Symbols and Numerics